# THE
# ASCENSION
# OF
# AUTHORSHIP

HARVARD STUDIES IN COMPARATIVE LITERATURE
FOUNDED BY WILLIAM HENRY SCHOFIELD
49

# THE
# ASCENSION
# OF
# AUTHORSHIP

Attribution and Canon Formation in Jewish,
Hellenistic, and Christian Traditions

## JED WYRICK

Harvard University Department of Comparative Literature
Distributed by Harvard University Press
Cambridge, Massachusetts, and London, England
2004

PRINTED IN THE UNITED STATES OF AMERICA

FIRST PRINTING

ISBN 0-674-01611-0 (cl.)
ISBN 0-674-01662-9 (pa.)
Library of Congress Control Number: 2004111129

To Lenny and Greg,
for loving old traditions and creating new ones

# CONTENTS

# PREFACE

This work began as a doctoral dissertation in Comparative Literature at Harvard University. A comparison of the dissertation title (*The Genesis of Authorship: Legends of the Textualization of Homeric Epic and the Bible*) with the title of the present work reveals the essence of its development since then. *The Ascension of Authorship* no longer represents a search for an absolute origin or genesis, but rather investigates the ways that our present day notions of authorship "rose up" as a transformation and synthesis of conflicting ancient views of attribution and authoritativeness. Rather than merely treating selected episodes in the interpretive afterlife of the Homeric epics and the Hebrew Bible/Old Testament, it now deals significantly with trends in interpretation and textual history in three cultural contexts: the Judaisms of the Second Temple and rabbinic periods, Hellenistic civilization, especially as it flourished in Alexandria, and early conceptualizations of Christianity, culminating with St. Augustine. Legends about the imagined textual provenance or textualization of foundational cultural documents continue to be a subject of analysis, but they are increasingly highlighted here as windows into culturally specific views about the perceived role of individuals in textual production, salvation, and contamination. Most significantly, *The Ascension of Authorship* articulates a new claim: that the dynamic of canon formation in all three traditions is closely tied to ancient norms of attaching names to texts after composition, subsequent assessments of inherited attributions, the weight of past valuations of the faithfulness and sacredness of texts, and the supposed trustworthiness of their textualization and transmission.

The fast moving world of scholarship in canon formation has not been idle since this work was submitted for publication. Important contributions to the field can be found in three new edited collections: Lee Martin McDonald and James A. Sanders, eds., *The Canon Debate* (Peabody, Massachusetts: Hendrickson Publishers, 2002); J. M. Auwers and H. J. de Jonge, eds., *The Biblical Canons* (Leuven: Peeters, 2003); and Margalit Finkelberg and Guy G. Stroumsa, eds., *Homer, the Bible, and Beyond: Literary and Religious Canons in the Ancient World* (Leiden, Boston: Brill, 2003). New discussions on the canonical significance of 4QMMT (a Dead Sea Scrolls text) have also appeared in print. I would like to address these works, as well as the valuable insights of Robert McQueen Grant's *Heresy and Criticism: The Search for Authenticity in Early Christian Literature* (Louisville: Westminster/J. Knox Press, 1993), in future publications.

During the many years in which *The Ascension of Authorship* has developed, I have been fortunate to receive support from what must be the most congenial group of colleagues anywhere: the Department of Religious Studies at California State University, Chico. I would especially like to thank Micki Lennon, Andrew Flescher, Bruce Grelle, and Joel Zimbelman for their ideas and suggestions. I would also like to acknowledge the support of Sam Edelman and the Modern Jewish and Israel Studies program at Chico State.

Important parts of this book, relating to the history of the interpretation of Proverbs 25:1 and the idea of a succession of prophets, were presented at annual meetings of the Association for Jewish Studies. The Humanities Center at Chico State kindly invited me to present my research on authorship, St. Augustine, and ancient views of the individual. I am grateful to Steve Mason, Maurice O'Sullivan, and other members of Ioudaios-L, the First Century Judaism Discussion Forum, for helping me to resolve difficult questions in the interpretation of early Judaism, and for providing a scholarly community. My warmest appreciation goes to Susan Hayes for her patience and expertise in editing the manuscript. I would also like to thank Kathy George for facilitating the editorial process, and Mary Mortensen for her excellent index. I am deeply indebted to David Stern for his detailed criticism and for helping me pinpoint the most convincing conclusions of my analysis. And my sincerest thanks to the following for their aid in the final proof-reading: Ron Hendel, Carlos Lopez, Fred Porta, Alisa Regelin, Margot Williams, and Eric Wyrick. All remaining errors are, of course, my own.

At the earliest stages of this work, I was greatly helped by the advice of my dissertation reader James Kugel, whose methodology has endlessly inspired me, and Albert Henrichs, whose aid was essential in gaining access to the literary culture of Alexandria. I cannot describe how much I admire them and have learned from them. I would also like to thank Bernard Septimus, who was kind enough to help me in many a late night conversation at the Harvard gym. And I am extremely grateful to the Department of Comparative Literature at Harvard for providing a space in which I could investigate the textual and poetic dimensions of Hellenism and Judaism.

Looking back on the period in which I composed my dissertation, I understand how much its ideas were shaped through interaction with my fellow students. They include Carlos Lopez, Patricia Barbeito, George Syrimis, Fred Porta, Sumi Furiya, and Timothy Power. I would especially like to thank Steven Nelson for getting me to put my ideas onto paper, and Carlos Lopez, who was the sounding board for the creation of this work, and helped me to understand the differences between text, scripture, and canon. Thanks also to my friends from Chico and Boston who have been supportive since that time: Michael Bohrer, Joe Perry, Juliane Wise, and Rebecca Yadegar.

My parents, Ann and Warren, have been generous and enthusiastic in helping me build a life and career, and are a constant source of enjoyment. Lance Ferris helped me through the last stages of this process, and has been nurturing and loving in every way. Finally, Greg Nagy has been present at every stage of the development of this book, and served as advisor to the dissertation that came before it. I cannot thank him enough for his boundless insight, his tireless scrutiny of my writing, and the heartfelt encouragement he provides his current and former students, including me.

June 15, 2004
Sacramento, California

# A NOTE ON TRANSLATIONS
# AND TRANSLITERATIONS

Passages in Greek, Hebrew, and Latin have been given in the original language and in English translation. Translations have been credited to their original translator, even if they have been slightly modified. All unmarked translations from Hebrew, Greek, and Latin are my own, with the exception of unmarked translations from Josephus' *Against Apion*, which are from the Loeb edition and translation by H. St. J. Thackeray.

### A note on transliterations

Greek and Hebrew words crucial to the argument of the text have been transliterated for the benefit of readers who are not familiar with either or both languages.

### Greek transliteration:

The following table indicates the transliterated equivalents of Greek letters and letter combinations. In spelling Greek names, I have used the familiar Latinized forms for names of well-known individuals (Callimachus, Peisistratus, Crates), established English and Latin designations for well-known texts (*Frogs, Certamen Homeri et Hesiodi*), and a more consistent system of transliteration for less familiar Greek names and texts (Hellanikos, Kynaithos, *Karneonikai*).

| Greek | Transliteration | Greek | Transliteration |
|---|---|---|---|
| A α | a | O o | o |
| B β | b | Π π | p |
| Γ γ | g | P ρ | r (rh with initial rough breathing) |
| Δ δ | d | Σ σ ς | s |
| E ε | e | T τ | t |
| Z ζ | z | Υ υ | u or y |
| H η | ê | Φ φ | ph |
| Θ θ | th | X χ | kh |
| I ι | i | Ψ ψ | ps |
| K κ | k | Ω ω | ô |
| Λ λ | l | ʿ | h (rough breathing) |
| M μ | m | γγ | ng |
| N ν | n | γκ | ngk |
| Ξ ξ | x | γχ | ngkh |

## Hebrew transliteration:

I have used the most familiar spellings for well-known names and texts (Baba Bathra, Aboth deRabbi Nathan, Breshit Rabbah, Qoheleth). Other Hebrew transliterations, including less familiar Hebrew names or texts, do not follow the standard of the Society for Biblical Literature (which is fully reversible but unwieldy for transliterating rabbinic Hebrew) nor the system utilized by the Encyclopedia Judaica (which I found to be under-precise), but rather a composite form indicated by the table of consonantal equivalents below. Hebrew vowels are loosely transliterated with their approximate English equivalents.

| Hebrew | Transliteration | Hebrew | Transliteration |
|---|---|---|---|
| א | ' (or disregarded) | ל | l |
| ב | b | מ final ם | m |
| ב | v | נ final ן | n |
| ג | g | ס | s |
| ד | d | ע | ʿ |
| ה | h | פ | p |
| ו | v (only if a consonant) | פ final ף | f |
| ז | z | צ final ץ | z̧ |
| ח | ḥ | ק | q |
| ט | ṭ | ר | r |
| י | y (or disregarded) | שׁ | sh |
| כ | k | שׂ | ś |
| כ final ך | kh | ת | t |

# THE
# ASCENSION
# OF
# AUTHORSHIP

# INTRODUCTION

Finally, I realize how much the specificity of the French intellectual field may have contributed to the conception of this book, in particular to its perhaps immoderate ambition of giving a scientific answer to the old questions of Kant's critique of judgment, by seeking in the structure of the social classes the basis of the systems of classification which structure perception of the social world and designate the objects of aesthetic enjoyment. But in an age when the effects of a premature division of labor separate anthropology from sociology, and within the latter, the sociology of knowledge from the sociology of culture, not to mention the sociology of food or sport, it is perhaps the advantage of a world still haunted by the ultimate and total questionings of the prophetic intellectual that one is led to refuse the self-induced myopia which makes it impossible to observe and understand everything that human practices reveal only when they are seen in their mutual relationships, that is, as a totality.
— Pierre Bourdieu, *Distinction: A Social Critique of the Judgement of Taste*

The modern, Western idea of authorship is at heart an amalgamation of contrasting ideas about individuals and their role in the origins of traditional or sacred texts deriving from Greek and Jewish civilizations. The Greek world valorized the creations of individual poets, orators, and philosophers, and immortalized their achievements in stone and archive. Jewish traditions de-emphasized individual composition, and articulated instead a doctrine of divine authorship, based upon a vision of the writer of scripture that took the prophet as its model.

Authorship is also the product of contrasting valuations of individuals credited with the textualization and physical transmission of literary works. Jewish traditions recognized authoritative writings as guaranteed by the prophetic status of their scribes or the mythical status of the figure that had first given utterance to the work, and tended to ignore other texts. In the ancient Greek tradition, the name of a writer or even of an editor served as a standard to assess the value and authoritativeness of texts. However, this name was far from a foolproof indication. Even when the attribution was deemed authentic, editors were frequently accused of having tampered with the texts they claimed to preserve or rescue. Hellenistic Greek scholars, assured that all documents were equally subject to abuse and neglect, instituted a methodology by which an array of potential flaws in the transmission process could be corrected.

This book represents a comparative study of the literature of the ancient world. In particular, it focuses on ancient literary history — not the literary history that scholars of the modern age have written about the classical and biblical traditions, but the histories that these traditions have told about themselves. I will explore how Jewish exegetes, curious about the transmission history of the Bible, attempted to use clues from the Bible itself to fill in the gaps in their knowledge. These clues were found in the brief and often ambiguous headings that introduce individual compositions or biblical sections. Interpreting these headings was typically a matter of fitting them into pre-existing Jewish ideas about biblical composition.

Hellenistic Greek scholarship attempted to utilize a scientific methodology to repair texts and arrive at the correct author. However, the textual emendations of Greek scholars were sometimes based on subjective considerations or on a faulty understanding of the nature and origin of the text in question. Similarly, the aetiologies developed by Greek traditions to account for the current form of age-old Greek documents were based on the creative interpretation of clues thought to be hidden in historical documents or in the texts themselves. These aetiologies thus resemble the conclusions of Jewish exegetes about the textual history of biblical books.

This study explores the surviving corpus of literary legends, not-quite-historical narratives told about the history of texts, from the Jewish, Hellenistic, and Christian traditions.[1] One type of legend found in all three traditions addresses a scenario involving textual destruction and restoration. These legendary textual traumas are used by each tradition to different ends. Early Jewish sources consistently argue that textual disasters occurred, but that they did not damage the legitimacy of the transmission of sacred texts. Some Jewish traditions have legends of miraculous feats of human memory as the solution for such disasters, and others present these events as the occasion of new divine revelation. Textual disaster is a moment of loss for the Greeks. Greek legends of textual destruction were used to explain poetic phenomena that were not really understood by Greek scholars. These included the simultaneous composition and performance of traditional works like the Homeric epics, or the accumulation of utterances attributed to legendary individuals and sacred sources, such as works attributed to Orpheus, Pythagoras, Hippocrates, Theognis of Megara, and the oracle at Delphi. Greek legends about textual disasters, as well as the frequent Greek speculation about forgery and literary fraud, are typically the justification and impetus for the development of scholarly techniques that restored the damaged original. While miraculous occurrences in textual transmission for early Judaism resulted from this tradition's desire to downplay human agency in textual composition, Greek scholars dwelt upon how transmission could be harmed by the excessive involvement of individuals.

These contrasting views on the role of individuals in textual creation and transmission are useful in tracing the development of Greek and Jewish canons, understood as definitive lists or finite collections of sacred scriptures or other quasi-sacred, authoritative texts. The investigation of the historical principles that regulate the formation and solidification of canons has in part animated my investigation of authorship. It seems clear that the establishment of criteria about the nature, status, or identity of writers of texts was a decisive factor in the formation and consecration of early Jewish, Hellenistic, and Christian canons alike. The writer was an essential organizing principle for the formation of both ancient religious and literary canons; the literary or prophetic status of the writer credited with a given text was a decisive element in evaluating the worth of the text itself in all three traditions.

Early Jewish interpreters developed a procedure for attaching names to sacred texts, although they stopped short of acknowledging human authorship. My analysis of the classical Jewish position on the authorship of the Torah reveals that rabbinic interpreters were interested in the individuals whose names were linked with biblical books solely in their role as copyists of these works. This analysis focuses on a well-known *baraita* (an anonymous teaching from the oldest strata of rabbinic tradition) preserved in the Babylonian Talmud, together with its accompanying commentary (B. Baba Bathra 14b–15a). In this passage, some prophets (like Job) did not have the requisite authority to copy down a biblical book; for such cases the *baraita* assigns an appropriate, contemporaneous Israelite.

Further investigation reveals that this rabbinic teaching represents the culmination of earlier Jewish approaches to the question. Early Second Temple biblical interpreters had attempted to find a given work's composers in order to remedy the anonymity of the work and rescue it from unauthoritative status, while subsequent Jewish interpreters like Josephus viewed scripture as having been recorded by a succession of prophets. Rabbinic exegetes, as represented in the *baraita* mentioned above, paid less attention to the individual's role in the composition of biblical writings. Instead, they focused on discovering the precise conditions of the textualization of biblical books and the individuals responsible for it. Nevertheless, all these interpreters shared a common approach: they organized, assessed, and rejected texts on the basis of the stature and legitimacy of the individuals with whom they were associated. The evidence suggests that authoritative texts had to be attached to a suitably authoritative composer, and later to an eligible scribe, in order to gain standing in any of the many versions of Judaism extant during the Second Temple period. Attribution was an essential component of a system that denied or downplayed individual composition yet utilized individuals to authenticate textual authority.

The writings of Josephus (b. 37/8 C.E.), who stands squarely between the early Second Temple period and rabbinic Judaism, serve as a focal point for this study. A Hellenized Jew of priestly lineage, trained by Essenes and associated with the Pharisees for the sake of political expediency, Josephus' approach to the question of attribution is representative of a variety of Second Temple period Jewish positions on the provenance of the Hebrew scriptures. His critique of Greek agonistic historiography also represents a point of departure for this study; not only did Josephus effectively sum up the differences between Jewish and Greek approaches to composition, but his writings on the subject apparently had a direct impact on the foundation of the Christian conception of authorship. Josephus' point that Hebrew scriptures were recorded by a "succession of prophets" represents an important moment in the evolution of Jewish approaches to attribution. Josephus' idea of a "succession of prophets" derives from a Jewish midrash on the transfer of authority from Moses to Joshua and from Elijah to Elisha. It also represents a rewording of Plato's description of Delphic oracular revelation. Further, Josephus' position with regard to the succession of prophets accords with the rabbinic approach to the textualization of the biblical books: biblical documents are guaranteed by certainty of the identification of the scribe who copied them down.

According to Josephus, the problem with Greek letters was the overly individualistic aims of Greek writers, and the inability of the Greek tradition to sustain an accurate written tradition. A different concern was exhibited among the Greeks themselves. In a culture where the ability of individuals to compose in their own names was a matter of course, the threat to this system was the potential for forgery and plagiarism — the deliberate misattribution of literary works with the intent to derive financial gain or social prestige. The Greeks developed a sophisticated grammatical technique for discovering whether a work was correctly attributed or not: *krisis poiêmatôn* 'attribution analysis'. This study will explore the history of attribution analysis through an examination of the texts in which it is described.

The legendary origin of the techniques of attribution analysis, together with an explanation of the forged elements that this analysis is meant to locate, are most elegantly presented in a Byzantine legend about Peisistratus preserved in the scholia to an Alexandrian grammatical treatise. This particular incarnation of the Peisistratus legend (there are others) conflates the Athenian tyrant

from the sixth century B.C.E., credited by some with the systematization of the Homeric epics, with figures involved in Homeric
scholarship from the third and second centuries B.C.E. It also incorporates elements of the Septuagint translation narrative (the story
of the translation of the Bible into Greek at the behest of Ptolemy,
king of Alexandria.) The resulting amalgamation constitutes an aetiology of the origin of forgery and the development of scholarly
techniques to distinguish genuine from fraud. It is also a legend
that ratifies the Alexandrian text of Homer as a quasi-scriptural
document. This element of the legend is clearly patterned on the
mythical ratification of the Septuagint by the Jews of Alexandria,
and marks yet another influential synthesis of Greek and Jewish
worldviews.

Common to both Jewish and Greek traditions was a fear that
texts could be destroyed and the knowledge contained within them
lost. The Peisistratus legend opened with such a textual disaster;
the result was the introduction of forged lines into Homer and the
soiling of the purity of the Homeric text. The heroes of this story
are the Homeric editors themselves, together with the methodology
they developed to restore the flawed text. A comparable disaster destroyed the Hebrew scriptures during the Babylonian exile, according to a story appearing in an esoteric Jewish text from the late first
century C.E. Although the entire Bible was lost, it was thereafter recalled by Ezra, word for word, together with a great number of
esoteric works intended for only the most worthy of readers. Christian exegetes took comfort in this non-mainstream Jewish legend
and used it to legitimize the authoritative status of works not contained in the Hebrew Bible. While textual destruction was the
occasion of literary fraud in the Greek tradition, it resulted in a pro-
liferation of textual authority for some Jews and many Christians.

Christian biblical exegetes combined Jewish and Greek views
on writers' relationships to texts to create a new concept — authorship as critically and ecclesiastically authenticated prophecy. The
principal component of this notion of authorship was the Jewish
belief of divine composition as recorded in writing by human
prophets. The Church Fathers took strong note of the positions of
major churches and past authorities on the value of a given text;
but they also promoted attribution analysis as a decisive factor in

authenticating prophecy. In effect, the Christian notion of authorship required that the writing had been accomplished truthfully (in
the author's own name), and that it be a vehicle for the divine truth
(the Word of God). For the Church Fathers, an authoritative composition represented the words of its author and the word of God at
one and the same time. The Christian conceptualization of authorship was crafted from a Jewish metal, but was shaped on the anvil
of Greek attribution analysis — the means by which a text was verified as having been composed by the writer to whom it was attributed. Significantly, this version of authorship did not require that the
contributions of human authors to a prophetic text be rigorously
separated from its sacred component; to the contrary, it depended
on the continuing amalgamation of human and divine.

My investigation is based in a number of postulates about the
nature of authorship. Inasmuch as these are premises, they belong
to this introduction — although there is a certain circularity here,
as they are to a certain extent conclusions that I wish to highlight
in a condensed manner before I turn to the examination of the evidence itself.

One premise of this work is that the term "authorship" is not
just an abstraction that describes and has always described what
authors share; it is a culturally and historically determined relationship by which writers are constantly being defined. As recent
theoretical discussions have argued, authorship is shaped and even
created by the discourses that have set out to describe, limit, evaluate, and remunerate the relationship between individuals and texts.
While my study affirms this basic premise (one that, frustratingly,
continues to be seen as threatening to philologists and scholars of
antiquity who have their teeth set on edge by post-Structuralist
thought), I will show that the ancient critical discourses about writers are only part of the story. Another of this study's premises is that
authorship is the product of a historical development featuring cultures with completely opposing views on the nature of the individual and the value of the writer. These cultures were fused together
by a tradition that was unfazed by the diverse and contradictory nature of Greek and Jewish approaches to attribution and composition. It might be added that the Western tradition remains unaware
of the contradictory assumptions inherent to its conception of

authorship, and that its view of the author is paradoxically sustained by the invisibility of the contradiction. Finally, my study points to a yet uncharted direction in the study of authorship, one in which developments in the history of authorship are understood in relation to previous incarnations of the discourse on authors. This itself derives from the premise that discourses are irrevocably tainted by the ways they have been deployed in past. Developments in the history of authorship can be best evaluated through consideration of the underlying dynamic called into being at the ascension of the discourse.

In part, the methodology for my study is informed by the most influential theoretical discussion of authorship in contemporary literary theory, Michel Foucault's essay, "What is an Author?".[2] While this essay (especially when paired with Roland Barthes' "The Death of the Author") has mostly been read as a manifesto on how authors of our own time ought to be evaluated, or even as a theoretical justification for abandoning all discussion of the author in general, it also contains powerful insights about intellectual history.[3]

From the perspective of someone interested in classical and biblical antiquity, Foucault's archaeology of authorship is useful not so much in describing what authorship in these periods is, but rather what it is not. By stripping away layers of theological and technological developments which have determined the nature of authorship in modern times, Foucault reveals that our own notions about what constitutes an author are only partly applicable to the era that preceded the introduction of the printing press and copyright laws. Yet despite the popularity of Foucault's essay in some circles, the realization that authorship in ancient Greece or Israel cannot be described in terms that are at all related to approaches to more recent writers has been slow to penetrate the work of contemporary classical and biblical philologists.

While one reading of Michel Foucault's essay (and of his work in general) leads to the conclusion that newly discovered radical discontinuities in intellectual history invalidate traditional diachronic studies, in another sense this particular essay seems to invite new historical research. Foucault credits St. Jerome (fourth century C.E.) as the individual who created a scheme for distinguishing inspired and non-inspired biblical books by the applica-

tion of biographical principles; he considers this an enduring element in the constitution of the modern author.[4] The fact that this
genealogy of authorship begins with Jerome, the scion of biblical
interpretive communities and Greek literary critics, suggested to
me that European authorship might derive from a theological
foundation in biblical interpretation, melded with approaches to
attribution perfected in Greece and Rome. Even if one admits the
importance of subsequent technological and legal developments
stressed in Foucault's investigation, this genealogy allowed me
(perhaps in an un-Foucauldian way) to postulate the existence of a
theological and cultural dynamic at the heart of the idea of modern
authorship. More to the point of this present work, Foucault's contribution to the discussion opened up new space for a history of
authorship that would not impose anachronistic ideas on ancient
literary culture.

"What is an Author?" is an essay with an interest in the historical construction of authorship, but it does not actually describe in
depth any particular historical moment. Perhaps this can be credited to what appears to be Foucault's real concern, the status of
"initiators of discursive practices" such as Marx and Freud. At the
end of his essay, Foucault asks the question "What matters who's
speaking?" There *is* an answer to this question, although it is perhaps not an answer that the defenders of authorial subjectivity
would like to hear. Historically speaking, the agent is important because it has always been used to assess the legitimacy, canonicity,
sacredness, and truth-value of the written message. Since the Renaissance, authorial agency has been the source of that mysterious
religious relic known as the *originality* of the work — the extent to
which an author can create *ex nihilo* what used to be considered inspired or divine.

Foucault places emphasis on the idea of transgression in the
formation of the author function.

First of all, discourses are objects of appropriation. The form of
ownership from which they spring is of a rather particular type,
one that has been codified for many years. We should note that,
historically, this type of ownership has always been subsequent
to what one might call penal appropriation. Texts, books, and

discourses really began to have authors (other than mythical, "sacralized" and "sacralizing" figures) to the extent that others became subject to punishment, that is, to the extent that discourses could be transgressive.[5]

The historical evidence from ancient Greece does not back up his claim that being subject to punishment came prior to individuals writing in their own names. To the contrary, the desire for public acclaim and the early habit of recording poetic victors in official lists at Argos, Elis, and Delphi, was sufficient to inaugurate this practice, without the existence of any legal strictures prohibiting false ascription. Perhaps one could highlight the transgressive nature of deliberate misattribution in the development of the author function. However, I would point out that innocence historically plays as great a role in the misnaming of works in ancient Greece as does intentional fraud. Ancient scholars were as much on guard against misattribution and homonymy as they were against literary deceit. In a purely innocent way, texts like the *Iliad*, the *Theogony*, the Hippocratic corpus, or the wise sayings of Megara were credited to a few, well-known culture heroes of Greece — Homer, Hesiod, Hippocrates, or Theognis.

On the other hand, the idea of forgery and plagiarism occupies a prominent place in the legendary narratives about textual corruption issued by the Hellenistic world. Literary fraud, both imagined and real, certainly propelled Hellenistic scholars to go to great lengths to investigate the attribution of their texts. But even here, it is likely that deliberate literary fraud was far less frequent than ancient critics imagined. Forgery and plagiarism served as an explanation for textual corruption (and perceived textual corruption) even when other factors were actually to blame.

If Foucault's theory of the transgressive origins of authorship fails to convince, perhaps a more abstract approach to the nature of the way names of writers function in general can be used to explain the appearance of "real authors" in place of legendary personae like Homer, Hesiod, and Hippocrates. This order of affairs would appear to follow from the semiotic properties of all writing, and in particular of the kind of writing that appears most straightforwardly to indicate the presence of the writer — the signature.

To some extent at least, the name of the author functions like any kind of signature. As Jacques Derrida states, "By definition, a written signature implies the actual or empirical non-presence of the signer."[6] But the distinctive semiotic qualities of the signature are even more complex: "In order to function, that is, in order to be legible, a signature must have a repeatable, iterable, imitable form; it must be able to detach itself from the present and singular intention of its production."[7] Because the writer's name can be alienated from its proper attachment to an individual's work (as happens in forgery, plagiarism, mislabeling, and misattribution), or even from the individual himself (as happens in mistaken identity or homonymy), the writer's name becomes analogous to the signature in two respects. First, the alienability of the name triggers a blossoming of a new awareness on the part of ancient literary critics and readers that the writer is a biological, linguistic, and stylistic unity, a single force that lurks behind the text and was initially responsible for it. When the form and content of a given piece of writing do not match ancient readers' preconceived *gestalt* of this writer, the name previously attached may be stripped from the work, and a new one supplied. What counts now is not that the writer is the creator of a work, but that a writer becomes *typified* as the originator of a *kind* of written form and content. In this way, the name of the writer is analogous to the signature, which, in Derrida's formulation, must have "a repeatable, iterable, imitable form." Second, the writer's name resembles the signature by virtue of its ability "to detach itself from the present and singular intention of its production." This name functions as a sign that is supposed to indicate the source of an utterance, and as a sign that allows utterances that approximate a kind of written form and content to be ventriloquized by a shadow writer. This predicament was created the moment the practice of affixing names to texts began, whether this consisted of a signatory seal affixed to the manuscript or a colophon or verse inserted into the first line of the work, at the end, or somewhere within the body of the text.

There are other aspects to the transformation of writers from legendary personae to real persons that must be considered. In part, this transformation can be explained by considering the ancient scholarly discourse on authors. The evidence from ancient

Greece suggests that the alienability of the name from the work contributed greatly to the interest in the person behind that work in the eyes of ancient readers. In other words, authorial biography became an object of study because ancient scholars realized that misattribution of all sorts was a possibility. It would be hard to separate the development of the idea of the writer in ancient Greece from this particular discourse on authors.

My approach has also been influenced by the work of anthropologist Maurice Bloch. Bloch's history of the circumcision ritual in Madagascar reveals that the ritual is tremendously conservative. Although it can be seen to promote certain momentary political agenda or to evolve in a number of minor ways, the ritual's symbolic structure has remained the same over the course of two hundred years. Inspired by Bloch's formulations on the relationship between ritual and history, I examine here the process of canon formation (that is, of the creation of authoritative lists or collections of sacred or authoritative documents) as a kind of ritual. Bloch's investigations reveal that ritual cannot be evaluated as if it were the product of historical circumstances.

> At the very least, a negative point has been made that the ritual has resisted direct modification in response to politico-economic change that many theories in the social sciences would have led us to expect. It is possible to say categorically that the symbolic aspects of this ritual, and probably others like it, are not products of the politico-economic conjuncture of a particular time. A demonstration of how the ritual fits in a politico-economic context would at any particular point in our historical sequence be quite convincing and indeed probably valid, but it would *not* be an explanation of the symbolic content of the ritual.[8]

The discipline of anthropology's critique of approaches that have sought to connect ritual to political and economic circumstances underscores the impracticality of attempting to find a causative link between the idea of the canon and the history of a social formation, synchronically or in the very short term. As Bloch puts it, the task of the investigator in studying the determination of the symbolic by the social is not to investigate initial creation, but to discover "the principles of transformation." I have learned from this that the formation of the canon of Hebrew scriptures, of the canon of the New Testament, or even of the lists of first-rate authors promulgated by Alexandrian scholars, cannot be tied to an all-powerful academy of rabbis, church council, or convocation of grammarians. These institutions are legendary and aetiological; even when they existed, they did not determine canons, but rather endorsed the collective decisions of the traditions that preceded them.

The same may be said of the notion of the author, which in both Greek and Jewish cultures derives from a sacral view of the originators of tradition. I have not sought to describe the origin of authorship. For, as Bloch puts it,

> History has no beginning: People always act in a world constructed by previous generations. What we are seeking, therefore, when we try to understand how events construct culture are not rules of formation from a zero point but rules of transformation of an already existing system.[9]

While it is impossible to pinpoint a decisive originary moment in the formation of a Western notion of authorship, it remains the case that authorship has changed. Thus Josephus, through cultural contact and polemic, identified the Greek idea of the writer as an innovator and gainsayer of tradition by observing Greek culture from without. He may have helped transform the Jewish perspective on writers as well. Prior to Josephus, the writer had served to guarantee the provenance of Jewish scriptures, just as his status served to indicate the work's value. In order to inoculate the writer from newly identified Greek attitudes, the Jewish writer became more than ever before a scribe who contributed nothing to the text. Similarly, it was the combinatory impulses of Christianity, led by the rigorous inquiry of St. Augustine in particular, that first made note of another key transformation in the history of authorship. Augustine, having inherited a Greek view of writers (as well as a Roman approach to lawgivers), understood that he had to account for the will and intention of the human authors of his own sacred tradition, something to be measured against the intent of the divine author and the meaning of the words themselves.

In the spirit of this search for the rules of transformation, I have entitled this study "The Ascension of Authorship." The ascension refers to the moment at the conclusion of the Gospel of Luke (and in the ending added to the Gospel of Mark) when the resurrected Jesus is carried up into heaven. The ascension of Jesus connects him to his types from the Old Testament, namely Enoch and Elijah, who were similarly transported to heaven in the flesh. The notion of ascension is not an origin; it is rather a lifting up, a change in location rather than in essence. The connection of "ascension" with Christianity is thus fitting for the thesis of this book — that Western authorship implies a Christian, archetypal assumption of Greek and Jewish views on the nature of writers. But to use Hegel's term, the ascension of authorship is also its "sublation" (*Aufhebung*). This word, although deriving from the simple notion of "lifting up" (German *heben,* Latin *tollo, tollere, -tuli, -latum*), actually implies that in the process something has become united with its opposite, or even canceled and abrogated.[10] Indeed, various aspects of Greek and Jewish assumptions about composition were originally suppressed as they were assumed into the culture of Christianity. These aspects included the Jewish refusal to consider the literary creation of writers outside the prophetic succession (early Christians, in contrast, allowed for individuals to write a variety of literary works in their own names). Meanwhile, the Greek idea of the *agôn* or contest as a compelling guide to the valuation of literary merit was vacated as an ideal, in favor of the discrimination of the church and its officials. But even as they were suppressed and cancelled, these features were also preserved (the other meaning of "sublated" or *aufgehoben*), to be reactivated under changing historical circumstances, aesthetic sensibilities, and religious beliefs. At length, it would be possible to say that the *agôn* had become responsible for choosing society's prophets — a not entirely felicitous turn.

The statement of Pierre Bourdieu quoted in the epigraph to this introduction makes me question the wisdom of attempting to call attention to the prophetic, Jewish element hidden (or sublated) within contemporary discourses of authorship and criticism alike. The prophetic pretensions of critical discourse are what enable

Bourdieu to examine societal structures as a totality rather than to fall prey to the mind-numbing imperative that produces specialists scared to tackle larger issues for fear of moving outside their field. Deprived of the idea that prophets continue to exist, it is possible that individual scholars will be not able challenge this imperative in the future.

Attempting to make meaningful and sound analyses of materials from a variety of disciplines is a humbling experience, in which scholars like myself must endure accusations of dilettantism and anxieties about qualifications. Such at least has been my own experience in the field of comparative literature, as a student of classical philology, biblical interpretation, Jewish texts, and modern literary theory. Would it be possible to dabble in so many fields if I had no pretense of a "vision" that could counteract my limitations in any one of these areas? The desire for acclaim, the *kleos* 'fame, glory' that is the reward of the scholarly *agôn*, is another element that propels this study. Though I am unable to escape these two sublated principles of Western authorship, I will nevertheless attempt to uncloak the continuing influence of prophecy and the *agôn* on literary and cultural discourse.

Also working against the possibility that an individual may challenge prevailing norms in our current society is a development that occurred in the past thirty or forty years — the attack on the cultural organizing principle called "the canon." Without the social function played by canonization in the ancient world, there is no socially legitimated collection of cultural artifacts that allows individuals the opportunity to assess our culture. While the broadest possible array of artifacts is now fortunately available for analysis, the sheer glut of cultural objects can only foster increasing specialization, rather than encourage more encompassing assessments of literature and the other arts. But contrary to popular belief, canons are not gone for good. We now have canonical lists of texts and authors that relate to the approaches of critical theory, rather than agreed upon canons of literary texts and authors that may be treated critically. The shift reflects a new power structure: individuals are increasingly expected to master a certain limited number of works of theory or criticism, or to attain mastery of a shrinking field of knowledge, but not both. Wholesale acceptance of this new canon of theory and criticism makes the ignorance of traditional, canonical knowledge forgivable for some, and encourages over-specialization in others. Thus, cultural forces have accomplished the elimination of one contribution of the ancient world which might have enabled scholars of the future the opportunity to have an impact on society — namely, the formation of an agreed upon set of works that embody what our culture is and to what it aspires.

I have sought to avoid the use of the word "author" to describe poets, rhetoricians, or historiographers in the Greek world, or the composers of biblical works. To do so would prove to be a difficult exercise in sifting out the Jewish or Greek elements of authorship, in order to avoid the evaluation of one culture in terms of the other. To some, it might seem that using the word "author" to describe literary composers in either Jewish or classical traditions could not possibly influence our understanding of either tradition in a negative way. Yet while the object of this study is not to purify literary analysis of anachronism or cultural imposition, it remains a fact that speaking of Greek poets or biblical composers as "authors" amounts to both. It would not hurt for the disciplines involved in the study of such traditions to be wary of speaking inaccurately about the composition process. This is not a quibbling over terms; it represents a plea for recognition of cultural and historical difference.

It has been observed that ancient Judaism doesn't have a notion of authorship equivalent to that of the modern world. James Kugel finds in rabbinic literature a profound lack of interest in comparing biblical with belletristic writers:

> There are many occasions in rabbinic writings when, without denigration, biblical authors might have been compared, if only by way of homespun analogy, to makers of poems or histories or orations (as indeed midrash often compares God to an ordinary king, Moses to a court-scribe, etc.). Surely Moses, David or Isaiah might have been described as "poets" (as they later were by Christian writers), if only to extol their technical prowesses beyond those of ordinary singers. But they were not; the whole rabbinic orientation was pitched against this.[11]

What might be more surprising is there is no single word in ancient Greek for "author." Hellenistic literary historians divided what we would call authors into a two basic categories, poets (*poiêtai*) and prose writers (*sungrapheis*). Even the words for "lines" were referred to differently by the Alexandrian scholars, according to whether they were lines of poetry (*epê*) or prose (*stikhoi*).[12] Poets were further distinguished into the categories of epic, elegiac, iambic, melic, tragic, and comic poets. Historians, together with geographers and novelists, were simply called *sungrapheis* 'prose writers' (this term has survived in Modern Greek as the unmarked term for 'author'). Others were labeled according to their area of expertise rather than by the formal characteristics of their writing — namely, philosophers, orators, physicians, and grammarians.

What's more, the word *poiêtês* 'poet' was initially not used by poets themselves, but implied a view of poetry as a mere craft. Prior to the fifth century B.C.E., composers were not differentiated from performers. The multiple meanings of the more prevalent and archaic designation, *aoidos* 'singer', indicate that performance and composition were viewed as inseparable facets of a single activity. Andrew Ford points out that the term *poiêtês* was known but avoided by fifth century tragedians and epinician poets.[13] Comic playwrights, however, with their ears attuned to contemporary jargon, represented poetry as a *tekhnê* 'craft' like any other, and mockingly employ the vocabulary of "making" in hyperextended compounds.[14] Ford concludes that the term *poiêtês* emphasizes the "maker's artful designs rather that his moral wisdom or divine inspiration," and suggests that it was employed by those who were not singers and who championed new forms of knowledge.[15]

To take another example, the situation with regard to the tragedians of fifth century Athens does not allow one to discern a straightforward equivalent to the idea of the author. Rudolf Blum's reconstruction of the content of Aristotle's influential list of tragic works called the *Didaskaliai* 'rehearsals, productions' is a case in point. In a most straightforward sense, the poet is referred to as a *didaskalos* 'teacher' rather than as a creator of tragic verses:

> It was customary that the poets produced and directed their new
> plays and dithyrambs themselves. This was called *didaskein* (liter-

ally "teaching"), and the authors of plays and dithyrambs were specifically called *didaskaloi* (literally "teachers"), as the lexicographer Harpokration (second century C.E.) explains.[16]

In the lingo of this genre (or at least of the criticism that dealt with this genre), the tragic playwright is given a label by metonymy that refers to one of his characteristic duties — that of teaching the chorus. This metonymy is in itself curious — why should the essential element highlighted in the label applied to the tragic poet be one that has only a tangential relationship to the activity of poetic composition? Were the tragedians considered primarily as choral directors rather than as poets because the status of this role overshadowed other social roles? The high-ranking status of "director" in contemporary film springs to mind as a comparison; scriptwriters (and "book" or "concept" authors, in cases where the script has been adapted) rarely, if ever, achieve the status or notoriety of the director.

The confusing metonymy is compounded by the fact that there were important cases in which the playwright did not serve as the director of his plays. While the three tragic playwrights directed their own plays during their lifetime, works left by Sophocles and Euripides were produced posthumously by their relatives. Aristophanes, the most famous comic playwright from Athens, may never have directed his own plays. Blum finds that the customary term continued to apply in such cases: "The author remained however even in these cases the *didaskalos* in the broader sense. The director who was commissioned and of course paid by the author was called a *hypodidaskalos* (literally "sub-teacher") in the fourth century."[17] So the terminology is adapted to changing circumstances that made the term *didaskalos* a dead metonymy. Apparently, no one saw fit to change the familiar label, but less accustomed roles had new terms coined that reflected the way the theater was practically organized.

I would also caution against the use of the terms "forgery" or "plagiarism" to describe the complex motivations in the Jewish world's composition of texts in the name of a prototypical individual. They derive from a Greek understanding of the inviolable connection between a work's composer and the text to which his or her name is affixed, and are out of place in describing Jewish textual production. In the Greek tradition, writers typically wrote in their own names, not in the names of their culture heroes. (There are of course exceptions, and certain discourses seemed to have a heightened tolerance for legendary authorship.) But writing a text in one's own name is, from the perspective of early Judaism, as disturbing a cultural habit as writing in the name of Moses or Ezra would be to us; it should be recognized as such, and not merely dismissed as the logical, default attribution procedure because it happens to be the practice of the twentieth century heirs of the Greek tradition. There is little that affected the development of individuality in European culture as much as the fact that we inherited a Greek approach to marking our own texts with our own names rather than the Jewish reticence towards speaking from one's own perspective *in propria persona*.

A final word on the kinds of sources this work investigates. The discussion of individual agency in composition is framed in two distinct approaches to literary study by ancient critics — theorization about the role of the individual in the creation of any kind of text, and a more historical treatment explaining the transmission and textualization of specific texts. My thesis focuses on recovering these cultures' traditions about the transmission and textualization of their chief literary documents — the Homeric epics and the Bible. At times these sources concern themselves with the narrowest form of textualization — the recopying of manuscripts or translation of texts — rather than the moment of their composition. However, it will become clear that traditions about transmission and textualization are often the occasion for theorization about the nature of composition itself, and contain valuable information about each culture's conceptualization of the relationship between texts and names.

# CHAPTER I

# THE SCRIBES OF THE HEBREW BIBLE

The classical Jewish explanation for the textual origin of biblical scriptures is encapsulated in a short passage found in the Babylonian Talmud, the pre-eminent canonical document of rabbinic Judaism that achieved written form ca. 600 C.E. The passage is found in the tractate Baba Bathra 'the Last Gate', which addresses concerns relating to property, inheritance, and real estate.[1]

Baba Bathra 14b–15a is a repository of rabbinic teachings about the human scribes of the Bible. It gives a complete account of the Jewish position on who wrote the books of the Bible. There is an interest in the lifespan of the putative transcriber of each biblical book; when the book describes the death of this transcriber, the text arrives at a candidate who recorded his death and finished copying out the book he had begun. In addition to being the most complete critical treatment of the process of textualization of the Bible in Jewish sources, this text's methodical discussion sheds light on the earliest Jewish positions on human agency in biblical composition.

This passage has been much discussed from the perspective of what it might reveal about the state of the canon in the early rabbinic period. It has been described as the definitive formulation of rabbinic attitudes towards authorship of the Bible; however, I will argue that "authorship" or human composition are not at all the concern of this text. Through a comparison of this text with other approaches to the textualization of the Bible in the Second Temple period, it is my contention that Baba Bathra 14a–15b is concerned with textual transmission of biblical books and the process whereby prophecies and histories achieved a written form, and does not ever assert that these texts had been composed by the individuals with whom they were linked.

The passage that I will discuss includes a received tradition (a *baraita* 'remainder' originating in the Tannaitic period, the earliest stratum of rabbinic literature) answering the question "who wrote the scriptures."[2] This *baraita* is followed by commentary (*gemara*) deriving from the Amoraic period (the second oldest stratum of rabbinic literature) and later. I cite the text here:

ומי כתבן? משה כתב ספרו ופרשת בלעם ואיוב: יהושע כתב ספרו ושמונה פסוקים שבתורה:
שמואל כתב ספרו ושופטים ורות: דוד כתב ספר תהלים ע״י עשרה זקנים: ע״י אדם הראשון,
על ידי מלכי צדק, ועל ידי אברהם, וע״י משה, ועל ידי הימן, וע״י ידותון, ועל ידי אסף,
ועל ידי שלשה בני קרח: ירמיה כתב ספרו וספר מלכים וקינות: חזקיה וסיעתו כתבו
(ימש״ק סימן) ישעיה, משלי, שיר השירים וקהלת: אנשי כנסת הגדולה כתבו (קנד״ג סימן)
יחזקאל ושנים עשר, דניאל ומגילת אסתר: עזרא כתב ספרו ויחס של דברי הימים עד לו.
מסייעא ליה לרב, דאמר רב יהודה אמר רב: לא עלה עזרא מבבל עד שיחס עצמו ועלה.
ומאן אסקיה? נחמיה בן חכליה. אמר מר: יהושע כתב ספרו ושמונה פסוקים שבתורה. תניא
כמאן דאמר: שמונה פסוקים שבתורה יהושע כתבן, דתני: (דברים ל״ד) וימת שם משה עבד
ה׳ - אפשר משה (מת) (מסורת הש״ס: [חי]) וכתב וימת שם משה? אלא, עד כאן כתב משה,
מכאן ואילך כתב יהושע, דברי ר״י, ואמרי לה ר׳ נחמיה; אמר לו ר״ש: אפשר ס״ת חסר אות
אחת? וכתיב: (דברים ל״א) לקוח את ספר התורה הזה אלא, עד כאן הקב״ה אומר ומשה
אומר וכותב, מכאן ואילך הקב״ה אומר ומשה כותב בדמע, כמו שנאמר להלן: (ירמיהו לו)
ויאמר להם ברוך מפיו יקרא אלי את כל הדברים האלה ואני כותב על הספר בדיו. כמאן
אזלא הא דא״ר יהושע בר אבא אמר רב גידל אמר רב: שמונה פסוקים שבתורה יחיד קורא
אותן? לימא, (ר״י היא) ודלא כר״ש אפילו תימא ר״ש, הואיל ואשתנו אשתנו. יהושע כתב
ספרו. והכתיב: (יהושע כ״ד) וימת יהושע בן נון עבד ה׳ דאסקיה אלעזר. והכתיב: (יהושע כ״ד)
ואלעזר בן אהרן מת דאסקיה פנחס. שמואל כתב ספרו. והכתיב: (שמואל א׳ כ״ח) ושמואל
מת דאסקיה גד החוזה ונתן הנביא. דוד כתב ספר תהלים על ידי עשרה זקנים. וליחשוב
נמי איתן האזרחי אמר רב: איתן האזרחי זה הוא אברהם, כתיב הכא: (תהלים פ״ט) איתן

האזרחי. וכתיב התם: (ישעיהו מ"א) מי העיר ממזרח צדק [וגו']. קא חשיב משה וקא חשיב
הימן. והאמר רב: הימן זה משה, כתיב הכא: הימן, וכתיב התם: (במדבר י"ב) בכל ביתי נאמן
הוא תרי הימן הוו. משה כתב ספרו ופרשת בלעם ואיוב. מסייעא ליה לר' לוי בר לחמא.
דא"ר לוי בר לחמא: איוב בימי משה היה, כתיב הכא: (איוב י"ט) מי יתן אפוא ויכתבון מלי.
וכתיב התם: (שמות ל"ג) ובמה יודע אפוא. ואימא: בימי יצחק, דכתיב: (בראשית כ"ז) מי אפוא
הוא הצד ציד ואימא: בימי יעקב: דכתיב: (בראשית מ"ג) אם כן אפוא זאת עשו ואימא:
בימי יוסף. דכתיב: (בראשית ל"ז) איפה הם רועים לא ס"ד. דכתיב: (איוב י"ט) מי יתן בספר
ויוחקו. ומשה הוא דאיקרי מחוקק, דכתיב: (דברים ל"ג) וירא ראשית לו כי שם חלקת מחוקק
ספון. רבא אמר: איוב בימי מרגלים היה, כתיב הכא: (איוב א') איש היה בארץ עוץ איוב
שמו. וכתיב התם: (במדבר י"ג) היש בה עץ. מי דמי? הכא עוץ. התם עץ הכי קאמר להו
משה לישראל: ישנו לאותו אדם, ששנותיו ארוכות כעץ ומגין על דורו כעץ.

I. [*Baraita*]: Who wrote [the scriptures]?

    A. Moses wrote his own book and the portion (*parashah*) of Balaam and Job.[3]

    B. Joshua wrote the book which bears his name and [the last] eight verses of the Pentateuch.

    C. Samuel wrote the book which bears his name and Judges and Ruth.[4]

    D. David wrote the Book of Psalms, including in it the work of ten elders, namely Adam "the first," Melchizedek, Abraham, Moses, Heman, Yeduthun, Asaph, and the three sons of Korah.

    E. Jeremiah wrote the book which bears his name, the Book of Kings, and Lamentations.

    F. Hezekiah and his colleagues wrote (Mnemonic YMSHK) Isaiah, Proverbs, the Song of Songs, and Ecclesiastes.

    G. The Men of the Great Assembly wrote (Mnemonic KNDG) Ezekiel, the Twelve Minor Prophets, Daniel, and the Scroll of Esther.

    H. Ezra wrote the book that bears his name and the genealogies of the Book of Chronicles up to his own time.

II. [*Gemara*]:

    A. 1. This confirms the opinion of Rab, since Rab Judah has said in the name of Rab: Ezra did not leave Babylon to go up to Ereẓ Yisrael until he had written his own genealogy.

2. Who then finished it [the Book of Chronicles]?
   a. Nehemiah the son of Ḥakhaliah.
B. The Master has said: Joshua wrote the book which bears his name and the last eight verses of the Pentateuch.
   1. This statement is in agreement with the authority who says that eight verses in the Torah were written by Joshua, as it has been taught: [It is written], "So Moses the servant of the Lord died there."
   2. Now is it possible that Moses being dead could have written the words, "Moses died there"?
      a. The truth is, however, that up to this point Moses wrote, from this point Joshua wrote. This is the opinion of R. Judah, or, according to others, of R. Nehemiah.
   3. Said R. Simeon to him: Can [we imagine the] scroll of the Law being short of one letter, and is it not written: "Take this book of the Law"?
      a. No; what we must say is that up to this point the Holy One, blessed be He, dictated and Moses repeated and wrote, and from this point God dictated and Moses wrote with tears, as it says of another occasion, "Then Baruch answered them, He pronounced all these words to me with his mouth, and I wrote them with ink in the book."
   4. Which of these two authorities is followed in the rule laid down by R. Joshua b. Abba which he said in the name of R. Giddal who said it in the name of Rab: The last eight verses of the Torah must be read [in the synagogue service] by one person alone?
      a. It follows R. Judah and not R. Simeon.
      b. I may even say, however, that it follows R. Simeon, [who would say that] since they differ [from the rest of the Torah] in one way, they differ in another.
   5. [You say that] Joshua wrote his book. But is it not written, "And Joshua son of Nun the servant of the Lord died"?
      a. It was completed by Eleazar.

6. But it is also written in it, "And Eleazar the son of Aaron died"?

   a. Phineas finished it.

C. [You say that] Samuel wrote the book that bears his name. But is it not written in it, "Now Samuel was dead"?

   1. It was completed by Gad the seer and Nathan the prophet.

D. [You say that] David wrote the Psalms, including the work of the ten elders.

   1. Why is not Ethan the Ezrahite also reckoned with?

      a. Ethan the Ezrahite is Abraham. [The proof is that] it is written in the Psalms, "Ethan the Ezrahite," and it is written elsewhere, "who hath raised up righteousness from the East (*mi-mizraḥ*)."

   2. [The passage above] reckons both Moses and Heman. But has not Rab said that Moses is Heman, [the proof being] that the name Heman is found here [in the Psalms] and it is written elsewhere [of Moses], "In all my house he is faithful"?

      a. There were two Hemans.

E. You say that Moses wrote his book[5] and the section (*parashah*) of Balaam and Job.[6]

   1. This supports the opinion expressed by R. Levi b. Laḥma who said that Job was contemporary with Moses.

      a. [The proof is that] it is written here [in connection with Job], "Who will give now (*'efo*) and will write my word?" and it is written elsewhere [in connection with Moses], "For in this now (*'efo*) shall it be known."

   2. But on that ground I might say that he was contemporary with Isaac, in connection with whom it is written, "Who now (*'efo*) is he that took venison?"

   3. Or I might say that he was contemporary with Jacob, in connection with whom it is written, "If so now (*'efo*) do this"? or with Joseph, in connection with whom it is written, "Where (*'efo*) they are pasturing?"

4. This cannot be maintained; [The proof that Job was contemporary with Moses is that] it is written [in continuation of the above words of Job], "Would that they were inscribed in a book," and it is Moses who is called "inscriber," as it is written, "And he chose the first part for himself, for there was the lawgiver's (= *meḥoqeq* 'inscriber') portion reserved."

5. Taba said that Job was in the time of the spies.

    a. [The proof is that] it is written here [in connection with Job], "There was a man in the land of Uz (*'uẓ*) Job was his name," and it is written elsewhere [in connection with the spies], "Whether there be wood (*'eẓ*) therein."

        1) Where is the parallel? In one place it is *'uẓ*, in the other *'eẓ* 'wood'?

            a. What Moses said to Israel was this: [See] if that man is there whose years are the years of a tree (*'eẓ*) and who shelters his generation like a tree (*'eẓ*).

Baba Bathra 14b–15a,<br>trans. Simon (outline form mine)

The passage contains discussions relating to a wide range of subject matter, all of which spring from the question, "Who wrote the scriptures." The *baraita* in fact begins before the passage quoted above, with a statement on the order of the Prophetic books of the Bible, followed by a statement on the order of the Hagiographa. The commentary on the *baraita* also flows into the contents of the discussion that follows — an extended interpretation of the historical setting and composition of the Book of Job in 15a–16b. Nevertheless, the question *mi ketavan* 'who wrote [the scriptures]?' applies in some form to the entire passage cited above, providing a certain coherency of motivation and allowing a description of the passage as a discrete unit.

Based on the presence of characteristics that resemble those of Akkadian colophons, H. M. I. Gevaryahu has proposed that the *baraita* in Baba Bathra 14b–15a was based on an earlier catalogue that detailed the names, chronology, and authorship of the books of the Bible.[7] He also proposes that the very "editors" of the headings in the Prophets, Wisdom books, and Psalms, made use of such catalogues. If catalogues of this sort indeed existed, the *baraita* may itself cast light on the Second Temple period during which the headings in the Prophets, Wisdom books, and Psalms were composed. However, "Who wrote the scriptures?" is in part derived from the peculiar wording of biblical headings, especially Proverbs 25:1. If it does reflect an older catalogue text, it is probably in a rather vague way.

The *baraita* sheds light on the passage from *Against Apion* by Josephus in which the failure of the 'succession' of the prophets after Artaxerxes is blamed for the fact that they "have not been deemed worthy of like trust." Conversely, Josephus' statement provides a backdrop on prophetic recordkeeping that is crucial to the Talmudic understanding of authorship. I quote the passage here:

καὶ τούτων πέντε μέν ἐστι Μωυσέως, ἃ τούς τε νόμους περιέχει καὶ τὴν ἀπ' ἀνθρωπογονίας παράδοσιν μέχρι τῆς αὐτοῦ τελευτῆς· οὗτος ὁ χρόνος ἀπολείπει τρισχιλίων ὀλίγῳ ἐτῶν. ἀπὸ δὲ τῆς Μωυσέως τελευτῆς μέχρι τῆς Ἀρταξέρξου τοῦ μετὰ Ξέρξην Περσῶν βασιλέως οἱ μετὰ Μωυσῆν προφῆται τὰ κατ' αὐτοὺς πραχθέντα συνέγραψαν ἐν τρισὶ καὶ δέκα βιβλίοις· αἱ δὲ λοιπαὶ τέσσαρες ὕμνους εἰς τὸν θεὸν καὶ τοῖς ἀνθρώποις ὑποθήκας τοῦ βίου περιέχουσιν. ἀπὸ δὲ Ἀρταξέρξου μέχρι τοῦ καθ' ἡμᾶς χρόνου γέγραπται μὲν ἕκαστα, πίστεως δ' οὐχ ὁμοίας ἠξίωται τοῖς πρὸ αὐτῶν διὰ τὸ μὴ γενέσθαι τὴν τῶν προφητῶν ἀκριβῆ διαδοχήν.

Of these [our 22 books], five are the books of Moses, comprising the laws and the traditional history from the birth of man down to Moses' death. This period falls only a little short of 3,000 years. From the death of Moses down to Artaxerxes who followed Xerxes as king of Persia, the prophets after Moses wrote the events of their own times in thirteen books. The remaining four books contain hymns to God and precepts for the conduct of human life. From Artaxerxes down to our own time, the complete history has been written, but has not been deemed worthy of like trust with the earlier records, because of the absence of an exact succession (*diadokhê*) of the prophets.

Josephus, Against Apion 1.39–42, trans. Thackeray

The nature of this *akribês diadokhê* 'exact succession' has been one of the most contested ideas in studies of the canon of the Hebrew Bible, precisely because there are so few texts that give reasons for the inclusion or exclusion of biblical books that predate the rabbinic corpus. This work proposes that the Tannaitic approach to the prophetic succession (as it appears in the *baraita* in Baba Bathra 14b–15a) can be used to understand the full meaning of Josephus' statement, and vice versa. Baba Bathra 14b–15a marks an extreme form of early Jewish exegetical approaches to the problem of human agency in the composition and transmission of the Bible. Both the passages from Josephus and Baba Bathra center on the succession of scribes who recorded biblical events. For Josephus, the succession of prophets is at the core of a system that distinguishes between authoritative and non-authoritative texts (see chapter 4). Baba Bathra 14b–15a specifies the succession of scribes who wrote down the Bible, employing internal biblical evidence to arrive at the names that made up this succession.

At first glance, the *baraita* does not differentiate between authorship and scribal activity. But there are a number of clues that indicate that authorship is not at all its concern. For example, Solomon, the traditional author of Proverbs, Song of Songs, and Ecclesiastes, is not included here. Instead, the works usually ascribed to him are linked to Hezekiah and his companions, who, according to Proverbs 25:1, merely transcribed this single book. A more detailed discussion from the verse in Proverbs will follow; for the moment, I will focus on Baba Bathra's interest in the role of Hezekiah at the expense of Solomon:

חזקיה וסיעתו כתבו (ימש״ק סימן) ישעיה, משלי, שיר השירים וקהלת. אנשי כנסת הגדולה כתבו (קנד״ג סימן) יחזקאל ושנים עשר. דניאל ומגילת אסתר:

Hezekiah and his colleagues wrote (Mnemonic YMSHK) Isaiah, Proverbs, the Song of Songs and Ecclesiastes. The Men of the Great Assembly wrote (Mnemonic KNDG) Ezekiel, the Twelve Minor Prophets, Daniel and the Scroll of Esther.

Baba Bathra 15a

Is biblical authorship to be considered the equivalent of the activity of scribes, copying out the word of God? Why aren't the real "authors" of these texts, who, at least in the case of Solomon, were well established and accepted by the rabbinic tradition, mentioned here? Why is it not worth mentioning that the prophets wrote their prophecies? These are questions that I will return to in the course of this study. What may be said here is that the *baraita* is more interested in writing as textualization than in writing as composition.[8]

Another seeming example of the lack of distinction between original authorship and copying out of a given text may be seen in Baba Bathra's description of David's role vis-à-vis the Psalms. The text states:

דוד כתב ספר תהלים ע"י עשרה זקנים. ע"י אדם הראשון. על ידי מלכי צדק. ועל ידי אברהם. וע"י משה.
ועל ידי הימן. וע"י ידותון. ועל ידי אסף ועל ידי שלשה בני קרח:

> David wrote the book of Psalms including in it the work of ten elders: Adam, Melchizedek, Abraham, Moses, Heman, Yeduthun, Asaph, and the three sons of Korah.
>
> Baba Bathra 14b–15a

This passage gives information about the contributors to the book of Psalms that conflicts with other rabbinic sources.[9] In addition, the uncommon usage of על ידי *'al yidey* (abbreviated ע"י) with an active verb in this passage has been a source of some confusion.[10] It has been interpreted as 'including in it' in several modern translations, an interpretation that seems to derive from Rashi's understanding of the expression.[11] A parallel use of *'al yidey* (normally the marker of agency in passive constructions) with active verbs sheds light on the problem. The expression is found in Mishnah Sheqalim 6–7:

ה שוקל על ידי כהן על ידי אשה על ידי עבד על ידי הטן פטור

> The man paying the shekel on behalf of (*'al yidey*) a priest, on behalf of a woman, on behalf of a slave, or on behalf of a minor, is exempt.

Here '*al yidey* with an active verb means 'on behalf of'. In light of this, the sentence from Baba Bathra should be translated: "David copied out the Psalms on behalf of ten elders." The usage suggests that David does for the ten elders what they could not do for themselves — put their psalms into writing and compile them. It does not indicate that he himself composed any Psalms, perhaps because this is assumed, or perhaps because Davidic authorship is not the main concern of the passage. This ellipsis of the role of David as composer of Psalms was not satisfactory for all rabbinic commentators. David is listed as one of the ten elders in Midrash Tehillim 1:6, in order to make plain that he also copied for the other elders and on his own behalf — that is, that he also copied down the psalms which he himself composed.

An interesting parallel to the list of the textualizers of the Bible in Baba Bathra 14b–15a is found in B. Sanhedrin 17b, where a comprehensive "crib sheet" for the identity of the nameless individuals who are credited with Talmudic teachings is laid out:

- למידין לפני חכמים - לוי מרבי. דנין לפני חכמים -
שמעון בן עזאי. ושמעון בן זומא. וחנן המצרי. וחנניא בן חכינאי. רב נחמן בר יצחק מתני
חמשה: שמעון. שמעון. ושמעון. חנן. וחנניה. רבותינו שבבבל - רב ושמואל. רבותינו
שבארץ ישראל - רבי אבא. דייני גולה - קרנא. דייני דארץ ישראל - רבי אמי ורבי אסי.
דייני דפומבדיתא - רב פפא בר שמואל. דייני דנהרדעא - רב אדא בר מניומי. סבי דסורא
- רב הונא ורב חסדא. סבי דפומבדיתא- רב יהודה ורב עינא. חריפי דפומבדיתא - עיפה
ואבימי בני רחבה. אמוראי דפומבדיתא - רבה ורב יוסף. אמוראי דנהרדעי - רב חמא.
נהרבלאי מתנו - רמי בר ברבי. אמרי בי רב - רב הונא. - והאמר רב הונא: אמרי בי רב -
אלא: רב המנונא. אמרי במערבא - רבי ירמיה. שלחו מתם - רבי יוסי בר חנינא. מחכו עלה
במערבא - רבי אלעזר. - והא שלחו מתם לדברי רבי יוסי בר חנינא - אלא איפוך: שלחו
מתם - רבי אלעזר. מחכו עלה במערבא - רבי יוסי בר חנינא.

[The following rules apply throughout the Talmud: The statement,] "It was argued before the Sages," refers to Levi who argued before Rabbi. "It was discussed before the Sages," refers to Simeon b. Azzai, Simeon b. Zoma, Ḥanan the Egyptian, and Ḥanania b. Ḥakinai. R. Naḥman b. Isaac taught that there were five: the three Simeons, Ḥanan [the Egyptian] and Ḥanania [b. Ḥakinai].

"Our Rabbis in Babylon" refers to Rab and Samuel.

"Our rabbis in Ereẓ Yisrael," to R. Abba.

"The judges of the Exile," to Qarna.

"The judges of Ereẓ Yisrael," to R. Ammi and R. Assi.

"The judges of Pumbeditha," to R. Papa b. Samuel.

"The judges of Nehardea," to R. Adda bar Minyomi.

"The elders of Sura," to R. Huna and R. Ḥisda.

"The elders of Pumbeditha," to Rab Judah and R. ʿAina.

"The keen intellects of Pumbeditha," to ʿEfa and Abimi, sons of Reḥabah.

"The Amoraim of Pumbeditha," to Rabbah and R. Joseph.

"The Amoraim of Nehardea," to R. Ḥama. [Where we read,] "Those of Neharbelai taught," it refers to Rammi b. Berabi.

"They said in the School of Rab," refers to R. Huna. But did not R. Huna himself say, "They said in the School of Rab"? — R. Hamnuna is therefore the one referred to.

"They said in the West," refers to R. Jeremiah.

"A message was sent from Palestine," to R. Jose b. Ḥanina. "They laughed at it in the West," to R. Eleazar. But do we not read: "A message was sent from Palestine: according to R. Jose b. Ḥanina . . ."? — Therefore reverse it: "A message was sent from Palestine" refers to R. Eleazar; "They laughed at it in the West," to R. Jose b. Ḥanina.

B. Sanhedrin 17b, trans. Shachter

This passage clearly indicates that namelessness in the promulgation of authoritative teachings is deemed by this stratum of rabbinic culture as a condition to be remedied. Every vague attribution is pinned down to a specific named individual. At the same time, Sanhedrin 17b calls attention to the fact that earlier rabbinic tradents had either not been able to identify their predecessors, or felt no need to do so, at least with the specificity encountered here. In the past, vague statements indicating the source of a given teaching were evidently felt to be sufficient. But at the time of the creation of the passage above, the relative anonymity of many attributions in the Talmud had evidently become a liability, and the authority of individual rabbis was felt to be an essential element of a given teaching.

## The History of the Interpretation of Proverbs 25:1

### RABBINIC INTERPRETATIONS

The notion of a "Hezekian Recension" of the Bible or of portions of the Bible has long been a subject for modern biblical interpretation.[12] However, in the process of trying to discover the historical reality behind this "Hezekian Recension" (and indeed through the evaluation of rabbinic documents as belated witnesses to this process), what has been neglected is an investigation into what rabbinic and Second Temple biblical interpreters *thought* Hezekiah's role in biblical transmission was. One text that takes its cue from Baba Bathra's description of the role of Hezekiah in the transmission of the Bible is Aboth deRabbi Nathan, a commentary to Pirke Aboth from the Mishnah.[13]

הוו מתונים בדין כיצד מלמד שיהא אדם ממתין בדין שכל הממתין בדין מיושב בדין שנאמר גם אלה
משלי שלמה אשר העתיקו אנשי חזקיה מלך יהודה (משלי כ״ה א׳) <u>ולא שהעתיקו אלא שהמתינו</u>
אבא שאול אומר <u>לא שהמתינו אלא שפירשו</u> בראשונה היו אומרים משלי ושיר השירים
וקהלת גנוזים היו שהם היו אומרים משלות ואינן מן הכתובים ועמדו וגנזו אותם
עד שבאו אנשי כנסת הגדולה ופירשו אותם שנאמר וארא בפתאים אבינה בבנים נער חסר לב
[וגו׳] והנה אשה לקראתו שית זונה ונצורת לב הומיה היא וסוררת בביתה לא ישכנו רגליה פעם
בחוץ פעם ברחובות ואצל כל פנה תארוב והחזיקה בו ונשקה לו העיזה פניה ותאמר
לו זבחי שלמים עלי היום שלמתי נדרי על כן יצאתי לקראתך לשחר פניך ואמצאך מרבדים
רבדתי ערשי חטבות אטון מצרים נפתי משכבי מור אהלים וקנמון לכה נרוה דודים עד הבקר נתעלסה
באהבים כי אין האיש בביתו הלך בדרך מרחוק צרור הכסף לקח בידו ליום הכסא יבא ביתו (משלי ז׳)
וכתיב בשיר השירים לכה דודי נצא השדה נלינה בכפרים נשכימה לכרמים נראה אם פרחה
הגפן פתח הסמדר הנצו הרמונים שם אתן את דודי לך (ז׳ י״א) וכתיב בקהלת שמח בחור
בילדותך ויטיבך לבך בימי בחורותיך והלך בדרכי לבך ובמראה עיניך ודע כי על כל אלה יביאך
האלהים במשפט (י״א ט׳) וכתיב בשיר השירים אני לדודי ועלי תשוקתו (ז׳ י״א) הוי לא שהמתינו
אלא שפירשו :

Be Deliberate in Judgment: what is that? This teaches that a man should take time in rendering judgment; for whoever takes time in rendering judgment is unruffled in judgment. As it is said, "These also are the proverbs of Solomon which the men of Hezekiah king of Judah copied out" (Prov. 25:1): <u>it is not that they copied them out *(he'etiqu)*, but that they took their time *(himtinu)*.</u>

Abba Saul says: <u>It does not mean that they took their time</u> (*himtinu*)<u>, but that they interpreted</u> (*pirshu*). Originally, they used to say that Proverbs, Song of Songs, and Ecclesiastes were suppressed (*genuzim hayu*); for since they were held to be parables and not part of the Holy Writings (*ketuvim*), they arose and suppressed (*ganzu*) them, until the Men of the Great Assembly[14] came and interpreted them.

For [in Proverbs] it is said,
[quotation of Prov. 7:7–20]
And it is written in the Song of Songs,
[quotation of Song 7:12–13]
And it is written in Ecclesiastes,
[quotation of Song 11:9]
And (again) it is written in the Song of Songs,
[quotation of Song 7:11]

This proves, not that they took their time (*himtinu*), but that they interpreted (*pirshu*).

Aboth deRabbi Natan, Version A,
trans. Goldin, with modifications

Many scholars of the history of the canon of the Hebrew Bible have attempted to find in this text some reflection of the actual state of affairs during the process of canonization.[15] However, the idea that Proverbs,[16] Ecclesiastes, and Song of Songs were ever under dispute as "canonical" books,[17] or that any of these books were ever *genuzim* 'stored away' or suppressed has not been accepted by all.

The passage from Aboth deR. Natan, as well as the entire rabbinic debate about the storing away of biblical books, hangs on the interpretation of an editorial heading that appears midway through the book of Proverbs. I cite the biblical verse here:

גַּם־אֵלֶּה מִשְׁלֵי שְׁלֹמֹה אֲשֶׁר הֶעְתִּיקוּ אַנְשֵׁי ן חִזְקִיָּה מֶלֶךְ־יְהוּדָה׃

These too are the Proverbs of Solomon which the men of Hezekiah, king of Judah, copied out (*he'etiqu*).

For modern biblical scholars, the interpretation of Proverbs 25:1 touches on some but not all of the questions which troubled rabbinic and other early biblical interpreters. The larger questions for modern scholars are: what was the activity of the "men of Hezekiah" with regard to the textual history of at least a portion of the book of Proverbs? What kind of social entity does the expression "men of Hezekiah" refer to? Answering the first question has involved trying to come up with a technical understanding of the verb *he'etiqu*, used nowhere else in the Bible in the sense it seems to have here.[18] The second has involved a broader sociological and historical focus, and lies outside the scope of the present inquiry.[19]

According to Michael Fishbane, "This text (Prov. 25:1) is a valuable witness to court-sponsored scribal activity in ancient Israel, although it is not certain whether the verb הֶעְתִּיקוּ indicates the transmission or transcription of literary sources."[20] Fishbane cites M. Weinfeld, who has proposed 'transmitted', comparing the Hebrew verb with Akkadian *šûtuqu* (from *etēqu*).[21] He also cites the evidence of the Septuagint and rabbinic sources to support the translation 'transcribed'. H. M. I. Gevaryahu thinks of the biblical heading in the context of the complete corpus of such notices in the Hebrew Bible that detail the biblical books and persons connected with them, and compares them to the corpus of Akkadian colophons that give information about scribes and the contents of the book. "Should my hypothesis be correct, we may conclude that the 'editors' of the headings in the Prophets, Wisdom books, and Psalms, made use of such catalogues."[22]

Proverbs 25:1 is the only place in the Bible where *he'etiq* means 'copied out'. Brown-Drivers-Briggs (BDB), explaining how this expression came to mean 'transcribe', interprets the verb thus: '*remove* from one book or roll to another' — because the *hiph'il* of the root '*tq* usually refers to moving or transferring something from one place to another. Although the Septuagint reading *exegrapsanto* possibly reflects this ancient meaning of the word, some later readers took *he'etiqu* literally to mean 'they removed' [from circulation], in other words that the men of Hezekiah 'stored away' these works.

A brief comment on the original meaning of this term: *he'etiq*, employed here in a late text (a title or chapter heading likely deriving from the Second Temple period) and nowhere else in this sense in the Bible, may be a neologism. It is analogous to a technical meaning of the Greek word *metapherô* 'copy from one scroll to another' (cf. Strabo 13.1.54 C 609, a meaning not listed in Liddell-Scott-Jones). The *hiphʿil* of the root עתק 'to move, advance' corresponds with the Greek prefix *meta-* 'across, over' added to the root *pherô* 'to bear, carry'.

The activity of transferring material from one scroll to another was obviously not unknown to the Israelites prior to the Hellenistic period; however, the coining of a word to represent precisely this activity — instead of the more normal *katav* 'write' — would indicate a critical awareness of the distinction between writing as composing and writing as copying the words of another author. Several of the ancient versions uphold the crucial distinction between write meaning 'compose' and write meaning 'transcribe.' Thus the Septuagint translates *exegrapsanto* 'they wrote out', adding the prefix *ex* to mark this writing as something other than composition. Jerome's Vulgate eschews the word 'write' in any form, and renders the word as *transtulerunt* from *transfero, -ferre, -tuli, -latum;* this is the precise equivalent of the Greek technical term *metapherô* 'transfer'.

Many scholars of the history of the canon of the Hebrew Bible have attempted to find in the passage from Aboth deR. Natan some reflection of the process of canonization.[23] It is my view that this passage and its parallels (B. Shabbath 30b,[24] Pesikta of Rab Kahana 68b = Leviticus Rabbah 28.1,[25] Tosefta Yadaim 2.14,[26] or St. Jerome's *Commentary on Ecclesiastes* 12.13 ff.[27]) dramatize the process of reconciliation of apparent self-contradictions in revered texts more than they reflect an actual historical debate. In other words, these passages must be examined as performative literary expressions of religious confidence in troubling biblical material, not just as historical records, if they can be considered records at all. It is quite possible that the midrashic explanations of the philological or logical problems presented by Ecclesiastes, Song of Songs, or Proverbs preceded and resulted in the creation of the legendary disputes they purport to record. Rabbinic interpretive doubt might have been retrojected into the hoary past, in order to legitimize the solutions the rabbis created.[28] Of course it is also possible that these passages convey a faint recollection of an ancient doubt about certain non-prophetic works, particularly the Solomonic corpus. These two possibilities, it should be added, are not mutually exclusive.

Against the hypothesis that these passages are reflections of a genuine historical debate, I will show that the idea of a historical dispute over these books derives from confusion over the interpretation of Proverbs 25:1. The passage that displays this process most clearly is Aboth deR. Natan, version A (cited above), which discusses the meaning of *he'etiqu* in Proverbs 25:1 at length. There are two viewpoints preserved in Aboth deR. Natan: 1) "It is not that they *he'etiqu* them, but that they took their time;" and 2) "It does not mean that they took their time, but that they interpreted." Saul Lieberman explains the first of these statements in version A as making the distinction between copying a complete text and copying a brief selection from a set of writings.[29] According to Lieberman's theory, Aboth deR. Natan's statement "It is not that they copied them out, but that they took their time" could be rephrased: it is not that they copied them [mindlessly like a scribe], but that they took their time [and chose from among other writings of Solomon]. In Lieberman's understanding, the word *he'etiq* in its "plain sense" seems to be linked with scribal activity. This "plain sense" of the word is challenged and replaced with an alternate interpretation — 'to take one's time'. According to Lieberman's reading, since the "plain sense" of *he'etiq* — 'copy out' — was unsatisfactory for understanding the true meaning of the verse, Aboth deR. Natan supplied a new definition.

But was 'copy out' the recognized "plain sense" of *he'etiqu* in rabbinic times? Of all the ancient versions of Proverbs 25:1, only the Septuagint clearly interprets *he'etiqu* to mean 'copy out'. All the other translations and commentaries attempt to extrapolate from the etymology of the verb to understand its meaning. These interpretations generally focus on two separate roots '*tq*, one meaning 'to move' and the other meaning 'old'. Breshit Rabbah 1:5 confirms that 'removed' or 'withheld' was a possible meaning of *he'etiq* in rabbinic Hebrew. Moreover, most of the ancient versions of Prov. 25:1 seem to have understood *he'etiqu* as meaning something other than copy out. I have been unable to find an example of *he'etiq* in the rabbinic corpus that clearly means 'copy out'.

In a word, the "plain sense" of *he'etiq* was problematic; two more satisfactory options (the anonymous *himtinu* 'they took their time' and Abba Saul's *pirshu* 'they interpreted') are supplied, but neither is definitively endorsed. I would argue that the "plain sense" meaning of he'etiq was 'remove'.[30] This interpretation explains why it was challenged by Abba Saul and the anonymous discussant: the plain sense was problematic, because it implied that biblical books had been suppressed. Thus the tradition that follows Abba Saul's statement ("originally, they used to say that Proverbs, Song of Songs, and Ecclesiastes were suppressed") presumes that he'etiq means 'remove' or 'store away'.

If I am correct that the word he'etiq meant 'remove' for most rabbinic interpreters, the verse ("These too are the proverbs of Solomon which the men of Hezekiah, King of Judah, removed") implied to these interpreters something very serious about the history of scripture. Did the men of Hezekiah remove them from circulation and store them in a geniza? And if so, who brought them back? The rabbinic interpreters who held the view that Proverbs 25:1 described the suppression of Proverbs, and perhaps other Solomonic works as well, were compelled also to create a story of their return to circulation. Interpretations piled up on top of each other, and the exegetes were no longer aware of the source of their stories. Some blamed the suppression on the men of Hezekiah (the plain sense interpretation of Proverbs 25:1). Some claimed the men of Hezekiah had actually brought these works back into circulation; others credited the Men of the Great Assembly (the manuscript reading of Aboth deR. Natan),[31] or the Academy of Yavne. Still others saw the entire debate about suppression of biblical books as taking place at the Yavne. Thus, some saw "interpretation" as the meaning of the confusing word in Proverbs 25:1 (implying that the men of Hezekiah had never suppressed these works), while others saw interpretation as the means by which the suppressed books were removed from the geniza at a much later date. I propose that this confusion lies at the heart of the many statements regarding the suppression of biblical books found throughout rabbinic literature.[32] I also propose that the same confusion resulted in the legend of a debate over the status of individual books of scripture supposedly accomplished by the Academy of Yavne.[33]

As the extended discussion in Aboth deR. Natan suggests, the meaning of he'etiqu was an interpretive problem for the rabbis. Far from having special insight into its historical reality in the time of

Hezekiah, they sought to define the word through an approach to interpretation fundamentally different from modern linguistic and philological methods.

## THE ANCIENT VERSIONS OF PROVERBS 25:1

The ancient translations of this verse reveal that the verse was a problem for other strands of Jewish interpretation. I list below the Hebrew text as pointed by the Masoretes, followed by the principal ancient Greek and Latin versions.[34]

Masoretic Text: גַּם־אֵלֶּה מִשְׁלֵי שְׁלֹמֹה אֲשֶׁר הֶעְתִּיקוּ אַנְשֵׁי | חִזְקִיָּה מֶלֶךְ־יְהוּדָה׃

Septuagint (LXX): αὗται αἱ παιδεῖαι Σαλωμῶντος αἱ ἀδιάκριτοι, ἃς ἐξεγράψαντο οἱ φίλοι Ἐζεκίου τοῦ βασιλέως τῆς Ἰουδαίας.

Theodotian: [αὗται αἱ] παραβολαὶ [Σαλωμῶντος, ἃς] ἐπαλαίωσαν [οἱ φίλοι Ἐζεκίου] τοῦ βασιλέως Ἰούδα.

Aquila: καίγε αὗται παραβολαὶ (Σαλωμῶντος), ἃς μετῆραν ἄνδρες Ἐζεκίου τοῦ βασιλέως Ἰούδα.

Symmachus: καὶ ἔτι αὗται παροιμίαι [Σαλωμῶντος, ἃς] ἐπαλαίωσαν [οἱ φίλοι Ἐζεκίου] τοῦ βασιλέως Ἰούδα.

Vulgate: Haec quoque parabolae Salomonis quas transtulerunt viri Ezechiae regis Iuda.

### Removed

In the Greek translation of Proverbs 25:1 by Aquila, the verb in question is translated as 'removed': "These too are the parables (of Solomon), which the men of Hezêkiah removed (metêran, from metairô 'take across')." The dual sense of the verb metairô, which can also mean 'repeal', as in to 'repeal a decree' (psêphisma) in Demosthenes 19.174, might have facilitated its employment in translating he'etiq, in that its own transference from literal 'removing' to metaphorical 'repealing' could be used to assert that a similar extension of meaning was implicit in *heʿetiq*. To Aquila's translation may be compared the interpretation of *heʿetiq*, in Aboth deR. Natan (A) that follows the opinion of Abba Saul: "Originally, it is said, Proverbs, Song of Songs, and Ecclesiastes were suppressed (*ganaz*); for since they were held to be mere parables and not part of the Holy Writings, they arose and suppressed them." The conclusion that *ganaz* is a gloss on *heʿetiq* in this passage is buttressed by the manuscript of Aboth deR. Natan, where it is understood that the Men of Hezekiah had stored away and that the Men of the Great Assembly reintroduced them into circulation. The equation of *heʿetiq* with *ganaz* 'store away in a geniza', like its translation by Aquila as *metêran* 'remove', seems to derive from reading the word *heʿetiq* in the way it is everywhere else employed in the Bible (Genesis 12:18; 26:22; Job 9:5; 32:16) — namely, in the sense 'to cause to move' or even 'to remove' (e.g. Job 9:5). In an effort to specify what this removal might entail, some early interpreters concluded that these works could only have been *removed from circulation*, and that Hezekiah and his men had stored them away.

An example of *heʿetiq* that may help explain how it came to be understood as an equivalent to *ganaz* 'stored away' is found in Breshit Rabbah:

ר׳ הונא בשם בר קפרא פתח (תהלים לא) תאלמנה שפתי שקר וגו׳ אתפרכן אתחרשן אשתתקן אתפרכן אתחרשן היך מה דאת אמר (שמות ד) או מי ישום אלם או חרש או פקח או עור הלא אנכי ה׳ ואומר (בראשית לז) והנה אנחנו מאלמים אלומים בתוך השדה והנה קמה אלומתי אשתתקן כמשמעו הדוברות על צדיק חי העולמים עתק שהעתיק בבריותיו בגאוה אתמהה בשביל להתגאות ולומר אני דורש במעשה בראשית ובוז אתמהה מבזה על כבודי

R. Huna quoted in Bar Qappara's name: "Let the lying lips be dumb — *teʾalamnah*" (Ps. 31:19): this means, 'Let them be bound, made dumb, and silenced'. 'Let them be bound', as in the verse, "For, behold, we were binding sheaves — *meʾallemim ʾallumim*" (Gen. 37:7); 'Let them be made dumb', as you read, "Or who made a man *ʾillem* 'dumb'" (Ex. 4:11); while 'Let them be silenced' is its literal meaning. "Which speak *ʿataq* 'arrogantly' against the righteous" (Ps. 31:19), meaning, [which speak] against [the will of] the Righteous One, who is the Life of all worlds, on matters which he has withheld (*heʿetiq*) from His creatures. 'With pride' (ibid.) in

order to boast and say, "I discourse on the Creation work (ma'aśeh)!"
'And contempt' (ibid.): to think that he contemns My Glory!

Breshit Rabbah 1.5, trans. Freedman and Simon

In this passage, R. Huna provides an interpretation of Psalm 31:19:

תֵּאָלַמְנָה שִׂפְתֵי שָׁקֶר הַדֹּבְרוֹת עַל־צַדִּיק עָתָק בְּגַאֲוָה וָבוּז׃

Let the lying lips be dumb (te'alamnah), which speak against
the righteous arrogantly ('ataq) with pride and contempt.

According to R. Huna, Psalm 31:19 is directed against those who
speak the esoteric proto-Kabbalistic mysteries of the Creation
work[35] in an attempt to increase their own glory, rather than according to rules which stipulate the number of listeners who may
hear such teachings (one), as well as their age (forty and above).
R. Huna speaks of God as having he'etiq 'withheld' the esoteric discourse on Creation. The choice of this word must have been pre-
cipitated by the use of the adjective 'ataq 'arrogant' (a meaning
which seems far from both roots 'tq presented above) in Psalm
31:19. This much is clear: he'etiq here serves as an equivalent to
ganaz, but in the sense of an esoteric teaching that has both been
hidden and which one is not permitted to discourse on in public.

The suggestion that biblical books had been stored away, in a
geniza or storeroom like other problematic extra-biblical books,
was not acceptable to all exegetes.

### Made Old

The Greek translations of Proverbs 25:1 by Symmachus and
Theodotian translate he'etiqu as ἐπαλαίωσαν epalaiôsan 'made old'
(palaios). Saul Lieberman explains the translation as originating
from another root spelled 'tq, as in the Aramaic and Hebrew word
עתיק 'old' (e.g., Daniel 7:9). Lieberman compares this translation
with the glossing of the word by the anonymous Tanna in the beginning of the Aboth deR. Natan's discussion as himtinu 'they took
their time'. According to Lieberman, he'etiqu was held by these in-

terpreters to derive from the *hiph'il* (causative) of a root meaning 'be old'.

I would add that the Greek translation turns the idea of 'making old' into something which little resembles 'taking one's time'; Greek *epalaiôsan* means 'to decay through lapse of time' (in the passive), and even 'to abrogate, cancel'.[36] Even should an interpreter conclude that *he'etiqu* derived from *'atiq* 'old', it was possible to infer that the works of Solomon were stored away in a *geniza* by the men of Hezekiah.

### Wrote

Of the translations or paraphrases we possess, only two interpret *he'etiqu* as 'wrote'. The Septuagint has ἐξεγράψαντο (*exegrapsanto*), which means 'wrote out' in the sense of 'copied'. The *baraita* preserved in Baba Bathra 14b, חזקיה וסיעתו כתבו 'Hezekiah and his companions wrote', echoes this understanding of *he'etiqu*. But the *baraita*'s rendering of *he'etiqu* in Proverbs 25:1 as *katvu* 'wrote' might be ambiguous in other ways. In particular, *katav* as used in Baba Bathra does not appear to distinguish between authorship and scribal activity; usually Solomon would be considered the "author" of Proverbs, not Hezekiah. But as I argue below, a closer look at the Baba Bathra passage reveals that its use of *katav* never implies authorship, but more narrowly indicates scribal activity. The *baraita* in Baba Bathra is concerned with the identity and status of the scribes who copied out the books of the Bible, and the scriptural evidence that allows their identity to be determined. The *baraita* methodically traces the textualization of the Bible through the agency of human scribes, not its authorship.

### Interpreted

It is possible that Abba Saul's understanding of *he'etiqu* as *pirshu* 'interpreted' is itself a "translation" of the term. If so, how does he understand the word? Saul Lieberman suggests that Abba Saul saw in *he'etiqu* the idea of the transference from meaning to meaning. Lieberman further compares Abba Saul's understanding of the

verb to the more usual term *haśa'ah* 'lifting', which is typically employed in Mishnah and Tosefta to describe a shift from language to
language or from subject to subject.[37]

The story about Song of Songs, Ecclesiastes, and Proverbs having their paradoxes or sexually explicit content interpreted away in
order to rescue them from the geniza is most likely a fiction. The
opinion attributed to Abba Saul represents an attempt to solve the
dilemma of two contradictory interpretations of the same passage
(actually of the same word, *he'etiq*). Abba Saul attempts to keep
both motifs, the "removed" motif and the "interpreted" motif, by
creating a scenario in which the storing away happened first, and
the reconciliation of difficult passages happened later. He supplies
appropriate passages from the three biblical books to justify the
storing away. Finally, he shows how the problems were ameliorated
and the books restored through interpretive solutions, which he details. None of this describes a historical event.

A passage from the Talmud (B. Sanhedrin 101b) takes the idea
of *he'etiq* as 'interpretation' one step further.

(משלי כ"א) גם אלה משלי שלמה אשר העתיקו אנשי חזקיה מלך יהודה. וכי חזקיה מלך יהודה לכל
העולם כולו <u>לימד</u> תורה, ולמנשה בנו לא לימד תורה?

> These are also the proverbs of Solomon, which the men of Heze-
> kiah king of Judah *he'etiqu*" (Prov. 25:1). Now would Hezekiah
> king of Judah have <u>taught</u> (*limmed*) the Torah to the whole world
> yet not to his own son Manasseh? . . .
>
> B. Sanhedrin 101b, trans. Freedman

In this passage, the verb *he'etiq* seems to be glossed *limmed* 'taught'
rather than 'copy out'.[38] If *limmed* 'taught' can indeed be read as a
gloss of *he'etiq*, it should be understood as extending the idea of
*piresh* 'interpreted' found in Aboth deR. Natan. In essence, this
gloss explains the practical implications of Hezekiah "interpreting"
Torah — namely, that this interpretation took place in a public context and was meant to convey information to others.

## Also

An explanation for the many points of divergence in the translation of Proverbs 25:1 cannot just be sought in the translation of *he'etiqu* itself. Another confusing issue for ancient interpreters was the Hebrew word *gam* 'also' which comes at the beginning of the sentence.

A survey of the ancient versions reveals a pattern, separating the translations that begin the sentence with 'also' from those that include an adjective to describe the proverbs which are to follow. What must be remembered about Proverbs 25:1 is that the information it conveys regarding the transmission of the book as a whole appears in the middle of the book, not at the beginning. All of the ancient interpreters seem to have been puzzled by the placement of such information two-thirds of the way through the book, beginning with the word *gam*. Several interpreters apparently asked themselves, if the heading were only to apply specifically to the proverbs which followed 25:1 (in other words, "The men of Hezekiah *he'etiqu* the following proverbs, but not the preceding ones"), in what way is *gam* to be understood as 'also' or 'in addition'? The answer for these interpreters: *gam* should be read with the verb as an adverb, not with the demonstrative *'eleh* 'these'.

The various translations have made an attempt to understand what the additional activity performed by the men of Hezekiah consisted of. The Septuagint concludes that these proverbs in particular were textually confusing and unassembled in a single manuscript (*adiakritoi*). Thus, the addition of the adjective *adiakritos* (a word that appears nowhere else in the Septuagint) resulted from an unwillingness to connect Proverbs chapters 1–24 with Proverbs 25:1 ff. The reason why the men of Hezekiah had to write these chapters out is that Proverbs 25 ff. required extra editorial work.

The Septuagint apparently does not translate *gam* 'also' at all; but it may be more accurate to say that it does not syntactically link the adverb to the word *'eleh* 'these', as does the Hebrew Masoretic Text by means the hyphen or *maqaf*. The Septuagint finds that Hezekiah and his men wrote out Proverbs 25:2 ff. in addition to doing something else.

It might be helpful here to consider the Alexandrian provenance of the Septuagint translation, and Alexandria's place in the development of textual criticism. One of Alexandria's legends concerns the figure Peisistratus, whose role in the textualization of the Homeric epics eerily resembles what the history of scholarship has made out of Hezekiah:

Ἦν δέ, ὥς φασιν, ἀπολόμενα τὰ τοῦ Ὁμήρου· τότε γὰρ οὐ γραφῇ παρεδίδοτο, ἀλλὰ μόνῃ διδασκαλίᾳ καὶ ὡς ἂν μνήμῃ μόνῃ ἐφυλάττετο. Πεισίστρατος δέ τις Ἀθηναίων τύραννος, ἐν ἅπασιν ὢν εὐγενής, καὶ ἓν τοῦτο θαυμαστὸν ἐβουλεύσατο· ἠθέλησε γὰρ καὶ τὴν Ὁμήρου ποίησιν ἔγγραφον διαφυλάττεσθαι. Προθεὶς δὲ ἀγῶνα δημοτελῆ καὶ κηρύξας καὶ δοὺς ἄδειαν τοῖς εἰδόσι καὶ βουλομένοις τὰ Ὁμήρου ἐπιδείκνυσθαι, καὶ μισθὸν τάξας στίχου ἑκάστου ὀβολόν, συνήγαγεν ὁλοσχερεῖς τὰς λέξεις καὶ παρέδωκεν ἀνθρώποις σοφοῖς καὶ ἐπιστήμοσιν . . .

It happened, as they say, that the works of Homer were destroyed. For at that time they were handed down not in writing, but by teaching/performance (*didaskalia*) alone, so that they might be kept through memory. Peisistratus, tyrant of Athens, was in every way of noble birth, and he contrived this one remarkable deed. He wished, in writing (*engraphos*), to maintain (*diaphulattô*) even the *poiêsis* of Homer. He established games (*agôn* pl.) at public cost, made a public proclamation, and granted amnesty for those who knew and wished to make a public demonstration of (*epideiknumi*) the works of Homer; and having fixed the price at an obol a line, he gathered together the readings (*lexis* pl.) in rough form (*holoskherês* pl.) and handed them over to men both clever and learned . . .

Scholia to Dionysius Thrax, *Scholia Vaticana* (cod. C), 5.11–25, ed. Hilgard p.179

The parallels in these legends are striking. The tenuous textual situation of Homeric epics parallels the loss of thousands of Solomon's utterances. Through the intercession of the remarkable tyrant Peisistratus, it was thought by Alexandrians that Homer had been saved. But notice the way that he accomplishes this action: he gathers together the transcripts of Homeric performers (presumably causing them to be written down), and hands them over to a group of editors. We know from other versions of the Peisistratus legend, and from the nature of Alexandrian scholarship, that part of the activity of these scholars was to create new editions of Homer, and part was to declare which lines were genuine and which were not. It is in this light that I would interpret the Septuagint choice of *adiakritoi* 'unassembled' and *exegrapsanto* 'they copied out': according to the Septuagint, Hezekiah and his companions were basically editors of a large chunk of Proverbs, on the order of the Alexandrian grammarians and their royal patrons.

The *baraita* in Baba Bathra 14b had a different interpretation of the 'also' in Proverbs 25:1, one which similarly did not connect the *gam* to *'eleh*. According to this tradition, Hezekiah and his companions wrote down *all* of the book of Proverbs, in addition to Ecclesiastes, Song of Songs, and the book of Isaiah too.[39] Thus, Proverbs 25:1 is used as evidence that Hezekiah *katav* 'wrote down' more than just Proverbs chapters 25 and following. Implicit in Aboth deR. Natan is the same contention — that the statement in Proverbs 25:1 applied not just to the book of Proverbs, but also to the other works traditionally ascribed to Solomon. Both traditions thus share in this important detail — whatever Hezekiah did was done to more than just Proverbs 25 ff.

One must conclude that Aboth deR. Natan and similar texts cannot be used as a record of a debate over the canonicity of Proverbs, Ecclesiastes, or Song of Songs, or even as a record of the fact that they were temporarily stored away. The opinion that these works had been stored away is based on a homiletical re-interpretation of the meaning of Proverbs 25:1, and does not derive from a true historical tradition.

## A CHRISTIAN INTERPRETATION OF PROVERBS 25:1

I have advanced the view that ancient interpreters focused on Proverbs 25:1 as a way of explaining the transmission history of at least portions of the Bible. The evidence suggests that versions of this history derived from syntactic and lexical exegesis rather than from independent historical information. This trend is continued in the writings of Hippolytus, Bishop of Portus (ca. 170–ca. 236 C.E.), who provides a midrashic-type exegesis of the Proverbs 25:1, focusing on a single confusing word in the Septuagint translation of the verse. Speaking of the vast number of works attributed to Solomon in 1 Kings 4:32, Hippolytus asks where they have vanished, or if they ever existed:

Καὶ ποῦ πᾶσα ἡ πλουσία αὕτη γνῶσις; ποῦ δὲ τὰ μυστήρια ταῦτα καὶ ποῦ αἱ βίβλοι; ἀναφέρονται γὰρ μόναι αἱ Παροιμίαι, καὶ ἡ Σοφία, καὶ ὁ Ἐκκλησιαστὴς, καὶ τὸ Ἆσμα τῶν ᾀσμάτων. Τί οὖν ψεύδεται ἡ Γραφή; μὴ γένοιτο. Ἀλλὰ πολλὴ μέν τις ὕλη γέγονε τῶν γραμμάτων, ὡς δηλοῖ τὸ λέγειν "Ἆσμα τῶν ᾀσμάτων·" σημαίνει γὰρ ὅτι, ἅπερ εἶχον αἱ πεντακισχίλιαι ᾠδαὶ ἐν τῷ ἑνὶ διηγήσατο· ἐν δὲ ταῖς ἡμέραις Ἐζεκίου τὰ μὲν τῶν βιβλίων ἐξελέχθησαν, τὰ δὲ περιώφθησαν. Ὅθεν φησὶν ἡ Γραφή· "Αὗται αἱ Παροιμίαι Σολομῶντος αἱ ἀδιάκριτοι, ἅς ἐγράψαντο οἱ φίλοι Ἐζεκίου τοῦ βασιλέως·" πόθεν δὲ ἐξελέξαντο, ἀλλ ἢ ἐκ τῶν τῶν ἐγκειμένων ἐν αἷς λέγει ταῖς τρισχιλίαις παραβολαῖς καὶ πεντακισχιλίαις ᾠδαῖς; Ἐξ αὐτῶν οὖν τούτων οἱ φίλοι Ἐζεκίου σοφοὶ ὑπάρχοντες ἐξελέξαντο τὰ πρὸς οἰκοδομὴν τῆς Ἐκκλησίας. Τάς τε βίβλους τοῦ Σολομῶντος τὰς περὶ τῶν Παραβολῶν καὶ Ὠδῶν, ἐν αἷς περὶ φυτῶν καὶ παντοίων ζώων φυσιολογίας, χερσαίων, πετεινῶν τε καὶ νηκτῶν, καὶ ἰαμάτων πάθους, πάντως γραφείσας αὐτῷ ἀφανεῖς ἐποίησεν Ἐζεκίας διὰ τὸ τὰς θεραπείας τῶν νοσημάτων ἔνθεν κομίζεσθαι τὸν λαόν, καὶ περιορᾷν αὐτῶν παρὰ θεῷ τάς ἰάσεις.

And where is all this rich knowledge? And where are these mysteries? And where are the books? For the only ones extant are Proverbs, and Wisdom, and Ecclesiastes, and the Song of Songs. What then? Does the Scripture speak falsely? God forbid. But the matter of his writings was of great quantity, as is shown in the phrase "Song of Songs;" which indicates that in this one book he digested the contents of the 5,000 songs. In the days of Hezekiah, some of the books were selected (eklegô), and others discarded. Whence the Scripture says, "These are the unselected (adiakritoi)

Proverbs of Solomon, which the friends of Hezekiah the king copied out." And from what books did they select (*eklegô*) them, if not out of the books containing the 3,000 parables and the 5,000 songs? Out of these, then, the wise friends of Hezekiah took those portions which bore upon the building up of the Church. But the books of Solomon on the "Parables" and "Songs," in which he wrote of the physiology of plants, and all kinds of animals belonging to the dry land, and the air, and the sea, and of the cures of disease, Hezekiah obliterated (*aphaneis epoiêsen*), because the people looked to these for the remedies for their diseases, and neglected to seek their healing from God.

Hippolytus, *On the Song of Songs* (PL 10.627–630), trans. Salmond[40]

The evidence for the missing works of Solomon is found by Hippolytus in Proverbs 25:1. We are to believe that Hezekiah had access to all of these works, but saved only proverbs beginning in chapter 25. According to Hippolytus, the activity of the companions of Hezekiah was not limited to transferring material from one scroll to another, but rather consisted of sifting through thousands of parables for "those portions which bore upon the building up of the Church."

This explanation contains elements implicit in some of the other interpretations of Proverbs 25:1 that we have seen above. The other songs and parables of Solomon are among the works that in Jewish terms might be 'stored away' (*ganaz*). Alternately, the critical activity of the men Hezekiah according to Hippolytus resembles the glossing of *he'etiqu* as *pirshu* 'they interpreted', for it postulates that a critical evaluation of the nature of each parable and its relation to "the building up of the Church" was the basis for the ultimate decision to copy out these parables in particular. According to Hippolytus, this was not a textual or philological procedure (such as might be discerned in the Septuagint's initial choice of the adjective *adiakritos*), but a procedure involving questions of the value of the content of these parables.[41]

Hippolytus' discussion makes plain that the debate over the meaning of Proverbs 25:1 continued to focus on the translation of individual words. For Hippolytus, the Septuagint's use of *adiakritoi* 'unselected' implied a process of sifting on the part of the early collectors of scripture, in which proverbs with a sacred focus were lifted out of a large body of works composed by Solomon with a purely secular content. Thus, at stake in the discussion of an individual word was the history of scripture. Like early Jewish interpreters, Hippolytus provides an interpretation of the broader implications of the verse, and attempts through this interpretation to gain a grasp of the transmission history of the works of Solomon.

### LATER JEWISH INTERPRETATIONS OF PROVERBS 25:1

Comparable attempts to understand Proverbs 25:1 in relation to the transmission history of the Bible were also made by medieval Jewish commentators. These exegetes pick up on precisely the same grammatical features of the verse that were at issue for the Septuagint, Symmachus, Theodotian, Aquila, the Vulgate, and texts like Baba Bathra 14b and Aboth deR. Natan.

The Targum to Proverbs 25:1 preserves two mutually exclusive interpretations of the word *gam* 'also'.

אַף אִלֵין מַתְלוֹי דִשְׁלֹמֹה עֲמִיקֵי דְכַתְבוּ רַחֲמוֹי דְחִזְקִיָה מַלְכָּא דִיהוּדָה

These also are his deep sayings which the friends of Hezekiah the king of Judah wrote down.

The Targum includes the adjective עֲמִיקֵי *'amiqe* 'deep', a functional equivalent of the Greek *adiakritoi* 'confusing' or 'unassembled'; however, it explicitly translates *gam* as *'af* 'also'. I would suggest that the Targum no longer recognizes the textual origin of the interpretive traditions it preserves, and restores to the original what was seen as a missing element in the text, without eliminating the received interpretation. In James Kugel's terms, this represents "overkill."[42]

In his commentary to Proverbs, Saadiah Gaon (882–942 C.E.) claims that Proverbs 25:1 refers to an oral tradition:

The words of the scribe. These teach us that many passages were preserved; our fathers handed them down, one to another, over a period of time without the use of writing, until they were written later, and thus he said in explanation that the proverbs were uttered by Solomon (may peace be with him), and they were preserved over the course of time without being written until the men of Hezekiah wrote them down (*katvum*).

Saadiah, ad loc.

Saadiah goes on to see in this oral tradition an analogy to and apologetic for the Oral Torah. Notable in the passage is his glossing of *heʿetiq* as *katav* 'write', a gloss that I have argued lies behind Baba Bathra 14b. Saadiah understands by this that the men of Hezekiah 'wrote down' proverbs from oral sources rather than copying the verse from another book.

Ibn Ezra (1089–1164) finds the word *gam* 'also' worthy of notice, just as earlier exegetes had. His solution is that *gam* has an almost concessive force:

This verse was spoken by the scribe; perhaps it was Shabna, since he was a scribe of King Hezekiah. He explained in it [this verse] the reason for the copying and the word *gam* to magnify the earlier [proverbs].

Ibn Ezra, ad loc.

In other words, Ibn Ezra understands that *gam* 'also' links Proverbs 25 ff. to Proverbs 1–24, and that 25:1 applies equally to the entire book. However, putting the verse midway through the book shows that Proverbs 1–24 are of greater quality or value. The word *gam* signals an admission that these additional Proverbs require special justification.

Levi ben Gershom (1288–1344), better known by his acronym "Ralbag," highlights the differences between Proverbs 1–24 and 25 ff. in a manner that focuses on their transmission rather than their inherent value:

The wise men of the generation of Hezekiah; it appears that this is the reason that they separated them [= Prov. 25 ff.] from the other proverbs: these wise men collected the one group [Prov. 25 ff.] from his proverbs, but the other group of proverbs that they recalled earlier [Prov. 1–24] were found in the manner mentioned in (among?) the words of Solomon (*be–divrey Shelomo*).

Ralbag, ad loc.

Ralbag seems to be saying that the two groups of proverbs had different transmission histories, and that Proverbs 25 ff. were collected by the wise men from another group of Solomon's proverbs. It is notable that Ralbag seems to gloss *he'etiq* as *hifrid* 'separate', likely another "plain sense" meaning of *he'etiq* for rabbinic and medieval Jewish exegetes.[43] In contrast, Rashi glosses *he'etiqu* as *heheziqu* 'they attached merit to', evidently deriving the word from the root *'tq*, a synonym of *hzq* 'be strong' (as in Psalm 31:19).

The interpretation of Proverbs 25:1 was taken in both new and old directions in the two eighteenth century commentaries on the *Ketuvim* 'Writings' by David Altschuler of Galicia.[44] *Mezudat David* 'Fortress of David' is a commentary that speaks to the general meaning of the text. With regard to the significance of *gam* 'also', the conclusion of this commentary is that while the word *gam* 'also' implies similarity to the preceding proverbs, the placement of the verse implies a difference between Proverbs 25 ff. and the preceding chapters.

> It appears that from the beginning of the book up to here they would copy (*ma'atiq*) by hand the whole thing; and from here to the end, they would not copy them out except by the hands of the men of Hezekiah king of Judah who copied out these words from the books of Solomon which they came across. And to this end it says "These too are Solomon's Proverbs" — this means, even though they had not been found in the hands of everyone from every place, these too are his utterances which the men of Hezekiah King of Judah copied out, and they were confirmed as originating from the mouth of Solomon.
>
> *Mezudat David*, ad loc.

In other words, all proverbs were copied out, but Proverbs 25 ff., not being widely available, were copied out only by the men of Hezekiah from the books of Solomon. According to *Mezudat David*, the verse also asserts that Proverbs 25 ff. are indeed Solomon's utterances, even though they were copied out only by the men of Hezekiah.

The commentary *Mezudat Zion* 'Fortress of Zion', composed by Altschuler as a companion to *Mezudat David*, was meant to give an explanation of individual words. It marks a turning point in the interpretation of the verse, by giving a sophisticated philological treatment of the word *he'etiq* that anticipated that of Leopold Zunz, one of the foremost practitioners of *Wissenschaft des Judentums* in the nineteenth century.

> *He'etiqu:* Writing words from book to book is called *ma'atiq* [the participle from *he'etiq*] because it appears as if one is moving (*ma'atiq*) and transferring words to write them in another [book]; although they remain in the first one, it in any event appears as if they had been transferred.
>
> *Mezudat Zion,* ad loc.

This explanation echoes the conclusions of modern biblical scholarship. Altschuler's painstaking analysis of the etymology of *he'etiq* is a powerful argument that 'copy out' was *not* the "plain sense" meaning for rabbinic interpreters, but rather had to be extrapolated by means of logic and the exegete's knowledge of scribal practices.

As we have seen, both ancient and traditional interpretations of Proverbs 25:1 derive a great deal of information about the nature of the transmission of the Solomonic books, and in some cases, about the textual history of the Bible as a whole, from exegesis of the syntax of the Hebrew verse. In turn, the historical hypotheses that energize each interpretation also affect the specific way that the words are translated into Greek and Aramaic or glossed in Mishnaic Hebrew.

## The Meaning of *katav* in Baba Bathra 14b–15a

While explicit references to the composition process in rabbinic literature are rare, they do exist.[45] Such references confirm that the modern metaphor that connects the activity of writing with the process of composition of literary works is not proper to rabbinic diction. The following is an example of the use of the verb *'omer,* which generally means 'say' or 'utter', to describe the composition of biblical poems or books.

דוד אמר דברים שנאמר (שמואל ב כג) ואלה דברי דוד האחרונים וגו׳ ושלמה אמר דברים

שנאמר (קהלת א) דברי קהלת בן דוד מלך בירושלים דוד אמר הבלים שנאמר (תהלים לט) אך כל הבל

כל אדם נצב סלה ושלמה אמר הבלים שנאמר (קהלת א) הבל הבלים אמר קהלת הבל הבלים הכל הבל

דוד אמר משלים שנא׳ (שמואל א כד) כאשר יאמר משל הקדמוני מרשעים יצא רשע וגו׳ ושלמה אמר

משלים שנא׳ (משלי א) משלי שלמה בן דוד מלך ישראל דוד כתב ספרים דתהלים נכתב על שמו ושלמה

כתב ספרים משלי קהלת שיר השירים.

. . .

דוד אמר שירים שנא׳ (משואל ב כב) וידבר דוד לה׳ את דברי השירה הזאת וגו׳ ושלמה אמר שירים שנאמר

שיר השירים אשר לשלמה.

David composed (*'amar*) 'words', as it says, Now these are the last words of David (2 Sam. 23:1), and Solomon composed (*'amar*) 'words', as it says, "The words of Qoheleth son of David, king in Jerusalem" (Eccl. 1:1). David spoke on the vanity of things, as it says, "Surely every man at his best estate is altogether vanity" (Ps. 39: 6), and Solomon spoke on the vanity of things, as it says, "Vanity of vanities, saith Qoheleth, vanity of vanities, all is vanity" (Eccl. 1: 2). David uttered (*'amar*) proverbs, as it says, "As saith the proverb of the ancients, Out of the wicked cometh forth wickedness" (1 Sam. 24: 14), and Solomon uttered (*'amar*) proverbs, as it says, "The Proverbs of Solomon son of David king of Israel" (Prov. 1:1). David wrote (*katav*) books, since the Psalms are written (*nikhtav*) in his name (*'al shemo*), and Solomon wrote (*katav*) books, Proverbs, Ecclesiastes, and the Song of Songs.

. . .

David composed (*'amar*) songs, as it says, "And David spoke (*va-yidabber*) unto the Lord the words of this song" (2 Sam. 21.1) and Solomon composed (*'amar*) songs, as it says, "The Song of Songs which is Solomon's."

Shir Ha-Shirim Rabbah 1.1.6, trans. Simon

The passage makes plain that rabbinic diction does allow for a distinction between composition and textualization. When David or Solomon are described in their role as composers, the verb employed is *'amar* 'uttered'. When the text wishes to specify that both David and Solomon were responsible for writing down works that they may or may not have composed, the verb *katav* 'wrote' is utilized. This is confirmed by the note that David wrote down (*katav*) the book of Psalms, which are therefore recorded (*nikhtav*) in his name (as in "the Psalms of David"). This passage is patently cognizant of the fact that David himself did not compose each and every one of the psalms that he copied out. Other examples (B. Megillah 7a,[46] B. Sanhedrin 100b,[47] Qoheleth Rabbah 9.13,[48] Eikha Rabbah 1.1,[49]) allow for further refinement of the meaning of the verb: *'amar* 'say, utter' refers to the moment of oral textual creation, although it does not necessarily imply that the creation is of human rather than divine origin.[50]

If the verb *'amar* is the usual way for rabbinic diction to refer to the composition process, what precisely is the meaning of *katav* 'write' in Baba Bathra 14b–15a? Scholarly investigation of Baba Bathra has been continuously led astray because it was assumed that *katav* must refer to the composition process of books. More to the point: scholarship has erred in assuming that rabbinic interpreters knew only of a composition process that made use of writing. The absence of an equation between writing and composition in the passage from Shir Ha-Shirim Rabbah quoted above may indicate what my analysis of Baba Bathra has been leading to all along: *katav* is a word which does not refer at all to the composition process in rabbinic documents.[51]

Sid Leiman states, "Although כתב (*katav*) is usually rendered 'write', the verb includes 'author' and 'edit' in its range of meaning, as is evident from (Baba Bathra 14b)."[52] However, this is not a necessary conclusion. I would argue that *katav* nowhere means 'to author' in this passage, and that 'edit' has a meaning too specialized to refer to the process of transcribing a traditional text. Leiman also finds possible Maurice Simon's suggestion that the word means 'publish'.[53] Further, Leiman endorses a misinterpretation of *katav* as 'canonize': "David Hoffman...and Willhelm Bacher...

correctly suggest that כתב (*katav*) in Baba Bathra 14b (in the case of Hezekiah and his colleagues, and the Men of the Great Assembly) is best rendered by 'canonize'."[54] The interpretation of Baba Bathra 14b by M. L. Margolis with which Leiman agrees appears to be the prevalent view of the meaning of *katav* in Baba Bathra:

> To understand aright the purport of this account it must at once be conceded that the term 'wrote' cannot possibly have been used with the same meaning throughout. Certainly in the case of Hezekiah and his company, who 'wrote' Proverbs, and of the Men of the Great Synagogue, who 'wrote' the Twelve, the intended meaning is that the books mentioned were completed and edited by these two bodies. The title to chapters 25 and following in the Book of Proverbs reads: 'These also are proverbs of Solomon, which the men of Hezekiah king of Judah copied out'. The collection of Solomonic proverbs was accordingly 'completed' in the days of Hezekiah, and the book then received its final form. So it is with the Twelve. The three concluding writings are those of Haggai, Zechariah, and Malachi, who are reckoned among the men of the Great Synagogue. The volume naturally became complete only with their inclusion. On the other hand, we have no right to carry this meaning into all the other instances. Certainly with reference to all those who wrote their own books, the meaning can be only that they actually 'wrote' them, that is, were the authors of them.[55]

I would contest this formulation on the grounds that it would be redundant for Baba Bathra to claim that Moses, Joshua, Samuel, Jeremiah, and Ezra "authored their own books" (this would be the supposed translation of משה כתב ספרו etc.). The prepositional suffix affixed to the word *sefer* (i.e., *sifro* 'his book') indicates some sort of possession. What kind of possession could have been implied here? There are two possibilities: *sifro* can mean 'the book named after him or associated with him', or it can mean 'the book that he composed'. In the case of Moses, *sifro* refers to the Torah or the Pentateuch. The Torah is sometimes referred to in the Bible by the name of Moses (תורת משה 'the Torah of Moses' [1 Kings 2:3], ספר

תורת משה 'the book [sefer] of the Torah of Moses' [Joshua 8:31, 32; 23:6; 2 Kings 14:6], and in the parallel passage בתורה בספר משה 'in the Torah in the book [sefer] of Moses' [2 Chronicles 25:4]). Most interesting is the expression ספר תורת יהוה ביד משה in 2 Chronicles 34:14, which seems to specify the Mosaic contribution as one of manual agency, likely in copying the book.[56] From the evidence of the Dead Sea Scrolls (4QMMT C 10–11 and 2Q 25:1), the expression ספר משה appears to have been an accepted way to refer to the Pentateuch during the Second Temple Period.[57] A less likely conclusion is that *sifro* 'his book' refers to 'the book he composed'. If this is true, it is meaningless to claim that a given biblical figure "composed (*katav*) the book he composed (*sifro*)." I would reject this understanding of *sifro*, moreover, on the grounds that Baba Bathra is not focused on human composition at all, but rather is interested in transmission.

The other meaning of the word advocated by Leiman — that *katav* sometimes means 'canonized' — is unwarranted. It is not likely that rabbinic interpreters were self-conscious enough about the idea of canonization to discuss it as a historical process, which it indisputably was. Canonization, a process whose exact meaning is admittedly under debate in modern scholarship, could not have occurred at a single moment, namely the moment these texts were written down. It is conceivable that the rabbis understood the process we term 'canonization' to consist of a single moment in time, the moment their authoritative texts were copied down and thus became scripture. Such an understanding of the way texts became authoritative does not, however, correspond to contemporary understandings of 'canonization'. If the meaning 'canonize' (in the rabbinic conception of the term) is to work, it must apply equally to all instances of the word *katav* in the passage from Baba Bathra. Finally, it is highly unlikely that the rabbis would have asserted that any action on the part of Hezekiah or the Men of the Great Assembly made a given text authoritative — whether a text was authoritative surely sprang from its inherent nature as the word of God. On the basis of this alone, *katav* could not have meant 'to make authoritative'.

The implications of this discussion concerning the meaning of *katav* in Baba Bathra hinge upon the interpretation of Proverbs

25:1. Baba Bathra 14b–15a has arrived at an understanding of the verb *heʿetiqu* 'copied out' that is similar to the understanding both of the Septuagint and modern critical interpretation of this verb. Unlike Aboth deR. Nathan, Baba Bathra is not concerned with conflicting interpretations of the verb as 'stored away' or 'interpreted'. Therefore, I propose that the text can be better understood by a single translation of *katav* as 'copied out', and that *katav* in Baba Bathra 14b was intended as a gloss of *heʿetiqu*.

How could Proverbs 25:1 ("Also these are the proverbs which the men of Hezekiah copied out") have been read by Baba Bathra to refer to the entire book of Proverbs, not to mention Ecclesiastes, Song of Songs, and Isaiah? The 'also' of the Hebrew text, a word which was the source of much controversy in the history of interpretation of Proverbs 25:1, has been interpreted by Baba Bathra in quite an original manner. According to this text, the men of Hezekiah *also* copied out many other books. Apparently, the placement of Proverbs 25:1 midway through the book provoked no resistance against a broad application of the verse. Intrigued by the one stated reference to the copying procedure by Hezekiah and his men, as well as by similar hints in 1 and 2 Chronicles, the *baraita* in Baba Bathra records the names of the individuals who had copied out the rest of the Bible.[58]

While there is no agreement among rabbinic exegetes on questions relating to the precise role of David with regard to the composition of the psalms, the view of him as a scribe who copied the psalms of others is not hard to find.

ד״א שיר השירים ר׳ איבו ור׳ יהודה ר״א אמר שיר חד השירים תרין הא תלתא ור״י בר סימון אמר

שה״ש כולה חד ואילין תרתין אחרניאתא מה את עבד לון שיר המעלות לשלמה וחד מזמור שיר חנוכת

הבית לדוד <u>סברין מימר דוד אמרן ואת תולה בדוד שנאמר כמגדל דויד צוארך אלא מה שה״ש שלמה</u>

<u>אמרה ותלה אותה בדוד</u>

Another explanation: THE SONG OF SONGS. R. Aibu and R. Judah [joined issue on this]. R. Aibu said: "Song" indicates one, "songs" two, making three in all. R. Judah b. Simon said: The whole of the Song of Songs makes one, and two referred to in the word "songs" are different. How do you specify them? One is, A song of ascents of Solomon (Ps. 127), and the other, A Psalm, a song at the dedication of the House of David (Ps. 30). <u>You would naturally think that David composed this, but in reality it is only ascribed to David in the same way as it says, "Like the tower of David is thy neck" (Song of Songs 4:4). So here, Solomon composed it and ascribed it to David.</u>

Shir Ha-Shirim Rabbah 1.1.10, trans. Simon

In this passage from the collection of interpretations on the Song of Songs, there is an awareness of the subtlety involved in explaining matters of attribution. Solomon was able to compose (*'omer*) a psalm and still attribute it to David (*toleh 'otah be-David*), just as he could compare an image to David's tower. This represents a way out from conflicting attributions; but what is significant here is that there is an acceptance of the notion that the attribution does not necessarily imply composition.

Another approach to solving the dilemma of conflicting attributions of the psalms is preserved in parallel passages from two collections of midrashim on the books of Solomon:

רבי הונא רמח ר׳ אחא אצ״פ שעשרה רוי אדח אמרו חפר תהליח מרלהון

לא נאמר על שמותם אלא על ידי דוד מלך ישראל משלו משל למה״ד לחבורה של אנשים שמבקשים לומר

הימנון למלך אמר להם המלך כלכם נעימים כלכם חסידים כלכם משבחין לומר הימנון לפני אלא איש

פלוני יאמר על ידי כלכם למה שקולו ערב כך בשעה שבקשו עשרה צדיקים לומר ספר התהלים אמר להם

הקדוש ב״ה כלכם נעימים וחסידים ומשובחים לומר הימנון לפני אלא דוד יאמר על ידי כלכם למה שקולו

ערב הה״ד (ש״ב כ״ג) ונעים זמירות ישראל

R. Huna said in the name of R. Aḥa: Although ten persons composed the Book of Psalms, the only one of them to whom it is ascribed is David king of Israel. To illustrate this a comparison was made to a company of men who sought to sing an ode before the king. Said the king to them: "You are all good singers, you are all loyal, you are all famous, and qualified to sing an ode before me. Still, let So-and-so say it on behalf of you all, because his voice is particularly sweet." So when the ten righteous men sought to utter the book of Psalms, the Holy One, blessed be He, said to them, "You are all of you poetical enough and pious enough and famous

enough to sing an ode before Me; still, let David say it on behalf of
you all. Why? Because his voice is sweet," as it says, "The sweet
one of the Songs of Israel" (2 Sam. 23:1).

> Shir Ha-Shirim Rabbah 4.4.1, trans. Simon
> (cf. Qoheleth Rabbah 7.31)

The exegetes here make the important distinction between composition of individual psalms and a broader question of the attribution of the whole corpus of psalms to David. Here, David is not seen
as the copyist of the book of Psalms, as he is in the *baraita* in Baba
Bathra 14b. Nevertheless, the midrash makes a distinction between
types of attributions, not all of which signify composition. The
parable, introduced in this passage to explain the difference between types of attributions, imagines David as the singer of all the
psalms, rather than their composer.

## The Biography of Job

The project of attributing unnamed texts to legendary figures
bears a certain resemblance to the project of creating biographies for
legendary characters in the Bible. In effect, the interpretive process
that views David and Solomon as biblical scribes is very much connected with the need to make their biographies coincide with their
textual creations. This process is an extension of the "escape from
anonymity" described by Joseph Heineman.[59] Not only are obscure
figures given names through identification with other characters, but
also the writings of David and Solomon are held to be related to moments in their lives described elsewhere in the Bible. Similar types of
exegesis are brought into play in order to bring Job, one of the Bible's
most fairytale-like characters, to life. However this is not the main
reason that Baba Bathra is concerned with the biography of Job.

There has been little discussion of the rationale behind the introduction of the extended speculation on Job's historical setting in
treatments of Baba Bathra 15. The sheer quantity of midrashic
questions relating to Job indicates that Baba Bathra 15 served as a
repository for floating midrashim that dealt with Job. This may explain the latter sections of the passage, which veer away sharply

from the question of biblical transmission that constitutes the focus of the *baraita*. Nevertheless, the question of how the biography of Job relates to biblical transmission still stands — why was a discussion of Job placed directly following passages on the order of the biblical books and the individuals who copied down the biblical books?

To begin, I quote from the portion of the *baraita* and commentary that precedes the section, "Who wrote the scriptures." This passage specifies the order of the books of the Hagiographa:

סידרן של כתובים: רות וספר תהלים, ואיוב ומשלי, קהלת, שיר השירים וקינות, דניאל ומגילת אסתר,
עזרא ודברי הימים. ולמ"ד: איוב בימי משה היה. ליקדמיה לאיוב ברישא אתחולי בפורענותא לא
מתחלינן. רות נמי פורענות היא פורענות דאית ליה אחרית: דאמר רבי יוחנן:למה נקרא שמה רות? שיצא
ממנה דוד שריווהו להקב״ה בשירות ותושבחות. ומי כתבן? משה כתב ספרו ופרשת בלעם ואיוב:

The order of the Hagiographa is Ruth, the book of Psalms, Job, Proverbs, Ecclesiastes, Song of Songs, Lamentations, Daniel, and the Scroll of Esther, Ezra, and Chronicles. Now on the view that Job lived in the days of Moses, should not the book of Job come first? — We do not begin with a record of suffering. But Ruth also is a record of suffering? — It is a suffering with a sequel [of happiness], as R. Joḥanan said: Why was her name called Ruth? — Because there issued from her David who replenished the Holy One, blessed be He, with hymns and praises. Who wrote down the scriptures? Moses wrote down his own book and the portion of Balaam and Job.

Baba Bathra 14b, trans. Simon

In the scheme laid out in the *baraita*, the order for the three categories of books (i.e., Pentateuch, Prophets, and Hagiographa) outranks other considerations. But within these categories, books are to be arranged more or less chronologically according to the scheme presented in the section *mi ketavan* — that is, according to the antiquity of their scribes. Thus Ruth (copied out by Samuel) precedes the texts copied out by later prophets, which are in turn followed by works copied out by the men of the Great Assembly. It would appear that the time that Job lived has relevance to the ordering of biblical books.

However, a truly chronological basis for the ordering of these texts is not strictly followed. The placement of Job following the scroll Ruth is a glaring anachronism. The explanation presented in the passage represents a *post facto* amelioration of chronological awkwardness, rather than an accurate explanation of the arrangement scheme. The text explains that a record of suffering should not open the Hagiographa; but surely this was not the original reason for Job's placement following Ruth. Some Tannaitic interpreters concluded that the ordering of the books must originally have reflected an alternative dating for Job. Conversely, modern biblical scholars might conclude that considerations other than chronological were at work in the ordering of the books.[60] Baba Bathra 14b attempts to find significance in a pre-existing order, apparently constructed on the basis of a variety of considerations, not simply chronological. Since it is clear that Job's date is not used in Baba Bathra 15 as a means of explaining the location of the book of Job in scripture, it may also be stated that the list of biblical books (Baba Bathra 14b) stands at odds with the discussion of Job's chronology in Baba Bathra 15.

The passage from Baba Bathra 15 that returns to the question of Job's date is quoted here:

יתיב ההוא מרבנן קמיה דר' שמואל בר נחמני. ויתיב וקאמר: איוב לא היה

ולא נברא אלא משל היה. א"ל. עליך אמר קרא: איש היה בארץ עוץ איוב שמו. אלא מעתה, (שמואל

ב' י"ב) ולרש אין כל כי אם כבשה אחת קטנה אשר קנה ויחיה וגו'. מי הוה? אלא משל בעלמא. הכא

נמי משל בעלמא. א"כ. שמו ושם עירו למה? רבי יוחנן ורבי אלעזר דאמרי תרווייהו: איוב מעולי גולה

היה. ובית מדרשו בטבריא היה. מיתיבי: ימי שנותיו של איוב. משעה שנכנסו ישראל למצרים ועד שיצאו

אימא: כמשעה שנכנסו ישראל למצרים ועד [שעה] שיצאו. מיתיבי: שבעה נביאים נתנבאו לאומות

העולם. ואלו הן: בלעם ואביו. ואיוב. אליפז התימני. ובלדד השוחי. וצופר הנעמתי. ואליהוא בן ברכאל

הבוזי (א"ל) וליטעמיך. אליהוא בן ברכאל לאו מישראל הוה? והא כתי' ממשפחת רם אלא אינבוי

אינבוי לאומות העולם. ה"נ איוב אינבוי אינבי [לאומות העולם]. אטו כולהו נביאי מי לא אינבוי לאומות

העולם? התם עיקר נביאותייהו לישראל. הכא עיקר נביאותייהו לאומות העולם. מיתיבי: חסיד היה

באומות העולם ואיוב שמו. ולא בא לעולם אלא כדי לקבל שכרו. הביא הקב"ה עליו יסורין התחיל

מחרף ומגדף. כפל לו הקב"ה שכרו בעוה"ז [כדי] לטרדו מן העולם הבא תנאי היא. דתניא. רבי אלעזר

אומר: איוב בימי שפוט השופטים היה. שנאמר: (איוב כ"ז) הן אתם כולכם חזיתם ולמה זה הבל תהבלו.

איזה דור שכולו הבל? הוי אומר: זה דורו של שפוט השופטים. רבי יהושע בן קרחה אומר: איוב בימי

אחשורוש היה. שנאמר: (איוב מ"ב) ולא נמצא נשים יפות כבנות איוב בכל הארץ. איזהו דור שנתבקשו

בו נשים יפות? הוי אומר: זה דורו של אחשורוש. ואימא: בימי דוד. דכתיב: (מלכים א' א') ויבקשו נערה

יפה התם בכל גבול ישראל. הכא בכל הארץ. רבי נתן אומר: איוב בימי מלכות שבא היה, שנאמר:
(איוב א׳) ותפל שבא ותקחם. וחכ״א: איוב בימי כשדים היה, שנאמר: (איוב א׳) כשדים שמו שלשה
ראשים. ויש אומרים: איוב בימי יעקב היה, ודינה בת יעקב נשא, כתיב הכא: (איוב ב׳) כדבר אחת
הנבלות תדברי, וכתיב התם: (בראשית ל״ד) כי נבלה עשה בישראל. וכולהו תנאי סבירא להו דאיוב
מישראל הוה, לבר מיש אומרים. דאי ס״ד מאומות העולם הוה, בתר דשכיב משה מי שריא שכינה על
עובדי כוכבים? והא אמר מר: בקש משה שלא תשרה שכינה על עובדי כוכבים ונתן לו, שנאמר: (שמות
ל״ג) ונפלינו אני ועמך.

One of the rabbis was in session before R. Samuel bar Naḥmani, and, in session, he stated, "Job never lived, but was merely a metaphor!"

He said to him, "Said scripture, 'There was a man in the land of Uz, Job was his name' (Job 1:1)!"

"Well what about this: 'The poor man had nothing but one poor ewe lamb, which he had bought and brought up' (2 Sam. 12:3). Is that anything but a metaphor? This too is a metaphor."

"Well, then, why say what his name was, and where he lived?"

Both R. Joḥanan and R. Eleazar say, "Job was among those who came up from the exile, and his house of study was located in Tiberias."

An objection was raised: "The length of Job's life was from the time that Israel entered Egypt until they left"!

Say: "As long as from the time they entered Egypt till they left."

An objection was raised: "Seven prophets prophesied to the nations of the world and these are they: Balaam and his father, Job, Eliphaz the Temanite, Bildad the Shuhite, Zophar the Naamathite, and Elihu son of Barachel the Buzite [so Job was a prophet to the gentiles].

"Well, wasn't Elihu son of Barachel an Israelite, since Scripture says that he came from the family of Ram (Job 32:2)? He's included on the list because he prophesied to the gentiles, and Job too is listed because he prophesied to the gentiles."

"Well, didn't all the prophets prophesy to the gentiles?"

"Well, they prophesied principally to Israel, but these turned principally to the gentiles."

An objection was raised: There was a certain pious man

among the gentiles whose name was Job. He thought that he came into this world only to receive his just reward. The Holy One, blessed be He, brought on him tribulations. He began to curse and blaspheme. So the Holy One, blessed be He, simply doubled his reward in this world, so as to torment him from the world to come.

Well, as a matter of fact, what we have is a conflict among Tannaite formulations, for it has been taught on Tannaite authority:

R. Eliezer says, "Job lived in the time that the judges ruled, in line with this verse: 'Behold, all you yourselves have seen it, why then are you altogether vain' (Job 27:12). Now which generation is the one that is altogether vain? You have to say, it is a generation in which judges have judged."

R. Joshua b. Qorḥah says, "Job lived in the days of Ahasuerus: 'Let there be sought for the king young virgins, fair to look on' (Est. 2:2). And it is written, 'And there were no women found so beautiful as the daughters of Job' (Job 42:15). Now what is the generation in which they went looking for beautiful girls? You have to say it was in the time of Ahasuerus."

But maybe it was in the time of David: "So they sought for a beautiful girl" (1 Kings 1:3)!

In the case of David it was "in all the borders of Israel," in the case of Ahasuerus, "in all the land."

R. Nathan said, "He lived in the time of the Queen of Sheba: 'And the Sabeans made a raid and took them away' (Job 1:15)."

Sages say, "He lived in the time of the Chaldaeans: 'The Chaldaeans made three bands' (Job 1:7)."

Some say, "Job lived in the time of Jacob and married Jacob's daughter, Dinah: 'You speak as one of the impious women speak' (Job 2:10), and elsewhere in the context of Dinah, 'Because he had wrought folly in Israel' (Gen. 34:7)."

All these Tannaite authorities take the view that Job was an Israelite, except for "some say." For if you should suppose that he was a gentile, after Moses died, did the Presence of God ever again rest upon gentiles? And lo, a master has said, "Moses asked that the Presence of God not rest on gentiles, and that was given to him: 'That we be separated, I and your people, from all the people that are upon the face of the earth' (Ex. 33:16)."

Baba Bathra 15a–15b, trans. Neusner

The most extreme position on the biography of Job is given at the beginning of the passage:

> One of the rabbis was in session before R. Samuel bar Nahmani, and, in session, he stated, "Job never lived, but was merely a metaphor!"
>
> He said to him, "Said scripture, 'There was a man in the land of Uz, Job was his name' (Job 1:1)!"
>
> "Well what about this: 'The poor man had nothing but one poor ewe lamb, which he had bought and brought up' (2 Sam. 12:3). Is that anything but a metaphor? This too is a metaphor."
>
> "Well, then, why say what his name was, and where he lived?"
>
> Baba Bathra 15a

A position such as that of "a certain sage" that "Job never was and never existed — he is no more than a parable," seems to be raised as a foil for those who find it necessary to date Job. In the face of this extreme argument of the anonymous sage, apparently voiced only to be shot down, the project of discovering the date of Job is endowed with a certain legitimacy. If one can be sure that Job was a real person who lived in a real town, it is logical according to early biblical interpreters and their understanding of the Bible as a cryptic and complete document that Job's date can be ferreted out.[61] This activity is crucial in establishing the authority of biblical written transmission.

The technique known as "midrashic identification" (the process by which well-known biblical figures become identified with lesser known ones by means of homiletic comparison of similarities between the figures in question) was one of the means by which ancient interpreters attempted to ascertain the date of Job. An example of midrashic identification is the equation of Job with Jobab, mentioned in the genealogy in Genesis 10:29 as a descendant of Shem and in the fifth generation after Noah (Abraham is in the tenth). The identification, found in the postscript to the Septuagint translation of the book of Job, further specifies that Job was an Edomite.[62] This identification of Job with Jobab follows a familiar pattern in midrashic exegesis — the identification of a lesser known character (usually mentioned briefly in a genealogical list or in one of the historical treatments of Israelite history) with a more well-known figure. This particular identification is developed in a fragment of a Greek historian named Aristeas.[63] It is impossible to state with certainty how widespread was the teaching that equated Job with Jobab, or whether it derived from the epilogue to the Septuagint translation of Job alone.[64] As will be seen below, it is significant that this epilogue assumes that Job (*qua* Jobab) was an Edomite and thus a gentile.[65]

In other rabbinic sources, a given dating of Job is used to explain other exegetically challenging passages:

(במדבר יג) ארץ אוכלת יושביה היא - דרש רבא, אמר הקב״ה: אני חשבתיה

לטובה והם חשבו לרעה. אני חשבתיה לטובה - דכל היכא דמטו, מת חשיבא דידהו, כי היכי דניטרדו

ולא לשאלו אבתרייהו. ואיכא דאמרי: איוב נח נפשיה, ואטרידו כולי עלמא בהספידא. הם חשבו לרעה

- ארץ אוכלת יושביה היא

It is a land that eateth up the inhabitants thereof. Raba expounded: The Holy One, blessed be He, said: I intended this for good but they thought it in a bad sense. I intended this for good, because wherever [the spies] came, the chief [of the inhabitants] died, so that they should be occupied [with his burial] and not inquire about them. (Others say that Job died then and the whole world was occupied with mourning for him.) But they thought it in a bad sense: It is a land that eateth up the inhabitants thereof.

B. Sotah 35a, trans. Cohen

In the midst of an explanation for why the scouts were mistaken as to the worth of the land of Canaan that the Israelites were about to enter, the story about the death of Job is interjected as a means for explanation. According to Judith Baskin's reconstruction of the legend, the instructions of Moses to the scouts (to see "whether there is good wood [*uz*] within" [Numbers 13:20]) was read by rabbinic exegetes as an inquiry into whether Job, a native of Uz, were still alive. If he were, then the Canaanites would have been shielded from Israelite attack by his virtue alone.[66]

Job is also depicted as a member of Pharaoh's court in a number of texts.[67] Job's lifespan was determined to be 210 years on the basis of the statement in Job 42:16 that "after this Job lived a hundred and forty years" and on Job 42:10, where it is stated that "the Lord gave Job twice as much as he had before." In Seder Olam Rabbah 3, Job's lifespan is a sign pointing to the number of years the Israelites spent in Egypt; it is symbolic evidence that Job's life spanned this period exactly, and that he was a contemporary of Jacob and Moses.[68] This story is consistent with the dating assumed in the *baraita* in Baba Bathra 14b, in which Moses is alive to copy down the events of Job's life as well as his words, presumably dictated by Job himself before he died.

It is preferable for the rabbinic authorities cited in Baba Bathra 15 to guess and guess wrongly about the time of Job than it is to say that he never lived. This midrash tolerates multiple answers, or at least a debate about the real answer, more than it tolerates a solution that challenges the rules of the game. Attempts to fix the figure of Job in a historical moment preserved in Baba Bathra include a midrashic identification of Job's second wife with Dinah (15a), which places Job's life in the generation of Jacob.[69] More to the point, the position articulated most often in Baba Bathra — namely, that Job lived in the generation of Jacob or Joseph and prior to the time of Moses — conforms to the *baraita*'s premise that Moses copied out Job's book.[70]

The other dates given for Job in Baba Bathra 15a–b run counter to the premise of a Mosaic transmission of his book. 1) R. Joḥanan and R. Eleazar state that Job was among those who returned from the Babylonian Exile; 2) R. Eliezer says that Job was in the days "of the judging of the judges"; 3) R. Joshua b. Qorḥah says that Job was in the time of Ahasuerus; 4) the hypothesis is given that he lived during the time of David; 5) according to the Sages, he lived in the time of the Chaldaeans.[71] The conclusion is reached that "All these Tannaim agree that Job was from Israel, except those who say [that he lived in the days of Jacob]." The passage continues:

[This must be so,] for if you suppose that [they regarded Job] as a gentile, [the question would arise,] after the death of Moses how could the Divine Presence rest upon a gentile, seeing that a master has said, Moses prayed that the Divine Presence should not rest on gentiles, and God granted his request as it says, "That we be separated, I and thy people, from all the people that are upon the face of the earth."

Baba Bathra 15b

The truth of the matter is that the date of Job and whether Job was an Israelite or a gentile are interrelated questions. All discussants appear to have agreed that the Presence of God never rested on a gentile after Moses, and that therefore only Moses could have textualized a gentile's prophecies, since he was the earliest textualizer of the Bible and wrote down everything significant in history prior to his death (see the related discussion of Josephus in chapter 4). Consequently, all post-Mosaic dates for Job must also include the assumption that Job was an Israelite.

To return to the beginning of the discussion of Job in Baba Bathra:

Both R. Yoḥanan and R. Eleazar say, "Job was among those who came up from the exile, and his house of study was located in Tiberias."

An objection was raised: "The length of Job's life was from the time that Israel entered Egypt until they left"!

Say: "As long as from the time they entered Egypt till they left."

An objection was raised: "Seven prophets prophesied to the nations of the world and these are they: Balaam and his father, Job, Eliphaz the Temanite, Bildad the Shuhite, Zophar the Naamathite, and Elihu son of Barachel the Buzite [so Job was a prophet to the gentiles].

"Well, wasn't Elihu son of Barachel an Israelite, since Scripture says that he came from the family of Ram (Job 32:2)? He's included on the list because he prophesied to the gentiles, and Job too is listed because he prophesied to the gentiles."

"Well, didn't all the prophets prophesy to the gentiles?"

"Well, they prophesied principally to Israel, but these turned principally to the gentiles."

An objection was raised: There was a certain pious man among the gentiles whose name was Job. He thought that he came into this world only to receive his just reward. The Holy One, blessed be He, brought on him tribulations. He began to curse and blaspheme. So the Holy One, blessed be He, simply doubled his reward in this world, so as to torment him from the world to come.

Well, as a matter of fact, what we have is a conflict among Tannaitic formulations, for it has been taught on Tannaitic authority . . .

Baba Bathra 15a–b, trans. Neusner

If we follow the dialectic presented here, we see that the initial premise of the Tannaim R. Yoḥanan and R. Eleazer (that Job was among those who came up from the exile, and is therefore an Israelite) is challenged by three objections. The second of these seeks to determine that Job is not an Israelite on the basis of a tradition that he prophesied to the nations of the world rather than to the Israelites. The objection is dismissed on the grounds that the addressees of a prophet do not determine the nationality of the prophet himself. The third objection quotes another Tannaitic teaching that describes Job as a gentile. But this objection is treated as merely one view among conflicting Tannaitic statements. In any event, the discussants are aware that Job's status as Israelite or gentile is secondary to his date.

Of all the dates offered for Job's life in this section, only the one which places him in the time of Jacob is consistent with the position offered in the *baraita* "Who wrote the scriptures?" — namely, that Moses copied out the book of Job. The *baraita* concludes that Job died during the life of Moses, and that Moses copied out his writings. Baba Bathra 15b merely concludes that even if Job lived after Moses, he was an Israelite, and therefore his prophecies are legitimate; the book is validated as authentic Israelite prophecy no matter what date is assigned to Job. Further, the latter discussion ignores the question of who wrote down Job. Thus the section relating to who wrote down the scriptures (14b–15a) stands at odds with the section relating to Job's biography (15b). The extended Job discussion was included together with the *baraita* "who wrote the scriptures?" and its commentary, merely because it too dealt with the dating and biography of Job.

An earlier attempt to anchor Job in Israelite history is found in Ben Sira, the apocryphal text also known as Sirach or Ecclesiasticus. Ben Sira states that Ezekiel not only narrated his own visions, but also "recalled" or "mentioned" the book of Job:

יחזקאל ראה מראה      ויגד זני מרכבה

וגם הזכיר את איוב נ.[].א̅      המכלכל כל ד[רכי צ]דק

> It was Ezekiel who saw the vision,
> And narrated the kinds of the chariot
> And he also mentioned Job, [a prophet],
> Who held fast to all the w[ays of righ]teousness.
>
> Ben Sira 49:8–9[72]

Job is in fact mentioned by Ezekiel: "Mortal, when a land sins against me by acting faithlessly, and I stretch out my hand against it. Even if Noah, Daniel, and Job, these three, were in it, they would save only their own lives by their righteousness, says the Lord God" (Ezekiel 14: 13–14; cf. 14: 20). Ben Sira finds this notice significant because it is only here that the figure of Job is cited by another biblical book, and perhaps more to the point, by an Israelite prophet. Ezekiel's comment is clearly seen by Ben Sira as an anchor for the prophecies of Job, whom he likely viewed as a gentile (the prophet Ezekiel is certainly not being praised for merely having mentioned Job). Ben Sira apparently could not establish the date of Job beyond this reference, and thus only makes mention of him in relation to Ezekiel. In contrast to the *baraita* in Baba Bathra, which legitimized Job by connecting him to the pen of Moses, Ben Sira concludes that Ezekiel vouches for the historicity of Job and the legitimacy of his book. This fascinating passage suggests that some early exegetes could be content with legitimating Job by showing that his utterances were known to authentic Israelite prophets, without being concerned about who had textualized them.

By the time of Josephus in the first century C.E., concern over the identity of the textualizers of the biblical books had come to the fore. Although he does not discuss the case of the book of Job, Josephus develops a line of thought consonant with the *baraita* in Baba Bathra, that Moses had written down the portion of Balaam.

Ὑπὸ δὲ ταύτης παροξυνθεὶς τῆς αἰτίας Μωυσῆς ἐπὶ τὸν Μαδιανιτῶν ὄλεθρον τὴν στρατιὰν ἐξέπεμπε. περὶ ὧν τῆς ἐπ' αὐτοὺς ἐξόδου μετὰ μικρὸν ἀπαγγελοῦμεν προδιηγησάμενοι πρῶτον ὃ παρελίπομεν· δίκαιον [γὰρ] ἐπὶ τούτου τὴν τοῦ νομοθέτου γνώμην μὴ παρελθεῖν ἀνεγκωμίαστον. τὸν γὰρ Βάλαμον παραληφθέντα ὑπὸ τῶν Μαδιηνιτῶν. ὅπως ἐπαράσηται τοῖς Ἑβραίοις, καὶ τοῦτο μὲν οὐ δυνηθέντα θείᾳ προνοίᾳ, γνώμην δὲ ὑποθέμενον, ᾗ χρησαμένων τῶν πολεμίων ὀλίγου τὸ τῶν Ἑβραίων πλῆθος διεφθάρη τοῖς ἐπιτηδεύμασι νοσησάντων δή τινων περὶ ταῦτα. <u>μεγάλως ἐτίμησεν ἀναγράψας αὐτοῦ τὰς μαντείας, καὶ παρὸν αὐτῷ σφετερίσασθαι τὴν ἐπ' αὐτοῖς δόξαν καὶ ἐξιδιώσασθαι μηδενὸς ἂν γενομένου μάρτυρος τοῦ διελέγξοντος. ἐκείνῳ τὴν μαρτυρίαν ἔδωκε καὶ τῆς ἐπ' αὐτῷ μνήμης ἠξίωσε.</u>

This was the reason why Moses was provoked to send an army to destroy the Midianites. Of its campaign against them we shall speak presently, when we have first related what we have omitted; for it is right not to pass over our legislator's due praise, on account of his conduct here. This Balaam, who had been summoned by the Midianites to curse the Hebrews, and when he was hindered from doing it by Divine Providence, did still suggest a plan which, being adopted by the enemy, had well nigh led to a demoralization of the whole Hebrew community and actually infected the morals of some — <u>this was the man to whom Moses did the high honor of recording his prophecies. And while it was in his power to take the credit for them himself, as there would have been no witness to convict him, he still gave Balaam this testimony and considered his memory worthy on its account.</u>

Josephus, *Antiquities* 4.156–158, trans. Thackeray and Marcus

In the view of Josephus, Moses knew Balaam had been responsible for leading the Israelites into fornication and idolatry. Nevertheless, he not only copied Balaam's blessings of Israel into the Torah, but also attributed them to Balaam. Josephus' narrative solves two interpretive problems: how did Balaam's words get into the Torah, and how could Balaam's villainy be reconciled with the inspired status of his blessing? The answer supplied by Josephus is that Moses had copied down the oracles of Balaam; hence their location in the Pentateuch. Furthermore, the confusion surrounding the status of these divinely inspired blessings is cleared up, according to Josephus, when one considers the magnanimity of Moses. By rightfully attributing these prophecies to Balaam, Moses had bestowed credit where credit was due. It should be added that the discussion of the textualizer of the Balaam episode does not yet amount to a specific concern on the part of Josephus with textualization *per se,* but rather indicates the way textualization was being employed to answer other sorts of exegetical problems (such as how to interpret the figure of Balaam).

One could argue that both Josephus and the *baraita* in Baba Bathra correctly understand a powerful undercurrent in the biblical text itself, shedding light on the ambivalence toward the appropriation of poetic traditions from Israel's pagan neighbors exhibited by the episode. The explanation that overcomes the ambivalence already appears in the biblical text in the protestations of Balaam, in which he states that he had intended to curse the Israelites, but could only bless them. Josephus amplifies on the implied argument of the episode, placing in the mouth of Balaam a theory of prophetic revelation as fully divine speech lacking the slightest human contribution.

"ὦ Βάλακε, φησί, περὶ τῶν ὅλων λογίζῃ καὶ δοκεῖς ἐφ' ἡμῖν εἶναί τι περὶ τῶν τοιούτων σιγᾶν ἢ λέγειν, ὅταν ἡμᾶς τὸ τοῦ θεοῦ λάβῃ πνεῦμα; φωνὰς γὰρ ἃς βούλεται τοῦτο καὶ λόγους οὐδὲν ἡμῶν εδότων ἀφίησιν. ἐγὼ δὲ μέμνημαι μὲν ὦντε καὶ σὺ καὶ Μαδιηνῖται δεηθέντες ἐνταυθοῖ με προθύμως ἠγάγετε καὶ δι' ἃ τὴν ἄφιξιν ἐποιησάμην, ἥν τέ μοι δι' εὐχῆς μηδὲν ἀδικῆσαί σου τὴν ἐπιθυμίαν. κρείττων δὲ ὁ θεὸς ὧν ἐγὼ χαρίζεσθαι διεγνώκειν· καὶ παντελῶς ἀσθενεῖς ο προγινώσκειν περὶ τῶν ἀνθρωπίνων παρ' ἑαυτῶν ὑπολαμβάνοντες, ὡς μὴ ταῦθ' ἅπερ ὑπαγορεύει τὸ θεῖον λέγειν, βιάζεσθαι δὲ τὴν ἐκείνου βούλησιν· οὐδὲν γὰρ ἐν ἡμῖν ἔτι φθάσαντος εσελθεῖν ἐκείνου ἡμέτερον. ἔγωγ' οὖν τὸν στρατὸν τοῦτον οὔτ' ἐπαινέσαι προεθέμην οὔτ' ἐφ' οἷς τὸ γένος αὐτῶν

ὁ θεὸς ἀγαθοῖς ἐμηχανήσατο διελθεῖν, ἀλλ' εὐμενὴς αὐτοῖς οὗτος ὢν
καὶ σπεύδων αὐτοῖς εὐδαίμονα βίον καὶ κλέος αὠνιον παρασχεῖν ἐμοὶ
τοιούτων ἀπαγγελίαν λόγων ὑπέθετο."

To which Balaam replied, "O Balak, if thou rightly considerest this
whole matter, canst thou suppose that it is in our power to be
silent, or to say any thing, when the Spirit of God seizes upon
us? — for he puts such words as he pleases in our mouths, and
such discourses as we are not ourselves conscious of. I well remember by what entreaties both you and the Midianites so joy-
fully brought me hither, and on that account I took this journey. It
was my prayer, that I might not put any affront upon you, as to
what you desired of me; but God is more powerful than the purposes I had made to serve you; for those that take upon them to
foretell the affairs of mankind, as from their own abilities, are entirely unable to do it, or to forbear to utter what God suggests to
them, or to offer violence to his will; for when he prevents us and
enters into us, nothing that we say is our own. I then did not intend to praise this army, nor to go over the several good things
which God intended to do to their race; but since he was so favorable to them, and so ready to bestow upon them a happy life and
eternal glory, he suggested the declaration of those things to me."

Josephus, *Antiquities* 4.119–123, trans. Thackeray and Marcus

In his discussion of the biblical passage that most forthrightly displays the incongruity between prophetic vessel and divine utterance,
Josephus ruminates on divine agency and human instrumentality.
For both Josephus and the *baraita* in Baba Bathra 14b, it is not the
identity of the prophet but rather that of the scribe that guarantees
the legitimacy of revelation.

## The Rabbinic View on the Textualization of Revelation

I have presented an interpretation of Baba Bathra that accounts for both its overriding purpose and contradictory elements.
The biography of Job is a topic of analysis for the Talmud above all
because it is crucial in ascertaining which prophet wrote down his

book. Since many interpreters thought that Job had lived in the time of the Patriarchs (rather than after Ruth as the order of the biblical books seemed to indicate), it was concluded that his book had been transcribed by Moses. The date of Job also had bearing on the discussion of the order of the Hagiographa in Baba Bathra 14b, which were thought of as being chronological, with the exception of Job. Finally, a quite different question, whether Job was a gentile or Israelite, became attached to the passage. This question involved considering various other options for dating Job, despite the fact that these options would not have allowed Moses to write down the book of Job.

The following translation of Baba Bathra 14b–15a most effectively summarizes the conclusions I have reached thus far:

> Who copied down the scriptures? Moses copied down his book (*sefer*) and the portion of Balaam and Job. Joshua copied down his book and [the last] eight verses of the Pentateuch. Samuel copied down his book and the Book of Judges and Ruth. David copied down the book (*sefer*) of Psalms, on behalf of ten elders, namely Adam, Melchizedek, Abraham, Moses, Heman, Yeduthun, Asaph, and the three sons of Korah. Jeremiah copied down his book, the Book of Kings, and Lamentations. Hezekiah and his colleagues copied down (Mnemonic YMSHK) Isaiah, Proverbs, the Song of Songs and Ecclesiastes. The Men of the Great Assembly copied down (Mnemonic KNDG) Ezekiel, the Twelve Minor Prophets, Daniel and the Scroll of Esther. Ezra copied down his book and the genealogies of the Book of Chronicles up to his own time. This confirms the opinion of Rab, since Rab Judah has said in the name of Rab: Ezra did not leave Babylon to go up to Erez Yisrael until he had written his own genealogy. Who then finished it [the Book of Chronicles]? — Nehemiah the son of Ḥakhaliah.
>
> The Master has said: Joshua copied down the book that bears his name and the last eight verses of the Pentateuch. This statement is in agreement with the authority who says that eight verses in the Torah were copied down by Joshua, as it has been taught: [It is written], "So Moses the servant of the Lord died there." Now is it possible that Moses being dead could have copied down the words, 'Moses died there'? The truth is, however, that up

to this point Moses copied, from this point Joshua copied. This is the opinion of R. Judah, or, according to others, of R. Nehemiah. Said R. Simeon to him: Can [we imagine the] scroll of the Law being short of one letter, and is it not written: "Take this book of the Law"? No; what we must say is that up to this point the Holy One, blessed be He, dictated and Moses repeated and copied, and from this point God dictated and Moses wrote with tears, as it says of another occasion, "Then Baruch answered them, He pronounced all these words to me with his mouth, and I copied them down with ink in the book." Which of these two authorities is followed in the rule laid down by R. Joshua b. Abba which he said in the name of R. Giddal who said it in the name of Rab: The last eight verses of the Torah must be read [in the synagogue service] by one person alone? — It follows R. Judah and not R. Simeon. I may even say, however, that it follows R. Simeon, [who would say that] since they differ [from the rest of the Torah] in one way, they differ in another.

[You say that] Joshua copied down the book that bears his name. But is it not written, "And Joshua son of Nun the servant of the Lord died"? — It was completed by Eleazar. But it is also written in it, "And Eleazar the son of Aaron died"? — Phineas finished it. [You say that] Samuel copied down the book that bears his name. But is it not written in it, "Now Samuel was dead"? — It was completed by Gad the seer and Nathan the prophet. [You say that] David copied down the Psalms, on behalf of the ten elders. Why is not Ethan the Ezrahite also reckoned with? — Ethan the Ezrahite is Abraham. [The proof is that] it is written in the Psalms, "Ethan the Ezrahite," and it is written elsewhere, "Who hath raised up righteousness from the East (mi-mizraḥ)."

Baba Bathra 14b–15a

To recapitulate: the discussion in Baba Bathra is concerned with the written transmission of biblical books rather than with composition. Baba Bathra totally ignores human agency in biblical composition.

A complementary approach to the textualization of the Bible is found in Josephus' Against Apion (see chapters 3 and 4). Josephus places the books whose events were textualized by prophets in one category, and the works of David and Solomon in another. Apparently, only those individuals who composed songs or precepts are acknowledged by Josephus as having any role in the creation (as opposed to mere textualization) of these works. If only the books of Psalms, Proverbs, Ecclesiastes, and Song of Songs were in some way the compositional products of individuals and not just copied, who did Josephus imagine to have composed the rest of the Bible? The answer to this question lies not in the who, but in the what. In Josephus' scheme, the remaining twenty books of the Bible are not compositions in any sense of the term. They are the historical account of Israel as transcribed by a *diadokhê* 'genealogy' or 'succession' of prophets. History, in the view of Josephus, is not to be confused with a more creative notion of historiography as an interpretation of events. Josephus partly takes as his model the works of Thucydides, who imagines the historian as someone who merely *xungraphei* 'collates' or 'records' events (cf. Thucydides 1.1). It goes without saying that the histories written down by the prophets are not authorial compositions in any sense of the term according to Josephus.

The rabbinic view on the textualization of revelation is somewhat different. Unlike Josephus, the rabbis did not consider any part of the Bible to consist of mere history. While the rabbinic notion of textualization is largely parallel to that of Josephus, these textualizers are not conceived as prophets who write down history, but rather as scribes who write down God's instruction or *torah*. On the whole, this process is left unexplained. But in their commentary on the *baraita* in Baba Bathra 14b, the rabbis spell out the role of Moses in the textualization of the Pentateuch. The following extract from the passage, stated to be the words of R. Simeon, spells out this role:

אלא. עד כאן הקב״ה אומר ומשה אומר וכותב. כאן ואילך הקב״ה אומר ומשה כותב בדמע. כמו שנאמר

להלן: (ירמיהו לו) ויאמר להם ברוך מפיו יקרא אלי את כל הדברים האלה ואני כותב על הספר בדיו.

> What we must say is that up to this point the Holy One, blessed be He, dictated (*'omer*) and Moses repeated (*'omer*) and copied down (*kotev*), and from this point God dictated (*'omer*) and Moses wrote

with tears, as it says of another occasion, "Then Baruch answered them, 'He pronounced (*yikre*') all these words to me with his mouth, and I copied (*kotev*) them down with ink in the book'" (Jeremiah 36:18).

Baba Bathra 15a, trans. Simon

R. Simeon, comparing the situation of Moses to that of Baruch the scribe, makes it very clear that Moses was to God what Baruch was to Jeremiah the prophet, at least when Moses was copying down the last eight verses of the Pentateuch. In this passage, the verbal action described by *kotev* is clearly differentiated from that of *'omer* (usually translated as 'speak'). There is no sense of either 'authoring' or 'canonizing', or even 'editing' here. Here then is the confirmation from the very text of Baba Bathra that *kotev* means 'to copy down'.

Ostensibly, R. Simeon seeks to prove that Moses copied down the entire Torah. He is not content with the possibility that Moses was not involved in every verse, even those verses that describe his death and burial. He imagines that Moses is being told about his impending death by God, and that, overcome with emotion, he copies down God's words but does not utter them aloud. These become the only verses in the Pentateuch that were not uttered by human voice during their revelation. For R. Simeon, having Joshua involved would have denigrated both Moses and the Law.

The passage also sheds light on the difficult problem of the role of the prophet in the production of his pre-transcribed utterances, something that Philo takes great pains to understand in *De Vita Mosis*. By using the verb *'omer* to describe both the activity of God in revealing the Torah and the activity of Moses in re-articulating it, Baba Bathra speaks of this revelation in a seemingly confusing manner. M. Simon's translation above attempts to make sense of the ambiguity by rendering the first *'omer* as 'dictate', and the second as 'repeat'. While this is a possible understanding of the sentence, and even a reasonable interpretation of the ideology of divine origination of humanly transmitted biblical writings, the fact remains that the text employs the same multi-purpose word for both. The ambiguity is complicated by the meaning of *'omer* discussed above, 'to utter a work without the use of writing'. The use of the word to describe Moses' role in the composition of the Pentateuch is qualified by its juxtaposition with the same verb applied to God: "up to this point the Holy One, blessed be He *'omer* 'utters' and Moses *'omer* 'utters' and 'copies down' (*kotev*)." The work is thought of as having two speakers — both God and Moses give voice to the words of the Torah, but God does so first. The passage thus admits to three separate processes in the composition of the holy scriptures: God utters, Moses utters, and Moses copies it down in writing.

It is notable that the sages quoted in Baba Bathra mention a tradition in which the last eight verses of the Pentateuch must be read by one person alone:

> The Master has said: Joshua copied down the book that bears his name and the last eight verses of the Pentateuch. This statement is in agreement with the authority who says that eight verses in the Torah were copied down by Joshua, as it has been taught: [It is written], "So Moses the servant of the Lord died there." Now is it possible that Moses being dead could have copied down the words, 'Moses died there'? The truth is, however, that up to this point Moses copied, from this point Joshua copied. This is the opinion of R. Judah, or, according to others, of R. Nehemiah. Said R. Simeon to him: Can [we imagine the] scroll of the Law being short of one letter, and is it not written: "Take this book of the Law"? No; what we must say is that up to this point the Holy One, blessed be He, dictated and Moses repeated and copied, and from this point God dictated and Moses wrote with tears, as it says of another occasion, "Then Baruch answered them, He pronounced all these words to me with his mouth, and I copied them down with ink in the book." Which of these two authorities is followed in the rule laid down by R. Joshua b. Abba which he said in the name of R. Giddal who said it in the name of Rab: The last eight verses of the Torah must be read [in the synagogue service] by one person alone (*yaḥid qore' 'otan*)? — It follows R. Judah and not R. Simeon. I may even say, however, that it follows R. Simeon, [who would say that] since they differ [from the rest of the Torah] in one way, they differ in another.
>
> Baba Bathra 15a, trans. Simon

The passage contains a difficult notion: Rab's requirement that a single individual read the last eight verses of Deuteronomy (*yahid qore' 'otan*) in the synagogue. There are a number of interpretations that have been advanced in the traditional Talmudic commentaries.[73] According to Rashi and the Shulkhan Arukh, these verses should not be divided between readers, but should be read in a single block by a single individual.[74] The Tosafists ('supplementers' of Rashi's commentary) say that the majority of rabbis concluded that the *shaliah zibor* (service leader) should not read these verses.[75] Joseph ibn Migash states that these eight verses must always be read by one person, silently, and that this person should not read any other parts of the Torah. The opinion of Maimonides (the student of Migash) is that there need not be a *minyan* 'quorum' of ten Jews at the reading of these verses. It is even argued that an illustrious scholar should read them (a view that Moses Isserles attributes to Ha-Mordekhai, and which was also held by Ha-Meiri).[76]

The practice of having two readers of Torah during synagogue services deserves some comment here. There is no rabbinic consensus on the origin of the practice. The Mishnah assumes that the second "reader" was typically an Aramaic translator (*miturgeman*), utilized for the benefit of those in the congregation whose mother tongue was Aramaic, and who couldn't understand Hebrew. Significantly, the Mishnah forbids a single individual from reading and translating the Torah by himself, although no reason is given.[77]

Dual recitation is sometimes validated as an expression of the initial circumstances of the revelation of the Torah to Moses. In a statement attributed to R. Samuel bar R. Isaac, the Jerusalem Talmud states that the Torah was given through an intermediary (*sirsur*) — namely, Moses. Likewise, it is forbidden for a single individual to read and translate what he has read.[78] Similarly, the relationship of Moses and Aaron, his spokesman to Pharoah, is occasionally compared to the relative position of Torah reader and *meturgeman*.[79]

After the practice of Aramaic translation declined, a new rationale was required to explain the practice of having two readers of Torah, which had outlived the Aramaic vernacular. The Tosafists reveal that it was common practice for a *shaliah zibor* to help read the Torah in the synagogue in their time. According to their interpretation of *yahid* in Baba Bathra 15a, the reason for having two readers is "in order not to embarrass someone who doesn't know how to read," implying that the second reader might be less than accomplished, if not illiterate, in Hebrew.[80] Eventually, the second reader could be given credit for reading the Torah merely by reciting the blessings required by the Mishnah (Megillah 4.1–2), while the *shaliah zibor* did the actual reading.[81]

The anonymous narrator of Baba Bathra 15a attempts to relate the practice of a *yahid* reading the last eight verses of Deuteronomy to the teaching of both R. Judah and R. Simeon. To reiterate, R. Judah claimed that Joshua copied down the last verses of the Pentateuch, while R. Simeon, comparing Moses to Baruch the scribe, argued that Moses ceased repeating the eight verses and copied out what God dictated "in tears." The narrator goes on to argue the practice of having a *yahid* read these verses mimics the change in the conditions of their textualization, regardless of the precise nature of that change.

According to Baba Bathra 15a, the dual recitation of Torah is not in essence a practical matter. It is neither viewed as a way of enabling the congregation to hear the Torah in a familiar language, nor is it explained as a practice whereby an inaccurate or illiterate reader could escape public shame. Instead, both R. Judah and R. Simeon consider dual readership to be a mimesis of the revelation of Torah through Moses. If R. Judah's teaching about Joshua is correct, the recitation of the Torah as a whole by two readers becomes a mimesis of God's utterance and Moses' textualization of his words. Accordingly, when Moses ceased copying down God's words, the second reader must fall silent. If R. Simeon's teaching is correct, the recitation of the Torah by two readers represents the voices of God uttering Torah and Moses repeating it. Either way, dual recitation is here envisioned as a performative display of the Jewish belief that the Torah was divinely dictated rather than humanly authored.[82]

To conclude: Baba Bathra 14b–15a, which could be described as a compact summary of the rabbinic position on the origin of the Bible, avoids the consideration of human agency in scriptural composition, and instead meditates on the textualization of the biblical text. In shifting the discussion to textualization and away from authorship, human agents are given as small a role as possible in the recording of revelation. Even the *baraita,* the oldest layer of Baba Bathra 14–15, downplays David's composition of the Psalms, and totally ignores the role of Solomon as an author. Emphasizing the creative role individuals in biblical composition is inimical to its view of the Bible as a divine compendium.

Can this interpretive approach of attaching a name to a text be considered in a history of authorship? In a sense, authorship, defined as human composition, is not what we see at work in the Talmud. One might say that a discussion of authorship is suppressed by this passage, as if it would distract from its primary goal of providing the definitive statement on biblical textualization, or even as if authorship were not a category with which to evaluate the Bible as a whole. Nevertheless, names are indeed attached to texts here, in a manner that is as circumscribed as possible. The approach to text-name attachment in the Talmud thus represents a nascent theorization about the relationship of individuals to texts, in the very fact that it avoids composition in favor of transmission. It also reveals that individualism in composition was antithetic to rabbinic theology.

CHAPTER 2

# ATTACHING NAMES TO
# BIBLICAL BOOKS

Attribution belongs to the realm of literary scholarship, and has little to do with the intentions of the composers of works. It isn't so much about what an author *did* write, but rather it is about what he *would have written* (or, from the perspective of ancient literary interpreters, what he must have written). This chapter describes three processes: the elimination of anonymity by means of attribution, the evolution and variety of Jewish positions on human agency in biblical composition, and the use of attribution as a means of determining whether a book was to be considered authoritative.

In Baba Bathra 14b, textual anonymity — the lack of the name of an individual accompanying a given text — was a condition waiting to be remedied by the careful investigation of candidates who had potentially copied each biblical book. Every biblical book is accounted for by this text; the identity of its human agents is carefully worked out on the basis of midrashic (homiletic) principles and strategies already present in pre-rabbinic biblical exegesis. The Bible's nature as a cryptic yet perfect document suggested that the clues for this attribution might be found within the text itself.[1] The very same principles that could be used in the solution of halakhic (legal) or other interpretive problems were therefore applicable to the quest for finding the human scribe for each biblical book.

## Human vs. Divine Authorship

I argued in chapter 1 that the position of the *baraita* in Baba Bathra 14b on the human agents of biblical textualization represented a rejection of human authorship. There are many rabbinic statements that similarly downplay the role of individuals in the composition of the Bible. Moses is sometimes figured as a scribe copying out the Torah verse by verse, but not at all contributing to the text.[2]

This tendency also resulted in a view that certain books usually assigned to later periods had been previously revealed to Moses. Thus, it is stated in the Jerusalem Talmud with regard to the book of Esther:

רב ור׳ חנינה ור׳ יונתן ור׳ ובר קפרא ור׳ יהושוע בן לוי אמרו המגילה הזות נאמרה למשה מסיני אלא

שאין מוקדם ומאוחר בוזה

Rab, R. Ḥaninah, R. Jonathan, Bar Qappara, and R. Joshua b. Levi said, "This scroll was stated to Moses at Sinai, for there is no chronological order in the Torah."

J. Megillah 1.5

The rabbis could derive the notion of the revelation at Sinai even of a book as late as Esther from tried and true exegetical principles like *'eyn muqdam u-me'uḥar be-torah* "there is no early or late in the Torah." The book of Ruth would also be described by the rabbis as divinely uttered (e.g. Ruth Rabbah 4.5, a restatement of the tradition in J. Megillah 1.5). Rabbinic discussions of the divine origin of the Song of Songs went to even greater lengths to argue against human authorship. It is stated that the Song of Songs, the "holiest of holies" according to some, was composed by God or by the angels, and that it too had been revealed to Moses at Mt. Sinai or at the Red Sea, even before the rest of the Torah.[3] Solomon's role is often entirely effaced in these discussions. The tendency that began in an effort to downplay the human composition of biblical books thus culminated in an affirmation of the Sinaitic revelation of at least three of the five *megillot* 'scrolls'.[4]

Apparently, the idea of the human authorship of scripture was already a source of discomfort for Philo of Alexandria in the first century C.E. Philo's view on human vs. divine authorship differs substantially from rabbinic positions on this question; nevertheless, it reveals that the compositional contribution of Moses could also be downplayed through an appeal to allegorical mysticism. Yehoshua Amir's exploration of the trope of Moses as "author" of the Pentateuch in the writings of Philo shows that Philo had a complex way of understanding Moses as prophet and philosopher. Amir concludes:

> [Philo's Moses] is both receiver and transmitter of the Divine teaching. As receiver he not only receives a knowledge of Divine teaching from without; he also receives from within a share of the Divine being, as Philo likes to explain in connection with the verse "Stand thou here with Me." Thus for Philo the word of Mikra [scripture] can be a word that comes to Moses and a word that proceeds from him, at one and the same time.[5]

Philo's scheme with regard to simultaneous human and divine agency is further complicated by the fact that he assumes a pagan vocabulary of oracular prophecy. Amir notes that Philo depends on Plato's treatment of the mantic utterance in the *Timaeus* (72a–b).[6] Philo's Moses is frequently taken over by divine possession like a pagan *prophêtês* 'prophet' and soothsayer: "The prophet . . . no longer being in himself was possessed by the divinity and foretold (*thespizô*) these things (ὁ δὲ προφήτης . . . οὐκέτ' ὢν ἐν ἑαυτῷ θεοφορεῖται καὶ θεσπίζει τάδε)" (*De Vita Mosis* 2.250). This possession by the divinity is described as a transformation to prophet status: "While his heart was still hot within him, burning with lawful indignation, inspiration came upon him, and, transformed into a prophet (*metabalôn eis prophêtên*), he foretold these words . . ." (*De Vita Mosis* 2.280). Philo constructs a threefold scheme of divine utterances, some of which are "spoken by God in his own person with

His prophet for interpreter," some in which "the revelation comes through question and answer between Moses and God," and a third category, in which the utterances were conceived by the human mind of Moses but which were nevertheless inspired by God. No matter how much Philo wishes to equate Moses with Greek philosophers, he always avoids granting him an unqualified role in composition.[7]

The approaches to this question taken by the earliest strata of Second Temple Jewish interpretation are less easy to grasp, although it is useful to compare them with later rabbinic approaches. As we shall see, one of the tendencies of biblical interpretation during the Second Temple period was to see certain individuals, especially David and Solomon, as human originators of psalms, songs, and didactic sayings.[8] There are two features which rabbinic and pre-rabbinic approaches to biblical attribution share. The first is a tendency to attach a name to each and every portion of the Bible, especially anonymous texts. The second is a process whereby texts attributed to an otherwise unknown figure were to be connected with a better-known individual. Both operations were accomplished by the use of "midrashic identification," the exegetical technique which shows that lesser-known or unnamed figures are in reality guises of more familiar figures.

Yiẓḥak Heineman was among the first to connect midrashic identification with textual attribution.[9] Heineman documents the various forms of midrashic *riḥuz* 'focusing', where unnamed characters in biblical narratives are identified with known characters that appear elsewhere in the Bible. He further explains that such identifications resulted in the pseudepigrapha — the corpus of falsely ascribed writings that circulated in Jewish circles. Perhaps in order to elevate the significance of these texts and to connect their contents to past authorities, the authors of these new teachings hung their texts on the support of a wise man known by name. But midrashic identifications could also arise out of complete naiveté, as a form of the same "escape from anonymity" that Heineman perceives to be at work throughout Jewish *midrash aggadah*. It is this tendency that he finds operative in the attribution of un-named texts to individuals in Baba Bathra 14b. In short, authorial attribution is a species of the procedure involved in the naming of any unnamed character. The unattributed text was simply a vacuum waiting to be filled.

Heineman's argument that biblical interpretation cannot tolerate a vacuum in its ascription of texts to individuals holds for both rabbinic and early Second Temple exegesis (with the exception of a heterodox stance towards attribution in some non-canonical texts — see below). But while the midrashic origin of textual attribution is convincing, I disagree with Heineman that textual attribution merely represents a meaningless application of a more general principle. As I will argue, attribution served as a means of ratifying the authoritativeness of biblical compositions that were not associated with an established prophet.

This discussion about the nature of biblical authorship resembles the formulation of the classical philologist Ulrich von Wilamowitz-Moellendorff. Wilamowitz speaks of a *horror vacui* 'horror of a vacuum' in the authorial ascription of Greek texts that began in the Hellenistic period, perhaps due to the pressure of the formation of the great libraries at Pergamum and Alexandria.[10] According to Wilamowitz, many collections of classical texts, grouped under a putative author, were begun in this fashion. Such works include the genealogical and didactic works of Hesiod, the Aesop Fables, the medical treatises of Hippocrates, and the magical and alchemistic works of Democritus.[11] The prevalence of this mode of textual interpretation in the classical world from the Hellenistic period onwards is suggestive for study of Jewish attribution techniques in the Second Temple period.

Perhaps the best known of the midrashic identifications was the set of maneuvers which enabled early Jewish interpreters to arrive at the notion of Solomon as the author of Proverbs, Ecclesiastes, and Song of Songs. In the case of Song of Songs, the attribution was clear (Song of Songs 1:1: "Song of Songs which is Solomon's" or "The best of Solomon's songs"). In contrast, Ecclesiastes nowhere states Solomon's name, but merely claims to be composed by a son of David who was king in Jerusalem. Solomon was the only person who fit the description, and the avoidance of his name seemed to provide a clue about other texts in which his presence could be detected. Thus, although Solomon was thought to have composed the book of Proverbs, several divisions in the collection seemed to be attributed to otherwise unknown individuals — Agur, Jakeh, Lemuel, and Ithiel. If Solomon could have alternate names, such as Jedidiah 'beloved of God' as Nathan called him, or Qoheleth as he was apparently referred to in Ecclesiastes 1:1, could not Agur and Lemuel too be names which referred to the same wise individual who had composed the other words of wisdom contained in the Bible? The following passage from Qoheleth Rabbah exemplifies the usefulness of "midrashic focusing" in attribution:

למה נקרא שמו קהלת שהיו דבריו נאמרין בהקהל על שם שאמר (מלכים א' ח') אז יקהל שלמה

. . .

שלש שמות נקרא לו ידידיה קהלת שלמה ר' יהושע אומר שבעה אגור יקה למואל איתיאל אמר שמואל עיקר אותנטייא שלהם ידידיה קהלת שלמה מודה ר' שמואל באילין ארבעה אלא שנתכנה בהן שלמה ושנתנו להדרש אגור שאגור בדברי תורה יקה שהיה מקיא בדבריו כספל הזה שמתמלא בשעתו ומתפנה בשעתו כך שלמה למד תורה בשעתה ושכחה בשעתה למואל שנם לאל בלבו ואמר אני יכול להרבות ולא לחטוא איתיאל שאמר אתי אל ואוכל בן דוד בן מלך בן מלך חכם בן חכם צדיק בן צדיק אבגינוס בן אבגינוס

Why was Qoheleth's name so called? Because his words were uttered in public (*hiqqahel*), as it is stated, "Then Solomon assembled (*yaqehl*) the elders of Israel" (1 Kings 8:1) . . .

He was called by three names: Jedidiah (2 Sam. 12:25), Qoheleth, and Solomon. R. Joshua said: He had seven names: Agur, Jakeh, Lemuel, Ithiel (cf. Prov. 30:1, 31:1) [in addition to the three mentioned]. R. Samuel said: The proper, authentic names among them are Jedidiah, Qoheleth, and Solomon. R. Samuel admits the other four, but [he maintains that] Solomon received them as surnames and they were given to him for expository reasons. He was called "Agur" because he was stored (*'agur*) with words of Torah. He was called "Jakeh" because he discharged (*meki'*) words [of wisdom] like a bowl that is filled at one time and emptied at another time; similarly did Solomon learn Torah at one time and forget it at another time. He was called Lemuel because he spoke against God in his heart, saying "I can multiply [wives] without sinning." He was called "Ithiel" because he said, "God is with me (*'itti'el*), and I can do so, seeing that I am David's son, a king and a king's son, a wise man and a wise man's son, righteous and the son of a righteous man, a nobleman and a nobleman's son."

Qoheleth Rabbah 1.2, trans. Cohen

A certain economy or thrift would seem to animate the move towards Solomonic authorship.[12] A unity in style aided in the identification of Solomon with the minor figures whose names had been attached to chapters of proverbs, although the category of biblical "wisdom" is more than just a style or even a single genre.[13] These types of homiletic techniques, by which multiple names could be seen as referring to a single writer, initially propelled the search for the composers of biblical works.

Just as interpreters of wisdom texts sought to whittle down the number of composers of these texts to a single well-known entity, some interpretive communities practically ignored psalmic attributions to figures other than David. However, one influential rabbinic view of psalmic attribution preserved in the *baraita* in Baba Bathra 14b concludes that there were ten composers of psalms, despite the fact the number of individuals who have been credited with psalm composition actually adds up to more than ten.[14] In order to keep the number of the composers of Psalms at ten, the *baraita* states that one of the lesser-known "authors" of the psalms is in reality just a name for a more well-known composer:

דוד כתב ספר תהלים על ידי עשרה זקנים. וליחשוב נמי איתן האזרחי אמר רב: איתן האזרחי

זה הוא אברהם. כתיב הכא: (תהלים פ"ט) איתן האזרחי. וכתיב התם: (ישעיהו מ"א) מי העיר ממזרח

צדק [וגו']. קא חשיב משה וקא חשיב הימן. והאמר רב: הימן זה משה, כתיב הכא: הימן. וכתיב התם:

(במדבר י"ב) בכל ביתי נאמן הוא תרי הימן הוו.

[*Baraita*] David wrote the Psalms, including the work of the ten elders. [*Gemara*] Why is not Ethan the Ezrahite also reckoned with? — Ethan the Ezrahite is Abraham. [The proof is that] it is written in the Psalms, "Ethan the Ezrahite," and it is written elsewhere, "Who hath raised up righteousness from the East (*mi-mizraḥ*)."

[The passage above] reckons both Moses and Heman. But has not Rab said that Moses is Heman, [the proof being] that the name Heman is found here [in the Psalms] and it is written elsewhere [of Moses], "In all my house he is faithful (*ne'eman*)"? — There were two Hemans.

Baba Bathra 14b, trans. Simon

Although Ethan the Ezrahite was thought to have composed Psalm 89 (according to its brief heading), removing him from the list of psalmic authors by equating him with Abraham helped keep the number of such composers down to the magic number ten. In the case of Moses and Heman, the *baraita* does not consider that these were one and the same person, although clearly rabbinic exegetes were capable of turning Heman into an incarnation of Moses if necessary.

Another intriguing authorial identification appears in B. Megillah 15a, the Targum to Malachi 1:1, and the preface to the Book of Malachi by St. Jerome. Each of these texts asserts that Malachi was another name for Ezra.[15] The identification has relevance for evaluating Josephus' claim that a "succession of prophets" (which included Ezra) was responsible for the recording of the biblical books. It was not outside of the arsenal of later Jewish interpretation to turn figures like David or Daniel into prophets, although they had never been considered such by earlier Israelite culture. Evidently, the technique of midrashic identification was used for the same purpose. Prophetic status was essential for legitimate biblical transmission, not just for Josephus, but in rabbinic circles as well. One may see this even in the Talmudic notice about the authorship of non-biblical prayers used in the Jewish daily liturgy: "One hundred and twenty elders, among them several prophets, composed the Eighteen Benedictions" (B. Megillah 17b). This body of one hundred and twenty elders was known as the Great Assembly. A key to its authority was that included in its number were the prophets Haggai, Zechariah, and Malachi.

## David and the Psalms

In Baba Bathra 14b, it is stated, "David wrote down the Book of Psalms, on behalf of (*'al yidey*) the ten elders, namely Adam, Melchizedek, Abraham, Moses, Heman, Yeduthun, Asaph, and the three sons of Korah." It was not thought worth mentioning that David copied out his own Psalms, although this locution had not been avoided in the case of Moses, Joshua, or Samuel (each were said to have copied out *sifro* 'his book'). What is the reason for the oversight, if it can be called that? Was there an attempt to downplay the role of David in the composition of the Psalms?

The theme of David as prophet and author has been explored by James Kugel in an important treatment of Second Temple notions of biblical authorship.[16] In several places in the New Testament and Qumran texts, as well as in rabbinic texts, David's name is linked with the Psalms as a whole; in the earliest of these texts, according to Kugel, the attribution suggests that David was conceived as the author of the Psalms. Eventually, David comes to be described not just as an author, but also as a prophet. In the Acts of the Apostles 2:29–30, David is plainly called a prophet. Elsewhere in early Christian texts, it is stated (somewhat more cautiously) that David prophesied (Acts 1:16 and 4:25, the Gospel of Mark 12:36–37, and the Epistle of Barnabas 12:10). The theme of David's gift of prophecy also appears in Josephus (*Antiquities* 8.109–110) and in the "List of David's Compositions" from the Dead Sea Scrolls. David's designation as prophet may have been aided by the fact that he was called *'ish ha-'elohim* 'a man of God' (in 2 Chronicles 8:14 and Nehemiah 12:24, 36), even though he is nowhere in the Hebrew Bible called a *nav'i* 'prophet'. One explanation offered by Kugel for the Chronicler's interest in making David an *'ish ha-'elohim* involved his desire to give the music elements of the Temple service a distinguished founder, perhaps because liturgical song and those responsible for its performance had not been given the respect the Chronicler felt they deserved.[17] The later attention to David's authorship of the songs performed in the Temple reflects a similar impetus.

It is clear that the notion of "David the poet" appeared prior to his achieving the status of prophet; David's prophetic status was a secondary phenomenon, and served to explain the presence of certain psalms (e.g., Psalm 137) that referred to a period far later than his own. Thanks to his prophetic abilities, the poet was able to foresee conditions centuries after his death. I would emphasize that outright descriptions of David as a prophet *per se* (rather than merely prophesying, being inspired by the Holy Spirit, or writing "in prophecy") can only be found in Acts 2:30 and in later rabbinic and Christian texts. Kugel speculates that the promotion of Israel's ancient texts to scripture was the occasion for ancient interpreters to seek a divinely inspired originator of these works rather than some anonymous historian or scribe. Authorial attribution and the elevation of sacred works to scripture do seem to share in their critical concern for the status of the person to whom each text was attributed. But rather than attempting to show that a work's status as scripture *precedes* the development of the idea of a known and established human composer, I would suggest that the authoritativeness of a work (and not necessarily its status as scripture) derived from and was ratified by its attribution.[18] Initially, interpreters thus sought merely to find a venerable originator of these works, rather than a prophetic one.

The earliest testimony of the role of David as poet is the "List of David's Compositions" found appended to a collection of Psalms from cave 11 at Qumran; the scroll is referred to as 11QPs[a].

2　ויהי דויד בן ישי חכם ואור כאור השמש וסופר

3　ונבון ותמים בכול דרכיו לפני אל ואנשים ויתן

4　לו י ה ו ה רוח נבונה ואורה ויכתוב תהלים

5　שלושת אלפים ושש מאות ושיר לשורר לפני מזבח על עולת

6　התמיד לכול יום ויום לכול ימי השנה ארבעה וששים ושלוש

7　מאות ולקורבן השבתות שנים וחמשים שיר ולקורבן ראשי

8　החודשים ולכול ימי המועדות ולים הכפורים שלושים שיר

9　ויהי כול השיר אשר דבר ששה ואבעים וארבע מאות ושיר

10　לנגן על הפגועים ארבעה ויהי הכול ארבעת אלפים וחמשים

11　כול אלה דבר בנבואה אשר נתן לו מלפני העליון

And David, the son of Jesse, was wise, and a light like the light of the sun, and literate (= *sofer* 'a scribe'), and discerning and perfect in all his ways before God and men. And the Lord gave him a discerning and enlightened spirit. And he wrote down (*va-yikhtov* from root *katav*) 3,600 psalms; and songs to sing before the altar over the whole-burnt perpetual offering every day, or all the days of the year, 364; and for the offering of the Sabbaths, 52 songs; and for the offering of the New Moons and for all the Solemn Assemblies and for the Day of Atonement, 30 songs. And all the songs that he spoke (*dibber*) were 446, and songs or making music over the stricken, 4. And the total was 4,050. All these he spoke (*dibber*)

through prophecy (*be-nevu'a*) which was given him from before
the Most High.

11QPs[a] column XXVII, lines 2–11, trans. Sanders

This note represents the most comprehensive instance of the critical attribution of texts to an individual on the part of Second Temple biblical interpreters found thus far. It is also the earliest literary
evidence of the association of David with the composition of
Psalms (if David's role in this text may be described as such).[19] In
the tradition of the biblical headings that precede and occasionally
follow individual psalms, sections in the case of Proverbs, and the
entire work in the case of Ecclesiastes and Song of Songs, this note
is affixed to the end of an entire scroll of Psalms.

The fact that this notice was discovered as part of a collection
of psalms at Qumran may mislead, however, as to its provenance.
Eileen Schuller cites recent research, including her own analysis of
psalms from Qumran, arguing that the "List of David's Compositions" was not itself a composition of the Qumran community, but
probably derived from "the common poetry of Persian/Hellenistic
Judaism," like the psalm collection 4QPs[f] as a whole and the other
psalms contained in 11QPs[a].[20]

The Persian or early Hellenistic date of this list and its non-
sectarian origin should be seen in conjunction with what James
Kugel has noted as a reticence on the part of 11QPs[a] to accord
David full prophetic status. As Kugel notes, David is called "wise"
and "luminous" — in other words, he is described as a sage but not
a prophet. Nevertheless, his works are said there to have been composed *be-nevu'a* 'in prophecy'. What was reason for the reticence in
assigning David the status of prophet, but not in attributing to him
the authorship of near or more than 3,600 Psalms and hundreds of
songs? Is there a distinction to be made between works composed
by a prophet and works composed "in prophecy"?

I would suggest that David's ultimate rise to prophet status in
the New Testament and rabbinic texts was a direct reaction to his
earlier standing as composer and poet. As we see from the "list of
compositions" in 11QPs[a], "David the composer" preceded "David
the prophet." There was no need at this stage to consider him a
prophet, even if it was clear that his works were composed "in

prophecy"; after all, it was Samuel and Nathan who were David's prophets.[21] Indeed, the non-canonical Psalm 151A that appears immediately after the "List of David's Compositions" states clearly that it is Samuel who is "God's prophet" (LXX Ps. 151:5, Q lines 8–9). The "List of David's Compositions" would thus conform with Josephus' view that the psalms and three books of an edifying sort (that is, the works of David and Solomon) were not textualized by prophets in the succession (see chapter 4).

The "List of David's Compositions" states that David 'wrote down' (*va-yikhtov*) 3,600 Psalms (*tehillim*), and that he 'spoke' (*dibber*) a total of 448 songs (*shir*); later in line 11 it states that he 'spoke in prophecy' (*dibber be-nevu'a*) all 4,050 compositions. Two different verbs are used to refer to David's role in the composition of the Psalms. According to J. A. Sanders, the text serves as a challenge to the immense literary output of Solomon as described in 1 Kings 5:12.[22] What is most noticeable about this comparison is that Solomon is only said to have uttered (*dibber*) proverbs, while David is lauded as both a composer and a textualizer of poetic works. I would therefore argue that *sofer* in line 1 must be understood in its literal sense as 'scribe' rather than 'literate' or 'scholarly' as suggested by Sanders. The choice of this word to describe David is thus consistent with the approach to David's role in the transmission of Psalms found in Baba Bathra 14b, where David is valued principally as a faithful copyist. The "List of David's Compositions" therefore represents the earliest treatment of David as a copyist of texts — in this case, the ones he himself composed.[23]

There is a lack of precision in the list, arguably intentional, as to the exact role of David *vis-à-vis* these psalms and songs. I would suggest that the "List of David's Compositions" represents an attempt to link David as *both* composer and scribe to the Psalms. The last line of the text (line 11) ("All these he spoke [*dibber*] through prophecy [*be-nevu'a*] which was given him from before the Most High") has a slightly different concern. The fact that "all these [psalms and songs] were spoken prophetically" may be yet a third way of legitimizing the authoritative status of the psalms in this scroll. The list appears to be taking no chances, as if the fact that they were both composed and copied by David were not sufficient.

The interest in the role of David as copyist of his own psalms can also be seen in one of the Septuagint psalm headings. The Septuagint translation of the heading to Psalm 151, unlike the heading in 11QPs^a 151 (the Hebrew *Vorlage* of LXX Psalm 151A) or the Syriac Psalm 151 in the Syro-Hexeplar (the Syriac Apocryphal Psalm I), contains the word ἰδιόγραφος (*idiographos*) 'self-copied' prior to the usual designation 'to David.' In addition, the Septuagint refers to the psalm in this same heading as *exôthen tou arithmou* 'supernumerary', and describes that it was uttered "when [David] fought Goliath in one-on-one combat."[24] Sanders states, "The protest evident in *idiographos* suggests, perhaps, a doubt about the authorship which the faithful at Qumran did not entertain. On the contrary, in the Qumran Psalter this psalm occurs in the last column in such a position as to suggest that it held great importance in Qumranian beliefs concerning both David and his musical ability."[25] The heading could thus be paraphrased: "Although this psalm is not included in the usual collections, we know it was composed *or at least copied* by David and therefore is included here."[26]

The attribution of a vast list of compositions to David has special significance with regard to those psalms found in the scroll that are not part of the book of Psalms in the canonical Hebrew Bible; in fact, the non-canonical psalms follow the "list of compositions." I would therefore suggest that the "List of David's Compositions" seeks to validate the psalms contained in the Psalms Scroll from Qumran Cave 11, rather than to serve as a kind of hagiography of David.

The evidence from Qumran indicates a tendency to link all the psalms to David in as many ways as possible. He is credited with their composition, but this composition process is simultaneously pictured as resulting from prophecy. The list of compositions also emphasizes that David is the scribe who copied out the psalms, guaranteeing their legitimacy in another important way.

At a certain point in the late Second Temple period, Jewish interpreters were divided about the old attribution of the psalms to David. For some, the attribution implied that David had perhaps composed all the psalms, a feat that could only have been accomplished if he were a prophet; this meant elevating him to full prophet status. For others, the Davidic attribution was interpreted as a reference to the textualization rather than composition of the psalms, seeing that many of the psalm headings spoke of other composers. The "List of David's Compositions" from Qumran contains both approaches *in nuce,* although for its own reasons. It elevates the scribal activities of David to outshine Solomon's accomplishments, as well as to give an extra guarantee of the legitimacy of the psalms in the scroll. Similarly, it introduces the idea of David's prophetic composition to validate the psalms in the scroll that were not a part of other collections in yet another way. That David is said in the Qumran text to have composed psalms and songs "in prophecy" foreshadows the transformation from David the king into a full-fledged prophet.

The list found at Qumran does not really speculate on whether psalms derive from a human or a divine source, and does not consider the extent to which both human and divine play roles in composition. While the force of the statement does indeed indicate that all these works were composed 'in prophecy' (*be-nevu'a*) and that David is speaking from a source outside himself, I would argue that the real intent of this list is to validate a body of liturgical and poetic works in as many ways as possible. The idea of prophecy represents an essential part of this legitimatization procedure; so does attribution to David in his role as composer and scribe of the psalms.

## The Psalm Headings

The key to authorial attributions of the Psalms was the Psalm headings.[27] These consist of short prose utterances regarding the type of psalm, the instruments that could be used to play it, and often a name (like David) preceded by an ambiguous preposition *le-* (usually this indicates an indirect object or possession, but in the headings it is sometimes referred to as the *lamed auctoris*). Occasionally the heading includes a short biographical notice describing when the psalm was first uttered.

Brevard Childs, one of the biblical scholars who has examined them most closely, sets the date for the psalm headings squarely in the Second Temple period. The *terminus a quo,* according to Childs, falls sometime after the Chronicler: "the lack of its (i.e. the heading or superscription's) occurrence in Chronicles — in distinction to Daniel or Ben Sira — is noteworthy because the material of the Chronicler would seem to lend itself admirably to the use of the superscription form if it had been available."[28] The *terminus ad quem* is provided by the date of the Qumran Psalm scroll, for in it, according to Childs, the style of the heading is fully developed.[29]

Much of the scholarly work on the Psalm headings has focused on the so-called *lamed auctoris* applied to David (*le-David*). According to Kugel, "Perhaps the least likely hypothesis about this mysterious phrase is that it was originally an attribution of authorship, but that is precisely the sense in which it came to be taken."[30] However, there remains the outside possibility that it was in fact added as an indication of authorship, just as it later came to be taken. This is in fact the conclusion of Childs: "Whatever the expression לדוד (*le-David*) may once have meant, the claim of authorship now seems most probable. This point is confirmed by the final clause in those titles which specify a particular historical incident in David's life as providing the occasion for composition."[31] The fact that the Psalmic redactors were ignorant as to the real author of each particular psalm does not invalidate their certainty that David, Asaph, or any of the others whose names they affixed to the Psalms were their true authors. Perhaps they relied on a tradition that linked a given name to the liturgical origins of that song in the temple cult. But as the "biographical" psalm headings indicate, in other cases this was a critical conclusion based on midrashic or hermeneutic exegesis. In other words, the redactors, working from a long-standing association of the name of David with the Psalms in general, were able to locate similarities of the wording of an individual psalm with events from the life of David as described in 1 and 2 Samuel. These psalms seemed to refer to the life of their composer in a particular way, documenting his spontaneous outpouring of emotion and thankfulness to God at particular moments in his life. It seems likely at least that the more terse designation *le-David* 'to/for/of David' predated the expanded headings.

More expansive are the Septuagint Psalm headings, which reflect a continuation of the tendency to add biographical information and even new composers. The most remarkable of the Septuagint headings are those that attribute their psalms to individuals who were not recognized in the rest of the Jewish tradition as being associated with Psalms. The Septuagint Psalms 145–148 (= MT Psalms 146, 147:1–11, 147:1–12, 148) are ascribed to Haggai and Zechariah, two of the minor prophets, while the Masoretic Text merely has the heading *Halleluyah* 'Praised be God'. Similarly, Septuagint Psalm 64 adds the names Jeremiah and Ezekiel, even though it already has the 'to David' attribution in the Hebrew text. The addition of these prophets in the Septuagint headings perhaps indicates a need to associate the psalms with known prophets.

What was the purpose of the psalm headings? According to Childs, "By placing a Psalm within the setting of a particular historical incident in the life of David, the reader suddenly was given access to previously unknown information. David's inner life was now unlocked to the reader, who was allowed to hear his intimate thoughts and reflections." Childs' final conclusion, however, is forced: "It therefore seems most probable that the formation of the titles stemmed from a pietistic circle of Jews whose interest was particularly focused on the nurture of the spiritual life."[32] While it is possible that a consideration of the mood and situation of David when he first gave voice to a song or prayer might constitute an interest in the emotional tone of the psalm, these headings might simply exhibit an interest in the original context of these prayers and the types of conditions that they originally addressed.

The most interesting recent work on headings in the Bible has come from scholars making comparisons with the colophon, a parallel literary formation found in cuneiform documents in Mesopotamia.[33] Hermann Hunger defines the colophon as "a notation of the scribe put at the end of the (cimesform) tablet of literary content. The colophon contains data concerning the tablet and persons who have some connection with the given text."[34] According to Hunger, there is not one colophon that can be demonstrated to contain an author's name.[35]

In his study of the similarities between the corpus of colophons and biblical headings, H. M. I. Gevaryahu locates an essential difference between the Babylonian and Israelite literary texts: the names of the authors of Akkadian literature were never recorded in the texts themselves, unlike biblical literature.[36] Nevertheless, Gevaryahu advances the hypothesis that the "editors" of the head-

ings in the Prophets, Wisdom books, and Psalms made use of catalogues resembling the Akkadian colophons; these presumably
detailed the names, chronology, and authorship of the books of the
Bible.[37]

Gevaryahu claims that the biographical elements of the headings of biblical texts and books derive from scribal practices from
the time of the exile and thereafter. He states:

> The change from anonymity to recording the names took place
> during the era of the Babylonian exile. That was the period when
> the status and prestige of the prophets rose: as many became con-
> vinced that "a prophet was indeed in their midst" [Ezekiel 33:33],
> that really a true word of the Lord had been spoken by Jeremiah
> of Anathoth, as well as by the other prophetic preachers. People
> became interested in prophetic books, and with it came the desire
> to know the names and the times of the prophets. This revival of
> interest may have begun at the end of the seventh or the beginning
> of the sixth century.[38]

According to Gevaryahu, the writings of Jeremiah were the earliest
that carried headings affixed to collections of prophetic utterances;
these included the name of the prophet. One interesting proposal
that Gevaryahu makes on the basis of practice of the Akkadian
colophonists is that the superscriptions and titles in the Bible were
originally at the end of the text, and were only later transferred to
the beginning of the text. He offers a comparison with Greek practices, where a shift from the unwieldy practice of recording information at the end of a scroll was later augmented by the technique
of recording the author's name and subject in the first line. Thus,
the utilization of scrolls may have influenced the shift. Its practical
result could be terribly confusing for subsequent interpreters.
Gevaryahu uses the relocation of colophonic information as an explanation for the melding of the utterances of Isaiah with those of
his school. These works, which might easily have been copied together, would have been easily confused when the colophon ending
the Isaiah material was removed from its position midway through
the scroll and repositioned at the beginning of the entire collection. The subsequent chapters, authored by "Isaiah's school" rather

than by Isaiah himself, came to be accepted as the authentic word of Isaiah the son of Amoz.[39]

To summarize the conclusions of scholars on biblical headings, it would appear that most agree they are the product of interpretive communities. Childs dates them sometime after the Chronicler and before the Qumran Psalm scroll. If Gevaryahu is correct, the origin of the biblical headings lies in copying practices that were learned during the Babylonian exile. Scholars are divided as to whether the expression *le-David* 'to/for/of David' originally was meant as a form of attribution. What seems clear is that the terse expressions (such as *le-David*) were soon augmented by headings that were supplied by early interpreters of the texts; it is likely that these were scribes. Expanded headings are attested in the Septuagint, where the tendency seems to have taken on momentum. These headings should also be seen as a species of a powerful impulse in the transmission of scripture: the need to attribute unnamed texts to known biblical figures. As I will show, the strength of this impulse can be seen in the way it continued to be productive in Jewish homiletical interpretation found in rabbinic documents. Attribution of unnamed texts is not a fossilized approach, but a generative one.

Despite their interest in the identity of the minor composers of the Psalms (at the expense of David), the rabbis maintained the general idea of the attribution of the Psalms as a whole to David. Alan Cooper comments that the motive was exegetical: "For the rabbis, the Davidic attribution of the Psalms serves as a productive interpretive strategy. It provides a firm anchor for the use of the psalms as either retrospective or prophetic accounts of the history of Israel."[40] It might be more accurate to say that the rabbis, having inherited the idea of Davidic attribution, sometimes chose to employ it for interpretive ends.

However, insisting on the Davidic authorship of the corpus of psalms was not the response of all or even most Jewish interpreters. As I have suggested, the *baraita* in Baba Bathra's approach to biblical attribution (that David wrote down the Psalms on behalf of ten elders) may represent an opposing tendency — to interpret the Davidic attribution of all the psalms as a matter of textualization rather than composition. Indeed, the rabbinic tradition did not object to the idea that individuals other than David had composed individual psalms, and whimsically continued to play the game of matching unattributed psalms to biblical figures.

Rabbinic and other early biblical interpreters employed homiletic techniques to arrive at acceptable figures that might have composed psalms. As we saw in chapter 1, Baba Bathra 14b identified Ethan the Ezrahite with Abraham. In other cases, the psalm attribution was not even hinted at in the psalm heading, but had to be deduced from the content of the psalm. Besides David, the psalm headings indicate an attribution of several different individuals: Moses (Ps. 90), Ethan the Ezrahite (Ps. 89), Solomon (Pss. 72, 127),[41] Haman (Ps. 88), Yeduthun (Pss. 39, 62, 77), Asaph (Pss. 50, 73–83), and the sons of Korah (Pss. 42, 44–49, 84–5, 87–8). Tradition also attributes psalms to individuals not mentioned in the headings. Despite the fact that Psalm 110 bore the heading "A Psalm of David," the mention of Melchizedek in verse 4 was enough to suggest that Melchizedek had composed the work: "Yahweh has sworn and will not repent: 'You are a priest forever in the manner of Melchizedek.'" The name was one and the same with the mysterious King of Salem and Priest of God Most High who blessed Abraham and to whom Abraham offers a tithe in Gen. 14:18–19a. A host of interpretations arose in ancient times to explain the generosity, the righteousness, or the divine nature of this puzzling figure.[42] Apparently, one interpretation was that the mention of Melchizedek in Psalm 110 indicated that the psalm itself had been composed by this heavenly priest.

Equally shocking is the attribution of Psalm 139 to Adam, despite the fact that the title to Psalm 139 reads "of David." The attribution appears in Baba Bathra 14b (where Adam is listed as one of the ten composers of psalms) as well as in the late collection, Midrash Tehillim:

ר׳ יהודה אומר המזמור הזה אדם הראשון אמרו . שנאמר ה׳ תקרתני ותדע שלא היה לי איפשר בלא

אשה לכך נאמר לא טוב היות האדם לבדו . לכך נאמר ה׳ הקרתני . אתה ידעת שבתי וקומי שבתי בג״ע

> R. Judah taught: This is a psalm (Ps. 139) that Adam composed, as is shown by the words "O Lord, Thou hast searched me, and known me" — known that it is impossible for me to be without a

wife. As Scripture says, "It is not good that the man should be alone; I will make him a help meet for him" (Gen. 2:18). Hence it is said "O Lord, Thou hast searched me, and known me," And, "Thou knowest my downsitting," my sitting at ease in the Garden of Eden.

Midrash Tehillim on Psalm 139, trans. Braude

The reason for the ascription to Adam is not at all the verse quoted above — "O Lord, thou hast searched me, and known me" (Ps. 139:1). This bit of exegesis springs from an already-established connection of the psalm to Adam, but probably did not itself elicit the connection. The midrash seeks to explain the first verse of the psalm in relation to its author. In other words, if Adam wrote the psalm, what exact event in his life was he referring to when he spoke these words?

The real source of the attribution to Adam can be seen in a portion of the psalm not quoted in the midrash:

כִּי־אַתָּה קָנִיתָ כִלְיֹתָי תְּסֻכֵּנִי בְּבֶטֶן אִמִּי <sup>13</sup>

אוֹדְךָ עַל כִּי נוֹרָאוֹת נִפְלֵיתִי נִפְלָאִים מַעֲשֶׂיךָ <sup>14</sup>

וְנַפְשִׁי יֹדַעַת מְאֹד׃

לֹא־נִכְחַד עָצְמִי מִמֶּךָּ אֲשֶׁר־עֻשֵּׂיתִי בַסֵּתֶר <sup>15</sup>

רֻקַּמְתִּי בְּתַחְתִּיּוֹת אָרֶץ׃

גָּלְמִי ׀ רָאוּ עֵינֶיךָ וְעַל־סִפְרְךָ כֻּלָּם יִכָּתֵבוּ יָמִים <sup>16</sup>

יֻצָּרוּ וְלֹא [וְלוֹ] אֶחָד בָּהֶם׃

<sup>13</sup>It was You who created my conscience,

You fashioned me in my mother's womb.

<sup>14</sup>I praise You,

for I am awesomely, wondrously made;

Your work is wonderful;

I know it well.

<sup>15</sup>My frame was not concealed from You

when I was shaped in a hidden place,

knit together in the recesses of the earth.

<sup>16</sup>Your eyes saw my unformed limbs;

they were all recorded in Your book;

in due time they were formed,

to the very last one of them.

Psalm 139:13–16, trans. JPS *Tanakh*

To early interpreters, the psalm described the creation of Adam (despite its mention of a "mother's womb"). Therefore, it must have originally been uttered by Adam. Psalm 92 is also ascribed to Adam by R. Levi in Vayikra Rabbah 10:5. Here it is stated that the psalm, composed after Cain had repented during his trial for the murder of Abel and was pardoned, represents Adam's recognition of the power of repentance.

The attribution of the Psalms provides an intriguing example of both the *horror vacui* of the unattributed text, as well as ideas of human agency in biblical composition. In general, unattributed psalms were ascribed to David; however this was not always the case.

אמר ר׳ לוי בשם ר׳ חנינה אחד עשר מזמורים שאמר משה בטכסים של נביאים אמרן . ולמה לא נכתבו
בתורה . לפי שאלו דברי תורה ואלו דברי נבואה .

R. Levi said in the name of R. Ḥanina: The eleven psalms uttered by Moses were uttered in a prophetic manner. And why were they not written in the Torah?[43] Because the latter includes only the words of Torah, and the former are words of prophecy.

Midrash Tehillim 90:4, trans. Braude

In the Masoretic Text, only Psalm 90 has a heading that refers to Moses. The origin of the idea that Moses wrote Psalms 90–100 seems to lie in an extrapolation about the significance of the heading to Psalm 90: תפלה למשה איש האלהים 'Prayer of Moses, a man of God'. Since Psalm 101 resumes the ascription to David,[44] and because the intervening psalms contain no name in their headings, it was deemed reasonable to make the title preceding Psalm 90 apply to the entire group.[45] Not all interpreters followed this procedure; in the Septuagint, only Psalm 91 (LXX 90) is attributed to Moses, while the rest (excluding the unattributed Psalm 100 [=LXX 99]) are "Psalms of David."

Another late midrashic exposition on these eleven psalms considers closely the prophetic role of Moses, bearing out the opinion of R. Ḥanina voiced in the passage cited above that these psalms were uttered prophetically.

אחד עשר מזמורים אמר משה כנגד אחד עשר שבטים ואלו הן

Moses composed eleven Psalms appropriate to eleven tribes, namely
the following.

Midrash Tehillim on Psalm 90:3, trans. Braude

The midrash goes on to specify that Psalm 90:1–3 is appropriate to
the tribe of Reuben, Psalm 91:1 is appropriate to the tribe of Levi,
Psalm 92:1 is appropriate to the tribe of Judah, Psalm 93:1,5 is appropriate to the tribe of Benjamin, Psalm 94:1 is appropriate to the
tribe Gad, and Psalm 95:1 is appropriate to the tribe of Issachar. At
this point, the passage ends the matching of psalms to tribes:

אמר ר יהושע בן לוי כאן שמעתי מכאן ואילך את הושב לעצמך

R. Joshua ben Levi said: Thus far have I heard [of the psalms appropriate to the several tribes]. From here on, reckon them out for
yourself.

Midrash Tehillim on Psalm 90:3, trans. Braude

The fact that there are eleven psalms in this group suggested to exegetes a correspondence with the eleven tribes that Moses blesses
in Deuteronomy 33. These are not given in the order of the blessings in Deut. 33, but rather are connected to the tribes on the basis
of perceived hints and allusions. It is interesting that this particular
midrash is less "user friendly" and more "do it yourself." The passage does not finish the one-to-one correspondence between psalm
and tribe that it begins; rather there is supplied an off-hand directive: "R. Joshua ben Levi said: Thus far have I heard of the psalms
appropriate to the several tribes. From here on, reckon them out
for yourself."

Just as a *horror vacui* inspired the ascription of Psalms 91–100
to Moses in the rabbinic tradition, it also resulted in the attribution
of the rest of the psalms with no name in their heading to David.
The Septuagint ascribes Psalms 92–100 to David; it does the same
for other unnamed songs in the Masoretic Text. It is possible that
this is the real import of the blanket connection of the Psalms to

David during the Second Temple period. The problem, as many early interpreters must have seen it, was to make sure that the anonymity of these texts was remedied, and thus to show that David was the prophetic composer of psalms in general. It was clearly disturbing for early biblical interpreters to consider the possibility that their sacred psalms might be undervalued because they had no attribution.

## Biblical Attribution: the Esoteric Position

At a certain point in the history of biblical attribution, Jewish interpreters began to reject even the information contained within the Bible that had always seemed to communicate explicitly that Solomon had composed the Song of Songs. Similarly, we saw in Baba Bathra that Solomon's role in composition was downplayed in favor of the men of Hezekiah, the individuals who were instrumental in the transmission of Solomon's books. These biblical interpreters seemed to ignore the written clues in the Bible as to the names with which these texts had been traditionally linked, either in the service of an ideology which held that God had authored the Bible, and in any event to discover the individuals who had copied out each work. Other interpreters, mostly of an apocalyptic or proto-esoteric bent, had a different view of biblical composition. On the one hand, the prophets were held by these interpreters to be more than copyists of existing texts or witnesses of historical events; they were also thought to have revealed new doctrines and additional texts. For these interpreters, the fact that a work was composed by Solomon did not vitiate its divine origin. On the other hand, a little mystery in the attribution process was tolerable; not only was there no *horror vacui* for esoteric interpreters towards texts that were patently authoritative, but a different attitude towards the relationship between scriptural authoritativeness and attribution obtained.

One such example of the heterodox position on authorship is the Martyrdom and Ascension of Isaiah, tentatively dated in the first century C.E. (the Martyrdom) and the third century C.E. (the Vision).[46] This text, likely a Christian reworking of older Jewish material relating the death of the prophet Isaiah at the hands of King

Manasseh by being cut in two with a wood saw, includes a vision of the life and death of the Beloved (Christ).[47] We can see from this text that in the late Second Temple period, the attribution of authorship of all the Psalms to David was no longer *de rigueur*:

> And the rest of the words of the vision are written in the vision of Babylon. And the rest of the vision about the Lord, behold it is written in parables in the words of mine that are written in the book which I prophesied openly. And the descent of the Beloved into Sheol, behold it is written in the section where the Lord says, "Behold, my son shall understand." <u>And all these things, behold they are written in the Psalms, in the parables of David the son of Jesse, and in the Proverbs of Solomon his son, and in the words of Korah and of Ethan the Israelite, and in the words of Asaph, and in the rest of the psalms which the angel of the spirit has inspired, (namely in those which have no name written),</u> and in the words of Amos my father and of Hosea the prophet, and of Micah, and of Joel, and of Nahum, and of Jonah, and of Obadiah, and of Habakkuk, and of Haggai, and of Zephaniah, and of Zechariah, and of Malachi, and in the words of the righteous Joseph, and in the words of Daniel.
>
> Martyrdom of Isaiah 4:19–22, trans. Knibb

For the author of Martyrdom of Isaiah, even unnamed biblical texts are inspired by the "angel of the spirit." This text finds no need to legitimize biblical texts by supplying an author figure when the Bible is silent — a position that differs from the other sources on attribution discussed above. There is also a willingness to recognize that the Psalm headings are to be understood literally and not using midrashic principles (i.e. that Ethan is Abraham or that Yeduthun is another name for David); the fact that no name is written on many Psalms is likewise to be interpreted literally, to mean that someone other than these three individuals had composed them.

Not only does this text highlight the role of minor figures involved with the composition of psalms, it also speaks for the first time about unattributed texts as exactly that. There is no need to prove by a dazzling example of midrashic exegesis that these texts were really composed by a well-known individual. Unattributed psalms can be perfectly acceptable as authoritative texts. The Martyrdom and Ascension of Isaiah derives from a time when the corpus of psalms has become so fixed that there was no need to validate each and every unnamed psalm with the name David.

The Martyrdom and Ascension of Isaiah may have a hidden agenda, however. Even if its toleration of anonymous psalms testifies to a stable and authoritative corpus of psalms, at the same time, this toleration is offered as proof that other anonymous and inspired works deserve the same veneration. In the above passage, a wide variety of canonical and non-canonical works is given equal weight. The Psalms, including the anonymous psalms, are held on equal footing with the works of the prophets, with the non-canonical "words of the righteous Joseph," with the book in which Isaiah prophesied openly (i.e. the Book of Isaiah), and more to the point, with the esoteric teachings of Isaiah contained in the Martyrdom and Ascension of Isaiah itself.

The last section of the work is crucial in ascertaining the position of the work as a whole on the question of anonymity and authorship. This section also contains one of the most striking declarations of the ideological principles at work in pseudepigraphic writings:

> And Isaiah told (them) to all those who were standing before him, and they sang praises. And he spoke to Hezekiah the king and said, "These things I have spoken. And the end of this world and all this vision will be brought about in the last generation." And Isaiah made him swear that he would not tell this to the people of Israel, and that he would not allow any man to copy these words. And then they shall read them. But as for you, be in the Holy Spirit that you may receive your robes, and the thrones and crowns of glory, which are placed in the seventh heaven. Because of these visions and prophecies, Sammael Satan sawed Isaiah the son of Amos, the prophet, in half by the hand of Manasseh. And Hezekiah gave all these things to Manasseh in the twenty-sixth year of this reign. But Manasseh did not remember these things, nor place them in his heart, but he became the servant of Satan and was destroyed.
>
> Martyrdom of Isaiah 11:36–43, trans. Knibb

Of interest in this conclusion to the pseudepigraphic text is a self-conscious statement about the text's status: "And Isaiah made him swear that he would not tell this to the people of Israel, and that he would not allow any man to copy these words." Here is the origin of the inspired works absent from the priestly collection of Hebrew scriptures, according to Martyrdom of Isaiah — the prophet himself exacts an oath of silence from his initial audience, one that includes refraining from the "copying out" of a text.[48] The explanation for how a work of Isaiah could appear centuries after the death of the prophet is that the text was a secret from the very beginning. It is no surprise therefore that these hidden oracles of a visionary concern deeds that would be meaningful only in later days. The text goes on: "And then they shall read them."[49] Part of the prophecy of this self-styled Isaiah is that people shall read this text when they can comprehend its message. The words and authority might be those of the Israelite prophet Isaiah, but the message is contemporary. In some sense the recognition and toleration of anonymity is tied to this esoteric agenda.

### Attribution and Authoritativeness

One common motif of Second Temple apocalyptic literature was the attempt to endow texts with an authoritative status by ascribing them to the earliest men that walked the earth. Enoch, a figure who was thought to have ascended to heaven while he was still alive, was credited with a vast knowledge of astrological lore and was figured as the writer of several non-canonical texts from this period.[50] In the text of 1 Enoch, he speaks to his son Methuselah like the narrator of Proverbs 1–9 addressing his son:

> [Enoch says:] And now, my son Methuselah, all these things I recount to you and write down for you. I have revealed to you and given you the book concerning all these things. Preserve, my son, the book from your father's hands in order that you may pass it to the generations of the world.
>
> 1 Enoch 82:1, trans. Isaac

The recognition that Enoch was the first man to have composed a book is made explicitly by the Book of Jubilees, another non-canonical and apocalyptic work from the first century C.E.:

> This one was the first who learned writing and knowledge and wisdom, from (among) the sons of men, from (among) those who were born upon earth. And who wrote in a book the signs of the heaven according to the order of their months, so that the sons of man might know the (appointed) times of the years according to their order, with respect to each of their months. <u>This one was the first (who) wrote a testimony and testified to the children of men throughout the generations of the earth</u>. And their weeks according to jubilees he recounted; and the days of the years he made known. And the months he set in order, and the sabbaths of the years he recounted, just as we made it known to him. And he saw what was and what will be in a vision of his sleep as it will happen among the children of men in their generations until the day of judgment. He saw and knew everything and wrote his testimony and deposited the testimony upon the earth against all the children of men and their generations.
>
> Jubilees 4:17–20, trans. Wintermute[51]

That Enoch was the first author is contradicted by the Christian appendix to the Latin version of the Life of Adam and Eve. Here it is stated: "Then Seth made tablets of stone and clay, and wrote in them the life of his father Adam and his mother Eve, what he had heard from them and his eyes had seen . . ." (Life of Adam and Eve 51:3). These tablets are later said to be discovered by "the wise Solomon," who was schooled by an angel to read the writing of Seth and his antediluvian prophecies of the coming of Christ. Solomon is also instructed to build the Temple in the place where Adam and Eve used to worship the Lord.[52]

Both Jubilees and the Life of Adam and Eve supply a mythical origin of authorship with figures that adhere to the requirements of their ideological aims. For Jubilees, the project of endorsing a solar calendar and showing that biblical history can be measured in periods of jubilees accorded well with the attribution of the origin of writing to Enoch. Enoch, in his role as the font of astrological lore, may have already been revered by the religious communities behind the text of Jubilees, with the calendrical agenda that they espoused. The Christian version of the Life of Adam and Eve, in contrast, attempts to legitimize itself by attributing its authorship to Seth, an eyewitness to the life of his parents. This text is not troubled by its creation of a new "first author" figure; more important was the impulse to legitimize a text with an appropriately legendary composer. Early figures like Noah and the pre-Mosaic Israelite patriarchs were also supposed to have written accounts and testaments. Rabbinic sources speak of a "book of Adam," referred to in Psalm 139:16.

It is with this backdrop that one must consider the statement of Josephus that ". . . it is not open to everybody to write the records . . . but the prophets alone had this privilege, obtaining their knowledge of the most remote and ancient history through the inspiration which they owed to God" (*Against Apion* 1.37). In distinct contrast to the apocalyptic position on attribution, Josephus presents Moses as being the first prophet to be given this privilege. Moses is for Josephus the only accredited individual capable of recording "the traditional history (*paradosis*) from the birth of man (*anthrôpogonia*) down to his own death" (*Against Apion* 1.39–40). Effectively, Josephus has articulated a scheme that makes authoritative biblical status dependent upon attribution. Only individuals that postdate Moses can have written authoritative books; all books written by individuals who precede Moses are *ipso facto* unauthoritative. The modern scholar J. C. H. Lebram similarly concludes that the designation of Moses as the earliest prophetic vessel in the succession was a strategy to de-legitimize apocalyptic works attributed to the earliest men who walked the earth.[53] A comparable conclusion is found in Tertullian's *Apologeticus*:

Auctoritatem litteris praestat antiquitas summa. Primus enim prophetes Moyses, qui mundi conditionem et generis humani pullulationem et mox ultricem iniquitatis illius aevi vim cataclysmi de praeterito exorsus est, per vaticinationem usque ad suam aetatem et deinceps per res suas futurorum imagines edidit, penes quem et temporum ordo digestus ab initio supputationem saeculi prasestitit.

Extreme antiquity gives books authority. For Moses was the first prophet. He began in the past with foundation of the world, the production of mankind, and later on the mighty cataclysm that avenged the iniquity of that age; by prophecy down to his own day and thereafter, in his own story he gave pictures of things yet to be. In this book the sequence of events set in order from the beginning has permitted the computation of the world's age.

Tertullian, *Apologeticus* XIX.1, Codex Fuldensis, trans. Glover[54]

While Tertullian calls Moses the first prophet and states that he recorded the events up to his own time, St. Augustine explicitly argues that authors more ancient than Moses are of questionable authenticity:

Iam vero si longe antiquiora repetam, et ante illud grande diluvium noster erat utique Noe patriarcha, quem prophetam quoque non immerito dixerim; si quidem ipsa arca quam fect it in qua cum suis evasit prophetia nostrorum temporum fuit. Quid Enoch septimus ab Adam, nonne etiam in canonica epistula apostoli Iudae prophetasse praedicatur? Quorum scripta ut apud Iudaeos et apud nos in auctoritate non essent nimia fecit antiquitas, propter quam videbantur habenda esse suspecta ne proferrentur falsa pro veris. Nam et proferuntur quaedam quae ipsorum esse dicantur ab eis qui pro suo sensu passim quod volunt credunt. Sed ea castitas canonis non recepit non quod eorum hominum qui Deo placuerunt reprobetur auctoritas sed quod ista esse non credantur ipsorum.

But to go back to matters of far greater antiquity, our patriarch Noah certainly was living even before the great Flood; and I should be quite justified in calling him a prophet, seeing that the very ark which he built and in which he and his family escaped was a prophecy of our times. Then again, Enoch, the seventh in descent from Adam, is said to have prophesied; and the authority for this is the canonical epistle of the apostle Jude (Jude 14).[55] But the excessive antiquity of the writings of those men has had the effect of preventing their acceptance, either by the Jews or by us, as authoritative; on account of their remoteness in time it seemed

<u>advisable to hold them suspect, for fear of advancing false claims to authenticity</u>. For there are some writings put forward as genuine works of those authors by those who without discrimination believe what they want to believe, as suits their inclination. But the purity of the canon has not admitted these works, not because the authority of these men, who God approved, is rejected, but because these documents are not believed to belong to them.

St. Augustine, *City of God* XVIII.38, trans. Bettenson

It is difficult to know whether the opinion of St. Augustine derives from a Jewish position rather than from his own extrapolation about the nature of the canon. In any event, his words demonstrate an awareness of a Jewish suspicion towards primeval writings attributed to the first generations after Adam.

On the other end of the timeline, Josephus' claim that the time of Artaxerxes was the temporal limit for the composition of the justly accredited books of the Bible effectively excluded works either set in the post-Persian period (such as 1 Maccabees) or written by individuals later than Malachi or Ezra. The Book of Ben Sira was a casualty of this restriction. As Kugel states, "Ben Sira's book was particularly beloved among the founders of rabbinic Judaism, but apparently because his identity was well known and the book was not attributed to some ancient worthy from the biblical past, they felt that it could not be included in the rabbinic canon of Scripture, and the original Hebrew version of it was therefore eventually lost."[56] Both Ben Sira's non-prophetic status and his late date made the book difficult to accept as canonical; added to this was the distinctly foreign practice of writing a Jewish book in one's own name. Ben Sira's "signature" speaks to the short-lived influence of Greek individualism on Jewish composition practices.

The attribution of the book made all the difference. In effect, early Jewish interpreters relied on attribution as a means of dating a book, and more to the point, as a means of determining whether it could be authoritative. A post-Artaxerxes, post-Ezra attribution was excluded from authoritative status just as easily as if the book had been ascribed to a pre-Mosaic composer.

It is difficult to arrive at firm conclusions as to the reason why attribution procedures developed as they did in the early and middle Second Temple period. It is certain that there existed a *horror vacui* with regard to the unattributed text. Unattributed texts were often assigned names or at least linked to individuals like David and Moses by Second Temple exegetes and later by the rabbis. The Qumran "List of David's Compositions" appears to indicate that Davidic attribution was used as a badge of authoritativeness for psalms that were already circulating anonymously or that were not part of the standard Psalter.[57] In the late Second Temple period, attributions were used to exclude as well as include works into a given group's canon. Because a text's attribution was seen as the most telling indication of its authoritativeness and legitimacy, certain works could be ruled out from the canon on the ground that they were not written down by an eligible prophet. In rabbinic documents, biblical attributions (both those explicit in the text and those that could be supplied through interpretation) could still imply that a human individual had composed the work. But eventually, they came to be used to explain how and at whose hands divinely authored scripture had achieved textual form.

CHAPTER 3

# THE JEWISH CRITIQUE OF
# GREEK LETTERS

Josephus composed *Against Apion,* an extensive refutation of the
arguments that had been raised by opponents of the Jews, sometime during the years 94–100 C.E., more than two decades after the
destruction of the Second Temple in Jerusalem. Defending the Jewish approach to the textualization of history is of crucial importance to Josephus in *Against Apion.* The larger purposes of this
work are to discredit the specific charges raised by pagan critics of
the Jews, and to set forth a competing version both of historical
events and Judaism in general that might appeal to readers from a
variety of traditions. But the success of this project hangs on the effectiveness of Josephus in distinguishing oriental record-keeping
from Greek historiography, and in setting forth the thesis that
Greeks and Jews have fundamentally differing national characters
and approaches to writing. In the process of critiquing Greek historiography, Josephus alleges that agonistic individualism among the
Greeks interferes with the accurate transmission of historical
records. It is difficult to imagine that such a critique of the individualistic tendencies of Greek writers could have been raised by the

Greeks themselves, since they lacked the perspective required to assess their own national character and its influence on their modes of thought.[1]

Josephus argues that a writer should have the kind of authority that can only be conveyed by a suppression of all ambition or desire to increase his prestige, as is the case for the writers of the Jewish historical documents. Josephus assumes that a true historical document should be written down by an eyewitness to the events themselves, and not by a later researcher.[2] He employs the insights of Greek attribution analysis to discredit literary documents of the Greek world, contending that many of the most esteemed Greek texts were not composed by the authors to whom they are attributed.[3] Josephus' recognition and critique of the individuality in Greek historical composition were both insightful and influential. His critique, although pejoratively stated, anticipates aspects of Christian authorship in its recognition of the creativity of the individual as well as in the value it places on the authenticity of the text. As I will later argue, his thoughts on these issues would serve as an important ingredient in the Christian definition of authorship.[4]

A brief summary of Josephus' treatment of historiography among the Greeks will reveal how much these questions are related to a development of the notion of authorship in the ancient world. Josephus begins *Against Apion* with the stated purpose of proving that the Jews were indeed as ancient as he had claimed in his *Antiquities*, a huge chronicle of Jewish history from Adam to Josephus' own time. In order to contradict arguments deployed by his rivals as to the relative modernity of the Jewish people, Josephus gives a catalogue of references to Jews in the literature of the Greeks. Not content with this, he wonders that only Greeks are to be trusted concerning antiquity (περὶ τῶν παλαιοτάτων ἔργων) while all other accounts are ignored; this flies in the face of the fact that the Greeks are actually newcomers to the world from "yesterday and the day before" (1.2.7).

As Josephus argues, Greek accounts are flawed because of their non-oriental approach to the relationship between the individual and history, and indeed between the individual and the creation of verbal records. For Josephus, the problem with Greek authors is that they try to outshine their rivals (1.5.25) and to show their skill with words. This manifests itself in the fact that the Greek accounts deviate wildly from the events themselves. What's more, Josephus claims, "they reach an end through their endeavors that is the very opposite of historical inquiry" (ὅλως δὲ τὸ πάντων ἐναντιώτατον ἱστορίᾳ πράττοντες διατελοῦσι 1.5.26). One cause of the ineffectiveness of historiography in reaching the valid goal of *historia* 'historical inquiry' is the Greek culture's reliance on competition as a means of determining historical truth. When historical truth is a commodity whose value is to be determined by a procedure of hawking and salesmanship, its innate worth is damaged. Each writer, vying to be considered the most veracious of all, uses all of the literary skills at his disposal to make unbelievable accounts believable; according to Josephus, it is the divergence of these accounts from those that precede them which creates the illusion of veracity. He sums up this thought, "While then for style and cleverness in using words (λόγων μὲν οὖν ἕνεκα καὶ τῆς ἐν τούτοις δεινότητος) we must yield the palm to the Greek historians, we have no reason to do so for veracity in the history of antiquity . . ." (1.27).

Josephus presents a case in which Greek historiography has no claim to authoritativeness, for the very reason that Greek historians are individualistic, competitive, and rebellious, not to mention that they are more interested in a turn of phrase or a satisfying denouement than in recounting events as they really happened. He presents a divide between Eastern (oriental) and Western (Greek) antiquarians, in which the Egyptians and Babylonians evince greater esteem for their chronicles (*anagraphai*). The Phoenicians are praised as having made the largest use of writing, for the governance of ordinary life, and for the commemoration of public events (1.28). The praise of oriental antiquarianism serves as a prelude for his treatment of Jewish reverence for the documents and traditions of the past, which surpasses even the value placed upon the written word by the Egyptians, Babylonians, and Phoenicians. "Not only did our ancestors in the first instance set over this business men of the highest character, devoted to the service of God, but they took precautions to ensure the priests' lineage should be kept unadulterated and pure" (1.30–31). As we shall see, the purity of the priests' lineage is not merely praised as a sign of the purity of the records whose authenticity they would guarantee. This lineage is itself a way of thinking about textual purity. The concern with the purity of the priestly lineage results from a very real fear that alterations to the text might be accomplished by communities wishing to mold the sacred text to their own beliefs and interests.

If there is any Greek genre of history writing that Josephus participates in, it is that of *arkhaiologia,* the exploration of the history of earliest events that Thucydides pioneered. Part of the assumptions of this approach were that this exploration of the remote past was inherently less accurate than events witnessed by the historiographer. With this unspoken caveat, Josephus attempts to briefly describe the earliest attempts at history and philosophy, in the service of his goal to vindicate the Jews and Jewish antiquity.

οἱ μέντοι τὰς ἱστορίας ἐπιχειρήσαντες συγγράφειν παρ' αὐτοῖς, λέγω δὲ τοὺς περὶ Κάδμον τε τὸν Μιλήσιον καὶ τὸν Ἀργεῖον Ἀκουσίλαον καὶ μετὰ τοῦτον εἴ τινες ἄλλοι λέγονται γενέσθαι, βραχὺ τῆς Περσῶν ἐπὶ τὴν Ἑλλάδα στρατείας τῷ χρόνῳ προύλαβον. ἀλλὰ μὴν καὶ τοὺς περὶ τῶν οὐρανίων τε καὶ θείων πρώτους παρ' Ἕλλησι φιλοσοφήσαντας, οἷον Φερεκύδην τε τὸν Σύριον καὶ Πυθαγόραν καὶ Θάλητα, πάντες συμφώνως ὁμολογοῦσιν Αἰγυπτίων καὶ Χαλδαίων γενομένους μαθητὰς ὀλίγα συγγράψαι, καὶ ταῦτα τοῖς Ἕλλησιν εἶναι δοκεῖ πάντων ἀρχαιότατα καὶ <u>μόλις αὐτὰ πιστεύουσιν ὑπ'</u> <u>ἐκείνων γεγράφθαι.</u>

Again, the Greeks who [first] essayed to write history, such as Cadmus of Miletus and Acusilaus of Argos and any later writers who are mentioned, lived but a short time before the Persian invasion of Greece. Once more, the first Greek philosophers to treat of celestial and divine subjects, such as Pherecydes of Syros, Pythagoras, and Thales, were, as the world unanimously admits, in their scanty productions the disciples of the Egyptians and Chaldeans. These are the writings which the Greeks regard as the oldest of all, and <u>they scarcely believe them to have been written</u> <u>by those people.</u>

Josephus, *Against Apion* 1.13–14[5]

In the spirit of the discussion over the meaning of Hebrew *katav* in Baba Bathra, it might be asked whether Josephus meant for *gegraphthai* to signify 'be composed' or 'be copied out' here. As trapped as we are in the modern metaphor of writing as composition, it is difficult to ascertain whether Josephus is reporting a challenge to the attribution of the oldest writings of the Greeks by Pherecydes, Pythagoras, or Thales, or whether he is making a comment as to the transmission of these texts, which might originally have been transmitted without the use of writing. Having some bearing on this question is the present day knowledge of the false ascription of much of the Pythagorean corpus.[6] From the one perspective, Pythagoras is less than Moses because he didn't copy out his own writings, but left that activity to his followers. From the other perspective, Pythagoras is a shell of a name that became attached to the works of others with a similar philosophy. The confusion is alleviated when we consider the issue from another perspective: for Josephus, these are two sides of the same coin. An untrustworthy transmission process is equal to doubt about the authenticity of the work. It is *because* Pythagoras, unlike Moses, did not copy out the words he spoke, that his name could be applied to the utterances of others.

The next sentence further elucidates Josephus' approach to this question:

Πῶς οὖν οὐκ ἔστιν ἄλογον τετυφῶσθαι τοὺς Ἕλληνας ὡς μόνους ἐπισταμένους τἀρχαῖα καὶ τὴν ἀλήθειαν περὶ αὐτῶν ἀκριβῶς παραδιδόντας;

Surely, then, is it not absurd that the Greeks should be so conceited as to think themselves the only ones understanding ancient things and the only accurate transmitters of its history?

Josephus, *Against Apion* 1.15

I propose that Josephus' notion of accurate transmission is in essence a preview of the approach to textualization of the biblical books found in Baba Bathra 14b–15a. Josephus is more attuned to the faithful transmission of information than he is to the origins of a text in an individual, and is only tangentially concerned with challenging the ascription of any given work to an individual in the entire course of *Against Apion*. His polemic against authorship is rarely based on the truth or falsehood of any particular connection of a name to a text,[7] but is more directed against the ill effects of an attribution process that does not include adequate transmission safeguards. Nevertheless, nestled within the notion of "inaccurate transmission of history" is the idea that inaccuracy consists of or leads to ungenuine additions to a text.

For Josephus, there are two basic reasons for the inconsistency of Greek history. The first is as follows:

Αἰτίαι δὲ τῆς τοιαύτης διαφωνίας πολλαὶ μὲν ἴσως ἂν καὶ ἕτεραι τοῖς βουλομένοις ζητεῖν ἂν φανεῖεν, ἐγὼ δὲ δυσὶ ταῖς λεχθησομέναις τὴν μεγίστην ἰσχὺν ἀνατίθημι. καὶ προτέραν ἐρῶ τὴν κυριωτέραν εἶναί μοι δοκοῦσαν· τὸ γὰρ ἐξ ἀρχῆς μὴ σπουδασθῆναι παρὰ τοῖς Ἕλλησι δημοσίας γίνεσθαι περὶ τῶν ἑκάστοτε πραττομένων ἀναγραφὰς τοῦτο μάλιστα δὴ καὶ τὴν πλάνην καὶ τὴν ἐξουσίαν τοῦ ψεύδεσθαι τοῖς μετὰ ταῦτα βουληθεῖσι περὶ τῶν παλαιῶν τι γράφειν παρέσχεν.

For such inconsistencies many other causes might possibly be found if one cared to look for them; for my part, I attach the greatest weight to the two which I proceed to mention. I will begin with that which I regard as the more fundamental. The main responsibility for the errors of later historians who aspired to write on antiquity and for the license granted to their mendacity rests with the original neglect of the Greeks to keep official records of current events.

Josephus, Against Apion 1.19–21

The Greeks were hampered by the lack of official records of current events, which Josephus considers to make up the lion's share of the biblical histories. He does not consider the books of the Bible to be the creative or even the scholarly work of individuals, but rather to consist of the eyewitness accounts of Israelite history recorded just as they occurred (τὰ δὲ καθ' αὑτοὺς ὡς ἐγένετο σαφῶς συγγραφόντων — 1.37) by the most trustworthy of the prophets (this additional safeguard of reliability is one which sets Israelite record-keeping apart from that of other nations). Josephus brings up the difference between Israelite and Greek record-keeping traditions as a way of explaining why the Greek histories are unreliable. But the dearth of Greek records on current events also is used to explain his second reason for the inferiority of Greek history writing — the tendency of history writers to be creative *literati* rather than impartial narrators. In short, there are two reasons for Greek inaccuracy: a lack of current recordkeeping and the phenomenon this leads to — rhetorical license.

The following passage delineates the offenses resulting from such rhetorical license:

"Ἄτε δὴ τοίνυν οὐδεμιᾶς προκαταβεβλημένης ἀναγραφῆς, ἣ καὶ τοὺς μαθεῖν βουλομένους διδάξειν ἔμελλεν καὶ τοὺς ψευδομένους ἐλέγξειν, ἡ πολλὴ πρὸς ἀλλήλους ἐγένετο διαφωνία τοῖς συγγραφεῦσι. δευτέραν δὲ πρὸς ταύτῃ θετέον ἐκείνην αἰτίαν· οἱ γὰρ ἐπὶ τὸ γράφειν ὁρμήσαντες οὐ περὶ τὴν ἀλήθειαν ἐσπούδασαν, καίτοι τοῦτο πρόχειρόν ἐστιν ἀεὶ τὸ ἐπάγγελμα, λόγων δὲ δύναμιν ἐπεδείκνυντο, καὶ καθ' ὅντινα τρόπον ἐν τούτῳ παρευδοκιμήσειν τοὺς ἄλλους ὑπελάμβανον, καὶ ὰ ΙΟῦΙΟΝ ἡρμόζοντο τινὲς μὲν ἐπὶ τὸ μυθολογεῖν τραπόμενοι, τινὲς δὲ πρὸς χάριν ἢ τὰς πόλεις ἢ τοὺς βασιλέας ἐπαινοῦντες· ἄλλοι δὲ ἐπὶ τὸ κατηγορεῖν τῶν πράξεων ἢ τῶν γεγραφότων ἐχώρησαν ἐνευδοκιμήσειν τούτῳ νομίζοντες. ὅλως δὲ τὸ πάντων ἐναντιώτατον ἱστορίᾳ πράττοντες διατελοῦσι· <u>τῆς μὲν γὰρ ἀληθοῦς ἐστι τεκμήριον ἱστορίας, εἰ περὶ τῶν αὐτῶν ἄπαντες ταὐτὰ καὶ λέγοιεν καὶ γράφοιεν.</u> οἱ δ' ε ταῦτα γράψειαν ἑτέρως, οὕτως ἐνόμιζον αὐτοὶ φανεῖσθαι πάντων ἀληθέστατοι. λόγων μὲν οὖν ἕνεκα καὶ τῆς ἐν τούτοις δεινότητος δεῖ παραχωρεῖν ἡμᾶς τοῖς συγγραφεῦσι τοῖς Ἑλληνικοῖς, οὐ μὴν καὶ τῆς περὶ τῶν ἀρχαίων ἀληθοῦς ἱστορίας καὶ μάλιστά γε τῆς περὶ τῶν ἑκάστοις ἐπιχωρίων.

It is, then, this lack of any basis of documentary evidence, which would have served at once to instruct the eager learner and to confute the liar, that accounts in the main for the inconsistencies between different historians. But a second reason must be added. Those who rushed into writing were concerned not so much to discover the truth, notwithstanding the profession which always comes readily to their pen, as to display their literary ability; and their choice of a subject was determined by the prospect which it offered them of outshining their rivals. Some turned to mythology, others sought popularity by encomiums upon cities or monarchs; others, again, set out to criticize the facts or the historians as the road to a reputation. In short, their invariable method is the very reverse of historical. <u>For the proof of historical veracity is universal agreement in the description, oral or written, of the same events</u>. On the contrary, each of these writers, in giving his divergent account of the same incidents, hoped thereby to be thought the most veracious of all. While, then, for eloquence and literary ability we must yield the palm to the Greek historians, we have no reason to do so for veracity in the history of antiquity, least of all where the particular history of each separate foreign nation is concerned.

Josephus, Against Apion 1.23–27

The attack by Josephus on the individualistic agenda of the Greek historians should not be collapsed into a supposed extension of the Platonic critique of sophistry in the writing of historical accounts. Josephus is not merely critiquing the subordination of truth to rhetorical display, or the sophist's ability to be an advocate for the truth of positions that he does not believe to be true or that are not in fact true. Far more troubling to Josephus is the Greek individualistic style and its total inappropriateness to the project of rendering truth statements about events. Josephus is not lambasting rhetorical eloquence (which on other occasions he praises) as much as he is rejecting the Greek temperament, its need to view history writing as an adversarial process in which the latest version is made to triumph over its predecessors in order to accrue praise for its author. Of course this resembles Plato's dismissal of sophistry in many regards; however, Josephus has refashioned Plato's critique into a battle between a Greek and Jewish worldview, rather than between that of competing philosophies within a single culture.

Josephus' statement, "For the proof of historical veracity is universal agreement in the description, oral or written, of the same events," may be said to encapsulate his philosophical premise or worldview. It applies not just to the evaluation of historiography (for as we will see, the genre of historiography as consisting of classical or classicizing texts with self-conscious historical narrators is not the genre that Josephus participates in) but to the validity of any text. Josephus' worldview about the nature of veracity, or at least about the *proof* of historical veracity (cf. τῆς μὲν γὰρ ἀληθοῦς ἐστι τεκμήριον ἱστορίας), is a stunning reversal of the Greek individualistic and agonistic conception of truth arising through a competition of sources and explanations, with the "best truth" winning out by force of its argumentation. Rather, it is the absence of such competition that is indicative of a veracious account.

The writer's most powerful critique of Greek historiography takes the form of an indictment of the fictionalizing of the past by Greeks who have not the slightest regard for their nations' archives. In contrast to the Israelites, who neither added, removed, nor altered [a syllable] (1.42) of their own chronicles, the Greeks have a propensity to add the equivalent of a shipwreck and a love-interest to every tale from the past.

ἢ τίς ἂν ὑπομείνειεν Ἑλλήνων ὑπὲρ αὐτοῦ; ἀλλ' οὐδ' ὑπὲρ τοῦ καὶ πάντα τὰ παρ' αὐτοῖς ἀφανισθῆναι συγγράμματα τὴν τυχοῦσαν ὑποστήσεται βλάβην· λόγους γὰρ αὐτὰ νομίζουσιν εἶναι κατὰ τὴν τῶν γραψάντων βούλησιν ἐσχεδιασμένους. καὶ τοῦτο δικαίως καὶ περὶ τῶν παλαιοτέρων φρονοῦσιν, ἐπειδὴ καὶ τῶν νῦν ἐνίους ὁρῶσι τολμῶντας περὶ τούτων συγγράφειν, οἷς μήτ' αὐτοὶ παρεγένοντο μήτε πυθέσθαι παρὰ τῶν εἰδότων ἐφιλοτιμήθησαν.

What Greek would endure as much for the same cause? Even to save the entire collection of his nation's writings from destruction he would not face the smallest personal injury. For to the Greeks they are mere stories improvised according to the fancy of their authors; and in this estimate even of the older historians they are quite justified, when they see some of their own contemporaries venturing to describe events in which they bore no part, without taking the trouble to seek information from those who know the facts.

Josephus, *Against Apion* 1.44–45

There are two flaws inherent to the Greek approach to the past. Greek records are seen as collections of mere stories; and these fictional events are introduced into the accounts by individuals who "according to their own desire or fancy" insert fallacious material. The notion of "improvising" (*skhediazô*) plays an interesting role in this condemnation. The word seems to designate the act of inventing stories, especially so-termed by Hellenistic historiographers (e.g. Polybius 12.4.4, Dionysius of Halicarnasus 1.7, Diodorus Siculus 1.23). It also refers to the process of improvisation or "speaking off the cuff," specifically as practiced in rhetoric (e.g. Philodemus, *Volumina Rhetorica* 1.100 S). In short, fiction is born through the excessive influence of imagination or of the "stream of consciousness" of the individual writer.

Josephus' analysis of the flaws of authorship rests not on a distinction between individual and tradition, but rather on the opposition between truth and fiction. In contrast to this fictionalizing author, Josephus speaks of the prophets who recorded the Israelite past as being extremely limited in their contribution to the narration of events. He views the prophetic individual as a guarantor of the veracity of a tradition, a faithful scribe and accurate witness to the events he describes, not separated from the events by an oral tradition or even a lapse of time (with the exception of the unique Moses, who wrote of events long before he lived). When a tradition is vouchsafed by a prophetic scribe, the likelihood of textual tampering through the intervention of a succession of bards or duplicitous historiographers is removed. These scribes are in a quite different category from the historiographers Josephus lambastes, even if their names are similarly attached to the events they witnessed. In his pejorative conceptualization of authorship, any writer who is also the originator of the information he conveys is involved in fabrication.

This view of the prophet as the authenticator of biblical history was anticipated in some of the latest historical material found in the Bible itself — 1 and 2 Chronicles. The Chronicler refers to twelve otherwise unknown sources that are attributed to ten prophets, including Samuel, Nathan, Gad, Ahijah, Jeddo, Shemaiah, Iddo, Jehu, Isaiah, and Hozai. According to Sara Japhet, in referring to all these prophetical works, what the Chronicler actually had in mind was the same comprehensive work with a general title, "the history of Israel." The respective parts of this work are thus ascribed to contemporary prophets, a most concrete expression of the view that it was the prophets of Israel who wrote the history of their time. The writing of history is thus seen as contemporary with the events, inspired, and of absolute authority.[8]

Japhet attributes the insight to Edward Curtis and Alonzo Madsen, who deftly explain the rationale for this conclusion:

> The prophetic writings [cited in 1 and 2 Chronicles] . . . are not in all probability distinct works, but are illustrations of the usual Jewish manner of citing sections of comprehensive works. As in the [New Testament] we read, "Have ye not read in the Book of Moses in the place concerning the Bush" (Mark 12:26), or more aptly, "Knew ye not what the scripture saith in Elijah" (Romans 11:2). The "histories" of Nathan, Gad, and the others are then the sections of which Nathan, Gad, etc., were the catchwords in the Book of Kings . . . This is proved first because the history of the prophet Jehu and the vision of Isaiah are expressly mentioned as in this Book of Kings, and secondly because the Chronicler never cites the authority of the Book of Kings and the history of a prophet for any one reign except where they are coupled together.[9]

As Paul's citation (in Romans 11:2) of "Elijah" makes plain, the names of individual prophets could stand for the parts of scripture that described their exploits. The example, as well as the other evidence adduced by Curtis and Madsen, lends credence to the claim that the Chronicler referred to Samuel and Kings as a compilation of works that had been recorded by contemporaneous prophets. Josephus' idea of the prophetic witnessing of biblical events is thus firmly part of Jewish tradition, rather than his own invention. Ironically, Chronicles itself might be used to contradict Josephus' larger claim, since it represents a history composed from past (albeit authoritative) sources rather than by witnesses of the events themselves. Josephus would doubtless respond that Chronicles in no

way contradicts these sources, and rather adds to them authoritative material that had been omitted (hence the Greek name of the
book, *paralipomena* 'things left out'). Moreover, in Josephus' view,
the entire work was guaranteed and legitimated by the prophet
who wrote it down (presumably Ezra, identified by Jewish tradition
as the prophet Malachi).

Having described a notion of creative authorship among the
Greeks that the Jews lack, Josephus proceeds to argue that reverence for truth among Jews outweighs their lack of interest in the
creative arts:

"Οθεν δὴ καὶ τὸ προφερόμενον ἡμῖν ὑπό τινων ἔγκλημα, τὸ δὴ μὴ
καινῶν εὑρετὰς ἔργων ἢ λόγων ἄνδρας παρασχεῖν, ἐντεῦθεν
συμβέβηκεν· οἱ μὲν γὰρ ἄλλοι τὸ μηδενὶ τῶν πατρίων ἐμμένειν
καλὸν εἶναι νομίζουσι καὶ τοῖς τολμῶσι ταῦτα παραβαίνειν μάλιστα
σοφίας δεινότητα μαρτυροῦσιν. ἡμεῖς δὲ τοὐναντίον μίαν εἶναι καὶ
φρόνησιν καὶ ἀρετὴν ὑπειλήφαμεν τὸ μηδὲν ὅλως ὑπεναντίον μήτε
πρᾶξαι μήτε διανοηθῆναι τοῖς ἐξ ἀρχῆς νομοθετηθεῖσιν. ὅπερ
εἰκότως ἂν εἴη τεκμήριον τοῦ κάλλιστα τὸν νόμον τεθῆναι· τὰ γὰρ μὴ
τοῦτον ἔχοντα τὸν τρόπον αἱ πεῖραι δεόμενα διορθώσεως ἐλέγχουσιν.

This, in fact, is the origin of the reproach brought against us by
some critics of <u>our having produced no inventors in crafts or lit-
erature</u>. In the eyes of the world at large there is something fine in
breaking away from all inherited customs; those who have the
temerity to defy them are credited with the possession of consummate ability. To us, on the other hand, the only wisdom, the only
virtue, consists in refraining absolutely from every action, from
every thought that is contrary to the laws originally laid down.
This may fairly be claimed as a proof of their excellent draftsmanship; codes which are not of this character are proved by experience to need amendment.

Josephus, *Against Apion* 2.182–183

"Inventors in crafts or literature" (καινῶν εὑρετὰς ἔργων ἢ λόγων
ἄνδρας) is as close as Josephus gets to defining authorship.[10] Yet despite this brief acknowledgment that authors — creators of works
with redeeming value — are on a par with the inventors of valuable

cultural items and practices in the Greek tradition, Josephus turns the acknowledgment on its head, making innovation into a sign of a lack of wisdom, virtue, and reverence for tradition.

Josephus makes plain his opinion that the fault of many histories is that they do in fact have "authors." This makes authorship into a pejorative: it consists of the individualistic rhetorical display at the service of winning personal acclaim. Authorship results in the abuse of truth, inasmuch as an individual's reputation and value is placed on a higher level than historical accuracy. In this too Josephus differs from Plato's critique of sophistry. Plato found fault with the teaching of skills in which the worse cause could win out over a better cause; these skills, especially since they could be taught to youngsters and in effect bought with money, were deemed to be immoral. Josephus objects to the motivation that generates originality in historiography — the desire to win personal acclaim; he does not object to rhetorical facility in and of itself, or to the fact that it may be bought with money or taught to the youth. He finds historiography's flaws to lie in the Greek hunger for *kleos* 'glory' through the composition of persuasive chronicles. Such is his idea of an author: a literary sophist out for his own glory at the expense of the veracity of the historical account he is composing.

In the view of Josephus, why then do the Israelites not have "inventors in crafts or literature"? And is not Josephus himself out for his own glory? Doesn't he employ rhetorical means to make his histories convincing, and doesn't he contradict the false accounts of others as a means of validating his own? Josephus appeals to the ideology of the transmission of biblical books as a means of explaining why authorship is not a part of the Israelite way of writing history. This ideology is the precursor of the doctrine of biblical textualization contained in Baba Bathra 14b–15a. The resemblance of Josephus' views to the approach of the Chronicler as well as to later rabbinic teaching indicates that this doctrine was entrenched in Jewish interpretive traditions, rather than something created by Josephus as a result of his training in Greek and Roman letters. And even though he accepts full credit for his own writing by speaking in his own name rather than anonymously, Josephus presents the idea of prophetic transmission, not Greek historiography, as a model for the composition of history.

Instead of inventors, the Jews have a succession of prophets, who recorded the history of Israel until the prophets were no longer able to trace their "lineage" back to Moses:

εἰκότως οὖν, μᾶλλον δὲ ἀναγκαίως, ἅτε μήτε τὸ ὑπογράφειν αὐτεξουσίου πᾶσιν ὄντος μήτε τινός ἐν τοῖς γραφομένοις ἐνούσης διαφωνίας, ἀλλὰ μόνον τῶν προφητῶν τὰ μὲν ἀνωτάτω καὶ παλαιότατα κατὰ τὴν ἐπίπνοιαν τὴν ἀπὸ τοῦ θεοῦ μαθόντων, τὰ δὲ καθ' αὑτοὺς ὡς ἐγένετο σαφῶς συγγραφόντων, οὐ μυριάδες βιβλίων εἰσὶ παρ' ἡμῖν ἀσυμφώνων καὶ μαχομένων, δύο δὲ μόνα πρὸς τοῖς εἴκοσι βιβλία τοῦ παντὸς ἔχοντα χρόνου τὴν ἀναγραφήν, τὰ δικαίως πεπιστευμένα. καὶ τούτων πέντε μέν ἐστι Μωυσέως, ἃ τούς τε νόμους περιέχει καὶ τὴν ἀπ' ἀνθρωπογονίας παράδοσιν μέχρι τῆς αὐτοῦ τελευτῆς· οὗτος ὁ χρόνος ἀπολείπει τρισχιλίων ὀλίγῳ ἐτῶν. ἀπὸ δὲ τῆς Μωυσέως τελευτῆς μέχρι τῆς Ἀρταξέρξου τοῦ μετὰ Ξέρξην Περσῶν βασιλέως <u>οἱ μετὰ Μωυσῆν προφῆται τὰ κατ' αὐτοὺς πραχθέντα συνέγραψαν</u> ἐν τρισὶ καὶ δέκα βιβλίοις· α δὲ λοιπαὶ τέσσαρες ὕμνους εἰς τὸν θεὸν καὶ τοῖς ἀνθρώποις ὑποθήκας τοῦ βίου περιέχουσιν. ἀπὸ δὲ Ἀρταξέρξου μέχρι τοῦ καθ' ἡμᾶς χρόνου γέγραπται μὲν ἕκαστα, πίστεως δ' οὐχ ὁμοίας ἠξίωται τοῖς πρὸ αὐτῶν <u>διὰ τὸ μὴ γενέσθαι τὴν τῶν προφητῶν ἀκριβῆ διαδοχήν</u>.

It therefore naturally, or rather necessarily, follows (seeing that with us it is not open to everybody to write the records, and that there is no discrepancy in what is written; seeing that, on the contrary, the prophets alone had this privilege, obtaining their knowledge of the most remote and ancient history through the inspiration which came to them from God, and committing to writing a clear account of the events of their own time just as they occurred), it follows, I say, that we do not possess myriads of inconsistent books, conflicting with one another; but our books, those which are justly believed, are only 22, and contain the record of all time. Of these, five are the books of Moses, comprising the laws and the traditional history (*paradosis*) from the birth of man down to Moses' death. This period falls only a little short of 3,000 years. From the death of Moses down to Artaxerxes who followed Xerxes as king of Persia, <u>the prophets after Moses wrote (*sunegrapsan*) the events of their own times</u> in thirteen books. The

remaining four books contain hymns to God and precepts for the
conduct of human life.

From Artaxerxes down to our own time, the complete history
has been written, but has not been deemed worthy of like trust
with the earlier records, <u>because of the absence of an exact ge-
nealogy/succession of the prophets</u>.

Josephus, Against Apion 1.36–42

I will return to this important passage in chapter 4. For now, it suf-
fices to point out that Josephus on the one hand places Israelite history as recorded by the prophets in a totally different category from
Greek historiography, and on the other, grants to Moses alone the
authority to record the *arkhaiologia* of Israel. The prophets who followed Moses are described as being contemporaneous with the
events they recorded, in contradistinction to Moses, whose books
included the laws and events "from the birth of man" which he had
not himself witnessed.

Without openly acknowledging his literary indebtedness to the
writing of Thucydides, Josephus echoes the famous justification by
Thucydides of his choice of a contemporary rather than temporally
distant topic in the Peloponnesian War.[11] Thucydides states that he
wrote ἀρξάμενος εὐθὺς καθισταμένου καὶ ἐλπίσας μέγαν τε ἔσεσθαι καὶ
ἀξιολογώτατον τῶν προγεγενημένων 'beginning the account at the
very outbreak of the war, in the belief that it was going to be a great
war and more worth writing about than any of those which had
taken place in the past' (1.1.1). Thucydides also says that it is impossible to know the events that happened prior to his own time:
"For the events prior to these and those still more ancient were impossible to discover clearly on account of the magnitude of time intervening" (1.1.3). Such praise of the value of personal witness as
opposed to speculative treatment of sources undertaken in other
historiographic approaches underlies Josephus' statements. Fashioning himself as a historian of a similar caliber to Thucydides, and
more to the point, of a piece with the prophets who recorded the
biblical events, Josephus states in the *Antiquities* that they committed to writing "a clear account of the events of their own time (τὰ
κατ᾽ αὐτοὺς πραχθέντα) just as they occurred." He describes his role
in the documenting of the Jewish War similarly: "I, on the contrary,

have written a veracious account, at once comprehensive and detailed, of the war, having been present in person at all the events" (*Jewish War* 1.47). Yet while Josephus finds a model in Thucydides, this is only as a Greek analog to chronographic principles that characterize his Jewish predecessors.

Discussions of the nature of poetic creation amid references to the plastic arts allow us to explore Josephus' views of the artistry of writing. His approach to the matter is wholly Platonic. He picks up the discussion directly from the *Republic*, as he later explicitly acknowledges (2.256).

Τί τοίνυν τὸ αἴτιον τῆς τοσαύτης ἀνωμαλίας καὶ περὶ τὸ θεῖον πλημμελείας; ἐγὼ μὲν ὑπολαμβάνω τὸ μήτε τὴν ἀληθῆ τοῦ θεοῦ φύσιν ἐξ ἀρχῆς συνιδεῖν αὐτῶν τοὺς νομοθέτας μήθ' ὅσον καὶ λαβεῖν ἠδυνήθησαν ἀκριβῆ γνῶσιν διορίσαντας πρὸς τοῦτο ποιήσασθαι τὴν ἄλλην τάξιν τοῦ πολιτεύματος, ἀλλ' ὥσπερ ἄλλο τι τῶν φαυλοτάτων ἐφῆκαν τοῖς μὲν ποιηταῖς οὕστινας ἂν βούλωνται θεοὺς εἰσάγειν πάντα πάσχοντας, τοῖς δὲ ῥήτορσι πολιτογραφεῖν κατὰ ψήφισμα τῶν ξένων θεῶν τὸν ἐπιτήδειον· πολλῆς δὲ καὶ ζωγράφοι καὶ πλάσται τῆς ἐς τοῦτο παρὰ τῶν Ἑλλήνων ἀπέλαυσαν ἐξουσίας, αὐτὸς ἕκαστός τινα μορφὴν ἐπινοῶν, ὁ μὲν ἐκ πηλοῦ πλάττων, ὁ δὲ γράφων, οἱ δὲ μάλιστα δὴ θαυμαζόμενοι τῶν δημιουργῶν τὸν ἐλέφαντα καὶ τὸν χρυσὸν ἔχουσι τῆς ἀεὶ καινουργίας τὴν ὑπόθεσιν.

Now, what is the cause of such irregular and erroneous conceptions of the deity? For my part, I trace it to the ignorance of the true nature of God with which their legislators entered on their task, and to their failure to formulate even such correct knowledge of it as they were able to attain and to make the rest of their constitution conform to it. Instead, as if this were the most trifling of details, they allowed the poets to introduce what gods they chose, subject to all the passions, and the orators to pass decrees for entering the name of any suitable foreign god on the burgess-roll. Painters also and sculptors were given great license in this matter by the Greeks, each designing from his own imagination (*epinoeô*) a figure (*morphê*), one molding (*plattô*) it of clay, another using paints. The artists (*dêmiourgoi*) who are the most admired of all use ivory and gold as the material for the novelties (*kainourgiai*) which they are constantly producing.

Josephus, *Against Apion* 2.251–253

Josephus blames poets and orators for the unscrupulous introduction of foreign gods into Greek life, as well as indiscretions of the gods themselves. More interesting for our argument, poets and orators are equated with painters and sculptors and are declared to be subject to the same sorts of abuses of the gods. There is even an element of blasphemy here: the sculptors and painters, "each one designing some *morphê* 'figure'," would seem to be a bad parody of God, who created man, not from his imagination but in his own image. The claim also resembles what Josephus says moments before about the personification and deification of abstract emotions: "They [the Greek poets] have even deified Terror and Fear, nay Frenzy and Deceit (which of the worst passions have they not sculpted [*anaplattô*] into the nature and shape [*morphê*] of a god? [εἰς θεοῦ φύσιν καὶ μορφὴν ἀνέπλασαν])" (2.248). The element of blasphemy is heightened by the juxtaposition of human and divine inspiration or intentionality, signified by the word *epinoia* 'intention': In the above passage, painters and sculptors "each design (*epinoeô*, the verb from which *epinoia* is derived) a figure of his own imagination (αὐτὸς ἕκαστός τινα μορφὴν ἐπινοῶν)." The notion of 'divine inspiration' or 'awareness' (κατὰ τὴν ἐπίνοιαν ἡ ἀπὸ τοῦ θεοῦ μαθόντων) from which the prophets alone obtained their knowledge of the most remote and ancient history (1.37) was similarly represented by *epinoia*.

Elsewhere Josephus has shown that the Bible has its own examples of poetry and oratory, apparently not subject to the charge that they are onerous to religious values. Why then is Greek poetry and rhetoric singled out here? Because in Greece these genres share more with painting and sculpture, which emphasize form and pleasure at the expense of religious or edifying content. Biblical meter is rather the adornment of the oracle and the prayer, the proper garb for the most elevated subject. More to the point, poetry and rhetoric are as misused in Greece as is historiography, more properly conceived of as a chronicle of events. In both cases, the influence of the individual artist or author has been to turn an acceptable genre into a showcase of stylistic ability and a place to show up the traditions of the forefathers for the sake of personal notoriety.

The influence of Plato on Josephus' formulation of this critique is apparent in his citation of the philosopher immediately after:

ἀφ' ἧς ὁρμηθεὶς ὁ Πλάτων οὔτε τῶν ἄλλων οὐδένα ποιητῶν φησι δεῖν εἰς τὴν πολιτείαν παραδέχεσθαι καὶ τὸν Ὅμηρον εὐφήμως ἀποπέμπεται στεφανώσας καὶ μύρον αὐτοῦ καταχέας, ἵνα δὴ μὴ τὴν ὀρθὴν δόξαν περὶ θεοῦ τοῖς μύθοις ἀφανίσειε. μάλιστα δὲ Πλάτων μεμίμηται τὸν ἡμέτερον νομοθέτην κἀν τῷ μηδὲν οὕτω παίδευμα προστάττειν τοῖς πολίταις ὡς τὸ πάντας ἀκριβῶς τοὺς νόμους ἐκμανθάνειν, καὶ μὴν καὶ περὶ τοῦ μὴ δεῖν ὡς ἔτυχεν ἐπιμίγνυσθαί τινας ἔξωθεν, ἀλλ' εἶναι καθαρὸν τὸ πολίτευμα τῶν ἐμμενόντων τοῖς νόμοις προυνόησεν.

From this standpoint Plato declares that no poet ought to be admitted to the republic, and dismisses even Homer in laudatory terms, after crowning and anointing him with unguents, in order to prevent him from obscuring by his fables the correct doctrine about God. In two points, in particular, Plato followed the example of our legislator. He prescribed as the primary duty of the citizens a study of their laws, which they must all learn word for word by heart. Again, he took precautions to prevent foreigners from mixing with them at random, and to keep the state pure and confined to law-abiding citizens.

Josephus, *Against Apion* 2.256–258

Plato is cited by Josephus in a similar way to Thucydides, as a Greek whose opinion and approach are worthwhile, precisely because they turn against the Greek poetic tradition and point out this tradition's structural weaknesses. Homer proves to be the bone of contention for Josephus, for his poetry is the only thing comparable to biblical scripture in the Greek world. One cannot help thinking that while Josephus here uses Plato against Homer, elsewhere he would not shrink from attacking Plato on the grounds that he does not have sufficient reverence for Homer, even though Plato crowns the poet and "anoints him with unguents."

The result of Josephus' attack on historiographical practices is that "authorship" becomes a charge of unreliability against a Greek by a Jew. Josephus, speaking as a literary critic, is the first in the Jewish tradition to present authorship as the writing of fiction. This formulation is the inadvertent byproduct of a critical analysis of texts. Josephus has arrived upon the idea of an author (though he doesn't have a word for it) — a person who has created the material he produces whole cloth — through a critical evaluation of the excesses of Greek historiographers.

Several critics have focused on the inconsistencies of Josephus' view of historiography. Through a hunt for the Greek sources of Josephus' approach, scholars have in a sense deconstructed *Against Apion*. Josephus is charged with making use of the very historical principles he decries. Moreover, in discrediting the works of Greek historians, he is claimed to belong firmly to the Greek tradition.

Tessa Rajak's article "The Sense of History in Jewish Intertestamental Writing" takes off from Josephus to provide an overarching scheme in which to evaluate all Jewish historians of this period. Rajak's scholarship on Hellenistic influences in Josephus' life and works provides a paradigm upon which all studies of Palestinian and Diasporic Judaism of the Greek and Roman periods should be based.[12] In the tradition of the work of Saul Lieberman, as well as the monumental work of Martin Hengel on Hellenism and Judaism, Rajak envisions the Palestine of Josephus to be profoundly influenced by Greek letters and culture, despite a rabid ideological opposition to Hellenism on the part of a significant portion of the Jewish population. While fully acknowledging the debt of my own approach to the work of Rajak, I wish to modify the terminology that Rajak uses to evaluate *Against Apion*.

Rajak states, "my interest lies not in what Josephus has to say about Greek history and historiography *per se,* but about the way he perceives the essential difference between the Greek and the Hebrew approach." The very phrasing of this description of Rajak's subject matter makes clear that the essential difference between Greek and Hebrew thought or worldview or culture is being analyzed in terms of the approach of both cultures towards historiography. However, the term "historiography" is by no means a neutral frame by which to evaluate Jewish texts; the use of the word pre-supposes that there is an approach to the writing of events that transcends cultural difference, when in fact we know that the practice of historiography is at its core Greek. Rajak goes on to say, "Josephus, however, expresses the plain view (we cannot help feeling that there is a touch of the Greek rhetoric schools about his neat presentation of it!) that contradiction must mean unreliability."[13] Rajak does not here show Josephus' logic to betray him, but merely points out the irony of employing Greek argumentation to defeat Greek writings.

In the debate over the origins of the thought of Josephus that takes place in the work of Rajak, Schwartz, Schäublin, and others, there is an overwhelming tendency to locate his Greekness at the very moments he attacks the Greeks. However, the terms of this debate have prejudiced its outcome. When Rajak ventriloquates Josephus — "contradiction must mean unreliability" — it is understood by her that contradiction in historiography is implied, while it must be noted that Josephus is speaking of contradiction of events or revelation, not in the Greek belletristic and individualistic narration of events that constitutes Greek historiography. Josephus' very argument is that historiography is not a universal principle, but a peculiar approach to the presentation of events from the past. Josephus exposes historiography as a Greek literary and rhetorical genre that is quite different from an Eastern chronicle. It is unfair to evaluate him as a historiographer when that is not at all what his work consists of, and when he has formulated a devastating critique of its very premises.

Rajak continues:

> He claims, in effect, that the Jews as a nation are distinguished for being historically minded, that their historical documents are qualitatively different from others' . . . and that their entire attitude to the past, above all the distant past, is unique. The formulation is one which suits his calling, as a Greek historian, and his purpose, to vindicate his *Antiquities* by taking on his critics. Without that challenge, and without the Greek orientation of the debate, he perhaps would not or even could not have formulated the matter thus.

While Rajak goes on to say that "there is a genuine fusion here of two cultures," she turns this into a matter of Jewish content and Greek method. However, Rajak's own formulation of the problem consists of a translation of Josephus' activities, as it were, into Greek. When she says, "their *historical* documents are qualitatively different," Rajak has turned Eastern records into the equivalent of Greek histories. If the entire attitude of the Jews towards the past is different from the Greeks, what makes it possible for this attitude to be described as "history," or Josephus as a "Greek historian"? If we assume that the Jews have *historical* documents and evaluate Josephus as a *Greek historian* before we even begin the debate, it should then be no surprise when we conclude that Jewish "historiography" was learned from the Greeks.

The hunt for Greek sources for Josephus' conception of "history" has gone beyond a quite real need to ascertain the impact of Greek literature on his presentation of Jewish topics, as if anything less than an espousal of the science of historiography on the part of Josephus would indicate that he were not a Hellenized Jew. An example of this approach is given by Shaye Cohen in an article entitled, "History and Historiography in the *Against Apion* of Josephus." Cohen states from the beginning, "But the *Against Apion* is not just an apology; it is also an essay in historiography and historical criticism."[14] The parallels to Josephus' critique of historiography adduced by Cohen lend to his argument a great deal of validity. Cohen claims that Josephus' book resembles a work of Josephus' contemporary, Plutarch, called *On the Malice of Herodotus,* especially because both authors reveal intentional distortion of the events of the past by means of "internal" evidence (citing *Against Apion* 1.4, 219, 226). He also adduces the historiographical theorization of Polybius, especially his criticism of the historians Timaeus and Duris, and his critique of "tragic history," a word coined by Polybius. Both these parallels have an incredible similarity to certain features of *Against Apion;* in particular, Josephus seems to substitute "(Greek) History" for Polybius' "tragic history" in his own exposition. However, a comparative approach to literary models and parallels is no substitute for analysis of a given text in itself; they will not interpret *Against Apion* for us.

Cohen reaches his version of Josephus — the hypocritical

Greek historian who doesn't credit his Greek sources for his own methods employed to attack the Greeks — by concluding that Josephus did not learn historical criticism from Jewish sources. That Josephus may not have been using *historical* criticism *per se* is not considered. When Josephus takes pains to note that history among the Greeks is an agonistic approach to the past created by an author, Cohen merely notes that both Josephus and Greek historians "write prefaces, talk about themselves, give their names, and, in general, reveal a self-consciousness completely missing from the biblical historians. They criticize each other and point out each other's errors." Yet Josephus distinguishes the kind of individual he is referring to from any sort of "self-conscious narrator" who gives his name and talks about himself. He describes an individual (what should be considered an "author") on a completely different order from himself. In addition, while Josephus may point out the errors of Greek historians or the chronicles of the Egyptians and Babylonians, he does not challenge the Hebrew records or correct them in any way in his *Antiquities,* even if he does augment scripture with the traditions of early biblical interpretation that he received along with the Hebrew text. Thus, while Josephus does act as a historian with regard to Greek sources, he does not treat Jewish sources with a similar skepticism; nor does he attempt to derive *kleos* 'glory' as an author, such as he claims to accrue when Greek historians discredit their predecessors and embellish their own accounts. His purpose is to set the record straight for the benefit of the Jews (whatever his intended readership), not for the sake of his own acclaim. For Josephus, Greek authors are not his predecessors, although he borrows liberally from their stylistic approach to narration and utilizes them as sources; Josephus likely considers himself to be another prophetic witness of the events experienced by the Jewish people.[15]

Cohen does not stop at the possibility that Josephus borrowed Greek arguments to challenge Greek historians; he goes on to claim that the arguments Josephus gives for the reliability of Jewish sources are also Greek arguments ("All of these pro-Jewish and anti-Greek arguments have Greek origins").[16] Thus, the claim that the Jews preserve their original constitution is said to derive from a Greek tradition of philosophical reflections on constitutions, found in Herodotus, Aristotle, and Polybius, among others. The idea of "argument from consensus" is held by Cohen to be responsible for Josephus' notions of an unchangeable and universally sanctioned Jewish canon, as well as his claims that Jews are famous for their concord and harmony. This "argument from consensus" is labeled a Greek invention,[17] and it is not acknowledged that Josephus might have actually arrived at these observations on his own, through observation of the quite real differences between Jewish and Greek treatments of the past — something which can be seen by anyone comparing the writing of Herodotus for example with 1 and 2 Samuel.

Where Josephus is acknowledged to have differences with Greek historiographers, he seems "absurd" to the Greeks and to us, according to Cohen. "No other ancient historian, as far as I have been able to determine, argues, as Josephus does, that disagreement among historians is invariably a sign of error and mendacity, and agreement is invariably a sign of truth and reliability. In fact, Josephus' argument would have seemed absurd to a Greek reader. Human knowledge is advanced through argumentation and through trial and error."[18] The need to question Josephus' claims from the perspective of the Greeks or from that of modern conceptions of how knowledge is advanced misses the point, and fails to understand Josephus on his own terms. Cohen paraphrases the worldview of Josephus, adding his own skepticism: "Historical truth is not created or discovered by human inquiry, since it exists as an 'objective' 'fact'." Trained in the niceties of Kantian philosophy and post-modern critique, or even general principles of historiography, we all know to draw back from a claim of "objective fact" that is uninfluenced by the conditions of its observation. But to frame the question this way, as both a matter of "*historical* truth" and "objective fact" is to impose a philosophical grid upon the writing of Josephus which interferes with the data.

Cohen goes further, claiming that the presumed contrast between Greeks and Jews "in reality mirrors an internal Greek debate," and collapses the distinction into a debate between Epicureans and Pythagoreans on the one hand (resembling the position of the Jews in *Against Apion*) and Greek philosophical schools (such as the Stoics, the Academics, and the Peripatetics) on the other.[19] In Cohen's view, the governing philosophical distinction between Jews and Greeks in *Against Apion* boils down to a dispute between philosophies loyal to the doctrines and words of their founders (Epicureans and Pythagoreans) and the far more innovative philosophies of the Stoics, Academics and Peripatetics. The distinction between Pharisees and Sadducees is portrayed as an "internal Jewish analog" of this Greek philosophical schism. *Against Apion,* for Cohen, becomes no more than the latest oriental attack on Greek culture, with the twist that it is really a Greek attack on Greek culture flavored by a Jewish belief in objective truth.[20]

Despite these scholars' attempts, Josephus' indictment of Greek historiography cannot be seen as detrimental to his own attempt at history writing. Such a view is not sufficiently sensitive to the project that Josephus sets for himself. Josephus takes great pains to distinguish his own approach to the retelling of past events from the approach of Greek historiography. History, according to Josephus, isn't a category of writing that should have an "author." It is rather, at its best, a transparent and faithful recording of events. In the most favorable of circumstances (such as is the case of his own record of the Jewish War or Thucydides' account of the Peloponnesian War) the account is recorded by a participant in the action. It is the duty of each culture to hand down its historical traditions by whatever means available; and while it is indeed possible for a historian to do research into events which he could not have witnessed, he must stake the veracity of his account upon the reliability of the records he employs.

The reluctance of Josephus to participate in the Greek literary arena (the *agôn*) helps explain the attitudes of Jewish writers both inside and outside the Greek world. The Jewish literary practice of pseudonymous composition (writing in the name of a legendary or prophetic authority) derives from a similar belief that the name of an individual detracts from the authority of the utterance. Rather than writing to get into the canon (problematically referred to as "canon consciousness" by some recent critics), the composers of these texts may have had no illusion that their texts could ever achieve the status of the "justly accredited" works of the Hebrew Bible as preserved by the priests of the Temple until its destruction.

These texts may have misled later readers, but there has been no convincing proof that they were all intended to do so. The prospect of writing the words as if a patriarch had spoken them was no more duplicitous than was the creation of speeches and dreams that did not exist in the Bible in Jewish literary midrash, or the creative re-enactment of speeches in the historical narratives of Thucydides and Josephus. Jewish exegetes insisted that the midrash *was* the text, after it had been properly filled in. But for a non-Hellenized Jew to write in his own name entailed a difficult proposition; authority did not properly issue in this world from individuals.[21]

Jewish writers who operated within the Greek sphere were relieved from the burden of some of these considerations, if only because they felt the need to communicate with Greek audiences using conventions with which they would be familiar. Of course, one cannot discount the possibility that Josephus, Philo, and other self-styled biblical exegetes and retellers of biblical events sought to attach unwilting glory to their names. In contrast, Jewish commentaries composed in Hebrew and Aramaic — the Mishnah, Talmud, and Midrash — are without exception anonymous until the middle ages, even if the judgments transmitted by these collections depend on the authority of both named and unnamed rabbinic authorities. Even then, these names attest not to the creativity of the individual rabbis, but rather to their insight in uncovering predetermined interpretations lying dormant in the Torah, and more important, to the lineage and authoritativeness of the traditions they transmit.

## CHAPTER 4

# BIBLICAL AND HOMERIC
# TEXTUALIZATION ACCORDING
# TO JOSEPHUS

### Josephus, Apion, and Hellenism

Josephus stands at the center of the debate about the extent of Hellenism in Jewish Palestine. He himself would appear to be the strongest example of a Hellenized Palestinian Jew; and yet, all his works were composed in Rome, and, in the case of the *Jewish War*, with the aid of assistants to help him with Greek. Although the ideas of Greek culture demonstrably permeate his conceptualization of Judaism, his example reveals that it was possible for one of the most Hellenized Jews to depict Judaism as being completely at variance with the Greek world. In the previous chapter, the extent of Josephus' opposition to Greek literary culture on an ideological level was explored. As I will argue here, Josephus contrasts the textualization and transmission of the Hebrew scriptures with that of the Homeric epics. Nevertheless, his discussion of the prophets' role in this process is suffused with Greek ideas.

A number of recent scholars in the debate over Hellenism in Palestine have questioned the extent of Greek influence in Palestine during the Hellenistic and Roman periods. These scholars have challenged the position articulated by Saul Lieberman and Martin Hengel, which had suggested a pervasive Hellenism in the Judaism of the area.[1] Some have maintained, for instance, that the "Judaizers," a group described vividly by Josephus in the *Jewish War*, successfully resisted all Hellenistic culture.[2] The lack of Greek literary texts composed by Jews in Palestine has been cited as evidence for this position. With the exception of the colophon to the Greek translation of Esther, the lost memoirs of Herod the Great, and two no longer extant works of Justus of Tiberias, rival of Josephus, no other original Greek texts survive that are unequivocally of Jewish Palestinian origin.

Similarly, the provenance of certain Greek works sometimes thought to have originated from Jewish Palestine has increasingly come under fire. For instance, it has been argued since Jacob Freudenthal's 1875 work on Alexander Polyhistor (a Greek historian who quoted surviving passages of many Jewish works in Greek) that Theodotus, composer of an epic featuring the city of Shechem composed in Greek dactylic hexameters, was a Samaritan rather than a Jew. Thus, the fact that Theodotus wrote in Greek dactylic hexameters does not speak to a thoroughly Hellenized Jewish Palestine.[3] More recently, it has been suggested that the epic of Philo the Elder was composed not in Palestine but rather in Alexandria, or that Eupolemus, author of a history of the Jews in the middle of the second century B.C.E., was not necessarily from Palestine or even Jewish.[4] The corpus of Greek inscriptions from Palestine has also been interpreted in various ways; the point is often made that such inscriptions do not speak to a widespread influence of Greek in every stratum of society, because they seemingly did not displace the numerous Hebrew and Aramaic inscriptions.[5]

I propose to consider this question employing a distinction between ideological Hellenism and cultural Hellenism. This distinction is admirably articulated by Shaye Cohen's description of his methodological approach to the problem:

> This approach attempts to get beyond the rhetoric of the Jews of antiquity. If various Jews of antiquity saw Judaism and Hellenism as antithetical, that hardly means that these entities

*were* antithetical . . . We cannot deduce from Maccabean and rabbinic ideology and rhetoric the real relationship of Judaism to Hellenism. Nor can we generalize from that very unusual Jew, Paul.

This conception of "Hellenism" leads to a redefinition of "Hellenistic Judaism." All the Judaisms of the Hellenistic period, of both the diaspora and the land of Israel, were Hellenized, that is, were integral parts of the culture of the ancient world. Some varieties of Judaism were more Hellenized than others, but none was an island into itself. It is a mistake to imagine that the land of Palestine preserved a "pure" form of Judaism and that the diaspora was the home of adulterated or diluted forms of Judaism. The term "Hellenistic Judaism" makes sense, then, only as a chronological indicator for the period from Alexander the Great to the Maccabees or perhaps to the Roman conquests of the first century B.C.E. As a descriptive term for a certain type of Judaism, however, it is meaningless, because all the Judaisms of the Hellenistic period were "Hellenistic."[6]

Cohen's comments provide a rubric by which even the Judaism of the strongest opponents to Greek culture can be evaluated. Even where Jewish political groups were successful in opposing Seleucid rule and resisting inroads of Greek language and Greek religion, the interpenetration of Greek and Jewish cultures could not be entirely avoided or willed away. Since Greek culture continued to be a powerful force during the Roman period, the approach is useful in understanding Palestine throughout late antiquity.

Josephus formulates his broadest views on the nature of Jewish letters in opposition to Greek culture. His description of the textualization of the Hebrew Bible and understanding of the process of its scripturalization are similarly formulated in response to Greek ideas about composition and textual transmission. Thus, Josephus focuses on a number of details that set biblical textualization apart from Hellenistic literary composition. Unlike Greek texts, the Bible is the product of a reliable transmission history — it was written down not only as the events occurred (see chapter 3), but by an unassailable succession of individuals with a divine dispensation to record both events and revelations. As I will argue, Josephus' model of the authoritative scribe, guaranteed by his place in a chain of succession, derives from traditional Jewish exegesis and a Platonic version of oracular revelation. It is shaped by a deliberate contrast with what Josephus could glean about Greek literary practices and authorship.

Josephus sets Homer in opposition to the Hebrew Bible in every respect. Homer was transmitted by memory, whereas the books of the Bible were written down by the prophets as soon as events occurred. Moses, alone of the prophets, is given the authority to record events that he did not witness, as his *paradosis* 'traditional history' goes back to Adam and the creation. While the Hebrew scriptures were always kept in a central location, the Homeric songs were scattered and not united until later. Josephus concluded that this had resulted in extreme textual variation, since many locales maintained their own idiosyncratic texts of Homer. A survey of the quotations of Homer in various ancient witnesses and from the so-called "eccentric papyri" reveals the validity of his charge. Equivalent discrepancies were totally lacking in the case of the Bible. Conveniently, Josephus does not acknowledge the differences in biblical manuscript families that have long been the subject of modern scholarly research, that were investigated by ancient scholars like Origen and St. Jerome, and that were decried by the rabbis and Jewish sectarians.

Josephus thinks of the textual stability of the Hebrew law code in terms borrowed from classical philology.

Ὅθεν δὴ καὶ τὸ προφερόμενον ἡμῖν ὑπό τινων ἔγκλημα, τὸ δὴ μὴ καινῶν εὑρετὰς ἔργων ἢ λόγων ἄνδρας παρασχεῖν, ἐντεῦθεν συμβέβηκεν· οἱ μὲν γὰρ ἄλλοι τὸ μηδενὶ τῶν πατρίων ἐμμένειν καλὸν εἶναι νομίζουσι καὶ τοῖς τολμῶσι ταῦτα παραβαίνειν μάλιστα σοφίας δεινότητα μαρτυροῦσιν. ἡμεῖς δὲ τοὐναντίον μίαν εἶναι καὶ φρόνησιν καὶ ἀρετὴν ὑπειλήφαμεν τὸ μηδὲν ὅλως ὑπεναντίον μήτε πρᾶξαι μήτε διανοηθῆναι τοῖς ἐξ ἀρχῆς νομοθετηθεῖσιν. ὅπερ εἰκότως ἂν εἴη τεκμήριον τοῦ κάλλιστα τὸν νόμον τεθῆναι· τὰ γὰρ μὴ τοῦτον ἔχοντα τὸν τρόπον αἱ πεῖραι δεόμενα διορθώσεως ἐλέγχουσιν.

This, in fact, is the origin of the reproach brought against us by some critics of our having produced no inventors in crafts or literature. In the eyes of the world at large there is something fine in breaking away from all inherited customs; those who have the temerity to defy them are credited with the possession of consummate ability. To us, on the other hand, the only wisdom, the only virtue, consists in refraining absolutely from every action, from every thought that is contrary to the laws originally laid down. This may fairly be claimed as a proof of their excellent draftsmanship; codes which are not of this character are proved by experience to need amendment (*diorthôsis*).

Josephus, Against Apion 2.182–183

The word Josephus here employs for amendment (*diorthôsis*) is in fact the technical term for the process of editing and correcting a manuscript. In the ancient world, this process achieved its most sophisticated form in the editing of the multiple and divergent Homeric manuscripts that had resulted from composition in performance or different performance traditions to be found in the versions of Homer from all over the Greek world.[7] The reference to Homeric scholarship is not at all a *non sequitur* here. The very person at whom Josephus directs his polemic in this work, Apion, was a Homeric philologist who was involved in the creation of such editions (*diorthôseis*).

In order to evaluate the basis of Josephus' knowledge about Greek literary scholarship of his day, it is necessary to examine this figure of Apion.[8] Apion was born in the oasis of El Kargeh in Upper Egypt in the second half of the first century B.C.E. He studied in Alexandria under Didymus Chalkenteros, a Greek grammarian and lexicographer, and succeeded Theon as head of the famous literary school in Alexandria. Later, he moved to Rome, where he became a professional grammarian. During Caligula's reign, he was honored by the city of Alexandria with its citizenship, and in 39 C.E. was appointed by the city as leader of its delegation to Rome in the conflict between Greeks and Jews a year earlier. Apion may have instigated the pogrom in 38 C.E. He is the first to promulgate a version of the Blood Libel, claiming that Jews ate a fattened Greek annually. He also asserted that the Jews keep the Sabbath because they had developed a tumor (Greek *sabbô* or *sabbatôsis*) in the groin on the seventh day after the exodus and were compelled to rest on that day. Josephus relates that Apion himself developed a

tumor or gangrene in his genitals, which resulted not only in surgi-
cal circumcision, but also in his death some time in the middle of
the first century C.E.

It seems clear that Apion was the most famous Homeric
scholar of his day, as is indicated by Seneca:

> Apion grammaticus, qui sub C. Caesare tota circulatus est Graecia
> et in nomen Homeri ab omnibus civitatibus adoptatus, aiebat
> Homerum utraque materia consummata, et Odyssia et Iliade,
> principium adiecisse operi suo, quo bellum Troianum complexus
> est. Huius rei argumentum adferebat, quod duas litteras in primo
> versu posuisset ex industria librorum suorum numerum conti-
> nentes.

> Apion, the scholar, who drew crowds to his lectures all over
> Greece in the days of Gaius Caesar and was adopted in the name
> of Homer by every state, used to maintain that Homer, when he
> had finished his two poems, the *Iliad* and the *Odyssey*, added a
> preliminary poem to his work, wherein he embraced the whole
> Trojan war. The argument which Apion adduced to prove this
> statement was that Homer had purposely inserted in the opening
> line two letters which contained a key to the number of his books.
> Seneca, *Epistle* 88.40, trans. Gummere

The letter of Seneca attests to the notoriety of Apion, independent
of Josephus; Apion is *tota circulatus est Graecia et in nomen Homeri
ab omnibus civitatibus adoptatus* 'well known in all of Greece and
adopted under the name of Homer by every state'. The exact meaning of the description of Apion as *in nomen Homeri . . . adoptatus*
'adopted under the name of Homer by every city-state' is unclear.
Suzanne Neitzel renders Seneca's statement employing a Greek ad-
jectival form: "[Apion] was assigned the honorary name 'Homer-
ikos' by the Greek city-states."[9] Whatever its precise meaning, the
expression speaks to the pervasiveness and bombast of Apion's reputation as a Homeric scholar. This bombast is also apparent in the
report of Pliny the Elder, who relates that the emperor Tiberius
called Apion "the world's cymbal" (*cymbalum mundi*).[10]

In Seneca's short description, Apion also claimed that Homer inserted the number of books that he composed in code within the first line of the *Iliad* (the letters MH from μῆνιν ἀείδε θεά 'Sing, goddess, the wrath . . .' are supposed to indicate that Homer composed 48 books, the numerical value of μη). In addition, he states that there was a *principium* 'proem' that summarized all the events that took place at Troy. This story is in counterpoint to the tradition Josephus relays about the twenty-four Hebrew books which neither increase nor decrease with the passing fancy of Alexandrian philological interpreters. I would argue that it is precisely this kind of information that gives Josephus ammunition in his polemic against Greek writings. Unlike the Homeric corpus, the contents of which vary according to the city one is in and the editor one follows as authoritative, there is no dispute over the number and identity of the Hebrew corpus of texts. Josephus, implicitly establishing a parallel between these works, uses his knowledge of the extreme variation in textual traditions of Homeric transmission as evidence of their historical inferiority.

The historian Pliny relates another story about Apion which reveals the grammarian's interest in the connection between the biography of Homer and his works. In an absurd demonstration of biographical criticism, Apion apparently attempted through necromancy to answer the age-old question of Homer's native country and parentage:

> quaerat aliquis, quae sint mentiti veteres Magi, cum adulescentibus nobis visus Apion grammaticae artis prodiderit cynocephalian herbam, quae in Aegypto vocaretur osiritis, divinam et contra omnia veneficia, sed si tota erueretur, statim eum qui eruisset mori, seque evocasse umbras ad percunctandum Homerum quanam patria quibusque perentibus genitus esset, non tamen ausus profiteri quid sibi respondisse diceret.

> One might well ask what were the lies of the old Magi, when as a youth I saw Apion the grammarian, who told us that the herb cynocephalia, called in Egypt Osiritis, was an instrument of divination and a protection from all kinds of sorcery, but if it were uprooted altogether the digger would die at once, and that he had called up ghosts to inquire from Homer his native country and the

name of his parents, but did not dare to repeat the answers which
he said were given.

Pliny, *Natural History* 30.6.18, trans. Jones

Pliny's information, attained through his personal acquaintance
with Apion during his youth, gives a striking picture of the Egyptian philologist. Not content with the multiplicity of answers to this
question as propounded by exegetes of the Homeric epics and the
biographers of the poet, Apion attempts to bypass the controversy
by appealing to the dead poet himself. His spooky refusal to repeat
the poet's response adds an interesting element to ancient scholarship's inability to ascertain this information. The answers were perceived as being harmful to the poet, the gods, Greece, or even Apion
himself. Apion felt they were best kept secret. Meanwhile, he elevated his own scholarly prestige by being in possession of such secret knowledge.[11]

Pliny's comment recalls Josephus' statement about Apion:
"Grammarian of Homer's poetry though he was, he could not definitively (διαβεβαιωσάμενος) say what his native land was, or even
that of Pythagoras, who lived, one might say, just the other day"
(*Against Apion* 2.14). The speculation as to the birthplace of Homer
was not just a matter of rivalry between Greek states anxious for
the prestige of this title by the time of the Alexandrian critics, even
if it had started out this way. Alexandria and Pergamum, homes of
the two greatest libraries and of the most authoritative editions of
Homer, staked their claims in part on the basis of legends about
Homer's birthplace. The philosophical schools of Pythagoras and
Zeno each had their own rendition of Homer's native land, one
which no doubt legitimated the bloodlines of these philosophies.
The collection at Alexandria was held to have sprouted from the
private library of Aristotle. Since the practice of composing *hupomnêmata*, commentaries dealing with minutiae of Homeric vocalization, word division, punctuation, and other linguistic matters, was
held to originate with Aristotle, Alexandria could lay claim to the
purest Homer around. Scholars of Pergamum countered that their
own library derived from the private store of the Peisistratids, sixth
century tyrants of the Athenian polis. Although the city couldn't compete with Alexandria's authoritative philological editions, Pergamum

claimed to have the text itself, or as close as one could get — the Homer of Peisistratus.

Apion's inability to declare the birthplace of Homer drew from a larger dilemma facing Alexandrian philology in his day. Pergamene allegorical analysis had gained ascendancy in Alexandrian Jewish exegesis since the time of Philo and the author of the Letter of Aristeas before him. The unequivocal affirmation of such methods of analysis on the part of Philo a century after Aristarchus indicates that Alexandria that was no longer unified behind the philological, non-allegorical criticism of Zenodotus and Aristarchus. Moreover, Alexandrian grammarians were now making full use of grammatical principles that had originally been developed by Crates of Mallos, the first librarian at Pergamum. Apion's recourse to necromancy in the determination of Homer's birthplace is thus another sign of the collapse of the scholarly divide between Alexandria and Pergamum (see chapter 5), for his inquiry cast doubt on the traditional Alexandrian narrative about Homer's life and birthplace.

It is worth noting that Apion's investigation of Homer's birthplace continued the Alexandrian emphasis on authorial biography as a matter lying at the heart of interpretive scholarship. In short, his approach to the solution of exegetical questions such as Homeric etymology (his specialty) was to ascertain the birthplace (and thus native dialect) of Homer. The preoccupation of Apion and Alexandrian criticism in general with authorial biography is in many ways comparable to the method Josephus used to vouch for the legitimacy of the books of the Hebrew Bible: ascertaining the status of the individuals who copied them out. Yet it also serves as a counterpoint to Josephus' literary approach, which critiques Greek historiography on the grounds of its excessive compositional individualism.

It must be emphasized that Apion was a consummate Alexandrian grammarian, and that his basic approach was informed by the views of this tradition. For instance, his position that Homer composed the *Iliad* and *Odyssey* in forty-eight books and was not the author of the cyclic poems represents a solid Alexandrian (and Aristotelian) viewpoint. He frequently cites the opinions of Aristarchus and other Alexandrian scholars by name, although occasionally in order to show how much more clever he was than they.[12] Later lexicographers and grammarians characterized his scholarly explanations as bad or ridiculous, but he must have been widely respected in his time to be appointed the head of the illustrious school of literary studies in Alexandria. Thus, it is important to realize that Josephus saw Apion not only as a bombastic, cartoon-like figure and intractable enemy of the Jews, but also as the foremost Alexandrian scholar of the day. Josephus likely learned much about Alexandrian scholarly approaches to the textual transmission of Homer in order to combat this bitter enemy.

### Josephus on Homer: What Homer Wrote

The main thrust of Josephus' argument in *Against Apion* is to delineate Greek authorship from the more limited activity of the biblical prophets who allegedly copied down the biblical books. Josephus utilized Greek poetics as a means of explaining why the prophets are not authors. His description of the handing down of biblical letters, their copying out and editing, intersected with similar legends of the transmission of the Homeric epics by the rhapsodes. These legends were deliberately contrasted by Josephus with the way that biblical events came to be recorded. In Josephus' critique of the transmission of Homeric epic, in his dismissal of the antiquity of the Greeks, and even in his implicit critique of the Jewish sect known as the Pharisees, he consistently undercuts the reliability and validity of oral transmission, bardic performance, and human memory as a means to preserve texts, traditions, or information of any sort.

For Homeric scholars since the eighteenth century, one of the most important witnesses to the formation of the Homeric poems appears in the course of Josephus' polemic against oral transmission in *Against Apion:*

καί φασιν οὐδὲ τοῦτον ἐν γράμμασι τὴν αὑτοῦ ποίησιν καταλιπεῖν, ἀλλὰ διαμνημονευομένην ἐκ τῶν ἀσμάτων ὕστερον συντεθῆναι καὶ διὰ τοῦτο πολλὰς ἐν αὐτῇ σχεῖν τὰς διαφωνίας.

> They say that he did not leave his poetry in writing, but, first trans-
> mitted by memory, the scattered songs were not united until later;
> to which circumstance the numerous inconsistencies of the work
> are attributable.
>
> Josephus, *Against Apion* 1.13

Homeric scholar Friederich August Wolf formulated his theory of
Homeric rhapsodic transmission largely on the basis of this statement of Josephus; Theodore Reinach calls it one of the "pierres an-
gulaires" of Wolf's *Prolegomena* to the Homeric poems.[13] Wolf's
exact words on Josephus are worth considering, and not just for
their enduring contribution to Homeric studies:

> But so far as I can determine, neither Eustathius nor any of the
> scholiasts tries to learn whether Homer himself knew the art [i.e.
> writing] that was unknown to his heroes; thus they neither affirm
> nor deny the matter categorically . . . This question doubtless ex-
> ercised the Alexandrian critics as well. And if there is any author-
> ity that we can set — given this great loss of ancient books —
> against the ambiguous silence of our scholia, it derives precisely
> from their disputations. This is how one must take the remarkable
> passage in Josephus, where he clearly says, "It is said that Homer
> did not use writing in composing poems, and that they were first
> revealed to the public and spread by memory; afterward, being
> consigned to writing, they took on this form and tenor." This is the
> only clear, authoritative testimony about the question. But it is
> weightier because it was written against the most learned Ho-
> meric commentator, and no ancient defender of a different or con-
> trary opinion survives.[14]

From the time of Wolf, Homeric scholars have read Josephus' statement as evidence for the Peisistratean recension of the *Iliad* and the
*Odyssey*. But recent interpretations, more sensitive to the way that
legends of textual transmission work, have recast Josephus' testimony with regard to the historicity of Peisistratus.

The Peisistratean recension has been explained as the "big
bang" cosmology of Homeric poetry. According to Gregory Nagy,
the story is essentially a myth of textual origins that was appropri-

ated as an instrument of propaganda for the Peisistratean dynasty.[15] Nagy states: "The idea of an 'assembling' of a text 'from the songs' suggests that the premise of Josephus' argumentation is the historical reality of a narrative tradition that told of a recension of the Homeric poems commissioned by the Athenian tyrant Peisistratus."[16] Josephus indeed refers to a charter myth that resembles the stories of Peisistratus in systematizing the works of Homer. As Nagy argues, this narrative tradition is a historical reality, although one which likely does not reflect the actual contributions of Peisistratus himself, as will be argued below. However, Peisistratus is not mentioned in Josephus' account. As I will argue, Josephus probably derives his account from Alexandrian sources that downplayed the role of Peisistratus in their ongoing rivalry with Pergamum.

In order to gain a more accurate view of Josephus' notions of Homeric transmission, it is necessary to reconsider the meaning of the utterance ἀλλὰ διαμνημονευομένην ἐκ τῶν ᾀσμάτων ὕστερον συντεθῆναι. Minna Skafte Jensen's treatment of the wording of the various reports of the Peisistratean recension is helpful here. Jensen states:

> But common to all versions is the idea that Homer originally composed an *Iliad* and an *Odyssey*, that they were subsequently scattered for some reason or other, and then finally collected again . . .
> In the sources this is generally revealed by a contraposition of the prefixes dia- *versus* sun-.[17]

Jensen interprets the *dia-* prefix everywhere to mean 'in different directions', in contradistinction to *sun-* 'together', although she also notes that it can carry the sense of 'transmitting'. However, it seems more obvious to translate the *dia-* as meaning 'through time'.[18]

I would therefore suggest that Josephus' statement (ἀλλὰ διαμνημονευομένην ἐκ τῶν ᾀσμάτων ὕστερον συντεθῆναι) should be translated: "But, having been recalled in the interim from songs, it *later* was assembled." As may be gleaned from Josephus' emphasis on archival writing as a safeguard of accurate transmission throughout *Against Apion,* his point is likely that the poetry of Homer was only later assembled *in writing,* an action contrasted with the role of memory alone in its previous preservation. The key word is ὕστερον 'later': Josephus is emphasizing the temporal gap between composition (understood to be composition by Homer himself) and its writing down. Josephus also highlights another negative aspect of Homeric transmission — its lack of a centralized transmission process.

Josephus does not refer to a Peisistratean assembly of a standardized Homeric text in so many words, but focuses rather on the mistakes resulting from the re-recording of Homer's exact words with writing. When he writes about a written text full of discrepancies ("to which circumstance the numerous inconsistencies of the work are attributable" [1.12]), Josephus is probably thinking of the written editions from Alexandria dating from the end of the third century B.C.E., full of athetized lines and questionable variants. Whether Josephus was aware of the Peisistratean legend at all is uncertain.[19] If Josephus knew of the stories of a Peisistratean recension, how could he have collapsed them into the formation of formalized written editions by editors like Aristarchus? The Peisistratus legend did not normally contain a message denigrating Peisistratus' text as being full of errors; such a message would have run counter to the idea that Peisistratus had established the definitive text of Homer of his time. Nevertheless, other stories of the Peisistratids contained such criticisms.[20]

The scholarship on Josephus' view of Homeric transmission has never questioned the assumption that the Jewish historian is referring to Peisistratean recension. Nagy, having determined that a Peisistratean-type legend is the background for Josephus' statement, and noting that the Peisistratean legends directly involve the use of writing, correctly concludes that Josephus is not really a good witness for rhapsodic transmission of Homer, despite the attempt of Wolf to use him as such.

> There is reason, then, for resisting what both Villoison and Wolf infer from the stories of the Peisistratian Recension. These stories center on the notion of a lost text, and they make no explicit reference to the reality of oral transmission by Homeric performers called rhapsodes. Although there is indeed evidence to support both Villoison and Wolf in their arguing for the concept of a rhap-

sodic phase in the history of Homeric transmission, the point is that the Alexandrian scholars argued for an altogether different concept: for them, especially for Aristarchus, the idea of an original written text of Homer was not so much a metaphor but a historical reality. For Aristarchus, it appears that Homer was an Athenian who lived around 1000 B.C., in the time of Athenian migrations (cf. scholia A to *Iliad* 13.197); moreover, the scholastic tradition stemming ultimately from Aristarchus implies that Hesiod actually had a chance to *read* them (scholia A to *Iliad* 12.22a) . . . Thus Wolf seems unjustified in thinking that the Homer scholars of Alexandria posited a phase of oral transmission to account for the variations they found in the history of the Homeric text. The problem is, Wolf does not make a distinction between earlier and later views of Homer in ancient criticism: the premise of Josephus reflects an earlier Homeric model, while that of Apion promotes a later one, of Aristarchean provenance (to repeat: Apion was a student of Didymus).[21]

Nagy concludes (citing Jensen) that Josephus reflects an earlier Homeric model of transmission theories in the ancient world.[22] According to this earlier model, Homer had originally composed an *Iliad* and an *Odyssey;* these poems were subsequently scattered, and then finally collected again.[23] I would specify that Josephus' model of Homeric transmission has as a premise the prevailing language of the Alexandrians, and it is plausible that Josephus got his information about Homer from the works of Apion himself. The Alexandrian school did allow for the involvement of rhapsodes in Homeric transmission (e.g. the writings of Dionysius Thrax — see chapter 5). But the key tenet of this school was that Homer literally "wrote" the *Iliad* and *Odyssey.*

I would argue that Josephus does indeed make explicit reference to a rhapsodic tradition, in which the Homeric texts, without the use of writing, were διαμνημονευομένην ἐκ τῶν ᾀσμάτων 'recalled from songs'. From this perspective, Josephus imagined that Homeric editors attempted to reclaim a lost Homeric text, but their only evidence was the less than trustworthy evidence of singers who had memorized the Homeric text and preserved it in the form of songs. The fact that Aristarchus thought of Homer as having written down his poem should not be contrasted with the statement of Josephus. However, stressing that the epics had been written down by Homer would not have been in the interest of Josephus' polemic.

Both Nagy and Richard Janko have pointed out that the Alexandrians fail to mention the Peisistratean recension. Nagy and Janko, however, differ in their interpretation of this phenomenon:

> The idea of a Peisistratean Recension, according to one expert, "was unknown in the heyday of Alexandrian scholarship" (Janko, *Books 13–16*, p.32). I would rather say "deliberately ignored" or at least underrepresented, not "unknown."[24]

Nagy goes on to emphasize that references to the Peisistratean Recension are wholly absent from the Iliadic A Scholia, which primarily reflect the Aristarchean tradition.[25] If Josephus derives his knowledge from Alexandrian Homeric scholars like Apion, but the Alexandrians themselves officially discounted or at least downplayed stories about the Peisistratean Recension (because these stories were the official legitimizing myth of the Pergamene library), it stands to reason that Josephus was not referring to Peisistratus *per se*, but to a comparable textualization myth.

In fact, Josephus does refer to Peisistratus in his account and uses him as a well-known figure to establish the date of Dracon.

τὸ γὰρ ἐξ ἀρχῆς μὴ σπουδασθῆναι παρὰ τοῖς Ἕλλησι δημοσίας γίνεσθαι περὶ τῶν ἑκάστοτε πραττομένων ἀναγραφὰς τοῦτο μάλιστα δὴ καὶ τὴν πλάνην καὶ τὴν ἐξουσίαν τοῦ ψεύδεσθαι τοῖς μετὰ ταῦτα βουληθεῖσι περὶ τῶν παλαιῶν τι γράφειν παρέσχεν. οὐ γὰρ μόνον παρὰ τοῖς ἄλλοις Ἕλλησιν ἠμελήθη τὰ περὶ τὰς ἀναγραφάς, ἀλλ' οὐδὲ παρὰ τοῖς Ἀθηναίοις, οὓς αὐτόχθονας εἶναι λέγουσιν καὶ παιδείας ἐπιμελεῖς, οὐδὲν τοιοῦτον εὑρίσκεται γενόμενον, ἀλλὰ τῶν δημοσίων γραμμάτων ἀρχαιοτάτους εἶναί φασι τοὺς ὑπὸ Δράκοντος αὐτοῖς περὶ τῶν φονικῶν γραφέντας νόμους ὀλίγῳ πρότερον τῆς Πεισιστράτου τυραννίδος ἀνθρώπου γεγονότος. περὶ μὲν γὰρ Ἀρκάδων τί δεῖ λέγειν αὐχούντων ἀρχαιότητα; μόλις γὰρ οὗτοι καὶ μετὰ ταῦτα γράμμασιν ἐπαιδεύθησαν.

The main responsibility for the errors of later historians who aspired to write on antiquity and for the license granted to their mendacity rests with the original neglect of the Greeks to keep official records of current events. This neglect was not confined to the lesser Greek states. Even among the Athenians, <u>who are reputed to be indigenous and devoted to learning, we find that nothing of the kind existed, and their most ancient public records are said to be the laws on homicide drafted for them by Dracon, a man who lived only a little before the despotism of Peisistratus</u>. Of the Arcadians and their vaunted antiquity it is unnecessary to speak, since even at a still later date they had hardly learned the alphabet.

Josephus, Against Apion 1.19–20

Despite the fact that Peisistratus was familiar to Josephus as a tyrant, he in no way connects him to the textualization of Homer. The discussion of the late date at which the Arcadians learned their letters that immediately follows the Peisistratus discussion highlights the missing connection between Peisistratus and the written recension of Homer. I would argue that Josephus avoids the Peisistratus legend because it was generally employed only by the Pergamenes, and was used by them as way of testifying to the accuracy of their Homeric texts, not as an attack on their veracity.

The other claim that had been made by Wolf about Josephus was that he believed that Homer had composed his epics orally, and that they were written down much later. As satisfying as it would be to find an ancient source that confirms our own knowledge about simultaneous performance and composition on the part of an epic singer (as theorized by Milman Parry and Albert Lord), Josephus actually provides no such information. To return to Josephus' statement:

καί φασιν οὐδὲ τοῦτον ἐν γράμμασι τὴν αὐτοῦ ποίησιν καταλιπεῖν, ἀλλὰ διαμνημονευομένην ἐκ τῶν ᾀσμάτων ὕστερον συντεθῆναι καὶ διὰ τοῦτο πολλὰς ἐν αὐτῇ σχεῖν τὰς διαφωνίας.

and they say, that he did not bequeath his poems in writing, but having been recalled from songs, it was later assembled, and for this reason has so many discordances.

Josephus, Against Apion 1.13

Josephus neither asserts nor denies that Homer wrote down the epics. By saying "he did not bequeath his poems in writing" (οὐδὲ τοῦτον ἐν γράμμασι τὴν αὐτοῦ ποίησιν καταλιπεῖν) he is merely commenting on the transition from Homeric times to a later period. The verb καταλιπεῖν 'to bequeath, to leave behind' is not at all a standard way to refer to the physical act of writing. It rather signifies the process of turning over property to an heir at death.

The point Josephus is attempting to make about Homer becomes clearer when contrasted with a remarkable passage from the *Antiquities*:

ἔπειτα ποίησιν ἑξάμετρον αὐτοῖς <u>ἀνέγνω, ἣν καὶ καταλέλοιπεν ἐν</u> <u>βίβλῳ ἐν τῷ ἱερῷ</u> πρόρρησιν περιέχουσαν τῶν ἐσσομένων, καθ' ἣν [καὶ] γέγονε [τὰ] πάντα καὶ γίνεται, μηδὲν ἐκείνου διημαρτηκότος τῆς ἀληθείας. ταῦτ' οὖν τὰ βιβλία παραδίδωσι τοῖς ἱερεῦσι καὶ τὴν κιβωτόν, εἰς ἣν καὶ τοὺς δέκα λόγους γεγραμμένους ἐν δυσὶ πλαξὶ κατέθετο, καὶ τὴν σκηνήν·

Then he <u>read aloud</u> to them a poem in hexameter verse, <u>which he</u> <u>has moreover bequeathed in a book preserved in the temple</u>, containing a prediction of future events, in accordance with which all has come and is coming to pass, the seer having in no whit strayed from the truth. All these books he consigned to the priests, together with the ark, in which he had deposited the Ten Commandments written on two tables, and the tabernacle.

Josephus, Antiquities 4.303, trans. Thackeray

Josephus' description of Moses' last song (identified as the "Ha'azinu" song in Deut. 32) as a *hexametra poiêsis* 'hexameter poem' is puzzling, considering that biblical Hebrew lacked a metrical system. James Kugel, who has explored the afterlife of this statement among later biblical scholars, postulates that Josephus meant to convey the epic quality of the composition: "by 'hexameter' Josephus may mean a heroic song, an epic speech such as those found in Homer."[26] One should keep in mind that the Delphic oracles were also composed in hexameters. It is thus a possibility that Josephus viewed the song as a poem composed in hexameters because he was convinced of the oracular quality of the song, or wished to convey to his Greek audience its prophetic nature as well as its poetic quality.

Comparison of the two passages reveals that Josephus implicitly contrasts Homer's failure to hand down a text with Moses' success. The verb *kataleipô* 'bequeath' appears in both accounts; it signifies the handing down of a written text upon the death of its composer. Josephus further specifies that Moses' song was "bequeathed" in a book or papyrus roll and deposited in the temple (ἐν βίβλῳ ἐν τῷ ἱερῷ).

Plutarch confirms that *kataleipô* was employed to refer to the handing down of a written body of works not composed by the transmitter.

> οἱ δὲ πρεσβύτεροι Περιπατητικοὶ φαίνονται μὲν καθ' ἑαυτοὺς γενόμενοι χαρίεντες καὶ φιλόλογοι, τῶν δ' Ἀριστοτέλους καὶ Θεοφράστου γραμμάτων οὔτε πολλοῖς οὔτε ἀκριβῶς ἐντετυχηκότες διὰ τὸ τὸν Νηλέως τοῦ Σκηψίου κλῆρον, ᾧ τὰ βιβλία κατέλιπε Θεόπραστος, εἰς ἀφιλοτίμους καὶ ἰδιώτας ἀνθρώπους περιγενέσθαι.

> The earlier Peripatetics, though they seem intrinsically sophisticated and scholarly, did not have access to many of the writings of Aristotle and Theophrastus, and what they did have was not accurate — all on account of the legacy of Neleus of Scepsis, to whom Theophrastus had bequeathed (*kataleipô*) the books. Because of that legacy, they [the books] had been handed down to men without any ambition or affiliation.
>
> Plutarch, *Life of Sulla* 26.2, trans. Nagy

In this passage, *kataleipô* 'bequeath' replaces *paradidômi* 'transmit' in Strabo's account of the same events (Strabo 13.1.54 C 609). Comparable passages confirm this sense of the word: Diogenes Laertius V.62 (Strato's Testament) καταλείπω δ' αὐτῷ καὶ τὸ βιβλία πάντα πλὴν ὧν αὐτοὶ γεγράφαμεν 'I bequeath to him (Lykon) also all the books, except for the ones which we ourselves wrote'. It is quite clear from this that *kataleipô* is regularly employed to indicate the handing down of texts as physical property, and seems not to refer to the act of simultaneous writing and composition.

By claiming that Homer failed to give his written text as an inheritance to his heirs, Josephus implicitly measures Homer against the model provided by Moses, who not only recorded his deathbed orations (contained in the book of Deuteronomy) but also placed them in the temple, safeguarding the text for future generations. Josephus is again driving home his claim that Greek culture is incapable of maintaining written records, because it lacks the oriental veneration for the archive, not to mention the safeguards used by Jews to protect their records. In short, Josephus believed that *none of Homer's written texts survived,* due to the failure of Greek culture to maintain a chain of succession of individuals who might care for this society's written texts. The contrast with Homer is heightened by the fact that the work of Moses in question is a poem (*poiêsis*) composed in hexameters — the meter of Greek epic poetry. The notion that Moses read the song from a written transcript also betters Homeric performance at its own game (keep in mind Moses is reading these hexameters aloud). As opposed to the Greek practice of unreliable bardic recitation or elaboration, Moses' speech act simply gives voice to the pre-existing text. For Josephus, Greek poets improvise, but Moses sticks to the script. Josephus again critiques Greek letters with the very judgments of Greek scholars about Homeric transmission. Even if Homeric performers from an earlier date would not have admitted that their recitation was modified *ad hoc,* by the fourth century at least, Greek teachers of rhetoric were fully endorsing the idea of improvisation in oratory, and described the Homeric rhapsodes as improvisators.[27] It should be added that Josephus openly maligns the Greek tendency to improvise (*skhediazein*) elsewhere in this same text (*Against Apion* 1.45).

As we have seen, Homeric scholars of our own era mistakenly concluded that Josephus' description of Homeric transmission assumed that Homer had *never* written down his epics. However, this sense of the word *kataleipô* is not supported by Josephus' typical use of the word. To the contrary, the process indicated by *kataleipô* in *Antiquities* 4.303, where Moses bequeathed his text in a written papyrus roll in the temple, is *preceded* by Moses *reading aloud* (*anagignôskô*) his poem from a written document. Thus, *kataleipô* does not refer to the process of writing down a poem because in this case the poem had *already* been written down at the moment of its utterance.

The error in the interpretation of Josephus goes back to Wolf. Since the *Prolegomena to Homer,* scholars have interpreted Josephus' words to refer to something these words do not even address — whether Homer "wrote down" the epics. Wolf's translation of Josephus' statement made the crucial error:

> This is how one must take the remarkable passage in Josephus, where he clearly says, "It is said that Homer did not use writing in composing poems, and that they were <u>first</u> revealed to the public and spread by memory; afterward, being consigned to writing, they took on this form and tenor" (*Homerum tradi scriptura usum non fuisse | in pangendis Carminibus, eaque <u>primo</u> memoriter prodita in vulgus et propagata, postea litteris mandata hanc formam et tenorem adscivisse*).

Wolf's Latin translation of Josephus inserts Homer's composition process (with the adverb *primo* 'at first') into a statement which was really only concerned with a period following composition. The sentence in Greek says only that Homer didn't leave behind (*katalipein*) his poems in writing, not that he had never employed writing. There is no equivalent of *primo* in Greek, referring to the moment of Homer's composition; there is only a *husteron* 'later' (translated as *postea* by Wolf) which indicates time following a period of ostensibly rhapsodic transmission. Josephus cannot be made into a proponent of Homer as an illiterate bard. His statement describes a period of time when writing *no longer* preserved the epics.

Wolf observed that the word *phasin* 'they say' indicates that Josephus is quoting a widely held belief on the part of Alexandrian critics.[28] This is in keeping with Josephus' "historiographical" technique of refuting the statements of Greek historians by their own words (e.g. "The authors of scurrilous and mendacious statements about us will be shown to be confuted by themselves" [1.1.4]). But this statement (that Homer didn't "bequeath" or "leave behind" a text to the world) seems on the surface to be a wholly different premise than Aristarchus' belief that Homer *wrote* and Hesiod *read* the *Iliad* and *Odyssey.* How do we reconcile these two opinions, or are they in fact antithetical? There are two interlocking theses of

Alexandrian Homeric scholarship represented here. The first is an assumption, formed by the inescapable influence of the metaphor of writing-as-composition in the time of Aristarchus: Homer wrote down the *Iliad* and the *Odyssey*. The second is methodological doctrine, and argues for the very need for editorial activity on the part of the Alexandrian critics: no manuscript written by Homer survived to reach the Alexandrian philologists intact. It is the second point that Josephus gives us, while he fails to mention the first, no doubt because it does not suit his purpose in *Against Apion*. Nevertheless, his goal is to refute the Alexandrians by their own words; this means assuming, for the sake of argument, that their claims about Homer's writing down the epics are correct. Josephus turns what seems to have been a well-known Alexandrian methodological dictum into an argument claiming that even what the Greeks wrote down they were not capable of preserving.

What I suggest as an Alexandrian methodological dictum, that Homer wrote down the *Iliad* and *Odyssey* but that these written texts did not survive, finds support in a late antique or Byzantine legend involving a Peisistratean/Ptolemaic recension of Homer. This legend, found in the Scholia to Dionysius Thrax (a student of Aristarchus), maintains that the books of Homer were destroyed by fire, flood or earthquakes, and were later reassembled from the memory of individuals in different locations. This element of the legend springs from the fusion of two separate traditions about Homeric transmission, a process described in chapter 5. One was the Peisistratean recension legend, initiated by the Peisistratids or their intellectual heirs both to glorify themselves and to set their mark on a standardized version of Homer. But another set of legends also existed, emphasizing a quite different aspect of Homeric transmission. In order to explain the many anomalies in the various Homers that existed *kata poleis* 'by city' in the *politikai* 'city editions', a legend about the scattering of the Homeric poems and their subsequent reassembly arose in Alexandrian circles.[29]

From the point of view of a critic of Greek letters like Josephus, Alexandrian claims that they had restored the original words of Homer were called into question by the Alexandrian methodological dictum (that no manuscript written by Homer survived), and by its correlate (physical texts are untrustworthy repositories of information, because they can be physically damaged by the elements or faulty editing). For Josephus, the original text cannot survive without a trustworthy archive, nor can it be restored by scholars.

The idea of the destruction of works of learning by the elements is not only assumed by Josephus' account, but his very mention of the works of Homer is preceded by reference to physical catastrophe.

τὸν δὲ περὶ τὴν Ἑλλάδα τόπον μυρίαι μὲν φθοραὶ κατέσχον ἐξαλείφουσαι τὴν μνήμην τῶν γεγονότων, ἀεὶ δὲ καινοὺς καθιστάμενοι βίους τοῦ παντὸς ἐνόμιζον ἄρχειν ἕκαστοι τῶν ἀφ' ἑαυτῶν, ὀψὲ δὲ καὶ μόλις ἔγνωσαν φύσιν γραμμάτων· ὁ γοῦν ἀρχαιοτάτην αὐτῶν τὴν χρῆσιν εἶναι θέλοντες παρὰ Φοινίκων καὶ Κάδμου σεμνύνονται μαθεῖν.

The land of Greece, on the contrary, has experienced countless catastrophes, which have obliterated the memory of the past; and as one civilization succeeded another the men of each epoch believed the world began with them. They were late in learning the alphabet and found the lesson difficult; for those who would assign the earliest date to its use pride themselves on having learnt it from the Phoenicians and Cadmus.

Josephus, *Against Apion* 1.10–11

This kind of catastrophe complements the stories of the destruction of texts described in the Peisistratus legend of the Scholia to Dionysius Thrax. Josephus derives this information from the story of the destruction of Atlantis described in Plato's *Timaeus*, which describes the loss of knowledge that this and other catastrophes entailed. Plato indicates that the Athenians had forgotten these events because they had not known the use of writing:

. . . οἳ πρῶτον μὲν ἕνα γῆς κατακλυσμὸν μέμνησθε πολλῶν ἔμπροσθεν γεγονότων, ἔτι δὲ τὸ κάλλιστον καὶ ἄριστον γένος ἐπ' ἀνθρώπους ἐν τῇ χώρᾳ παρ' ὑμῖν οὐκ ἴστε γεγονός, ἐξ ὧν σύ τε καὶ πᾶσα ἡ πόλις ἔστιν τὰ νῦν ὑμῶν, περιλειφθέντος ποτὲ σπέρματος βραχέος, ἀλλ' ὑμᾶς λέληθεν διὰ τὸ τοὺς περιγενομένους ἐπὶ πολλὰς γενεὰς γράμμασιν τελευτᾶν ἀφώνους.

To begin with, your people remember only one deluge, though there were many earlier; and moreover you do not know the bravest and noblest race in the world once lived in your country. From a small remnant of their seed you and all your fellow-citizens are derived; but you know nothing of it because the survivors for many generations died leaving no word in writing.

Plato, *Timaeus* 23b–c, trans. Cornford

In Plato's account, the Athenians have their population and government destroyed as well as their high level of civilization. Not surprisingly, Josephus employs this story in a manner that is critical of the Greeks and their lack of respect for historical records.

Josephus goes on to question whether the participants in the Trojan War knew the alphabet:

οὐ μὴν οὐδὲ ἄπω ἐκείνου τοῦ χρόνου δύναιτό τις ἂν δεῖξαι σωζομένην ἀναγραφὴν οὔτ' ἐν ἱεροῖς οὔτ' ἐν δημοσίοις ἀναθήμασιν. ὅπου γε καὶ περὶ τῶν ἐπὶ Τροίαν τοσούτοις ἔτεσι στρατευσάντων ὕστερον πολλὴ γέγονεν ἀπορία τε καὶ ζήτησις, ε γράμμασιν ἐχρῶντο, καὶ τἀληθὲς ἐπικρατεῖ μᾶλλον περὶ τοῦ τὴν νῦν οὖσαν τῶν γραμμάτων χρῆσιν ἐκείνους ἀγνοεῖν. ὅλως δὲ παρὰ τοῖς Ἕλλησιν οὐδὲν ὁμολογούμενον εὑρίσκεται γράμμα τῆς Ὁμήρου ποιήσεως πρεσβύτερον. οὗτος δὲ καὶ τῶν Τρωϊκῶν ὕστερος φαίνεται γενόμενος, καί φασιν οὐδὲ τοῦτον ἐν γράμμασι τὴν αὑτοῦ ποίησιν καταλιπεῖν, ἀλλὰ διαμνημονευομένην ἐκ τῶν ᾀσμάτων ὕστερον συντεθῆναι καὶ διὰ τοῦτο πολλὰς ἐν αὐτῇ σχεῖν τὰς διαφωνίας.

Even of that date [i.e. the time of Cadmus] no record, preserved either in temples or on public monuments, could now be produced; seeing that it is a highly controversial and disputed question whether even those who took part in the Trojan campaign so many years later made use of letters, and the true and prevalent view is rather that they were ignorant of the present-day mode of writing. Throughout the whole range of Greek literature no undisputed work is found more ancient than the poetry of Homer. His date, however, is clearly later than the Trojan War; and even he did not bequeath his poems in writing . . .

Josephus, *Against Apion* 1.11–12

The reason for the scholarly confusion regarding Josephus' statement about Homer not handing down his poems in writing derives from a misinterpretation of this passage: it was assumed Josephus was using Homeric transmission as evidence for the *ignorance* of alphabetic writing during this period, when in fact he is arguing that *the Greeks do not revere written records*. He cites the scholarly consensus of his time: the Greeks possessed the technology of writing, and had the capability to record what they wished. That this consensus derives from Alexandrian Homeric scholars is verified by a passage from the A Scholia (considered to be a repository for Aristarchian interpretations likely deriving from Alexandria). This passage describes the *sêmata lugra* 'baleful signs' of the Bellerophontes story in *Iliad* Book 6 as pictures or pictograms, rejecting the view that they should be interpreted as letters (A Scholia to *Iliad* 6.169).[30] Thus, the Alexandrians maintained that the alphabet was not known by the generation of Bellerophontes, who lived before the Trojan War, even if these pictograms were clearly able to state, "kill the bearer of this message." However, the Alexandrians also believed that Homer lived some 70 years after the Trojan War and after the alphabet had been borrowed, a fact that Josephus also assumes here. In short: according to Josephus, Homer's failure to pass on a written text even after the introduction of alphabetic writing resulted from the Greeks' lack of respect for record-keeping and textual preservation. Josephus does not claim that Homer had not written down his poems.

## The Idea of a Succession of the Prophets

Because of its relevance for the discussion of when the canon was closed, the statement of Josephus regarding the set number of books in the Hebrew Bible and the failure of the succession of prophets following the time of Artaxerxes has elicited an astounding degree of attention from scholars.

καὶ τούτων πέντε μέν ἐστι Μωυσέως, ἃ τούς τε νόμους περιέχει καὶ τὴν ἀπ' ἀνθρωπογονίας παράδοσιν μέχρι τῆς αὐτοῦ τελευτῆς· οὗτος ὁ χρόνος ἀπολείπει τρισχιλίων ὀλίγῳ ἐτῶν. ἀπὸ δὲ τῆς Μωυσέως

τελευτῆς μέχρι τῆς ᾿Αρταξέρξου τοῦ μετὰ Ξέρξην Περσῶν βασιλέως
οἱ μετὰ Μωυσῆν προφῆται τὰ κατ᾿ αὐτοὺς πραχθέντα συνέγραψαν
ἐν τρισὶ καὶ δέκα βιβλίοις· αἱ δὲ λοιπαὶ τέσσαρες ὕμνους εἰς τὸν θεὸν
καὶ τοῖς ἀνθρώποις ὑποθήκας τοῦ βίου περιέχουσιν. ἀπὸ δὲ
᾿Αρταξέρξου μέχρι τοῦ καθ᾿ ἡμᾶς χρόνου γέγραπται μὲν ἕκαστα,
πίστεως δ᾿ οὐχ ὁμοίας ἠξίωται τοῖς πρὸ αὐτῶν διὰ τὸ μὴ γενέσθαι
τὴν τῶν προφητῶν ἀκριβῆ διαδοχήν.

Of these [our 22 books], five are the books of Moses, comprising
the laws and the traditional history from the birth of man down to
Moses' death. This period falls only a little short of 3,000 years.
From the death of Moses down to Artaxerxes who followed Xerxes
as king of Persia, the prophets after Moses wrote the events of
their own times in thirteen books. The remaining four books contain hymns to God and precepts for the conduct of human life.
From Artaxerxes down to our own time, the complete history has
been written, but has not been deemed worthy of like trust with
the earlier records, because of the absence of an exact succession
(*diadokhê*) of the prophets.

Josephus, *Against Apion* 1.39–42

Josephus' statement — "From Artaxerxes down to our own time,
the complete history has been written, but has not been deemed
worthy of like trust with the earlier records" — presumably accords
with the state of the corpus of biblical writings in the first century
C.E.[31] This corpus would have included a fixed number of texts, but
not apocryphal works of history such as 1 and 2 Maccabees. Because "the proof of historical veracity is universal agreement in the
description, oral or written, of the same events," and because
the Apocrypha are not included in the same category of texts as the
books written down prior to the time of Artaxerxes, Josephus concludes that they are not worthy of equal trust.

There have been two scholarly perspectives on the origins of
this scheme. The first claim is that Josephus' idea of a succession
of prophets resembles the Jewish tradition describing the chain of
transmission of a tradition of the fathers, otherwise referred to as
the Oral Torah. It has even been suggested that the expression "the
*diadokhê* of the prophets" derives from an Aramaic expression, al-

though it is unattested.[32] The idea of "the tradition of the fathers" is most clearly articulated in a Mishnaic work that stands among the earliest of the writings in this legal corpus. The tractate Pirke Aboth "Sayings of the Fathers," a collection of proverbs and wise utterances, begins with the following statement about the succession of the deliverance of Torah from Moses down to the great rabbis Hillel and Shammai:

משה קבל תורה מסיני. ומסרה ליהושע. ויהושע לזקנים. וזקנים לנביאים. ונביאים מסרוה לאנשי כנסת

הגדולה. הם אמרו שלשה דברים. הוו מתונים בדין. והעמידו תלמידים הרבה. ועשו סיג לתורה:

> Moses received Torah from Sinai and delivered it to Joshua, and Joshua to the Elders, and the Elders to the Prophets, and the Prophets delivered it to the Men of the Great Synagogue. These said three things: Be deliberate in judging, and raise up many disciples, and make a hedge for the Torah.
>
> M. Pirke Aboth 1.1

The passage from Aboth details the chain of succession, beginning with Moses and ending (in a portion of the text not quoted) with the great rabbis. The handing down of "Torah" is meant to refer to the Oral Law. This process differs from the charge of the prophets according to Josephus — to record the history of Israel as they witnessed it. As I will argue, Josephus' understanding of a *diadokhê* of the prophets is not analogous to the transmission presented here.

Elias Bickerman noted that Josephus utilizes "succession" as a way of understanding the transmission of authority from one prophet to the next, in contradistinction to the Bible itself, which did not concern itself with such matters.[33] Comparing Josephus' statement to M. Pirke Aboth 1.1, Bickerman finds that professorial filiation is described as if it were a genetic lineage connecting ancestors to descendants.[34] The Aboth lineage, beginning with Moses and Joshua and ending with the Houses of Hillel and Shammai (schools of rabbinic interpreters claiming filiation of Hillel and Shammai), was established with the intention of ratifying the authority of Hillel and Shammai within this tradition.

Bickerman traces the substitution of a notion of professorial lineage for natural filiation, and concludes that this practice originates in the Greek academies (those of Plato, Aristotle, Epicurus, and Zeno) beginning in the fifth century B.C.E. As is clear from the writings of Diogenes Laertius, the author of one of the most important ancient works about ancient Greek philosophy that survives today, the Greeks arranged famous philosophers by schools and by the principle of *diadokhê* 'succession'. This amounted to a chronological focus that traced lines of philosophical development from teacher to pupil. Each founder designated an heir to carry on his teaching (and thus, Plato was succeeded by Speusippus, followed by Xenocrates and Polemon, while Aristotle was succeeded by Theophrastus, etc.). The word *diadokhoi* 'successors' was employed by the Greeks to refer to the professorial lineage of the heads of these schools. In imitation of this procedure, both Josephus and Aboth appeal to a lineage of "professors" that leads back to Moses, *fons et origo* of Jewish wisdom, as Bickerman puts it. Bickerman also sees the rabbinic "houses" of Hillel and Shammai as equivalents to these schools. By describing them as "houses," the rabbinic tradition lends these schools the legitimacy of Greek educational institutions.[35] The comparison between the notion of succession in the Greek schools and that of the rabbinic tradition is indeed enlightening, and helps explain this tradition's portrayal of the intellectual lineage of the schools of Hillel and Shammai (especially in Mishnah Pirke Aboth). The Greek parallels are also instructive in evaluating the significance of the textual transmission of the Mishnah and its oral commentaries. As Saul Lieberman has explained, the "publication" of the Mishnah was achieved without the use of writing, and was transmitted by the rote memorization accomplished by the Tannaim.[36] These individuals were, in effect, living books, whose function was to recite (the more mindlessly, the better), rather than explicate. In this context, the distinction between the schools of Hillel and Shammai in some respect included a battle over which editions of the Mishnah were to be considered binding.[37] Lieberman draws a parallel between the role of the Tannaim and the Homeric rhapsodes, who performed versions of the epics and expounded upon them in accompanying oral commentaries (*hupomnêmata*). In a later incarnation of this process, versions of the "texts" of Homer, together with commentary and notes (*hupomnêmata*), could be attributed to scholars like Aristotle, and were promulgated in his name. If Lieberman is correct, the Mishnahs of Hillel and of Shammai were very much like the Homer of Aristotle.[38]

But while the comparison with the Greek schools satisfies as an explanation for the transmission of the Mishnah, it is not as applicable to the use of *diadokhê* in Josephus to refer to written scriptures. Despite Bickerman's claim, Josephus does not make the notion of succession figurative in a way precisely analogous to the professorial notion of succession. Nor does he admit to the existence of competing manuscript versions of scripture, although recent research has discovered three manuscript families of the Hebrew Bible in existence during the time of Josephus.[39]

There is crucial difference between the *diadokhê* of the prophets and the *diadokhê* of the fathers. The fathers handed down the oral law, which would later be textualized in the Mishnah and the Talmud. In contrast, the object handed down by the *diadokhê* of the prophets was the *dispensation* to record events in authoritative *written* documents — the books of the Bible.

The second theory about Josephus' use of the expression "succession of prophets" is aptly summarized by Rebecca Gray:

> In fact, the theory of a continuous prophetic succession seems to be *derived from* the existence of such a set of writings, in something like the following way: Josephus believed that only prophets, inspired by God, were capable of writing perfectly accurate history; there existed what he regarded as perfectly accurate histories for each successive period from Moses to Artaxerxes; therefore, he concluded, there must have been a prophet in each successive generation throughout this period who recorded the history of his own day.[40]

Gray's argument is that Josephus is not a valid witness for the process of authorization of some biblical books as opposed to others, because his observations are extrapolated from a pre-existing canon. I disagree with Gray's interpretation of the value of Josephus on the question of the state of the canon, although her research on the specificity of Josephus' prophetic vocabulary is indispensable.[41] As I will argue, Josephus did not derive his notion of continuous prophetic succession from the biblical texts themselves, no more than he found anything to be admired in the Pharisaic (and later rabbinic) ideology of the traditions of the fathers and the Oral Torah. Instead, Josephus' description of a succession of prophets derives from a conceptualization of a prophetic office originating in the Jewish tradition. The theory of a continuous prophetic succession is merely the clearest articulation of a widespread Jewish belief about the textualization of the Hebrew scriptures extant during the late Second Temple period. It is formulated using a vocabulary in part derived from Plato's description of oracular revelation.

As I have suggested above, Josephus employs popular accounts of the transmission of Homer's epics as a foil for biblical textual transmission. A suggestive use of *diadokhê* in the language of the Hellenistic scholia may help explain what Josephus means. According to a scholion to Pindar's Nemean Odes, the Homeric rhapsodes belonged to a clan that traced itself by succession back to Homer himself:

"ὅθεν περ καὶ Ὁμηρίδαι ῥαπτῶν ἐπέων . . . ἀοιδοί": Ὁμηρίδας ἔλεγον τὸ μὲν ἀρχαῖον τοὺς ἀπὸ τοῦ Ὁμήρου γένους, οἳ καὶ τὴν ποίησιν αὐτοῦ <u>ἐκ διαδοχῆς</u> ᾖδον· μετὰ δὲ ταῦτα καὶ οἱ ῥαψωιδοὶ οὐκέτι τὸ γένος εἰς Ὅμηρον ἀνάγοντες ἐπιφανεῖς δὲ ἐγένοντο οἱ περὶ Κύναιθον, οὕς φασι πολλὰ τῶν ἐπῶν ποιήσαντας ἐμβαλεῖν εἰς τὴν Ὁμήρου ποίησιν. ἦν δὲ ὁ Κύναιθος τὸ γένος Χῖος, ὃς καὶ τῶν ἐπιγραφομένων Ὁμήρου ποιημάτων τὸν εἰς Ἀπόλλωνα γεγραφὼς ὕμνον ἀνατέθεικεν αὐτῶι. οὗτος οὖν ὁ Κύναιθος πρῶτος ἐν Συρακούσαις ἐραψώιδησε τὰ Ὁμήρου ἔπη κατὰ τὴν ξθ ὀλυμπιάδα (504/1), ὡς Ἱππόστρατός φησιν.

"Whence also the Homeridai, the bards of sewn-together verses, begin . . ." (Pindar, *Nemean* 2). They used to say that the Homeridai were of the lineage (*genos*) of Homer long ago, and sang his poetry <u>by succession</u> (*ek diadokhês*). Afterwards the rhapsodes, no longer clearly tracing (*anagô*) their lineage (*genos*) back to Homer, became the followers of Kynaithos, who it is said composed many of the verses and inserted them into the poetry of Homer. Kynaithos was a native of Chios, and in addition to the poems inscribed by Homer wrote the Hymn to Apollo and dedicated it to him. This Kynaithos was the first to rhapsodize the epics of Homer in Syracuse at the 58th Olympiad, as Hippostratos says.[42]

Scholia to Pindar, *Nemean* 2, Ic (=*FGrHist* 568 Hippostratus)

In this scholion, the word *diadokhê* appears to be used to clarify what is meant by the idea that a clan or *genos* can be said to have inherited Homeric epics. The use of *diadokhê* in the Pindar scholion speaks to a technical meaning. The Pindar scholion's use of the word implies a quasi-ownership of the Homeric text that is based on a principle of patrimony — that the text is handed down either as property or as a birthright from ancestor to descendant. Texts obviously cannot be handed down in genetic code; thus the phrase 'by succession' (*ek diadokhês*) implies that descendants had been repeatedly anointed to carry on the tradition, and had been taught this poetry as a special privilege of their office over the course of multiple generations. In other words, the phrase explains the claim of certain clans or families to have inherited certain texts by birthright.

The testimony of Kynaithos, found in the Pindar scholion above, has often been taken at face value. These particular individuals are thus often assumed to have been linked to each other by a genetic or quasi-genetic bond (they are Homeridai, the descendants or patriliny of Homer), and it is a given that the epics could be traced back to the individual who composed them (Homer).[43] However, new research into the question has showed that the title "Homeridai" most probably did not originate as a true patronymic. M. L. West states that there are many collective names with this ending, like the Hermokopidai (the mutilators of the Hermai), that do not imply a filial relationship (and thus there can be no question that they are the descendants or followers of a man called "Hermokopos").[44] He also questions the idea of a true genetic relationship, stating that the "title 'Homeridai' sounded as if it meant the descendants of Homer. So they told the story that the Homeridai had originally been one clan, but had subsequently admitted others who were not related."[45]

West also suggests the true origin for the name Homer: "it is conceivable that the Homeridai correspond in the same way to a

Phoenician prototype *beney 'omrim, 'sons of speakers', that is, tale-tellers as a professional class."[46] The word beney, though it literally means 'sons of', often refers to a non-genetic bond in Hebrew (e.g. beney ha-nevi'im 'members of a prophetic guild'). Homeridai would therefore be the Greek translation of this term; it was later misinterpreted in the exact way that beney 'sons of' could be misinterpreted in Hebrew. West's conclusion is that the existence of an individual named "Homer" is a fictitious extrapolation from the existence of the guild of Homeridai, which thus preceded this invention. Because the suffix -idai implied genetic filiation going back to an ancestor named in the word's root, the Homeridai were assumed to be the descendants of an imaginary individual called Homer. This individual was then credited with the poems that were the charge of the Homeridai.[47]

The stipulation that the heirs of Homer hand down the epic composed by their ancestor Homer ek diadokhês is in part a periphrastic explication of the perceived genetic link between the Homeridai and Homer. The expression emphatically restates and conceptualizes the link between a given tradent and his predecessors. It also conceptualizes the link between any given tradent and epic: if a text can be inherited in a manner that is analogous to the handing down of a title, the right to such a text takes on the characteristics of titled ownership. As such, the expression attests to a notion of rights to a text — rights that cannot be sold but only handed down from heir to heir. Finally, the expression suggests a link between textual ownership and textual accuracy. The epea 'words, epic poetry' of the Homeridai are figured as the actual words of Homer, as opposed to the words of other groups who merely claim to have Homer but cannot have inherited him.

Josephus often employs a literal notion of 'succession' as the inheritance of a title to kingship, and even more narrowly, the passing on of genetic traits. As noted above, the primary referent of diadokhê is the notion of genetic succession or paternity, and so it is useful to begin with the most literal sense of the term. Thus, Josephus writes about the descendants of Cain:

ἔτι δὲ ζῶντος Ἀδάμου Κάϊος τοὺς ἐγγόνους πονηροτάτους συνέβη γενέσθαι <u>κατὰ διαδοχὴν καὶ μίμησιν</u> ἄλλον ἄλλου χείρονα τελευτῶντα·

Thus, within Adam's lifetime, the descendants of Cain went to depths of depravity, and, <u>as a result of inheritance and imitation,</u> each ended worse than the last.

Josephus, *Antiquities* 1.66

The word *diadokhên* 'inheritance' is paired with *mimêsin* 'imitation'. This pair of terms is used to refer to a nature vs. culture distinction: *diadokhê* indicates the passing on of genes, while *mimêsis* (clearly in the sphere of culture) refers to the emulation of deeds.

What happens to the term *diadokhê* when it ceases to refer to its primary referent (that of a human lineage of ancestors and descendants) and acquires a more extended meaning? To use Josephus' own terms, what I am exploring here is a κρίσις τοῦ διαδόχου 'crisis of the *diadokhê*' (*Antiquities* 17.247). A crisis — both in the sense of a moment of critical decision and in the sense of a moment of doubt — accompanies every use of *diadokhê* in the sense of 'line of political succession' as narrated in Josephus' *Antiquities*. These crises involve a question of how to choose a new leader when the mechanism for the determination of such a leader (namely, the *diadokhê* 'succession') has broken down. In the spirit of the discussion over the meaning of Hebrew *katav* in chapter 1, the "crisis" is for us a dilemma about how to interpret the meaning of the word *diadokhê* as it applies to the prophets involved in the transmission of biblical books. It is also an exploration into the way that, for Josephus, a *diadokhê* doesn't last forever, and is eventually always in doubt. In other words, *diadokhê* is the word that is used above all in a negative situation, when there is no longer any genetic continuity to which it could apply. While its meaning denotes a presence, its usage more often than not connotes an absence — a line that is exhausted or at best unknown, a dead tradition, a severed link.

Josephus employs the term *diadokhê* to describe the regulations (*nomima*) handed down by the Pharisees through the "tradition of the fathers." As Steve Mason has shown, the reputed accuracy of Pharisaic interpretation, as well as their tradition of the fathers, is consistently impugned by Josephus throughout his works.[48] In the following passage, however, Josephus attempts to describe the philosophical school (*hairêsis*) of the Pharisees in as neutral terms as possible:

νῦν δὲ δηλῶσαι βούλομαι ὅτι νόμιμά τινα <u>παρέδοσαν</u> τῷ δήμῳ οἱ Φαρισαῖοι <u>ἐκ πατέρων διαδοχῆς</u>. ἅπερ οὐκ ἀναγέγραπται ἐν τοῖς Μωυσέος νόμοις. καὶ διὰ τοῦτο τὸ τῶν Σαδδουκαίων γένος ἐκβάλλει. λέγον ἐκεῖνα δεῖν ἡγεῖσθαι νόμιμα τὰ γεγραμμένα. <u>τὰ δ' ἐκ παραδόσεως τῶν πατέρων</u> μὴ τηρεῖν.

For the present I wish merely to explain that the Pharisees <u>had handed down</u> (*paredosan,* verb form of *paradosis*) to the people certain regulations <u>from the lineage (*diadokhê*) of the fathers</u>, which were not recorded in the Laws of Moses, for which reason they are rejected by the Sadducean group (*genos*), who hold that only those regulations should be considered valid which were written down, but that those which had been handed down <u>from the tradition (*paradosis*) of the fathers</u> need not be observed.

Josephus, Antiquities 13.297, trans. Marcus

In this passage, the word *diadokhê* is semantically parallel to *paradosis* 'tradition/traditional history'. The well-known context of this passage — the difference between the Pharisees and the Sadducees on the validity of non-scriptural tradition — allows us to specify the nature of the conception of "tradition" that is being referred to here. The unwritten *nomima* 'legal materials' which the Sadducees do not observe would in time be considered the Oral Law (*torah she-ba'al peh*). The adherence to such a body of unwritten laws and authoritative interpretations separated the Pharisees from the Sadducees, and would become the defining feature of rabbinic Judaism.

It is possible that Josephus here employs *paradosis* 'tradition' to explain why the Sadducees reject Pharisaic tradition. Meanwhile, despite his attempt at neutrality, he undercuts the Pharisees on his own behalf by showing that they lay claim to the validity of their traditions on the basis of their *diadokhê* 'succession' from the fathers. The term *diadokhê* (from *dekhomai* "receive") contrasts etymologically with *paradosis* (from *didômi* 'give'). In contrast to *diadokhê, paradosis* appears to refer to tradition handed down like a gift rather than like a bloodline or office.[49] In the above quotation, the Sadducees reject the *nomima* 'laws, regulations' of the Pharisees which have been handed down through the *paradosis* of the fathers, probably because they are unwritten, and because they do not consider that a *paradosis* 'tradition' is a trustworthy transmission device. Josephus may be implying his own criticism of the Pharisees in his use of the term *diadokhê* (succession by birthright) to describe the tradition of the fathers. In other words, it seems possible that he doubts the legitimacy of their claim that they are successors of Moses and the patriarchs. This would amount to a succession parallel to the succession of prophets, which he had already concluded was no longer certain.

The word *diadokhê* is used to refer to non-literal genetic succession in two places in Josephus' works — the passage about the prophets and the one about the traditions of the fathers touted by the Pharisees. Josephus describes the prophetic *diadokhê* as a dispensation to record events and prophecies; once it has run out (as all successions other than the bloodline of the priests eventually do in his writing), no new books can be awarded the same trust.

Can a metaphor of genetic succession accurately describe the succession of prophets? In order to answer this question, it is useful to examine Josephus' description of the *diadokhê* of priests. The succession of priests represents perhaps the only succession that is valued by Josephus as secure and unimpeachable through the course of time. The legitimacy of this succession is essential, because it stands as a seal of the authenticity of the unadulterated official manuscripts of the Hebrew scriptures, maintained in the archives of the Temple by these priests.

(1.30–1) οὐ γὰρ μόνον ἐξ ἀρχῆς ἐπὶ τούτων τοὺς ἀρίστους καὶ τῇ θεραπείᾳ τοῦ θεοῦ προσεδρεύοντας κατέστησαν. ἀλλ' ὅπως τὸ γένος τῶν ἱερέων ἄμικτον καὶ καθαρὸν διαμενεῖ προυνόησαν. δεῖ γὰρ τὸν μετέχοντα τῆς ἱερωσύνης ἐξ ὁμοεθνοῦς γυναικὸς παιδοποιεῖσθαι καὶ μὴ πρὸς χρήματα μηδὲ τὰς ἄλλας ἀποβλέπειν τιμάς. ἀλλὰ τὸ γένος ἐξετάζειν ἐκ τῶν ἀρχαίων λαμβάνοντα τὴν διαδοχὴν καὶ πολλοὺς παρεχόμενον μάρτυρας.

(1.36) τεκμήριον δὲ μέγιστον τῆς ἀκριβείας· οἱ γὰρ ἀρχιερεῖς οἱ παρ' ἡμῖν ἀπὸ δισχιλίων ἐτῶν ὀνομαστοὶ παῖδες ἐκ πατρὸς εἰσὶν ἐν ταῖς ἀναγραφαῖς.

(1.37–38) εἰκότως οὖν. μᾶλλον δὲ ἀναγκαίως. ἅτε μήτε τὸ ὑπογράφειν αὐτεξουσίου πᾶσιν ὄντος μήτε τινὸς ἐν τοῖς γραφομένοις ἐνούσης διαφωνίας, ἀλλὰ μόνον τῶν προφητῶν τὰ μὲν ἀνωτάτω καὶ παλαιότατα κατὰ τὴν ἐπίπνοιαν τὴν ἀπὸ τοῦ θεοῦ μαθόντων, τὰ δὲ καθ' αὑτοὺς ὡς ἐγένετο σαφῶς συγγραφόντων, οὐ μυριάδες βιβλίων εἰσὶ παρ' ἡμῖν ἀσυμφώνων καὶ μαχομένων . . .

(1.30–1) Not only did our ancestors in the first instance set over this business men of the highest character, devoted to the service of God, but they took precautions to ensure that the priests' lineage should be kept unadulterated and pure . . . a member of the priestly order must marry a woman of his race . . . but he must investigate her pedigree, obtaining the genealogy (*tên diadokhên*) from the archives and producing a number of witnesses . . .
(1.36) But the most convincing proof of our accuracy in the matter is that the high priests are named in the records, father to son, going back two thousand years . . .
(1.37–8) It therefore naturally, or rather necessarily, follows (seeing that with us it is not open to everybody to write the records, and that there is no discrepancy in what is written; seeing that, on the contrary, the prophets alone had this privilege, obtaining their knowledge of the most remote and ancient events according to the inspiration [*epinoia*] which they owed to God) . . . it follows that we do not possess myriads of inconsistent books, conflicting and militating against each other.

Josephus, Against Apion 1.30–38, excerpted

The prophets and the priests are contrasted here, which helps to explain the distinction between priestly *diadokhê* and prophetic *diadokhê*. In the case of the priests, genealogical succession is literalized. The legitimacy of the priestly succession is guaranteed by strict scrutiny over marriage practices, involving witnesses and ultimately the testimony of the archives themselves and the lists of names they contain. These priests were charged with the keeping of records (*anagraphai*); their lineage ensured that the manuscripts of the Hebrew scriptures remained pure, just as the scriptures demanded that their lineage remained pure.

When applied to prophets, who were called by God rather than chosen by birth, the word *diadokhê* assumes a non-literal value. However, unlike the majority of scholars who have discussed this passage, I do not assume that because it is metaphorical it represents a lack of clarity in the thought of Josephus. The metaphor 'prophetic *diadokhê*', at once opaque but apparently clear enough for scholars not to have troubled over it, is an extension of literal succession. In some way its use is analogous to the technical use of the word found in the scholion to Pindar. There, the Homeridai, the guild of rhapsodes who performed the *Iliad* and the *Odyssey,* are spoken of as having a *diadokhê.* In the Pindar scholion, the word implied a transfer of textual ownership from heir to heir; this transfer took on the qualities and validity of literal (genetic) succession, even though it was probably transferred from master to apprentice. Similarly, the succession of prophets in Josephus (as long as it lasted) had the legitimacy of the genetic continuity of priests.

Josephus thus combines several ways of thinking about guaranteeing textual accuracy. Biblical history was written down by the very people who witnessed it. As a result, the Bible is superior to the writings of Homer and Pythagoras. Moreover, the prophets are conceived of as belonging to a quasi-lineage going back to Moses, a lineage that guarantees their capacity to be faithful witnesses. Finally, the sequence of the "pure" lineage of the priests (1.30–36) guarantees the accuracy of these chronicles after they ceased to be recorded, storing them in the Temple archives and preventing them from being altered. No writings of subsequent prophets outside the succession are accorded equal treatment.

Having summarized Josephus' understanding of the succession of prophets, I return to an argument that has been raised by some scholars who have discussed Josephus' words. The argument may be stated as follows: Josephus is merely giving his own idiosyncratic position on the nature of the Hebrew scriptures, one that is derived from the scriptures themselves, rather than from a Jewish tradition. To the contrary, I propose that Josephus' notion of a prophetic succession may already be seen in the perspective on the transfer of prophetic authority present in the book of Ben Sira, both in the Hebrew original and especially in its Greek translation. In turn, Ben Sira arrives at a concept of succession by considering two examples of the transfer of prophetic authority in the Bible: the succession from Moses to Joshua, and from Elijah to Elisha. Josephus adds a twist to the tradition: the succession can be used to explain the presence and absence of texts in the Temple archives.[50] In arriving at this conclusion (ironically with the aid of the ideas of a Greek philosopher), he had succeeded in laying bare the very principles by which the canon of scriptures had been generated.

Israelite practice, as reconstructed by modern biblical scholars, confirms that "prophet" was indeed an "office," which ideally would be occupied by a single individual. When the monarchy ceased, so did the notion of a single prophetic office; but its legend may have spurred early interpreters to attempt to locate the idea of prophetic succession in the biblical text itself. Such a legend may be seen in the traditions about the earliest prophets as found in 1 and 2 Kings. The expression *beney ha-nevi'im* (found in 1 Kings 20:35, 2 Kings 2:3, 5, 7, 15; 4:1, 38; 5:22; 6:1 and 9:1) would seem to denote a sort of prophetic guild whose membership is not necessarily genetically determined. Nevertheless, its literal translation ('sons of the prophets') may have led early interpreters to consider the prophetic office as subject to a line of succession in some way analogous to that from father to son.

The clearest (and perhaps only) example of a transfer of prophetic authority recorded in the Bible is that from Elijah to Elisha. Early biblical interpreters searched for other occurrences of the type of transfer of authority so clearly exhibited in the Elijah narratives, assuming that what held true for these two prophets must have held true for every other. The transition from Moses to Joshua was an obvious candidate for the instantiation of the practice. In fact, Numbers chapter 27 (cf. Deut. 34:9) describes God directing Moses to lay his hands upon Joshua, so that he might give him "some of his authority," and that all the Israelites would obey him; his office is also validated by the Urim "before the Lord." Nevertheless, Joshua is never described as assuming a specifically prophetic office.

The text of Ben Sira, a second century B.C.E. apocryphal work composed in the sapiental mode, reveals the hermeneutic assumptions behind the idea of a prophetic succession from Moses to Joshua. Joshua is remembered in two guises — as a military leader (as is plainly evident in his role in the book of Joshua) and as a "servant of Moses in prophecy":

משרת משה בנבואה        גבור בן חיל יהושע בן נון

> Joshua son of Nun was mighty in war
> and was the servant (*mesharet*) of Moses in prophecy
>
> Ben Sira 46:1[51]

The language employed by Ben Sira is biblical; Joshua is described as the *mesharet* 'servant' of Moses in Ex. 33:11, Num. 11:28, and Joshua 1:1. In the biblical idiom, the root *š-r-t* can be used to indicate higher domestic service (e.g. Joseph) or royal officers (in late texts). However, it is also used to describe special service in worship, particularly on the part of the Levites or priests. But while Joshua is several times described as *mesharet* of Moses, this service is never qualified as being *be-nevu'a* 'in prophecy'. How did Ben Sira arrive at an understanding of the prophetic quality of Joshua's service to Moses?

The answer likely lies in Joshua 1:1. In this passage, God speaks to Joshua, described significantly as the *mesharet* of Moses:

וַיְהִי אַחֲרֵי מוֹת מֹשֶׁה עֶבֶד יְהוָה וַיֹּאמֶר יְהוָה אֶל־יְהוֹשֻׁעַ בִּן־נוּן מְשָׁרֵת מֹשֶׁה לֵאמֹר:

> After the death of Moses, servant (*'eved*) of the Lord, the Lord
> spoke to Joshua son of Nun the servant (*mesharet*) of Moses, saying:
>
> Joshua 1:1

Because this passage combines two different terms for "servant," it may have called out to interpreters like Ben Sira for explanation. Obviously Moses is not a servant of God in the same way that Joshua is the servant of Moses; not only would this offend all propriety, but the difference in the two terms apparently implied that two different types of servanthood were indicated.

Joshua also appears as the servant of Moses in a passage in Exodus:

וְדִבֶּר יְהוָה אֶל־מֹשֶׁה פָּנִים אֶל־פָּנִים כַּאֲשֶׁר יְדַבֵּר אִישׁ אֶל־רֵעֵהוּ וְשָׁב אֶל־הַמַּחֲנֶה וּמְשָׁרְתוֹ יְהוֹשֻׁעַ בִּן־נוּן נַעַר
לֹא יָמִישׁ מִתּוֹךְ הָאֹהֶל:

And the Lord spoke to Moses face to face, just as a man speaks to
his companion; and he would return to the camp; but his servant
(*mesharto*), Joshua son of Nun, did not leave the tent.

Exodus 33:11

At the very moment that Moses' face to face encounters with God
are detailed, the passage specifies the whereabouts of Joshua, again
described as Moses' *mesharet* 'servant'. Again, Joshua is being distinguished from Moses; he is not privy to Moses' conversation of
God, and was not even able to leave the tent when they would con-
verse. How then could a passage like this support the understanding that Joshua is a servant "in prophecy"?

Evidence from the midrashic tradition reveals that other Jewish interpreters had concluded that *mesharet* implied a special kind
of servant. In Bamidbar Rabbah to Numbers 12:9, Joshua's status
as *mesharet* is explicated as an indication that he had taken over
Moses' prophetic office:

ד"א ביום כלות ביום הקים אין כתיב כאן אלא ביום כלות ביום שכלו המזיקין

מן העולם ויהי ביום כלות משה וגו' הה"ד (משלי כז) נוצר תאנה יאכל פריה

וגו' מדבר ביהושע שהוא שימש את משה כמה דתימא (שמות לג) ומשרתו

יהושע בן נון נער לא ימיש מתוך האוהל למה נמשלה תורה כתאנה שרוב

האילנות הזית הגפן התמרה נלקטים כאחת והתאנה נלקטת מעט מעט וכך

התורה היום לומד מעט ולמחר הרבה לפי שאינה מתלמדת לא בשנה ולא

בשתים עליו נאמר נוצר תאנה מהו יאכל פריה של תורה מלכות ושרות

שנאמר (משלי ח) בי מלכים ימלוכו בי שרים ישרורו וכן אירע ליהושע שלא

ירשו בניו של משה מקומו אלא יהושע ירש מקומו כמה דתימא (במדבר כז)

קח לך את יהושע בן נון וגו' (משלי כז) ושומר אדוניו יכובד זה יהושע שהיה

משמש את משה ביום ובלילה כמה דתימא (שמות לב) לא ימיש מתוך האהל

ואומר (במדבר יא) אדוני משה כלאם לפיכך כבדו הקב"ה מה כבוד עשה לו

הקב"ה לפי שכך אמר ליהושע (שם כז) ולפני אלעזר הכהן יעמד ושאל לו

במשפט האורים וגו' ולפי ששמש אדוניו זכה לרוח הקודש שנא' (יהושע א)

ויהי אחרי מות משה וגו' שאין תלמוד לומר משרת משה למה נאמר לומר לך

לפי שהיה משרת משה זכה לנבואה הוי יכובד

"And it came to pass on the day that Moses had made an end."
This bears on the text, "Whoso keepeth the fig-tree shall eat the
fruit thereof; and he that waiteth on his master shall be honoured"

(Prov. 27:18), which applies to Joshua, who served (*shimesh*) Moses; as you read, "But his minister Joshua, the son of Nun, a young man, departed not out of the Tent" (Ex. 33:11). Why was the Torah likened to a fig-tree? Because most trees — the olive, the vine, the date — are picked all at once, while the fig-tree is picked little by little. It is the same with the Torah. One learns a little of it one day and more the next; for it cannot be learned all in one year or in two. Of such a man it says, "Whoso keepeth the fig-tree." What is meant by "Shall eat the fruit thereof"? The fruit of the Torah is kingly and princely rank; as is borne out by the text, "By me kings reign, and princes decree justice" (Prov. 8:15). This is what actually happened to Joshua; for it was not the sons of Moses who succeeded (*yarshu*) their father, but Joshua succeeded (*yarash*) him; as you read, "Take thee Joshua the son of Nun . . . and lay Thy hand upon him," etc. (Num. 27:18). "And he that waiteth on his master shall be honored" alludes to Joshua who ministered (*meshamesh*) to Moses by day and by night; as is proved by the text, "Joshua departed not out of the Tent" (Ex. 33:11), and by what it further says, "Joshua . . . said: My lord Moses, shut them in" (Num. 11: 28). Consequently the Holy One, blessed be He, honored him. What honor did the Holy One, blessed be He, confer upon him? He said of Joshua as follows: "He shall stand before Eleazar the priest, who shall inquire for him by the judgment of the Urim," etc. (Num. 27: 21). And because he served his master he attained to the privilege of receiving the Holy Spirit; as it says "Now it came to pass after the death of Moses . . . that the Lord spoke unto Joshua," etc. (Josh. 1:1). There was, surely, no need for Scripture to state "The minister (*mesharet*) of Moses"! What then is the purpose of the statement "The minister of Moses"? To tell you that he was awarded the privilege of prophecy because he was the minister of Moses. Thus we have explained, "Shall be honored."

Bamidbar Rabbah 12:9, trans. Slotki

The passage relates to a number of hypotheses advanced in the preceding discussion. It provides independent confirmation of the idea that scripture's description of Joshua as the *mesharet* of Moses was understood by Jewish exegetes to relate to something other than his position as Moses' manservant. Second, it reveals that early interpreters assumed Moses transferred not just his chieftain-like authority to Joshua, but the privilege of prophecy as well. Finally, it corroborates the notion of a prophetic dispensation being handed down through divine election rather than by blood, seeing as the sons of Moses might have been expected to receive the honor if human rather than divine practices had held sway. The basis for this reading seems to be the following reasoning: what does the word "servant" imply, if not that Joshua "follows after" Moses figuratively (that is, "in prophecy"), just as a servant follows his master? As Moses was felt to be more than just a master, so Joshua was interpreted as more than a simple manservant.

Other evidence that Ben Sira understands *mesharet* 'servant' as referring to a transition in prophetic authority to the office of prophet can be seen in his description of Elijah. From the perspective of later Judaism, it is obvious that the mantle of the prophet Elijah, assumed by Elisha, embodies the Jewish ideal of prophetic succession, and that Elisha's vision of Elijah's assumption into heaven in the fiery chariot validates his status. But for early biblical interpreters, a great deal of finesse was required to demonstrate that this particular transfer of authority implied similar occasions for the other prophets in the Bible.

The intricacies of this process may be traced by first examining the Hebrew of Ben Sira 48:8, the first half of which is admittedly difficult:

ונביא תחליף תחתיך     המושח מלא תשלומות

You [Elijah] are an anointer who is full of retribution
and you will appoint a prophet after you

Ben Sira 48:8[52]

This passage largely derives from an interpretation of 1 Kings 19:16:

וְאֵת יֵהוּא בֶן־נִמְשִׁי תִּמְשַׁח לְמֶלֶךְ עַל־יִשְׂרָאֵל וְאֶת־אֱלִישָׁע בֶּן־שָׁפָט מֵאָבֵל מְחוֹלָה תִּמְשַׁח לְנָבִיא תַּחְתֶּיךָ׃

You will anoint Jehu son of Nimshi as king over Israel, and Elisha son of Shaphat of Abel-meholah you will anoint as prophet after you.

The first half of the Ben Sira 48:8 may originally have read המושח
מלכי תשלומות 'You [Elijah] are one who anoints *kings* of retribution'.[53]
In any event, what is really at issue here is the second portion of the
line. Ben Sira describes the activity of Elijah as choosing or ap-
pointing rather than anointing Elisha: "you will appoint (*taḥlif*) a
prophet after you." In biblical texts, the word *taḥlif* (the Hiph'il
[causative] of חלף 'pass on or away, pass through') can mean 'substitute, i.e., cause to succeed' (cf. Isaiah 9:9). Ben Sira changes verbs
from *timshah* 'you will anoint' of 1 Kings 19:16 to *taḥlif* 'you will
cause to succeed' in order to make plain the significance of Elisha's
consecration by Elijah. According to Ben Sira, the expression
*timshah* was thus meant to imply that Elijah would instantiate his
successor in the office of prophecy, even though this transition of
authority was not accomplished by anointment with oil (the ritual
implied in the Hebrew verb ממש). Ben Sira's rephrasing of 1 Kings
19:16 was perhaps influenced by the passage a few verses later
(1 Kings 19:21), where it is stated that Elisha went after Elijah and
וישרתהו *va-yeshartehu* 'attended to him' (from the same root as *mesharet*). This would be consistent with the view already expressed
by Ben Sira, that 'serving' a prophet (or being a *mesharet* 'servant'
of a prophet) amounted to becoming his prophetic disciple.

The Greek translation of the text of Ben Sira connects the
transfer from Moses to Joshua and Elijah to Elisha by using the
term *diadokhos* 'successor' to describe the nature of the office held
by these prophets. At Ben Sira 46:1, the text states:

κραταιὸς ἐν πολέμῳ ᾽Ιησοῦς Ναυη
καὶ διάδοχὸς Μωυσῆ ἐν προφητείαις

Mighty in war is Joshua son of Nun
and the successor (*diadokhos*) of Moses in prophecies

Ben Sira 46:1

In essence, the Greek translation has attempted to clarify the notion
of "servant of Moses in prophecy" by eliminating the metaphor "servant" altogether. The notion of Joshua as prophetic successor, implicit in the Hebrew original of Ben Sira, achieves its ultimate form

here in the Greek. The grandson's translation is in all likelihood the source of Josephus' use of the term *diadokhos* to describe Joshua:

Μωυσῆς δὲ γηραιὸς ἤδη τυγχάνων διάδοχον ἑαυτοῦ Ἰησοῦν καθίστησιν ἐπί τε ταῖς προφητείαις καὶ στρατηγὸν εἴ που δεήσειε γενησόμενον, κελεύσαντος καὶ τοῦ θεοῦ τούτῳ τὴν προστασίαν ἐπιτρέψαι τῶν πραγμάτων. ὁ δὲ Ἰησοῦς πᾶσαν ἐπεπαίδευτο τὴν περὶ τοὺς νόμους παιδείαν καὶ τὸ θεῖον Μωυσέος ἐκδιδάξαντος.

Moses, already advanced in years, now appointed Joshua as his successor (*diadokhos*) both in his prophetical functions and as commander-in-chief, whensoever the need should arise, under orders from God himself to entrust the direction of affairs to him. Joshua had already received a thorough training in the laws and in the divine (*to theion*) under the tutelage of Moses.

Josephus, *Antiquities* 4.165, trans. Thackeray

Soon after this passage, Josephus states that Joshua "prophesied" (*proephêteuse*) in the presence of Moses (*Antiquities* 4.311). Neither idea is to be found in scripture; nevertheless, Ben Sira, his grandson, and Josephus alike promoted the concept of Joshua as the prophetic successor of Moses.

The Greek translation of Ben Sira 48:8 was also influential in the way the abstract concept of succession (*diadokhê*) would be realized in Josephus. The translation speaks of Elijah as establishing multiple prophetic successors, although this is not a feature of the Hebrew original:

ὁ χρίων βασιλεῖς εἰς ἀνταπόδομα
καὶ προφήτας διαδόχους μετ᾽ αὐτόν

You [Elijah] are one who anoints kings to inflict retribution,
And prophets as successors after him [Elisha]

Ben Sira 48:8

The Greek has returned to the term "anoint" (from 1 Kings 19:16 תִּמְשַׁח לְנָבִיא תַּחְתֶּיךָ 'you will anoint [Elisha] (*timshaḥ*) as prophet after you'), despite the fact that Ben Sira had employed *taḥlif* 'choose as successor'. But again, it has made the notion of succession explicit in the text, adding to the Hebrew original in a significant way.

The pluralization of both *prophêtas* 'prophets' and *diadokhous* 'successors' in the Greek translation also represents an attempt to amplify on the significance of the transfer of authority from Elijah to Elisha. The plural specifies that Elijah did not just choose Elisha, but instituted a process whereby prophetic successors would thereafter be chosen by subsequent prophets. The change in person ('after him' rather than 'after you', implying after Elisha) similarly pictures Elijah as instituting a succession rather than choosing a single successor.[54]

Josephus' conception of a prophetic succession thus clearly derives from Ben Sira, and was highly influenced by the Greek version of Ben Sira in particular. While it is difficult to say for sure, the idea that prophets had succeeded one another may have been widespread. It seems clear, at least, that the idea of Joshua and Elisha as successors to Moses and Elijah was not the invention of Josephus.

It is also likely that Josephus developed his idea of "the succession of prophets" under the influence of a description of prophecy from Plato's *Timacus*, a text referred to several times in *Against Apion*. We have seen in chapter 2 that Philo of Alexandria made use of the vocabulary of the *Timaeus* to expound on the Bible using the language of Greek philosophy. In particular, Philo utilized Plato's comments on the process of oracular divination in order to explain the divine revelation to Moses at Sinai.[55] I argue here that Josephus, approaching the problem of the qualitative difference between the Bible and the less sacred (apocryphal) works, found that the Jewish tradition's approach to the written records of the prophets was fully consistent with Plato's description of the oracle at Delphi, at which had been established a "lineage (*genos*) of declarers (*prophêtês* pl.) as judges (*kritês* pl.) over the inspired (*entheos* pl.) mantic utterances (*manteia* pl.)." I would suggest that Josephus employed Plato's description in order to make sense of the difference between justly accredited writings and unauthoritative writings in the Jewish tradition. In so doing, he affirmed the then current Jewish belief that the authoritativeness of a given book of the Bible could only be evaluated by consideration of the status of its human agent. Plato's formulation is a further aid in deciphering Josephus' use of words like *diadokhê* 'lineage' and *prophêtês* 'prophet'. Moreover, I would suggest that Plato's notion of prophets as "judges (*kritês* pl.) over inspired mantic utterances" is the essence of Josephus' formulation of the relationship between Israelite prophets and the canonization of scripture.

The significance of Plato's *Timaeus* for Greek education in the time of Josephus was such that it had an unparalleled impact on the thought of Jews like Philo and Josephus. David Runia writes:

> It would be a serious mistake, however, to conclude that the *Timaeus* was only read and studied by professional philosophers or students of philosophy. The very fact that it was regarded as the "Platonists' Bible" meant that its influence inevitably filtered down to men of letters and even those who had received only a smattering of learning. Indeed the *Timaeus* was the only Greek prose work that up to the third century A.D. every educated man could be assumed to have read. This is well illustrated by the citations and allusions in early Christian writers such as Clement of Rome, Athenagoras, Justin, Theophilus, the author of the *Cohortatio ad Graecos*, Minucius Felix, few of whom one would wish to describe as genuine students of philosophy.[56]

It is in the context of the definitive statement on the nature of prophetic authority in the most widely read Greek prose text of antiquity that Josephus' words on biblical prophets must be placed. As I argued above, Josephus cites evidence about Greek civilization derived from the *Timaeus* several times in *Against Apion;* what is new here is that the language of the *Timaeus* is employed by Josephus to help articulate Jewish doctrine.

The passage from the *Timaeus* in question is one of the few places in surviving Greek literature in which the oracular experience is described in detail. I quote the entire passage here:

ἱκανὸν δὲ σημεῖον ὡς μαντικὴν ἀφροσύνῃ θεὸς ἀνθρωπίνῃ δέδωκεν· οὐδεὶς γὰρ ἔννους ἐφάπτεται μαντικῆς ἐνθέου καὶ ἀληθοῦς, ἀλλ' ἢ καθ' ὕπνον τὴν τῆς φρονήσεως πεδηθεὶς δύναμιν ἢ διὰ νόσον, ἢ διά τινα ἐνθουσιασμὸν παραλλάξας. ἀλλὰ συννοῆσαι μὲν ἔμφρονος τά

τε ῥηθέντα ἀναμνησθέντα ὄναρ ἢ ὕπαρ ὑπὸ τῆς μαντικῆς τε καὶ
ἐνθουσιαστικῆς φύσεως, καὶ ὅσα ἂν φαντάσματα ὀφθῇ, πάντα
λογισμῷ διελέσθαι ὅπῃ τι σημαίνει καὶ ὅτῳ μέλλοντος ἢ παρελθόντος
ἢ παρόντος κακοῦ ἢ ἀγαθοῦ· τοῦ δὲ μανέντος ἔτι τε ἐν τούτῳ
μένοντος οὐκ ἔργον τὰ φανέντα καὶ φωνηθέντα ὑφ' ἑαυτοῦ κρίνειν,
ἀλλ' εὖ καὶ πάλαι λέγεται τὸ πράττειν καὶ γνῶναι τά τε αὑτοῦ καὶ
ἑαυτὸν σώφρονι μόνῳ προσήκειν. ὅθεν δὴ καὶ τὸ τῶν προφητῶν
γένος ἐπὶ ταῖς ἐνθέοις μαντείαις κριτὰς ἐπικαθιστάναι νόμος· οὓς
μάντεις αὐτοὺς ὀνομάζουσίν τινες, τὸ πᾶν ἠγνοηκότες ὅτι τῆς δι'
αἰνιγμῶν οὗτοι φήμης καὶ φαντάσεως ὑποκριταί, καὶ οὔτι μάντεις,
προφῆται δὲ μαντευομένων δικαιότατα ὀνομάζοιντ' ἄν.

That divination is the gift of heaven to human unwisdom we have
good reason to believe, in that no man in his normal senses deals
in true and inspired divination, but only when the power of understanding is fettered in sleep or he is distraught by some disor-
der or, it may be, by divine possession. It is for the man in his
ordinary senses to recall and construe the utterances, in dream or
in waking life, of divination or possession, and by reflection to
make out in what manner and to whom all the visions of the seer
betoken some good or ill, past, present, or to come. When a man
has fallen into frenzy and is still in that condition, it is not for him
to determine the meaning of his own visions and utterances;
rather the old saying is true, that only the sound in mind can at-
tend to his own concerns and know himself. Hence it is the custom to appoint the lineage of declarers to be judges over the
inspired mantic utterances. These are themselves given the name
of diviners by some who are quite unaware that they are exposi-
tors of riddling oracle or vision and best deserve to be called, not
diviners, but spokesmen of those who practice divination.

Plato, Timaeus 71e–72b, trans. Cornford

Plato separates the act of divination into two separate realms — the
mantic and the prophetic. The point here is that "prophecy" is not
really what many have thought it to be, for they have conflated divination itself and its poetic embodiment in hexameters into a single
event governed by a single individual.

Plato's concern in this passage is to stress the distinction between the *prophêtai*, these 'judges of inspired mantic utterances', and the *mantis*, a man who has fallen into a frenzy and who could not determine the meaning of his own visions and utterances. The key for our purposes here is that prophets were thought of as having a *genos* 'lineage' in this *locus classicus* of Greek theorization of the pragmatics of oracular performance. The idea of a prophetic *genos* will help us understand why Josephus chose to imagine that biblical prophets had a *diadokhê*.

It would appear that Plato's idea of a *genos* 'lineage' of unrelated individuals who prophesize is in accord with other Greek descriptions of the activity of prophets. The T Scholia to Homer, for example, preserve a description of the *genos* of priests of Zeus at Dodona, reputedly the oldest Greek oracle:

⟨Σελλοί⟩ "'Ελλοί", ἀπὸ 'Ελλοῦ τοῦ Θεσσαλοῦ. οὕτω δὲ ὁ ποιητὴς καὶ οἱ παλαιοί. τινὲς δὲ Σελλοί, ἀπὸ Σελλήεντος τοῦ ποταμοῦ, ὃς νῦν †ως καλῶσ† καλεῖται. ἐὰν δὲ εἴπωμεν Σελλοί, ἔσονται περὶ πᾶσαν τὴν Δωδώνην οἰκοῦντες, οὐ περὶ τὸ τέμενος τοῦ θεοῦ· καὶ βέλτιον· <u>ἐν Δωδώνῃ γὰρ τὸ γένος ἐστὶ τῶν ἐρέων τοῦ Διὸς κατὰ διαδοχήν</u>. κοινὸν δὲ τοῖς πᾶσι 'Έλλησι τὸ ἐνταῦθα ἱερόν. <u>σημειωτέον ὅτι ἄνδρας φησὶν αὐτόθι προφητεύειν</u>.

<Selloi> "Helloi," from Hellos of Thessaly; so it was called by the poet and the ancients. Some use the term Selloi, from the river Sellêes, as it is now called. If we say Selloi, this refers to those who inhabit the entire Dodona, not merely the sacred precinct of the god. And better: <u>in the Dodona is the tribe (*genos*) of the priests of Zeus by succession (*kata diadokhên*)</u>. The sanctuary there is held in common by all Greeks. <u>One should note that men claim to prophesize (*prophêteuein*) in that place</u>.

T Scholia to *Iliad* 16.234

It would appear that this *genos* of priests is maintained by succession (*kata diadokhên*) rather than by familial descent. What is especially remarkable about this description is the fact that these priests claim to prophesize. Not only does this accord with Plato's description of the prophets at Delphi, but it also reveals that the idea of a *diadokhê* 'succession' was likely implicit in Plato's notion of the *genos* of prophets.

As Gray's research has shown, Josephus employs the term *prophêtês* even in his history of the period after Artaxerxes; in fact, Josephus at one point describes himself as a prophet. According to Josephus, prophecy did not die out after the time of Artaxerxes, as was claimed by later rabbinic interpreters. Rather, the *diadokhê* 'succession' of prophets, or to use the Platonic term, the *genos* 'lineage' of prophets, was no longer capable of being accurately determined. I would suggest that Josephus replaced Plato's word *genos* with *diadokhê*, a term that was integral to a perhaps widespread Jewish conceptualization of the Israelite prophets, as represented in the Greek translation of Ben Sira. Whereas Plato's term *genos* implied 'clan', 'race', or even 'tribe' (Josephus even uses *genos* to describe the Sadducean group), the word *diadokhê* could now be understood as the Jewish divinely sanctioned transfer of prophetic authority. Josephus takes Plato's rules for proper oracular textualization seriously, because it appears to accord with Jewish descriptions of the prophetic succession such as found in the Greek translation of Ben Sira. The influence of the Platonic description of oracular utterance may also be seen in Josephus' claim that Moses composed his last speech to the Israelites in hexameters — the meter in which the Delphic *prophêtai* 'spokesmen' verbalized the divine revelations. Josephus' explanation for the lack of trust in late texts recorded by individuals who lived after the time of Artaxerxes may best be explained by considering the function of prophets in Plato's terms — to serve as "judges over the inspired utterances." Wasn't this what the Jewish tradition had always said about the prophets — that they vouched for the legitimacy of the histories and utterances they had copied out? Both Plato's notion of the *genos* 'tribe' of prophets and the metaphor of succession provided Josephus with a powerful metaphor to describe the end of scriptural authority — the end of a bloodline. This element, at least, was new, for Jewish tradition does not appear to have described the end of its prophecies in such a way prior to Josephus.

To summarize: for ancient Greek scholars of literature since Plato, the idea of a *genos* or *diadokhê* constituted a way of thinking about the passing down of texts (Homeric epics, the oracles of Delphi and the Dodona) by social groups (the Homeridai, prophets, priests). The terms *genos* and *diadokhê* indicated the passing down of rights to these texts, but where *genos* attributes this to a literal bloodline, *diadokhê* indicates election and, in the case of the prophets, a metaphorical bloodline. Both the Pindar scholion and Josephus agree that *diadokhê* refers to the passing down of textual rights from successor to successor. But the nature of these textual rights differs in both traditions. For the Greek scholiast to the Pindaric Ode, these rights amount to ownership rights over Homer. For Josephus, they consist of the privilege to record historical events and prophetic utterances in writing. On another level, *diadokhê* refers to the works themselves. The transmitters of these traditions are being described as if they were a line of priests or prophets; yet the metaphor attests to the purity of the tradition, not to the gene pool of the transmitters.

The object handed down by the *diadokhê* of the prophets was the *dispensation* to record events and prophetic utterances in authoritative *written* documents — the books of the Bible. For Josephus at least, the limits of the canon of scriptures are explained by the withdrawal of this dispensation, which could no longer be granted when the "paternity" of the prophets became unsure. This dispensation constitutes a singular moment of authorship among the Jews, as limited as this notion of authorship was. No individual could be granted a similar dispensation thereafter, even though he should himself be a prophet, and even if he (like Josephus) could write an accurate account without personal embellishment and without contradicting the "justly accredited" works of the prophets before him.

As I have discussed, the key difference between Jewish letters and the traditions of the Greeks, according to Josephus, was that the Jews wrote down events as they occurred, and did not attempt to contradict the information accurately recorded in their inviolable archives. The Greeks, in contrast, embellished their accounts for personal acclaim, did not properly preserve their traditions and history in writing, and relied on the unreliable evidence of oral performance. It now seems certain that Josephus did not value the Pharisaic traditions of the fathers, the equivalent to the rabbinic *torah she-ba'al peh,* the Oral Torah revealed on Mt. Sinai to Moses and passed down through a channel of prophets and later wise men, for similar reasons. Josephus thus acknowledges a succession of prophets up to a certain date, together with the succession of priests who maintain the archives, even as he discounts the succession of the fathers and the validity of oral tradition in any form.

## The Closing of the Canon of the Hebrew Bible

The question of the date of the settling of the canon of the Hebrew Bible is as much of an old chestnut as can be found in biblical studies. While fully cognizant of the pitfalls involved in re-opening this question, I hope to provide a different approach, in order to decipher one of the most important statements about the status of the Hebrew Bible in pre-rabbinic times. This approach is informed by the anthropological study of ritual as formulated by Maurice Bloch; it also focuses on the prophetic scribe responsible for textualization. As I will argue, early biblical interpreters considered the status of the individual credited with textualizing a work as an all-important gauge of scriptural legitimacy.

Bloch points out that there is a need to evaluate the historical causation resulting in symbolic formations (such as "ritual" or even "canon"), but from a diachronic rather than synchronic perspective:

On a short time-scale it is quite clear that the social does not bring about the symbolic, and to suggest that it does, as is done in functionalist theories, is, as [Victor] Turner clearly sees, wrong. This does not mean, however, that the establishment of a causative link between the history of the social formation and the ritual cannot be attempted. It is simply that the connection cannot be understood either synchronically, or in the very short term. Indeed, this book will show that for the Merina circumcision ritual, two hundred years are quite insufficient for doing more than beginning to understand the nature of determination. The reason is not far to seek. People act in terms of what they know and what they know is the product of their historically constructed culture. *They may transform and change this culture but they do not do it from a zero starting base.* Because of this the study of determination must be not a study of initial creation, but of the principles of transformation.[57]

Unfortunately, the process of canon formation has often been approached as a study of its initial genesis, rather than a study of the principles of its transformation. Josephus is a witness for a moment in the transformation of a set of texts on their journey to eventual canonization under the auspices of a formalized Jewish (or Christian) religion. It is also possible that he is a player in the process, or that he is describing the actions of others that played a role in the evolving status of the texts belonging to the Hebrew scriptures.

A study of Josephus' testimony, according to the principles outlined by Bloch, will not be helpful in ascertaining the date of canon formation, if only because the notion of "canon" lies in the realm of the symbolic. The critique of formalism and Marxism in the field of anthropology has led to the firm conclusion that the social cannot determine symbolic formations in the short term. In other words, a single moment or a single agent is incapable of originating a society's complex symbolic formations. Nevertheless, as Bloch's method outlines, an approach that addresses multiple moments in the interaction between the social and the symbolic diachronically will have the opportunity to articulate the principles of transformation of symbolic formations. The study of Josephus' conceptualization of a fixed body of Hebrew writings and his reasons for viewing them as sacred reveals one such historical moment, as well as the principles of the transformation of this collection of texts into a canon.

The long-held dispute over "open" and "closed" canons in part results from a logical conundrum inherent to the very notion of the canon.[58] "Closed" and "open" are academic shorthand for an early or late date for the closing of the biblical canon. That is, the "open" canon position claims that the canon was *finally, once and for all* decided only at the end of the first century c.e. According to this view, the canon was decided by an all-powerful rabbinic council (the so-called Council of Yavne); at this council, it is claimed that biblical works were both chosen and rejected (Ben Sira or Ecclesiasticus is one work which these critics consider to have been rejected by the rabbis).[59] The "closed" position argues rather that the canon of the Hebrew scriptures as a whole had already been *finally, once and for all* settled as early as the second century B.C.E. Scholars articulating both views promote much earlier dates for the closing of the Torah and Prophets, portions of scripture that were composed at earlier dates.

The idea of an "open canon" attributes a sense of meaning to the choice of which texts were to be included in the Bible. This choice represents a historical determinability, a comprehensibility achievable by humans, as well as an answer to the question "why are *these books in particular* present in the Bible?" Those of the "closed" side reject the sense of strong human agency involved in such a process; the "closed" side wants the Bible to be "closed" before human consciousness almost, before the advent of the distinct rabbinic personalities with the human implications that name and personality entail. Moreover, the "closed" side seeks to go back to the first, *originary moment* of finality (the formation of the canon), to the moment when finality was first and definitively set. The "open" side recognizes that finality can only possibly be determined by the *last* moment at which it was determined, hence its emphasis on statements about the Hebrew writings found in the Talmud.

If there really was a debate over the sacredness of biblical books at the Council or Academy of Yavne, this would indicate that the question was still open in some respects at least. However, there is much evidence that such a council did not make significant decisions about biblical books. It should be noted that Bloch's cross-cultural studies suggest that it would be unparalleled for a council of religious leaders to countermand tradition and the assumptions of earlier authorities on matters relating to the very basis of their religious system.

But the "closed" position is also somewhat misleading. It appears that the priests who collected scriptures and safeguarded them in the Temple *thought* the canon had been closed since the time of Artaxerxes and the generation that had experienced the exile. (On this point, I would argue that Josephus represents the prevailing view in Jewish society for centuries prior to his own time.) Thus the "closed" position does not adequately describe the process by which the elite of this society stopped including works in the official collection of scriptures. The archivists throughout the Second Temple period may not have known that scriptural books in their collection postdated Artaxerxes. If any "newly discovered" works were included in the collection, it was likely because they thought such writings derived from prophets of Artaxerxes' time or before.

According to scholars of the "closed" position, Judah Maccabee was the individual who may have closed the canon.[60] However, it is likely that Judah did not exactly decide to stop including "newly discovered" works that were thought to derive from the eligible prophets. As I will discuss below, Judah (or at least, the individual who recorded his deeds in 2 Maccabees) believed that Nehemiah had been the last to add to the collection. If this hypothesis is accurate, Judah and his contemporaries did not know he himself had closed the canon, because it was thought that Nehemiah had already done so.

The "closed" position must also confront evidence from Josephus and elsewhere indicating that Jewish exegetes did not view each and every biblical book or all three sections of the collection with equal reverence until the time of the rabbis. The relative authority of individual scriptures, as well as the extent to which scripture was viewed as inspired, continued to evolve during the rabbinic period.

Canonization cannot be seen from the perspective of "the beginning of the end" versus "the end of the end," but rather as a theological conundrum that escapes analysis. There are moments of decision, but these are always moments of impotency, times when previous decisions are unassailable. To take a significant example, it has been claimed that the rabbis' declaration that Ben Sira is not inspired represents the closing of the canon. But the very fact that Ben Sira could be excluded from the biblical canon enacts this impotency — for if it could be excluded, it was not sacred, and therefore the decision was merely a reflection of its lack. The exclusion of Ben Sira in no way proves that decision-making was possible, but might be said to indicate the reverse. If a sacred work could be excluded from the biblical canon, then it could be said that real decision was possible; and of course this is *a priori* an impossibility.

The date of canon formation can never be determined unless one is to take a position on the absurd question of whether finality is achieved at its beginning or at its end. In terms of agency, the formation of the canon escapes all human touch, which nevertheless is instrumental in its construction. Recognition of the nature of forces involved undercuts the possibility that the date (and accordingly the rationale) for canonization can be determined, for it challenges the possibility that decisions as to canonicity were ever really made. The authenticity of the scriptural work, as determined by tradition (this is a vague term for all the previous endorsements of a text) as well as its transmission history, indicated its sacredness or inspiration. Individuals were only instrumental in casting off the inauthentic and uninspired, which in actuality excluded themselves. The Council of Yavne could merely ratify the inspired and exclude the uninspired, and thus *negatively* determine inspiration. The Chief Rabbinate of Jerusalem could today declare that the works of Philo of Alexandria are uncanonical and uninspired. Does this indicate that the canon is still open? From the perspective of the tradition itself, individuals do not decide canonicity and inspiration but only declare it. The canon was closed long before its contents were delimited; moreover, it was never truly "open." It is this dialectic which is at the heart of the notion of the biblical canon.

Some of the debate's confusion has been generated by contrasting definitions of the term "canonical." According to Sid Leiman, "a canonical book is a book accepted by Jews as authoritative for religious practice and/or doctrine, and whose authority is binding upon the Jewish people for all generations. Furthermore, such books are to be studied and expounded in private and in public."[61] Adding another layer, Leiman speaks of the biblical canon as being made up of books that are *both* canonical *and* inspired. (The rabbinic conception of the sacredness of scripture is designated by the notion of *kitvey ha-qodesh* 'Holy Scriptures'; all holy scriptures "defile the hands" through their sacredness or inspiration by the *ruah ha-qodesh* 'holy spirit'.) He claims that it was possible for a book to be canonical and uninspired (such as Ben Sira and Megillath Taanith), as well as inspired and uncanonical (unfortunately for his theory, there are no examples of books that fit this category).[62]

Leiman argues that rabbinic debates over the status of biblical books were a matter of the inspiration rather than the canonicity of these books, which was already secure by this time.

As Leiman concludes, the rabbis did not think of scripture as deriving its canonicity from its inspiration. They may have been right, in that historical canonization did not necessarily require a formal declaration of the work's inspiration. From a diachronic perspective, a book's inclusion in the Temple archives (for instance, a work of history or a collection of proverbs) may not have depended on whether it had been declared inspired. However, it is impossible to know for sure the extent to which inspiration or sacredness was already viewed as a property of each and every one of these texts.

If we employ the rabbinic definition of the biblical canon as consisting of canonical works that have been declared sacred, then it is the rabbis who created this canon, because there is no evidence of any such declarations prior to rabbinic documents. To be sure, the rabbis did not make real decisions on the sanctity or inspiration of individual works of scripture, as I have argued. The story that the book of Proverbs (or Ecclesiastes, or the Song of Songs) had been stored away and then was later declared sacred is a myth. Nevertheless, it was the rabbis who constructed the biblical canon (so defined), either by having real discussions about their mythical reconstructions of the history of certain biblical books, or by reminiscing about fictional discussions at which inspiration was pronounced. Either way, inspiration was *declared* by the rabbis, even if it wasn't *decided* by them.

## Josephus and the Threefold Division of Scripture

Josephus' understanding of human agency in the composition of biblical books has important implications on our understanding of the threefold nature of the *tanakh*, Judaism's designation for the Bible. The term *tanakh* is an acronym composed of three Hebrew letters (*tnk*) that indicate its three component parts (*torah* 'Law', *nevi'im* 'Prophets', and *ketuvim* 'Writings'). As was discussed above, the idea of a threefold division of scripture is thought by many scholars to predate the specific rabbinic designation of the contents of categories. But the significance of the second and third of these categories was originally quite unlike the shape it would later take during the rabbinic period.

A threefold division of biblical books has been observed in the Prologue to the Greek version of Ben Sira, 2 Maccabees, the "Halakhic Letter" (4QMMT) from the Dead Sea Scrolls, Philo, the Gospel of Luke, and *Against Apion* of Josephus. This threefold division can be traced back at least to the middle of the second century B.C.E., but its stability has been over-emphasized by most scholars. In a recent survey of the collection of the Hebrew scriptures, A. van der Kooij argues convincingly that the arrangement given by Josephus is not an *ad hoc* construction suited only to his apologetic interests in *Against Apion*, but corresponds to the early development of the biblical collection (150 B.C.E. to 100 C.E.).[63] It is his view that events between 164 and 150 B.C.E. (namely, the Maccabean revolt) gave impetus to the collection, which he interprets as part of a process of reestablishing ancestral traditions after a serious threat. But van der Kooij judiciously points out that the collection that arose during this period should not necessarily be seen as a definitive collection; not only had the text not been standardized, but the arrangement was not the same as that of later Judaism.[64] I would add that the arrangement of Josephus represents a coming to fruition of ideas represented in prior divisions of scripture; it represents one moment in the process, rather than the only pre-rabbinic position.

The earliest evidence of a threefold division of scripture indicates that the three categories in rabbinic Judaism were unlike their earlier counterparts with regard to the specific contents of each category. Surprisingly, some important Second Temple period sources speak to a fourfold division of the archives in which scriptures were housed, while several others indicate a twofold division.

The Prologue to the Greek version of Ben Sira speaks of the Hebrew scriptures as consisting of a finite number of books or scrolls falling into three sections, only two of which have definitive designations. The passage, which derives from the second half of the second century B.C.E., describes rather than labels the third category:

ὁ πάππος μου Ἰησοῦς ἐπὶ πλεῖον ἑαυτὸν δοὺς εἴς τε <u>τὴν τοῦ νόμου</u> <u>καὶ τῶν προφητῶν καὶ τῶν ἄλλων πατρίων βιβλίων</u> ἀνάγνωσιν καὶ ἐν τούτοις ἱκανὴν ἕξιν περιποιησάμενος προήχθη καὶ αὐτὸς συγγράψαι τι τῶν εἰς παιδείαν καὶ σοφίαν ἀνηκόντων . . . οὐ γὰρ σοδυναμεῖ αὐτὰ ἐν ἑαυτοῖς Ἑβραϊστὶ λεγόμενα καὶ ὅταν μεταχθῇ εἰς ἑτέραν γλῶσσαν· οὐ μόνον δὲ ταῦτα, ἀλλὰ καὶ <u>αὐτὸς ὁ νόμος καὶ αἱ προφητεῖαι καὶ τὰ</u> <u>λοιπὰ τῶν βιβλίων</u> οὐ μικρὰν ἔχει τὴν διαφορὰν ἐν ἑαυτοῖς λεγόμενα.

My Grandfather Jesus, who had devoted himself for a long time to the study of <u>the Law, the Prophets, and the other hereditary books</u>, and developed a thorough familiarity with them, was prompted to write something himself in the nature of instruction and wisdom . . . For things recited in their original Hebrew, do not have the same force even when they are translated into another language. That is true not only of these words; but also <u>the Law itself, the Prophets, and the remainder of the books</u> have no small difference when they are recited in their own language.

The Prologue to the Greek Translation<br>of Ben Sira, 7–12 and 21–26

The third category is here referred to as *ta alla patria biblia* 'the other hereditary books' and *ta loipa tôn bibliôn* 'the remainder of the books'. The expression 'the other hereditary books' indicates the origin of all the books (they have been handed down as an inheritance, and do not derive from the here-and-now, but are rather the legacy of the ancestors). It also describes the books in question as lacking the particularity of the first two groups. The expression 'the remainder of the books' indicates that the whole is of a finite quantity (hence the word *loipa* 'remainder'), and reiterates the lack of particularity of the category. It is in no way possible to be certain of the contents of this category, or even of the category "Prophets." But I am inclined to agree with the assessment of van der Kooij, who claims that "it is probable that 'the Prophets' of the Prologue comprised the same books as those in Josephus."[65] I will return to this question below.

Two of the passages that have been adduced as evidence of a threefold division of scripture actually speak to an archive divided into four categories. Such an archive is depicted in 2 Maccabees, where Judas Maccabee is claimed to have reassembled a collection of scrolls originally gathered by Nehemiah.

ἐξηγοῦντο δὲ καὶ ἐν ταῖς ἀναγραφαῖς καὶ ἐν τοῖς ὑπομνηματισμοῖς τοῖς κατὰ τὸν Νεεμιαν τὰ αὐτὰ καὶ ὡς καταβαλλόμενος βιβλιοθήκην ἐπισυνήγαγεν τὰ περὶ τῶν βασιλέων βιβλία καὶ προφητῶν καὶ τὰ τοῦ Δαυιδ καὶ ἐπιστολὰς βασιλέων περὶ ἀναθεμάτων. ὡσαύτως δὲ καὶ Ιουδας τὰ διαπεπτωκότα διὰ τὸν γεγονότα πόλεμον ἡμῖν ἐπισυνήγαγεν πάντα, καὶ ἔστιν παρ' ἡμῖν· ὧν οὖν ἐὰν χρείαν ἔχητε, τοὺς ἀποκομιοῦντας ὑμῖν ἀποστέλλετε.

These facts are set out in the official records and in the memoirs of Nehemiah. And further (it is found in them) how Nehemiah, laying up a library, collected the scrolls concerning the kings and prophets, and the scrolls of David, and letters of the kings about sacred offerings. In the same way Judas also has collected all the books that had been lost (*diapiptô*) as a result of the recent war; and they are in our possession. If you should have need of them, you should send word to us to convey them to you.

2 Maccabees 2:13–14

Judah's activities may have been a response to the attempt of Antiochus IV to destroy the Law, as described in 1 Maccabees 1:56–57. His efforts at collecting books are compared to Nehemiah's activity in gathering books about the kings and prophets (a category sometimes equated with the *nevi'im* 'Prophets'), together with the books of David (presumably the Psalms) and letters of the kings about offerings.[66] It is assumed by this text that the Torah or 'Law' had already been collected in the Temple prior to the time of Nehemiah (and that the Torah was already canonical; this is the position of Leiman). Nehemiah's activity thus consisted of assembling three additional categories of materials, two of which were already or would later become part of Hebrew scriptures. One category is labeled *ta peri tôn basileôn biblia kai prophêtôn* 'the scrolls concerning the kings and the prophets'. This expression has generally been seen as indicating their subject matter (they are scrolls which are *peri tôn basileôn . . . kai prophêtôn* 'concerning kings . . . and prophets'). But it is possible that it describes both their subject matter ('the scrolls concerning the kings') and their provenance (*kai prophêtôn* 'and of the prophets'). The other category consists of the scrolls of David (τὰ τοῦ Δαυιδ), namely, the scrolls of Psalms, which seem to be the sole contents of the category at this time. Nehemiah also gathered an additional category of texts that was of archival interest only.

According to van der Kooij, "it has been rightly argued that this typology is meant to legitimize the claims of the Hasmoneans regarding their prerogatives in the temple and the cult."[67] The collection, if historical, must have occurred shortly after the death of Antiochus IV (164–163 B.C.E.). However, as van der Kooij states, "The tradition about Nehemiah founding a library is generally assumed to be fictional." Nevertheless, Judas is imagined as a latter-day Nehemiah.[68] The action of collecting scriptures by Judas is thus downplayed as merely the continuation of a practice initiated by his predecessor. Here is the key point: according to the text, Judas is not initiating anything or deciding to close the collection, but is merely gathering books to reconstitute a pre-existing library that was associated with Nehemiah.

The grouping found in 2 Maccabees is almost identical to the four categories of scripture found in the "Halakhic Letter" from the Dead Sea Scrolls.

[כתב]נו אליכה שתבין בספר מושה ו[ב]ספר[י] הנ[ב]יאים ובדוי[ד . . .]. [במעשי] דור ודור

We have [written] to you so that you may study (carefully) the book of Moses and the books of the Prophets and in David [and the] [annals of] each generation.

4QMMT C:10–11[69]

This recently published work views scripture again in four categories: the Torah (*sefer Moshe* 'the book of Moses'), Prophets (*sifrey ha-nevi'im* 'the books of the prophets'), Psalms (labeled only "David"), and a fourth, almost secular category (*ma'asey dor ve-dor* 'the annals of each generation'). It is significant that only the first two groups contain the word *sefer* 'book' or 'scroll', as if to imply that the third and fourth categories lack certain qualities of the first two.

Philo speaks of a division of scriptures employed by the sect of the Theraputae that is virtually identical to the scheme offered in Josephus. It consisted of "laws, oracles prophesied through the prophets, psalms, and the other books in which understanding and piety were increased and came to fruition."[70] Like Josephus, Philo's sect considered psalms and wisdom literature as separate from the law and the books of the prophets. Whether the sect's scriptures had three or four categories is uncertain.

It was also possible to refer to the Hebrew scriptures merely by speaking of two categories only. Hence in the New Testament, the biblical books are sometimes referred to as "Moses and all the prophets" (Luke 24:27).[71] Similarly, in 4 Maccabees 18:10, "the Law and the Prophets" appears to refer to the whole collection of biblical books.[72] When three categories are mentioned, they tend to consist of "the Law of Moses, the Prophets, and the Psalms," as in Luke 24:44.[73] However, it is worth recalling that in the Prologue to the Greek version of Ben Sira the third and final category is called "the other hereditary books" and "the remainder of the books."[74]

In short, the evidence suggests an evolving division of scriptures, expanding and shrinking from two to four groups of texts. I wish to discuss how this evolution affected the governing premise of the second category in particular. It is my contention that the second element of the threefold rabbinic designation for the Hebrew Bible — nevi'im 'Prophets' — did not originally derive from the fact that these books were in part about prophets. Nor did this designation stem from the fact that these books were dominated by the utterances of prophets (as if the category included only the books of Isaiah, Jeremiah, Ezekiel, and the Twelve Minor Prophets minus Jonah). I propose that the term nevi'im properly designated those books that had been copied out by a prophetic witness, and originally had nothing to do with their contents or dramatis personae. I would add that the distinction between "former" and "latter" prophets (made in the Septuagint translation as well as by the rabbis) derives from a time when the category "Prophets" no longer applied to works it had originally covered. The modifiers "former" and "latter" served to remedy the lack of coherence of the new contents of the category by dividing the books into period-defined genres or types of revelation.[75]

Josephus originally applies the concept (i.e. books of prophecy) to all of the books of the Bible other than the Law (the Torah), with the exception of the Psalms (traditionally associated with David) and three books of instruction (most scholars agree these consisted of the works traditionally associated with Solomon). Despite the fact that David was described as a prophet both in rabbinic documents and in one New Testament book (Acts of the Apostles 2:30), Josephus apparently does not consider David as part of the prophetic succession.[76] His reticence was at least in part shared by the "List of David's Compositions" (11QPs[a]) from the Dead Sea Scrolls, where David is described as having uttered all the psalms "in prophecy," but is not called a prophet *per se*.[77] Similarly, as Solomon apparently never achieved prophetic status (at least prior to rabbinic exegesis), it stands to reason that his words of wisdom could not be included in the category of works copied out by prophets. For Josephus (and the tradition he is here giving voice to), the category "Prophets" would appear to include only those books written down by actual prophets.[78]

The meaning of the second category is quite different in the *baraita* in Baba Bathra 14b, which originates sometime before 200 C.E. but after the time of Josephus. In contrast to Josephus, the *baraita* does not take special note of the prophetic status of the copyists of books that appear in the category *nevi'im* 'Prophets'. As I have stressed, this *baraita* is interested in rectifying the anonymity of the scribes, rather than in stipulating that each copyist was a prophet — even if the book (like that of Isaiah) patently belonged in the category *nevi'im*.[79] In short, the meaning of the category "Prophets" is no longer understood to refer to the textualizers of the books it includes.

There is some evidence to suggest that rabbinic exegetes would later attempt to restore the prophetic status of those textualizers of biblical books. The "Men of Hezekiah," who are said in the *baraita* to have copied out the works of Solomon and Isaiah, seem to be the most troubling entity, since they do not appear to have included a prophet in their number.[80] Although an exegetical remedy was available (2 Chronicles 33:19 could be read to suggest that the men of Hezekiah had included a number of anonymous seers during the reign of Manasseh), midrashic sources prior to Rashi offer no confirmation that such a solution was ever employed.[81] A more drastic attempt is in evidence in traditions that developed around Baba Bathra 14b–15a. Parallel passages preserved in medieval manuscripts credit the prophet Isaiah rather than Hezekiah and his colleagues with copying out Song of Songs, Proverbs, Ecclesiastes, and Isaiah, presumably because Isaiah's prophetic status was more satisfactory.[82] This manuscript variant may be evidence of an attempt to re-endow the textualizers of the biblical books with prophetic status, a matter that had been of little concern to the *baraita*.

In the New Testament, Luke records a speech delivered by Peter in which David is called a prophet (Acts of the Apostles 2:30). Similarly, in the final stages of the evolution of Jewish views about the works of Solomon, rabbinic texts bypassed the question of the status of the men of Hezekiah, and reconstituted Solomon as a prophet.

ד"א דברי קהלת בן דוד <u>שלשה נביאים</u> ע"י שהיה נבואתן דברי קנתרין נתלת נבואתן בעצמן קِיאלו הן דברי

קהלת (עמוס א') דברי עמוס (ירמיה א') דברי ירמיהו

> Another interpretation of "The words of Qoheleth the son of David": <u>There were three prophets</u> to whom, because it consisted of words of reproach, their prophecy was attributed personally, viz. "The words of Qoheleth," "The words of Amos" (Amos 1:1), and "The words of Jeremiah" (Jer. 1:1).
>
> Qoheleth Rabbah 1:2, trans. Cohen

As may be seen from this and other examples that abound in the midrashim, rabbinic exegetes eventually chose to elevate Solomon (in this case in his guise as Qoheleth) as well as David to prophet status.[83] Through such interpretive gestures, *all* the books of the Bible could be said to have been uttered rather than merely written down by prophets. But the consequence was that the original distinction between the second and third categories of scripture was lost.

The reason that these categories began to change can be found in the evolving status of the third category of scriptural books, referred to by Josephus as "psalms and edifying books." In time, the Psalms and the works of Solomon (especially the Song of Songs) achieved a level of sacredness that rivaled even the prophetic books. Consequently, the third category (eventually known as *ketuvim*

'Writings') could no longer be considered of lesser authority than the second. At the same time as the new status of Psalms and the Song of Songs began to rub off on the category in which they were placed, works from the second category that seemed most to resemble the contents of the third category drifted towards it. Thus Job (the stylized story of the misfortunes of an upright man), Ruth (a saga about the ancestress of King David), Lamentations (a set of laments about the destruction of Jerusalem), Daniel (the account of a seer who is never actually termed a prophet), Esther (a narrative about the miraculous salvation of an oppressed diaspora community), Ezra and Nehemiah (the eyewitness accounts of the return from exile), and 1 and 2 Chronicles (a retelling of Israelite history) were re-classified as "Writings" rather than works copied by prophets. This category subsequently took on the sacredness of its component works like the Song of Songs; the Greek *hagiographa* 'Holy Writings', a translation of Hebrew *ketuvim*, is instructive in considering the significance of the redefined third category.

Rabbinic literature records discussion about the elevation of these texts from being merely works recorded by prophets to works that were themselves holy. For example, the *baraita* in Baba Bathra 14b states that Esther was copied out by the Men of the Great Assembly. This body was said to have included not only the last three prophets in the prophetic succession, but also Mordechai, one of the principal characters in the narrative. It is he that Jewish tradition credits with retelling the story. A discussion about the scroll found in the Talmud seems to record doubt about the sacredness of the book:

אמר רב יהודה אמר שמואל: אסתר אינה מטמאה את הידים. למימרא דסבר שמואל אסתר

לאו ברוח הקודש נאמרה? והאמר שמואל: אסתר ברוח הקודש נאמרה - נאמרה לקרות ולא נאמרה ליכתוב

> Rab Judah said in the name of Samuel; [The scroll] of Esther does not make the hands unclean. Are we to infer from this that Samuel was of opinion that Esther was not composed under the inspiration of the holy spirit? How can this be, seeing that Samuel has said that Esther was composed under the inspiration of the holy spirit? — It was composed to be recited [by heart], but not to be written.
> B. Megillah 7a, trans. Simon

It is true that the scroll has a special place in the Jewish liturgy that involves its recitation during the holiday of Purim. Nevertheless, the Talmud's explanation of Samuel's qualification of the scroll does not ring true. While many scholars have considered this discussion as a real debate about the canonicity of Esther during Samuel's time, the preceding analysis suggests an alternative explanation. Perhaps the works originally found in the second and third categories were not at first considered to "make the hands unclean" like the Torah. Samuel's statement would thus testify to a period prior to the sacralization of works that were originally classified as "recorded by prophets," even if this had nothing to do with Esther's canonical status.

When works that had been grouped in the category "Prophets" began to migrate to the third category, not only their degree of holiness but even the imagined conditions of their composition were drastically altered. So while the *baraita* in Baba Bathra 14b records Esther as having been copied out by the Men of the Great Assembly, the Jerusalem Talmud relates a different version of the scroll's creation:

רב ור׳ חנינה ור׳ יונתן ור׳ ובר קפרא ור׳ יהושוע בן לוי אמרו המגילה הזות נאמרה למשה מסיני אלא
שאין מוקדם ומאוחר בתורה

Rab, R. Ḥaninah, R. Jonathan, Bar Qappara, and R. Joshua b. Levi said, "This scroll was stated to Moses at Sinai, for there is no chronological order in the Torah."

J. Megillah 1:5[84]

As was the case with the Song of Songs, the book of Esther ultimately acquired a level of holiness that outstripped its previous status. This meant re-evaluating the occasion of its composition; henceforward it was considered as being part of the revelation at Sinai, and thus became equal in stature to the Torah itself.

The remaining books, containing utterances of the prophets (Isaiah, Jeremiah, Ezekiel, the Twelve Minor Prophets), as well as the historical accounts that sometimes happened to foreground narratives *about* prophets (Joshua, Judges, 1 and 2 Samuel, 1 and 2 Kings), remained in the default category *nevi'im.* I would therefore argue that the category "Writings" is a more coherent grouping (inasmuch as it is based on literary considerations) than the final form of the category "Prophets." To return to the words of Josephus, "the prophets after Moses wrote the events of their own times in thirteen books" (*Against Apion* 1.40); this formulation describes a content (the events of their own time) that was marked by the individuals who recorded this content (the prophets after Moses). As the category became robbed of the breadth of works that initially gave it significance, it would henceforward be seen as a set of texts including both history and prophetic utterances, but having nothing to do with the identity of those who had recorded these books.

Previous scholarship has arrived at a consensus on Josephus as a Hellenized Jew in a way that validates its own scholarly objectives and assumptions. Josephus' scanty references to the Hebrew Bible as an unchangeable corpus of sacred "scripture," even as a "canon," were held to arise from a pre-existing corpus of works that he sought to explain. His critique of Greek history was little more than a ploy to validate his own work, using a methodology heavily borrowed from the Greek historians he found objectionable.

I have argued that Josephus thinks about history like a Jew. The reluctance of Jews to participate in historiographical writing after the fall of the Second Temple is well known.[85] Perhaps this later Jewish reticence did not appear *ex nihilo,* but recapitulated an old resistance to the Greek approach to the past, a resistance voiced by Josephus. To say that Josephus thinks about history "as a Jew" is not to claim that the origins of his critique lie in an ingrained rejection of Greek historiography in Jewish sources. To the contrary, Josephus arrives at his position on Greek historiography through his own understanding of Judaism and his own reading of the differences between Hebrew accounts of the past and those of Herodotus, Hecataeus and others. Nevertheless, what is crucial is that his notion of the Jewish approach towards history is arrived at through a dialectic process involving a rejection of an essentialized view of Greek letters. Josephus' notion of Jewish history amounts to a synthesis of oriental and biblical precedents together with Greek approaches that buck the trend of his caricature of Greek historiography (such as the approach of Thucydides).

Josephus' expansive additions to biblical events were once considered to have arisen from the Hellenistic world, known for its novelistic treatments of mythological events. Recently, however, these expansions have been recognized as deriving from a store of interpretations of the Bible, perhaps handed down orally, rather than from Greek literary models. It is thus more accurate to say that Josephus derived his knowledge of the status of the texts belonging to the Hebrew Bible from such a storehouse of Second Temple Jewish traditions.

Nevertheless, these traditions fell under the influence of Hellenic ideas. While Josephus' version of the Jewish writing of history is formulated in contrast to his view of Hellenistic historiography, it also replicates the historiographical ideal of Thucydides, and seems to echo Hellenistic critiques of mendacious Greek historians. Josephus employs Platonic formulations to describe the mechanics of Jewish prophecy. Even when he rejects the Greek way of doing things, his very discussion betrays Greek influence. He is apparently familiar with the Greek obsession with attribution analysis (the procedure by which the attributions of texts were authenticated), although he seems to conclude that Hebrew writings could never require such techniques, since their transmission attests to the validity of their attributions. He contrasts the Jewish oral tradition with Greek improvisation. Greek inventiveness in crafts or literature, as well as the Greek desire to defy and break away from all inherited customs, is compared unfavorably with Jewish obedience to a law deemed unchangeable and needing no amendment. Further, his understanding of the textualization of the Bible is deliberately contrasted with the Alexandrian position on the textualization of the Homeric epics.

For the purposes of this study, one of the most intriguing aspects of *Against Apion* is the way that it clashes with the Greek conceptualization of composition, and yet still manages to afford a decisive role to "writers" of texts. Josephus appeals to the human textualizers of the Hebrew Bible in order that, through them, he might explain the Jewish differentiation between sacred and non-sacred writings. According to Josephus, those writings with a suitable prophetic witness were determined to be sacred texts, while writings attributed to individuals who could not be vouched for were left off the list. As was discussed in chapter 2, this view accords with the attribution practices of the early Second Temple period, and would appear to lie at the heart of the formation of the biblical canon. Josephus' location of Greekness and Jewishness in approaches to textualization sets the stage for a notion of authorship that would be developed first by the Church Fathers and later by European literary and legal discourse. Josephus is responsible for bringing discrepancies between agonistic and prophetic, individualistic and veristic modes of composition to the awareness of early Christian scholars and to their discourse on authorship. These discrepancies have rested uneasily at the heart of the European conceptualization of authorship for the past two thousand years.

It is possible to say that authorship represents a disjunction of Greek and Jewish approaches to individual agency in the production of written records. The notion of the author (not yet designated by a single term) as an agonistic fictionalizer of history could only be formulated from the perspective of a tradition with quite a different reverence for its chronicles — that is, at the margins of the Greek world. Christian theologians like Eusebius, St. Jerome, and St. Augustine took up the classical world's approach to writerly agency. This agency amounted to a willingness to affix a signature to one's own work; thus, the classical world's valuation of the writer's signature overpowered the Jewish dislike of individual agency.[86] But from Judaism they inherited the idea of authors as individuals given the dispensation to speak a truth that transcends the individual — a dispensation granted only by God to a prophet. This aspect of authorship remains alive in the reverence we grant our own canonical literary authors. It may be seen in our panegyrics to their genius and conscious mastery of their art. It is even visible in our post-modern belief that texts, without the conscious knowledge and intent of their authors, are able to convey the truth about the world and offer clairvoyant conclusions about how things really are.

# CHAPTER 5

# PEISISTRATUS AND PTOLEMY

When the epic works of Homer were written down,
many educated Greeks were unpleasantly surprised.
— Rudolph Blum, *Kallimachos*

It is instructive to consider historical legends (essentially myths told about real people) in the particular settings, both historical and literary, in which they are most fully articulated. An investigation of the legend of the textualization of the Homeric Epics by the sixth century B.C.E. Athenian tyrant, Peisistratus, reveals that this story meant a great deal to a culture that valued the thousand-year-old literary legacy of ancient Greece. The Peisistratus legend plays a crucial role in the self-legitimization of the late-antique discourse of grammar, an important discipline that formed the basis for education for much of antiquity and the middle Ages. I will argue that the Peisistratus legend is employed by grammatical discourse to justify and promote its highest aim — to locate and label inauthentic literary works and portions of works. This discourse is able to articulate its agenda through the Peisistratus legend because it came to serve as one of ancient scholarship's most plausible aetiologies of forgery.

During the legend's long development, the figure of Peisistratus was frequently confused with Ptolemy II, a Hellenistic ruler of

Egypt in the third century B.C.E. As I will argue, the conflation of
Ptolemy II with Peisistratus was brought about by the fact that
both rulers provided competing origins for literary imposture. According to one strand of Greek scholarship, the Peisistratids (the
dynasty that included Peisistratus) were the earliest forgers of literary documents. Other Greek scholars found that the Ptolemaic period provided a more convincing origin, because it allowed them to
attribute forgery and plagiarism to economic and psychological
factors rather than personal and political motives.

The fusion of the Peisistratus and Ptolemaic legends would
eventually result in the conflation of the textual histories connected
with both individuals. Jewish legend credited Ptolemy II with
bringing about the translation of the Hebrew Bible into Greek, a
story that was remarkably similar to the account of Peisistratus' efforts in gathering the Homeric epics. During the development of
the Peisistratus legend, the story of the textualization of the Homeric epics took on attributes of the Ptolemaic translation of the Hebrew Bible into Greek.

The fusion process allows us to examine the radical incongruity of Greek and Jewish views on the nature of literary authority,
belying the ease of their conflation. It also affords the present study
of the relationship between texts and individuals with the author's
foil — the textualizer. As if he were a kingly patron of the scribes of
the Hebrew Bible, Peisistratus was often lauded for saving the
Homeric epics from destruction by having them transcribed when
they were in danger of being lost. In other words, for some communities, his name became the guarantor of an authentic version
of the text. But other strands of the Greek tradition were not averse
to labeling him a literary criminal whose efforts had modified the
authoritative documents of Athenian and Greek culture. The story
of Peisistratus was thus transformed into a call to search for the
true words of Homer. Around the crime of the textualizer, the notion of the true author coalesces. This process has continued into
modern times. Like Hezekiah, declared by modern biblical scholars
to be the promoter of an edition or recension of the Hebrew Bible,
Peisistratus is often seen by modern scholars as the patron of the
"official" recension of Homer, on the basis of little more than legendary evidence.

## The Peisistratus Legend in the Scholia to Dionysius Thrax

Dionysius Thrax 'the Thracian' (ca. 170–ca. 90 B.C.E.) was a pupil of Aristarchus in Alexandria and later a teacher of grammar and literature at Rhodes. He wrote the *Tekhnê Grammatikê*, an epitome of pure grammar that classifies accents, stops, letters, and syllables and defines the parts of speech. His definitive summary of Alexandrian grammatical learning, augmented by Stoic principles of grammar such as *analogia* 'analogy' that were the hallmarks of the Pergamene grammar which had been developed by Crates of Mallos, was highly influential on Latin grammar, and through it, on most of the modern grammars of Europe. In Hellenistic, Roman, and Byzantine times a number of lengthy commentaries began to supplement the grammar of Dionysius Thrax. Referred to as the Scholia to Dionysius Thrax, these commentaries represent a high point in the literary and linguistic scholarship of the late antique and Byzantine world. The Scholia to Dionysius Thrax exist in several distinct traditions that loosely resemble each other in content, arrangement, and style.[1]

Nested within these late antique or Byzantine Scholia to Dionysius Thrax is a legend concerning Peisistratus and the destruction and re-assembly of the Homeric epics. This legend, although late and historically inaccurate (it appears to make the claim that Peisistratus, Zenodotus, and Aristarchus all lived at the same time), is usually included in discussions of Homeric text fixation and the so-called "Peisistratean Recension." It is generally acknowledged at most to be no more than a late echo of a questionable historical event that occurred in the sixth century B.C.E. In fact, however, even the oldest Peisistratus legends are not attested further back than the first century B.C.E. The earliest surviving account comes from Cicero. Rudolf Pfeiffer speculates that Cicero's source for the Peisistratus legend was probably Asclepiades of Myrlea (second/first century B.C.E.) in his *Peri Grammatikôn*.[2] Pfeiffer also asserts that it is a "reasonable assumption" that Asclepiades, who may have been the student of Dionysius Thrax, was the ultimate source of the Scholia to Dionysius Thrax; through these scholia, he may have served as the source of material found in later Byzantine excerptors like Tzetzes.[3]

The legend appears in chapter 6 of three versions of the Scholia; this chapter is entitled *Peri Rhapsodias* 'On the Art of the Rhapsodes', and is a commentary to the section of the grammar of Dionysius Thrax bearing the same designation. The context for a discussion of the role of Peisistratus is the discussion over the definition of the word "rhapsody." One version of the scholia begins with the terse formulation of Dionysius Thrax himself, and then gives an alternative explanation:

'Ραψῳδία ἐστὶ μέρος ποιήματος ἐμπεριειληφός τινα ὑπόθεσιν. Ἐπειδὴ οἱ ἀρχόμενοι ἀναγινώσκειν παῖδες πρὸ πάντων τῶν βιβλίων ἅπτονται τῶν Ὁμηρικῶν, τὰ δὲ Ὁμηρικὰ ποιήματα τέμνεται εἰς ῥαψῳδίας, βούλεται διδάξαι καὶ τοὺς παῖδας αὐτὸ τοῦτο, τί ἐστι ῥαψῳδία, καί φησι τὸν ὅρον τοῦτον. Ποίημα μὲν γάρ ἐστι τὸ ὅλον βιβλίον, ὡς ἡ Ἰλιὰς καὶ ἡ Ὀδύσσεια, τὰ δὲ τμήματα αὐτῶν ῥαψῳδίαι καλοῦνται·

*"Rhapsody is part of the poiêma that is taken up with some plot (hupothesis)."*[4] Since pupils starting to read begin with Homeric compositions before all other books, and the Homeric *poiêmata* are cut into rhapsodies, it is advised to teach the pupils what rhapsody is. Many give (*phêsi*) this definition (*horos*): *poiêma* is the whole book, such as the *Iliad* and the *Odyssey*, but their divisions (*tmêmata*) are called "rhapsodies."

*Commentarius Melampodis seu Diomedis* chap. 5,
ed. Hilgard p. 28

After giving examples of rhapsodies (these correspond to the titles of Homeric sections as listed in Aelian, *Varia Historia* 13.14[5]), the scholiast goes on to cite two etymologies of "rhapsode" that Dionysius of Thrax himself had put forward. The first is that the word derives from ἡ ἐπὶ ῥάβδῳ ᾠδή *hê epi rhabdôi ôidê* 'the song (*ôidê*) upon the staff (*rhabdos*)', as if the word were ῥαβδῳδία *rhabdôidia*. The scholiast defends this etymology with a fact relating to epic performance: "for, those who sang the Homeric *poiêmata* sang them holding a staff of laurel, the symbol of Apollo." The second etymology, equivalent to the derivation found in Pindar *Nemean* 2, is that *rhapsôidia* stems from ῥάπτειν *rhaptein* 'to sew together', which the scholiast in turn derives from ῥῶ *rhô*, a verb meaning 'mend'.

The portion of the scholia that relays the Peisistratus legend follows what appears to be a well-known premise of Alexandrian scholarship on the transmission of Homer. A catastrophe had destroyed the physical text of Homer: "it happened, as they say, that the works of Homer were destroyed." The element of reportage, ὡς φασιν *hôs phasin* 'as they say', is a typical way to introduce a commonly held position in the language of the scholia. Three versions of the legend are quoted below:

1. Ἦν δέ, ὥς φασιν, ἀπολόμενα τὰ τοῦ Ὁμήρου· τότε γὰρ οὐ γραφῇ παρεδίδοτο, ἀλλὰ μόνῃ διδασκαλίᾳ καὶ ὡς ἂν μνήμῃ μόνῃ ἐφυλάττετο. Πεισίστρατος δέ τις Ἀθηναίων τύραννος, ἐν ἅπασιν ὢν εὐγενής, καὶ ἐν τοῦτο θαυμαστὸν ἐβουλεύσατο· ἠθέλησε γὰρ καὶ τὴν Ὁμήρου ποίησιν ἔγγραφον διαφυλάττεσθαι. Προθεὶς δὲ ἀγῶνα δημοτελῆ καὶ κηρύξας καὶ δοὺς ἄδειαν τοῖς εἰδόσι καὶ βουλομένοις τὰ Ὁμήρου ἐπιδείκνυσθαι, καὶ μισθὸν τάξας στίχου ἑκάστου ὀβολόν, συνήγαγεν ὁλοσχερεῖς τὰς λέξεις καὶ παρέδωκεν ἀνθρώποις σοφοῖς καὶ ἐπιστήμοσιν, ὡς καὶ τὸ ἐπίγραμμα αὐτοῦ δηλοῖ·

> Τρίς με τυραννήσαντα τοσαυτάκις ἐξετίναξε
> δῆμος Ἀθηναίων, καὶ τρὶς ἐπηγάγετο,
> τὸν μέγαν ἐν βουλῇ Πεισίστρατον, ὃς τὸν Ὅμηρον
> ἤθροισα, σποράδην τὸ πρὶν ἀειδόμενον.
> Ἡμέτερος γὰρ κεῖνος ὁ χρύσεος ἦν πολιήτης,
> εἴπερ Ἀθηναῖοι Σμύρναν ἀπῳκίσαμεν.

It happened, as they say, that the works of Homer were destroyed. For at that time they were handed down not in writing, but by teaching/performance (*didaskalia*) alone, so that they might be kept through memory. Peisistratus, tyrant of Athens, was in every way of noble birth, and he contrived this one remarkable deed. He wished, in writing (*engraphos*), to maintain (*diaphulattô*) even the *poiêsis* of Homer. He established games (*agôn* pl.) at public cost, made a public proclamation, and granted license for those who knew and wished to make a public demonstration of (*epideik-*

*numi*) the works of Homer; and having fixed the price (*misthos*) at an obol a line, he gathered together the readings (*lexis* pl.) in rough form (*holoskherês* pl.), and handed them over to men both clever and learned, as the epigram makes clear:

Thrice I reigned as tyrant, and as many times
did the people of Erekhtheus expel me and thrice
recall me, Peisistratus, great in council, who
collected Homer, formerly sung in scattered form (*sporadên*).
For that man of gold was our fellow-citizen,
if we Athenians colonized Smyrna.

*Scholia Vaticana* (cod. C), 5.11–25, ed. Hilgard p.179

2. Ἀναγκαῖον δὲ μετὰ τὴν ἐτυμολογίαν τῆς ῥαψῳδίας μνησθῆναι κἀκείνου, ὅτι ἔν τινι χρόνῳ τὰ Ὁμήρου ποιήματα παρεφθάρη ἢ ὑπὸ πυρὸς ἢ ὑπὸ ὑδάτων ἐπιφορᾶς ἢ ὑπὸ σεισμοῦ, καὶ ἄλλων ἄλλως τῶν βιβλίων διασκεδασθέντων καὶ φθαρέντων ὕστερον εὑρέθη ὁ μὲν ἔχων τυχὸν ἑκατὸν στίχους Ὁμηρικούς, ὁ δὲ χιλίους, ἄλλος διακοσίους, ἄλλος ὅσους ἂν ἔτυχε· καὶ ἤμελλε λήθῃ παραδίδοσθαι ἡ τοιαύτη ποίησις. Ἀλλὰ Πεισίστρατός τις Ἀθηναῖος στρατηγός, θέλων καὶ ἑαυτῷ δόξαν περιποιήσασθαι καὶ τὰ τοῦ Ὁμήρου ἀνανεῶσαι, τοιοῦτόν τι ἐβουλεύσατο· ἐκήρυξεν ἐν πάσῃ τῇ Ἑλλάδι τὸν ἔχοντα Ὁμηρικούς στίχους ἀγαγεῖν πρὸς αὐτόν, ἐπὶ μισθῷ ὡρισμένῳ καθ' ἕκαστον στίχον. Πάντες οὖν οἱ ἔχοντες ἐπέφερον καὶ ἐλάμβανον ἀδιαστρόφως τὸν ὁρισθέντα μισθόν· οὐκ ἀπεδίωκε δὲ οὐδὲ τὸν φέροντα οὓς ἤδη προειλήφει παρ' ἑτέρου στίχους, ἀλλὰ κἀκείνῳ τὸν αὐτὸν ἐπεδίδου μισθόν· ἐνίοτε δὲ καὶ πλείους· ὅθεν τις ἔσθ' ὅτε καὶ ἰδίους παρεισέφερε, τοὺς νῦν ὀβελιζομένους. Καὶ μετὰ τὸ πάντας συναγαγεῖν παρεκάλεσεν ἑβδομήκοντα δύο γραμματικούς, συνθεῖναι τὰ τοῦ Ὁμήρου ἕκαστον κατ' ἰδίαν, ὅπως ἂν δόξῃ τῷ συνθέντι καλῶς ἔχειν, ἐπὶ μισθῷ πρέποντι λογικοῖς ἀνδράσι καὶ κριταῖς ποιημάτων, ἑκάστῳ δεδωκὼς κατ' ἰδίαν πάντας τοὺς στίχους ὅσους ἦν συναγαγών. Καὶ μετὰ τὸ ἕκαστον συνθεῖναι κατὰ τὴν ἑαυτοῦ γνώμην, εἰς ἓν συνήγαγε πάντας τοὺς προλεχθέντας γραμματικούς, ὀφείλοντας ἐπιδεῖξαι αὐτῶν ἕκαστον τὴν ἰδίαν σύνθεσιν, παρόντων ὁμοῦ πάντων. Οὗτοι οὖν ἀκροασάμενοι οὐ πρὸς ἔριν, ἀλλὰ πρὸς τὸ ἀληθὲς καὶ πᾶν τὸ τῇ τέχνῃ ἁρμόζαν, ἔκριναν πάντες κοινῇ καὶ ὁμοφρόνως, ἐπικρατῆσαι τὴν σύνθεσίν τε καὶ διόρθωσιν

'Αριστάρχου καὶ Ζηνοδότου· καὶ πάλιν ἔκριναν τῶν δύο συνθέσεών τε καὶ διορθώσεων βελτίονα τὴν 'Αριστάρχου. 'Επειδὴ δέ τινες τῶν συναγαγόντων τοὺς 'Ομηρικοὺς στίχους πρὸς τὸν Πεισίστρατον διὰ τὸ πλείονα μισθὸν λαβεῖν καὶ ἰδίους στίχους, ὡς προείρηται, σκεψάμενοι προσέθηκαν, καὶ ἤδη ἐν συνηθείᾳ ἐγένοντο τοῖς ἀναγινώσκουσιν, οὐκ ἔλαθε τοῦτο τοὺς κριτάς, ἀλλὰ διὰ μὲν τὴν συνήθειαν καὶ πρόληψιν ἀφῆκαν αὐτοὺς κεῖσθαι, ὀβελίσκους δὲ ἑκάστῳ τῶν ἀδοκίμων καὶ ἀλλοτρίων καὶ ἀναξίων τοῦ ποιητοῦ στίχων παρατιθέμενοι τοῦτο αὐτὸ ἐνεδείξαντο, ὡς ἀνάξιοί εἰσι τοῦ 'Ομήρου. Φέρεται δὲ ἐπίγραμμα εἰς τὸν Πεισίστρατον ὡς σπουδάσαντα συναγαγεῖν τὰ τοῦ 'Ομήρου τοιοῦτον·

Τρίς με τυραννήσαντα τοσαυτάκις ἐξετίναξε
    δῆμος 'Αθηναίων, καὶ τρὶς ἐπηγάγετο,
τὸν μέγαν ἐν βουλῇ Πεισίστρατον, ὃς τὸν "Ομηρον
    ἤθροισα, σποράδην τὸ πρὶν ἀειδόμενον.
'Ημέτερος γὰρ κεῖνος ὁ χρύσεος ἦν πολιήτης,
    εἴπερ 'Αθηναῖοι Σμύρναν ἀπῳκίσαμεν.

It is necessary, following the etymology of "rhapsody," to make mention of the following. At some time the *poiêmata* of Homer were destroyed, either by fire [or by an influx of water (*Comm. Melam. seu Diom.*)] or by earthquake, and, since the scrolls had been scattered and destroyed in every direction, one would be found having by chance a hundred Homeric lines each, another having thousands, another two hundred, while another, however much it happened to have; and it was likely that the *poiêsis* in such a state would be given over to forgetfulness. But Peisistratus the *stratêgos* of Athens, wishing to acquire for himself a reputation and to revive (*ananeoomai*) the works of Homer, devised this course of action. He announced thought the whole of Greece that anyone in possession of Homeric lines should bring them to him for a fixed premium per single line. As a result, everyone who had lines returned them, and they invariably received the set premium. Nor did he chase away even someone holding lines which he already prejudged (*prolambanô*) as originating from another author, but to him too he gave the same premium. Some among them found one or two superfluous (*perittos*) lines, others even more. From which it happened that now and then someone brought forward his own lines (which are now marked with the obelisk), and after gathering together all the lines they summoned 72 experts (*grammatikoi*) to assemble the works of Homer, each one in private, in whatever manner he might consider the assemblage would be best. He summoned them for a premium (*misthos*) that was fitting for intellectual (*logikos* pl.) men and critics of *poiêmata*, and to each was given all the lines in isolation (*kat' idian*), as many as had been gathered together. And after each one compiled it according to his best judgment into a single entity, he [Peisistratus] assembled (*sunêgage*) all the chosen experts (*grammatikoi*), who were required to make him a public display of (*epideixai*) their individual (*idios*) compilations, with everyone being present. These listened, not for competition's sake but rather with a view to the truth and the skillful marriage (*harmozon*) [of the fragments] in general; and they all decided, in common and unanimously, that the compilation and correction (*diorthôsis* pl.) of Aristarchus and Zenodotus had prevailed. And again they decided that of the two compilations and editions the best was the one of Aristarchus. Indeed, some of those who were combining Homeric lines for Peisistratus, in order to get a bigger premium, added lines, which, as also has been said, they recognized as being peculiar (*idios*); and already these lines were habitual to the readers. This, however, did not escape the judges' notice, but owing to habituation (*sunêtheia*) and their preconceived ideas (*prolêpsis*) they let them lie. Adding obelisks for each of the lines which were unauthorized (*adokimos*) and alien (*allotrios*) and unworthy of the poet, they made a display of (*epideiknumi*) it as this, for [these lines] are unworthy of Homer. The story is also related by this epigram, dedicated to Peisistratus zealously assembling the works of Homer:

> Thrice I reigned as tyrant, and as many times
> did the people of Erekhtheus expel me and thrice
> recall me, Peisistratus, great in council, who
> collected Homer, formerly sung in scattered form (*sporadên*).
> For that man of gold was our fellow-citizen,
> if we Athenians colonized Smyrna.

> *Commentarius Melampodis seu Diomedis* (cod. C), ed. Hilgard
> pp. 29–30, = *Scholia Marciana* (VN), ed. Hilgard p. 316

3. Φασὶ δὲ ὡς ἀπώλοντο τὰ τοῦ Ὁμήρου· τότε γὰρ οὐ γραφῇ παρεδίδοτο, ἀλλὰ μόνη ἐφυλάττετο· καὶ ἤδει ὁ μὲν τυχὼν ἑκατὸν στίχους, ὁ δὲ πεντήκοντα, ἄλλος δὲ ὅσους ἂν ἔτυχε· καὶ ἤμελλε λήθῃ παραδίδοσθαι ἡ τοιαύτη ποίησις. Ἀλλὰ Πεισίστρατος θέλων καὶ ἑαυτῷ δόξαν περποιήσασθαι *etc.* (= *Commentarius Melampodis seu Diomedis* and *Scholia Marciana*).

They say that the works of Homer were destroyed. For at that time they were handed down not in writing, but by performance (*didaskalia*) alone, and however it might be preserved through memory alone. And he knew that one person happened to have a hundred lines, and another fifty, another having however many he happened to have. And it was likely that the *poiêsis* in such a state would be given over to forgetfulness. But Peisistratus, wishing to acquire a reputation for himself *etc.* (see 2 above).

Scholia Londinensia, ed. Hilgard p. 481

Although there are obvious differences in these versions of the legend, it is immediately apparent that there is a close relationship between the two basic versions of the Peisistratus legend and the epigram. Each version of the legend constitutes a homiletic expansion of the details of the epigram, and is designed to answer key questions about this open-ended and apparently ambiguous poem. The motivation is simple: there existed little trustworthy evidence of Peisistratus' role in transmitting the Homeric poems, and this evidence was seized on by scholars eager to legitimate their own philological agenda. This process is analogous to the interpretation and translation of Proverbs 25:1, the verse which documents the efforts of Hezekiah in the transmission of at least one part of a book of the Bible (see chapter 1). The figures of Hezekiah and Peisistratus thus stand as parallels in the story of literary history, inasmuch as both are reconfigured by exegetical tradition as pre-eminent textualizers on the basis of tantalizingly slim evidence.

As interpretations of the epigram about Peisistratus, the versions cited above boil down to conflicting interpretations of a single utterance: what is the meaning of the phrase, "Peisistratus *êithroisa* 'gathered/collected/strung together' Homer"? From the perspective of the composers of this legend, "gathering Homer" could only imply editorial activity; modern scholars, in contrast, are more inclined to consider Peisistratus as a figure involved in the standardization of epic performance at the Athenian Panathenaia. But while editing was the most probable interpretation of the epigram's notion of "gathering Homer," other information about Peisistratus did not lend credence to the conclusion that Peisistratus himself was capable of creating an edition of Homer. The dilemma is solved by the *Scholia Vaticana* with the construction of a biography of Peisistratus in which the tyrant is portrayed as gathering together Homeric fragments:

Πεισίστρατος δέ τις ᾽Αθηναίων τύραννος, ἐν ἅπασιν ὢν εὐγενής, καὶ ἓν τοῦτο θαυμαστὸν ἐβουλεύσατο· ἠθέλησε γὰρ καὶ τὴν ῾Ομήρου ποίησιν ἔγγραφον διαφυλάττεσθαι. Προθεὶς δὲ ἀγῶνα δημοτελῆ καὶ κηρύξας καὶ δοὺς ἄδειαν τοῖς εἰδόσι καὶ βουλομένοις τὰ ῾Ομήρου ἐπιδείκνυσθαι, καὶ μισθὸν τάξας στίχου ἑκάστου ὀβολόν, συνήγαγεν ὁλοσχερεῖς τὰς λέξεις καὶ παρέδωκεν ἀνθρώποις σοφοῖς καὶ ἐπιστήμοσιν . . .

Peisistratus, tyrant of Athens, was in every way of noble birth, and he contrived this one remarkable deed. He wished, in writing (*engraphos*), to maintain (*diaphulattô*) even the *poiêsis* of Homer. He established games (*agôn* pl.) at public cost, made a public proclamation, and granted license for those who knew and wished to make a public demonstration of (*epideiknumi*) the works of Homer; and, having fixed the price at an obol a line, he gathered together (*sunêgagen*) the readings (*lexis* pl.) in rough form (*holoskherês* pl.), and handed them over to men both clever and learned . . .

*Scholia Vaticana* (cod. C), 5.11–25, ed. Hilgard p. 179

The *Scholia Vaticana* specify that the readings (*lexis* pl.) which Peisistratus gathers together are in rough form (*holoskherês*) only; these readings are later supplied to learned scholars. Evidently, the interpreter of the epigram, having fixed upon a suitable object for Peisistratus to gather (i.e. Homeric verses), is concerned that Peisistratus had no reputation as an editor. Thus, according the *Scholia*

*Vaticana,* Peisistratus collected and transcribed the works of Homer, but he gave his rough draft to learned men who edited it.

The other versions of the legend (*Commentarius Melampodis seu Diomedis* and *Scholia Marciana*) depict Peisistratus as founding not a Panathenaic festival at which rhapsodes competed in performance of epic, but rather a contest of Homeric editors:

ὅθεν τις ἔσθ᾽ ὅτε καὶ ἰδίους παρεισέφερε, τοὺς νῦν ὀβελιζομένους. Καὶ μετὰ τὸ πάντας συναγαγεῖν παρεκάλεσεν ἑβδομήκοντα δύο γραμματικούς, συνθεῖναι τὰ τοῦ Ὁμήρου ἕκαστον κατ᾽ ἰδίαν, ὅπως ἂν δόξῃ τῷ συνθέντι καλῶς ἔχειν, ἐπὶ μισθῷ πρέποντι λογικοῖς ἀνδράσι καὶ κριταῖς ποιημάτων, ἑκάστῳ δεδωκὼς κατ᾽ ἰδίαν πάντας τοὺς στίχους ὅσους ἦν συναγαγών. Καὶ μετὰ τὸ ἕκαστον συνθεῖναι κατὰ τὴν ἑαυτοῦ γνώμην, εἰς ἓν συνήγαγε πάντας τοὺς προλεχθέντας γραμματικούς, ὀφείλοντας ἐπιδεῖξαι αὐτῶν ἕκαστον τὴν ἰδίαν σύνθεσιν, παρόντων ὁμοῦ πάντων.

From which it happened that now and then someone brought forward his own lines (which are now marked with the obelisk), and after gathering together all the lines they summoned 72 experts (*grammatikoi*) to assemble the works of Homer, each one in private, in whatever manner he might consider the assemblage would be best. He summoned them for a premium (*misthos*) that was fitting for intellectual (*logikos* pl.) men and critics of *poiê-mata,* and to each was given all the lines in isolation (*kat' idian*), as many as had been gathered together. And after each one compiled it according to his best judgment into a single entity, he [Peisistratus] assembled (*sunêgage*) all the chosen experts (*grammatikoi*), who were required to make him a public display of (*epideixai*) their individual (*idios*) compilations, with everyone being present.

> *Commentarius Melampodis seu Diomedis* (cod. C), ed. Hilgard pp. 29–30, = *Scholia Marciana* (VN), ed. Hilgard p. 316

According to this version, Peisistratus gathers not just the Homeric verses, but also the seventy-two grammarians who would establish the definitive Homer text. This additional element has its origin in genuine historical detail (the nature of Alexandrian Homeric scholarship) and mythological precedent (the story of the translation of the Septuagint). As I will argue, it is animated by a concern to document the origins of attribution analysis by the Alexandrian grammarians.

All three versions of the legend interpretations begin with a similar premise. The statement, "It happened, as they say, that the works of Homer were destroyed" (found in the *Scholia Vaticana*) is embellished in the other versions:

ἔν τινι χρόνῳ τὰ Ὁμήρου ποιήματα παρεφθάρη ἢ ὑπὸ πυρὸς ἢ ὑπὸ ὑδάτων ἐπιφορᾶς ἢ ὑπὸ σεισμοῦ . . .

At some time the *poiêmata* of Homer were destroyed either by fire or by influx of water or by earthquake . . .
> *Commentarius Melampodis seu Diomedis* (cod. C), ed. Hilgard
> pp. 29–30, = *Scholia Marciana* (VN), ed. Hilgard p. 316

I have argued that the belief that the text of Homer was destroyed is a scholarly dictum that was promulgated by the Alexandrian grammarians. I suggested that this dictum was expressed in Josephus' *Against Apion* in a slightly sarcastic form: "They say that even he [Homer] did not bequeath his *poiêsis* in writing" (1.12). I also proposed that the reigning view in Alexandrian Homeric criticism was that Homer had indeed written his text, but that this text did not survive for Alexandrian "moderns" and so had to be painstakingly reconstructed through philological analysis. If my argument is correct, the Scholia to Dionysius Thrax preserve an alloform of Josephus' version of the Alexandrian dictum: the Homeric text was destroyed prior to the time of Peisistratus and therefore did not survive intact for (modern) readers.

Evidence suggests that the story of Peisistratus with regard to his role in reshaping of the Homeric text eventually became an aetiological myth that glorified the city of Pergamum and its library. The story was likely propagated by the librarian and chief Pergamene Homeric scholar, Crates of Mallos, a Stoic philosopher who had been lured to Pergamum by the Attalid dynasty to head their new library.[6] Pergamene ideology traced the library at Pergamum back to the private collection of Peisistratus, a tyrant of Athens who had charge of the official Athenian texts during his rule.[7] Thus, a story of a Peisistratean version of Homer was an indirect way of praising the Pergamene school headed by Crates, and amounted to a boast that the Attalids had the best edition of Homer, the very one that Peisistratus had gathered or put together. It also may have been used to legitimate the hermeneutic approach to Homer known as allegory, an approach to the epics based on Stoic cosmology and made famous by Crates himself.[8] If this analysis is correct, the aetiology was originally directed against the Alexandrian school of Aristarchus, which was ideologically opposed to turning Homer into a cosmological allegory, and which claimed to have the tools to reconstruct the original text of Homer.[9]

It should not be concluded that the Pergamum-Alexandria scholarly debate presents an uncomplicated lesson for modern advocates of literary theory in their opposition to philology. In contemporary theoretical circles, philology is often dismissed because it alone naively advocated a return to the "real" text. However, in the ancient version of this debate, both sides claimed to have the real text. The Pergamene cosmological or allegorical approach to Homeric interpretation was founded upon the myth that the city had inherited the true text of Homer, while the Alexandrians pursued the true text because it was always out of reach, tainted by human tampering and textual decay.

If the story of Peisistratus was indeed a Pergamene trademark, a means of mythically substantiating Pergamum's text of Homer, as well as Pergamene views on Homeric interpretation, what then is the significance of a legend which appeals to the figures of both Zenodotus and Aristarchus, the pre-eminent Homer interpreters of Alexandria, and conflates them with the myth of Peisistratus' reformulation of the Homeric text? I will return to this question later.

It is difficult to date any of these versions of the legend other than in the vaguest terms. They derive from a period far enough from the time of the Alexandrian library that Aristarchus and Zenodotus can be made into contemporaries of Peisistratus. The Scholia to Dionysius Thrax achieve their current form at earliest in the seventh century C.E., but it is certain that the legend precedes them, and should be dated somewhere between the third and the seventh centuries C.E. One indication that the legend precedes the Scholia to Dionysius Thrax lies in the differing definition of key literary terms. Thus, Dionysius Thrax claims that *lexis* 'word' is "the small-est part of language (*logos*) with regard to syntax (*kata suntaxin*)." The scholia contest this, claiming that the letter (*stoikhos*) is the smallest part, and that *lexis* is rather the smallest part of meaning (*dianoia*); it is the next step up from the letter and the syllable, which had been treated by Dionysius in the immediately preceding units. In other words, for both the scholiast and Dionysius Thrax, *lexis* means 'word'. The author of the Peisistratus legend employs the term in a wholly different manner. In the legend, Peisistratus takes the *lexis* (pl.) which are in rough form (*holoskherês* pl.) and gives them to learned men. What must be meant is the rough "writ-ten dictations" or "readings" that Peisistratus is depicted (in the *Scholia Vaticana*) as having transcribed with his own hand.

A similar piece of evidence can be seen in the variety of inter-pretations given for the words *poiêma* and *poiêsis* in these passages. In the *Scholia Vaticana*, the Peisistratus legend closes with a quota-tion from Dionysius Thrax himself — "rhapsody is part of the *poiêma*" — which the scholiast proceeds to dispute, based on his own understanding of the difference between *poiêma* and *poiêsis*:

"'Ραψῳδία ἐστὶ μέρος ποιήματος." Ποιήσεως ἐχρῆν εἰπεῖν, οὐ ποιήματος· ποίησις γὰρ ἡ πᾶσα Ἰλιάς, ποίημα δὲ ἑκάστη ῥαψῳδία. Διαφέρει δὲ ποίημα καὶ ποίησις καὶ ποιητικὴ καὶ ποιητής· ποιητικὴ μὲν γάρ ἐστιν ἡ ἕξις, ποιητὴς δὲ ὁ μετέχων ποιητικῆς, ποίημα δὲ ὁ στίχος καὶ τὸ σύνταγμα τὸ ἐν ταὐτῷ ἀρχὴν καὶ τέλος ἔχον, ὁποῖόν ἐστι τὸ Κ τῆς Ἰλιάδος ἡ νυκτεργεσία καλουμένη· ποίησις δέ ἐστιν ἥτις ἀρχὴν μὲν οὐκ ἔχει ἐν τοῖς προτέροις, τὸ δὲ νόημα ἐν τοῖς ἐχομένοις ἀποτελεῖ· ἢ ποίημά ἐστι φράσις ἔμμετρος καὶ εὔρυθμος, ἀρχαιοτέρα καὶ σεμνοτέρα τῆς λογικῆς συντάξεως, κατὰ τῶν ὑποκειμένων πραγμάτων ἢ ὡς ὑποκειμένων τιθεμένη, ὑποκειμένων μὲν θείων τε καὶ ἀνθρωπίνων, ὡς ὑποκειμένων δέ, οἷον Σκύλλης, Χιμαίρας καὶ τῶν ὁμοίων.

"*Rhapsody is part of the* poiêma." One should rather say of the *poiêsis*, not of the *poiêma*. For *poiêsis* refers to the entire *Iliad*, but *poiêma* refers to each rhapsody. There is a difference between *poiêma* and *poiêsis* and *poiêtikê* and *poiêtês* 'poet'. *Poiêtikê* is proficiency (*hexis*); the *poiêtês* 'poet' is the one who has a share of the *poiêtikê; poiêma* is the line and arrangement which has a beginning and an end in the same, such as Book 10 of the *Iliad*, which is called "The Night Assembly." *Poiêsis* does not have a beginning in previous events, but brings to completion a thought within its action. But *poiêma* is a thought in meter and with pleasing rhythm, and is more ancient and august than spoken (*logikos*) syntax, concerning matters that are presumed factual or set forth as if they were. It concerns things assumed factual about gods and men on the one hand, and things presented as if they were factual on the other, such as Scylla, Chimera, and the like.

*Scholia Vaticana,* ed. Hilgard pp. 179–80

The scholiast's distinction between the two terms is interesting (*poiêsis* according to the scholiast is a word that describes an entire epic poem, while *poiêma* refers to the smaller divisions as were sung by the rhapsodes), but incorrect as an interpretation of the meaning of these words in the legend. It also gives two definitions of the term: *poiêma* is both a distinct unit within epic, but also means 'poetic language' and 'poetic convention'.

The terms *poiêsis* and *poiêma* have completely different meanings in the Peisistratus legend preserved in the Scholia to Dionysius Thrax. A compendium of the passages from the legend in which these words appear is given below:

He wished, in writing, to maintain the *poiêsis* of Homer.

It is said that the *poiêmata* of Homer were stitched together by Peisistratus the Athenian tyrant.

. . . since at some time the *poiêmata* of Homer were destroyed either by fire or by earthquake [or by an influx of water], and when the scrolls (*ta biblia*) had been scattered and destroyed in every direction . . .

and it was likely that the *poiêsis* in such a state would be given over to forgetfulness.

critics of *poiêmata*
> *Commentarius Melampodis seu Diomedis* (cod. C), ed. Hilgard
> pp. 29–30, = *Scholia Marciana* (VN), ed. Hilgard p. 316

Modern researchers have long recognized that the terms *poiêsis* and *poiêma* have no consistent meaning in the writing of ancient literary scholars.[10] According to the idiosyncratic understanding of the terms in the Peisistratus legend found in the Scholia to Dionysius Thrax, *poiêsis* refers to the Homeric works prior to the activity of Peisistratus, and also describes Homer *in an ideal state*. In contrast, *poiêma* is more than just the text that his efforts bring about; it also refers to distinctly written and perishable documents that contain the *poiêsis*. In other words, *poiêsis* is the Platonic "form" of the Homeric poetry, while *poiêmata* (the plural of *poiêma*) are the written "copies" or "imprints" of this *poiêsis*. So while the *poiêmata*, "the written texts," have been destroyed, the *poiêsis* — "Homer itself" — remains, scattered about, and in danger of being lost through lack of attention. Thus the critics of *poiêmata* are those who involve themselves with the written trace of Homer's *poiêsis*. This conception of Aristarchus and his school as critics of *poiêmata* who are attempting to recover the *poiêsis* (viewed as being the true Homer) is thus very much at the heart of the legend — not only in its narrative, but in its terminology.

To return to the Dionysius Thrax statement and the scholiast's correction, one can locate successive stages in the understanding of these terms.

> "'Ραψῳδία ἐστὶ μέρος ποιήματος." Ποιήσεως ἐχρῆν εἰπεῖν, οὐ ποιήματος· ποίησις γὰρ ἡ πᾶσα'Ιλιάς, ποίημα δὲ ἑκάστη ῥαψῳδία.

> *"Rhapsody is part of the* poiêma." One should rather say of the *poiêsis*, not of the *poiêma*. For *poiêsis* refers to the entire *Iliad*, but *poiêma* refers to each rhapsody.
> *Scholia Vaticana*, ed. Hilgard p. 179[11]

The layers of meaning can be distinguished in temporal terms. I will discuss these in order, from most recent to most distant.

For the Scholia to Dionysius Thrax, *poiêma* is a synonym for "book" (as in Book 10 of the *Iliad* — compare French *chant*); *poiê-sis* is a word used to describe the entire *Iliad* or *Odyssey*. "Rhapsody" is in turn understood simply as referring to one of the customary divisions of epic, such as the Doloneia.

For the legend (which must precede the Scholia to Dionysius Thrax yet postdates the treatise of the Alexandrian grammarian himself[12]), *poiêsis* refers to the Platonic type of the works of Homer, their ideal form in contrast to the imperfect reflection of that form when compiled by Peisistratus. The word *poiêma* indicates the written and imperfect reflection of this perfect Homer. It also has a temporal dimension, for it is the word appropriate to describe the state of the text of Homer following the time of Peisistratus.

For Dionysius Thrax (author of the utterance "rhapsody is part of the *poiêma*"), *poiêma* is a synonym for the epic as a whole. "Rhapsody," on the other hand, is one of the customary divisions that comprise the whole epic, such as the Doloneia. It is interesting to note that this definition of "rhapsody" can be combined with other testimonia about the performance of Homer at the Panathenaia to arrive at a convincing understanding of the original meaning of the term. "Rhapsody" may be the name of an arcane poetic unit for Dionysius Thrax, because it derives from the standardized portion of epic performed by a single rhapsode at the Panathenaia.

In each of these three stages certain poetic terms are understood, and others explicated. In the first stage, Dionysius Thrax explains the meaning of "rhapsody" as a unit of the *Iliad* or *Odyssey* (termed *poiêma*). In the second stage, the Peisistratus legend articulates a distinction between *poiêsis* and *poiêma*, in which *poiêma* is now the imperfect image, the written and error-laden text, while the Platonic "idea" of Homer is called the *poiêsis*. In the third stage, the scholiast now understands *poiêma* to mean either a book of the *Iliad* or *Odyssey*, or one of the rhapsodic divisions that represent a complete action (such as the Doloneia). Accordingly, the best example of *poiêma* is found when these two divisions coincide (such as Book 10 of the *Iliad*, which is identical in content to the *Doloneia*). The word *poiêsis* has also been reinterpreted (possibly due to an idiosyncratic understanding of the Peisistratus legend that the scholiast relates) to refer to the *Iliad* or *Odyssey* in their entirety. In sum, the scholiast and Dionysius Thrax do not disagree on the meaning of "rhapsody," but rather on the meanings of *poiêma* and *poiêsis*. Further, the temporal distinction between pre- and post-Peisistratean "Homers," which is in essence a qualitative distinction between perfect ideal and imperfect copy, is found in the Peisistratus legend but in neither Dionysius Thrax nor the scholiastic discussions of his work. It should be concluded from this evidence that the legend was not originally composed by the scholiasts who recorded it.

As has been stressed, the story of Peisistratus was deliberately avoided by the Alexandrian grammarians, and is not found in the quotations of Dionysius Thrax. Even if the Alexandrians considered that a single individual could be credited with the re-textualization of Homer, they seem not to have spoken of Peisistratus. The idea of the re-textualization of Homer during the sixth century B.C.E. could be advanced by foregrounding other individuals, such as Solon the lawgiver.[13]

### Un-Homeric Lines and the Aetiology of Forgery

Dionysius Thrax had distinguished six characteristics of grammar that grammar should investigate.[14] Receiving the place of honor among these six forms of grammatical evaluation was *krisis poiêmatôn* 'poetic analysis' or 'attribution analysis'. As is clear from the following passage, *krisis poiêmatôn* was taken by later interpreters, if not by Dionysius Thrax himself, as the term for distinguishing authentic texts from forgeries. In the Scholia to Dionysius Thrax, attribution analysis is given a Byzantine twist: the location of forgeries in the classical tradition is training for the search for inauthentic documents among the works of the New Testament.

" "Εκτον κρίσις ποιημάτων, ὃ δή κάλλιστόν ἐστι πάντων τῶν ἐν τῇ τέχνῃ." Κρίσις ποιημάτων μὲν ἡ ἀκριβὴς γνῶσις τῶν ποιημάτων λέγεται· ταύτῃ τῇ ἠκριβωμένῃ γνώσει χρώμενος ὁ γραμματικὸς δεῖ γινώσκειν τὰ βιβλία τῆς ἐκκλησίας πάντα, τουτέστιν τὴν παλαιὰν καὶ καινὴν διαθήκην, ἵνα ὅταν ἀκούσῃ φωνὴν ξένην καὶ σύγγραμα ἢ ποίημα ψευδές, μὴ δέξηται αὐτὸ ὡς ἀληθινόν, ἐπειδὴ ἔστιν εὐαγγέλιον κατὰ Θωμᾶν λεγόμενον. Δεῖ δὲ γινώσκειν τὸν γραμματικὸν τὰ ὀνόματα καὶ τὰς φωνὰς τῶν εὐαγγελιστῶν, ἵνα μὴ ἀλλότριον καὶ ψευδὲς εὐαγγέλιον δέξηται· ἀλλὰ καὶ ὁμώνυμα καὶ ψευδῆ συγγράμματα εἰσίν, οἷον ἡ λεγομένη Ἀποκάλυψις τοῦ ἁγίου Παύλου· οὐ γάρ ἐστιν τοῦ ἁγίου Παύλου, ἀλλ᾽ ἑτέρου Παύλου αἱρετικοῦ τοῦ Σαμωσατέως, ὅθεν οἱ Παυλικιανοὶ κατάγονται· καὶ ἑτέρα Ἀποκάλυψις ἡ λεγομένη τοῦ θεολόγου· οὐκ ἔστι δὲ τοῦ θεολόγου· οὐ λέγομεν δὲ τὴν ἐν Πάτμῳ τῇ νήσῳ, μὴ γένοιτο· αὕτη γὰρ ἀληθεστάτη ἐστίν, ἀλλὰ τὴν ψευδώνυμον καὶ ἀλλοτρίαν. Δεῖ δὲ τὸν γραμματικὸν καὶ τὰ Ἑλληνικὰ βιβλία γινώσκειν· εἰσι γὰρ καὶ ἐν αὐτοῖς ὁμώνυμα βιβλία ψευδῆ, οἷον ἡ Ἀσπίς Ἡσιόδου καὶ τά Θηριακά Νικάνδρου· οὐ γάρ ἐστιν ἡ Ἀσπίς Ἡσιόδου οὐδὲ τὰ θηριακὰ Νικάνδρου· ἑτέρων γάρ εἰσιν ποιητῶν, ἐχρήσαντο δὲ οἱ συγγραφεῖς τῇ ὁμωνυμίᾳ Ἡσιόδου καὶ Νικάνδρου, ἵνα ἄξια κριθῶσιν ἀναγνώσεως. Δεῖ δὲ τὸν γραμματικὸν ταῦτα πάντα καλῶς ἐπίστασθαι, καὶ οὕτως λέγεσθαι καὶ εἶναι γραμματικόν.

*"The sixth [part of grammar] is poetic analysis, which is the fairest of all the uses of the art."* By 'poetic analysis' is meant the accurate appraisal of poetic works. The scholar (*grammatikos*) who makes use of such accurate appraisal must know all the books of the Church, among these the Old and New Testaments, so that whenever he hears a strange style (*phônê xenê*) and false historical or poetic works, he will not consider [it] as if it were truthful, such as the so-called Gospel according to Thomas. The scholar should know the vocabulary and the tone (*phônê*) of the gospels, so that he should not accept a foreign (*allotrios*) and false gospel. But there are also gospels which have the same names as authentic works (= which are *homônumos*) but are false, such as the so-called Apocalypse of St. Paul. This is not in fact of St. Paul, but of another Paul, a heretic from Samosata, and the Paulanicians (*Paulikianoi*) get it from here. There is also another Apocalypse of Theologos, which is not in fact of Theologos. We are not speaking of the one on the island of Patmos, God forbid. For that is certainly authentic; rather, of the pseudonymous and foreign (*allotrios*) one. It is necessary for the scholar to know the Greek books also. False books which share valid names (= which are *homônumos*) are also found here, such as the Shield of Hesiod

and the Theriaka of Nicander. The Shield is not of Hesiod nor is the Theriaka of Nicander; these are of other poets, but their authors used the same name (*homônumia*) as Hesiod and Nicander, so that they might be judged worthy of being read. A scholar should know all these examples well, and thus he is and can be called a scholar (*grammatikos*).

*Commentariolus Byzantinus*, ed. Hilgard p. 568

The study of forged works from the classical Greek tradition is meant to help teach the grammarian how to do his real task — discovering the correct authorship of questionable documents in the New Testament tradition. The basis of this activity is thought to belong to the analysis of grammar, especially vocabulary and *phônê* 'tone, voice'. The problem lies with homonymous works. The term *homônumos* (adjective or *homônumia* noun) here describes works falsely attributed to a well-known author (it elsewhere indicates a work correctly attributed to an author who happens to share the same name with another well-known author). The term implies that the grammarian should keep an open mind about the legitimacy of the work, and should not be unduly influenced by the name it happens to bear.

The phrase *krisis poiêmatôn,* variously translated as 'literary criticism' (Pfeiffer), *Echtheitskritik* (Speyer), or 'attribution analysis' (Blum/Wellisch), is alluded to in the Peisistratus legend.

ἐπὶ μισθῷ πρέποντι λογικοῖς ἀνδράσι καὶ κριταῖς ποιημάτων, ἑκάστῳ δεδωκὼς κατ᾽ ἰδίαν πάντας τοὺς στίχους ὅσους ἦν συναγαγών.

[Peisistratus summoned them] for a premium that was fitting for intellectual men and critics of *poiêmata* (*kritais poiêmatôn*), and to each were given all the lines in isolation, as many as had been gathered together.

*Commentarius Melampodis seu Diomedis* (cod. C), ed. Hilgard
pp. 29–30, = *Scholia Marciana* (VN), ed. Hilgard p. 316

Our understanding of what is meant by this expression has to take into consideration the legend's distinctive terminology. Because the word *poiêma* means something different in the legend than it does in the scholia, the meaning of *kritai poiêmatôn* (= those who perform *krisis poiêmatôn*) also has to be modified. Instead of "poetic analysis" or "attribution analysis" (its sense in the scholia), the phrase here must have the connotation of the kind of critical activity that can be performed upon the imperfect copies (*poiêmata*) of the original Homeric poetry (= *poiêsis*). Accordingly, the *kritai poiêmatôn*, from the perspective of the legend, are those who recover the *poiêsis* of Homer from the *poiêmata*. In other words, they are individuals who reconstruct the original text from the imperfect evidence of surviving written copies.

Another version of the Scholia to Dionysius Thrax brings up the identity of Dionysius Thrax himself and his authorship of the grammatical treatise:

Ζητοῦμεν δὲ καὶ τὸν συγγραφέα, ἵνα τὸ ἀξιόπιστον ἢ μὴ τοῦ συγγραψαμένου καταλάβωμεν· τοῦτο δὲ διὰ τὰ ψευδεπίγραφα τῶν βιβλίων, ὡς ἔχει ἡ Ἀσπὶς Ἡσιόδου· ἑτέρου γάρ ἐστιν, ἐπιγραφῇ δὲ καὶ ὀνόματι ἐχρήσατο τῆς Ἡσιόδου, ἵνα τῇ ἀξιοπιστίᾳ τοῦ ποιητοῦ ἀξία κριθῇ ἀναγνώσεως. Θέλουσιν οὖν τινες μὴ εἶναι γνήσιον τοῦ Θρακὸς τὸ παρὸν σύγγραμμα, ἐπιχειροῦντες οὕτως, ὅτι οἱ τεχνικοὶ μέμνηνται Διονυσίου τοῦ Θρακός, καὶ λέγουσιν ὅτι διεχώριζε τὴν προσηγορίαν ἀπὸ τοῦ ὀνόματος καὶ συνῆπτε τὸ ἄρθρον καὶ τὴν ἀντωνυμίαν· ἄρα οὖν οὐκ ἐστι Διονυσίου τοῦ θρακὸς τὸ παρὸν σύγγραμμα. Ἔστιν οὖν εἰπεῖν, ὅτι ἄλλος ἦν ἐκεῖνος ὁ Διονύσιος < ὁ > Θρᾷξ, καὶ ἄλλος ὁ ποιήσας τὸ παρὸν σύγγραμμα, ἐκεῖνος μὲν μαθητὴς Ἀριστάρχου, οὗτος δὲ ὁ τοῦ Πηροῦ.

One should investigate also the writer, so that we may check the trustworthiness of that which has been written. This is owing to the false ascription of books, just as is the case with Hesiod's *Shield*. This was composed by someone else, but employs both the epigraph and name of Hesiod, so that by the trustworthiness of that poet it might be judged worthy of reading. Some want the present treatise not to be genuine Dionysius Thrax. They make this attempt in the following way. Since the grammarians (*tekhnikoi*) make mention of Dionysius Thrax and say that he separated his address from his name and joined the article and an exchanged name (*hê antônumia*), that the present treatise is not of Dionysius Thrax. In other words, it is as if that person was another Dionysius Thrax, and was a different person from the one who composed the present treatise; the first was a pupil of Aristarchus, and the present writer is the son of Peros.

*Scholia Vaticana*, ed. Hilgard, p. 124

The identity of the true author of the work attributed to Dionysius Thrax is outside the scope of this study.[15] What should be emphasized is that the scholia advocate a methodology allowing forgery and authentic documents to be distinguished, and employ this methodology to ascertain the authenticity of their source text. This turn indicates the extent to which the search for authenticity animates the discourse of grammar: the discourse goes so far as to advocate investigating the identity of its founder.[16]

The discussion of authorship thus makes an appearance in the Scholia to Dionysius Thrax on three important occasions. First, the scholia explain that Dionysius Thrax had made the location of forgery (the chief duty of poetic analysis) the most noble (*kallistos*) goal of grammar. The principles involved were to be sought in the criticism of ancient Greek works and applied to documents associated with New Testament authors. Second, the scholia discuss the veracity of their textual point of departure — the grammatical work known under the name of Dionysius Thrax. Third, they cite an ancient legend that not only displays the motivations for forgery in ancient times during the textual transmission of the most important literary monument of the Greeks, but also validates the critical approach by which inauthentic additions may be located. In this way, the Peisistratus legend functions on an ideological level as an aetiological myth legitimating the highest purpose of Dionysius Thrax's grammar according to the Byzantine scholiastic tradition.

A weakness of the story would seem to be its contention that certain lines had become habitual for the readers that had only just received them. These lines had been added to the epics during Peisistratus' campaign to reassemble all of Homer, and could only have been read for the first time after he gathered them together. The legend's compression of this process is not limited to making

Aristarchus and Peisistratus contemporaries. Having Zenodotus (born ca. 325 B.C.E.) and Aristarchus (ca. 216–144 B.C.E.) be competitors at the same editorial convention is similarly anachronistic, though on a less dramatic scale.

The event is portrayed as if it were a poetic contest between rhapsodes, such as that formalized by Peisistratus in sixth century Athens, or as a contest been tragedians, as took place in the City Dionysia at Athens beginning in the fifth century. Here, the contestants are Alexandrian editors, putting their editorial precision and the ability to spot a spurious line up to public scrutiny. Although the event is pointedly described as non-competitive in nature (they compete οὐ πρὸς ἔριν ἀλλὰ πρὸς τὸ ἀληθὲς καὶ πᾶν τὸ τῇ τέχνῃ ἁρμόζον 'not for competition's sake but rather with a view to the truth and the skillful marriage (harmozon) [of the fragments] in general'), this is nevertheless an agôn in the fullest sense of the term.

Two technical concepts from Hellenistic grammar and philosophy are found in the legend. The terms sunêtheia and prolêpsis are used to account for the preservation of forged lines in the Alexandrian Homer editions:

> Ἐπειδὴ δέ τινες τῶν συναγαγόντων τοὺς Ὁμηρικοὺς στίχους πρὸς τὸν Πεισίστρατον διὰ τὸ πλείονα μισθὸν λαβεῖν καὶ ἰδίους στίχους, ὡς προείρηται, σκεψάμενοι προσέθηκαν, καὶ ἤδη ἐν συνηθείᾳ ἐγένοντο τοῖς ἀναγινώσκουσιν, οὐκ ἔλαθε τοῦτο τοὺς κριτάς, ἀλλὰ διὰ μὲν τὴν συνήθειαν καὶ πρόληψιν ἀφῆκαν αὐτοὺς κεῖσθαι . . .

Indeed, some of those who were combining Homeric lines for Peisistratus, in order to get a bigger premium, added lines, which, as also has been said, they recognized as being peculiar (idios); and already these lines were habitual (en sunêtheiâi) to the readers. This, however, did not escape the judges' notice, but owing to habituation (sunêtheia) and their preconceived ideas about Homer (prolêpsis) they let them lie.

> Commentarius Melampodis seu Diomedis (cod. C), ed. Hilgard
> pp. 29–30, = Scholia Marciana (VN), ed. Hilgard p. 316

The legend would appear to be explaining why athetized lines of Homer remain in the official editions. The term sunêtheia 'habitua-

tion' seems to indicate that the people had already developed a tolerance or even a taste for the incorrect text. The judges were used
to the un-Homeric lines and were unwilling to dispense with them.
The term derives from Stoic grammar, and was a Pergamene term
for spoken language or dialect.[17] The concept of *sunêtheia* privi-
leged the wide variety of grammatical forms preserved in various
spoken dialects of Greek over the relative monoglossia of standard
written Greek. Attention to spoken Greek or *sunêtheia* had been
championed by the Pergamene Homer interpreter, Crates. His approaches on this particular topic at least were welcomed by the
Aristarchian school, otherwise the archrival of the Pergamene
school. The legend seems to criticize the use of *sunêtheia* in editing
Homer, and may thus contain a jab at the Pergamene penchant for
preserving anomalous forms in written editions of Homer.

A similar point may be made about *prolêpsis*. The word, of
Epicurean or Stoic provenance, refers to a "preconception, mental
picture or scheme into which experience is fitted."[18] In the legend,
the editions of Homer produced by the seventy scholars assembled
by Peisistratus are contaminated by a methodological flaw: they decide what Homer ought to include based on preconceived notions.
One wonders whether this was intended as a defense of the Alexandrian insistence on having manuscript evidence for textual emendations.

While Peisistratus is also said to "prejudge" lines of Homer, he
dutifully ignores his first instincts so as not to taint the process of
editing unfairly:

οὐκ ἀπεδίωκε δὲ οὐδὲ τὸν φέροντα οὓς ἤδη προειλήφει παρ' ἑτέρου
στίχους, ἀλλὰ κἀκείνῳ τὸν αὐτὸν ἐπεδίδου μισθόν·

Nor did he chase away even someone holding lines which he already prejudged (*prolambanô*) as originating from another author, but to him too he gave the same premium.
*Commentarius Melampodis seu Diomedis* (cod. C), ed. Hilgard
pp. 29–30, = *Scholia Marciana* (VN), ed. Hilgard p. 316

In this case, *prolambanô* (the verb from which *prolêpsis* derives) is
used not as a pejorative, but indicates that Peisistratus himself did

everything in his power to leave the decision for scholars more in the know. Peisistratus is responsible for retaining un-Homeric lines, even those that he had "prejudged" (*prolambanô*) as belonging to another author. He thus recognizes that *prolêpsis* is not sufficient grounds for textual criticism.

## Ptolemy Philadelphus and the Origins of the Peisistratus Legend

The Peisistratus legend shares many elements with an account about the history of Aristotle's library relayed by Strabo. Strabo's story identifies Aristotle's collection of books as the core of the Alexandrian library, and explains the ideology of the Alexandrian library and the goal of philology.

Ἐκ δὲ τῆς Σκήψεως οἵ τε Σωκρατικοὶ γεγόνασιν Ἔραστος καὶ Κορίσκος καὶ ὁ τοῦ Κορίσκου υἱὸς Νηλεύς, ἀνὴρ καὶ Ἀριστοτέλους ἠκροαμένος καὶ Θεοφράστου, διαδεδεγμένος δὲ τὴν βιβλιοθήκην τοῦ Θεοφράστου, ἐν ᾗ ἦν καὶ ἡ τοῦ Ἀριστοτέλους· ὁ γοῦν Ἀριστοτέλης τὴν ἑαυτοῦ Θεοφράστῳ παρέδωκεν, ᾧπερ καὶ τὴν σχολὴν ἀπέλιπε, πρῶτος ὧν ἴσμεν συναγαγὼν βιβλία καὶ διδάξας τοὺς ἐν Αἰγύπτῳ βασιλέας βιβλιοθήκης σύνταξιν. Θεόφραστος δὲ Νηλεῖ παρέδωκεν· ὁ δ' εἰς Σκῆψιν κομίσας τοῖς μετ' αὐτὸν παρέδωκεν, ἰδιώταις ἀνθρώποις, οἳ κατάκλειστα εἶχον τὰ βιβλία οὐδ' ἐπιμελῶς κείμενα· ἐπειδὴ δὲ ᾔσθοντο τὴν σπουδὴν τῶν Ἀτταλικῶν βασιλέων ὑφ' οἷς ἦν ἡ πόλις, ζητούντων βιβλία εἰς τὴν κατασκευὴν τῆς ἐν Περγάμῳ βιβλιοθήκης, κατὰ γῆς ἔκρυψαν ἐν διώρυγί τινι· ὑπὸ δὲ νοτίας καὶ σητῶν κακωθέντα ὀψέ ποτε ἀπέδοντο οἱ ἀπὸ τοῦ γένους Ἀπελλικῶντι τῷ Τηΐῳ πολλῶν ἀργυρίων τά τε Ἀριστοτέλους καὶ τὰ τοῦ Θεοφράστου βιβλία· ἦν δὲ ὁ Ἀπελλικῶν φιλόβιβλος μᾶλλον ἢ φιλόσοφος· διὸ καὶ ζητῶν ἐπανόρθωσιν τῶν διαβρωμάτων εἰς ἀντίγραφα καινὰ μετήνεγκε τὴν γραφὴν ἀναπληρῶν οὐκ εὖ, καὶ ἐξέδωκεν ἁμαρτάδων πλήρη τὰ βιβλία. συνέβη δὲ τοῖς ἐκ τῶν περιπάτων τοῖς μὲν πάλαι τοῖς μετὰ Θεόφραστον οὐκ ἔχουσιν ὅλως τὰ βιβλία πλὴν ὀλίγων, καὶ μάλιστα τῶν ἐξωτερικῶν, μηδὲν ἔχειν φιλοσοφεῖν πραγματικῶς, ἀλλὰ θέσεις ληκυθίζειν· τοῖς δ' ὕστερον, ἀφ' οὗ τὰ βιβλία ταῦτα προῆλθεν, ἄμεινον μὲν ἐκείνων φιλοσοφεῖν καὶ ἀριστοτελίζειν, ἀναγκάζεσθαι μέντοι τὰ πολλὰ εἰκότα λέγειν διὰ τὸ πλῆθος τῶν ἁμαρτιῶν. πολὺ δὲ εἰς τοῦτο καὶ ἡ Ῥώμη προσελάβετο· εὐθὺς γὰρ μετὰ τὴν Ἀπελλικῶντος τελευτὴν Σύλλας ᾖρε τὴν Ἀπελλικῶντος βιβλιοθήκην ὁ τὰς Ἀθήνας ἑλών. δεῦρο δὲ κομισθεῖσαν Τυραννίων τε ὁ γραμματικὸς διεχειρίσατο φιλαριστοτέλης ὢν. θεραπεύσας τὸν ἐπὶ τῆς βιβλιοθήκης. καὶ βιβλιοπῶλαί τινες γραφεῦσι φαύλοις χρώμενοι καὶ οὐκ ἀντιβάλλοντες. ὅπερ καὶ ἐπὶ τῶν ἄλλων συμβαίνει τῶν εἰς πρᾶσιν γραφομένων βιβλίων καὶ ἐνθάδε καὶ ἐν Ἀλεξανδρείᾳ.

From Scepsis came the Socratic philosophers Erastus and Coriscus and Neleus the son of Coriscus, this last a man who not only was a pupil of Aristotle and Theophrastus, but inherited (*diadekhomai*) the library of Theophrastus, which included that of Aristotle. At any rate, Aristotle bequeathed (*paradidômi*) his own library to Theophrastus, to whom he also left his school; and he is the first man, so far as I know, to have collected books and to have taught the kings in Egypt how to arrange a library. Theophrastus bequeathed (*paradidômi*) it to Neleus, who brought it home (*komizô*) to Scepsis and bequeathed (*paradidômi*) it to his followers, non-affiliated (*idiôtais*) men, who kept the books locked up but not carefully stored. When they found out about the ambition (*spoudên*) of the Attalid kings (the city was under their control) in searching for books for the collection of the Library in Pergamum, they hid the books underground in a kind of hollow. Later, after the books had already been damaged by moisture and moths, their descendants sold them — both the books of Aristotle and those of Theophrastus — to Apellicon of Teos for the price of a large sum of money. Apellicon was more of a bibliophile than a philosopher, and so, seeking a restoration of the parts that had been eaten through (*diabromatos* pl.) he transferred (*metapherô*) the writings into new copies (*antigrapha*), filling in the lacunae (*anaplêroô*) not very well, and the books that he published [= made an *ekdosis* of] were full of errors (*hamartia* pl.). So this is how it came about that the earlier members of the Peripatos, the ones that came after Theophrastus, had no books at all, except for a few, which were mostly exoteric, and thus they were able to engage in philosophical discourse about practically nothing, but only to talk frivolously about commonplaces (*lêkuthizein*). As for the later members [of the Peripatetic school], starting from the time when these books appeared in published form (= *proerkhomai*), it was easier to philosophize and "aristotelize," but they were forced to call most of their statements verisimilitudes because of the large mass of errors. Rome was in large part responsible for this: after the death of Apellicon, Sulla, who had captured Athens, had carried off Apellicon's library. After it was brought home (*komizô*) here [= to Rome], Tyrannion the *grammatikos*, who was a pro-Aristotelian, took it in hand, having successfully cultivated the man in charge of the library. Booksellers also took it in hand, but they used inferior (*phaulos* pl.) scribes and did not collate (*antiballô*) — something that also happens to other books too that are copied for sale, both here and in Alexandria.

Strabo, Geography 13.1.54C 609, trans. Nagy

This story about the library being bequeathed to a line of successors of Aristotle is extremely pessimistic about the possibilities for textual transmission. The line of succession rots out just as surely as the actual texts, which were buried in a kind of hollow in order to escape the notice of the Pergamenes. The successors to Aristotle do even more damage than had been accomplished by the moths and mold: Apellicon buys the library and fills the missing parts of the texts with errors and false conjectures. Copied afresh into new editions, these errors are nearly impossible to spot. The philosophers who used them, originally trained to speak commonplaces about nothing owing to the fact that they had no books, were now subject to speaking plain nonsense, because the books they were referring to had been compromised by a dilettante of an editor. The condition of Alexandrian scholarship presented by Strabo thus explains the intellectual mission of the grammarians.

It is also possible that Strabo's story is a parody of the Alexandrian claims to possess Aristotle's books. Whatever the truthfulness of the claim that Aristotle's books form the basis of the Alexandrian collection, it is generally conceded by scholars that the methodology of Aristotle had a great deal of influence on the Alexandrian school. The Alexandrians obviously took pride in their library's association with Aristotle, just as the Attalid library at Pergamum was apparently validated by the legend that it had in its possession the very text of Homer that had been assembled by Peisistratus. Other stories confirm that Alexandria prided itself on possessing the best manuscripts from Greece, if not the actual books found in Aristotle's personal library.[19] Galen tells how the Alexandrian library gained possession of the Athenian state's official manuscripts of the three great tragedians — Aeschylus, Sophocles, and Euripides. The story relates that Ptolemy rented the Athenian city edition of the three playwrights, and, having authorized the texts to be copied, returned the copies to Athens rather than the originals, shedding few tears about forfeiting his fifteen talent deposit.[20] But Strabo's story casts doubt on the value of Aristotle's books, as well as Alexandrian claims to possess untainted original documents from Athens.

In the foreword of John Philoponus to Aristotle's treatise *In Categorias* "On the Categories," a fascinating story about Ptolemy Philadelphus and his zeal to gather the works of Aristotle appears amidst a discussion about how to distinguish genuine from spurious works of the philosopher. Seven commentaries on the works of Aristotle composed by Philoponus survive, despite the fact that he was anathematized in 680 C.E. on account of his unorthodox Christian Neoplatonist theology. Philoponus, who lived ca. 490–570 C.E., was known as "Grammaticus"; two of his works on grammar survive. He resided in Alexandria, making his comments on both Aristotelian forgery and Ptolemaic book gathering particularly resonant for the discussion of the history of the Peisistratus legend.

Πασῶν δὲ τῶν ᾽Αριστοτέλους πραγματειῶν τὰ προλέγεσθαι ὀφείλοντα ἕξ ἐστιν, ὁ σκοπὸς τὸ χρήσιμον ἡ αἰτία τῆς ἐπιγραφῆς ἡ τάξις τῆς ἀναγνώσεως ἡ εἰς τὰ κεφάλαια διαίρεσις <u>καὶ εἰ γνήσιον τοῦ φιλοσόφου τὸ βιβλίον</u>. καὶ ὁ μὲν σκοπός ἐξαπομάττει τῆς πραγματείας τὴν φύσιν καὶ ὥσπερ ἕξιν τῷ ἀναγινώσκοντι παρέχει πῶς νοεῖν ἕκαστον δεῖ· παρασκευάζει γὰρ ἕκαστον τῶν λεγομένων πρὸς τὸν σκοπὸν ἀπευθύνειν τοῦ συγγράμματος· ὁ γὰρ τὸν σκοπὸν ἀγνοῶν ἔοικε τυφλῷ, οὐκ εἰδότι ὅποι φέρεται, καὶ μάτην πάντα νομίσει τὰ πρὸς τὸν σκοπὸν τείνοντα ὑπὸ τοῦ ἀρχαίου λέγεσθαι. τὸ δὲ χρήσιμον σπουδὴν καὶ προθυμίαν τῷ ἀκροατῇ ἐντίθησι· δεῖ γὰρ τὸν μέλλοντά τινος ἄρχεσθαι μανθάνειν πρότερον τὸ ἀπ᾽ ἐκείνου χρήσιμον, εἰς τί αὐτῷ λυσιτελεῖ. τὴν δὲ αἰτίαν τῆς ἐπιγραφῆς, ἐπειδὴ ἐπί τινων συγγραμμάτων ἔστιν ὅτε ἀδήλου τῆς ἐπιγραφῆς οὔσης χρὴ ζητεῖν δι᾽ ἣν αἰτίαν οὕτως ἐπιγέγραπται, ὡς ἐν ταῖς Κατηγορίαις καὶ ἐν τῷ Περὶ ἑρμηνείας καὶ ἐν ἄλλοις· ἐν γὰρ τῷ Περὶ οὐρανοῦ ἢ ἐν τῷ Περὶ ψυχῆς οὐ δεῖ τὴν αἰτίαν τῆς ἐπιγραφῆς ζητεῖν· αὐτόθεν γὰρ τὸ σαφὲς ἔχει. ζητοῦμεν δὲ καὶ εἰ γνήσιον τοῦ συγγραφέως τὸ βιβλίον· τρεῖς γὰρ ἀφορμαὶ γεγόνασι τοῦ νοθεύεσθαι τὰ συγγράμματα τοῦ Ἀριστοτέλους, μία μὲν ὁμωνυμία <τῶν συγγραφέων> (γεγόνασι γὰρ καὶ ἕτεροι Ἀριστοτέλους, ὧν τὰ συγγράμματα διὰ τὴν ὁμωνυμίαν τινὲς ἐνόμισαν τοῦ Ἀριστοτέλους), δευτέρα δὲ ἡ τῶν συγγραμμάτων ὁμωνυμία (οἱ γὰρ μαθηταὶ αὐτοῦ Εὔδημος καὶ Φανίας καὶ Θεόφραστος κατὰ ζῆλον τοῦ διδασκάλου γεγράφασι Κατηγορίας καὶ Περὶ ἑρμηνείας καὶ Ἀναλυτικά), ἡ δὲ τρίτη τοιαύτη ἐστί· Πτολεμαῖον τὸν Φιλάδελφον πάνυ ἐσπουδακέναι φασὶ περὶ τὰ Ἀριστοτέλους συγγράμματα, ὡς καὶ περὶ τὰ λοιπά, καὶ χρήματα διδόναι τοῖς προσφέρουσιν αὐτῷ βίβλους τοῦ φιλοσόφου. ὅθεν τινὲς χρηματίσασθαι βουλόμενοι ἐπιγράφοντες συγγράμματα τῷ τοῦ φιλοσόφου ὀνόματι προσῆγον· ἀμέλει φασὶν ἐν τῇ μεγάλῃ βιβλιοθήκῃ εὑρῆσθαι Ἀναλυτικῶν μὲν τεσσαράκοντα βίβλου, Κατηγοριῶν δὲ δύο. ἐκρίθη δὲ ὑπὸ τῶν ἐξηγητῶν Κατηγοριῶν μὲν τοῦτο εἶναι γνήσιον τοῦ Ἀριστοτέλους Ἀναλυτικῶν δὲ τέσσαρα. ἐκρίθη δὲ ἔκ τε τῶν νοημάτων καὶ τῆς φράσεως καὶ τῷ ἀεὶ ἐν ταῖς ἄλλαις πραγματείαις μεμνῆσθαι τούτου τοῦ βιβλίου τὸν φιλόσοφον. τάξιν δὲ ζητοῦμεν ἀναγνώσεως, ἵνα μὴ τοῖς μείζοσι πρῶτον ἐγχειρῶμεν καὶ ὧν εἰς τὴν γνῶσιν ἕτερα ὀφείλει προλαμβάνεσθαι, ἀγνοοῦντες τὰ ἡμῖν πρῶτον γινώσκεσθαι ὀφείλοντα. τὴν δὲ εἰς τὰ μόρια διαίρεσιν, διότι δεῖ τὸν ἀκριβῶς βουλόμενον τὴν τοῦ ὅλου φύσιν μαθεῖν τὰ τούτου μέρη ἀκριβῶς ἐπεσκέφθαι, οἷον ὁ τὸν ἄνθρωπον ἀκριβῶς εἰδέναι βουλόμενος ὀφείλει τούτου κεφαλήν τε καὶ χεῖρας καὶ πόδας καὶ τὰ ἄλλα ὁμοίως εἰδέναι μέρη. οὕτως οὖν καὶ ἑκάστου συγγράμματος δεῖ τὰ μέρη πρότερον εἰδέναι, εἰς πόσα καὶ ποῖα διαιρεῖται.

For all the treatises of Aristotle, the matters which should be spoken of first are six: the aim (*skopos*), its usefulness (*to khrēsimon*), the reason for the title (*epigraphē*), the order of the reading, the work's division into main points, <u>and if the book of the philosopher is genuine (*gnēsios*)</u>. The aim (*skopos*) gives a measure of the nature of the treatise, and, like skill/proficiency (*hexis*),[21] explains to the reader how he should understand each part. For each of the things spoken of contrives to guide towards the aim of the work. Whoever is ignorant of the aim is like a blind man, who doesn't know where he is taken, and considers whatever is directed towards that aim to have been said by the ancient one for no purpose. The usefulness [of a work] puts zeal and eagerness into the person listening. For it is necessary for someone about to begin something first to learn from its usefulness, to what end it avails him. The reason for the title: because with respect to some of the works it happens now and then that, when the title is unclear, it is necessary to inquire for what reason it is entitled thus, such as in the case of the *Categories* and *Concerning Interpretation* and in the case of other works. In *About the Heavens* or in *About the Soul* it is not necessary to inquire after the reason for the title, for it is clear from the title itself. We inquire also if the book is genuine. There are three occasions for considering the writings of Aristotle spurious. The first is homonymy <of the writers> (for there have lived other Aristotles, whose writings some have considered Aristotle's, on account of homonymy). The second is homonymy of the works (for his pupils Eudemos and Phanias and Theophrastus wrote *Categories* and *Concerning Interpretation* and the *Analytics* on account of their admiration for their teacher). The third is the following. They say (*phasin*) that Ptolemy Philadelphus was altogether zealous concerning the works of Aristotle, just as he was for others, and that he gave money to those offering him books of the philosopher. On which account some, wishing to be reimbursed, brought him works, which they inscribed (*epigraphô*), with the name of the philosopher. And indeed they say that in the great library forty books of the *Analytics* were found, and two books of the *Categories*. It was decided (*krinô*) by the exegetes of the *Categories* that the present work is genuinely Aristotle's, and four books of the *Analytics*. This was decided (*krinô*) from the design (*noêma*) and the style (*phrasis*) and because the philosophy of this book was always recalled in his other works. We consider the arrangement of the readings, so that we don't first attempt greater ones and others of these readings which, in respect to knowledge, ought to be preceded, being ignorant of the things which ought to be known by us first. The division into parts — since it is necessary that one considering the exact nature of the whole learn to consider its parts, just as he who wishes to know a human being accurately ought to know the head, hands, feet, and the other parts equally. Thus it is also necessary to know first the parts of each work, the quantities and qualities into which it is divided.

Philoponus (olim Ammonius), *In Aristotelis Categorias Commentarium*, ed. Busse, pp. 7–8

The commentary appeals to a grammatical methodology that is already familiar from the work of Dionysius Thrax and the scholia thereto. It directs the scholar to undertake six inquiries with regard to evaluating Aristotle's works, the last of which is the evaluation of the authenticity of the work (this work employs a vocabulary derived from kinship, *gnêsion* 'legitimate' and *nothos* 'illegitimate'). The analysis of the work's authenticity is further subdivided into three categories: the homonymy of the author, the homonymy of the work, and straight-out forgeries resulting from Ptolemy's activity in gathering the library. The first two categories (homonymy of author and work) attempt to resolve the confusion and misattribution resulting from accidental similarity in names or the fact that titles name the subject of a work rather than a unique entity. With regard to both forms of homonymy, the intent to deceive is not a factor. The third category employs the story of Ptolemy II as an aetiology of intentional literary fraud.

As this sixth century C.E. commentary on Aristotle reveals, the figure of Ptolemy II was employed by the Byzantine tradition to account for and historicize both textual fixation and the existence of inauthentic works. There can be little doubt that the Peisistratus of the Scholia to Dionysius Thrax legend is modeled on Ptolemy; the substitution would explain the fact that Peisistratus is conceived as being a contemporary of Aristarchus.

The tradition that blames Ptolemy II for the introduction of literary fraud is found already in the work of Galen (born 129 C.E.), a physician and scholar.[22]

Αὐτὸ μὲν τὸ Περὶ φύσεως ἀνθρώπου βιβλίον ἐν τῷ προτέρῳ τῶνδε τῶν ὑπομνημάτων ἐξήγημαι. νυνὶ δὲ τὰ προσκείμενα κακῶς αὐτῷ προχειριοῦμαι. συγκείμενα καὶ αὐτὰ μετὰ διασκευῆς. ἓν μὲν γάρ ἐστι μικρὸν βιβλίον, ἐν ᾧ περὶ τῆς τῶν ὑγιαινόντων διαίτης γέγραπται, καὶ δοκεῖ Πολύβου εἶναι σύγγραμα τοῦ Ἱπποκράτους μαθητοῦ. τὸ δὲ μεταξὺ τούτου τε καὶ τοῦ Περὶ φύσεως ἀνθρώπου διεσκεύασται, παρεγγεγραμμένον ὑπὸ τοῦ πρώτου συνθέντος εἰς ταὐτὸν τὰ δύο ταῦτα βιβλίδια, τὸ Περὶ φύσεως ἀνθρώπου τοῦ Ἱπποκράτους αὐτοῦ σύγγραμμα καὶ τὸ τοῦ Πολύβου Περὶ διαίτης ὑγιεινῆς. ἐν γάρ τῷ κατὰ τοὺς Ἀτταλικούς τε καὶ Πτολεμαϊκοὺς βασιλέας χρόνῳ πρὸς ἀλλήλους ἀντιφιλοτιμουμένους περὶ κτήσεως βιβλίων ἢ περὶ τὰς ἐπιγραφάς τε καὶ διασκευὰς αὐτῶν ἤρξατο γίνεσθαι ῥαδιουργία τοῖς ἕνεκα τοῦ λαβεῖν ἀργύριον ἀναφέρουσιν ὡς τούς βασιλέας ἀνδρῶν ἐνδόξων συγγράμματα. μικρῶν οὖν ὄντων ἀμφοτέρων τῶν βιβλίων, τοῦ Περὶ φύσεως ἀνθρώπου καὶ τοῦ Περὶ διαίτης ὑγιεινῆς, εὐκαταφρόνητον ἑκάτερον τούτων εἶναί τις δόξας διὰ τὴν σμικρότητα συνέθηκεν εἰς ταὐτὸν ἄμφω. καί τις ἴσως ἄλλος ἢ καὶ αὐτὸς ὁ πρῶτος αὐτὰ συνθεὶς παρενέθηκέ τινα μεταξὺ τῶν δύο ταυτὶ τὰ νῦν προχειρίζεσθαι μέλλοντα.

In the first of these commentaries, I provide an exegesis of the book *Concerning the Nature of Man*. But now, I will discuss these works which mistakenly lie next to it, having been put together through this edition (*diaskeuê*). For one is a little book, in which a healthful life is written about; the treatise appears to be by Polybius, a student of Hippocrates. But the work which appears between the latter work [i.e. that of Polybius] and *Concerning the Nature of Man* was compiled together with them, these two small books (the treatise *Concerning the Nature of Man* of Hippocrates himself and the *Concerning a Healthful Diet* by Polybius) having been interpolated (*parengraphô*) by the first writer (*sunthetês*) into the same work. For in the time when the Attalid and Ptolemaic Kings tried to outdo each other in their zeal (*pros allêlous antiphilotimoumenous*) for the possession of books, fraudulence (*rhadiourgia*) concerning their ascriptions (*epigrahê* pl.) and editions (*diaskeuê* pl.) came in to being (*gignomai*), perpetuated by people who would present the kings with writings as if they were composed by generally approved (*endoxos*) men in order to make profit. Because both of these are small books (*Concerning the Nature of Man* and *Concerning a Healthful Diet*), someone, considering either of them to be negligible owing to their brevity, combined them both into a single work. And perhaps someone else, or even the first author himself, having put them together, inserted something between these two works, which are about to be discussed.

Galen, *Commentaria In Hippocratis De Natura Hominis* I.44 [8 L.], p. 57

Galen's historical thesis, that forgery originates with the efforts of the Pergamene and Alexandrian book buyers, appears several pages earlier in his commentary on Hippocrates' work:

πρὶν γὰρ τοὺς ἐν᾿Αλεξανδρείᾳ τε καὶ Περγάμῳ γενέσθαι βασιλεῖς ἐπὶ κτήσει παλαιῶν βιβλίων φιλοτιμηθέντας, οὐδέπω ψευδῶς ἐπεγέγραπτο σύγγραμα. λαμβάνειν δ᾿ ἀρξαμένων μισθὸν τῶν κομιζόντων αὐτοῖς συγγράμματα παλαιοῦ τινος ἀνδρὸς οὕτως ἤδη πολλὰ ψευδῶς ἐπιγράφοντες ἐκόμιζον. ἀλλ᾿ οὗτοι μὲν οἱ βασιλεῖς μετὰ τὸν ᾿Αλεξάνδρου γεγόνασι θάνατον, ὁ δὲ Πλάτων ἀνωτέρω τῆς ᾿Αλεξάνδρου βασιλείας ἐγεγράφει ταῦτα μηδέπω πεπανουργευμένων τῶν ἐπιγραφῶν, ἀλλ᾿ ἑκάστου βιβλίου τὸν ἴδιον γραφέα διὰ τοῦ προγράμματος δηλοῦντος.

Most especially, Plato was born very near to the time of the disciples of Hippocrates; if this book were of one of these, the name of its composer would have been inscribed. For prior to the advent of the kings of Alexandria and Pergamum who vied with each other (*philotimeomai*) for the honor of the possession of ancient books, not yet were works falsely ascribed. But since those conveying to them writings of some ancient individual began to take a reward (*misthos*), they thus introduced at that time many which were falsely ascribed.

Galen, *Commentaria In Hippocratis De Natura Hominis* I.44 [8 L.], p. 55[23]

Galen asserts that forgery began as a result of the formation of libraries at both Alexandria and Pergamum, employing a reasonable argument in defense of this proposition. However, the argument fails to convince modern researchers, who point out that literary fraud in the Greek works existed long before the existence of libraries at Alexandria or Pergamum.

Galen's argument was equally unconvincing to other ancient scholars, perhaps because they had read about forgeries being committed as early as the sixth century B.C.E. Onomacritus, an Athenian diviner and protégé of the Peisistratid dynasty, had been accused of interpolating or inserting (*empoieôn*) inauthentic verses into the oracles of Musaeus, probably to promote a manipulative political agenda (Herodotus, *Histories* 7.6). Herodotus also describes Onomacritus as revealing only selected portions of the oracles of Musaeus in the Peisistratids' attempt to get the king of Persia to invade Greece, passing over the oracles that spelled disaster for the venture. Pausanius, who states that the works of Musaeus are almost all forgeries, thinks that Onomacritus is responsible, although he stops short of accusing him of having composed the entire corpus (1.22.7). Aristotle also claimed that Onomacritus had forged the poems that were known under the name of Orpheus (according to Philoponus, in his commentary on Aristotle's *De Anima*).[24] The Peisistratids were also the focus of a fourth century polemic between the Megarans and the Athenians over the ownership of the island of Salamis. The Athenians used evidence from the Homeric epics to validate their own claims over the island, but the very verses they cited were contested by the Megarans as forged lines that had been inserted by the Peisistratids.[25]

I propose that ancient scholars who followed Galen reconfigured legends pertaining to the Attalid and Ptolemaic dynasties. These scholars apparently attributed the introduction of forgery to a more ancient set of rulers — the dynasty of Peisistratus — in accord with important ancient authorities like Aristotle. The harmonization of legends relating to Peisistratus and Ptolemy proceeded not only out of an interest to document the harm brought by their manipulation of manuscripts, but also out of a desire to praise the promotion of learning accomplished by both rulers. One such example is found in the opening pages of Athenaeus' *Deipnosophistai*:

ἦν δέ, φησί, καὶ βιβλίων κτῆσις αὐτῷ ἀρχαίων Ἑλληνικῶν τοσαύτη
ὡς ὑπερβάλλειν πάντας τοὺς ἐπὶ συναγωγῇ τεθαυμασμένους,

Πολυκράτην τε τὸν Σάμιον καὶ Πεισίστρατον τὸν ᾿Αθηναίων τυραννήσαντα Εὐκλείδην τε τὸν καὶ αὐτὸν ᾿Αθηναῖον καὶ Νικοκράτην τὸν Κύπριον ἔτι τε τοὺς Περγάμου βασιλέας Εὐριπίδην τε τὸν ποιητὴν ᾿Αριστοτέλην τε τὸν φιλόσοφον καὶ Θεόφραστον καὶ τὸν τὰ τούτων διατηρήσαντα βιβλία Νηλέα· παρ οὗ πάντα, φησί, πριάμενος ὁ ἡμεδαπὸς βασιλεὺς Πτολεμαῖος, Φιλάδελφος δὲ ἐπίκλην, μετὰ τῶν ᾿Αθήνηθεν καὶ τῶν ἀπὸ ῾Ρόδου εἰς τὴν καλὴν ᾿Αλεξάνδρειαν μετήγαγε.

[Athenaeus says that] he [Larensis] had possession of so many ancient Greek books that he surpassed all who have been admired for their collections, including Polycrates of Samos, Peisistratus the tyrant of Athens, Nicocrates of Cyprus, the kings of Pergamum, Euripides the poet, Aristotle the philosopher, Theophrastus, and Neleus, who preserved the books of the two last named [=Aristotle and Theophrastus]. From him [ = Neleus], he says, our own king Ptolemy, surnamed Philadelphus, purchased them, and he transported them, along with the books from Athens and Rhodes, to our fair city of Alexandria.

Athenaeus, Deipnosophistai 1.3a–b, trans. Nagy

This passage focuses primarily on the transmission of Aristotle's books to Ptolemy II, but lists Peisistratus as a pre-eminent predecessor of both. It claims, on dubious evidence, that Peisistratus was among the most distinguished collectors of books.

According to Gellius, Peisistratus was the first leader to supply books for public consumption. He also points out that this tradition was continued by Ptolemy:

Libros Athenis disciplinarum liberalium publice ad legendum praebendos primus posuisse dicitur Pisistratus tyrannus. Deinceps studiosius accuratiusque ipsi Athenienses auxerunt; sed omnem illam postea librorum copiam Xerxes Athenarum potitus urbe ipsa praeter arcem incensa abstulit asportavitque in Persas. Eos porro libros universos multis post tempestatibus Seleucus rex, qui Nicanor appelatus est, referendos Athenas curavit. Ingens postea numerus librorum in Aegypto ab Ptolemaeis regibus vel conquisitus vel confectus est ad milia ferme voluminum septingenta; sed ea omnia bello priore Alexandrino dum diripitur ea civitas, non sponte neque opera consulta, sed a militibus forte auxiliaris incensa sunt.

Peisistratus, the Tyrant, is said to have been the first to make books concerning the liberal arts available to the public to read. Afterwards, the Athenians themselves built up the collection with care and toil. But when Xerxes occupied Athens and burned the city apart from the Acropolis, he stole all this wealth of books and took them away with him to Persia. Much later King Seleucus, known as Nicanor, had all these books restored to Athens. Afterwards a very great many books were collected or made in Egypt, by the Ptolemies; as many as seven hundred thousand scrolls. But in the course of the first war of Alexandria, during the sack of the city, all these thousands of scrolls were given to the flames: not spontaneously, to be sure, nor by intention, but accidentally, by the auxiliaries.

Gellius, Noctes Atticae VII.17, trans. Rolfe[26]

The connection between Peisistratus and Ptolemy as lovers of learning and advocates of the public's right to whatever literature they might desire to read is found also in Tertullian:

Ptolemaeorum eruditissimus, quem Philadelphum supernominant, et omnis litteraturae sagicissimus, cum studio bibliothecarum Pisistratrum, opinor, aemularetur, inter cetera memoriarum, quibus aut vetustas aut curiositas aliqua ad famam patrocinabatur, ex suggestu Demetri Phalerei grammaticorum tunc probatissimi, cui praefecturam mandaverat, libros a Iudaeis quoque postulavit, proprias atque vernaculas litteras, quas soli habebant. Ex ipsis enim et ad ipsos semper prophetae peroraverant, scilicet ad domesticam dei gentem ex patrum gratia. Hebraei retro qui nunc Iudaei. Igitur et litterae Hebraeae et eloquium. Sed ne notitia vacaret, hoc quoque a Iudaeis Ptolemaeo subscriptum est septuaginta et duobus interpretibus indultis, quos Menedemus quoque philosophus, providentiae vindex, de sententiae communione suspexit. Adfirmavit haec vobis etiam Aristaeus. Ita in Graecum stilum experta monumenta reliquit. Hodie apud Serapeum

Ptolemaei bibliothecae cum ipsis Hebraicis litteris exhibentur.
Sed et Iudaei palam lectitant. Vectigalis libertas; vulgo aditur sab-
batis omnibus.

The most learned of the Ptolemies, whom they surname Philadelphus, most acute in all literature, the rival (I would say) of Peisistratus in love of libraries, in addition to the other documents
which age or art recommended to fame (it was Demetrius of
Phalerum that gave him the hint, of all scholars of that day most
expert, chief librarian of the King) — Ptolemy, then, asked the
Jews also for their books, their own literature in their own tongue,
which they alone possessed. Of the Jews had the prophets come;
to the Jews had the prophets ever preached as to the race and
household of God, in accordance with the grace shown to their fathers. Hebrews of old they were, who now are Jews; so the books
are called Hebrew and the language. But that understanding of
their books might not be wanting, the concession was made to
Ptolemy by the Jews, and seventy-two interpreters were given to
him — men, whom Menedemus, himself a philosopher, champion
of belief in Providence, esteemed for their sharing this dogma
with him. Aristeas has told you the story, too. So he left the
records open to all in Greek. To this day in the temple of Serapis,
Ptolemy's library is displayed together with the Hebrew originals.
Why, yes! And the Jews openly read the books. They have that freedom in return for a tribute. Every Sabbath day there is common
access to those books.

Tertullian, Apologeticus XVIII.5–8, trans. Glover

The Ptolemy who is contrasted favorably with Peisistratus is not
the Ptolemy whose efforts resulted in literary fraud or deceit, but
rather it is the sanitized Ptolemy of Jewish/Christian apology. Here,
Tertullian's source is the Letter of Aristeas, although, he was doubtless aware of other stories that relayed the zeal of Ptolemy in gathering together Greek books.

Tertullian was attracted to the comparison between Ptolemy
and Peisistratus in his account of the translation of the Hebrew
scriptures into Greek specifically with regard to Ptolemy's magnanimity in allowing the Jews access to the library. Tertullian's story

about Ptolemy leaving the library open for Jews to read the Greek translations of the Hebrew Bible would appear to be consistent with the magnanimous figure that Ptolemy II cuts in the Letter of Aristeas. But because his public magnanimity appears nowhere in the sources dealing with the Septuagint, as Moses Hadas has pointed out, I would suggest that the motif derives from stories about Peisistratus that depict him as the father of a succession of library patrons who are lovers of public learning.[27] The idea that the Peisistratids were the first to put books on display for the public appears not only in the Gellius passage quoted above, but also in Plato's treatment of Hipparchus (a member of the Peisistratid dynasty). According to Plato (*Hipparchus* 228c), Hipparchus wished to educate the citizens of Athens. He accomplished this by introducing the public performance of the works of Homer at the Feast of the Panathenaia, by retaining as a follower Simonides of Keos, the choral lyric poet, and by inscribing his own elegiac renditions of wise utterances on public monuments as a display of his acumen.[28]

While the preceding examples praise Peisistratus and Ptolemy for their promotion of knowledge, it is easy to see the flip side of a desire for ever-more knowledge. In Strabo's account of the books of Apellicon discussed above, the zeal (*spoudê*) of the Attalids leads to the hiding of manuscripts:

ἐπειδὴ δὲ ἤσθοντο τὴν σπουδὴν τῶν ᾿Ατταλικῶν βασιλέων ὑφ᾿ οἷς ἦν
ἡ πόλις. ζητούντων βιβλία εἰς τὴν κατασκευὴν τῆς ἐν Περγάμῳ
βιβλιοθήκης. κατὰ γῆς ἔκρυψαν ἐν διώρυγί τινι·

When they found out about the ambition (*spoudê*) of the Attalid kings (the city was under their control) in searching for books for the collection of the Library in Pergamum, they hid the books underground in a kind of hollow.

Strabo, *Geography* 13.1.54 C 609, trans. Nagy

The zeal of the Attalids results in a sequence of events in which the books of Aristotle are damaged and forgery is born. It is the key element in the chain of causation, the psychological motivation that explains the sorry state of textual preservation in later times. Excessive zeal in the Attalids' search for books here actually contributes to fraudulence and the demise of the trustworthiness of the manuscripts they seek to collect.

The "zeal" of Ptolemy in gathering together books for his library is a vivid detail that appears frequently in the accounts of Ptolemy's book gathering. Athenaeus highlights Ptolemy's zeal: πολλῶν δὲ ὁ Φιλάδελφος βασιλέων πλούτῳ διέφερε καὶ περὶ πάντα ἐσπουδάκει τὰ κατασκευάσματα φιλοτίμως 'But from all these kings, Ptolemy Philadelphus differed in wealth and zealously pursued (*spoudazô*) all devices, being a lover of honor (*philotimôs*)' (Athenaeus V.203C). In Eusebius' version of the account of the translation of the Hebrew Bible into Greek, this motif is also apparent.

γράφει δὲ ταῦτα ᾿Αρισταῖος, ἀνὴρ λόγιος μὲν ἄλλως, οὐ μὴν ἀλλὰ καὶ παρατυχὼν τοῖς πραχθεῖσι κατὰ τὸν δεύτερον Πτολεμαῖον, τὸν ἐπικληθέντα Φιλάδελφον, καθ᾿ ὃν τὰ τῆς ἑρμηνείας τῶν ᾿Ιουδαϊκῶν γραφῶν διὰ σπουδῆς τοῦ βασιλέως γενόμενα τῶν κατὰ τὴν ᾿Αλεξάνδρειαν βιβλιοθηκῶν ἠξιώθη.

Aristeas, a reasonable man in other respects, writes these things, alluding to none other than the actions at the time of Ptolemy II, called Philadelphus. According to him, the events of the translation of the Jewish writings in the library at Alexandria as a result of the zeal of the king were deemed worthy.

Eusebius, *Praeperatio Evangelica* VIII.1.8

Eusebius also records Demetrius of Phalerum as saying:

σπουδάσω δ᾿ ἐν ὀλίγῳ χρόνῳ πρὸς τὸ πληρωθῆναι πεντήκοντα μυριάδας τὰ λοιπά.

I will be zealous in completing the remaining five hundred thousand in a short period of time.

Eusebius, *Praeperatio Evangelica* VIII.2.1

Comparison between this passage and the Letter of Aristeas is instructive. Eusebius, in other respects keeping the wording of his source, replaces the verb πληρώσω *plêrôsô* 'to fill' with σπουδάσω *spoudasô* 'hasten, be zealous'. The choice of verbs was obviously felt necessary to convey the extraordinary effort Ptolemy took in securing an additional 500,000 volumes for his library. It also provides another example of the way Ptolemy is epitomized by this single word. Galen and others speak of Ptolemy in a related way, as *philotimos* 'ambitious' (cf. the Athenaeus passage above). Through such motifs, scholars were able to provide a single psychological explanation for a widespread phenomenon — the prevalence of inauthentic literary works that had been made quite apparent during the formation of the catalogues of the great libraries at Pergamum and Alexandria.

It was suggested in the discussion above that the epigram found in the Peisistratus legend in the Scholia to Dionysius Thrax served as the kernel around which the various versions of the legend coalesced. Accordingly, the "zeal" motif sheds new light on the conflation of Peisistratus with Ptolemy II. The scholiast (version 1 above) characterizes the zeal of Peisistratus in the epigram as similarly resulting in damage to texts: φέρεται καὶ ἐπίγραμμα εἰς τὸν Πεισίστρατον σπουδάσαντα συναγαγεῖν τὰ Ὁμήρου τοιοῦτον 'The story is also related by this epigram, dedicated to Peisistratus, who was zealous (*spoudasas*) in assembling the works of Homer'. It would appear that the reputation of Peisistratus as being a zealot in the gathering of Homeric lines might have rubbed off from his association with Ptolemy.[29] The message of the "zeal" motif (namely, that excessive thirst for knowledge has negative consequences) provided the story about Homeric forgery with its psychological motivation, just as it had explained the damage to Aristotle's books.[30]

The figure of Ptolemy may have been suitable to explain the existence of forged books, but he did not qualify to explain other sorts of literary fraud, recognized to have been in existence since the sixth century B.C.E., and often connected with the Peisistratid dynasty. Ptolemy could not therefore stand at the center of a legendary aetiology of literary attribution analysis. Instead, Peisistratus was linked with the origin of literary fraud. However, Peisistratus' notorious reputation had to be reconciled with accounts that featured him as a collector of books and preserver of knowledge (qualities that he had absorbed from his association with Ptolemy). To this end, the story of Peisistratus was refashioned into a narrative that promoted attribution analysis as the highest purpose of the discourse of grammar. In a twist of fate, the first forger became the legendary founder of the ancient art of distinguishing genuine authorship and literary fraud.

## The Literary Contest and the Motivations for Literary Fraud

According to Galen, forgery did not exist prior to the advent of significant literary markets for books, caused by the rivalry of the Attalids and Ptolemies. Another interesting legend involving Ptolemy considers an additional factor in assessing the causes of literary fraud — the lure of fame and the negative impact of the literary contest.

Vitruvius' preface to his seventh book begins with a paean to "the ancients" who transmitted their thoughts to posterity in treatises, out of a selfless desire to ensure that ensuing generations should not lack the benefit of their ideas. Vitruvius singles out the concrete knowledge of the deeds of the past recorded in these volumes, as well as the thoughts of physicists about nature, the ethical rules of the philosophers, and the motives of kings of the past as analyzed by the historiographers. His praise of the writers of the past is followed closely by his broad condemnation of literary theft — the inappropriate use of the wisdom of the ancients. He adds that the ancients had their own ways to detect and prevent fraud, describing the vigilance of Aristophanes in this regard at length.

Reges Attalici magnis philologiae dulcedinibus inducti cum egregiam bybliothecam Pergami ad communem delectationem instituissent, tunc item Ptolomaeus infinito zelo cupiditatisque incitatus studio non minoribus industriis ad eundem modum contenderat Alexandriae comparare. cum autem summa diligentia perfecisset, non putavit id satis esse, nisi propagationibus inseminando curaret augendam. itaque Musis et Apollini ludos dedicavit et, quemadmodum athletarum, sic communium scriptorum victoribus praemia et honores constituit.

His ita institutis, cum ludi adessent, iudices litterati, qui ea probarent, erant legendi. rex, cum iam sex civitatis lectos habuisset nec tam cito septumum idoneum inveniret, retulit ad eos, qui supra bybliothecam fuerunt, et quaesiit, si quem novissent ad id expeditum. tunc ei dixerunt esse quendam Aristophanen, qui summo studio summaque diligentia cotidie omnes libros ex ordine perlegeret. itaque conventu ludorum, cum secretae sedes iudicibus essent distributae, cum ceteris Aristophanes citatus, quemadmodum fuerat locus ei designatus, sedit.

Primo poetarum ordine ad certationem inducto cum recitarentur scripta, populus cunctus significando monebat iudices, quod probarent. itaque, cum ab singulis sententiae sunt rogatae, sex una dixerunt et, quem maxime animadverterunt multitudini placuisse, ei primum praemium, insequenti secundum tribuerunt. Aristophanes vero, cum ab eo sententia rogaretur, eum primum renuntiari iussit, qui minime populo placuisset.

Cum autem rex et universi vehementer indignarentur, surrexit et rogando impetravit, ut paterentur se dicere. itaque silentio facto docuit unum ex his eum esse poetam, ceteros aliena recitavisse; oportere autem iudicantes non furta sed scripta probare. admirante populo et rege dubitante, fretus memoriae certis armariis infinita volumina eduxit et ea cum recitatis conferendo coegit ipsos furatos de se confiteri. itaque rex iussit cum his agi furti condemnatosque cum ignominia dimisit, Aristophanen vero amplissimis muneribus ornavit et supra bybliothecam constituit.

The Attalid kings, impelled by their delight in literature, established for general perusal a fine library at Pergamum. Then Ptolemy, moved by unbounded jealousy and avaricious desire, strove with no less industry to establish a library at Alexandria after the same fashion. When he had completed it with great diligence, he did not think it enough unless he should provide for its increase by sowing and planting. So he consecrated games in honor of the Muses and Apollo, and established prizes and honors for the successful writers of the day, in the same way as for successful athletes.

When the arrangements were completed, and the games were at hand, learned judges had to be chosen to examine the competitors. When the king had chosen six persons from the city and could not quickly find a seventh person suitable, he consulted the governors of the library whether they knew anyone prepared for such a duty. They gave the name of Aristophanes, who read each book in the library systematically day by day with comprehensive ardor and diligence. Therefore at the assemblage for the games special seats were allotted to the judges, and Aristophanes, being summoned with the rest, took his seat in the place allotted to him.

The competition for poets was first on the list; and when their poems were recited, the whole multitude by its utterances warned the judges what to approve. When, therefore, the judges were asked one by one, the six agreed and gave the first prize to the poet who, they observed, most pleased the audience; the second prize to the person who came next in their approval. Aristophanes, however, when his opinion was asked, voted that the first place should be given to the candidate who was least liked by the audience. When the king and all the company showed great indignation, he rose and obtained permission to speak.

Amid a general silence he informed them that only one of the competitors was a true poet; the others recited borrowed work (*aliena recitavisse*), whereas the judges had to deal with (= judge [*probare*]) original compositions (*scripta*), not with plagiaries (*furta*). The assembly was surprised and the king was doubtful. Aristophanes relying upon his memory produced a large number of papyrus rolls from certain bookcases, and comparing these with what had been recited (*ea cum recitatis conferendo*) he compelled the authors to confess they were thieves. The king then ordered them to be brought to trial for theft. They were condemned and dismissed in disgrace, while Aristophanes was raised to high office and became librarian.

Vitruvius, *De Architectura* 7.1–10, trans. Granger

The Greek *agôn* was a dubious means of arriving at textual authoritativeness, as this story of Vitruvius reveals. Plato rails against what he calls *theatrokratia* 'the rule of the theater' as a form of democratic abuse that is capable of resulting in immoral literary compositions (*Laws* 3.701a).[31] Similarly, the present narrative reveals that while a literary contest might be valuable as a means of choosing the best literary work, it is worthless in demanding that the rules of the contest be upheld. According to this story, public artistic contests may even have encouraged literary theft. The *agôn* is devised to reward the poet who most pleases the audience with his poetry. But the poem does not belong to the person who claimed to have composed it — it has been plagiarized.

The newfangled technology of the Library at Alexandria and its stodgy librarian-to-be emerge as the heroes of this tale. It should be noted that Aristophanes does not rely solely on his knowledge in reaching a decision as to the authenticity of the play. Aristophanes' suspicions that he had seen the work sometime before are verified by the library's extensive holdings, accessible through its effective shelving system. The message of the anecdote seems to be that while democratically judged poetic contests encouraged literary fraud, the library and its grammarians had the technology and wherewithal to respond effectively.

The story about Aristophanes has an analogue in the stories preserved about Aristarchus in the Scholia to Dionysius Thrax. According to these scholia, Aristarchus had the reputation of being able to recite all tragedy by heart. In recognition of this feat, his pupil, Dionysius Thrax, is said to have painted him with an image of the tragic Muse over his heart.[32] The analogies between the Vitruvius story and the scholiast's anecdote perhaps indicate a common source, glorifying one or another of the Alexandrian grammarians and his prodigious memory. By comparison with this story about Aristarchus, the Vitruvius anecdote's subordination of the grammarian's memory to the enterprise of attribution analysis and the technology of the catalogue or shelving system stands out in stark relief.

The use put to the story about Aristophanes by Vitruvius demonstrates another essential point with regard to ancient theories of forgery and its origin. The development of authorship in the classical world is closely tied to discussions of literary fraud and other forms of abuse. Vitruvius relates his story about plagiarism and its detection in the midst of his encomium to ancient writers, to his literary predecessors and to the sources he has used in compiling his own treatise. Authors are seen as "the ancients" (*maiores*), not as contemporaries; they are authorities (*auctoritates*), not rivals to be challenged in a battle of wits. Further, an appropriate relationship with the author means not stealing from him, but acknowledging one's debt openly, even as one borrows from his wisdom. This peculiar definition of the author as an ancient authority to be revered and not challenged is thus inseparable from the discourse on literary fraud and the ethical directives proscribing inappropriate behavior against the ancients.

The contest and the desire for fame, as well as the sophistication of the Alexandrian "card-catalogue" system and its librarian, are used by Vitruvius to explain the existence (as well as the detection) of literary fraud. As was discussed above, there was also an economic explanation of forgery; Galen had attributed the rise of forgery to the literary market created by the competition between the Ptolemies and the Attalids. In the Peisistratus legend in the Scholia to Dionysius Thrax, the economic explanation for the existence of forged lines in Homer is retrojected back to the time of Peisistratus.

There are two moments in this legend when the premium interferes with the reconstruction of the original text. In the first, Peisistratus announces through all of Greece that anyone who has Homeric lines (τὸν ἔχοντα Ὁμηρικοὺς στίχους) should bring (ἀγαγεῖν) them to him for a fixed *misthos* 'premium' or 'monetary compensation'. The legend specifies that there was no hedging by Peisistratus on the rewarding of the premium (ἐλάμβανον ἀδιαστρόφως τὸν ὁρισθέντα μισθόν 'they <u>invariably</u> received the set premium'). Even lines "prejudged" (*prolambanô*) by Peisistratus as belonging to another author are included in the rough draft he assembles; their owners given the same sum (*misthos*) as those supplying authentic lines.

The premium is also a factor in the second stage of Homeric re-textualization, according to the legend. The "intellectual men and critics of *poiêmata*" also receive a premium for their labors, a premium that is keyed to their status, rather than fixed. Nevertheless, the temptation to get a higher premium for more lines remains: "Some of those who were combining Homeric lines for Peisistratus, in order to get a bigger premium, added lines, which, as also has been said, they recognized as being peculiar (*idios*)." Perhaps it was not originally intended that money should interfere at this stage in the editing process; if these scholars had been given a wage appropriate to their status, there would not have existed any motivation to add lines. Accordingly, it would appear that the *misthos* was understood in both contexts as 'price-per-line'. The premium-per-line was fixed (*horisthenta*) for the common people, but scholars could demand a higher fee. This motif thus provides an aetiology for the existence of lines in the text of Homer that are considered superfluous (*perittos,* equivalent to what other Homeric scholars call *polustikhoi* 'plus verses').[33]

The explicit references to money in the Peisistratus legend are easily matched by the strength of economic imagery in other aspects of the story. The Greek word *adokimos* 'unauthorized' as used in the legend conveys an even more profound economic imagery:

. . . ὀβελίσμους δὲ ἑκάστῳ τῶν ἀδοκίμων καὶ ἀλλοτρίων καὶ ἀναξίων τοῦ ποιητοῦ στίχων παρατιθέμενοι . . .

. . . they added obelisms for each of the lines which were unauthorized (*adokimos*) and alien (*allotrios*) and unworthy of the poet (*anaxios tou poiêtou*).

The legend speaks of three factors that were considered by Aristarchus and Zenodotus in their evaluation of individual lines which are listed on equal footing with their origination: whether a line is *adokimos* 'unauthorized', whether it is *allotrios* 'foreign', or whether it is *anaxios tou poiêtou* 'unworthy of the poet'.

The word *adokimos* signifies either 'that which is not excellent (*dokimos*)' in the sense that its pleasing surface is at odds with its interior, or 'that which has not been sanctioned/held good after a trial' (from the verb *dokimazô*), i.e. 'illegitimate' or 'unauthorized'. Two passages from Plato's *Laws* illustrate intriguing aspects of this ostensibly vague word, as well as revealing something about the perception of the nature of forgery and authorship prior to the Hellenistic period.

πρὸς τούτοις δ' ἔτι νόμος ἕπεται πᾶσι τούτοις, μηδ' ἐξεῖναι χρυσὸν μηδὲ ἄργυρον κεκτῆσθαι μηδένα μηδενὶ ἰδιώτη, νόμισμα δὲ ἕνεκα ἀλλαγῆς τῆς καθ' ἡμέραν, ἣν δημιουργοῖς τε ἀλλάττεσθαι σχεδὸν ἀναγκαῖον, καὶ πᾶσιν ὁπόσων χρεία τῶν τοιούτων μισθοὺς μισθωτοῖς.

δούλοις καὶ ἐποίκοις, ἀποτίνειν. ὧν ἕνεκά φαμεν τὸ νόμισμα κτητέον αὑτοῖς μὲν ἔντιμον, τοῖς δὲ ἄλλοις ἀνθρώποις ἀδόκιμον· κοινὸν δὲ Ἑλληνικὸν νόμισμα ἕνεκά τε στρατειῶν καὶ ἀποδημιῶν εἰς τοὺς ἄλλους ἀνθρώπους, οἷον πρεσβειῶν ἢ καί τινος ἀναγκαίας ἄλλης τῇ πόλει κηρυκείας, ἐκπέμπειν τινὰ ἂν δέῃ, τούτων χάριν ἀνάγκη ἑκάστοτε κεκτῆσθαι τῇ πόλει νόμισμα Ἑλληνικόν. διώτῃ δὲ ἂν ἄρα ποτὲ ἀνάγκη τις γίγνηται ἀποδημεῖν, παρέμενος μὲν τοὺς ἄρχοντας ἀποδημείτω, νόμισμα δὲ ἄν ποθεν ἔχων ξενικὸν οἴκαδε ἀφίκηται περιγενόμενον, τῇ πόλει αὐτὸ καταβαλλέτω πρὸς λόγον ἀπολαμβάνων τὸ ἐπιχώριον· ἰδιούμενος δὲ ἄν τις φαίνηται, δημόσιόν τε γιγνέσθω καὶ ὁ συνειδὼς καὶ μὴ φράζων ἀρᾷ καὶ ὀνείδει μετὰ τοῦ ἀγαγόντος ἔνοχος ἔστω, καὶ ζημίᾳ πρὸς τούτοις μὴ ἐλάττονι τοῦ ξενικοῦ κομισθέντος νομίσματος.

Furthermore, upon all this there follows also a law which forbids any private person to possess any gold or silver, only coin for purposes of such daily exchange as it is almost necessary for craftsmen to make use of, and all who need such things in paying wages to hirelings, whether slaves or immigrants. For these reasons we say that our people should possess coined money (*nomisma*) which is legal tender (*entimos*) among themselves, but valueless (*adokimos*) elsewhere. As regards the universal Hellenic coinage, for the sake of expeditions and foreign visits . . . it is necessary that the State should always possess Hellenic money. If a private citizen ever finds himself obliged to go abroad, he may do so, after first getting leave from the magistrates; and should he come home with any surplus of foreign money, he shall deposit it with the State, and take for it an equivalent in home coinage (*epikhôrios*); but should anyone be found out keeping it for himself, the money shall be confiscated, and the man who is privy to it and fails to inform, together with the man who has imported it, shall be liable to cursing and reproach, and, in addition, to a fine not less than the amount of the foreign money brought in.

Plato, Laws 5.741e–742e, trans. Bury

This elaborate law involves the relation between an internal currency (of "paper money" as it were, rather than coined with gold or silver) and external systems of exchange which employ precious metals. The community is being protected from the dangers of the excess of moneymaking, because "what is called contemptible vulgarity perverts a liberal character." In this passage, the homegrown monetary currency has a certain agreed-upon exchange value (it is *entimos*) rather than inherent value, but only in the context of the society Plato is describing; elsewhere it is of no use (*adokimos*), not only illegitimate as currency but also lacking the precious metal which would give it practical exchange value.

The tokens that Plato describes are in effect an ancient version of modern paper money. Marc Shell explains the lure of the metaphor of paper money in expressing an ideal symbolic system:

> During its historical metamorphosis from commodity (a lump of gold) to a coin (a commodity impressed with the stamp of the state) to paper money (a mere impression), *solid* metal undergoes and participates in culturally and philosophically subversive changes. The widespread use of coins, which are both symbols and commodities, may precipitate some conceptual misunderstanding of the relationship between signs and things, but it does not encourage its users to believe that symbol and commodity, or word and concept, are entirely separable . . . Paper money, on the other hand, does appear to be a symbol entirely disassociated from the commodity that it symbolizes.[34]

The Greek adjective *dokimos* is meant to describe the legitimacy of this "paper" money, and, in effect, the authenticity of the inscription stamped upon the worthless metal. Plato's vision of a society employing metal-free money is one in which the stamp of the state (as *dokimos* 'legitimate') is final, meaningful, and unequivocal, having no recourse to the value of the metal on which it would otherwise be imprinted.

As Shell points out in his reading of Goethe's *Faust*, paper money always refers to a commodity (such as gold) but masks its relationship:

> Focusing on the relationship between paper money and coin, Faust comes to believe that numismatic validity, which is pro-

posed by a coin (as its own inscription) is derived from the coin itself (as ingot), yet in the end he discards this belief when he comes
to consider paper money and inflation . . . In *Faust* paper money is
more subversive than coin insofar as it appears to represent the
value of the commodity directly. Paper money is a token of gold,
but it appears to be a token of exchange value. This value appears
to exist only in the commodity and to be expressed by the price.
Paper money thus doubly enforces the illusion that exchange
value has an independent existence.[35]

In the case of a coin, value derives from its exchange value (determined by the inscription) as well as from the physical metal of the
coin (by a process of metonymy, a relationship of contiguity). Paper
money, on the other hand, only represents the commodity (as a
metaphor) and therefore appears to have no use value and only exchange value. It embodies the notion that exchange value has an independent existence, both by its inscription, designating a fixed
value (negating the idea of market fluctuation in buying power),
and by its illusory independence from the commodity. Similarly, a
state outlawing metal currency asserts the independence of agreed-
upon (exchange) value from inherent (use) value. Plato chooses
the word *adokimos* in order to theorize the particular predicament
of the value of "paper" money outside a community that recognizes
its buying power. In other words, that which is *adokimos* has no
value when dislocated from the context that gave rise to it. In another location it is worthless because the inscription is invalid,
doubly so because it had never metonymically derived value from
its metal (gold). All that is left is its metaphorical relationship to the
commodity — a link that is not recognized by outsiders because it
is arbitrary, and has no meaning outside of its proper context. Thus
there is no possibility of moneychanging outside his utopia.

A second passage from the *Laws* relates the word *adokimos* to
types of poetry that are illegitimate in certain contexts:

ποιητὴς δὲ ἔστω τῶν τοιούτων μὴ ἅπας, ἀλλὰ γεγονὼς πρῶτον μὲν
μὴ ἔλαττον πεντήκοντα ἐτῶν, μηδ᾽ αὖ τῶν ὁπόσοι ποίησιν μὲν καὶ
μοῦσαν ἱκανῶς ἱκεκτημένοι ἐν αὑτοῖς εἰσιν, καλὸν δὲ ἔργον καὶ

ἐπιφανὲς μηδὲν δράσαντες πώποτε· ὅσοι δὲ ἀγαθοί τε αὐτοὶ καὶ
τίμιοι ἐν τῇ πόλει, ἔργων ὄντες δημιουργοὶ καλῶν, τὰ τῶν τοιούτων
ᾀδέσθω ποιήματα, ἐὰν καὶ μὴ μουσικὰ πεφύκῃ. κρίσις δὲ αὐτῶν ἔστω
παρά τε τῷ παιδευτῇ καὶ τοῖς ἄλλοις νομοφύλαξι, τοῦτο
ἀποδιδόντων αὐτοῖς γέρας, παρρησίαν ἐν μούσαις εἶναι μόνοις, τοῖς
δὲ ἄλλοις μηδεμίαν ἐξουσίαν γίγνεσθαι, μηδέ τινα τολμᾶν ᾄδειν
<u>ἀδόκιμον</u> μοῦσαν μὴ κρινάντων τῶν νομοφυλάκων, μηδ' ἂν ἡδίων ᾖ
τῶν Θαμύρου τε καὶ Ὀρφείων ὕμνων, ἀλλ' ὅσα τε ἱερὰ κριθέντα
ποιήματα ἐδόθη τοῖς θεοῖς, καὶ ὅσα ἀγαθῶν ὄντων ἀνδρῶν ψέγοντα
ἢ ἐπαινοῦντά τινας ἐκρίθη μετρίως δρᾶν τὸ τοιοῦτον. τὰ αὐτὰ δὲ
λέγω στρατείας τε πέρι καὶ τῆς ἐν ποιήσεσι παρρησίας γυναιξί τε
καὶ ἀνδράσιν ὁμοίως γίγνεσθαι δεῖν.

Along with sacrifices, they must continually devise noble games,
to serve as festival contests, modeled as closely as possible on
those of war. At each of these they must distribute prizes and
awards of merit, and compose for one another poems of praise
and blame, according to the character each one exhibits not only
in the contests, but in his life generally, magnifying him who is accounted most good and blaming him who is not. Not everyone
shall be allowed to be a poet; for, first, no one who is under fifty
years old shall compose one, and further, no one shall do so who,
though he may be fully proficient in poetry and music, has not as
yet performed any noble or notable deed. But, even though they be
not musical, those poems shall be sung which are composed by
men who are personally good and honored in the State as performers of noble deeds. The adjudication of these shall lie with the
Educator and the rest of the Law-wardens, who shall grant them
the sole privilege of free speech in song; whereas to the others no
permission shall be given; nor yet shall anyone venture to sing an
<u>illegitimate (*adokimos*)</u> song — not even should it be sweeter than
the hymns of Thamyras or of Orpheus, but only such sacred poems as have won the judges' approval and have been presented to
the gods, or those by good men which have been adjudged to have
duly distributed praise or blame. I intend the same regulations to
apply to men and women alike, both as regards military excur-
sions and freedom to compose unsupervised.

Plato, *Laws* 8.829c–e, trans. Bury

Plato's ideal society includes a law about authorship, which encourages the moral excellence of the authors (and the sacredness of their poetry) and totally disregards pure poetic ability and aesthetic value. Consequently, all poetry that is not composed by a societally sanctioned author is to be deemed *adokimos*. Plato takes pains to elaborate that, contrary to one's expectations about the etymology of *adokimos* as 'that which is not excellent', aesthetic excellence is not to be considered in the sanctioning process, and is therefore irrelevant as a criterion in determining what is sanctioned poetry.

Translating this set of relationships into the vocabulary of monetary exchange, one might say that the "paper" money is equivalent to Plato's ideal poetry — it has an inscription but does not derive its value from universally recognized aesthetic value. The inscription on the money is represented by the poet (and one should recall that both the inscription on a coin and the name of the poet inscribed upon a text are designated by the word *epigraphê*). The commodity (gold) is figured as enduring artistic value (such as that of the songs of Orpheus and Thamyras). This artistic value is excluded from playing a role in the determination of poetry's worth. These songs appear to have only exchange value, determined by the inscription (= the poet, the force that authorizes the songs) rather than the going rate in artistic judgment. The independence of coinage from metal — of exchange from use value — proposed by Plato is thus equivalent to his idealized version of literary composition. In the society he describes, the artistic object is *dokimos* 'legitimate' because its composer has been approved by the state, not because of the intrinsic aesthetic worth of the composition.

Both Orpheus and Thamyras, poetic innovators from the mythical past of Greek literature, are cited by Plato as examples of poets whose acknowledged aesthetic merits should not be allowed to substitute for recognizable moral strengths and societal stature.[36] With regard to Thamyras, Plato appears to dislike the poet because he stands for the agonistic underpinnings of Greek poetry. In a passage from the catalogue of ships in the *Iliad*, the mortal Thamyras boastfully challenges the Muses to a contest, and upon his defeat, is maimed and loses both his divine gift of singing and his ability to play the lyre (*Iliad* 2.594–600). Andrew Ford's compelling analysis of this episode focuses on the fact that Homer's poems attempt to efface all mention of competition between human poets. Nevertheless, the agonistic element surfaces: "where all horizontal relationships between poets are ignored, interpoetic strife can be played out only along the vertical axis of the Muse-poet."[37] As Ford notes, Thamyras is the only named and identified singer in the *Iliad*, and stands in that poem for preceding poets. But in a sense he also stands for the hubris of the individual attempting to make a name for himself at the expense of the tradition, embodied in the persons of the Muses: "Thamyras' attempt to take on the Muses is also a battle to claim priority and authority for the single singer against the tradition."[38]

Plato's dismissal of the *adokimos* 'illegitimate' song, even if it should be better than the hymns of Orpheus or Thamyras, is made more comprehensible through an understanding of the Thamyras reference.

μηδέ τινα τολμᾶν ᾄδειν ἀδόκιμον μοῦσαν μὴ κρινάντων τῶν νομοφυλάκων, μηδ' ἂν ἡδίων ᾖ τῶν Θαμύρου τε καὶ Ὀρφείων ὕμνων, ἀλλ' ὅσα τε ἱερὰ κριθέντα ποιήματα ἐδόθη τοῖς θεοῖς, καὶ ὅσα ἀγαθῶν ὄντων ἀνδρῶν ψέγοντα ἢ ἐπαινοῦντά τινας ἐκρίθη μετρίως δρᾶν τὸ τοιοῦτον.

. . . nor yet shall anyone venture to sing an illegitimate (*adokimos*) song — not even should it be sweeter than the hymns of Thamyras or of Orpheus, but only such sacred poems as have won the judges' approval and have been presented to the gods, or those by good men which have been adjudged to have duly distributed praise or blame.

Plato, *Laws* 8.829d–e, trans. Bury

Just as in the *Iliad*, Thamyras here stands for the kind of poetic individualism that Plato would rather not recognize in the hypothetical running of a state, not just a composer of beautiful poetry. Plato would have the poet be less than the society (a viewpoint that echoes his critique of poetry in the Republic and confirms his place outside the prevailing economics of Greek agonistic poetics), rather than a genius whose skill and hubris would compel him to challenge the authority of tradition or community.

A similar point may be made about Plato's mention of Orpheus. In Plato's *Symposium,* Orpheus is unfavorably compared to Alcestis:

οὕτω καὶ θεοὶ τὴν περὶ τὸν ἔρωτα σπουδήν τε καὶ ἀρετὴν μάλιστα τιμῶσιν. Ὀρφέα δὲ τὸν Οἰάγρου ἀτελῆ ἀπέπεμψαν ἐξ Ἅιδου, φάσμα δείξαντες τῆς γυναικὸς ἐφ' ἣν ἧκεν, αὐτὴν δὲ οὐ δόντες, ὅτι μαλθακίζεσθαι ἐδόκει, ἅτε ὢν κιθαρῳδός, καὶ οὐ τολμᾶν ἕνεκα τοῦ ἔρωτος ἀποθνῄσκειν ὥσπερ Ἄλκηστις, ἀλλὰ διαμηχανᾶσθαι ζῶν εἰσιέναι εἰς Ἅιδου. τοιγάρτοι διὰ ταῦτα δίκην αὐτῷ ἐπέθεσαν, καὶ ἐποίησαν τὸν θάνατον αὐτοῦ ὑπὸ γυναικῶν.

In this manner even the gods give special honor to zeal and courage in concerns of love. But Orpheus, son of Oeagrus, they sent back with failure from Hades, showing him only a wraith of the woman for whom he came; her real self they would not bestow, for he was accounted to have gone upon a coward's quest, too like the minstrel that he was, and to have lacked the spirit to die as Alcestis did for the sake of love, when he contrived the means of entering Hades alive. Wherefore they laid upon him the penalty he deserved, and caused him to meet his death at the hands of women.

Plato, *Symposium* 179d, trans. Lamb

Both heroes descended to the underworld on a quest for the life of another; but Alcestis does not do so with the aim of continuing to live, as did Orpheus. Consequently, Orpheus is rewarded only with the wraith (*phasma*) of the person he seeks to save; this wraith is all surface and no substance.[39] For Plato, Orpheus' cowardice cannot compare with the virtue of Alcestis, who truly saves her husband from death. Orpheus is for Plato a symbol of artistic skill absent of true moral integrity. It is thus fitting that the sweetness of Orpheus' hymns is irrelevant to their legitimization.

Plato's literary criticism in the *Laws* renegotiates the terms by which literary excellence is to be determined. Building upon a system of representation in which inherent commodity value is metaphorically replaced, Plato describes a situation in which controlling the access to authorship has become the most effective means of creating a body of texts that reflects the society's ethical standards. As in Plato's critique of poetry in the *Republic*, the aesthetic value of poetry is subordinated to its moral value. A poem that is *adokimos* is one whose author has violated moral norms or ideals. It is through a process of weeding out unacceptable poets that a poem's value can be most effectively monitored and controlled. The stature of the poet is the sole factor in determining the acceptability of the poetic object.

For Plato, a fraudulent work is the product of a censored author. By this definition, he sets the stage for the impersonation of legitimate authors by authors wishing to enter this closed system. This has nothing to do with textual originality, for the discussion assumes that all texts are original. The passage also says nothing about the legal conditions under which a name may be properly attached to a text. It speaks only to the conditions under which a named text is legal, or more accurately, when a poet is to be given societal dispensation to compose new works.

In deemphasizing the value of originality or beauty, Plato's treatment of poetic composition shares some features with Vitruvius' critique of the abuses of *theatrokratia* 'rule of the theater'. In the Vitruvius story, the audience endorses poetry that pleases it and that presumably has the highest aesthetic value. This story could easily have turned out otherwise; Aristophanes of Byzantium might have revealed to the audience that the great works of the past are more enjoyable than the latest fad. Instead, he functions in the narrative as a voice of authority advocating originality and proper attribution at the expense of beauty. Vitruvius, unlike Plato, is not interested in the moral attributes of the poet, but only in the accuracy of the link between name and text. But both writers are similarly opposed to rewarding aesthetic value for its own sake, without regard to the conditions under which the work was composed.

We have seen how the word *adokimos* in Plato describes a currency that is valueless outside of the society that accepts it and a song composed by an unacceptable author. The word bespeaks a concern with the conditions under which a name or an inscription may be properly associated with a text or a value. This helps us understand what is meant in the Peisistratus legend when inauthentic Homeric lines are athetized on the ground that they are *adokimos*. A poetic line only has value in the context from which it arose; elsewhere it is *allotrios* 'foreign' and illegitimate tender. Moreover, the inauthentic Homeric line is *adokimos* because its composer is not on the moral level of Homer (hence it is also described as *anaxios* 'unworthy' of Homer), but not because it is aesthetically inferior.

Plato's approach to attribution and composition resonates with some Jewish views on these questions. His delineation of a system in which poets are determined to be morally acceptable or rejected as such recalls Josephus' idea of a succession of prophets, where only texts written by an authorized individual are to be considered authoritative. Philo, a Hellenistic Jew who saw himself as a practitioner of Plato's philosophy, both narrows and expands Plato's notion of testing for literary authoritativeness.

λόγιον οὖν ἐστιν ἐν ἡμῖν τὸ φωνητήριον ὄργανον, ὅπερ ἐστὶν ὁ γεγωνὼς λόγος· οὗτος δὲ ἢ ἀκριτόμυθός ἐστι καὶ ἀδόκιμος ἢ κεκριμένος καὶ δόκιμος· εἰς ἔννοιαν δ' ἡμᾶς ἄγει λόγου τοῦ κατὰ διάκρισιν· τὸ γὰρ λόγιόν φησιν οὐ τὸ ἄκριτον ἢ κίβδηλον, ἀλλὰ τὸ τῶν κρίσεων, ἴσον τῷ διακεκριμένῳ καὶ ἐξητασμένῳ

The "oracle," then, is in us the organ of speech, which is the uttered word: and this may either be rejected (*adokimos*) as spoken at random (*akritomuthos*) or may be approved (*krinô*) as well-judged (*dokimos*). But the sacred writer [the writer of Exodus 28:30] is leading us to think of the word spoken with judgment and discernment (*kata diakrisin*); for he tells us that the oracle is not the untested (*akritos*) or counterfeit (*kibdêlos*) one, but "the oracle of the judgments," an expression tantamount to "well tested (*diakrinô*) and examined."

Philo, *Allegorical Interpretation* iii.119, trans. Colson

Philo here explicates the phrase from the Septuagint translation of Exodus 28:30, τὸ λόγιον τῶν κρίσεων 'the oracle of the judgments', and concludes that it refers to those oracles which have been tested and approved, as opposed to those oracles which are untested, *adokimos,* and counterfeit. In other words, not all oracles are valid; some are to be rejected through discernment and examination (verbs *krinô* and *diakrinô*). Philo does not consider the writer as decisive in testing the validity of an oracle, for a single individual is assumed able to speak both authoritative and non-authoritative utterances.

It seems likely that Philo is aware of the Platonic understanding of *dokimos* and *adokimos* in this passage. Both contexts of Plato's use of *adokimos* in the *Laws* — the realms of monetary and textual authenticity — are found in this passage. There is a straightforward reference to the semantics of coinage in *kibdêlos* 'counterfeit'. While Philo does not refer to the status of the writer in his evaluation of valid and invalid oracles, his focus on the difference between acceptable and unacceptable oracles echoes Plato's focus on the difference between poetry that is sanctioned and unsanctioned by the state.

Philo's distinction between authoritative and non-authoritative prophetic utterances also recalls Plato's discussion of the judging of oracles in the *Timaeus* of Plato.

> τοῦ δὲ μανέντος ἔτι τε ἐν τούτῳ μένοντος οὐκ ἔργον τὰ φανέντα καὶ φωνηθέντα ὑφ' ἑαυτοῦ κρίνειν. ἀλλ' εὖ καὶ πάλαι λέγεται τὸ πράττειν καὶ γνῶναι τά τε αὐτοῦ καὶ ἑαυτὸν σώφρονι μόνῳ προσήκειν. ὅθεν δὴ καὶ τὸ τῶν προφητῶν γένος ἐπὶ ταῖς ἐνθέοις μαντείαις κριτὰς ἐπικαθιστάναι νόμος·

> When a man has fallen into frenzy and is still in that condition, it is not for him to determine the meaning of his own visions and utterances; rather the old saying is true, that only the sound in mind can attend to his own concerns and know himself. Hence it is the custom to appoint the lineage (*genos*) of declarers (*prophêtês* pl.) to be judges (*kritês* pl.) over the inspired (*entheos* pl.) mantic utterances (*manteia* pl.)

> Plato, *Timaeus* 72a–b, trans. Nagy

According to Plato, because the *mantis* 'seer' is in a frenzy, he cannot determine the meaning of his utterances. A *genos* 'line' of prophets is thus appointed as judges (*kritês* pl., from the same root as *krinô*). Philo transforms this statement to reflect the Jewish understanding of the prophet as the individual who is inhabited by God (rather than the *mantis* as Plato has it). The Jewish prophet is not able to "judge" the authoritativeness of his utterances. The expression in Exodus 28:30, τὸ λόγιον τῶν κρίσεων 'the oracle of the judgments', thus refers to a subsequent process of judging (*krinô* and *diakrinô*) on the part of some societally sanctioned party.

Philo's use of *diakrinô* may shed some light on another interpretive problem that was at issue in chapter 1. In the Septuagint's translation of Proverbs 25:1 ("These too are the proverbs of King Solomon which the men of Hezekiah copied out"), the adjective *adiakritoi*, qualifying the word *paideiai* 'proverbs' or 'maxims', is inserted into the Greek translation. The word, which appears nowhere else in the Septuagint, might have been intended to refer to the fact that these works were unedited and somehow formless, hence Symmachus' use of the word to translate "formless" in Genesis 1:2 ("the earth was formless [*adiakritos*] and void"). Alternately, it could have been meant to indicate that Proverbs 25–29 had been mixed with other works (the understanding of pseudo-Hippolytus). For Philo, the verb *diakrinô* 'well-tested' seems to refer to the process by which authenticity of an oracle is determined. Assuming that Philo's Alexandrian Jewish diction gives special insight into the meaning of the Septuagint's *adiakritoi paideiai*, I propose that the expression should be translated "untested maxims", or "maxims whose prophetic authoritativeness has not been determined." This translation expresses some of the same doubts about Proverbs 25–29 found in some other ancient interpretations of the verse. It assumes a tested oracular legitimacy for the Proverbs 1–24, and articulates the provisional and unverified status of the utterances found in the rest of the book.

We have seen that the Peisistratus legend participates in the varied and complicated ancient literary discourse that considered the nature of proper and improper literary utterances. The legend relates to a variety of traditions that aetiologize literary fraud, but also taps into normative discussions found in Platonic treatments of poetic and oracular composition. Both strands of ancient literary discussions of authorship are intriguing in their own right, and shed light on the eventual integration of critical and normative dimensions of authorship by early Christians.

## The Peisistratus Legend and the Septuagint

Scholars have long been aware that the Peisistratus legend in the Scholia to Dionysius Thrax was "contaminated" by the legend of the translation of the Septuagint. Many of the features of the legend are acknowledged to originate from the Septuagint translation accounts, including the presence of seventy-two interpreters found in the Peisistratus legend, the motif of the seclusion of the editors, the final public convocation of the editors, and their ratification of an agreed-upon text.

The translation of the Septuagint at the behest of Ptolemy is reported in the Letter of Aristeas and in a host of later references. In this Alexandrian Jewish tradition, the number of elders is given variously as either seventy or seventy-two. In the Peisistratus legend, the choice of seventy-two (as opposed to seventy) can be partly attributed to the "obelizing" of the ungenuine lines of Homer. The number seventy-two, written in the Ionic alphabet οβ', was perhaps mnemonically influenced by the most vivid words in the narrative. Both the obolos coin that Peisistratus pays for each Homeric verse (in the first version of the legend), and the obelos or the dagger-like editorial markings invented by Zenodotus and used by the Alexandrian critics to mark inauthentic lines of Homer begin with these letters. The legend clearly seeks to explain the significance of the seventy-two editors, inherited from the Septuagint translation account, through this wordplay.[40]

Ancient versions of the Septuagint translation vary in their employment of the number of Jewish elders that performed the translation. The oscillation between seventy and seventy-two in the various accounts of the translation of Hebrew scriptures is aptly explained by Gilles Dorival as a matter of the symbolic character of these numbers, rather than of a true historical discrepancy.[41] This idea hearkens back to Exodus 24, where the biblical blueprint for a deliberative body composed of seventy elders and headed by two preeminent leaders (Moses and Aaron) is found. Accordingly, either "70" or "72" can be used to refer to this same political entity, variously conceived as including its leaders within its number or not.

The "contamination" of the Peisistratus legend by the Septuagint translation story is also visible in a motif that runs through many of the versions of tale. According to a number of these versions, the Greek translation of the Hebrew Bible is authoritative and miraculous because all seventy experts arrive at an identical version without having consulted with each other. In the Dionysius Thrax legend, the unedited transcripts of Homer that had been collected by Peisistratus are given to the seventy-two editors individually rather than while assembled ("and to each were given all the lines individually [*kat' idian*]"). The presence of this element is meant to convey that their editorial decision-making was not influenced by group dynamics, but was the product of individual scrutiny.[42] However, it is certain that the motif derives from the Septuagint tale and was later fitted to its new context.

In several of the accounts of the translation of the Bible into Greek that postdate the Letter of Aristeas (the earliest example of the story of the translation), it is claimed that the translations of the seventy or seventy-two elders were miraculously identical. This miraculous identity derives from a midrashic-style interpretation of a single verse in the Greek Bible (Exodus 24:11) by Hellenized Jewish exegetes. The key word in the Septuagint version of Ex. 24.11, according to Moses Hadas, is *diaphônein* 'to disagree':

> At Ex. 24:11 where the elders are spoken of and where the Hebrew gives "And upon the nobles of the children of Israel He laid not His hand," the LXX gives "And of the chosen ones of Israel not one perished." The verb used is *diaphônein*, of which the common meaning is 'disagreed'. Such a homonym is ideal material for midrashic ingenuity. The context in Exodus is the solemn transmission of the Law, for which the elders represented the people. No better verse could be imagined to prove the unanimity and demonstrate the authority of a new transmission of the Law.[43]

The universal agreement of the seventy interpreters, according to Hadas, derives from a homiletic reading of a verse in the Septuagint, which, even in its plain sense, represents an alteration of the Hebrew original. Why should Hellenized Jewish interpreters of the Septuagint seek to perform midrash on the Greek version of this one particular verse in Exodus? The matter may be explained by attention to the role this verse played in the polemic between Greek-speaking Jews who viewed the Septuagint as authoritative, and Jews from Palestine or Babylonia who argued that the Septuagint was invalid because it mistranslated Hebrew verses.[44] Among the verses that the rabbis allege were altered by the translators for King Ptolemy (these number from seven to twenty verses according to the various rabbinic sources), one can find Exodus 24:11.

The Hebrew Masoretic Text of Ex. 24:11 is markedly different from its Greek translation, although not precisely in the way imagined by rabbinic detractors of the Septuagint:

MT:  וְאֶל-אֲצִילֵי בְּנֵי יִשְׂרָאֵל לֹא שָׁלַח יָדוֹ וַיֶּחֱזוּ אֶת-הָאֱלֹהִים וַיֹּאכְלוּ וַיִּשְׁתּוּ׃

MT translation: Against <u>the nobles</u> of the Israelites <u>he did not send his hand</u>; and they beheld the Lord and they ate and drank.

LXX: καὶ <u>τῶν ἐπιλέκτων</u> τοῦ Ισραηλ <u>οὐ διεφώνησεν οὐδὲ εἷς·</u> καὶ ὤφθησαν ἐν τῷ τόπῳ τοῦ θεοῦ καὶ ἔφαγον καὶ ἔπιον.[45]

LXX translation: And of <u>the chosen</u> of Israel <u>not a single one failed to answer</u> (diaphônêsan); and they were seen in the place of the Lord, and they ate and drank.

Rabbinic version of the LXX translation:[46]
... ואל זטוטי בני ישראל לא שלח ידו

Translation of rabbinic version: Against <u>the youths</u> of the Israelites he did not send his hand ...

The anomalous Septuagint translation of Ex. 24:11 has not yet been adequately explained by scholars. What is certain is that the verse played a role in the debate between Jewish communities as to the validity of the Greek translation itself. One of the most striking elements in the Greek version is the inexplicable οὐ διεφώνησεν οὐδὲ εἷς 'not a single one failed to answer'. As Hadas pointed out, *diaphônein* was interpreted by ancient exegetes to mean "disagree" (thus making the verse read, "not a single one disagreed"). This interpretation of the verse went on to influence the growth of the Septuagint translation legend.

The rabbis who focused on the verse make the point that the Masoretic text's *hapax legomenon* אֲצִילֵי *'aziley* 'nobles' is given the Greek equivalent of זָטוּטֵי *zaṭuṭey* 'youths'. However, the Septuagint in fact employs the word *epilektoi* 'chosen ones'; and in any event, this word is not by any means the most objectionable part of its rendering of the verse. (The confusion exhibited by these Tannaitic legends would appear to spring from a similar verse in the same chapter [Ex.24:5], where the Septuagint correctly translates וַיִּשְׁלַח אֶת־נַעֲרֵי בְּנֵי יִשְׂרָאֵל 'he sent the youths of the Israelites'.) The rabbis had a tradition that acknowledged translation flaws in the Septuagint, even if the precise nature of these differences was not a matter of firsthand knowledge, due to their ignorance of the Greek language. The rabbis may have focused on this verse in particular because Hellenistic Jews employed the verse to promulgate an argument about the inspired quality of the Septuagint. By discerning a hidden message in the key word in this verse, advocates of the Septuagint argued that the translation was perfectly accurate or even miraculously inspired. The attention given to this passage in both Talmudic and Alexandrian Jewish exegesis suggests that the verse was a nexus of an ideological dispute between the two communities. The Alexandrians used it to vouch for the legitimacy of their translation; the rabbis found it indicative of the kinds of errors in translation that were to be found all over the Septuagint.

In Josephus' criticism of Homeric transmission, he makes use of a metaphor of harmful textual "discrepancies" or "discordances" that is elucidated through comparison with the Septuagint translation of Ex. 24:11:

καί φασιν οὐδὲ τοῦτον ἐν γράμμασι τὴν αὐτοῦ ποίησιν καταλιπεῖν, ἀλλὰ διαμνημονευομένην ἐκ τῶν ᾀσμάτων ὕστερον συντεθῆναι καὶ διὰ τοῦτο πολλὰς ἐν αὐτῇ σχεῖν <u>τὰς διαφωνίας</u>.

and they say, that he [Homer] did not bequeath his poems in writing, but having been recalled from songs, it was later assembled, and for this reason has so many <u>discordances (*diaphônia*)</u>.

Josephus, *Against Apion* 1.13

According to Josephus, Homeric inaccuracies result from a lack of respect of the written word and a haphazard and untrustworthy oral tradition. He describes these inaccuracies as *diaphôniai* 'discordances'. The significance of "discordances" may be best seen from the Septuagint version of Ex. 24:11 ("not a single person was discordant [*diaphônêsan*]"). The state of the Homeric epics could not be further from Josephus' description of the unambiguous univocality of the Hebrew manuscripts of the Bible. In the eyes of the Hellenistic Jewish community in Alexandria, the lack of discordance or multiformity in the textualization of the Bible extended even to its translation. This assurance embodied the deep faith among even the most Hellenized Jews in the unequivocal textual trustworthiness of scripture.

In his own account of the translation of the Septuagint, Josephus does not claim that the translation of the Septuagint was a mystical and prophetic process; nor does he claim that the Septuagint is a perfect translation. It is, however, a single agreed-upon text, rather than one that exists in a bewildering array of divergent manuscripts.

οἱ δ' ὡς ἔνι μάλιστα φιλοτίμως καὶ φιλοπόνως ἀκριβῆ τὴν ἑρμηνείαν ποιούμενοι μέχρι μὲν ὥρας ἐνάτης πρὸς τούτῳ διετέλουν ὄντες . . . Μεταγραφέντος δὲ τοῦ νόμου καὶ τοῦ κατὰ τὴν ἑρμηνείαν ἔργου τέλος ἐν ἡμέραις ἑβδομήκοντα καὶ δυσὶν λαβόντος, συναγαγὼν ὁ Δημήτριος τοὺς Ἰουδαίους ἅπαντας εἰς τὸν τόπον, ἔνθα καὶ μετεβλήθησαν οἱ νόμοι, παρόντων καὶ τῶν ἑρμηνέων ἀνέγνω τούτους.τὸ δὲ πλῆθος ἀπεδέξατο μὲν καὶ τοὺς διασαφήσαντας πρεσβυτέρους τὸν νόμον, ἐπήνεσεν δὲ καὶ τὸν Δημήτριον τῆς ἐπινοίας ὡς μεγάλων ἀγαθῶν αὐτοῖς εὑρετὴν γεγενημένον, παρεκάλεσάν τε δοῦναι καὶ τοῖς ἡγουμένοις αὐτῶν ἀναγνῶναι τὸν νόμον, ἠξίωσάν τε [πάντες] ὅ τε ἱερεὺς καὶ τῶν ἑρμηνέων οἱ πρεσβύτεροι καὶ τοῦ πολιτεύματος οἱ προεστηκότες, ἐπεὶ καλῶς τὰ τῆς ἑρμηνείας ἀπήρτισται, καὶ διαμεῖναι ταῦθ', ὡς ἔχοι, καὶ μὴ μετακινεῖν αὐτά. ἀπάντων δ' ἐπαινεσάντων τὴν γνώμην ἐκέλευσαν, εἴ τις ἢ περισσόν τι προσγεγραμμένον ὁρᾷ τῷ νόμῳ ἢ λεῖπον, πάλιν ἐπισκοποῦντα τοῦτο καὶ ποιοῦντα φανερὸν διορθοῦν, σωφρόνως τοῦτο πράττοντες, ἵνα τὸ κριθὲν ἅπαξ ἔχειν καλῶς εἰς ἀεὶ διαμένῃ.

Thereupon they set to work as ambitiously and painstakingly as possible to make the translation accurate, continuing at their work until the ninth hour . . . Now when the Law had been transcribed and the work of translation brought to an end in seventy-two days, Demetrius assembled all the Jews at the same place where the laws had been rendered, and <u>in the presence of the translators read them aloud</u>. Thereupon the people expressed their approval of the elders who had interpreted the Law, and also praised Demetrius . . . and all of them, including the priest and the eldest of the translators and the chief officers of the community, requested that, since the translation had been so successfully completed, it should remain as it was and not be altered. Accordingly, when all had approved this idea, they ordered that, if anyone saw any further addition made to the text of the Law or anything omitted from it, he should examine it and make it known and correct it; in this they acted wisely, that what had once been judged good might remain for ever.

Josephus, Antiquities, 12.104.107–109, trans. Marcus

According to Josephus, the Septuagint is ratified in a constitutional process that inspires the fullest faith and confidence in the validity of the text. The translation is read aloud in the presence of the seventy-two translators, none of whom express discord or disapproval, and in the presence of the entire assembled Jewish populace of Alexandria. All agree to the validity of the translation. Accordingly, it is declared that it should never be altered, although on an ironic note, scholars are encouraged to correct any errors they might discover later on. The process is deliberately modeled on the assent to and ratification of the covenant by the Israelites at Mt. Sinai, when Moses reads the book of the covenant, in a ritual conceived as being valid for all subsequent generations (Ex. 24:7). But the process is also a kind of parody of a Greek *agôn*, and is perhaps imagined as an improvement on the tragic contests at which a number of playwrights submitted their works to be performed before the city-state and were evaluated by a panel of judges.[47] Here there is only a single entry, and there is only unanimity among the seventy-two erstwhile translators, who now serve in their function as a council of elders.

The accounts of the translation of the Septuagint employ a number of narrative embellishments that are present in the Peisistratus legend in the Scholia to Dionysius Thrax. As Naomi Janowitz perceptively observes, the versions of the Septuagint translation legend do not coalesce around a kernel of historical truth, but expand and contract according to various theological or literary agenda of the texts in which they are found: "in each case the basic plot is fine-tuned to suit each exegete's own ideas about how the Torah was written, how the text and its translation should be read and interpreted, and by whom."[48] The elements shared by the Peisistratus legend can thus be deciphered according to their function in the versions of the Septuagint translation from which they derive.

In Philo's version of the translation of the Septuagint, the idea of "harmonization," already implicit in the passage from *Aristeas* quoted above and apparently in the Septuagint of Ex. 24:11 itself, is magnified and elaborated.

καθίσταντες δ' ἐν ἀποκρύφῳ καὶ μηδενὸς παρόντος ὅτι μὴ τῶν τῆς φύσεως μερῶν, γῆς ὕδατος ἀέρος οὐρανοῦ, περὶ ὧν πρῶτον τῆς γενέσεως ἔμελλον ἱεροφαντήσειν (κοσμοποιία γὰρ ἡ τῶν νόμων ἐστὶν ἀρχή), καθάπερ ἐνθουσιῶντες προεφήτευον οὐκ ἄλλα ἄλλοι, τὰ δ' αὐτὰ πάντες ὀνόματα καὶ ῥήματα, ὥσπερ ὑποβολέως ἑκάστοις ἀοράτως ἐνηχοῦντος.

Sitting here in seclusion with none present save the elements of nature, earth, water, air, heaven, the genesis of which was to be the first theme of their sacred revelation, for the laws begin with the story of the world's creation, they became as it were possessed, and under inspiration, wrote, not each scribe something different, but the same, word for word, as though invisibly dictated to each by a prompter.

Philo, *De Vita Mosis* 2.37, trans. Colson

The story is infused with Platonic language — both in the presence of the elements of nature, and in the notion of a prompter (*hupoboleus*) who invisibly dictates (*aoratôs enêkhountos*) behind the stage curtain, as it were. The idea of the *hupoboleus* 'prompter' recalls both the prompter or *souffleur* in a theater (cf. Plutarch

2.813) and the legislation of Solon, who enacted that the poems of Homer should be recited from a cue (ἐξ ὑποβολῆς / *ex hupobolês*, Scholia B to *Iliad* 19.80).[49] Most striking is Philo's description of the event in miraculous and prophetic terms. The translators sit in seclusion (*en apokruphôi*), become almost possessed (*enthousiôntes*), and prophesy (*prophêteuô*) to each other the same translation, word for word. Philo describes the event as a religious mystery, in which the Greek translation is vouchsafed by nature, God, and, I would add, the strictest Alexandrian editorial procedures, by which individuals are freed from group pressures. This description accords with the faith Philo places in the very words, images, and metaphors of the Septuagint translation, as well its veneration by the Alexandrian Jewish community.

Christian accounts of the translation further expand on the notion of privacy and the lack of communication between the seventy translators:

προσέταξεν αὐτοῖς . . . ἐπὶ τῷ ἕκαστον ἰδίᾳ καθ' ἑαυτὸν τὴν ἑρμηνείαν πληρῶσαι. προστάξας τοῖς ἐφεστῶσιν ὑπηρέταις πάσης μὲν αὐτοὺς θεραπείας τυγχάνειν. εἴργεσθαι δὲ τῆς πρὸς ἀλλήλους ὁμιλίας. ἵνα τὸ τῆς ἑρμηνείας ἀκριβὲς καὶ διὰ τῆς τούτων συμφωνίας γνωσθῆναι δυνηθῇ. Ἐπεὶ δὲ ἔγνω τοὺς ἑβδομήκοντα ἄνδρας μὴ μόνον τῇ αὐτῇ διανοίᾳ ἀλλὰ καὶ ταῖς αὐταῖς λέξεσι χρησαμένους . . . ἐκπλαγεὶς καὶ θείᾳ δυνάμει τὴν ἑρμηνείαν γεγράφθαι πιστεύσας . . .

[Ptolemy] directed them . . . to complete the translation by themselves apart from each other, charging the attendant ministers to render them every service, but also to keep them from communicating with each other, in order that even through the agreement (*sumphônia*) of the translators, the accuracy of the translation might be known. When he found that the seventy men had rendered not only the same meaning (*dianoia*) but even the very same phraseology (*lexis* pl.) . . . he, being astounded, believed the books to be written by divine agency . . .

Pseudo-Justin, *Exhortation to the Greeks* 13

As opposed to the version found in the Letter of Aristeas, in Pseudo-Justin the process of collation (cf. *antiballô* 'collate' in the Letter of

Aristeas) comes after the translation, and succeeds in demonstrating to the pagan Ptolemy that the texts are divine.

The rabbinic tradition adds an embellishment that resembles Philo's version. According to a Talmudic legend, the translators worked in isolated cells.

דתניא: מעשה בתלמי המלך שכינס שבעים ושנים זקנים. והכניסן בשבעים ושנים בתים. ולא גילה
להם על מה כינסן. ונכנס אצל כל אחד ואחד ואמר להם כתבו לי תורת משה רבכם. נתן הקדוש
ברוך הוא בלב כל אחד ואחד עצה. והסכימו כולן לדעת אחת.

> It has been taught: "It is related of King Ptolemy that he brought together seventy-two elders and placed them in seventy-two [separate] rooms, without telling them why he had brought them together, and he went in to each one of them and said to him, 'Translate for me the Torah of Moses your master.' God then prompted each one of them and they all conceived the same idea . . ."
>
> B. Megillah 9a, trans. Simon[50]

The rabbinic oscillation between positive and negative views of the translation of the Torah into Greek has been the subject of much scholarship, but is outside the scope of this study. The positive version of the legend seems to echo Philo's account, but embellishes on the notion of the translators being in seclusion (*en apokruphôi*), by having them be placed in separate cells, as if in a jail. This idea is echoed by St. Augustine:

> Qui si, ut fertur multique non indigni fide praedicant, singuli cellis etiam singulis separati cum interpretati essent, nihil in alicuius eorum codice inventum est quod non isdem verbis eodemque verborum ordine inveniretur in ceteris, quis huic auctoritati conferre aliquid, nedum praeferre audeat? Si autem contulerunt ut una omnium communi tractatu iudicioque vox fieret, ne sic quidem quemquam unum hominem qualibet peritia ad emendandum tot seniorum doctorumque consensum aspirare oportet aut decet.

> And if, as is reported, and as many not unworthy of confidence assert, they were separated during the work of translation, each man

being in a cell by himself, and yet nothing was found in the manuscript of any one of them that was not found in the same words
and in the same order of words in all the rest, who dares put anything in comparison with an authority like this, not to speak of
preferring anything to it? And even if they conferred together with
the result that a unanimous agreement sprang out of the common
labor and judgment of them all; even so, it would not be right or
becoming for any one man, whatever his experience, to aspire to
correct the unanimous opinion of many venerable and learned men.

      Augustine, *De Doctrina Christiana* II.15.22, trans. Shaw

Although Augustine knows the tradition of the private cells, he
doesn't feel compelled to choose this version over the idea of a public assembly at which the translation was harmonized. In his view,
both variants equally validate the legitimacy of the Septuagint.

One of the contemporaries of Augustine who openly disputed
the facticity of such elements in the translation legend was St.
Jerome. Jerome challenged the veracity of Philo's notion of the
translators being prophets, as well as the claim that they had been
put in cells (a detail that possibly derived from the rabbinic tradition, as represented in B. Megillah 9a).[51]

Et nescio quis primus auctor septuaginta cellulas Alexandriae
mendacio suo exstruxerit, quibus divisi eadem scriptitarent, cum
Aristeas ejusdem Ptolemaei ὑπερασπιστής, et multo post tempore
Josephus, nihil tale retulerint: sed in una basilica congregatos,
contulisse scribant, non prophetasse. Aliud est enim vatem, aliud
esse interpretem. Ibi Spiritus ventura praedicit: hic eruditio et verborum copia, ea quae intelligit, transfert.

I do not know who was the first author who through his lie built
seventy cells in Alexandria in which they [the translators] were
separated and yet all wrote the same words; whereas Aristeas,
champion of the same Ptolemy, and long after him Josephus have
related nothing of the sort, but write that they were assembled in
a single hall and conferred together, not that they prophesied. For
it is one thing to be a prophet and another to be an interpreter; in
one case the Spirit foretells future events, in the other erudition

and command of language translate those things which it understands.

St. Jerome, *Preface to the Pentateuch (Genesi)*

(*PL* 28.150–1), trans. Braverman

From the perspective of Jerome (a sometime critic of the Septuagint and champion of the Hebrew original of the Old Testament),
the individual cells and the public assembly in which the translators conferred are incompatible.

The account of Irenaeus combines the ideas of individual
scrutiny and the notion of a deliberative body to assess the translation.

ὁ μὲν Θεὸς ἐδοξάσθη, αἱ δὲ γραφαὶ ὄντως θεῖαι ἐγνώσθησαν, τῶν
πάντων τὰ αὐτὰ ταῖς αὐταῖς λέξεσιν καὶ τοῖς αὐτοῖς ὀνόμασιν
ἀναγορευσάντων ἀπ' ἀρχῆς μέχρι τέλους, ὥστε καὶ τὰ παρόντα ἔθνη
γνῶναι ὅτι κατ' ἐπίπνοιαν τοῦ Θεοῦ εἰσιν ἡρμηνευμέναι αἱ γραφαί.

God was indeed glorified, and the Scriptures were acknowledged
as truly divine. For all of them read out of the common translation
[which they had prepared] in the very same words and the very
same names, from beginning to end, so that even the Gentiles
present perceived that the Scriptures had been interpreted by the
inspiration of God.

Irenaeus, *Against Heresies* 3.212, trans. Roberts and Rambaut

This version echoes Philo's account in respect to its depiction of the
translation as a matter of divine inspiration, adding the conspicuous presence of gentiles. It would appear that Irenaeus' account
stands close to the Peisistratus legend in the Scholia to Dionysius
Thrax. If Irenaeus' account indeed served as a model for the Peisistratus legend, it contains an extra element — the idea of inspiration
governing the activity of the translators. But it is certainly reasonable that the latter should omit the notion of divine inspiration in
describing the reconstruction of Homer's epics.

It is interesting to note that the relationship between legends
of Homeric transmission and the translation of the Bible are not

entirely one-sided. The Letter of Aristeas, the earliest source for the stories of the translation of the Septuagint, employs the vocabulary of Homeric textual scholarship in its description of the translation process:

οἱ δὲ ἐπετέλουν ἕκαστα σύμφωνα ποιοῦντες πρὸς ἑαυτοὺς ταῖς ἀντιβολαῖς· τὸ δὲ ἐκ τῆς συμφωνίας γινόμενον πρεπόντως ἀναγραφῆς οὕτως ἐτύγχανε παρὰ τοῦ Δημητρίου.

And so they proceeded to carry it out, making all details harmonize by mutual comparisons (*antibolê* pl.). The appropriate result of the harmonization (*sumphônia*) was reduced to writing (*anagraphê*) under the direction of Demetrius.

Letter of Aristeas 302, trans. Hadas

The key concepts in this passage, as in later dependent versions such as that of Pseudo-Justin (quoted above), are *sumphônia* 'harmonization' (parallel to the *diaphônia* 'discordance' of Josephus' statement about Homeric texts) and *antibolê* 'the process of comparison of manuscripts' or 'collation'.[52] Translation is described as if it were a species of the process of the creation of an edition from manuscripts within the same language!

As might be expected, the Peisistratus legend removes supernatural and prophetic elements from the Septuagint translation accounts, even as it incorporates other significant details into its narrative. The accounts of Irenaeus and Josephus contain an essential element present in the Peisistratus legend — the public reading and ratification of the text. Philo's colorful element — that the translators sat in seclusion (*en apokruphôi*) — strongly resembles the fact that the editors in the Peisistratus legend are given Homeric transcripts *kat' idian* 'individually'. Pseudo-Justin's phrasing of this motif (ἐπὶ τῷ ἕκαστον ἰδίᾳ καθ' ἑαυτὸν 'by themselves apart from each other') is suggestively close. On the other hand, the detail of the seventy cells, as found in the versions of the rabbis and St. Jerome, represents an embellishment of this element, and thus these versions did not directly influence the Peisistratus legend.

Both the Letter of Aristeas and Pseudo-Justin speak of the translation of Hebrew scriptures as a process involved with the harmonization (*sumphônia*) of details through collation (*antibolê*). This description resonates strongly with the editorial mission of the convocation of seventy-two grammarians in the Peisistratus legend. These versions of the translation legend, and especially that of Pseudo-Justin, should be considered as the source of the Septuagintal motifs found in the Peisistratus legend in the Scholia to Dionysius Thrax.

Why was the Peisistratus version augmented by elements from the Septuagint translation legend? Was this simply a matter of the conflation of Ptolemy II with Peisistratus, or was there some more pressing reason? The Alexandrian Jewish community's certainty in the unequivocal textual trustworthiness of their version of scripture embodied their desire to remain Jewish in a Greek context. This deep faith was inherited by early Christianity, which promulgated the Septuagint translation account and embellished it with the aim of increasing its wonder. The Jewish-Christian Septuagint narrative presented a striking contrast with the Greek view of its own documents, for the scholars of Alexandria openly admitted to the uncertain textual form of their esteemed literary works. It seems possible that the Greek community at Alexandria attempted to subvert the most powerful narrative of Alexandrian Judaism and Christianity by claiming the narrative properly applied to Homer, the conveyor of Greek *paideia*, rather than to the Bible.

Not all the elements of the story of translation of the Septuagint were applicable to the Peisistratus legend. The state of Septuagint manuscripts was far less troubled than the Homeric epics, found in a bewildering array of divergent manuscripts.[53] Accordingly, while the motif of the universal consent of the Septuagint translators is present in the Peisistratus legend, it is modified in important ways. For example, the editors depicted in the Peisistratus legend create manuscripts that are slightly imperfect; individually, their editorial skills are flawed. It is their collective judgment that most resembles the universal consent motif. In a democratic display of unity, they endorse the edition of Aristarchus, the most renowned Homeric scholar of antiquity.

## Greek vs. Jewish Views of Textualization and Literary Authority

Josephus' account of the translation of scripture into Greek reveals a qualitative difference between Greek and Jewish approaches to granting authority to texts. In his account, the rendering of the Torah into Greek results in a text whose status is subordinate to the Hebrew original. There are none of the miraculous or prophetic overtones of the translation found for instance in the writing of Philo of Alexandria; instead, the passage speaks soberly about procedures by which the text might be altered should inadequacies be discovered. Although his description is directly modeled on the Israelite ratification of the Book of the Covenant at Mt. Sinai in Exodus 24, Josephus has picked a biblical model that most resembles Greek political decision-making:

οἱ δ' ὡς ἔνι μάλιστα φιλοτίμως καὶ φιλοπόνως ἀκριβῆ τὴν ἑρμηνείαν ποιούμενοι μέχρι μὲν ὥρας ἐνάτης πρὸς τούτῳ διετέλουν ὄντες . . . Μεταγραφέντος δὲ τοῦ νόμου καὶ τοῦ κατὰ τὴν ἑρμηνείαν ἔργου τέλος ἐν ἡμέραις ἑβδομήκοντα καὶ δυσὶν λαβόντος, συναγαγὼν ὁ Δημήτριος τοὺς Ἰουδαίους ἅπαντας εἰς τὸν τόπον, ἔνθα καὶ μετεβλήθησαν οἱ νόμοι, <u>παρόντων καὶ τῶν ἑρμηνέων ἀνέγνω τούτους</u>. τὸ δὲ πλῆθος ἀπεδέξατο μὲν καὶ τοὺς διασαφήσαντας πρεσβυτέρους τὸν νόμον, ἐπήνεσεν δὲ καὶ τὸν Δημήτριον τῆς ἐπινοίας ὡς μεγάλων ἀγαθῶν αὐτοῖς εὑρετὴν γεγενημένον, παρεκάλεσάν τε δοῦναι καὶ τοῖς ἡγουμένοις αὐτῶν ἀναγνῶναι τὸν νόμον, ἠξίωσάν τε [πάντες] ὅ τε ἱερεὺς καὶ τῶν ἑρμηνέων οἱ πρεσβύτεροι καὶ τοῦ πολιτεύματος οἱ προεστηκότες, ἐπεὶ καλῶς τὰ τῆς ἑρμηνείας ἀπήρτισται, καὶ διαμεῖναι ταῦθ', ὡς ἔχοι, καὶ μὴ μετακινεῖν αὐτά. ἁπάντων δ' ἐπαινεσάντων τὴν γνώμην ἐκέλευσαν, εἴ τις ἢ περισσόν τι προσγεγραμμένον ὁρᾷ τῷ νόμῳ ἢ λεῖπον, πάλιν ἐπισκοποῦντα τοῦτο καὶ ποιοῦντα φανερὸν διορθοῦν. σωφρόνως τοῦτο πράττοντες, ἵνα τὸ κριθὲν ἅπαξ ἔχειν καλῶς ἐς ἀεὶ διαμένῃ.

Thereupon they set to work as ambitiously and painstakingly as possible to make the translation accurate, continuing at their work until the ninth hour . . . Now when the Law had been transcribed and the work of translation brought to an end in seventy-two days, Demetrius assembled all the Jews at the same place where the laws had been rendered, and <u>in the presence of the translators read them aloud</u>. Thereupon the people expressed their approval of the elders who had interpreted the Law, and also praised Demetrius . . . and all of them, including the priest and the eldest of the translators and the chief officers of the community, requested that, since the translation had been so successfully completed, it should remain as it was and not be altered. Accordingly, when all had approved this idea, they ordered that, if anyone saw any further addition made to the text of the Law or anything omitted from it, he should examine it and make it known and correct it; in this they acted wisely, that what had once been judged good might remain for ever.

Josephus, Antiquities 12.104, 107–109, trans. Marcus

Josephus mentions neither the inspired quality of the translations nor the comparison of translations at the end of the day. If the Septuagint is figured as a competitor at a contest, there are no other contestants. Josephus thus provides a means for bridging the deep divide between Greek and Jewish methods for granting authority to worthy texts. This public reading is no contest, but grants authority to the translation in a manner that is consonant with the Greek *agôn* and the democratic ideal. The language of prophecy and miracle is avoided. By modeling the translation of the Septuagint on the most democratic moment in Israelite history, Josephus offers a compromise between the Greek reliance on the *agôn* and Jewish belief in divine revelation.

The work that may not be altered has a fallback clause that allows it to be modified should any discrepancy with the original later be detected. The assembly ratifies the text and pronounces that what was deemed good at one time should be valued at another. But future generations will value the translation because of the very fact that the text may be altered should need arise:

ἁπάντων δ' ἐπαινεσάντων τὴν γνώμην ἐκέλευσαν, εἴ τις ἢ περισσόν τι προσγεγραμμένον ὁρᾷ τῷ νόμῳ ἢ λεῖπον, πάλιν ἐπισκοποῦντα τοῦτο καὶ ποιοῦντα φανερὸν διορθοῦν, σωφρόνως τοῦτο πράττοντες, ἵνα τὸ κριθὲν ἅπαξ ἔχειν καλῶς εἰς ἀεὶ διαμένῃ.

Accordingly, when all had approved this idea, they ordered that, if anyone saw any further addition made to the text of the Law or anything omitted from it, he should examine it and make it known and correct it; in this they acted wisely, that what had once been judged good might remain for ever.

Josephus, *Antiquities* 12.109, trans. Marcus

Unlike the more Hellenized versions of the translation, Josephus describes a Septuagint that is probably not a perfect rendering of the Hebrew original. In *Against Apion*, he had argued that the Jewish scriptures are unalterable, especially since they are safeguarded from change by the lineage of priests which has sole access to the text. Here, he concludes that the Septuagint will retain its worth *because* it can be altered. The entrance of a Jewish text into the Greek world entails the corruption of oriental and especially Jewish esteem for the inalterability of sacred documents. In effect, Josephus' description amounts to a compromise between Greek and Jewish modes of textual validation.

While Josephus envisioned errors as a possible byproduct of translation, the rabbis found the Septuagint's errors to be unforgivable. In several passages found in the Talmud, the rabbis impugn the legitimacy of the Greek translation by lambasting a number of passages the translators garbled or deliberately misunderstood. Their knowledge of the Septuagint's errors is not based on firsthand evidence, but likely derives from a pre-rabbinic tradition opposed to Alexandrian Judaism and its version of scripture.

In the Peisistratus legend, modeled after the Septuagint translation scene, a quite different approach to textual legitimacy is manifested. Greek agonistic culture values individual contribution above universal agreement, although the deleterious efforts of individuals on textual transmission are not dismissed. Thus, on the one hand, faulty editing procedures are blamed for the introduction of errors into the text of Homer. On the other, the final edition of Aristarchus is approved by the collective wisdom of the assembled editors, despite the fact that each was unable to apply this wisdom effectively in creating his own edition. In the legend, individual contribution plays a role in both the augmentation and diminution of the authoritativeness of the text.

In the rabbinic critique of the Septuagint and the writings of Josephus is revealed a consistent theme in the Jewish conception of textual legitimacy. The Jewish sphere lays claim to a universal endorsement of its sacred scriptures, safeguarded from subsequent error by the vigilance of the tradition. In contrast, Greek scholarship is well aware of the shortcomings of its literary documents, and attributes such shortcomings to individuals motivated by greed, power, zeal, desire for glory, or bad scholarship. But the Greek world, especially in the Alexandrian tradition, also evinces a faith that the scholarship of a small number of perspicacious individuals may remedy the harm done to these texts over the course of time.

## Conclusion

The formation of the Peisistratus legend in the Scholia to Dionysius Thrax in one respect begins with King Ptolemy Philadelphus. Ptolemy was considered by Galen to be the person who first brought about literary fraud by his zeal to create a world-class library. Later Greek scholars did not agree with Galen, and concluded that Peisistratus, member of a dynasty accused of forgery by Aristotle and Herodotus, was a better candidate. The legends that had grown up around Ptolemy were reconfigured around the figure of Peisistratus, although Peisistratus had preceded Ptolemy by centuries. Several of these accounts had described Ptolemy II as a "modern-day" Peisistratus. In reality, Peisistratus was being imagined as an ancient Ptolemy II. The equation of Peisistratus and Ptolemy II represented a projection of the recent, Hellenistic past onto the sixth century B.C.E.[54]

Included among the Ptolemaic legends was the account of his role in commissioning the Septuagint. Like the other details of Ptolemy's career that had already been attributed to Peisistratus, aspects of the Septuagint legend were incorporated into the account of the textualization of the Homeric epics. Aristarchus and Zenodotus were made parallel to the two most important Jewish elders from Jerusalem, and the textualization of Homer was imagined as a process akin to the translation of the Septuagint.

The conflation of Peisistratus and Ptolemy II was ideologically anachronistic, in that it confused warring library traditions, based in Pergamum and Alexandria. The appearance of the Peisistratus legend in the scholia to the work of an Alexandrian grammarian speaks to a time when the intellectual rivalry between Alexandrian and Pergamene scholarship had been resolved or had disappeared. Originally, the story of Peisistratus had probably been a badge of pride for the Pergamene library and its approach to Homeric interpretation. In contrast, Alexandrian scholars imagined that the city's library had originated from the personal collection of Aristotle, a more recent and scholarly progenitor. Moreover, Alexandrian scholars did not credit Peisistratus with any role in the textualization of Homer.

As the old conflict disappeared, the Peisistratus legend from Pergamum began to be used to validate Alexandrian textual scholarship. The Peisistratus legend in the Scholia to Dionysius Thrax could now be employed to celebrate the process by which the text of Homer, contaminated through natural disaster and human greed, could be re-established through the skills of the grammarian. It could also now serve as an aetiology and theoretical explanation for literary fraud. In the context of the Scholia to Dionysius Thrax, it functions to promote the evaluation of authenticity of biblical books by means of the approach developed to establish the text of the greatest classical authors. The legend thus serves to legitimate *krisis poiêmatôn* 'attribution analysis' as the highest principle of grammar.

Both Peisistratian and Ptolemaic aetiologies of forgery presented themselves as a scene for a theoretical discussion about the reasons that literary fraud is committed. These discussions thus participate in a broader ancient theoretical discourse evaluating the nature of legitimate authorship and contrasting it with what each text considers improper literary composition. Ancient writers who engage in this kind of speculation hold that literary fraud can be committed not only out of a desire for profit, but also to receive public acclaim. According to Galen, forgery results from economic stimuli (the book trade) and psychological stimuli (the excessive zeal for books that promoted this trade). The story relayed by Vitruvius argues that literary contests and the desire for authorial fame have the potential to encourage literary fraud. Other ancient writers attempted to describe a literary system that would correct such flaws (Plato) or that had already corrected them (Philo). Plato envisions a state in which aesthetic considerations are not the final word in poetic composition. He is less concerned with locating inauthentic works than in the possibility of the conveyance of the author's improper morals onto society, and advocates the establishment of a panel of elders to ascertain who is fit to compose in the new state. Philo, in contrast, depicts a literary culture (that of the ancient Hebrews) that evaluated the utterances of its prophets who had already been chosen by God. These utterances could be ratified or dismissed, on the ground that not every prophetic utterance was worthy to be treated as authoritative. In short, Galen, Vitruvius, and Alexandrian scholarship in general depend on scholarly evaluation to purge the world of inauthentic works. Plato and Philo envision a system where judges assess the moral suitability of the writer or the validity of the prophet's utterances.

The Peisistratus legend combines elements from each of these traditions. It confusedly speculates on the reasons for excising verses from the final version of Homeric epic. Three rationales are given. The line may be removed because it is *adokimos* 'unseemly' or 'untested', a term implying a moralistic test worthy of Plato's panel of judges who evaluate the character of the would-be author. Conversely, the term signifies that it is merely 'illegitimate' like illegal tender. It may be declared *anaxios tou poiêtou* 'unworthy of the poet', a blatant value judgment informed by aesthetics but perhaps also moral considerations. Or it may be removed on the ground that it is *allotrios* 'foreign'. This final term implies that does not fit in with the others (with the notion of what "fits" based in some way upon an aesthetic judgment).[55] It also amounts to a speculation of the reason it does not fit — that it originates with another poet, not Homer.

In the legend of Peisistratus, evaluation of forgery is moral and aesthetic (it is a matter of what is *axios* 'worthy' of the poet, or what is *dokimos* 'seemly' or 'tested'). It is legal or financial (com-

parable to the other use of *adokimos* by Plato). It is also epidemio-
logical (distinguishing that which is *allotrios* 'foreign' from native;
'foreign' evokes notions of citizenship, ethnicity, language, and culture). Distinguishing forged from genuine lines is accomplished by
two supremely perspicacious individuals. These are chosen and
ratified by the seventy grammarians, just as the translation of the
Pentateuch was ratified by the seventy-two Jewish elders sent to
King Ptolemy by the High Priest of Jerusalem.

The legend found in the Scholia to Dionysius Thrax is thus a
remarkably complex aetiology of forgery, one that speculates on the
causes of literary imposture as well as on the procedures that should
be used to spot it. It proclaims the message is that it is possible to
distinguish genuine from forgery at the level of micro-criticism,
even if in the end the text must remain sullied by foreign contamination. The legend achieves this goal first by legitimating two
individuals by means of elaborate democratic procedures at the
conference called by Peisistratus. Having established the creden-
tials of its two heroes, the legend proceeds to its central theme: that
literary and grammatical investigation is capable of separating spurious from authentic and recreating the text of Homer. Because it is
known that forged lines can be accurately located, it is possible to
speak with confidence that the remaining Homer owes its origination to that one individual. A true text becomes one that has been
liberated from false additions. The legend draws from the critical
judgments of Aristotle, who taught that only some works normally
attributed to Homer were actually composed by him. But it takes a
step further, advocating that even the *Iliad* and *Odyssey,* genuine
Homeric works according to Aristotle, be culled of un-Homeric lines.

By the time of Aristarchus, textual criticism had reached a
peak. It is thus fitting that the Zenodotus and Aristarchus of the
Peisistratus legend become mythic heroes of the discourse that establishes an authentic, universally agreed-upon text. Their names
stand for attribution analysis, a process that distinguishes between
genuine and forged ultimately on aesthetic, stylistic, and moralistic
grounds — summed up in the notion of "that which is worthy of the
poet."

The history explored here demonstrates the increasing attention paid by ancient grammarians to the textualizers of literary

works, out of an effort to explain features of the works themselves that they could not imagine to derive from their composers. This chapter thus describes an important stage in the scholarly focus on the connection between individuals and texts. In some respects, the conception of authorship revealed by these ancient sources is negative, since the authentic Homer amounts to the remainder left over from the grammatical surgery performed on his text. When the accomplishments of the textualizer had been located and removed, the author could truly be seen in his words. Or, was it that the textualizer was to be blamed for elements that didn't accord with scholars' preconceptions about the author?

# CHAPTER 6

# ARISTOTLE AND EZRA

## TWO POLES IN THE EARLY CHRISTIAN APPROACH

## TO TEXTUAL HISTORY

Textual histories composed by early Christian scholars took shape under the influence of two contrasting models or ways of thinking about the transmission of texts — the literary analysis of Aristotle and legendary prophetic textualization, typified by the legend of Ezra as re-textualizer of the Bible which had been burned and destroyed by Babylonian invaders. Aristotelian literary analysis consisted of a scholarly, almost scientific methodology; this methodology found its highest exponents in the scholars of Ptolemaic Alexandria. The approach is first exemplified in the lists of poetic victors compiled by Aristotle in the fourth century B.C.E. It remains a central part of literary analysis for St. Jerome in the fifth century C.E.; Jerome employs Arisitotelian literary methodology in the formation of his own list of the life and works of ecclesiastical authors. The Ezra legend, in contrast, is anything but scientific, since it centers on a narrative of the destruction and miraculous re-textualization of the Hebrew Bible. While opposing religious traditions later utilized the Ezra legend to attack Christian and Jewish claims about the antiquity and authenticity of their scriptures, the dramatic version of

Ezra's deeds was initially employed by Christian and Jewish groups to expand their scriptural canon and to promote the authoritativeness of its constituent parts. Both methodology and legend have important thematic and historic ties to the narratives featuring Peisistratus and Ptolemy that were explored in chapter 5.

These two models promote inherently opposing versions of the value of the received text. Nevertheless, they are reconciled by Christian scholars. The Aristotelian approach becomes a preferred technique for Christian scholars like Eusebius to establish and challenge the authenticity of the name traditionally attached to a given text of scripture, teaching, or commentary that did not accord with catholic, orthodox Christianity. The Ezra narrative, in contrast, is used to assert the authenticity of scriptural texts (especially the Septuagint translation of the Hebrew Bible) that had been impugned by opposing sects or religions. For Christian scholarship, attribution analysis (the Aristotelian approach) becomes the preferred means to undercut the canonical collections of rival religious movements, while stories about the miraculous reconstruction of the text (featured in the Ezra legend) are a technique for defending works alleged by outsiders to be flawed or even forged.

### Aristotelian Literary Scholarship

While ancient scholars credited the invention of attribution analysis to the efforts of Peisistratus or Ptolemy, modern researchers have discovered that the interest in attribution and in the effectiveness of the methods used to detect improperly attributed texts more properly derives from Aristotle. The evidence for the connection between Aristotle and Alexandria is strong. It would appear that Alexandria's library was composed, at least in part, from the personal collection of Aristotle.[1] Alexandria and Pergamum likely argued the antiquity of their documents by tracing them back to the scholarly activities of Aristotle and Peisistratus, respectively. Pergamum's claim — that the city was in possession of copies of the very text of Homer that Peisistratus had commissioned — was probably felt by some to have the greater cachet. But while Aristotle was the more recent progenitor, the accounts of his role in shaping the Alexandrian collection also were somewhat more plausible. Aristotelians had an extremely effective argument contesting the claims of Pergamum about the Peisistratian origin of their edition of Homer: in fact, Aristotle himself had accused the Peisistratids of forging the works of Orpheus, and probably other works as well.[2] A line of intellectual descent connecting the textual investigations of Aristotle with those of Callimachus and the other Alexandrian scholars seems certain. Under Callimachus' scholarly evaluation of the holdings of the Alexandrian library, the science of attribution analysis (*krisis poiêmatôn*), together with the Aristotelian approach to the documentation of literary history, seem to have progressed furthest. In turn, the research methods and approaches to literary scholarship established in Alexandria by Callimachus and others had a direct influence on the literary investigations of the Church Fathers like Eusebius, St. Jerome, and St. Augustine. The Alexandrian scholars and the Church Fathers who followed them were in fact refining Aristotle's approach.

Aristotle had recognized that research was required to establish the identity of the individual that had composed the text. Such research was necessary even in cases where it could be confirmed that the name borne by the text was correct. After all, certain Greek names were extremely popular. Because of confusion over identical names, an individual could be incorrectly credited with a text composed by his namesake. This predicament was termed "homonymy" by ancient scholars.[3] The work of Diogenes Laertius, an author who investigated the lives and opinions of famous philosophers in antiquity, testifies to the difficulties faced by ancient literary critics due to the popularity of certain ancient Greek names. Diogenes lists namesakes for twenty-nine of the eighty-two philosophers that he surveys. Most of the twenty-nine had been authors themselves. He lists an average of five to six homonyms for each of the twenty-nine, but in one case he lists fourteen namesakes (for Herakleides), and for the names Demetrios and Theodoros he lists twenty homonyms each.[4]

Attribution analysis was necessitated by homonymy as well as by the perpetration of intentional literary fraud, which included plagiarism, forgery, and literary ventriloquism. But unintentional errors in the transmission of a written text, or textual variations that owed their existence to the oral tradition, were also evaluated according to this methodology. Such phenomena were often explained by ancient scholars as being the products of plagiarism or forgery, when in reality they had nothing to do with fraud. It should be noted that the history of the investigation of illusory literary fraud is as important as the advances in locating actual imposture. The methods devised to correct illusory literary fraud had a profound and lasting impact on the development of literary criticism. Because of the fear that properly attributed texts had become corrupted, ancient scholars began to promulgate a microscopic textual investigation process that culminated in a line-by-line or word-by-word correction of texts.

The affinity between investigations of the authenticity of a line or word and investigations of the genuineness of an entire text is demonstrated by Quintilian, the Roman writer on style and rhetoric:

> enarrationem praecedit emandata lectio et mixtum his omnibus iudicium est, quo quidem ita severe sunt usi veteres grammatici, ut non versus modo censoria quadam virgula notare et libros, qui falso viderentur inscripti, tamquam subditos submovere familia permiserint sibi, sed auctores alios in ordinem redegerint, alios omnino exemerint numero.

> The explanation is preceded by the reading and correction, and the critical evaluation (*iudicium*) is mixed with all three. The old grammarians were so severe in their critique that they not only permitted to mark verses [which they thought to be not authentic] with a critical mark, and to expel books from the family that appeared under a false title, as if they had been changelings (*subditos*), but they also included some authors in the list [of classics] (*ordo*) while excluding others altogether.
>
> Quintilian, *Institutiones Oratoriae* I.4.3, trans. Blum

Quintilian reveals how the process of evaluating the authenticity of verses was part of a more general attribution analysis. His comment indicates that the search for the inauthentic lay at the heart of the formation of a list (*ordo*) of first-rank authors.

Quintilian notes that the Alexandrians expelled illegitimate books as *subditi* 'changelings, babies switched at birth' from their "family" of books. His use of the language of human kinship to describe Alexandrian scholarship is not only an apt metaphor, but is echoed in the actual language of Alexandrian scholarship itself. Thus Diogenes Laertius concludes his chapter on Plato with a list of the *nothoi* 'illegitimate' or 'bastard' texts. Genuine works were regularly called *gnêsioi* 'legitimate, authentic', in the sense that children are legitimate offspring of a parent.[5]

An important chapter in the history of the development of the tools of literary criticism is represented by what Rudolf Blum calls the "biobibliography," the technical term for a compilation of book lists containing biographical data about their composers. According to Blum, the first task for the Alexandrian scholar was to distinguish between a writer's genuine works and those falsely ascribed to him. Instead of simply setting the inauthentic works in a different category, some early practitioners of attribution analysis attempted to find the real authors of spurious works; scholars who did not do so were castigated for leaving the job unfinished. Blum, following Pfeiffer, calls this entire process "literary criticism" rather than "critical evaluation of authenticity," which would only describe the more limited investigation (i.e. distinguishing between genuine and inauthentic works).[6] However, it is not certain that *krisis poiêmatôn* 'attribution analysis' (the term that Pfeiffer translates 'literary criticism') necessarily included the relatively sophisticated and perhaps risky attempt to find the real author of a disputed work.

## THE LIST

The biobibliography, as perfected by Callimachus and put to ecclesiastical use by St. Jerome in his *De Viris Illustribus*, derives from Aristotle's lists of poetic victors. But Aristotle's genre also has a prehistory. According to Blum, the first comprehensive works of literary history took the form of lists. The historian Hellanikos of Lesbos (second half of the fifth century B.C.E.) made a list of the *Karneonikai*, the victors in the Karneian contests at Sparta; the festival of the Karneia, devoted to Apollo, included not just athletic games but poetical and musical contests. Hellanikos also compiled a list of the mythical and historical priestesses of Hera in Argos (*Hiereiai Tês Hêras Hai En Argei*).[7]

Blum's assessment of the import of the genre of the list and significance of the Greek interest in recording victorious poetic contests is essential for understanding the origin of the genre of biobibliography:

> With his *Karneonikai* Hellanikos laid the foundations for a typically Greek form of literature (in the widest sense), akin to chronicles, whose form was the *pinax* (literally tablet, list): the list of victors. This expressed, quite apart from parochial pride, the passion of all Greeks for games (first observed by Jacob Burckhardt), a passion so strong that they wanted to preserve the memory of the great games and their victorious participants for eternity.[8]

The genre of the list of victors helps explain the Greek interest in literary history in general and the particular approach to literary scholarship employed by Aristotle and his successors. First, the agonistic mentality of the ancient Greeks clearly lies behind the interest and the efforts of scholars like Hellanikos to record the victors of poetic contests. These lists not only provided the evidence for scholars like Aristotle who were interested in documenting past literary history, but they also created a scholarly climate that led these scholars to continue to produce lists, the accepted genre of literary investigation. Aristotle and his successors were persuaded to write updated and ever more complete lists. These new lists must have attracted scholars who sought the illusion of completeness or even mastery over their fields. They reeked of authoritativeness, being charter documents of the history of each city-state. They were unencumbered by personal opinion or critical invective. The poets in each list had been validated by a contest that was in actuality a religious event; even the dutiful and reverent actions of the list-maker attest to the seriousness of the occasion.

Following the model of Hellanikos, Hippias of Elis wrote the *Olympionikôn Anagraphê*, a list of the victors in the games at Olympia.[9] The Olympic games were the most important of the games in Greece and a hallmark of Pan-Hellenism, the sense of national Greek consciousness also embodied in the universal veneration for the oracle at Delphi and the epics of Homer. While this list in itself has little relevance for the trajectory of ancient literary studies, its importance in establishing a chronology for ancient Greece as a whole is well known. The list of Olympic victors served as a dating system in antiquity, and remains the basis for all dates that we now possess.[10]

Four works of Aristotle take the form of the list, the genre that originated with Hellanikos and Hippias: the *Olympionikai, Pythionikai, Nikai Dionysiakai,* and the *Didaskaliai.* The *Olympionikai* were likely nothing more than a revised and enlarged new edition of the work by Hippias. The *Pythionikai,* probably commissioned by the Amphiktyones, listed lyric poets who had won in the artistic competitions (the most important of the Pythic games) as well as successful athletic contestants. The *Nikai Dionysiakai* (the full title according to Hesychios was *Nikai Dionysiakai Astikai Kai Lênaikai* 'Victories [in the dramatic contests] of the City and Lenaean Dionysia') appears to have been a list of victories at these contests.

The most influential of Aristotle's works in the genre of the list was the *Didaskaliai,* which means 'rehearsals' or 'productions'. This work listed the productions of plays at the Athenian festivals of the City Dionysia and the Lenaea. Aristotle apparently derived the information for his lists from public records. Since ca. 500 B.C.E., when the state began to arrange performances and contests, the responsible archons kept records and housed them in their archives, not out of an interest in literary history, but to document expenses. These archives enabled Aristotle to keep track of key details about the production of each work. While the *Didaskaliai* haven't survived into modern times, one of the inscriptions found on the Acropolis (called the *Fasti* by Wilamowitz) lists information that, according to many scholars, derived from Aristotle's *Didaskaliai.* On the basis of this evidence, it seems clear that Aristotle kept track of the following information:

- the *archôn epônymos* 'archon under whose name the contest had occurred';
- the *phylê* 'tribe' whose chorus of boys had won a victory in the boys' dithyramb contest;

- the *phylê* whose chorus of men had won a victory in the men's dithyramb contest;
- the *khorêgoi* 'leaders of the chorus' who had paid the two choruses;
- the *khorêgos* and *didaskalos* 'author/director' of the winning comedy;
- the *khorêgos* and *didaskalos* of the three winning tragedies;
- beginning in 447 B.C.E., the victorious principle actor of tragedies.

It also seems clear that Aristotle's list conveyed information of interest purely to the literary scholar, such as when someone other than the author had produced and directed a play, or when a poet had produced a previously unsuccessful play in a revised version. He distinguished between contemporary poets and actors of the same name by adding "the elder" or "the younger," and it is possible that he occasionally added annotations. While this list does convey some information of a literary character, it is essentially an antiquarian document motivated by religious and cultural veneration for the contests themselves. The devotional quality of these lists is visible not only in their model, the list of priestesses of Hera at Argos compiled by Hellanikos, but in the way they commemorate the concept of victory itself, rather than the poet or the composition.

It appears that Aristotle's *Didaskaliai* was not intended to accompany a corresponding set of texts, and it does not seem to be keyed to a library. It subordinates the poet to the contest, and makes an unwieldy tool to compile a list of a given author's works. Blum also notes that no authors of dithyrambs are mentioned. "The contest of dithyrambs, unlike that of plays, was not a competition of individuals, poets, and actors, but one of collective bodies, the *phylai* and their choruses."[11] While Aristotle may have neglected to mention the poet in the dithyramb contest because it had not been recorded in the Athenian archives, this fact nevertheless speaks to subordination of information of a literary character to the list's principle function as a medium to commemorate the victors, whatever role they had played in the production of the work. What mattered is that these individuals or groups had been immortalized by Athenian society in the course of its religious observances.

As Blum points out, the *Didaskaliai* were unwieldy for certain investigations, which is why they were revised by Callimachus. Aristotle had listed victories in chronological order, making it difficult to compile a list of compositions or victories of a given author. Callimachus used Aristotle's work as the basis for his poet-centered bibliography of the Attic playwrights (called the *Pinax*).

Callimachus' *Pinax* of Attic playwrights was a preliminary study to another work, his *Pinakes* of Greek authors. It listed information by poet rather than by year of the contest at the City Dionysia or at the Lenaea. By this very fact, the writer of tragedies became the center of scholarly attention. This structure bears witness to the Alexandrian scholarly world's interest in investigating the works of a given playwright, and speaks to a decline in interest in the dynamics of the contests themselves. Scholars now wanted to search out and take account of all the works of a given author, a difficult task when a given playwright's works could be lurking at various points along Aristotle's list. Callimachus and his generation were no longer interested in memorializing each victory — its historical conditions, who had competed, and which tribe, actor, poet had won what prizes — as scholars had been in the past.

While the principles by which collections of books had previously been organized are unclear, the arrangement of scrolls in the Alexandrian library suggests an intensification of scholarly focus on the writer. Scrolls were arranged first by authors and then alphabetically by title (although only by the first letter of each title, as full alphebetization would have proved unmanageable in a library in which scrolls were stacked in heaps within cubby holes). The sheer volume of works at the Alexandrian library may have led to the development of interest in second and third-tier writers, as well as increased attention to the question of attribution, animated by a debate as to where individual scrolls should be shelved.

In contrast to Callimachus' *Pinax* of Attic playwrights, his *Pinakes* of Greek authors served as a catalogue of the entire Alexandrian library. This list too was arranged by author. The new work was made necessary by the fact that the works of a given author might not necessarily be shelved together, since sometimes scrolls might contain works of more than one author and were shelved according to the author of the first work in the scroll. It also seems likely that Callimachus produced a summary of the *Pinakes,* a catalogue of the extant works of the library (that was simultaneously a *de facto* catalogue of works of all Greek literature), rather than merely being a catalogue of copies that documented extra copies and noted where they were shelved. This new work was not keyed to the library, but, as a virtual bibliography of Greek works, could be used as a reference work by anyone interested in the field, regardless of their ability to access this particular library. It also conveyed information of a biographical nature; hence, it is referred to by Blum as "biobibliography" and "national author lexicon."

Callimachus' scholarly activities mark a distinct transformation in the Greek world's approach to textual scholarship and conceptualization of authorship. As Blum states, Callimachus' predecessor, Zenodotus, seems to have been interested solely in the reconstruction of the original text.[12] Callimachus, in contrast, wanted to ascertain which works of a given author were in fact authentic. He did so in a methodical and comprehensive manner, and is perhaps the key figure in the development of *krisis poiêmatôn* 'attribution analysis'. This method marks the culmination of the Greek fascination with the list as a means of keeping civic records, marking time, commemorating religious events, and memorializing individual feats of glory. It also represents a watershed in the Greek investigation of the authenticity of literary documents.

The *Pinakes* of Callimachus were emulated by Jerome — the first in a long line of Christian authors of such lists. He took material largely from the *Ecclesiastical History* of Eusebius. The title of the work, *De Viris Illustribus* 'On Illustrious Men', was taken from Suetonius, who used the term *viri illustres* solely for authors.[13] But in form, *De Viris Illustribus* is a biobibliography (the genre invented by Callimachus with his *Pinakes*). Jerome himself states that his principle models in this endeavor were Hermippos of Smyrna, known as "the Callimachean," and Suetonius.[14] According to Blum, the biobibliography (an authoritative list of works that included biographical information) was one of the mechanisms by which Greek attribution analysis was transmitted to Christianity. By choosing to employ this genre for *De Viris Illustribus*, and by relying on evidence from Eusebius, a practitioner of Alexandrian philology in his own right, Jerome fashioned himself as the heir to the Alexandrian tradition.

## Authorial Biography

Greek authorial biography, while not exclusively an Aristotelian endeavor, also had a significant impact on the status of the writer and the change in sensitivity towards the historical conditions of literary creation. Ancient Greek biography, which begins with Theagenes in the sixth century (in his lost treatise on the life of Homer), seems to have started as a form of literary exegesis, and derives its insights about the writer from the texts themselves.[15] In the second century B.C.E., a new type of author biography appeared that was more list-like than its Peripatetic precursors. The Alexandrians from this period called the biography *bios* 'life' or *genos* 'descent'. These works were grammatical in interest and terse in style, and did not have the more anecdotal and rhetorical form of the earlier Peripatetic biographical works. They listed (in varying sequence and length) name, author class, birthplace, family, teachers, *akmê* 'period of flourishing', contemporaries, place of activity, unusual events, inventions (innovations), conspicuous characteristics, death, age, and works.[16] According to Blum, these were probably originally biographical sections of articles in handbooks.

As the genre developed in the Hellenistic period, it began to investigate which works had really been written by a given writer, and became a medium in which authentic works were distinguished from spurious ones.[17] Unlike the Peripatetic biographies, the Alexandrian biographies did not have a list of genuine works at the end, likely because the table of contents of an edition itself served as a bibliography of works. Their compact style and focus on only the sparest of details reveal a new approach to the personality of the writer. By eschewing the legendary treatments of earlier biographers in favor of a more sober catalogue of details about the author's life, the Alexandrian biographers transformed the author from a mythologized, full persona into a more plausible individual whose life could only be summarized by the few salient facts that were known on "good evidence" (that is, often from the works themselves).

## Christian Attribution Analysis

Christian scholars proved to be enthusiastic practitioners of the Greek methods to determine the authenticity of church readings, and whether they had been properly ascribed to the composer with whom they had been traditionally linked. The following passage from the Scholia to Dionysius Thrax reveals the extent to which the connection between this methodology and pagan Greek literature in general provided the basis for scholarly education during the Byzantine period:

" "Ἕκτον κρίσις ποιημάτων, ὃ δή κάλλιστόν ἐστι πάντων τῶν ἐν τῇ τέχνῃ." Κρίσις ποιημάτων μὲν ἡ ἀκριβὴς γνῶσις τῶν ποιημάτων λέγεται· ταύτῃ τῇ ἠκριβωμένῃ γνώσει χρώμενος ὁ γραμματικὸς δεῖ γινώσκειν τὰ βιβλία τῆς ἐκκλησίας πάντα, τουτέστιν τὴν παλαιὰν καὶ καινὴν διαθήκην, ἵνα ὅταν ἀκούσῃ φωνὴν ξένην καὶ σύγγραμα ἢ ποίημα ψευδές, μὴ δέξηται αὐτὸ ὡς ἀληθινόν, ἐπειδὴ ἔστιν εὐαγγέλιον κατὰ Θωμᾶν λεγόμενον. Δεῖ δὲ γινώσκειν τὸν γραμματικὸν τὰ ὀνόματα καὶ τὰς φωνὰς τῶν εὐαγγελιστῶν, ἵνα μὴ ἀλλότριον καὶ ψευδὲς εὐαγγέλιον δέξηται· ἀλλὰ καὶ ὁμώνυμα καὶ ψευδῆ συγγράμματα εἰσίν, οἷον ἡ λεγομένη Ἀποκάλυψις τοῦ ἁγίου Παύλου· οὐ γάρ ἐστιν τοῦ ἁγίου Παύλου, ἀλλ᾽ ἑτέρου Παύλου αἱρετικοῦ τοῦ Σαμωσατέως, ὅθεν οἱ Παυλικιανοὶ κατάγονται· καὶ ἑτέρα Ἀποκάλυψις ἡ λεγομένη τοῦ Θεολόγου· οὐκ ἔστι δὲ τοῦ Θεολόγου· οὐ λέγομεν δὲ τὴν ἐν Πάτμῳ τῇ νήσῳ, μὴ γένοιτο· αὕτη γὰρ ἀληθεστάτη ἐστίν, ἀλλὰ τὴν ψευδώνυμον καὶ ἀλλοτρίαν. Δεῖ δὲ τὸν γραμματικὸν καὶ τὰ Ἑλληνικὰ βιβλία γινώσκειν· εἰσι γὰρ καὶ ἐν αὐτοῖς ὁμώνυμα βιβλία ψευδῆ, οἷον ἡ Ἀσπὶς Ἡσιόδου καὶ τά Θηριακά Νικάνδρου· οὐ γάρ ἐστιν ἡ Ἀσπὶς Ἡσιόδου οὐδὲ τὰ θηριακὰ Νικάνδρου· ἑτέρων γάρ εἰσιν ποιητῶν, ἐχρήσαντο δὲ οἱ συγγραφεῖς τῇ ὁμωνυμίᾳ Ἡσιόδου καὶ Νικάνδρου, ἵνα ἄξια κριθῶσιν ἀναγνώσεως. Δεῖ δὲ τὸν γραμματικὸν ταῦτα πάντα καλῶς ἐπίστασθαι, καὶ οὕτως λέγεσθαι καὶ εἶναι γραμματικόν.

*"The sixth [part of grammar] is poetic analysis, which is the fairest of all the uses of the art."* By 'poetic analysis' is meant the accurate appraisal of poetic works. The scholar (*grammatikos*) who makes

use of such accurate appraisal must know all the books of the Church, among these the Old and New Testaments, so that whenever he hears a strange style (*phônê xenê*) and false historical or poetic works, he will not consider [it] as if it were truthful, such as the so-called Gospel according to Thomas. The scholar should know the vocabulary and the tone (*phônê*) of the gospels, so that he should not accept a foreign (*allotrios*) and false gospel. But there are also gospels which have the same names as authentic works (= which are *homônumos*) but are false, such as the so-called Apocalypse of St. Paul. This is not in fact of St. Paul, but of another Paul, a heretic from Samosata, and the Paulanicians (*Paulikianoi*) get it from here. There is also another Apocalypse of Theologos, which is not in fact of Theologos. We are not speaking of the one on the island of Patmos, God forbid. For that is certainly authentic; rather, [we are speaking] of the pseudonymous and foreign (*allotrios*) one. It is necessary for the scholar to know the Greek books also. False books which share valid names (= which are *homônumos*) are also found here, such as the Shield of Hesiod and the Theriaka of Nicander. The Shield is not of Hesiod nor is the Theriaka of Nicander; these are of other poets, but their authors used the same name (*homônumia*) as Hesiod and Nicander, so that they might be judged worthy of being read. A scholar should know all these examples well, and thus he is and can be called a scholar (*grammatikos*).

*Commentariolus Byzantinus*, ed. Hilgard p. 568

This grammatical treatise conveys important information about the prevalence of attribution analysis in the Christian world of the Byzantine period. What is especially intriguing about the passage is its pedagogical legitimization of the study of Classical Greek texts as a body of information on which skills that would later be redirected to New Testament documents could be honed.

Attribution analysis of documents relating to New Testament figures was necessitated by the anonymity of many New Testament books. It has generally been accepted that the titles of the Gospels were added by later editors, and do not constitute the "signatures" of their authors. These simple attributions (for example, *Kata Matthaion* 'From Matthew' or 'According to Matthew') are, in any event, slightly ambiguous: do these traditions or teachings derive from Matthew's disciples? Do the titles imply that the text was dictated by the evangelist, or that it was written down by his own hand? Moreover, a close reading of many of the New Testament documents on their own reveals that these texts are deliberately anonymous and that their authors had reservations about revealing their identities openly. These texts stand in stark contrast to the letters of Paul, Peter, James, and Jude, and the Revelation of John, all of which describe or name their author within the document.

In a fascinating study, David Trobisch has analyzed how the Canonical Edition of the New Testament (that is, the authoritative form or version in which the collection was first published) represents an attempt by editors to solve questions of attribution and rectify the apparent anonymity of many New Testament books. Trobisch's argument needs to be summarized here, because it is crucial in understanding the development of the Christian view on the writers of the New Testament. Trobisch argues that the editors of the New Testament intended a specific reading experience that would lead the reader to knowledge of the composers of each text, despite the fact that many of these writers had wished to remain anonymous. The Canonical Edition provides instructions to the implied reader through interconnecting redactional signals and cross-referencing. Even if the name given in the book's title is taken as an explicit statement of authorship, these redactional signals "stimulate the curiosity of the readers and direct them to specific text passages in other writings of the Canonical Edition," thus providing a fuller and more satisfying portrait of the author than could possibly be conveyed by the title alone.[18] Moreover, the titles "are the result of a deliberate redactional effort typical for anthologies to direct the interest of the readers to what the editors feel is the central message of the collection."[19]

By means of these signals, Trobisch skillfully analyzes how the Canonical Edition directs readers to fill in biographical details of this author by combing the collection for references. For example, the title of the Gospel "According to Matthew" leads the readers to the story of a tax collector named Matthew who followed Jesus when called (Matthew 9:9). This tax collector is called Levi in Mark 2:14 and Luke 5:27. Trobisch finds that the name change to Matthew was to be understood as an autobiographical note and a correction of a misleading tradition.[20] Through this reference, the Canonical Edition reveals the identity of the author of the Gospel and establishes a link between Matthew and the Gospels of Mark and Luke.

Readers learn about Mark, the author of the Gospel according to its title, not from the Gospel itself, but from a variety of references in Acts and the letters of Peter and Paul. Trobisch suggests that these interlocking references create a biography of Mark. This biography features a quarrel with Paul and a later reconciliation between the two apostles. Mark is the cause of Paul's split with the missionary Barnabas, Mark's uncle (reported in Acts 15:37–41). The dispute involved whether Paul and Barnabas should include Mark in their mission, since he had abandoned them during a previous venture to Pamphylia. However, the reader learns that Paul and Mark later made peace, when Paul asks the congregation of the Colossians to welcome him (Colossians 4:10). Mark is also mentioned as a member of Paul's ministry in 2 Timothy 4:11 and as a co-worker in Philemon 24, leading the reader to conclude that the conflict is over. According to Trobisch, this reconciliation also serves to link together Peter and Paul, since Mark was closely associated with Peter, who refers to him as "my son" in 1 Peter 5:13.

The Canonical Edition functions in much the same way with regard to Luke. The book of Acts does not mention the name of Luke or describe his identity; nor does Luke's Gospel, apart from its title. Instead, the Canonical Edition highlights a number of clues found within Luke-Acts as well as elsewhere for its readers to digest. The use of the first-person plural in Acts indicates that its author was a companion of Paul. The common addressee "Theophilus" in both the Gospel of Luke and Acts signifies that they are both compositions of the same author. The reader is directed to passages in Paul's letters that refer to Luke (Colossians 4:14; 2 Timothy 4:11; Philemon 23–24); here it is learned that Luke was Paul's favored disciple. Together with the title "According to Luke" affixed to the Gospel, these clues indicate the identity of the author of Acts and help the reader to paint his portrait.

The name John is the source of much confusion. It could potentially refer to two different individuals called John mentioned in the Gospel itself (namely, John the Baptist and John the father of

Peter, both of whom are unlikely candidates for author). The confusion is furthered by the Gospel's deliberate attempt to avoid stating the identity of its author openly. Instead, the reader is merely told in John 21:20 that the author (described merely as the disciple "whom Jesus loved") is the same individual who had reclined next to Jesus at the Last Supper and asked who would betray him. This anonymous individual is presumably one of the three disciples that Jesus occasionally confided in (namely, Peter and the two sons of Zebedee, John and James — see Matthew 17:1, 26:37, and Mark 5:37). The context of John 21 reveals that the disciple "whom Jesus loved" cannot possibly be Peter. Further, Acts 12:2 informs the reader that James son of Zebedee had died early, while John 21:23 reveals that the author of the Gospel had lived to a great age. What is even more remarkable is the way that the editors who added the appendix to John (chapter 21) point readers to John 13 to help them identify the author. Trobisch concludes, "In a way the editors of John's Gospel respect the anonymity by not mentioning the author's name in John 21. They refer the readers to specific text passages, but the name John is given only in the title."[21] Through these interlocking references, the anonymity of the author of the fourth Gospel is solved for the reader who cares to investigate further.

In like fashion, the letters of John reveal their authorship subtly, by emphasizing terms that appeared in John's Gospel (such as "beginning," "word," and "life"). They depict an author who had reached a great age (such as referring to his addressees as "my little children"). Trobisch presents a situation in which readers are encouraged by the Canonical Edition to accept the title of the letters of John, but also to validate its provenance for themselves. He also suggests that readers will have no doubt over the author of 2 and 3 John, as the other numbered letters of the New Testament also imply they were written by the same person. Similarly, Revelation contains the name John both in its title and within the text (Revelation 1:1, 4, 9; 22:8). The assumption is that John son of Zebedee is the author of this text, in addition to the Gospel and the letters, although the ancestry of the John mentioned in Revelation is never specified.

Some of the letters that explicitly name their authors within the text (those of Peter, James, and Jude) provoke readers to probe specific passages in which these authors are identified in more detail. Peter is one of the main characters in the New Testament, and is mentioned over 150 times; there is little doubt over his identity. But there are five individuals in the New Testament called James (the son of Zebedee, the son of Alphaeus, the brother of the lord, James "the younger," and the father of the disciple Jude). The interlinking references of the Canonical Edition, claims Trobisch, show the way to the identity of this James. Comparison between Jude 1 and James 1:1 reveals that Jude and James refer to themselves in interlinking ways. Jude calls himself a "servant of Jesus Christ and brother of James" (Jude 1), while James describes himself "a servant of God and of the Lord Jesus Christ" (James 1:1). Neither call themselves apostles of Jesus Christ, as had Paul and Peter. The fact that the content of the letters of James contradicts the teaching of Paul (on the important question of whether a person is justified by faith alone as Paul claimed, or by works as well, as argued James) leads readers to suppose that the James mentioned is the one who had at first opposed Paul (as mentioned in Galatians 1:19 and 2:12). It is not difficult for the reader to conclude that James and Jude are those mentioned as brothers of Jesus in the Matthew 13:55. I would add that the letter of Jude may have been included in the Canonical Edition in part because it is crucial in establishing the identity of the author of the letters of James.

These cross-references function to construct a narrative of an ultimately harmonious relationship between the authors of the New Testament, a narrative that might otherwise be lost in the descriptions of their conflicts. As Trobisch asserts, "The names of the alleged gospel authors Mark and Luke refer the readers to passages in Acts, 1 Peter, and to the letters of Paul, which indicate harmony and cooperation between the Jerusalem authorities and Paul."[22] After reading about a dispute between Paul and James, or between Paul and Mark (cf. Acts 15:37–41), the Canonical Edition provides clues that indicate a reconciliation between all parties.

The Canonical Edition thus communicates two distinct messages. The first message is that the twenty-seven books in the New Testament were composed by eight writers, each with a distinct portraiture and biographical identity revealed by the collection as a whole, and not merely by the works they composed. These include

Matthew, the tax collector and disciple of Jesus; Mark, the associate of Peter and co-missionary with Paul; Luke the physician and favored disciple of Paul; John, the son of Zebedee, known as the disciple "whom Jesus loved"; Paul, formerly Saul, apostle to the gentiles; James, the brother of Jesus; Simon Peter, the apostle of Jesus; and Jude, another brother of Jesus. The second message is narrative in nature, consisting of a story of harmonious resolution between Paul and the Jerusalem apostles that was achieved after an initial divide. These two interrelated messages rest on the assumption that the documents in the collection were composed by the individuals to whom they are attributed.

At some point following the publication of the Canonical Edition, Christian scholars would accept these attributions as fact. As the text from the scholia to Dionysius Thrax cited above reveals, the trustworthiness of the attributions in the Canonical Edition of the New Testament stood in stark contrast to the status of other works circulating in early Christian communities. The authenticity of works in the collection could even be taken to suggest that the attributions of *none* of these other works were legitimate. But did the Canonical Edition create a standard of authenticity, or was it created by such a standard? (Whether "Canonical Edition" was a one-time textual "printing" or is merely a heuristic concept remains a subject for debate.)

An overview of explicit statements regarding the attributions of works credited to the followers of Jesus shows that it was fully within the authority of noted scholars to challenge their authenticity. Early Christian scholars also challenged the Old Testament canon, but in a different manner. Even if the attributions of Old Testament scriptures were correct, as the Church fathers were apparently willing to admit, could they be sure that authentic scriptures had not been left out of the collection? A variety of approaches to these matters can be seen in the works of Tertullian (152–222 C.E.), Origen (ca. 184–254 C.E.), Eusebius (260–339 C.E.), and St. Jerome (347–420 C.E.). Their differences aside, these scholars often defend the legitimacy of doubtful Old Testament books, but boldly attack suspicious writings attributed to New Testament figures. The approach of these scholars to both Old and New Testament attribution analysis reveals the degree to which Aristotelian methodology left its mark on Christianity.[23] Moreover, the application of attribution analysis to potentially inspired documents by early Christians had a tremendous impact on the development of the idea of authorship, as well as on the way scripture would henceforward be viewed.

## TERTULLIAN

The debate between Tertullian and Marcion represents a significant chapter in the history of Christian attribution analysis. Marcion, the founder of a Gnostic version of Christianity who believed that Jesus and the God of the Old Testament were two separate gods, had voiced theories about the contamination of New Testament documents by the first followers of Jesus and Paul. From his perspective, these followers had adulterated the message of Jesus; thus he rejected all parts of the New Testament that linked Christ in any way to the creator God, the God of Israel. Marcion's charge was that "false apostles had falsified (*interpolaverunt*) the truth of the Gospels" (*Adversus Marcionem* IV.4). Marcion also rejected the entire Old Testament, although his complaint was not that it was inauthentic, but rather that it was non-Christian.

Marcion's canon (the first known authoritative list of Christian writings) included an expurgated version of the Gospel of Luke, together with ten epistles of Paul, which were apparently edited to remove references to the Old Testament. He concluded that his gospel had been written down by Christ himself, not by St. Luke. According to Tertullian, Marcion in his *Antitheses* accuses the Gospel of Luke of having been falsified by the upholders of Judaism. They had done so in order to combine the gospel in one body with the law and the prophets, and so that they could pretend that Christ had a Jewish origin.

For his part, Tertullian argues that Marcion's gospel is itself adulterated (*adulteratus*), and that he has made it his own by interpolation (*interpolando*). In opposition to Marcion, who claimed that the title (*titulum*, the equivalent of Greek *epigraphê*) of Luke's Gospel (i.e., "According to Luke") was falsified, Tertullian articulates a theory about the process by which the works of the New Testament achieved written form at the hands of individual *auctores* 'authors' or 'agents':

> Constituimus inprimis evangelicum instrumentum apostolos auctores habere, quibus hoc munus evangelii promulgandi ab ipso domino sit impositum ... Contra Marcion evangelio, scilicet suo, nullum adscribit auctorem

> I lay it down to begin with that the documents of the gospel have the apostles for their authors (*auctores*), and that this task of promulgating the gospel was imposed upon them by our Lord himself ... Marcion on the other hand attaches (*adscribit*) to his gospel the name of no author (*auctor*).
>
> Tertullian, *Adversus Marcionem* IV.2, trans. Evans

The word *auctor* here implies a more limited notion of activity than is conveyed by our notion of "author." Nevertheless, as Tertullian makes plain, the designation of the correct *auctor* for each gospel is essential to the authority of the gospels. Thus, the absence of a human agent in Marcion's gospel amounts to a violation of a central premise of Tertullian's ideas about the nature of the biblical text and its origin.

Tertullian presents the debate between Marcion and Christianity as a quandary over how to judge a dispute in which identical charges are levied by both sides.

> Ego meum dico verum, Marcion suum. Ego Marcionis affirmo adulteratum, Marcion meum. Quis inter nos determinabit, nisi temporis ratio, ei praescribens auctoritatem quod antiquius reperietur, et ei praeiudicans vitiationem quod posterius revincetur? In quantum enim falsum corruptio est veri, in tantum praecedat necesse est veritas falsum.

> I say that my [New Testament] is true; Marcion says the same for his. I say that Marcion's is falsified; Marcion says the same of mine. Who shall decide between us? Only such a reckoning of dates, as will assume that authority belongs to that which is found to be

older, and will prejudge as corrupt that which is convicted of having come later. For in so far as the false is a corruption of the true, to that extent must the truth have preceded that which is false.

Tertullian, *Adversus Marcionem* IV.2, trans. Evans

Tertullian's reasoning is sound, at least from the perspective of attribution analysis: the document that can be demonstrated to be prior is more authentic than the later version. But from Marcion's perspective (as far as it can be reconstructed from the attacks of Tertullian and others), relative priority is no claim to authenticity.[24] What is most striking about this debate is the way that the religious confrontation between two competing versions of Christianity takes place, in large part, within the discourse of attribution analysis.

### ORIGEN

A good example of the earliest stages of Christian attribution analysis can be seen in the discussion surrounding the book of Susanna in Origen's *Letter to Africanus*. Susanna, a Jewish composition preserved in the Greek translation of the Septuagint as an addendum to the book of Daniel, would eventually be classified as Deuterocanonical on account of the fact that it was not included in the Hebrew scriptures. Africanus had concluded from this fact that Susanna could not have been written by Daniel. Origen asks in response:

Ὥρα τοίνυν, εἰ μὴ λανθάνῃ ἡμᾶς τὰ τοιαῦτα, ἀθετεῖν τὰ ἐν ταῖς ἐκκλησίαις φερόμενα ἀντίγραφα, καὶ νομοθετῆσαι τῇ ἀδελφότητι ἀποθέσθαι μὲν τὰς παρ᾽ αὐτοῖς φερομένας ἱερὰς βίβλους, κολακεύειν δὲ Ἰουδαίους καὶ πείθειν ἵνα μεταδῶσιν ἡμῖν τῶν καθαρῶν καὶ μηδὲν πλάσμα ἐχόντων;

Is it now necessary, if these things should not just escape our notice, to athetize the copies in use in the Church, and to order the community to reject the sacred books in usage among them, and to flatter the Jews and to persuade them to give us, in their place, pure texts without any fabrication (*plasma*)?

Origen, *Letter to Africanus* 8

When Origen endorses the study of the Hebrew manuscripts, it is not to find a truer version of scripture, but to prepare for the controversies which would arise between Christians and Jews. His goal, here and elsewhere, is to expand the canon of Old Testament scriptures, or as he puts it, to prevent it from being shrunk by either the censorship of the Jews or the mistaken Christian practitioners of attribution analysis like Africanus.

In specific, Origen claims the Jews were in the habit of excising portions of scripture now kept in the Apocrypha that spoke poorly of their figures of authority. His reasoning is of course questionable; the Hebrew Bible is hardly a book filled only with role models or authority figures that are beyond moral reproach. Nevertheless, Africanus' charge, as well as Origen's able response, is instructive in evaluating the scope of Greek attribution analysis in the early stages of Christianity. Africanus evaluates the book of Susanna on the all-important ground of Greek attribution analysis: was the book of Susanna in fact composed by Daniel, as tradition held? Origen, in turn, claims that Jewish attribution analysis had been faulty: Jews had excluded the book on moral rather than philological grounds.

Origen is not above accusing the Jews of having excised other passages from their own manuscripts on account of a desire to preserve the reputation of their esteemed figures.

Λεκτέον δὲ πρὸς ταῦτα ὅτι ὅσα δεδύνηνται τῶν περιεχόντων κατηγορίαν πρεβυτέρων καὶ ἀρχόντων καὶ κριτῶν περιεῖλον ἀπὸ τῆς γνώσεως τοῦ λαοῦ, ὧν τινὰ σώζεται ἐν ἀποκρύφοις.

One must say with regard to these questions that as much as they were able, they have lifted from the knowledge of the people all passages containing accusations against the elders and rulers and judges, of which some are saved in the Apocrypha.

Origen, *Letter to Africanus* 13

Origen gives the example of the story about Isaiah being tortured to death by the Jews, as found in both the Letter to the Hebrews (from the New Testament) and the pseudepigraphical *Martyrdom of Isaiah*. He suggests that the latter text was perhaps intentionally damaged (*rheradiourgêtai*) by the Jews, through insertion of improper words into the text, so that the whole would be suspect (*Letter to Africanus* 13). Another of his examples of Jewish tampering with the text of the Old Testament concerns Jesus' speech to the Pharisees and hypocrites, that had they lived in the days of their fathers, to whom they claim to be joined "in the blood of the prophets" (Matthew 23:29–36). Jesus asserts that the Pharisees in so doing give testimony to the fact that they are in fact the sons of those who killed these prophets. Yet because scenes of Jews killing the prophets are not found in the Old Testament in its present shape, Origen concludes that the Jews have bowdlerized their scriptures (*Letter to Africanus* 14).[25] On this basis, Origen sums up his argument to Africanus:

> Καὶ οἶμαι δὲ ἀποδεδειχέναι ἐν τοῖς προκειμένοις ὅτι οὐδὲν
> ἄτοπόν ἐστι γεγονέναι μὲν τὴν ἱστορίαν, καὶ τὴν μετὰ πολλῆς
> ἀκολασίας ὠμότητα τετολμῆσθαι τοῖς τότε πρεσβυτέροις κατὰ
> τῆς Σουσάννας, καὶ γεγράφθαι μὲν προνοίᾳ τοῦ πνεύματος,
> ὑπεξαιρεῖσθαι δέ, ὡς ἂν εἴποι τὸ πνεῦμα, ὑπὸ τῶν ἀρχόντων
> Σοδόμων.

> I think I have demonstrated in what precedes that it is not absurd to say the following: the story took place, the ancients of that epoch dared this cruel act of savagery against Susanna, and the account was written with the intention of the Holy Spirit, but was removed, as the Holy Spirit might say, by "the rulers of Sodom" (Isaiah 1:10).
>
> Origen, *Letter to Africanus* 15

Although fully conversant with the procedures involved in attribution analysis, Origen seemed to prefer to refute charges of false ascription than to employ the technique to discount the inspired status of works of scripture. Thus, whenever the topic of the apocrypha or pseudepigrapha arises, Origen rushes to their defense.

Similarly, Origen supports the Pauline ascription of the Letter to the Hebrews, much challenged by other early Church authorities (see *Letter to Africanus* 14). In the *Ecclesiastical History* of Eusebius, Origen's position on Hebrews is quoted:

ὅτι ὁ χαρακτὴρ τῆς λέξεως τῆς Πρὸς Ἑβραίους ἐπιγεγραμμένης ἐπιστολῆς οὐκ ἔχει τὸ ἐν λόγῳ ἰδιωτικὸν τοῦ ἀποστόλου, ὁμολογήσαντος ἑαυτὸν ἰδιώτην εἶναι τῷ λόγῳ, τοῦτ᾽ ἐστὶν τῇ φράσει, ἀλλ᾽ ἐστὶν ἡ ἐπιστολὴ συνθέσει τῆς λέξεως Ἑλληνικωτέρα, πᾶς ὁ ἐπιστάμενος κρίνειν φράσεων διαφορὰς ὁμολογήσαι ἄν. πάλιν τε αὖ ὅτι τὰ νοήματα τῆς ἐπιστολῆς θαυμάσιά ἐστιν καὶ οὐ δεύτερα τῶν ἀποστολικῶν ὁμολογουμένων γραμμάτων, καὶ τοῦτο ἂν συμφήσαι εἶναι ἀληθὲς πᾶς ὁ προσέχων τῇ ἀναγνώσει τῇ ἀποστολικῇ.

ἐγὼ δὲ ἀποφαινόμενος εἴποιμ᾽ ἂν ὅτι τὰ μὲν νοήματα τοῦ ἀποστόλου ἐστίν, ἡ δὲ φράσις καὶ ἡ σύνθεσις ἀπομνημονεύσαντός τινος τὰ ἀποστολικὰ καὶ ὥσπερ σχολιογραφήσαντός τινος τὰ εἰρημένα ὑπὸ τοῦ διδασκάλου. εἴ τις οὖν ἐκκλησία ἔχει ταύτην τὴν ἐπιστολὴν ὡς Παύλου, αὕτη εὐδοκιμείτω καὶ ἐπὶ τούτῳ· οὐ γὰρ εἰκῇ οἱ ἀρχαῖοι ἄνδρες ὡς Παύλου αὐτὴν παραδεδώκασιν. τίς δὲ ὁ γράψας τὴν ἐπιστολήν, τὸ μὲν ἀληθὲς θεὸς οἶδεν, ἡ δὲ εἰς ἡμᾶς φθάσασα ἱστορία ὑπὸ τινῶν μὲν λεγόντων ὅτι Κλήμης, ὁ γενόμενος ἐπίσκοπος Ῥωμαίων, ἔγραψεν τὴν ἐπιστολήν, ὑπὸ τινῶν δὲ ὅτι Λουκᾶς, ὁ γράψας τὸ εὐαγγέλιον καὶ τὰς Πράξεις.

In the epistle entitled *To the Hebrews* the diction does not exhibit the characteristic roughness of speech or phraseology admitted by the Apostle himself; the construction of the sentences is closer to Greek usage, as anyone capable of recognizing differences of style would agree. On the other hand the matter of the epistle is wonderful, and quite equal to the Apostle's acknowledged writings: the truth of this would be admitted by anyone who has read the Apostle carefully.

If I were asked my personal opinion, I would say that the matter (*noêma*) is the Apostle's but the phraseology and construction are those of someone who remembered the Apostle's teaching and like a scholiast recording what his master had said. So if any church regards this epistle as Paul's, it should be commended for so doing, for the primitive Church had every justification for handing it down as his. Who wrote the epistle is known to God alone: the accounts that have reached us suggest that it was either Clement, who became Bishop of Rome, or Luke, who wrote the gospels and the Acts.

Origen (cited by Eusebius), trans. Williamson[26]

Origen again employs attribution analysis for the purpose of solid-ifying the canonical status of a document rather than impugning the validity of doubtful works. His reasoning seems to echo the fre-quently cited opinion of Tertullian on attribution: *capit magistorum videri quae discipuli promulgarint* 'it is allowable that that which disciples publish should be regarded as their masters' work'.[27] Ter-tullian employs this reasoning to justify the apostolicity of the anonymous gospels associated with Mark and Luke by tradition. Similarly, Origen justifies Hebrews, concluding that the *noêma* 'thought' of Hebrews betrays its origin in Paul, even if it was for-mulated and interpreted by a disciple acting as a "scholiast."[28] This kind of creative approach to saving works accused of being forger-ies by appealing to legitimate extenuating factors in attribution is typical of Origen's approach.

## EUSEBIUS

The most impressive example of early Christian use of attribu-tion analysis is found in the writings of Eusebius (260–339 C.E.). Eusebius regularly cites discussions of the authenticity of church writings by his predecessors, and engages in his own speculations on the subject.[29] Eusebius closes his description of each of the lives of apostles and disciples with a list of their works. In Alexandrian fashion, he evaluates the authenticity of the documents that have been attributed to the individual in question. For example, in his discussion of James brother of Jesus, he states the following:

τοιαῦτα καὶ τὰ κατὰ Ἰάκωβον, οὗ ἡ πρώτη τῶν ὀνομαζομένων καθολικῶν ἐπιστολῶν εἶναι λέγεται· ἰστέον δὲ ὡς νοθεύεται μέν, οὐ πολλοὶ γοῦν τῶν παλαιῶν αὐτῆς ἐμνημόνευσαν, ὡς οὐδὲ τῆς λεγομένης Ἰούδα, μιᾶς καὶ αὐτῆς οὔσης τῶν ἑπτὰ λεγομένων καθολικῶν· ὅμως δ᾽ ἴσμεν καὶ ταύτας μετὰ τῶν λοιπῶν ἐν πλείσταις δεδημοσιευμένας ἐκκλησίαις.

Such is the story of James, to whom it is said that the first of the epistles called "catholic" belongs. One should know that it is con-sidered spurious (*notheuetai*, from *nothos* 'bastard, forgery'), and that few early writers refer to it at any rate, any more than to the one said to be Jude's, which is also one of the seven called catholic. Nevertheless, we understand that these two, together with the others, have been widely accepted in many churches.

Eusebius, *Ecclesiastical History* II.23, trans. Williamson

In this passage, Eusebius sets the received wisdom about the authenticity of the epistles of James and Jude against the practice of the churches. A challenge to the authenticity of a document is apparently outweighed by the opinion of the churches as to the merits of the document. However, I would suggest that Eusebius does not consider the opinion of the churches to negate scholarly consensus about the authorship of a work and the validity of its attribution. Even though he never admits that church practice can by itself authenticate the attribution of a work of doubtful authorship, it would appear that the decision of the ecclesiastical community can at least validate the content of the work and provide the decisive factor regarding its acceptance.

The frequent citations of preceding generations of Christian scholars (Clement, Origen, Dionysius), as well as the more vague allusions to scholarly consensus, are typical of Eusebius' approach to attribution analysis. But Eusebius also displays a considerable degree of confidence in the merits of his own judgements as to the authenticity of a document, as may be seen in the following discussion of the entire category of inauthentic works associated with the New Testament.

ἐν τοῖς νόθοις κατατετάχθω καὶ τῶν Παύλου Πράξεων ἡ γραφὴ ὅ τε λεγόμενος Ποιμὴν καὶ ἡ Ἀποκάλυψις Πέτρου καὶ πρὸς τούτοις ἡ φερομένη Βαρναβᾶ ἐπιστολὴ καὶ τῶν ἀποστόλων αἱ λεγόμεναι Διδαχαὶ ἔτι τε, ὡς ἔφην, ἡ Ἰωάννου Ἀποκάλυψις, εἰ φανείη· ἥν τινες, ὡς ἔφην, ἀθετοῦσιν, ἕτεροι δὲ ἐγκρίνουσιν τοῖς ὁμολογουμένοις. ἤδη δ' ἐν τούτοις τινὲς καὶ τὸ καθ' Ἑβραίους εὐαγγέλιον κατέλεξαν, ᾧ μάλιστα Ἑβραίων οἱ τὸν Χριστὸν παραδεξάμενοι χαίρουσιν. ταῦτα δὲ πάντα τῶν ἀντιλεγομένων ἂν εἴη. ἀναγκαίως δὲ καὶ τούτων ὅμως τὸν κατάλογον πεποιήμεθα, διακρίνοντες τάς τε κατὰ τὴν ἐκκλησιαστικὴν παράδοσιν ἀληθεῖς καὶ ἀπλάστους καὶ ἀνωμολογημένας γραφὰς καὶ τὰς ἄλλως παρὰ ταύτας. οὐκ

ἐνδιαθήκους μὲν ἀλλὰ καὶ ἀντιλεγομένας, ὅμως δὲ παρὰ πλείστοις
τῶν ἐκκλησιαστικῶν γινωσκομένας, ἵν᾽ ε᾽δέναι ἔχοιμεν αὐτάς τε
ταύτας καὶ τὰς ὀνόματι τῶν ἀποστόλων πρὸς τῶν αἱρετικῶν
προφερομένας ἤτοι ὡς Πέτρου καὶ Θωμᾶ καὶ Ματθία ἢ καί τινων
παρὰ τούτους ἄλλων εὐαγγέλια περιεχούσας ἢ ὡς Ἀνδρέου καὶ
Ἰωάννου καὶ τῶν ἄλλων ἀποστόλων πράξεις· ὧν οὐδὲν οὐδαμῶς ἐν
συγγράμματι τῶν κατὰ τὰς διαδοχὰς ἐκκλησιαστικῶν τις ἀνὴρ εἰς
μνήμην ἀγαγεῖν ἠξίωσεν. πόρρω δέ που καὶ ὁ τῆς φράσεως παρὰ τὸ
ἦθος τὸ ἀποστολικὸν ἐναλλάττει χαρακτήρ, ἥ τε γνώμη καὶ ἡ τῶν
ἐν αὐτοῖς φερομένων προαίρεσις πλεῖστον ὅσον τῆς ἀληθοῦς
ὀρθοδοξίας ἀπᾴδουσα, ὅτι δὴ αἱρετικῶν ἀνδρῶν ἀναπλάσματα
τυγχάνει. σαφῶς παρίστησιν· ὅθεν οὐδ᾽ ἐν νόθοις αὐτὰ κατατακτέον,
ἀλλ᾽ ὡς ἄτοπα πάντη καὶ δυσσεβῆ παραιτητέον.

Among spurious (*nothoi*) books must be placed the "Acts" of Paul,
the "Shepherd," and the "Revelation of Peter"; also the alleged
"Epistle of Barnabas," and the "Teachings of the Apostles," together
with the Revelation of John, if this seems the right place for it: as
I said before, some reject (*athetein*) it, others include (*engkrinein*) it
among the agreed upon books. Moreover, some have found a place
in the list for the "Gospel of the Hebrews," a book which has a spe
cial appeal for those Hebrews who have accepted Christ. These
would all be classed with the Disputed Books, but I have been
obliged to list the latter separately, distinguishing (*diakrinein*)
those writings according to the tradition of the Church are true,
genuine (*aplastoi*), and recognized, from those in a different category, not canonical (*endiathêkoi*) but disputed, yet familiar to
most churchmen; for we must not confuse these with the writings
published by heretics under the name of the apostles, as containing either Gospels of Peter, Thomas, Matthias, and several others
besides these, or Acts of Andrew, John, and other apostles. To
none of these have any of the churchmen in the [recognized] successions (*kata tas diadokhas*) considered it worth referring in their
writings. Again, nothing could be farther from apostolic usage
than the type of phraseology employed, while the ideas and implications of their contents are so irreconcilable with true orthodoxy
that they stand revealed as the fictions (*anaplasmata*) of heretics.

It follows that so far from being classed even among spurious books (*nothoi*), they must be thrown out as impious (*dussebê*) and beyond the pale (*atopa*).

Eusebius, *Ecclesiastical History* III.25, trans. Williamson

F. F. Bruce assumes that Eusebius did not mean to challenge that the Shepherd was not actually written by Hermas, and therefore was asserting that this work and the others listed with it were "uncanonical" (*nothos* pl.).[30] I would argue that Eusebius understands the term *nothos* 'illegitimate' in its usual critical sense as 'spurious' (i.e. that the work was not composed by the individual to whom it is attributed). Nevertheless, Eusebius does not argue that all spurious works are necessarily "impious and beyond the pale" (*dussebês* and *atopos*). It would appear that authenticity is only one of the considerations by which New Testament writings may be declared authoritative, in his view. Other considerations include the use made of the documents by early Church writers, and the legitimacy of content of the works, especially as determined by the majority of ecclesiastical communities.

A significant component of the Christian approach to the determination of the contents or canon of scripture can be said to derive from Josephus. Like Josephus, Eusebius thinks of the legitimacy of the apostles as deriving from the notion of a succession (*diadokhê*); the term appears sixty-nine times in the *Ecclesiastical History* alone. Like Ben Sira, Eusebius speaks of Joshua as the *diadokhos* 'successor' of Moses.[31] He appears to understand by this that Joshua is a type of his namesake Jesus, who succeeded to his authority over the "true and most pure religion." Eusebius also quotes the Josephus passage (*Against Apion* 1.8) about the Hebrew scriptures containing no *diaphonia* 'discrepancies'.[32] It seems likely that scholars like St. Jerome and St. Augustine bolstered their appreciation for Josephus and his ideas in part because of the value Eusebius places on Josephus' conceptualization of the Hebrew scriptures.

## ST. JEROME

St. Jerome is a transitional figure in the Christian adoption of Greek attribution analysis. He is among the first biblical critics to

consider the biography of the author in determining the authenticity of the work.[33] Jerome argues for the genuineness of a New Testament epistle (the Pauline Letter to Philemon) on the grounds that
the letter was written at the same time as others of Paul's letters
that most critics considered authentic. It is interesting that such
considerations were not an obstacle for Jerome when he discusses
whether Moses could have written a psalm that refers to Samuel.
Jerome concludes that the reference to Samuel is prophetic (*Ep.*
140.4.3 ff.) and does not necessitate an attribution of the psalm to
David.

Jerome's reticence in using Greek attribution analysis on potentially authoritative works seems to derive from the uncertain
status he had been given in putting forth his own ecclesiastical
views. On the one hand, Jerome was esteemed as a translator of the
Greek Bible, yet on the other, he was admonished by the Church hierarchy for his growing allegiance to the Hebrew original, as opposed to the Septuagint. While he wanted to revamp the Latin
translation of the Old Testament on the basis of the *hebrica veritas*
'Hebrew truth', he claimed that he did not wish to abandon the Septuagint, which he called "the house of the Lord." In fact, Jerome understood its significance to Christian communities, and perhaps
did not feel powerful enough to speak against Church doctrine. As
he became convinced that the Hebrew Bible was superior to the
Septuagint, he seems to have become more uncertain as to the validity of his judgements on doctrinal questions. The challenge he
faced lay in how to militate against the Septuagint without staking
out an ecclesiastically untenable position regarding its lack of
value. In a pinch, he would appeal to New Testament citations from
the Old Testament that diverged significantly from the Septuagint
version, claiming that the Septuagint translators were patently on a
lower level than the Apostles, and that the Septuagint had obviously not been the version that they had used. "Let the Septuagint
be the *true interpretation* which the Apostles approved," he stated.
In other words, he argued that it should be considered authoritative on account of the Apostles, and not because of a miraculous or
prophetic translation legend, which he explicitly rejects.

Many of Jerome's ideas about the concept of the canon appear
to derive from Josephus, whose complete works Jerome seems to

have read, and which influenced Eusebius, the source of much of Jerome's information about the canon of the New Testament.[34] Jerome was particularly impressed by *Against Apion*, and by Josephus' knowledge of both Hebrew sacred writings and "the whole library of the Greeks."[35] As has been explored in chapter 3, *Against Apion* criticizes much of Greek literature on account of the inconsistencies and contradictions found in it, as well as owing to the fact that many of the earliest authorities typically cited by the Greeks are not considered to have written the texts ascribed to them (e.g. *Against Apion* 1.13–14). Thus, Jerome's attribution analysis may have been colored by Josephus' thoroughly Jewish critique of Greek letters. For its part, Josephus' critique was informed by an internal Greek debate about proper methods in historiography, the correct use of historical sources, and the value of *autopsia* 'seeing with one's own eyes'.[36]

An example of Jerome's use of a Josephus' approach to evaluating authenticity may be seen in the following treatment of John, the apostle and evangelist:

> Praetermisso itaque anno, cuius acta a tribus fuerant exposita, superioris temporis, antequam Iohannes clauderetur in carcerem, gesta narravit, sicut manifestum esse poterit his qui diligenter quattuor evangeliorum volumina legerint. Quae res et διαφώνιαν, quae videtur Johannis esse cum ceteris, tollit.

> So, skipping this year [i.e. the year of Jesus' life] which had been set forth by these [i.e. Matthew, Mark, and Luke], he [John] related the events of the earlier period before John was shut up in prison, so that it might be manifest to those who should diligently read the volumes of the four Evangelists. This also takes away the διαφωνία *diaphônia* 'discrepancy' which seems to exist between John and the others.
>
> Jerome, *De Viris Illustribus* 9.3, trans. Halton

Jerome harmonizes the discrepancies between the gospel of John and the other gospels in a fashion consistent with Jewish interpretation, yet using a Greek methodology that can only be characterized as authorial biography. But what stands out for the present argument is his use of the Greek word *diaphônia* 'discrepancy' or 'discordancy'. I would suggest that Jerome is here making use of Josephus' claims about the consistency of Jewish scripture:

εἰκότως οὖν, μᾶλλον δὲ ἀναγκαίως, ἅτε μήτε τὸ ὑπογράφειν αὐτεξουσίου πᾶσιν ὄντος μήτε τινὸς ἐν τοῖς γραφομένοις ἐνούσης διαφωνίας, ἀλλὰ μόνον τῶν προφητῶν τὰ μὲν ἀνωτάτω καὶ παλαιότατα κατὰ τὴν ἐπίπνοιαν τὴν ἀπὸ τοῦ θεοῦ μαθόντων, τὰ δὲ καθ᾿ αὑτοὺς ὡς ἐγένετο σαφῶς συγγραφόντων, οὐ μυριάδες βιβλίων εἰσὶ παρ᾿ ἡμῖν ἀσυμφώνων καὶ μαχομένων . . .

It therefore naturally, or rather necessarily, follows (seeing that with us it is not open to everybody to write the records, and that there is no discrepancy [*diaphônia*] in what is written; seeing that, on the contrary, the prophets alone had this privilege, obtaining their knowledge of the most remote and ancient events according to the inspiration [*epinoia*] which they owed to God) . . . it follows that we do not possess myriads of inconsistent books, conflicting and militating against each other . . .

Josephus, *Against Apion* 1.38

Jerome's biobibliography is used in concert with a fundamentally Jewish doctrine of the consistency of scripture. Jerome derives this doctrine from his knowledge of Judaism, but especially from the concept of *diaphônia,* as articulated by Josephus.

The genre of the biobibliography was employed by Jerome in *De Viris Illustribus* to cover a new area — ecclesiastical authors. In essence, no writer had yet catalogued the literary output of the figures influential to the church. Jerome states that the work was intended to do for ecclesiastical writers what Tranquillus, a Latin bibliographer, had done for eminent secular authors. He thereby hoped to refute the charges of Celsus, Porphyry, Julian, and other enemies of the church that it had no philosophers, no orators, and no men of learning. Much of Jerome's information on matters of authenticity was derived from Eusebius' *Ecclesiastical History,* although he chose another form to convey this material. What is certainly interesting about the work in terms of the present study is the fact that Jerome had no qualms about listing himself among the famous ecclesiastical authors. This indicates his self-awareness as a writer and "illustrious man," surely an important ingredient in later European culture's understanding of the idea of authorship. It also contrasts with the Alexandrian reticence towards ranking contemporaneous authors in their list of first-class writers; according to Quintilian, Aristarchus and Aristophanes did not include Apollonius in the highest rank of poets, since they included no one from their own time.[37]

Jerome's attribution analysis, as it appears in *De Viris Illustribus*, stands as an example of the lesser scope of Christian attribution analysis, when compared to that of his Greek predecessors. Jerome comments on New Testament writings (epistles as well as the gospels) together with writings of lesser authority yet still of interest to the Church, but avoids all secular authors. Moreover, he presents the debate over authenticity as merely a matter of reporting the claims of other scholars, and does not go into the merits of each (a feature typical of the work of his main source, Eusebius). Jerome is remarkably reticent in stating his own view.

Jerome's treatment of Simon Peter exemplifies his approach to the attribution analysis of biblical writings, as is seen in the following excerpt:

> Scripsit duas epistulas, quae catholicae nominantur; quarum secunda a plerisque eius negatur propter stili cum priore dissonantiam. Sed et evangelium iuxta Marcum, qui auditor eius et interpres fuit, huius dicitur. Libri autem, e quibus unus actorum eius inscribitur, alius evangelii, tertius praedicationis, quartus ἀποκαλύψεως, quintus iudicii inter apocryphas scripturas repudiantur.

> He [Simon Peter] wrote two epistles which are called Catholic, the second of which, on account of its difference from the first in style, is considered by many not to be his. Then, too, the Gospel according to Mark, who was his disciple and interpreter, is ascribed to him. On the other hand, the books of which one is entitled his *Acts*, another, his *Gospel*, a third, his *Preaching*, a fourth, his *Revelation*, a fifth, his *Judgment*, are rejected as apocryphal.
>
> Jerome, *De Viris Illustribus* 1.3–5, trans. Halton

Jerome here supplies no citation of the scholars who are ascribing or rejecting the works of Simon Peter (although elsewhere, he cites both Tertullian and Eusebius).[38] With regard to the Second Epistle, he points out that stylistic considerations are at work in these anonymous scholars' conclusions about its authenticity, but does not elaborate.[39] Jerome does not add his weight to the opinions of any of these scholars, but merely reports the questions that have been raised.

At other times, however, Jerome is more forthcoming in the stylistic grounds employed to ascertain the authenticity of an ascription. With regard to Clement the Bishop, he states:

> Scripsit ex persona ecclesiae romanae ad ecclesiam Corinthiorum valde utilem epistulam et quae in nonnullis locis etiam publice legitur, quae mihi videtur characteri epistulae, quae sub Pauli nomine ad Hebraeos fertur, convenire; sed et multis de eadem epistula non solum sensibus, sed iuxta verborum quoque ordinem abutitur; et omnino grandis in utraque similitudo est.

> He wrote in the name of the Roman church a most useful *Letter to the Church of Corinth*, which in some places is even read publicly, which seems to me to correspond to the style of the *Epistle to the Hebrews* ascribed to the authorship of Paul, and uses many expressions from that same epistle which not merely agree in sense but even in word order, and there is an altogether great similarity between the two.
>
> Jerome, *De Viris Illustribus* 15.2–3, trans. Halton

It is unclear what Jerome is implying about the relationship between Clement's Letter to the Church of Corinth and the Epistle to the Hebrews, since he argues later that Hebrews is correctly attributed to Paul. Nevertheless, his stylistic focus and sophistication is remarkable.

Linguistic considerations also come into play in Jerome's evaluation of authenticity. In discussing the authenticity of Paul's letter to the Hebrews (challenged by Tertullian and others), he considers the language of composition as a crucial factor in stylistic evaluation:

... scripserat autem ut hebraeus hebraice, id est, suo eloquio dis-
ertissime — ea quae eloquenter scripta sunt in hebraeo, et elo-
quentius vertisse in graecum et hanc esse causam, quod a ceteris
Pauli epistulis discrepare videatur. Legunt quidam Laodicenses,
sed ab omnibus exploditur.

[Paul] being a Hebrew wrote Hebrew, that is, his own tongue and
most fluently, while the things which were eloquently written in
Hebrew were more eloquently turned into Greek, and this is the
reason why it seems to differ from other epistles of Paul. Some
read also a letter *To the Laodiceans,* but it is rejected by everyone.
Jerome, *De Viris Illustribus* 5.10–11, trans. Halton

Jerome appeals to linguistic factors (that the letter was originally
composed in Hebrew) to counteract charges of inauthenticity that
rested on stylistic arguments.

With regard to James, brother of Jesus, Jerome states:

unam tantum scripsit epistulam, quae de septem catholicis est,
quae et ipsa ab alio quodam sub nomine eius edita asseritur, licet
paulatim tempore procedente obtinuerit auctoritatem.

He [James] wrote a single epistle, which is reckoned among the
seven Catholic Epistles, and even this is claimed by some to have
been published by someone else under his name, and gradually as
time went on to have gained authority.
Jerome, *De Viris Illustribus* 2.2, trans. Halton

In a most dispassionate way, Jerome reports the fate of this text, the
debate over its authenticity, and the process by which the epistle
came to gain authority through time rather than through certainty
of its attribution. For Jerome, the correctness of the ascription is of
purely academic interest, and has no bearing on whether the text is
to be considered "catholic" or not. Alternately, it might be said that
Jerome is merely presenting the fruits of his research as it relates to
each entry in the biobibliography; conclusions are left for others.

Jerome reports the prevalence of scholarly doubt about the legitimacy of the epistle of Jude (it quotes a passage from Enoch, uni-

versally recognized as apocryphal, and is therefore rejected "by many"). Jerome ends this particular entry with a statement that reveals the principal grounds upon which canonicity is determined in his eyes: "Nevertheless, by age and use it has gained authority and is reckoned among the Holy Scriptures" (Jerome, *De Viris Illustribus* 4.1–2). Like his predecessor Eusebius, Jerome does not see authenticity as a necessary factor in determination of the status of a biblical book; rather, the opinion of "age and use" is decisive. Jerome's practice of attribution analysis seems to be consistent with his stance as compiler of biographical and literary information; he makes no definitive statements about attributions, nor does he make recommendations on the basis of the conclusions that would seem to follow.

The preceding overview provides a partial picture of the Aristotelian methodology employed by Tertullian, Origen, Eusebius, and Jerome. The fact that they openly discussed and even challenged the authenticity of New Testament works like the epistles of James, Peter, Jude, the Letter "to the Hebrews," and Revelation needs to be recognized as a critical element in discussions of canonization. As I will explore in chapter 7, the very creation of a New Testament canon was determined in part by the Aristotelian methodology as mediated by Alexandrian scholarship. Origen, a Christian scholar with great expertise in (pagan) Alexandrian criticism, provided a crucial link. The importance of attribution analysis in New Testament canon formation may be seen in the implicit recognition by Eusebius that attribution analysis was one among several methods by which the value and inspiration of a scriptural work could be evaluated. The same conclusion would be stated openly in the writings of St. Augustine.

## Ezra and the Retextualization of the Bible

The premise of the Peisistratus legend found in the Scholia to Dionysius Thrax was that the texts of Homer had been destroyed. I have suggested that this principle informed the philological methodology of Alexandrian Homeric criticism. I also suggested that Josephus' critique of the faulty transmission of Homer's epics was motivated by this same assumption. I have called this assumption an Alexandrian methodological dictum.

The hopeless lack of uniformity of Homeric manuscripts during the third to first centuries B.C.E. likely led to the formulation of this dictum. In addition, it is possible that the tradition of a cataclysmic event, such as the destruction of Atlantis described by Plato in the *Timaeus*, also lurked behind the development of this editorial principle. This is evidenced by Josephus' reference to Plato's legend as he critiqued the lack of written records among the Greeks. For Josephus as well as the Alexandrian scholars, speculation about such cataclysmic events may have appealed as an explanation for the sorry state of Greek documents from ancient times.

The tale of a catastrophe befalling the text of Homer is paralleled in the biblical world by a similar set of legends surrounding the Hebrew Bible associated with the figure of Ezra.[40] The story of the destruction of the Bible during the Babylonian captivity and its subsequent prophetic reconstruction by Ezra is remarkably similar to the claim that the texts Homer himself had written did not survive.[41] These stories were omitted in rabbinic texts, but were an important part of the attempt on the part of other post-70 C.E. Jewish groups to validate their traditions. Some mystical and apocalyptic strands of Judaism employed the Ezra story to legitimate texts absent from the canon of scripture — the former contents of the Temple archives. Stories about Ezra also became prominent in Christian discussions of the authenticity of its religious documents, as well as in pagan critiques of the authenticity of scripture. As Josephus reveals, Ezra was among the very last composers of biblical books recognized by the most conservative elements in the Jewish tradition — the Israelite priests who kept the Temple archives. Thus, it is not an accident that he was a focal point of later debates about the authenticity of tradition.

Common to accounts of textual conflagration and retextualization in both the Jewish and the classical spheres is an anxiety about the authoritativeness and legitimacy of the reconstituted text. Is the reconstituted text the same as the one that had been destroyed? Did the process of retextualization result in the introduction of extraneous material that did not derive from the original document? In the classical world, such anxieties could be remedied by the mode of inquiry known as attribution analysis, which could laboriously ask this question of a text, line by line.

Judaism dealt with the anxiety about the legitimacy of the reconstituted text in a number of ways. One strand of the tradition concluded that miraculous agreement was at play in the translation (a kind of retextualization) of the Bible by the seventy elders. Through an appeal to doctrines or religious beliefs (such as the prophetic inspiration or universal agreement of the translators), accurate retextualization was not an impossibility. Another strand (that of rabbinic Judaism) found incriminating errors in the Greek translation, denied its legitimacy, and ignored the possibility that textual destruction had ever occurred.[42]

The story of Ezra as a retextualizer of the destroyed Hebrew Bible owes something to widespread accounts of library conflagrations in the ancient world. Gellius' story of the burning of the library at Alexandria is an example of the type of narrative that helped spawn similar stories about Ezra. The narrative, discussed earlier in the context of this relationship between the Septuagint translation and the Peisistratus legend, actually describes two library conflagrations:

> Libros Athenis disciplinarum liberalium publice ad legendum praebendos primus posuisse dicitur Pisistratus tyrannus. Deinceps studiosius accuratiusque ipsi Athenienses auxerunt; sed omnem illam postea librorum copiam Xerxes Athenarum potitus urbe ipsa praeter arcem incensa abstulit asportavitque in Persas. Eos porro libros universos multis post tempestatibus Seleucus rex, qui Nicanor appellatus est, referendos Athenas curavit. Ingens postea numerus librorum in Aegypto ab Ptolemaeis regibus vel conquisitus vel confectus est ad milia ferme voluminum septingenta; sed ea omnia bello priore Alexandrino dum diripitur ea civitas, non sponte neque opera consulta, sed a militibus forte auxiliaris incensa sunt.

> Peisistratus, the Tyrant, is said to have been the first to make books concerning the liberal arts available to the public to read. Afterwards, the Athenians themselves built up the collection with care and toil. But when Xerxes occupied Athens and burned the city apart from the Acropolis, he stole all this wealth of books and

took them away with him to Persia. Much later King Seleucus, known as Nicanor, had all these books restored to Athens. Afterwards a very great many books were collected or made in Egypt, by the Ptolemies; as many as seven hundred thousand scrolls.[43] But in the course of the first war of Alexandria, during the sack of the city, all these thousands of scrolls were given to the flames: not spontaneously, to be sure, nor by intention, but accidentally, by the auxiliaries.

Gellius, Noctes Atticae VII.17, trans. Rolfe<br>(cf. Isidorus, Etymologiae VI.3.3–5)

Despite the fact that Athens probably never had a library, and that the story that its books were stolen by Xerxes and returned by Seleucus Nicanor is fictional, Gellius depicts Seleucus Nicanor as a patron to Athenian books and restorer of its library.[44]

In contrast to this report, the Armenian Mar Ibas (second century B.C.E.) records that Seleucus "had all the books in the world burned, because he wanted the calculation of time to begin with himself."[45] Zosimos of Ashkelon embellished on the idea that the Seleucids had destroyed rather than saved the Athenian collection of books. In his *Life of Demosthenes*, Zosimos recounts how the Athenian orator saved the writings of Thucydides from disaster:

ἐζήλωσε δὲ μάλιστα τῶν πρὸ αὐτοῦ τὸν συγγραφέα Θουκυδίδην καὶ τὰ πλεῖστα ἐκ τῶν ἐκείνου λόγων ἐπὶ τὸ πολιτικώτερον μετέφρασε· καὶ οὕτως λέγεται αὐτὸν ἐκμεμαθηκέναι ὥστε φέρεσθαί τι τοιοῦτον περὶ αὐτοῦ. ὅτι ποτὲ καείσης τῆς βιβλιοθήκης ἐν Ἀθήναις καὶ συγκαεισῶν τῶν Ἱστοριῶν Θουκυδίδου αὐτὸν μόνον ἀπομνημονεῦσαι πασῶν καὶ οὕτως μεταγραφῆναι ποιῆσαι.

[Demosthenes] especially emulated the writings of Thucydides and paraphrased most of his speeches on political topics. Thus it is said that he learned the work so thoroughly that he carried it in such a way with him; so that when the library in Athens burned and the *Histories* of Thucydides burned with it, he alone recalled the entire text and thus was able to rewrite it.

Life of Demosthenes, in Oratores Attici II, ed. Karl Müller, p. 523

This panegyric biography of Demosthenes appeals to the legend of the destruction of the Athenian library in order to heighten its presentation of the orator. The story celebrates the orator's prodigious memory and dedication to preserving knowledge; it is not meant to denigrate the textual accuracy of manuscripts of Thucydides that post-date the conflagration. It seems possible that the Ezra story had an influence on the account of Zosimos. However, the idea of textual destruction and reconstitution need hardly be said to have originated in a single tradition.[46]

Like the story of the destruction of an Athenian library by Xerxes, the tradition of the destruction of the Torah during the time of the Babylonian exile may have originated in an anachronistic retrojection. According to both Sulpicius Severus (*Chronica* II.19.8 *sacra etiam legis et prophetarum volumina igni cremata* 'the sacred volumes of the laws and prophets were burned by fire') and 1 Maccabees 1:56, copies of the Hebrew scriptures were destroyed by Antiochus Epiphanes in 167 B.C.E. This event may have been colored by accounts of the destruction of the first Temple in 586 B.C.E. through a belief that events of the present were a replaying of the highly significant event of the destruction of the Temple described in scripture. Alternately, the retrojection was born out of a desire to magnify the textual and apocalyptic significance of the figure of Ezra, who was likely associated with the end of the succession of biblical prophets long before Josephus.

The story of Ezra's deed is not biblical in origin, but assumes that the biblical accounts of the destruction of the Temple had hinted that scripture had been destroyed. The narrative hangs on a key biblical moment — Ezra's public reading of the Torah depicted in Nehemiah 8–10.[47] If Ezra's deed did not simply amount to the institution of public recitation of Torah for the first time, what might it have consisted of? For most early interpreters, it must have seemed out of the question that public reading of scriptures wasn't a part of Israelite observance from time immemorial. The description must then have referred to some other deed, such as the reestablishment of the Torah itself (according to rabbinic interpreters). A more extreme answer was supplied by non-rabbinic, non-Pharisaic Jewish circles. This interpretation took special note of Ezra's frequent designation as "scribe," which was no longer understood as a bureaucratic designation or as a special sort of teacher and interpreter of scripture.

The legend of the destruction of the Bible and the role of the prophet Ezra in recalling the entire text from memory is found in 4 Ezra, a work originally composed in Hebrew that dated from the period immediately following the destruction of the Second Temple (69–96 C.E.; other scholars date it at 100 C.E.).[48] The story that the physical copies of the Bible were destroyed and rewritten by Ezra is a drastic one, but then so too was the destruction of the Second Temple itself, a traumatic event for all Jews, and especially for the author of 4 Ezra. As a miracle story, the reconstruction of the Bible following the Babylonian captivity would certainly have appealed to Jews facing the end of Israelite religion as it had been known. The tale does not accord with the rabbinic position on the textual transmission of the Bible, which arrived at its own version of the deeds of Ezra.

Rabbinic tradition did praise Ezra as a figure associated with the reinvigoration of the Torah. According to this tradition, Ezra was a second Moses, who had a special relationship to the Torah and its re-establishment, as may be seen in the Jerusalem Talmud:

תני רבי יוסי אומר ראוי היה עזרא שתינתן תורה על ידו אלא שקדמו דור משה אע״פ שלא ניתנה התורה

על ידו אף הוא ניתן כתב ולשון על ידו

> It has been taught: R. Yose says, "Ezra was worthy to have the Torah given through him, but the generation of Moses came first." Even though the Torah was not given through him, through him was given the accepted form of writing and of speech.
>
> J. Megillah 1.9

Although Ezra was worthy of the revelation of Torah, his role in the promulgation of the Torah is considerably less than in the miracle stories. The Jerusalem Talmud goes on to specify that his role was confined to changing the script in which the Torah was written.

The connection between Ezra and Moses achieves a fuller form in a parallel passage from the Babylonian Talmud:

תניא. רבי יוסי אומר: ראוי היה עזרא שתינתן תורה על ידו לישראל, אילמלא (לא) קדמו משה..

במשה הוא אומר (שמות י"ט) ומשה עלה אל האלהים, בעזרא הוא אומר (עזרא ז') הוא עזרא עלה מבבל.

מה עלייה האמור כאן תורה - אף עלייה האמור לחלן תורה. במשה הוא אומר (דברים ד') ואתי צוה

ה' בעת ההיא ללמד אתכם חקים ומשפטים, בעזרא הוא אומר (עזרא ז') כי עזרא הכין לבבו לדרש את תורת

ה' (אלהיו) ולעשת וללמד בישראל חק ומשפט. ואף על פי שלא ניתנה תורה על ידו - נשתנה על

ידו הכתב. שנאמר(עזרא ד') וכתב הנשתון כתוב ארמית ומתרגם ארמית וכתיב (דניאל ה') לא

כהלין כתבא למקרא ופשרא להודעה למלכא . וכתיב (דברים י"ז) וכתב את משנה התורה הזאת -

כתב הראוי להשתנות. למה נקרא אשורית - שעלה עמהם מאשור.

It has been taught: R. Jose said: Had Moses not preceded him, Ezra would have been worthy of receiving the Torah for Israel. Of Moses it is written, "And Moses went up unto God" (Ex. 19:3), and of Ezra it is written, "He, Ezra, went up from Babylon" (Ezra 7: 6). As the going up of the former refers to the [receiving of the] Law, so does the going up of the latter. Concerning Moses, it is stated: "And the Lord commanded me at that time to teach you statutes and judgments" (Deut. 4:14); and concerning Ezra, it is stated: "For Ezra had prepared his heart to expound the law of the Lord [his God] to do it and to teach Israel statutes and judgments" (Ezra 7:10). And even though the Torah was not given through him, its writing was changed through him, as it is written: "And the writing of the letter was written in the Aramaic character and interpreted into the Aramaic [tongue]" (Ezra 4:7). And again it is written, "And they could not read the writing nor make known to the king the interpretation thereof" (Daniel 5:8).[49] Further, it is written: "And he shall write the copy (*mishneh*) of this law" (Deut. 17:18) — in writing which was destined to be changed (*lehishtanot*). Why is it called Ashur [script]? — Because it came with them from Assyria.

B. Sanhedrin 21b–22a, trans. Shachter

Ezra is again associated with the use of the square Aramaic script as opposed to the Hebrew (Phoenician) letters for writing the Bible. The rabbinical tradition, which links a change in script with Ezra's new religious and political authority, has a true ring to it. This simple maneuver has been elsewhere imposed to great effect in establishing a powerful basis for authority.[50] However, the tradition of a modest change in script rather than a wholesale retextualization of a destroyed Bible may be a concession or alternative to the

Palestinian tradition preserved in 4 Ezra. As such, the traditions that accord Ezra a more limited role in the transmission of the physical text may have served to combat the charge that the Torah had been physically restored through him.

Another Talmudic passage credits Ezra with a significant role in the history of the biblical text without claiming that he had recited it from memory. According to this tradition, the Torah, prior to the intercession of Ezra, had been promulgated not only in the square Ashur (Assyrian) script but in the Aramaic tongue as well.[51]

אמר מר זוטרא ואיתימא מר עוקבא: בתחלה ניתנה תורה לישראל בכתב עברי ולשון הקודש. חזרה

וניתנה להם בימי עזרא בכתב אשורית ולשון ארמי. ביררו להן לישראל כתב אשורית ולשון הקודש.

והניחו להדיוטות כתב עברית ולשון ארמי. מאן הדיוטות? - אמר רב חסדא: כותאי. מאי כתב עברית? -

אמר רב חסדא: כתב ליבונאה.

> Mar Zutra or, as some say, Mar ʿUkba said: Originally the Torah was given to Israel in Hebrew characters and in the sacred [Hebrew] language; later, in the times of Ezra, the Torah was given in Assyrian script and Aramaic language. [Finally], they selected for Israel the Assyrian script and Hebrew language, leaving the Hebrew characters and Aramaic language for the common people (*hedyoṭot*). Who are meant by the *hedyoṭot*? — R. Ḥisda answers: The Cutheans. And what is meant by Hebrew characters? — R. Ḥisda said: The *libuna'ah* script [i.e. the Samaritan characters].
>
> B. Sanhedrin 21b, trans. Shachter

Other references to Ezra succeed in glorifying his value as a teacher rather than textualizer of Torah:

שבתחלה כשנשתכחה תורה מישראל עלה עזרא מבבל ויסדה, חזרה ונשתכחה עלה הלל הבבלי ויסדה, חזרה

ונשתכחה עלו רבי חייא ובניו ויסדוה.

> For in ancient times when the Torah was forgotten from Israel, Ezra came up from Babylon and established it. [Some of] it was again forgotten and Hillel the Babylonian came up and established it. Yet again was [some of] it forgotten, and R. Ḥiyya and his sons came up and established it.
>
> B. Sukkah 20a, trans. Slotki

This passage presents Ezra's activity as part of a campaign to reinvigorate Torah study as an institution, and downplays any mention of the biblical text itself. But elsewhere, he is said to have committed to writing a pure copy of the scriptures and to have deposited it in the Temple courts.[52]

It would appear that the rabbinic world could not completely deny the tradition that Ezra had special role *vis-à-vis* the physical document of the Torah. Nevertheless, Ezra's actions according to rabbinic accounts fall considerably short of rewriting the Bible word for word when all of its copies had been physically destroyed. These accounts make plain that Ezra was not given the revelation of Torah because Moses had already been accorded this honor, and thus appear to contest the veracity of the legends about the re-revelation to Ezra.

The text of 4 Ezra represents the tradition that the above mentioned rabbinic traditions attempt to combat. In this passage, the story of Ezra is employed to broaden the corpus of scriptural works:

> Et respondi et dixi coram te, domine, Ecce enim ego abibo, sicut praecepisti mihi, et corripiam praesentem populam: qui autem iterum nati fuerint, quis commonebit?
>
> > Positum est enim saeculum in tenebris,
> >
> > et qui inhabitant in eo sine lumine;
>
> Quoniam lex tua incensa est, propter quod nemo scit quae a te facta sunt vel quae incipient operari. Si enim inveni gratiam coram te. Inmitte in me spiritum sanctum, et scribam omne quod factum est in saeculo ab initio, quae errant in lege tua scripta, ut possint hominess invenire semitam, et qui voluerint vive in novissimis vivant. Et respondit ad me et dixit: vadens congrega populum et dices ad eos, ut non te quaerant doebis XL. Tu autem praepara tibi buxos multos et accipe tecum Saream, Dabriam, Selemiam, Ethanum et Asihel, quinque hos quia parati sunt ad scribendum velociter; Et venies hic, et ego accendam in corde tuo lucernam intellectus, quae non extinguetur quoadusque finiantur quae incipies scribere. Et cum perfeceris, quaedam palam facies, quaedam sapientibus absconse trades: in crastinum enim hac hora incipies scribere.

¹⁸I responded as follows: Let me speak before you, Lord. ¹⁹If I proceed, as you ordered me [to do], to instruct the people now living,
who will admonish those yet to be born?

²⁰For the world lies in darkness,

And those who live in it [are] without light.

²¹Because your law has been burned, no one knows what has been
done by you or what is yet to be done. ²²If you please, now, grant
me your holy spirit that I may write down everything that has
been done in the world from the beginning, the things that were
written in your law, so that men may be able to find [their] way
and that, in the last times, those who want to live may do so. ²³He
replied to me as follows: Go, call the people together, and tell them
not to look for you for forty days. ²⁴In the meantime equip yourself with a good supply of writing tablets and engage Saraiah,
Dabriah, Shelemiah, Elkanah, and Ariel — those five because they
can write rapidly. ²⁵Then you shall come here and I will light the
lamp of understanding in your heart; it will not be extinguished
until what you are to write is finished. ²⁶When you are through,
you must publish the earlier ones but deliver the seventy others in
secret to the wise men. Tomorrow at this time you must begin to
write.

4 Ezra 14:18–26, trans. Myers

This version of Ezra's deeds stands in sharp contrast to priestly and
rabbinic definitions of the canon of the Hebrew Bible. Although the
author of 4 Ezra does not challenge standard Jewish notions of the
distinction between authoritative books (the twenty-four books)
and those dismissed or ignored by the tradition, the text nevertheless advocates an extremely liberal perspective with regard to the
value of non-canonical texts.⁵³ This clashes with the rabbinic prohibition on reading outside works, although it may accord with an
undercurrent of appreciation for esoteric ideas that was present
even in rabbinic culture.⁵⁴

The number 'seventy' is mentioned as the number of books
that Ezra was to give to the wise (*sapientes*). Seventy was a number
employed since biblical times as a figure standing for legitimacy
and authority (see chapter 5). But to Christian scholars from the

second century C.E. on, the idea of seventy books being given to the wise suggested an equation between the stories of Ezra and the Septuagint.

While Ezra's re-creation of the Bible is used to argue that the Septuagint translation was a miracle of scholarly consensus, the story of Ezra is also employed to broaden the limits of the Jewish biblical canon, or even to critique the legitimacy of this canon. Thus, the story was used by Christian scholars to account for verses of the Old Testament that could not be said to derive from the original prophet who recorded each biblical book. The author of 4 Ezra, followed by several Christian writers, appealed to the story to argue that certain esoteric or marginal works could in fact be inspired. Surprisingly, pagan writers used the story of Ezra's role in the retextualization of the Law to impugn Mosaic authorship; Ezra rather than Moses was declared to have composed the Law.

Clement of Alexandria (150–215 C.E.) justifies the inspired nature of the translation of the Bible into Greek on the grounds that Ezra's rewriting of the Bible proved that inspired and faithful versions of the original were indeed possible.

οἱ δὲ ἅτε ἔτι ὑπακούοντες Μακεδόσι τῶν παρὰ σφίσιν εὐδοκιμωτάτων περὶ τὰς γραφὰς ἐμπείρους καὶ τῆς Ἑλληνικῆς διαλέκτου εδήμονας ἑβδομήκοντα πρεσβυτέρους ἐκλεξάμενοι ἀπέστειλαν αὐτῷ μετὰ καὶ τῶν θείων βίβλων. ἑκάστου δὲ ἐν μέρει κατ᾽ ἰδίαν ἑκάστην ἑρμηνεύσαντος προφητείαν συνέπνευσαν αἱ πᾶσαι ἑρμηνεῖαι συναντιβληθεῖσαι καὶ τὰς διανοίας καὶ τὰς λέξεις· θεοῦ γὰρ ἦν βούλημα μεμελετημένον εἰς Ἑλληνικὰς ἀκοάς. <u>οὐ δὴ ξένον ἐπιπνοίᾳ θεοῦ τοῦ τὴν προφητείαν ἐνεργεῖσθαι, ἐπεὶ κἂν τῇ ἐπὶ Ναβουχοδονόσορ αἰχμαλωσίᾳ διαφθαρεισῶν τῶν γραφῶν ἐπίπνους Ἔσδρας ὁ Λευίτης ὁ ἱερεὺς γενόμενος πάσας τὰς παλαιὰς αὖθις ἀνανεούμενος προεφήτευσε γραφάς.</u>

They, being Macedonian subjects, chose from among their most reputed people seventy experts in the Scriptures who were familiar with the Greek language, and sent them to him with their sacred books. Each translated every individual prophecy separately. When they were compared, all the translations agreed in both sense and diction! It was God's will to achieve a result for Greek ears. <u>Nothing strange that the inspiration of the God who granted the original prophecy should direct the translation to make it a kind of Greek prophecy. On the captivity under Nebuchadnezzar, the Scriptures were destroyed. In the time of Artaxerxes, king of Persia, the Levite and priest Esdras (Ezra) was inspired to a prophetic restoration of all the old documents.</u>

Clement, Stromateis I.22.149, trans. Ferguson

To Clement's mind, the inspired and accurate translation of scripture is less strange than Ezra's word-for-word re-creation of the scriptures without consultation of the original. The miraculous translation of the Bible is figured as a variety of textual re-creation *ex nihilo.*

The same comparison may be seen in the writing of Irenaeus (ca. 135–200 C.E.):

Πρὸ τοῦ γὰρ Ῥωμαίους κρατῦναι τὴν ἀρχὴν αὐτῶν, ἔτι τῶν Μακεδόνων τὴν Ἀσίαν κατεχόντων, Πτολεμαῖος ὁ Λάγου, φιλοτιμούμενος τὴν ὑπ' αὐτοῦ κατεσκευασμένην βιβλιοθήκην ἐν Ἀλεξανδρείᾳ κοσμῆσαι τοῖς πάντων ἀνθρώπων συγγράμμασιν ὅσα γε σπουδαῖα ὑπῆρχεν, ᾐτήσατο παρὰ τῶν Ἱεροσολυμιτῶν εἰς τὴν Ἑλληνικὴν διάλεκτον σχεῖν αὐτῶν μεταβεβλημένας τὰς γραφάς. Οἳ δέ, ὑπήκουον γὰρ ἔτι τοῖς Μακεδόσι τότε, τοὺς παρ' αὐτοῖς ἐμπειροτάτους τῶν γραφῶν καὶ ἀμφοτέρων τῶν διαλέκτων ἑβδομήκοντα πρεσβυτέρους ἔπεμψαν Πτολεμαίῳ, ποιήσαντος τοῦ Θεοῦ ὅπερ ἠβούλετο. Ὁ δὲ ἰδίᾳ πεῖραν αὐτῶν λαβεῖν θελήσας εὐλαβηθείς τε μήτι ἄρα συνθέμενοι ἀποκρύψωσι τὴν ἐν ταῖς γραφαῖς διὰ τῆς ἑρμηνείας ἀλήθειαν, χωρίσας αὐτοὺς ἀπ' ἀλλήλων ἐκέλευσε τοὺς πάντας τὴν αὐτὴν ἑρμηνείαν γράφειν, καὶ τοῦτ' ἐπὶ πάντων τῶν βιβλίων ἐποίησεν. Συνελθόντων δὲ αὐτῶν ἐπὶ τὸ αὐτὸ παρὰ τῷ Πτολεμαίῳ καὶ συναντιβαλόντων ἑκάστου τὴν ἑαυτοῦ ἑρμηνείαν, ὁ μὲν Θεὸς ἐδοξάσθη, αἱ δὲ γραφαὶ ὄντως θεῖαι ἐγνώσθησαν, τῶν πάντων τὰ αὐτὰ ταῖς αὐταῖς λέξεσιν καὶ τοῖς αὐτοῖς ὀνόμασιν ἀναγορευσάντων ἀπ' ἀρχῆς μέχρι τέλους, ὥστε καὶ τὰ παρόντα ἔθνη γνῶναι ὅτι κατ' ἐπίπνοιαν τοῦ Θεοῦ εἰσιν ἡρμηνευμέναι α γραφαί. Καὶ οὐδέν γε θαυμαστὸν τὸν Θεὸν τοῦτο ἐνηργηκέναι, ὅς γε καὶ ἐν τῇ ἐπὶ Ναβουχοδονόσορ αἰχμαλωσίᾳ τοῦ λαοῦ διαφθαρεισῶν τῶν γραφῶν καὶ μετὰ ἑβδομήκοντα ἔτη τῶν Ἰουδαίων ἀνελθόντων εἰς τὴν χώραν αὐτῶν, ἔπειτα ἐν τοῖς χρόνοις Ἀρταξέρξου τοῦ Περσῶν βασιλέως ἐνέπνευσεν Ἔσδρᾳ τῷ ἱερεῖ ἐκ τῆς φυλῆς Λευὶ τοὺς τῶν προγεγονότων προφητῶν πάντας ἀνατάξασθαι λόγους καὶ ἀποκαταστῆσαι τῷ λαῷ τὴν διὰ Μωϋσέως νομοθεσίαν.

For before the Romans strengthened their dominion, the Macedonians being yet owners of Asia, — Ptolemy the Son of Lagus, ambitious of adorning the Library which he had founded in Alexandria with the writings of all, as many at least as were good for any thing, requested of the people of Jerusalem, that he might have their scriptures translated into the Greek language. But they (for they were then yet subject to the Macedonians) sent unto Ptolemy those among them who were best versed in the Scriptures, and in both the languages, being seventy elders: wherein God wrought the thing which He would. But he, desiring to make trial of them separately, and fearing lest haply they should upon some compact hide by their translation the truth as it is in the Scriptures, separated them one from another, and bade them all write the same passage translated; and this he did in all the books. And when they came together in Ptolemy's palace, and offered for comparison each his own translation, both God was glorified, and the Scriptures proved truly divine, all of them having set forth the same things in the same sentences and the same terms from beginning to end: so that the very Gentiles which were present might know, that the Scriptures were translated by inspiration of God. And no wonder surely that God should have wrought this; even as, when the Scriptures were corrupted in the captivity of the people under Nebuchadnezzar, and the Jews after 70 years had returned unto their own land, He did afterwards in the times of Artaxerxes King of the Persians inspire Esdras (Ezra), the Priest of the tribe of Levi, to arrange all the sayings of the Prophets which went before, and restore to the people the Code which came by Moses.

Irenaeus, *Against Heresies* 3.2, trans. Roberts and Rambaut

As in Clement, Irenaeus' point is that if Ezra could restore the Code (that is, the Law) of Moses, then by all means the miraculous translation of the scriptures into Greek, verified by the universal consent of the seventy translators, was certainly feasible. The connection made between the Ezra story and the Septuagint legend is here too no more than a suggestive parallel meant to uphold the value of the Greek Bible. But it still derives from a midrashic-type reading of 4 Ezra that focused on the nature of the seventy books handed over to the wise by Ezra.

The story of the destruction of the Law is more pointedly associated with the Septuagint translation in a startling text of pseudo-Hippolytus, surviving only in an Arabic manuscript. Here, Ezra is absent from the story, and Ptolemy II has become the villain who sought to damage the physical text of the Law:

> Armius, author of the book of *Times*, has said: in the nine-teenth year of the reign of King Ptolemy, he ordered the elders of the children of Israel to be assembled, in order that they might put into his hands a copy of the law, and that they might each be at hand to explain its meaning.
>
> The elders accordingly came, bringing with them the most excellent law. Then he commanded that every one of them should interpret the book of the law to him.
>
> But he dissented from the interpretation, which the elders had given. And he ordered the elders to be thrust into prison and chains. And seizing the book of the law, he threw it into a deep ditch, and cast fire and hot ashes upon it for seven days. Then af-terwards he ordered them to throw the filth of the city into that ditch in which was the book of the law. And the ditch was filled to the very top.
>
> The law remained seventy years under the filth in that ditch, yet did not perish, nor was there even a single leaf of it spoilt.
>
> In the twenty-first year of the reign of King Apianutus they took the book of the law out of the ditch, and not one leaf thereof was spoilt.
>
> Pseudo-Hippolytus, *Preface to the Pentateuch*
> (*PL* 10.704–5), trans. Salmond[55]

While the figure of Ezra is missing here, Pseudo-Hippolytus pro-vides an Ezra-type story that would have had some relevance to the culture of Greek Christianity, replete with a culturally tailored

Bible destruction narrative. In the Christian, Greek-speaking East, the Septuagint had a value that superseded the Hebrew text of the Bible. Accordingly, a story that related the near-destruction and miraculous recovery of the Bible's physical text was more poignant when applied to the Greek version revered by the story's author. Key for this discussion is the expansion of the connection between Ezra and the Septuagint that we have seen already in the writings of Irenaeus, Clement, and Tertullian.[56]

Not all the Christian scholars who commented on the Ezra story read it as an object lesson on the value of the Septuagint. Ezra was a useful figure for Christian scholars to explain the authenticity of scriptures that were not accepted by the Jews. For example, Priscillian (d. 385 C.E.) perceptively notes that 4 Ezra presents a challenge to certain notions of canonicity that were prevalent among Jews as well as Christians.

> Denique in antiquis librorum monumentis cum testamentum scribturarum diabolos invideret, Hierusalem capta polluto altario domini distrui templum satis non fuit; nam quia facile erat, ut quae manufacta erant in manufactis homo redderet, arca incensa est testamenti, sciente diabolo quod facile natura hominum oblig ata saeculo fidem perderet, si ad praedicationem divini nominis scribturarum testimonia non haberet. Sed argutior divini mysterii natura quam diabuli, quae, ut quid deus in homine posset ostenderet, reseruari Hesdram voluit qui illa quae fuerant incensa rescribsit. Quae si uere incensa et uere credimus fuisse rescribta, quamuis incensum testamentum legatur in canone, rescribtum ab Hesdra in canone non legitur, tamen, quia post incensum testamentum reddi non potuit nisi fuisset scribtum, recte illi libro fidem damus, qui Hesdra auctore prolatus, etsi in canone non ponitur, ad elogium redditi diuini testamenti digna rerum ueneratione retinetur; in quo tamen legimus scriptum spiritum sanctum ab initio saeculi et hominum et rerum gesta retinentem cor electi hominis intrasse et, quod vix ad humanam memoriam scribti forma retineret, ordine numero ratione repetita, cum *per diem loquens at nocte non tacens* scriberet, omnia quae gesta uidentur esse uel legimus scribta ad humanam memoriam condidisse. In quo libet exclamare: est! liceat! qualiter, rogo, pauca ex his leg-

entes culpabiles sumus, cum magis ob hoc rei sumus, quod omnia quae de deo sunt profetata non legimus? Non dubito autem quemquam ex his qui calumnias potius quam fidem diligunt esse dicturum: ultra nihil quaeras! sufficit te legere quod in canone scribtum est.

Finally the Devil cast an evil eye on the testament in the ancient monuments of the biblical books, since it was not enough that Jerusalem had been captured, the altar of the Lord polluted, and the Temple destroyed, because it stood to reason that man might replace the things made by hand with things made by hand. Therefore the Ark of the Covenant was burned, for the Devil knew how easily the nature of men having been tied down for a generation would lose faith, if it did not have the testimonies of the scriptures for the publication of the divine name. But the nature of the divine mystery is more cunning than that of the Devil, since, in order that that which God is capable [of accomplishing] through man be revealed, it willed Ezra, who rewrote those works which had been burned, to be spared. These are books which, if they were truly burned, we also believe they were truthfully rewritten. But although the burned testament may be read in the canon, the testament rewritten by Ezra is not. Nevertheless, after being burned, the testament could not have been restored unless it too was copied [by Ezra]. We rightly put trust in that book which was revealed by the authority of Ezra, even if it is not put in the canon. It is preserved in worthy veneration with regard to its pleasing account (*elogium*) of the restored divine testament. In it, we read recorded that the Holy Spirit, preserving the deeds both of men and of things from the beginning of the age, entered the heart of the chosen man [Ezra]. It is a fact that the imprint of a written text adheres to human memory hardly at all, even when repeated at the right time in sequence. Thus when Ezra wrote "speaking through the day and not being silent at night" (4 Ezra 14:43; Ps. 21:3), we read in written form all things which appear to be accomplished or conveyed to human memory. At which one might want to exclaim: it is allowable! Let it be permitted! I ask, how are we who read a few pages from these works at fault? Are we not more blameworthy on this account, if we do not read all the things that were prophesied about God? I do not however doubt that whoever esteems false accusations rather than faith will say: you should seek no further [writings]! It is sufficient for you to read what is written in the canon.

Priscillian III.67–8

The problem as Priscillian sees it is that some of the ninety-four books mentioned in 4 Ezra were not put into the canon, while others were. Some of the works attributed to Ezra (namely, Ezra, Nehemiah, and 1 and 2 Chronicles) for example are canonical, while works such as 3 and 4 Ezra (= 1 and 2 Esdras) are not. Priscillian understands that the twenty-four books in 4 Ezra refer to the canonical Bible, while the seventy meant only for the worthy (*digni*) include the *testamentum* 'testament' of Ezra — that is, the account known as 4 Ezra.

Priscillian acknowledges that the *testamentum* of Ezra is not canonical, but nevertheless insists that it is deserving of faith on two counts: (1) if it too was miraculously restored, it must have existed before the destruction, and may have been included in the canon before it was burned; and (2) it mentions the story of the Holy Spirit entering into Ezra, enabling him to remember all the events of the Bible which had been destroyed. For Priscillian, the authoritativeness of the text of 4 Ezra springs from its testimony of a divine revelation given to Ezra. Priscillian establishes ground-rules for the discussion: "If we believe that the works which were in fact (*vere*) burned were also accurately (*vere*) rewritten." According to these rules, it is a given that Ezra accurately rewrote the works which had been destroyed.[57] That 4 Ezra is the only witness of such a revelation is seen by Priscillian as an argument for the validity of the text, not as an argument against the trustworthiness of the revelation.

It is no accident that Priscillian chooses the example of 4 Ezra to challenge the Jewish canon on the grounds that it is excessively narrow. 4 Ezra itself vigorously defends the principle that the seventy books meant for the "worthy" alone are no less inspired than the works traditionally labeled as canonical. The priestly canon of twenty-four books is not the sole measure of worthiness of a text, for all the works rewritten through the agency of Ezra are valid. If the Church accepts the 4 Ezra as valid, it cannot but give weight to the rest of the apocryphal (deuterocanonical) literature not accepted by the Jews.

Tertullian takes a similar approach to the story of Ezra's restoration of the Jewish scriptures. His account testifies to a widespread Christian belief in the legend of Ezra that seems to have transcended more narrow questions over the authoritativeness of the book of 4 Ezra. Tertullian seeks to show that the works of Enoch could have been transmitted by his descendant Noah, the sole survivor of antediluvian culture. But even if this is not the manner in which Enoch's works were transmitted, it is equally plausible that the Enochian works were restored by Noah after the Flood *à la* Ezra after the Babylonian Captivity:

> Scio scripturam Enouch, quae hunc ordinem angelis dedit, non recipi a quibusdam, quia nec in armarium Iudaicum admittitur. Opinor, non putaverunt illam ante cataclysmum editam post eum casum orbis omnium rerum abolitorem alvam esse potuisse. Si ista ratio est, recordentur pronepotem ipsius Enoch fuisse superstitem cataclysmi Noë, qui utique domestico nomine et haereditaria traditione audierat et meminerat de proavi sui penes deum gratia et de omnibus praedicatis eius, cum Enoch filio suo Matusalae nihil aliud mandaverit, quam ut notitiam eorum posteris suis traderet. <u>Igitur sine dubio potuit Noë in praedicationis delegatione successisse, vel quia et alias non tacuisset tam de dei conservatoris sui dispositione quam de ipsa domus suae gloria. Hoc si non tam expedite haberet, illud quoque assertionem scripturae illius tueretur. Proinde potuit abolefactam eam violentia cataclysmi in spiritu rursus reformare, quemadmodum et Hierosolymis Babylonia expugnatione deletis omne instrumentum Iudaicae litteraturae per Esdram constat restauratum.</u> Sed cum Enoch eadem scriptura etiam de domino praedicarit, a nobis quidem nihil omnino reiciendum est quod pertineat ad nos. Et legimus omnem scripturam aedificationi habilem divinitus inspirari. A Iudaeis potest iam videri propterea reiecta, sicut et cetera fere quae Chris-

tum sonant. Nec utique mirum hoc, si scripturas aliquas non re-
ceperunt de eo locutas quem et ipsum coram loquentem non erant
recepturi. Eo accedit, quod Enoch apud Iudam apostolum testi-
monium possidet.

I am aware that the Scripture of Enoch, which has assigned
this order [of action] to angels, is not received by some, because it
is not admitted into the Jewish canon (*armarium*) either. I suppose they did not think that, having been published before the
deluge, it could have safely survived that worldwide calamity, the
abolisher of all things. If that is the reason [for rejecting it], let
them recall to their memory that Noah, the survivor of the deluge,
was the great-grandson of Enoch himself; and he, of course, had
heard and remembered, from domestic renown and hereditary
tradition, concerning his own great-grandfather's "grace in the
sight of God," and concerning all his preachings; since Enoch had
given no other charge to Methuselah than that he should hand on
the knowledge of them to his posterity. Noah therefore, no doubt,
might have succeeded in the trusteeship of [his] preaching, or, had
the case been otherwise, he would not have been silent alike concerning the disposition [of things] made by God, his Preserver,
and concerning the particular glory of his own house.

If [Noah] had not had this [conservative power] by so short a
route, there would [still] be this [consideration] to warrant our assertion of [the genuineness of] this Scripture: he could equally
have renewed it, under the Spirit's inspiration, after it had been
destroyed by the violence of the deluge, as, after the destruction of
Jerusalem by the Babylonian storming of it, every document of
the Jewish literature is generally agreed to have been restored
though Ezra.

But since Enoch in the same Scripture has preached likewise
concerning the Lord, nothing at all must be rejected by us which
pertains to us; and we read that "every Scripture suitable for edifi-
cation is divinely inspired" (2 Tim. 3:16). By the Jews it may now
seem to have been rejected for that [very] reason, just like all the
other [portions] nearly which tell of Christ. Nor, of course, is this
fact wonderful, that they did not receive some Scriptures which

spake of Him whom even in person, speaking in their presence, they were not to receive. To these considerations is added the fact that Enoch possesses a testimony in the Apostle Jude (Jude 14, 15).
Tertullian, *De Cultu Feminarum* I.3, trans. Thelwall

Tertullian's point that the Jews refuse to believe that a work of Enoch could have survived the Flood would appear to be a misrepresentation of actual Jewish criteria for accepting the authenticity of a biblical book. More conservative circles in Second Temple Judaism seem not to have challenged the works of Enoch or Shem on the grounds that these works were destroyed, but rather on the grounds that Moses was the first and only individual to have been given the dispensation to record biblical prehistory. But Tertullian quickly moves on to a more damning criticism: the Jews should not be the ultimate authority on the worthiness of scripture, because they do not accept the scriptures that speak of Christ. Incidentally, Tertullian speaks of the Jewish "canon" as an *armarium* 'bookcase' rather than as an authoritative list (Nahum Sarna argues that *armarium* is the Latin term for the "booklocker" in which the biblical scrolls had actually been filed in the Temple).[58] It is possible that he intends to denigrate the Jewish canon by employing this term, as if to imply that the Jewish canon is a piece of furniture, and is thus limited by its pure physicality.

Both Priscillian and Tertullian appeal to the story of Ezra in order to make a plausible case for the legitimacy of works not allowed into the Jewish Bible. As much as these theologians rail against the limits of the Jewish canon, they work with a Jewish vocabulary in their evaluation of the authoritativeness of a given work. Both authors speak of Ezra's restoration of the Law as a miraculous event, not as a story documenting textual instability or unreliability.

Priscillian cannot countenance the possibility that Ezra is not the composer of his *testamentum*. Tertullian's use of the legend, in contrast, suggests that he is consciously addressing Greek anxieties about attribution — that is, that the name affixed to a text might not be the name of its true composer. In seeking to expand the Jewish canon by including texts attributed to Ezra and Enoch, the only criticism of these works Tertullian can imagine is that Enoch might not have written the text attributed to him. In this, Tertullian is conforming to the Greek preoccupation with attribution analysis rather than to the Jewish view on acceptable and unacceptable individuals to whom a text might be attributed. But he answers Greek doubt as to the validity of the Enoch attribution with his faith in Ezra's miracle. Moreover, he utterly ignores the possibility that any part of these documents is inauthentic.

Because Greek attribution analysis was so successful at evaluating the authoritativeness of literary works, it was only a matter of time before Christian exegetes who had been exposed to classical philology began to consider the Bible under philology's purview. For example, Origen demonstrates a profound dependence on attribution analysis in his evaluation of the Septuagint. This was only to be expected from the architect of the *Hexapla*, the multi-columned Bible which juxtaposed the Hebrew original (both in its proper Aramaic script and transliterated) with four different Greek translations, in order to make informed judgments about any given biblical verse, if not to arrive at the "original" or "most authoritative" text.[59]

Origen often endows the Septuagint's asterisked passages (marking those passages that occur in the Septuagint translation but not in the original Hebrew text) with a legitimacy in keeping with this translation's auspicious origins. Accordingly, his attribution analysis does not always point to translation as the key moment in the introduction of textual anomalies. At least in one case, Origen cites Ezra's reconstruction of the Law as an explanation for a passage in the Septuagint that is not found in the Hebrew text. The Ezra legend is employed to explain how an event that must have occurred after the death of Joshua could legitimately appear in a work that Joshua wrote out.

οὕτως ἐποίησεν Ὀζάν. ἐκ τούτου δείκνυται ὡς οὐκ Ἰησοῦς ὁ τοῦ Ναυῆ. ἀλλ' ἕτερός τις μετὰ πολλὰς γενεὰς ταῦτα συνέγραψε. καὶ ἀληθὲς μὲν νοηθέν. οὐκ ἐναντίον δὲ οἷς πρότερον εἰρήκαμεν. ἔγραψε γὰρ ὁ Ἰησοῦς τὰ ἐπ' αὐτοῦ γεγονότα. ἢ ἀποκαλυφθέντα. ὥσπερ καὶ Μωυσῆς τὰ κατὰ τοὺς ἐπ' αὐτοῦ χρόνους. μετὰ δὲ ταῦτα τοῦ ναοῦ οκοδομηθέντος ἤδη ὑπὸ τοῦ σοφοῦ Σολομῶντος, καὶ τοῦ λαοῦ ὑποκλίναντος ες πολλὴν ἀσέβειαν, καὶ τοῦ Θεοῦ τὸν ναὸν ἔρημον καταλιπόντος ὡς μόλις εὑρεθῆναι τὸ Δευτερονόμιον ἐρριμμένον ὡς ἔτυχε· διάτοι τοῦτο τοῦ λαοῦ τὴν Βαβυλωνικὴν αἰχμαλωσίαν ὑποστάντος, Ἔσδρας νομικώτατος ὤν, καὶ ἀποστομίζων πᾶσαν τὴν Παλαιὰν Διαθήκην, ἔγραψε τὸν νόμον, καὶ ἕτερά τινα τὰ γεγονότα καὶ ἀποκαλυφθέντα. ταῦτα πάλαι μὲν προερρέθη, μετὰ δὲ ταῦτα γέγονε. τοιοῦτόν ἐστι δήπου καὶ ὁ νῦν ἐμνημονεύσαμεν.

"And this is what Hosea did" (LXX Joshua 6:26). From this is shown how not Joshua son of Nun, but someone else many generations later recorded these things. And it was remarked truthfully, not in opposition to the things we said earlier. For Joshua son of Nun wrote the events of his own time (*ta ep' autou gegonota*), or the things which were revealed to him (*apokaluphthenta*), just as Moses did for the events of his own time. After these things, when the temple was already built by Solomon the wise, and since the people had slid into much impiety, and the Lord left behind the temple abandoned, so that the copy of the law (*to deuteronomion*), having been cast away by chance, could scarcely be found.[60] For which reason when the people had endured the Babylonian captivity, Ezra being exceedingly learned in the Law (*nomikôtatos*), and reciting the entire Old Testament from memory, he copied out the Law (*nomos*), and other things which both occurred (*ta gegonota*) and were revealed (*apokaluphthenta*). These things were preordained long ago, but afterwards they came to fruition. Of this sort is [the verse] which we just mentioned.

Origen, Selecta In Jesum Nave vi.26 (PG XII.824B)

The part of Joshua 6:26 quoted here by Origen is a verse that is present in the Septuagint but is missing in the Hebrew Masoretic Text (MT). The MT verse reads: "At that time Joshua pronounced this oath: 'Cursed of the Lord be the man who shall undertake to fortify this city of Jericho: he shall lay its foundations at the cost of his first-born, and set up its gates at the cost of his youngest.'" The Septuagint goes on to give biographical information about the man whom Joshua cursed: "And this is what Hosea son of Baithel did.

Upon his first-born Abiron he laid its foundations, and upon his last-born who had been saved he set up its gates." As Origen notices, it was impossible that Joshua, the reputed scribe who copied out the events relayed in the book of Joshua, could have written that a certain individual fulfilled the conditions of his curse several generations later.

Apparently, Origen was not dismayed by the need to revise the standard Jewish line on biblical transmission, a doctrine which he seemed to have gained knowledge of through Josephus' *Against Apion*.[61] The Septuagint of Joshua 6:26 appeared to contradict the idea that in the book of Joshua, both the events of his own time (*ta ep' autou gegonota*) and the things which were revealed to him (*apokaluphthenta*) were written down by Joshua himself. Origen explains that Ezra inserted the verse when he re-recorded the book of Joshua, seeing as Ezra too had been given the prophetic dispensation to record the events of his own time as well as the things that were revealed to him. According to Origen, the Ezra legend does not contradict the Jewish version of biblical transmission, and can be used to explain accretions in the Septuagint text.

From the perspective of attribution analysis, the Ezra story had dangerous implications. It seemed possible to conclude that Moses and the other prophets did not write the Bible, but that Ezra did. In the hands of pagan critics of Christianity, the Ezra legend could provide potentially devastating evidence against Mosaic "authorship" of the Torah. One such text is *Against the Christians*, recorded in the *Apocriticus* of Macarius Magnes, but probably authored by Porphyry (234–ca. 305 C.E.), a pagan scholar and philosopher.[62]

ἔτι δὲ πολλῆς μοι γέμον τῆς ἀβελτηρίας φαίνεται τὸ λεχθέν· εἰ ἰἐπιστεύετε Μωσεῖ, ἐπιστεύετε ἂν ἐμοί· περὶ γὰρ ἐμοῦ ἐκεῖνος ἔγραψεν. ὅμως δὲ Μωσέως οὐδὲν ἀποσώζεται· συγγράμματα γὰρ πάντα συνεμπεπρῆσθαι τῷ ναῷ λέγεται· ὅσα δ' ἐπ' ὀνόματι Μωσέως ἐγράφη μετὰ ταῦτα, μετὰ χίλια καὶ ἑκατὸν καὶ ὀγδοήκοντα ἔτη τῆς Μωσέως τελευτῆς ὑπὸ Ἔσδρα καὶ τῶν ἀμφ' αὐτὸν ⟨οὐκ ἀκριβῶς⟩ συνεγράφη. εἰ δὲ καὶ Μωσέως δοίη τις εἶναι τὸ γράμμα, οὐ δυνατὸν δειχθῆναι ὡς θεόν που λελέχθαι ἢ θεὸν λόγον τὸν Χριστὸν ἢ δημιουργόν. ὅλως ⟨δὲ⟩ Χριστὸν σταυροῦσθαι τίς εἴρηκεν;

The saying appears to me to be full of stupidity: "If you believed Moses, then you would believe me. For he wrote about me" (John 5.46–7). Nevertheless no works of Moses have survived. For it is said that all of his writings were destroyed together with the Temple. All the things written in the name of Moses came after these; eleven hundred and eighty years after the death of Moses they were <inaccurately> recorded by Esdra and his companions. But even if one should grant that the law was by Moses, it does not prove that it was said that Christ was a god or Christ the divine logos or the creator. Further: who [among the Jews] has claimed that Christ was crucified?

Porphyry, *Against the Christians* frag. 68, ed. Harnack

Porphyry's doubt about the Mosaic authorship of the Law might be compared to the writings of pagans such as Celsus, who claimed that Moses had really copied stories from Greek myths when he was writing Genesis. Celsus argued that Moses had corrupted the story about the sons of Aloeus when he wrote about the tower of Babel, as well as the story of Deucalion in describing the Flood; he also maintained that the story of Phaethon was the origin of the tale of Sodom and Gomorrah.[63] Such claims about the priority of Greek civilization over that of the Israelites (which provoked extravagant claims in the other direction) were in any event common since the late Hellenistic period. What is new in the case of Porphyry is that this challenge takes the form of an attack against the attribution to Moses. On the basis of evidence presented by the Jewish tradition itself (i.e. the story of Ezra's rewriting of the Bible), Porphyry presents the possibility that the Law was a forgery of Ezra's. Such a charge effectively undercut Jewish writers who, since Artapanus in the third century B.C.E., had argued that Moses predated the earliest of the Greek poets and philosophers.

The pagan employment of Greek attribution analysis against the Jewish scriptures probably goaded Christians into articulating a defense of Ezra. Pagan polemics against the figure of Ezra also may have helped to inspire later Islamic criticisms.[64] Some Islamic stories revere the figure of Ezra (or 'Uzayr as he is called in Arabic).

In a version of the story by Al Tha'labī, Ezra learns the Torah by heart before the destruction of the Temple, remembers it 100 years later, and dictates it anew. The sages take the original Torah out of its hiding place and compare the two. When they did so, "They did not find a missing verse or a [missing] letter, and they were greatly amazed and said: Allah did not give the Torah to the heart of any one of us after it was lost, but only to him [to 'Uzayr], for he is His son. Therefore the Jews say 'Uzayr son of Allah."[65] In this text, Ezra also writes with all his fingers; he is a kind of magical *sofer mahir* 'quick scribe' who is almost equal to the divine scribe of Indian epic, Ganesha.

Some Islamic treatments of Ezra were blatantly critical. The Spaniard Ibn Ḥazm (d. 1064 C.E. ) claimed that the Torah was intentionally falsified and corrupted by Ezra the Scribe; Ibn Ḥazm could not accept the existence of any contradiction or imprecision in a text bearing God's word. The Jewish apostate to Islam, Samau'al al-Maghribī (d. 1175 C.E.), went further; he claimed that Ezra had invented tales of incest involving King David's ancestors to further his aim of preventing the rule of the Davidic dynasty during the days of the Second Temple. Samau'al insisted that Ezra had only patched and falsified the Torah from his own memory and that of other priests. For this reason, the Torah is called *Kitāb 'Azrā* 'the Book of Ezra', and not *Kitāb Allāh* 'the divine book of God'.[66]

It seems probable that the Samaritans absorbed some of their polemics against Ezra from Islamic intermediaries like Ibn Ḥazm and Samau'al. But they also had ample reason to dislike him on behalf of their own tradition. From the perspective of the later Samaritans, the dominant motive of Ezra's actions as recorded in the Bible was to make a final break with the Samaritans. Ezra transcribed the Hebrew text from the old characters that the Samaritans still use today into the square Aramaic script; according to Moses Gaster, this was done to eliminate the Samaritan text from circulation among the Jews.[67] The Samaritans claimed that Ezra had falsified the text of the Pentateuch by changing the name of a mountain in Deuteronomy 27:4 and eliminating the tenth commandment (two features of the Samaritan Pentateuch which serve as the charter for the Samaritan altar at Mt. Gerizim and its priesthood). Ezra's attack on intermarriage is also described by Gaster as an attempt to remove the risk posed by intermarriage with Samaritans and the abandonment of Zion and Jerusalem.[68]

It is in this context that a Samaritan anti-Ezra polemic should be read. The Chronicle Adler, a Samaritan historical account that achieved written form in the nineteenth century, states:

> . . . and [Ezra and his priests] wrote the book of the Holy Torah in the tongue of the Assyrians and in their letters, and he altered many things in the text of the Holy Torah out of hatred for the community of the children of Israel who are Observers of the Truth . . . Moreover many errors were made by him in the book of the Torah; which neither he nor his people perceived or understood. In addition to this he gathered many sayings and writings composed by former authors and prophets, such as suited his aims and desires . . .[69]

While the Chronicle is late, it certainly derives from older traditions. Whatever its provenance, it gives voice to a Samaritan polemic against the trustworthiness of the biblical text. This polemic focused on Ezra.[70] The Chronicle also blames Ezra for the inclusion of Prophets and Writings, which the Samaritans did not accept, in the Jewish Bible.

Both Islamic and Samaritan treatments of the idea of biblical falsification often relate in some way to the translation of the Septuagint by Ptolemy. Thus Ibn Ḥazm's polemic against interpolations resembles the rabbinic polemic against the mistranslations in the Septuagint; even the motif of comparison of old and new textual versions in Al Thaʿlabī's account of Ezra's translation may be said to derive from the philological themes which pervade the Septuagint translation legends. Similarly, Abu'l Fath's Chronicle (dating from the fourteenth century C.E.) uses the legend of the Septuagint translation under king Ptolemy (called Faltama in this Samaritan text composed in Arabic) to highlight the differences between the Jewish and Samaritan Pentateuch.[71] In this text, a virtual Samaritan Letter of Aristeas replete with a philosophical symposium scene, the translation of both the Jewish and Samaritan Pentateuch into Greek allows an impartial third party (Ptolemy) to confirm that the Samaritan document is more perfect.

The figure of Ezra became a locus for employing attribution analysis on biblical texts by critics of Judaism and Christianity. Jews responded by creating a number of midrashim that described Ezra's marked but limited contribution to biblical transmission. Perhaps this is the force of the comment found in Breshit Rabbah:

וישכן באהלי שם אין שכינה שורה אלא

באהלי שם בר קפרא אמר יהיו דברי תורה נאמרים בלשונו של יפת בתוך אהלי שם רבי יודן אמר מכאן
לתרגום מן התורה הה״ד (נחמיה ט) ויקראו בספר תורת האלהים זה המקרא מפורש זה תרגום ושום שכל אלו
הטעמים ויבינו במקרא אלו ראשי הפסוקים רבי הונא בן לוליאני אומר אלו ההכרעות והראיות רבנן דקסרין
אמרי מיכן למסורת רבי זעירא ורבי חננאל בשם רבי אפי׳ אדם רגיל בתורה כעזרא לא יהא קורא מפיו
וכותב והא תני מעשה שהיה ר״מ באסייא ולא היה שם מגילת אסתר וקרא לו מפיו וכתבה תמן אמרין שתי
מגילות כתב גנז את הראשונה וקיים את השנייה:

"And he shall dwell in the tents of Shem" (Genesis 9:27): the Shekhinah dwells only in the tents of Shem. Bar Qappara explained it: Let the words of the Torah be uttered in the language of Japheth [Greek] in the tents of Shem. R. Judan said: From this we learn that a translation [of the Bible is permitted]. Thus it is written, And they read in the book, in the Law of God (Nehemiah 8: 8): this refers to Scripture; distinctly (ibid.): to a translation; And they gave the sense (ibid.) — i.e. the punctuation accents; And caused them to understand the reading (ibid.) — this refers to the beginnings of the verses. R. Huna b. Lulianus said: It refers to the grammatical sequence [of words]. The rabbis of Caesarea said: Here we have an allusion to the traditional text. R. Zera and R. Ḥananel said: Even if a man is as well versed in the Torah as Ezra, he must not read it from memory and write it. But it was taught: It once happened that R. Meir visited Asia Minor, and finding there no scroll of Esther, he read it from memory and wrote it? There [in Babylonia] they say: He wrote two Scrolls, suppressed the first and kept the second as valid [for use].

Breshit Rabbah 36.8, trans. Freedman and Simon

Rabbinic tradition obliquely responds to those who would defame Ezra, or turn his legend into a miracle, by stipulating that rewriting the Bible from memory is forbidden. This statement occurs in the midst of an explication of the meaning of "God shall enlarge Japheth, and he shall live in the tents of Shem" in Genesis 9:27. R. Judan employs the description of Ezra's practice of public recitation and translation of the Bible depicted in Nehemiah 8:8 in order to argue that the verse in Genesis was meant to legitimate the practice of translation of the Bible into Greek, a practice elsewhere bewailed by the rabbis. But the subsequent mention of Ezra in conjunction with a prohibition of reading and writing the Torah from memory explains the motives of the rabbis in interpreting Nehemiah 8:8 in this manner. They are determined to explain the interpretive activity of Ezra as a matter of translation, establishing punctuation, the delineation of scriptural verses, the reading of words or phrases in ambiguous locations, *qere* vs. *ketib* readings, or accentuation and vocalization. In part, the goal of this litany of operations is meant to dispel the possibility that Ezra had recited the text from memory; the passage is in effect arguing that there is no room for such an interpretation of the verse. Parallels to this interpretation of Nehemiah 8:8 appear also in the Talmud. In B. Megillah 3a and B. Nedarim 37b, Ezra is not explicitly mentioned, and the acknowledgment of treatments of Ezra as a retextualizer of the Bible is suppressed even more than it is in the passage from Breshit Rabbah.

For Christians, the Ezra legend enabled early scholars to combine two very different versions of authority — Jewish prophetic authority (speaking in God's name), and the Greek notion of authority as deriving from proper attribution. These Christian thinkers were adept at deflecting unwelcome attempts at attribution analysis on biblical texts, even before they were raised (by Muslims or Samaritans, for instance). There was a distinction to be made between authorship and textualization, according to these interpreters. Allowing for such a distinction gave Christian scholars a tremendous advantage over latecomers to Greek attribution analysis. Ezra's role in textualization was prophetic, yet he contributed nothing to the text as an author. As we have seen, these Christians used the story of Ezra as a defense of the Septuagint and as an argument for their expanded canon. On another level, the success of the amalgamation of Greek and Jewish approaches to authority in explaining Ezra's accomplishment signaled the development of a very new notion of authorship.

CHAPTER 7

# FROM CANON TO AUTHORSHIP

Attribution analysis, which developed from the literary investigations of Aristotle and from the activity of Callimachus in creating a
catalogue of the holdings of the Alexandrian library, was an essential component in the scholarship on ecclesiastical writers of early
church luminaries like Tertullian, Origen, Eusebius, and St. Jerome.
This tradition of Greek scholarship also left its mark on St. Augustine, probably the most influential voice in the delineation of the
Christian biblical canon and in the creation of procedures by which
competing claims to canonicity could be reconciled. Augustine's
role in solidifying the canon of both the Old and New Testaments
should be evaluated not only as a continuation of Jewish practices
in the collection of authoritative documents of the Hebrew Bible,
but also as an outgrowth of Alexandrian scholarship's approach
towards the enumeration of "first-rate" Greek authors.

Augustine's delicate balancing of Greek and Jewish approaches
to the authoritative list parallels his unique and unprecedented
fusion of Greek and Jewish valuations of the role of individuals in
literary composition. I will argue that this fusion represents yet

another lasting Augustinian contribution to the history of both sacred and non-religious literature. Just as Augustine is largely responsible for articulating the orthodox position on the principles involved in the formation of the Christian Bible, he should also be given credit for laying the groundwork for the Western conception of the author. He accomplished this by applying Greek methods of attribution analysis and his own notion of writerly intentionality to a set of scriptural documents that, in a Jewish vein, he assumed to have been created ultimately by God.

## The Greek and Christian Concept of Canon

The ancient Greek obsession with determining the relative merits of writers is most clearly visible in the comedy of Aristophanes, the *Frogs*, produced in 405 B.C.E. The play went significantly further than that other remarkable poetic competition, the *Certamen Homeri Et Hesiodi* 'Contest of Homer and Hesiod'. This archaic, hexametric Greek poem records a singing match (an *agôn*) between the two preeminent epic poets (Homer and Hesiod) during their lifetime. In contrast, the *Frogs* does not depict a contest between living, contemporaneous poets (as Homer and Hesiod were imagined in the *Certamen*), but enacts a contest between two dead tragedians. The theme of intergenerational poetic contestation and of a contest between poets rather than their works had up to this point escaped the purview of the tragic and comic contests at the City Dionysia and the Lenaea in Athens. Playwrights could compete with each other every year, but a maximum of three tragedians and five comedians were eligible for any given contest. There was no societal mechanism available for comparing poet against poet, since a single year's entry (for tragedians, this included a tragic trilogy plus a stylized fourth play called a Satyr drama) could only be judged against the entries submitted at the same festival. Moreover, a poet could never be pitted against a deceased predecessor. To solve this new conundrum, Aristophanes introduces a new venue for assessing the relative value of playwrights that would never compete at Athens — Hades. The contest to end all contests, from the perspective of Athens at the end of the fifth century B.C.E., was Aeschylus vs. Euripides. The "weight" of all their plays was literally put in the balance — not merely a tragic tetralogy on each side.

Less whimsical treatments of this problem are attested soon after the *Frogs*. In the fourth century B.C.E., Heraclides Ponticus wrote *Peri Tôn Triôn Tragôdopoiôn* 'Concerning the Three Tragedians', presumably settling the debate about which were the preeminent tragedians.[1] Plutarch relates that Lycurgus, the fourth century orator, instituted a law that bronze statues of the poets Aeschylus, Sophocles, and Euripides be erected, and that their tragedies be written out and kept in a public depository. Lycurgus also made it law that the clerk of the state read the official "transcripts" of each tragedy to the actors who were to perform their plays, for comparison of the texts. Moreover, he declared it illegal to depart from the authorized text in performance (Plutarch, *Life of Lycurgus* 841). This anecdote suggests that Athenian identity was so forcefully connected to the works of its esteemed playwrights that state law was felt necessary to safeguard the prestige and textual integrity of this triad — that is, to institute an authoritative treatment for authoritative writers.

The evidence from late antiquity reveals that the relative merits of other types of writers were also assessed from the fourth century on. Quintilian (X.1.66) lists the three foremost (*praecipui*) comic poets — Eupolis, Cratinus, and Aristophanes; the same grouping is conveyed in the first line of Horace's fourth satire. Alexandrian scholars Eratosthenes and Aristophanes of Byzantium had considered the comic playwright Pherecrates as their equal.[2] Above all others, the Alexandrians were especially renowned as connoisseurs of the relative merits of the poets of the past — Aristarchus and Aristophanes are called *poetarum iudices* 'judges of the poets' by Quintilian (X.1.54).

The verb signifying a judgment of the preeminence of a writer is ἐγκρίνειν (*engkrinein*), defined by Rudolf Pfeiffer as 'to select authors and register them in the selective list'. In fact, there is only evidence of this term being employed with regard to Greek orators.[3] For Cicero, this became a matter of "classes;" thus, he placed the Stoic philosophers in the fifth class, as opposed to Democritus and others.[4] As Pfeiffer states, "it became the Roman way to call the ἐγκριθέντες 'classici' which means writers of the first class, 'primae classis' in the political and military language."[5] Such writers were classified as *engkrithentes* 'registered in the selective lists' initially on aesthetic or philosophical grounds. They later became πραττόμενοι (*prattomenoi*) 'treated' writers, whose works were repeatedly copied, taught in schools, and read by the educated public. While these works were saved (especially on account of their pedagogical value), the ἐκκριθέντες (*ekkrithentes*) 'writers judged out' were left to perish.[6] Alternative ways of expressing the idea of a hierarchy of writers also existed in the ancient world: the Roman rhetorician Quintilian used *ordo* 'rank', a metaphor derived from the sphere of social classification.

While there exists a term for complete lists of authors and their works (*pinakes*), there was no Greek or Latin word for selective lists of works or writers that had been determined to be of the first class, or that were judged worthy of inclusion. David Ruhnken coined the term "canon" (in Latin) in 1768 to stipulate the selective Alexandrian lists of the most highly respected ancient Greek orators.[7] From then on, it became popular in the European vernaculars to employ "canon" to refer to a list of secular authors or works from any period whose quality could be established by discerning critics. The term "canon" was suggested to Ruhnken from the tradition of the Church Fathers, where it signifies a list of biblical books accepted as genuine and inspired. There is little doubt that its use to refer to a list of secular authors was stimulated by the continuing influence of the Church's use of the word, as well as the mistaken belief that it had always been the accepted term among ancient Alexandrian literary scholars.

Biblical scholars who have investigated the concept of the New Testament canon typically begin from the Greek word *kanôn*, hopeful that the word, its etymology and historical deployment, might yield up the mysteries of the symbolic. H. W. Beyer's article on *kanôn* sets the pattern.[8] Noting that Greek *kanê* 'a cover woven from reeds' (related to Greek *kana*, *kaneon*, and *kaneion* 'a basket woven from reeds') is a loanword from the Semitic (e.g. Hebrew *qaneh* 'reed'), many scholars apparently conclude that there is really a single concept of a canon that spread from the Semitic to the Hellenic world together with this word. For these scholars, it is significant that the Semitic *qaneh* takes on a figurative cast (it often means 'straight rod or staff' in the Hebrew Bible). Implausibly, this development is thought to explain how Greek-speaking Christians came to use *kanôn* in a figurative sense as 'measuring rod', 'ruler', and 'plumbline'.

The history of the word in Greek reveals a subtle development of a concept focusing on the semantic sphere of the model or exemplary. In the realms of sculpture and music, the word began to imply a concept of "the ideal," in other words, that which is perfect, balanced, and harmonious. Legal thinkers understood *kanôn* as a binding principle and *kanones* as specific ideals. Among the Epicureans, *kanôn* meant the basis or logical criteria by which the truth-value of a statement might be judged. A most suggestive development is found in Greek mathematics, astronomy, and historical science, where the term *kanones* (plural of *kanôn*) was used for lists or tables (as in *khronikoi kanones* 'timetables to fix historical events').

New Testament scholars take special note of Paul's use of the word *kanôn*, especially in Galatians 6:16 where it signifies "the norm of true Christianity." In the first three centuries, the term served to designate an inner law and binding norm for Christianity. The word was transposed into Latin as *canon* (for example, by Cicero), although the Greek expression *kanôn tês pisteôs* 'canon of faith' was typically translated into Latin as *regula fidei* 'rule of faith' (see the discussion of the phrase in Augustine's *De Doctrina Christiana* below). The word was employed in such expressions as *kanôn tês alêtheias* 'the rule of truth', *kanôn tês ekklêsias* 'the canon of the church', and *ekklêsiastikos kanôn* 'the ecclesiastical canon'. Long before the word "canon" was ever used of scripture, the "rule of faith" and the "canon of the Church" meant much the same thing: the ideal of Christian faith as exemplified by church practice and teaching.[9]

Some of the earliest examples of the post-biblical Christian usage of *kanôn* are connected to Origen (ca. 184–254 C.E.) and the city of Alexandria where he resided. Eusebius (260–339 C.E.) describes Origen as bearing witness to a New Testament canon of four gospels only (*Ecclesiastical History* VI.25.3).[10] The Latin translation of Origen by Rufinus of Aquileia (345–411 C.E.) employs the notion of a canon (the Latin term is *canon*) of scripture.[11] Some twenty-five years after Eusebius' text (in about 350 C.E.), Athanasius, bishop of Alexandria, used the word to denote a selective list. He also regularly employs the verb *kanonizô* to mean 'include in the canon'.[12] Incidentally, Athanasius is also the first to list the twenty-seven books of the New Testament in its ultimate form without hesitating as to the relative value of its components.[13] Nevertheless, Athanasius' notion of a canon of scripture is likely influenced by Origen, if not by Eusebius as well. The overall importance of Origen and Alexandria in the formation of the concept of *kanôn* as a selective list of scriptures seems clear.

Despite the almost certain Alexandrian provenance of the term as applied to a list of scriptures, Beyer argues that "the use of *kanôn* in this sense was not influenced by the fact that Alexandrian grammarians had spoken of a canon of writers of model Greek."[14] In part this seems fair; the development of the concept in Christian circles was most likely ignited by Paul's use of the word. But the assumption that pagan Alexandrian scholars (such as Zenodotus, Aristophanes of Byzantium, or Aristarchus) had used *kanôn* to apply to their selective lists of first-rate authors is not accurate. In fact, the term *kanôn* was never actually used in this sense by non-Christian Alexandrians. For Aristophanes of Byzantium, *kanones* meant the 'rules' that apply to a given grammatical declension, by which one can predict the way a given word gets its grammatical endings. The idea of such rules thus participated in the grammatical principle of analogy, much favored by the Alexandrians. In addition, Aristophanes described particular authors and their style as *kanôn*, a 'model' or 'exemplar'.[15] The term apparently was also frequently used in ethics in the sense of 'rule' or 'model'. It seems that the application of the term *kanôn* to a list of works is the work of Christian scholars from Alexandria (especially Origen) who were influenced by their pagan scholarly predecessors.

The use of the term *kanôn* by early Christians to refer to the list of scriptural books is a testament to the process by which Alexandrian grammar was redeployed by early Christians to evaluate scriptural inspiration. In addition to being used to denote the grammatical "rules" that could be predicted by the principle of analogy, the term was eventually used by the Alexandrians in a more extended sense to describe the style of an orator, since any given orator was a 'model' or 'exemplar' for students to emulate. The transference of meaning from grammar to stylistics echoes the actual history of ancient classical scholarship: through the insights of grammar, the stylistic devices of the writer were laid bare to scholars. Instruction in the techniques of distinguishing between true and false ascription and teaching the writer's style were important parts of the Alexandrian school curriculum, and became central to the Alexandrian conceptualization of the nature of the writer. What's more, the writer became identifiable as a discrete and coherent entity through the process of being the object of the discourse of grammar, and to the extent that his or her style and content were iterable and might be replicated.[16] Unfortunately, student expertise in writing in the style of a given orator or poet also resulted in spurious works that were difficult to spot, spawning yet more rounds of attribution analysis.

For early Christian writers, *kanôn* signifies the more or less defined list of inspired biblical books. The concept of the work's iterability, that which may be copied, may also lie behind the extension of the term to describe the list of inspired biblical works. The term *kanôn* applied to the scriptures was perhaps meant to convey their *iterability of character* — that the figures or messages presented in New Testament writings, and indeed that these texts themselves, could serve as models or exemplars for Christians.

As I have discussed, the formation of the Christian *kanôn* or selective inspired list also derived from Alexandrian scholarship through the Christian employment of attribution analysis. The Church Fathers had a deep appreciation of the Alexandrian techniques to evaluate the authenticity of the authoritative documents of the Church. In fact, attribution analysis played a much more crucial role for Christians than it had in the opinions of the Alexandrian critics with regard to which authors were to be considered *engkrithentes* 'writers judged in'. According to Pfeiffer, the Alexandrian selective lists were lists of first class *authors*. In contrast, the Christian canon was a list of inspired *works*. The inspiration of a New Testament book rested in part on the status of its author and especially on the fact that it had been correctly attributed to the individual whose name it bore. The list of *engkrithentes* 'first-rate classical writers' that the Alexandrians had made, whatever they called this list or however formalized it was, never achieved the status of the biblical lists. Membership on this list in no way depended on attribution analysis. Whether a given work by an ancient Greek writer had been correctly attributed had little or no bearing on whether a poet, orator, or philosopher belonged to the first rank. In contrast, the Christian canon, which consisted of *works* that had been demonstrated as genuine, was in part defined by the possibility of forgery. It was, in effect, a list of inspired works that had not been faked and that were recognized by the majority of churches and significant church scholars.

The observations that were made in chapter 4 with regard to the canon of Hebrew scriptures apply to a large extent to the creation of the canon of the New Testament. I have argued throughout that a single moment or a single agent is incapable of originating a society's complex symbolic formations. Hypotheses about the role of the Council of Yavne in the formulation of the canon of the Hebrew Bible appear to have resulted in part from the misinterpretation of Proverbs 25:1, one of the few biblical verses that contained any information about the textual history of biblical books (see chapter 1). Similarly, it would appear that no ecclesiastical council made a final determination on the contents of New Testament scriptures, for the contents of the Christian scriptures were already stable.[17]

Augustine's guidelines for determining the stature of a scriptural work reveal the weight of previous generations and the practice of the entire Christian world making such decisions:

> Tenebit igitur hunc modum in scripturis canonicis, ut eas quae ab omnibus accipiuntur ecclesiis catholicis praeponat eis quas quidam non accipiunt. In eis vero quae non accipiuntur ab omnibus, praeponat eas quas plures gravioresque accipiunt, eis quas pauciores minorisque auctoritatis ecclesiae tenent. Si autem alias invenerit a pluribus, alias a gravioribus haberi, quamquam hoc invenire non possit, aequalis tamen auctoritatis eas habendas puto.

> Among the canonical scriptures he [the interpreter of scripture] will judge according to the following standard: to prefer those that

are received by all the catholic churches to those which some do not receive. Again, among those which are not received by all, he will prefer such as are sanctioned by the greater number of churches and by those of greater authority to such as held by the smaller number and by those of less authority. If, however, he finds that some books are held by the greater number of churches, and others by the churches of greater authority (although this is not a very likely thing to happen), I think that in such a case the authority on the two sides is to be considered as equal.

Augustine, *De Doctrina Christiana* II.8.12, trans. Shaw

This sliding scale confirms that church practice rather than ecclesiastical pronouncement was the deciding factor in the process of canonization. As F. F. Bruce concludes, "It is plain from [this passage] that, when Augustine wrote, no ecclesiastical council had made a pronouncement on the canon which could be recognized as the voice of the church."[18] It is interesting to note that in this particular passage Augustine does not mention attribution analysis as a test of the authenticity of individual scriptures. I would suggest that Augustine, like Eusebius (*Ecclesiastical History* III.25; see chapter 6), considered attribution analysis to be one factor among others in the evaluation of the canonicity of a work.

In 393 C.E., a church council held in Augustine's see of Hippo set forth the contents of the canonical books that Augustine had advocated. The lost proceedings of this council were summarized in the proceedings of the Third Council of Carthage (397 C.E.).[19] F. F. Bruce's evaluation of this process echoes the general principle in canon formation that I have articulated throughout this study: "[The proceedings of these councils] did not impose any innovation on the churches; they simply endorsed what had become the general consensus of the churches of the west and of the greater part of the east."[20] The statements of Augustine about the New Testament canon indicate that lingering confusion over the contents of the New Testament was over prior to these councils; in Bruce Metzger's view, it only remained for someone to say that the "great debate" was over.[21] Yet in considering the process as a debate or these councils as the official ending of the canonization process, there is a tendency to view the canonization process as equivalent to a Greek *agôn.*[22] As Harry Gamble concludes, these councils were local in nature and of limited authority, and thus, "no ecumenical authority of the ancient church ever rendered a formal decision for the church at large as to the exact contents of Christian scripture."[23] The idea that canons are determined by individuals or institutions in the short term has to be abandoned. To put it another way, the Greek poetic contest is not the model by which the drawing up of definitive lists of scriptures can be analyzed.[24]

### Augustine and the Attributions of the Old Testament

As I will argue, Augustine is a key figure in the development of the idea of the author. In part, this may be seen in the boldness of his application of Greek attribution analysis to books sometimes considered as scripture. Other Christian interpreters, foremost among them Eusebius and St. Jerome, had already considered the legitimacy of the attributions of biblical texts. However, Eusebius and Jerome both seem content to report the opinions of others, and are reluctant to apply a rigorous methodology to test individual books, stemming from their deference to established Church practice and the opinions of their predecessors. In Augustine's reflections one notices a greater self-assuredness. He applies attribution analysis to biblical books without the fear that he is about to overstep his bounds as an authority in these matters. Undoubtedly, he and his works have had the greater influence.[25] Augustine's attribution analysis is especially prominent in his attempt to establish the limits of the canon of the Old Testament. In contrast, the examples of attribution analysis we have seen from Eusebius and Jerome tend to focus on Christian documents and ecclesiastical works.

The most straightforward examples of Augustine's use of attribution analysis in the critical evaluation of extra-canonical scriptures are found in his *City of God.* With regard to the canonicity of the writings of Enoch, Augustine, like Tertullian (see chapter 6), cites the authority of a New Testament work (in this case, Jude 14–15) in order to argue that a text composed by Enoch is inspired. But Augustine does not recognize the possibility that Enoch might have been excluded from the Jewish canon because Enoch himself lacked a certain requisite authority or prophetic dispensation. Rather, the grounds for rejection involve ascertaining whether Enoch is the true author of the work attributed to him.

Iam vero si longe antiquiora repetam, et ante illud grande diluvium noster erat utique Noe patriarcha, quem prophetam quoque non immerito dixerim; si quidem ipsa arca quam fecit in qua cum suis evasit prophetia nostrorum temporum fuit. Quid Enoch septimus ab Adam, nonne etiam in canonica epistula apostoli Iudae prophetasse praedicatur? Quorum scripta ut apud Iudaeos et apud nos in auctoritate non essent nimia fecit antiquitas, propter quam videbantur habenda esse suspecta ne proferrentur falsa pro veris. Nam et proferuntur quaedam quae ipsorum esse dicantur ab eis qui pro suo sensu passim quod volunt credunt. Sed ea castitas canonis non recepit non quod eorum hominum qui Deo placuerunt reprobetur auctoritas sed quod ista esse non credantur ipsorum.

Nec mirum debet videri quod suspecta habentur quae sub tantae antiquitatis nomine proferuntur, quando quidem in ipsa historia regum Iuda et regum Israel quae res gestas continet de quibus eidem scripturae canonicae credimus commemorantur plurima quae ibi non explicantur et in libris dicuntur aliis inveniri quos prophetae scripserunt, et alicubi eorum quoque prophetarum nomina non tacentur nec tamen inveniuntur in canone quem recepit populus Dei.

Now if I may recall far more ancient things, our patriarch Noah certainly was living even before the great Flood; and I should be quite justified in calling him a prophet, seeing that the very ark which he built and in which he and his family escaped was a prophecy of our times. Then again, Enoch, the seventh in descent from Adam, is said to have prophesied; and the authority for this is the canonical epistle of the apostle Jude [Jude 14].[26] But the excessive antiquity of the writings of those men has had the effect of preventing their acceptance, either by the Jews or by us, as authoritative (*in auctoritate non essent*); on account of their remoteness in time it seemed advisable to hold them suspect, for

fear of advancing false claims to authenticity. For there are some
writings put forward as genuine works of those authors by those
who without discrimination believe what they want to believe, as
suits their inclination. But the purity of the canon (*castitas canonis*) has not admitted these works, not because the authority of
these men, whom God approved, is rejected, but because these
documents are not believed to belong to them.

It should not, indeed, appear surprising that writings put
forward under a name of such antiquity are regarded with suspicion; for in the actual history of the kings of Judah and Israel, the
contents of which we believe in as historical on the authority of
the same canon of Scripture, there are frequent references to matters not fully treated there which, we are told, can be found in
other books written by the prophets, and in some cases the names
of those prophets are not suppressed; yet these books are not
found in the canon accepted by the people of God.

Augustine, *City of God* XVIII.38, trans. Bettenson

Augustine acknowledges the prevalence of forgery and literary
fraud in the attribution of works of scripture to figures of obvious
authority. He subordinates what he represents as the Jewish position (that the Jews tolerated no authority prior to that of Moses in
the canon) to a more straightforward Aristotelian evaluation (they
are incorrectly attributed). Like Jerome, he is capable of condemn-
ing a work as doubtful, but unlike Jerome, he does not shy away
from the potential impact of his verdict. Augustine is among the
first to subscribe to the belief that all canonical texts have achieved
their place in the canon by passing the test of attribution analysis.
As I discussed in chapter 4, an assumption of the authenticity of the
authorial ascriptions of biblical books certainly rested at the heart
of the Jewish veneration of scripture. Such authenticity was felt by
Josephus (who speaks for commonly held Jewish values in this regard) to have been achieved as a result of the vigilance of the priests
who continually guarded the Temple archives against the introduction of inauthentic works. But faith in the institution of the Temple
archive, together with the certainty that Jews lacked the agonistic
mentality of the Greeks, allowed Jewish scholarship to remain free

of a scientific approach to attribution analysis. Christian scholars were under no such dispensation.

In considering the works of the Old Testament, Augustine arrives at the position on the excessive antiquity of pre-Mosaic scriptures that I have argued lies at the heart of late Second Temple period Jewish views on the canon. Typically, Augustine assumes that the Jews tolerated no authority prior to that of Moses in the canon because the tradition could not vouch for the correct attribution of such ancient works:

> Sed non frustra non sunt in eo canone scripturarum qui servabatur in templo Hebraei popul succedentium diligentia sacerdotum, nisi quia ob antiquitatem suspectae fidei iudicata sunt, <u>nec utrum haec essent quae ille scripsisset poterat inveniri, non talibus proferentibus qui ea per seriem successionis reperirentur rite servasse. Unde illa quae sub eius nomine proferuntur et continent istas de gigantibus fabulas quod non habuerint homines patres recte a prudentibus iudicantur non ipsius esse credenda, sicut multa sub nominibus et aliorum prophetarum et recentiora sub nominibus apostolorum ab haereticis proferuntur, quae omnia nomine apocryphorum ab auctoritate canonica diligenti examinatione remota sunt.</u>

> But these writings are with good reason not included in the canon of scripture which was carefully kept in the temple of the Hebrew people by a succession of priests. For they were judged of dubious authenticity because of their age. <u>It was also impossible to ascertain whether they were what Enoch had written since they were not presented by men who were found to have kept them with proper ceremony through successive generations. Hence discerning authorities are right in their judgment that the writings presented under Enoch's name with those tales about giants not having human fathers should not be attributed to him. In like manner, many writings are presented by heretics under the names of the apostles, but all these too have been excluded after careful examination from canonical authority and go under the name of apocrypha.</u>

> Augustine, City of God XV.23, trans. Bettenson

Augustine's conclusions correctly reflect Jewish beliefs in one sense, but are not accurate in another. Judaism's canon does indeed begin with works revealed to Moses; as I have suggested, it ends with the works written down by his prophetic successors who had lived during the Babylonian Exile. But the importance of the idea of a prophetic succession beginning with Moses as an organizing principle for this collection is now clear. For Augustine, Moses achieved a central position in this collection because the validity of the textual transmission of works composed by individuals prior to him could not be ascertained. Augustine thus incorrectly assumes that authenticity had always been foremost in the minds of the Jews who had created the canon of the Old Testament. Moreover, he concludes that attribution analysis is the most persuasive means for testing the canonicity of biblical books in general.

Augustine makes another striking proposition that could never have been articulated by Jewish exegetes like Josephus. He claims that the writings of biblical prophets in their capacity as historical researchers must have less authority than the revelations of these same prophets when inspired to speak forth the words of God. Augustine maintains that this distinction can be used as a means of explaining the difference between canonical and deuterocanonical works:

Cuius rei, fateor, causa me latet, nisi quod existimo etiam ipsos quibus ea quae in auctoritate religionis esse deberent sanctus utique Spiritus revelabat alia sicut homines historica diligentia alia sicut prophetas insipratione divina scribere potuisse, atque haec ita fuisse distincta, ut illa tamquam ipsis ista vero tamquam Deo per ipsos loquenti iudicarentur esse tribuenda, ac sic illa pertinerent ad ubertatem cognitionis, haec ad religionis auctoritatem in qua auctoritate custoditur canon, praeter quem iam si qua etiam sub nomine verorum prophetarum scripta proferuntur, nec ad ipsam copiam scientiae valent, quoniam utrum eorum sint quorum esse dicuntur incertum est; et ob hoc eis non habetur fides, maxime his in quibus etiam contra fidem librorum canonicorum quaedam leguntur, propter quod ea prorsus non esse apparet illorum.

The reason for the omission [of the deuterocanonical works], I confess (*fateor*), escapes me; except that I conceive that even those writers to whom the Holy Spirit unquestionably revealed matters which were rightly accorded religious authority, may have written sometimes as men engaged in historical research, sometimes as prophets under divine inspiration. And the two kinds of writing were so distinct that it was decided that the first kind should be attributed to the writers themselves while the other kind was to be ascribed, as we might say, to God speaking through them. Thus one sort was concerned with the development of knowledge, the other with the establishment of religious authority; and the canon was carefully guarded as bearing this authority. Outside the canon, though works may now be issued under the names of genuine prophets, they are of no value even as adding to our supply of knowledge, since it is uncertain whether they are authentic works of the authors to whom they are ascribed. That is why no reliance is placed on them; and this is particularly true of those in which statements are found that actually contradict the reliable evidence of the canonical books, so that it is immediately apparent that they are not authentic (*prorsus . . . illorum*).

Augustine, *City of God* XVIII.38, trans. Bettenson

With regard to the deuterocanonical books (the books of the Apocrypha), Augustine can only suppose that these were written by the prophets "as men engaged in historical research" whose goal was "the development of knowledge" rather than "the establishment of religious authority." This two-tiered edifice of prophetic composition, where a prophet is capable of inspired utterance at some times, but merely gives voice to human discourse at others, clearly moves beyond the schema developed by other Christian writers, although it echoes the understanding of Philo with regard to oracular utterances (see chapter 5). In chapters 3 and 4, I explored Josephus' notion of biblical narrative as the witnessing of history by the prophets. The historical writing of prophets, although dissimilar to prophetic revelation in its nature, was the prerogative of those within the prophetic succession, and was no less valid as scripture. This view was inherited by Origen (see chapter 6). In his discussion of the acceptability of Ezra's historical writings, Origen concluded that his status as prophet granted him the privilege to in-

terject references to current events in the older works he was copying. Augustine's position is thus new, since it negates the faith
placed in the historical research carried out by prophets, which
characterized the view of both Josephus and Origen.

The passage also demonstrates that Augustine understood
canonization to rest on the determination of the text as forgery or
correctly attributed. Further, if statements in the deuterocanonical
works contradict those in the canon, these texts, according to Augustine, are patently inauthentic. This methodology depended on
the belief that the Bible is a perfectly consistent document. Augustine had already given voice to this sentiment earlier in the *City of
God:* "There is indeed some truth to be found in these Apocrypha;
but they have no canonical authority on account of the many falsehoods they contain" (*City of God* XV.23). By falsehoods Augustine
could only mean contradictions with established scriptures. This
sentiment had itself been manifested in the writing of Africanus (as
reported by Origen), who challenged the veracity of Susanna on the
grounds that it contradicted other Old Testament works.

Augustine's knowledge of Jewish principles in canon formation may be seen both in his distinction between historical research
and revelation, and in his acknowledgment of a prophetic succession. A more telling reference to the Jewish ideology of prophetic
transmission may be seen in Augustine's use of the notion of the
succession of prophets, which was anything but an intuitive notion.

> Omittamus igitur earum scripturarum fabulas quae apocryphae
> nuncupantur eo quod earum occulta origo non claruit patribus, a
> quibus usque ad nos auctoritas <u>veracium scripturarum certissima
> et notissima successione</u> pervenit. In his autem apocryphis etsi in-
> venitur aliqua veritas, tamen propter multa falsa nulla est canon-
> ica auctoritas.

> We may then pass over the tales contained in the scriptures which
> are called "Apocrypha" because their origin is obscure and was
> not clear to the fathers, from whom the authority of the true
> Scriptures has come down to us <u>by a well-defined and well-known
> line of succession (*certissima et notissima successione*).</u> There is

indeed some truth to be found in these Apocrypha; but they have no canonical authority on account of the many falsehoods they contain.

Augustine, City of God XV.23, trans. Bettenson

Here, Augustine prevaricates, asserting that both a test of falsehood (to be ascertained by measuring a disputed text against the known truths of accepted canonical documents) and the integrity of the prophetic succession are useful in rejecting apocryphal texts. But it would appear that the purpose in testing the truth-value of a given deuterocanonical work is only to affirm what the "well-known line of succession" has already made manifest. This idea of a succession, I would argue, derives, either directly or indirectly, from Josephus.

In another passage that also likely derives from Josephus, Augustine also appeals to the notion of a succession of fathers (termed *diadokhê tôn paterôn* in Josephus' Greek):

Non itaque credendum est, quod nonnulli arbitrantur, Hebraeam tantum linguam per illum qui vocabatur Heber, unde Hebraeorum vocabulum est, fuisse servatam, atque inde pervenisse ad Abraham, Hebraeas autem litteras a lege coepisse quae data est per Moysen, sed potius per illam successionem patrum memoratam linguam cum suis litteris custoditam.

Now it is not to be believed, as some people suppose, that it was only as a spoken language that Hebrew was preserved by Heber (whose name is the origin of the name 'Hebrews') and that from him it passed on to Abraham, whereas the written language started with the Law given through Moses. We should rather believe that the recorded language, along with its literature, was safeguarded by that succession of fathers (*per illam successionem patrum*).

Augustine, City of God XVIII.39, trans. Bettenson

Augustine's knowledge of the line of succession or of a succession of fathers might derive from rabbinic doctrine or some other avenue; however, it is far more likely to originate with his assimilation of ideas from Josephus. Although it is uncertain whether he had read Josephus' works himself, the key passages were in any event preserved in the writings of Eusebius, Jerome, and others. It is also likely that *Against Apion* was a literary model for the genre of archeological investigation of the antiquity of Judeo-Christian civilization exemplified in the *City of God*.[27]

Other references to passages in Josephus' work are more easily seen in Augustine's comparison of philosophical contentiousness to the harmony of scriptures:

> ... cur dissenserunt et a magistris discipuli et inter se condiscipuli nisi quia ut homines humanis sensibus et humanis ratiocinatibus ista quaesierunt?
>
> Ubi quamvis esse potuerit et studium gloriandi quo quisque alio sapientior et acutior videri cupit nec sententiae quodam modo addictus alienae sed sui dogmatis et opinionis inventor, tamen ut nonnullos vel etiam plurimos eorum fuisse concedam quos a suis doctoribus vel discendi sociis amor veritatis abruperit ut pro ea certarent quam veritatem putarent, sive illa esset sive non esset; quid agit aut quo vel qua ut ad beatitudinem perveniatur humana se porrigit infelicitas, si divina non ducit auctoritas?
>
> Denique auctores nostri, in quibus non frustra sacrarum litterarum figitur et terminatur canon, absit ut inter se aliqua ratione dissentiant. Unde non immerito, cum illa scriberent, eis Deum vel per eos locutum ...

> How is it then, that disciples have disagreed with teachers, and fellow-disciples with one another? Must it not be because they sought the answers to these questions as men relying on human senses and human powers of reasoning?
>
> Now it may be that there was here also the concern for self-glorification, which makes each man desire to seem wiser and cleverer than the rest and not to be a kind of retainer, pledged in loyalty to another's opinions, but rather the originator (*inventor*) of a doctrine, holding views of his own. However, I am prepared to admit that some philosophers, perhaps even the majority of them,

broke away from their teachers or fellow pupils simply from the love of truth so as to fight for what they conceived to be the truth, whether they were mistaken or not. Be that as it may, what does it matter in what direction or by what way the unhappy state of man sets out on its pursuit of felicity, if it is not guided by divine authority?

It is to be noted that our authors (*auctores*) do not disagree with one another in any way. Perish the thought! It is not for nothing that they provide the fixed and final canon of sacred literature. This agreement justifies the belief that when they wrote these books God was speaking to them, or perhaps we should say through them.

Augustine, *City of God* XVIII.41, trans. Bettenson

When Augustine speculates on the differences between the philosophers and the writers of scripture, we can hear the echoes of Josephus' critique of Greek letters. The discourse of Christian exegesis had certainly not accomplished the full assimilation of Greek agonistic poetics (this would have to wait until the Renaissance).[28] Thus, the excoriation of Greek individuality that had been articulated by Josephus was useful to describe Augustine's dislike of excessive individualism. Of course, Augustine does not entirely agree with Josephus that all disputation is bad, especially if it arises out of a search for truth. His confusion reflects the fragility of the compromise between Hellenism and Judaism that he has begun to work out.

The careful weighing of the claims for and against the legitimacy of apocryphal books in Augustine's discussion is indicative of his mastery of Greek as well as Jewish approaches to testing the legitimacy of a text.

Omittamus igitur earum scripturarum fabulas quae apocryphae nuncupantur eo quod earum occulta origo non claruit patribus, a quibus usque ad nos auctoritas varaicium scripturarum certissima et notissima successione pervenit. In his autem apocryphis etsi invenitur aliqua veritas, tamen propter multa falsa nulla est canonica auctoritas. Scripsisse quidem nonnulla divine illum Enoch, septimum ab Adam, negare non possumus cum hoc in epistula canonica Iudas apostolus dicat. Sed non frustra non sunt in eo canone scripturarum qui servabatur in templo Hebraei popul succedentium diligentia sacerdotum, nisi quia ob antiquitatem suspectae fidei iudicata sunt, nec utrum haec essent quae ille scripsisset poterat inveniri, non talibus proferentibus qui ea per seriem successionis reperirentur rite servasse. Unde illa quae sub eius nomine proferuntur et continent istas de gigantibus fabulas quod non habuerint homines patres recte a prudentibus iudicantur non ipsius esse credenda, sicut multa sub nominibus et aliorum prophetarum et recentiora sub nominibus apostolorum ab haereticis proferuntur, quae omnia nomine apocryphorum ab auctoritate canonica diligenti examinatione remota sunt.

Let us then pass over the tales of those writings which are called apocrypha because their origin was hidden and uncertain to the fathers, from whom the authority of the true scriptures has come down to us by a very sure and well-known line of transmission. Although some truth is found in these apocrypha, yet they contain much that is false, and, for that reason have no canonical authority. Now we cannot deny that some things were written under divine inspiration by Enoch, who belonged to the seventh generation from Adam, since the apostle Jude says this in a canonical letter. But these writings are with good reason not included in the canon of scripture which was carefully kept in the temple of the Hebrew people by a succession of priests. For they were judged of dubious authenticity because of their age. It was also impossible to ascertain whether they were what Enoch had written since they were not presented by men who were found to have kept them with proper ceremony through successive generations. Hence discerning authorities are right in their judgment that the writings presented under Enoch's name with those tales about giants not having human fathers should not be attributed to him. In like manner, many writings are presented by heretics under the names of the apostles, but all these too have been excluded after careful examination from canonical authority and go under the name of apocrypha.

Augustine, *City of God* XV.23, trans. Bettenson

Augustine states the works are called *apocrypha* 'hidden' because their origin was hidden and uncertain to the fathers. As was noted above, he attributes the validity of scripture to the "very sure and well-known line of transmission," in true Jewish fashion. He can admit in principle the idea that authentic teachings of Enoch have survived, inasmuch as they are referred to in an inspired work of scripture (the book of Jude). However, this does not lead him to abandon the truest guide to the authenticity of Old Testament books — their preservation "with proper ceremony through successive generations." Augustine is aware of one of the principles that Jewish apologists like Josephus employ to authenticate the contents of the Hebrew Bible in the face of claims by competing groups: documents of excessive age are not reliable. One thinks of Josephus' claim that the succession of prophets begins with Moses, and that only Moses had the dispensation to record events that he had not himself witnessed and that predated his life. Finally, Augustine articulates the premises by which similar judgments may be made as to New Testament writings — namely, testing whether the apostolic attribution of the work is authentic.

Josephus may be said to have puzzled out a definition of authorship, without having a term for it. It amounted to a pejorative designation, an accusation thrown at the Greeks from the culturally distant literary world of the Jews.[29] The effectiveness of this accusation did not lie in the accuracy of its description of the differences between Greeks and Jews. Rather, it was effective because it enabled Christian exegetes like Augustine to separate the distasteful aspects of non-scriptural authors from their prophetic counterparts.

By using the Greek methodology of attribution analysis to endorse texts attributed to legendary individuals, Augustine and his predecessors had combined two very different ways of looking at both the connection between names and texts, and the connection between individuals and authority. Upon a belief system based on Jewish ideas of divine agency and prophetic revelation, they reinstantiated Greek individualism and the practice of writing in one's own name.

## Augustine's Idea of Authorship

> The purpose of scripture's Divine Author appeared clearly to Augustine, but the aims of its human author remained elusive. He did not find mysterious the fact that the infinite Being, source of all truths accessible to man, was able to express a number of these truths in one simple sentence, whose simplicity conveyed so much. It struck him as baffling, however, that a human author was allowed to share in this privilege.
>
> Bertrand de Margerie[30]

A scholarly consensus has emerged in the past century that Augustine stood on the threshold of a dramatic intellectual transformation in western society. Albrecht Dihle, a prominent figure in the study of ancient philosophy, states, "It is generally accepted in the study of the history of philosophy that the notion of will, as it is used as a tool of analysis and description in many philosophical doctrines from the early Scholastics to Schopenhauer and Nietzsche, was invented by St. Augustine."[31] According to the ancient historian and philologist, Arnaldo Momigliano, "The first work which combines autobiographical information and self-awareness perfectly is of course St. Augustine's *Confessions.*"[32] This view had already begun with G. Misch, who in 1907 claimed that no man before St. Augustine had enough "inner life" to write an authentic autobiography.[33] (Misch, though Jewish, confirmed the view of his teacher, Wilhelm Dilthey, that interiority as well as personality began with Christianity, and that personality, in the sense of an inner life, was unknown to pagans and Jews.)[34] Augustine has been awarded a key role in the development of the introspective conscience by the scholar of Christianity, Krister Stendahl, and has been described as the first individual by the French classicist, Jean-Pierre Vernant.[35] Recently, Phillip Cary has argued that he invented the concept of private inner space, combining Plotinus' idea of an inner world within the soul that was common to all with Christianity's idea of God dwelling within the temple of the body. The result was a notion of the inner self as a capacious private space in which God may be found yet which is separate from God. Augustine is also spoken of as having laid the groundwork for much of modern semiotics and theory of language.[36] The confluence of the conclusions of these scholars on Augustine may of course represent nothing more than an unfortunate stampede and scholarly pile-up, but if one gives credence to the notion of the paradigm shift in the history of science and the idea of radical discontinuities or epistemic breaks in the history of ideas, these scholars' assessment of the importance of the Augustinian moment cannot be easily dismissed.

Augustine is the culmination of Greek and Jewish approaches to the individual as signified by a name and biography. In the complexity of his approach to authorship, he moves beyond his Christian predecessors. His description of the author for the first time conceives of the writer not just as a biographic entity but also as a human individual with an intention and a will who is capable of transmitting eternally valid information.

Augustine's contribution to the ascension of authorship as a dominant paradigm in the Western tradition stems from a hermeneutic dilemma — how can one ascertain the correct meaning of scripture when not only the will of God but also the will of the text's human author must be taken into consideration? If the intent of the divine author can be established through the rule of faith, the prevailing practice of the established churches of the day, or through comparison with other scriptures, can the intent of the human author of scripture be similarly established? What precisely is the relationship between divine will or intent, and the intent of the human author? Does the intent of the human author, if it can be established, trump other meanings of a passage that a reader may arrive at, if these meanings are consistent with the rule of faith or correct Christian belief? It is my premise that Augustine's focus on will or intent of both human and divine author signals a new chapter not only in the history of exegesis (as has already been documented by scholars like Bertrand de Margerie), but also in the very development of the notion of the writer.

In assessing Augustine's discussion of the author as possessing a will or intent, it is essential to review the scholarly assessment of Augustine as the individual responsible for introducing the notion of the will into the philosophical tradition. Albrecht Dihle's analysis of Augustine's accomplishment represents an important survey of the elements that helped Augustine formulate this conception. The word Augustine uses for will (*voluntas*) of course precedes his own radical understanding of the concept. As Dihle shows, the term *voluntas* was already being used by Neoplatonic theologians in the third and fourth centuries C.E. to render in Latin the Greek words that had been used to denote the will of God. It is especially significant for the present study that *voluntas* was also a concept that had been specifically formulated to describe the relationship between legal writers and their texts. Augustine transformed the term from the sphere of theology and hermeneutics to the field of psychology, in order to describe the motivations of individuals.

Dihle partly attributes Augustine's development of a concept of the will to his self-examination. The *Confessions,* which testify to the intensity of Augustine's introspection, provided the vehicle for this new conception of will (*voluntas*); thus it is mainly by Augustine's unprecedented self-scrutiny that he surpassed the conceptual system of Greco-Roman culture. He concentrated on what was going on in the human mind during the act of cognition. For the first time, the same notion of will could be applied in both theological and anthropological contexts, to man and God alike. Dihle points out that this corresponds to the implicit outlook of the Hebrew Bible, where the human will is the only means man has of responding to God's intention or will, as it is made clear in His orders and commandments.

According to Dihle, the Latin language itself facilitated the classical world's assimilation of the implicit biblical conception of will. In contrast to classical and post-classical Greek, Latin is not over-specific in its terminology. Latin has a group of words that conveys the idea of impulse or intention to act, but does not divide these concepts according to whether they originate from rational or from irrational factors in the human soul, as does Greek. Thus the words *velle* and *voluntas* are not tied to distinct theories about the origins of the will, like their corresponding Greek terms. Because these over-specific Greek theories did not correspond to the biblical notion of will, the Greek terms were unable to incorporate the biblical conception, and were eclipsed in the western philosophical debate.

If Latin had a fortuitous way of translating the Greek philosophical terms (such as *boulêsis, proaieresis,* or *hormê,* which correspond to various distinct shades of the notion of "will"), why didn't Roman philosophers like Cicero arrive at the notion of will prior to Augustine? In Dihle's view, Roman philosophy rested completely within the confines of the Greek tradition, and despite linguistic factors, Greek modes of thinking reigned supreme. While the Latin language had a set of terms that could have been used to render a voluntaristic concept, Greek intellectualism totally dominated psychological and ethical reflection, hindering new insights into the nature of the will until the Greek philosophical paradigm could be transcended.

Another ingredient in Augustine's invention was the articulation of a notion of the will in the field of Roman law. The legal concept of "will" was fundamentally unlike the Greek legal notion of "intentionality" (*ekousion* or *pronoia*). Aristotle, for example, thought that the strict construction of the law (*akribodikaion*) had to be permanently corrected by the idea of "fairness" or "equity" (*epieikês*), not by assessing the true intent of the lawmaker and ascertaining what his response to a current situation might be. Any Greek evaluation of the will of the author behind a written text of legal importance inevitably could only raise a single question: had the author acted or formulated "knowingly"?[37] In the main, the will of the author in Greek law was irrelevant to a decision of a case, which mainly rested on the question of what was "fair," at least to the extent that it could be coupled with a persuasive rendition of the meaning of the law. Could the strict interpretation of a written document coexist with a sense of what was fitting, fair, or just? These were the principle questions that Greek law would address in a case.

The Romans, who had little confidence in legislation, preferred to rely on the interpretation and reinterpretation of a few laws and legal formulas or fixed procedures. Laws, although they tended to remain unchanged by new legislation in Rome, were adapted to the changing conditions of social and economic life. The praetor, who had unrestricted legal powers, was entitled to make use of every conceivable application, interpretation, or suspension of legal prescripts. His new applications or interpretations of existing and unchanging law were adopted by his successor if they turned out to be useful and practicable. For the Romans, laws, actions, formulas, and statements of legal intercourse always needed interpretation in order to clarify the intentions (*voluntas*) of the persons involved. Preference was often given to *voluntas*, the will of the lawgiver, rather than to the actual wording of the text (*verba*). Only words that were absolutely unmistakable in meaning and intention superseded the search for and evaluation of *voluntas*.

No Roman juristic text speculates on whether "will" originates from reason or from emotion, the usual inquiry that accompanied any speculation on will in Greek thought. The legal abstraction of "the will of the lawgiver" discarded these motivations, according to Dihle, because they would have been useless in the practice of legal argumentation. Since the Latin vocabulary of Cicero and the other translators of Greek philosophy had no separate terms to render the nuanced Greek vocabulary for "will originating from reason," as opposed to "will originating from emotion," the Roman legal abstraction of *voluntas* had no ties to these same Greek ethical questions.

But the new abstraction was not automatically applied to describe the nature of human will in general by the Romans, nor did Roman philosophers extrapolate from legal discourse to come to a new understanding of human behavior in which motivation for the will would be irrelevant. Thus, the juristic term *voluntas* remained a hermeneutic rather than an anthropological concept.

One might say that the concept of will, which explains the motivations of all human beings, was partially derived from the idea of the "will of the lawgiver" — the force of will that precedes and continues to determine the meaning of the dead letter of a written legal document. But Dihle stresses that there are multiple causes for Augustine's invention of the concept of the will. These include the use of the term in Neoplatonic theological speculation, its use in rendering Greek ethical concepts, the underlying prevalence of an idea of will in the biblical tradition, and even Augustine's penchant for introspection and self-analysis. The confluence of these causes precludes a single interpretation of the significance of his invention.

As Dihle makes plain, the word for the new concept of "the pure will of man" was now able to describe precisely the voluntarism that underlies the biblical tradition. What enabled Augustine's discovery of the will was his opportunity to articulate biblical theology from the perspective of a language and culture that could put into words the psychological premises of the Hebrew Bible and early Judaism. His personal addition was to shift the discussion from theology to consider his own motivations: Augustine employed the idea of will not to talk about God, but to talk about man.

The implications of Augustine's conception of the will for understanding his articulation of authorial hermeneutics are profound. His conceptualization of the will of the author is disturbingly complex. These matters are addressed in *De Doctrina Christiana* 'On Christian Instruction', Books 1–2 and most of Book 3 of which were written in 396–397 C.E., while Books 3 and 4 were completed in 426 C.E. They are taken up in extended form at the end of the *Confessions*, begun in 397 C.E.[38] *De Doctrina Christiana* is an essay on how to interpret scripture; it sets out guidelines for the approach to scriptural interpretation found in the *Confessions*. In the *Confessions*, the discussion on the will or intention of the author appears in an extended interpretation of the beginning of the book of Genesis that follows the narration of his life. Although such insights might be out of place in a modern autobiography, it was common for ancient writers to engage in a practical application of the insights they derived from real experience at the end of a narrative.

Hitherto, scholars of Augustine have addressed Augustine's claim that a single sentence might have multiple meanings, without addressing what multiple meanings imply about the nature of the author.[39] According to Bertrand de Margerie, scholars of Augustine from Thomas Aquinas to Séraphin Zarb thought that he had distinguished a primary literary sense, intended by the inspired human author of the text, from those other meanings intended by God that were visible in derived and adapted senses of the same passage.[40] De Margerie considers the matter differently, asking whether Augustine believed that a biblical author himself could have intended multiple understandings of a single sentence. Building on this perspective and considering the subject from another angle, the present study suggests that Augustine's acknowledgement of the existence of meanings unintended by the author, no less than his frequent recourse to the notion of intent in itself, represents a dramatic step in the history of authorship.

Augustine treats scriptural ambiguity as a logical problem to be resolved by following a number of steps in order. First come the initial phases of troubleshooting: a reconsideration of punctuation and pronunciation (these are especially important when dealing with a text written without word breaks or where punctuation is uncertain). Then, the reader should consult the *regula fidei* 'the rule of faith', itself arrived at through consultation with clearer passages from the Bible and with the authoritative teaching of the church. After these steps have been taken, two or more possible readings of the text may remain viable. If neither sense impedes faith (*uterque autem sensus fidem non impedit*),[41] he allows that the parts of the text that precede and follow the passage at hand (in other words, the context) should be consulted in order to resolve the question.[42] Thus far, Augustine's contribution suggests nothing unorthodox. However, he leaves room for the reader after such steps have been exhausted, as the following discussion of punctuation reveals:

> Ubi autem neque praescripto fidei neque ipsius sermonis textu ambiguitas explicari potest, nihil obest secundum quamlibet earum quae ostenduntur, sententiam distinguere . . . Tales igitur distinctionum ambiguitates in potestate legentis sunt.

> Where, however, the ambiguity cannot be cleared up, either by the rule of faith or by the context, there is nothing to hinder us from punctuating the sentence according to any method we choose of those that suggest themselves . . . Ambiguities in punctuation of this kind are therefore in the power of the reader.
>
> Augustine, *De Doctrina Christiana* III.2.5, trans. Shaw

The point is clear, although it is made in a relatively innocuous discussion of punctuation: the reader is to be given authority or power to resolve certain kinds of interpretive dilemmas that cannot be resolved by any other means. However, to over-emphasize Augustine's approval of the discretion of the reader as a suitable means to resolve ambiguity would be to misunderstand his true concern. Augustine does not wish to vault the reader over the authority of text or orthodox tradition. Instead, his valuation of the reader is merely a feature of his approach to attempting to ascertain the meaning of the text as its writer (*scriptor*) intended it to be understood.

The notion of authorial intent appears frequently in Augustine's writing. Sometimes the term used is *sensus auctoris* 'the sense of the writer' (*De Doctrina Christiana* II.13.19), or *scriptorum intentio* 'the intent of the writers' (*De Doctrina Christiana* III.4).[43] The idea is also described in a more roundabout fashion. In *De Genesi Ad Litteram,* Augustine speaks of choosing the interpretation that the author had in mind (*sensisse*).[44] He also describes intent as "what the Apostle wished to say (*quid voluerit dicere . . . apostolus*)" (*De Doctrina Christiana* IV.7.11).

The recourse to the intent of the writer is fascinating in its own right. But the significance of this category is heightened by the fact that readers sometimes lack sufficient information from the passage to grasp this intent. The category of "intent" is arguably raised here as a central concern for hermeneutics in general and not merely for Roman jurisprudence for the first time. It is not surprising that the category evokes a correspondingly new epistemological difficulty: what if the intent cannot be ascertained from the passage? One suggestive passage from *De Doctrina Christiana* indicates the steps a reader should take in such a circumstance:

> Quando autem ex eisdem scripturae verbis non unum aliquid, sed duo vel plura sentiuntur, etiam si latet quid senserit ille qui scripsit, nihil periculi est, si quodlibet eorum congruere veritati ex aliis locis sanctarum scripturarum doceri potest, id tamen eo conante qui divina scrutatur eloquia, ut ad voluntatem perveniatur auctoris per quem scripturam illam sanctus operatus est spiritus, sive hoc assequatur, sive aliam senteniam de illis verbis quae fidei rectae non refragatur exsculpat, testimonium habens a quocumque alio loco divinorum eloquiorum. Ille quippe auctor in eisdem verbis quae intellegere volumus, et ipsam sententiam forsitan vidit et certe dei spiritus, qui per eum haec operatus est, etiam ipsam occursuram lectori vel auditori sine dubitatione praevidit, immo ut occurreret, quia et ipsa est veritate subnixa, providit. Nam quid in divinis eloquiis largius et uberius potuit divinitus provideri quam

ut eadem verba pluribus intellegantur modis, quos alia non minus divina contestantia faciant approbari?

When, again, not some one interpretation, but two or more interpretations are put upon the same words of Scripture, even though the meaning the writer intended remain undiscovered, there is no danger if it can be shown from other passages of Scripture that any of the interpretations put on the words is in harmony with the truth. And if a man in searching the Scriptures endeavors to get at the intention of the author through whom the Holy Spirit spoke, whether he succeeds in this endeavor, or whether he draws a different meaning from the words, but one that is not opposed to sound doctrine, he is free from blame so long as he is supported by the testimony of some other passage of Scripture. For the author perhaps saw that this very meaning lay in the words which we are trying to interpret; and assuredly the Holy Spirit, who through him spoke these words, foresaw that this interpretation would occur to the reader, nay, made provision that it should occur to him, seeing that it too is founded on truth. For what more liberal and more fruitful provision could God have made in regard to the Sacred Scriptures than that the same words might be understood in several senses, all of which are sanctioned by the concurring testimony of other passages equally divine?

Augustine, *De Doctrina Christiana* III.27.38, trans. Shaw

Augustine concludes that the author may have foreseen how his writing could be interpreted. Even if he didn't, the Holy Spirit "who through him spoke these words" not only foresaw the reader's interpretation but caused it to occur to him. Augustine acknowledges that the writer's intent is key to interpretation. Simultaneously, he doubts that intent can be discovered, and refuses to treat authorial intent as the final goal of all interpretation. This constellation of responses to intentionality reveals what is at stake in his new understanding of authorship. When authorial intent becomes a discrete category of exegesis, an important factor and yet not the ultimate concern, we can be sure that notion of authorial intentionality has arrived.

What is so fresh about Augustine's notion of authorship is his skepticism for hermeneutic endeavors that are narrowly conceived as attempts to ascertain the will or intention of the author. Augustine questions the ability of the interpreter to access this will, as well as the role any narrow determination of the scope of this authorial will should play in answering difficult interpretive questions.

> Sed quis nostrum sic invenit eam inter tam multa vera, quae in illis verbis aliter atque aliter intellectis occurrunt quaerentibus, ut tam fidenter dicat hoc sensisse Moysen atque hoc in illa narratione voluisse intellegi, quam fidenter dicit hoc verum esse, sive ille hoc senserit sive aliud?

> But which of us all can find out this full meaning, among those so many truths which the seekers shall everywhere meet with in those words, sometimes understood this way, and sometimes that way, so that he might confidently affirm, This Moses thought, and this would he have understood in that story, as he says confidently, This is true, whether he thought this or that?
>
> Augustine, *Confessions* XII.24, trans. Chadwick

Augustine has a sophisticated understanding of the problems involved in attempting to ascertain the meaning of the writings of Moses. The words of Moses are thought to contain multiple truths, from which each interpreter may be able to grasp less than the total. Augustine rejects the premise that these truths may be objectively tested according to the yardstick of "what Moses had in mind and what he meant us to understand by his words." The truer question is "what meanings can [the words of Moses] bear," rather than which of the several possible interpretations can be verified as having been intended by Moses.

It is interesting that the question of intention is being applied at all to the Bible. In fact, it is probable that the author's intention had been of little concern to ancient Greek scholarship. Even the Sophists described by Plato in the *Ion* as interested in ascertaining the *dianoia* of Homer probably did not conceive of this term as 'intention' or the implicit will that animated his verses. "Homer's *dianoia*" more likely applied to the general significance of a given passage, with "Homer" functioning as a kind of metonymy for epic as a whole. Authorial intention was hardly a matter that occupied early Jewish interpreters of scripture either. However, the question of authorial intention does appear to precede Augustine, and was the obsession of his fellow Christians, as the discussion in the *Confessions* reveals. This must have been facilitated by Roman legal discourse, where ascertaining the intention of a lawgiver or author plays a crucial role in the framing of legal argument and decision. The hermeneutic transfer from legal discourse to biblical interpretation was made easy by the fact that Moses was considered by Christians as the pre-eminent lawgiver. The shift in the hunt for intention from a legal sphere to a biblical one thus likely represents a development that is at once Roman and Christian.

It is important to put Augustine's sophisticated discussion in the context of ancient scholarship, rather than to consider it as a lost corrective to a modern Romantic fascination with the intention of the author of any sort of document. Augustine's gesture challenges the questions his early Christian compatriots were asking of the Bible. Unlike these individuals, Augustine is attempting to argue that Moses' writings are qualitatively different from the standard will or testament. The writings of Moses contain a multiplicity of meanings. Presumably Augustine would affirm the importance of ascertaining the intention of the writer of a legal testament or will. Thus, Augustine is not making a point about hermeneutics in general, but rather about the kind of hermeneutics that should be applied to the Bible. Moses' writings are too complicated and rich in truths to justify an approach that arbitrarily attempts to limit their possible interpretations, as if they had been composed on the order of a legal document. In other words, a complicated text calls for complicated interpretive techniques.

These matters really disturb Augustine, and he is not reticent in explaining the reasons why:

Nemo iam mihi molestus sit dicendo mihi: "non hoc sensit Moyses, quod tu dicis, sed hoc sensit, quod ego dico." Si enim mihi diceret: "unde scis hoc sensisse Moysen, quod de his verbis eqiu eloqueris?" aequo animo ferre deberem, et responderem fortasse, quae superius respondi vel aliquanto uberius, si esset durior. Cum vero dicit: "non hoc ille sensit, quod tu dicis, sed quod ego dico" neque tamen negat, quod uterque nostrum dicit, utrumque verum esse, o vita pauperum deus meus, in cuius sinu non est contradictio, plue mihi mitigationes in cor, ut patienter tales feram; qui non mihi hoc dicunt, quia divini sunt et in corde famuli tui viderunt quod dicunt, sed quia superbi sunt nec noverunt Moysi sententiam, sed amant suam, non quia vera est, sed quia sua est. Alioquin et aliam veram pariter amarent, sicut ego amo quod dicunt, quando verum dicunt, non quia ipsorum, sed quia verum est: et ideo ament illud, quia verum est, iam et ipsorum est et meum est, quoniam in commune omnium est veritatis amatorum. Illud autem, quod contendunt non hoc sensisse Moysen, quod ego dico, sed quod ipsi dicunt, nolo, non amo, quia etsi ita est, tamen ista temeritas non scientiae, sed audaciae iest, nec visus, sed typhus eam peperit. Ideoque, domine, tremenda sunt iudicia tua, quoniam veritas tua nec mea est nec illius aut illius, sed omnium nostrum, quos ad eius communionem publice vocas, terribiliter admonens nos, ut nolimus eam habere privatam, ne privemur ea. Nam quisquis id, quod tu omnibus ad fruendum proponis, sibi proprie vindicat, et suum vult esse quod omnium est, a communi propellitur ad sua, hoc est a veritate ad mendacium. Qui enim loquitur mendacium, de suo loquitur.

Let no one irritate me further by saying, "Moses did not mean what you say. He meant what I say." If anyone were to ask me "How do you know that Moses meant his words to be taken in the way the you explain them?" it would be my duty to listen to the question with composure, and in answer I should give the explanation which I have already given, perhaps rather more fully if the questioner were slow to understand. But when a man says "Moses did not mean what you say, but what I say," and yet does not deny that both his interpretation and mine are consistent with the truth, then, O Life of the poor, O my God, in whose bosom there is no contradiction, I beg you to water my heart with the rain of forbearance, so that I may bear with such people in patience. They speak as they do, not because they are men of God or because they have seen in the heart of Moses, your servant, that their explanation is the right one, but simply because they are proud. They have no knowledge of the thoughts of his mind, but they are in love with their own opinions, not because they are true, but because they are their own. If this were not so, they would have equal respect for the opinions of others, provided that they were consistent with the truth, just as I respect their opinions when they do not depart from the truth, not because the opinions are theirs, but because they are within the truth. And in fact for the very reason that they are true, these opinions are not their own property.

Augustine, *Confessions* XII.25, trans. Chadwick

The objection to this approach to interpretation is that its practitioners take pride from their own statements about the text, as if they were property, and derived from the interpreter rather than from the text.[45] Further, Augustine laments that the intention of Moses is equated with a single possible interpretation, rather than with all the possible interpretations that are consistent with the truth, or do not depart from it.[46]

Augustine even goes so far as to imagine what Moses might say if he were living today. His caveat is reminiscent of Paul's distrust of the evidence derived from an angel from heaven or even from Paul himself, should either proclaim a gospel contrary to what had already been revealed (as appears in Galatians 1:8).

> Si ipse Moyses apparuisset nobis atque dixisset: "hoc cogitavi," nec sic eam videremus, sed crederemus?

> Even if Moses himself were to appear to us and say "This is what I meant," isn't it true that we would not merely by him saying so see his point, but rather take his point on faith?
> Augustine, *Confessions* XII.25, trans. Chadwick

Moses isn't the best interpreter of his own writing, according to Augustine, even if his own interpretation would have to be accepted by virtue of trust in his stature rather than after having been convinced by argument.

Augustine's answer to biblical hermeneutics is that the text is fully capable of accommodating multiple interpretations:

Ita cum alius dixerit: "hoc sensit, quod ego," et alius: "immo illud, quod ego," religiosius me arbitror dicere: cur non utrumque potius, si utrumque verum est, et si quid terium et si quid terium et si quid quartum et si quid omnino aliud verum quispiam in his verbis videt, cur non illa omnia vidisse credatur, per quem deus unus sacras litteras vera et diversa visuris multorum sensibus temperavilt? Ego certe quod interepidus de meo corde pronuntio, si ad culmen auctoritatis aliquid scriberem, sic mallem scribere, ut, quod veri quisque de his rebus capere posset, mea verba resonarent, quam ut unam veram sententiam ad hocapertius ponerem,ut excluderem ceteras, quarum falsitas me non posset offendere. Nolo itaque, deus meus, tam praeceps esse, ut hoc illum virum de te meruisse non credam. Sensit ille omnino in his verbis atque cogitavit, cum ea scriberet, quidquid hic veri potuimus aut nondum potuimus, et tamen in eis inveniri potest.

For this reason, although I hear people say "Moses meant as I do" or "Moses the very same that I do," I think it more truly religious to say "Why should he not have meant it as you both mean, if both are true?" And if others see in the same words a third, or a fourth, or any number of true meanings, why should we not believe that Moses saw them all? There is only one God, who caused Moses to write the Holy Scriptures in the way suited to the minds of great numbers of men who would all see truths in them, though not the same truths in each case. For my part I declare resolutely and with all my heart that if I were called upon to write a book which was to be vested with the highest authority (*auctoritas*), I should prefer to write it in such a way that my words might carry the sound of any truth with them that anyone could discern concerning these matters. I would rather write in this way than impose a single true meaning so explicitly that it would exclude all others, even though they contained no falsehood that could give me offence. I will not be so rash, my God, as to not assume that so great a man as Moses deserved as much. As he wrote these words, he was aware of all that they implied. He was conscious of every truth that we can deduce from them and of others besides that we cannot, or cannot yet, find in them, but can nevertheless there be found.

Augustine, *Confessions* XII.31, trans. Chadwick

The passage clearly puts scripture on a different plane than other texts, and makes clear that Augustine's debate is not about interpretation in general but about biblical hermeneutics in particular. Nevertheless, the ability of Augustine to put himself in the shoes of the inspired prophets who wrote down scripture is remarkable, and represents a shift from the relatively uncomplicated speculation on such matters by Origen or Jerome. There's a kind of gentleman's nod to the reader here, as if Augustine is willing to countenance that readers are not slaves to writers (even writers of scripture), and should be allowed to find meaning where it had not been noticed before. At the same time, he promotes an omniscient vision of the author (in contrast to his speculation in *De Doctrina Christiana* III.27.38, cited above) as having intended all possible legitimate interpretations.

What prevents this procedure from resulting in an abuse of the text by the interpreter is the heartfelt desire to make all interpretations accord with the truth or what is correct:

> Omnes quidem, qui legimus, nitimur hoc indagare atque conprehendere, quod voluit ille quem legimus, et <u>cum eum veridicum credimus, nihil, quod falsum esse vel novimus vel putamus, audemus eum existimare dixisse.</u> Dum ergo quisque conatur id sentire in scripturis sanctis, quod in eis sensit ille qui scripsit, quid mali est, si hoc sentiat, quot tu, lux omnium veridicarum mentium, ostendis verum esse, <u>etiamsi non hoc sensit ille, quem legit, cum et ille verum nec tamen hoc senserit?</u>

> In Bible study all of us are trying to find and grasp the meaning of the author we are reading, and <u>when we believe him to be revealing truth, we do not dare to think he said anything which we either know or think to be incorrect.</u> As long as each interpreter is endeavoring to find in the holy scriptures the meaning of the author who wrote it, what evil is it if an exegesis he gives is one shown to be true by you, light of all sincere souls, <u>even if the author he is reading did not have that idea and, though he had grasped a truth, had not discerned that seen by the interpreter?</u>
>
> Augustine, *Confessions* XII.18, trans. Chadwick

Augustine's approach to this question is not perfectly consistent; the author is at one point aware of all possible interpretations, and at another point, he does not necessarily have such knowledge.[47] Nevertheless, the overall effect is clear. Biblical interpretation should not consist of an attempt to use the author's intent to foreclose other true and meaningful interpretations.

The location of Augustine as a pioneer of the concept of authorship might be thought to fall down on several counts. He doesn't address the situation of authors of non-biblical works. He doesn't consider himself as an author worthy of the same hermeneutic scrutiny as Moses, apart from a hypothetical statement about what his mind-frame would be if he were to write holy scripture.[48] Thus Moses and the other prophets would appear to be the only individuals worthy of consideration as authors.[49] He never formulates a conception of the author as the governor of his work, as the individual who stands apart from it and to whose will or intention it is entirely subject. He never promulgates a theory of authorship in which originality rather than traditional authoritativeness is the measure of the writer; nor does he arrive at a doctrine of artistic *creatio ex nihilo*, of imagination and genius, or of a conception of the human author as analogous to the divine. Each of these belongs to successive stages in the development of authorship in Western civilization.[50] Nevertheless, Augustine, while denying that the will of the author reigns supreme over the work, has formulated an idea of the writer as having a will or intention that interpretation must take into account in determining the meaning of the text. A number of different historical processes would be required for this startlingly new notion to manifest itself in ways that suggest the over-ripeness of the author concept to postmodern sensibilities — ways that Augustine never intended.

Central to Augustine's creation of authorship stands the idea of the writer with an intention or will, and of a text, demonstrated to have originated at the hands of a named writer of stature, conveying truths at least in part consistent with this will, although quite possibly at odds with it. This idea of the will derived from Roman legal hermeneutics and Greek ethical and theological discourse, and was honed on Augustine's biblical and autobiographical investigations. Augustine employs the notion of will to ascertain the intent of the Jewish writer of scripture, originally conceived merely as a prophetic scribe who had been given the dispensation to record divine and human truths. But he could not help viewing the writer through a Hellenistic lens, marked by its concern for ascertaining the authenticity of textual ascriptions, and its penchant for memorializing the literary accomplishments of victorious poets in lists, libraries, and canons.

# CONCLUSION

The institution of authorship in the Western tradition results from an amalgamation of Jewish views on the provenance of scripture and Hellenistic attribution analysis, accomplished by early Christian hermeneutics. Since they were taken up by Christian scriptural interpretation, Jewish and Hellenistic exegetical traditions that assigned names to texts and investigated the nature of the relationship of individuals to texts, either as composers or textualizers, have had a impact on both sacred and profane thought in the Western tradition. The trajectory of this ascension of authorship — an ascension in the sense of a rise to prominence under the aegis of Christianity — is worth reviewing here.

I have traced the history of Jewish traditions exploring the relations between text formation or transmission and individuals, beginning with the editorial statements found within the biblical text that mark off books and chapters of the Bible. The Psalm headings, which have been dated to the early Second Temple period, provide a case and point. They reveal an early interest in attaching names to anonymously composed texts on the part of biblical editors and scribes. Scholars have suggested that they were preceded by cata-logues resembling Akkadian colophons, and were reformatted by biblical editors in a way that sometimes resulted in confusion on the part of later interpreters.

The interpretive history of the Psalms also provides an exam-ple of the evolution and variety of Jewish perspectives on individual composition during the Second Temple period and thereafter. The corpus of Psalms, although likely anonymous at the start, was linked to David at an early date; however, the precise nature of David's input was frequently re-evaluated. It seems likely that David was initially conceptualized as a singer and composer of songs, but gradually came to be viewed as a prophet or a scribe. Davidic attri-bution was used as a badge of authoritativeness for psalms that cir-culated in religious communities such as Qumran or that were not part of the standard Temple Psalter (those psalms kept in the Tem-ple archives by the priests). The evidence from Qumran indicates that some Jewish interpreters attempted to link David in as many ways possible both to the standard Psalter as well as to other psalms that only circulated outside the Temple archives.

Judging from the testimony of Josephus, attributions were used as justification for exclusion as well as inclusion of works into the Temple archives. Some Jewish interpreters evidently relied on attribution as a means of dating a book, and more to the point, as a means of determining whether it could be authoritative. A post-Artaxerxes (post-Ezra) attribution precluded a work from attaining authoritative status, much as if it had been ascribed to a pre-Mosaic composer.

It should be emphasized that anonymous literary composition was originally acceptable in Israelite literary culture, at least when it came to what were initially regarded as non-revelatory mediums — historical accounts, songs, or proverbs. But for the majority of late Second Temple Jewish exegetes, no authoritative text was able to remain unattributed. Textual attributions were invariably deduced from clues in the text, using midrashic techniques; genre consider-ations would also play a role. All texts that were part of the priestly archive of authoritative biblical documents were claimed to have originated with individuals of repute. Josephus refined this idea, claiming that scripture had been textualized by a succession of prophets who alone had been given the dispensation to record historical events. Josephus arrived at the notion of a succession of prophets on the basis of earlier Jewish models like Ben Sira, through comparison with Plato's description of the Greek oracles.

Josephus is a witness for a moment in the transformation of a set of texts from one stage of canonization to another. As anthropologist Maurice Bloch has shown, the social (that is, a process initiated by individuals or institutions) cannot determine a society's symbolic formations (including rituals and religious traditions) in the short term or at a single moment in time. However, attention to individual actors and moments in time can reveal the principles of transformation of these symbolic formations. An approach to canonization that addresses a variety of historical periods in which scripture was reconceptualized is thus able to articulate the principles of transformation by which a canon is constructed, although it is inadequate in making claims about the origin of the canon. Bloch's observation explains why the scholarly debate over whether the canon of Hebrew scriptures was closed in the second century B.C.E. or at the end of the first century C.E. overvalues the capability for the social to determine the symbolic. Both sides of the debate choose a single moment in time as the origination for a complex symbolic system — the collection of a body of texts representing revelation, history, law, wisdom, ritual, and liturgy. They draw from ancient accounts, which often aggrandize the role of legendary individuals (such as Ezra, Nehemiah, Judas Maccabee, and Rabbi Akiva) or institutions (the Great Assembly or the academy at Yavne) in canon formation. Accordingly, modern scholarly reconstructions tend to overvalue both these individuals and institutions, but underemphasize the powerlessness that individuals and institutions must have felt in making real decisions about the contents of scripture. Extrapolating on Bloch's insight, I would argue that no individual made a decision to close the canon, although they clearly made other sorts of decisions that made its closing a *fait accompli*.

Bloch's approach thus suggests that there is no moment at which canon formation can have been fixed, or even at which it was decided that books could not be added to the collection. In all probability, at no point did the collectors of scriptures make any sort of decision about the contents of the scriptures other than ascertaining the prophetic status of the text's scribe, the time in which he lived, and the authenticity of this attribution. They never decided to close the canon, but only ceased to recognize newly discovered works on the grounds that their prophetic provenance was unacceptable or their textual history was suspect. The collectors of the Hebrew scriptures evidently believed that all the scriptures in the Temple archives had been recorded by the prophet Moses and his successors, ending with the destruction of the first Commonwealth in 586 B.C.E. and with those prophets who had lived through the exile. Nevertheless, biblical books were patently composed later than the time of the return from the Babylonian exile, and were included in the archives because they were perceived to derive from an acceptable source.

Possibly, a change did take place by the time of Judas Maccabee, who is described as reassembling "Nehemiah's library." It would appear that Judas thought of himself as preserving a finite quantity of texts that all derived from the time of Nehemiah, little recognizing that "Nehemiah's library" might have designated the *archive* Nehemiah had instituted or the scrolls he had begun to gather.[1] Thus, it was likely Judas who unwittingly redefined the living archive as a closed collection, since he thought it had been closed centuries ago. By the time of Josephus, trust in the Temple archives themselves made all inquiries about textual history moot; only those works guaranteed to by the archives and the priests that kept them could be demonstrated as deriving from the prophets to whom they were attributed.

The three-letter rabbinic acronym for the Hebrew scriptures, *tanakh* (*tnk*), represents a threefold designation for scripture; it has long been understood that this threefold form pre-dated rabbinic Judaism. I have argued that although the Judaism of Josephus' day shared a threefold categorization of scripture with rabbinic Judaism, the contents and meaning of two of their respective categories had only a superficial similarity. The category represented by the "n" in *tanakh* (standing for *nevi'im* 'Prophets') included far more books during the Second Temple period than it did in later Jewish lists of scriptures. By the time of the composition of the *baraita* in Baba Bathra 14b (prior to 200 C.E.), many of these books had migrated to the third category, *ketuvim* 'Writings', which had begun to acquire a heightened sacredness in rabbinic exegesis. I have suggested that the term *nevi'im* 'Prophets' originally designated those books that had been copied out by a prophetic witness, rather than books about prophets or which merely included their utterances.

From the evidence of Josephus (who speaks with knowledge about a variety of sectarian positions on this question), late Second Temple Judaism considered all of the books of the Bible to be "books of the prophets," with the exception of the Psalms (traditionally associated with David) and three "edifying books" (most scholars agree these consisted of the works traditionally associated with Solomon). David was considered by some to be a composer of the Psalms, but he was not recognized as part of the prophetic succession by Josephus. In fact, while David was sometimes described as prophesying, he is openly called a prophet only in Acts 2:30. It wasn't until the rabbinic period that David and Solomon were both regularly considered prophets. Their initial status as kings rather than prophets explains why neither David's Psalms nor Solomon's books could be included in Josephus' category of prophetic books. For Josephus, the category "books of prophecy" meant those books written down by individuals in the prophetic succession, imagined as a quasi-genetic lineage of prophets who designated a successor prior to death.

In contrast to Josephus, the *baraita* in Baba Bathra 14b ("Who wrote the scriptures?") does not take special note of the prophetic status of the copyists of books that appear in the category *nevi'im* 'Prophets'. As I have stressed, this *baraita* is interested in assigning scribes to books, but not in claiming that each scribe is part of the prophetic succession. In short, the meaning of the category *nevi'im* is no longer understood by the *baraita* as referring to the textualizers of the books it comprises. By elevating David and Solomon to prophet status, rabbinic exegetes reconceptualized the books of the Bible. It was now assumed that all biblical books had been *uttered* by prophets, and thus ultimately by God; these books could no longer be considered as historical events or prayers or wise words that were trustworthy because they had been *recorded* by prophets. Accordingly, the original distinction between the Second Temple period analogues to the categories *nevi'im* 'Prophets' and *ketuvim* 'Writings' was lost.

The reason that these categories began to change partly lies in the evolving status of the third category, the books Josephus classifies as "psalms and edifying books." When the Psalms and the works of Solomon (especially the Song of Songs) came to be viewed as sacred scripture, the third category (eventually known as *ketuvim* 'Writings') could no be longer considered of lesser authority than the second. Works from the second category that seemed most to resemble the contents of the third category could now be grouped together. These works were reclassified as "Writings" rather than works copied by prophets. Works from the third category were even described as having been initially uttered or composed at Mt. Sinai; they were no longer to be considered merely books describing historical events.

Josephus, speaking as a literary critic, is the first in the Jewish tradition to present authorship (which he had no name for) as the writing of fiction or inaccurate history. His critique of Greek letters represents an astute commentary on the nature of Greek competitiveness. Indeed, Greek literary culture was thoroughly influenced by the passion of all Greeks for games and for achieving victory in ritual contests. This passion also manifested itself in the scholarly penchant for preserving the memory of the great games and their victorious participants for eternity in the form of lists. These lists commemorated the concept of victory itself, rather than the poet or the composition, and subordinated the poet to the contest.

The advent of Alexandrian scholarship brought about a new approach, although it was one that had been anticipated by the fourth century Athenian heroization of Aeschylus, Sophocles, and Euripides, and the scripturalization of their works. Alexandrian scholars demonstrated an interest in investigating the works of a given playwright, rather than in the dynamics of the contests themselves (this may be seen in the Callimachus' revision of the Aristotelian lists of victors at the tragic and comic contests in Athens). Moreover, these scholars saw the figure of the poet as instrumental in assessing and organizing literary works. The very arrangement of scrolls in the Alexandrian library led to and was the product of an intensification of scholarly focus on the writer. This period marks an increase in interest directed towards second and third-tier writers, as well as a refinement of the Aristotelian approach to the investigation of literary attributions. In part, the sharp increase in interest in attribution analysis was animated by a debate as to where individual scrolls should be shelved and how they should be listed in the library catalogues.

The genre of authorial biography was also influenced by the Hellenistic scholarly approach to writers. Since the sixth century B.C.E., authorial biographies had derived their insights about the writer from the texts themselves. But in the second century, authorial biography began to investigate which works had really been written by a given writer. These new biographies eschewed legendary treatments of writers in favor of a more sober catalogue of details about the author's life garnered from independent research.

The discourse of grammar itself helped bring about the new view of the writer. Through the insights of grammar, the stylistic devices of the writer were laid bare to scholars. These devices became part of the curriculum, for literary style was a fundamental feature of the 'exemplar' or 'model' that students composing speeches were required to emulate. Grammar focused on the literary style peculiar to each author, in order that students might improve their literary abilities and compose in the manner of past masters. The study of an orator's style became a central part of the Alexandrian conceptualization of the nature of the writer. Concurrently, the writer became identifiable as a discrete and coherent entity in part by being the object of the discourse of grammar.

The focus on style was also required to locate the spurious works that resulted from the student's more successful attempts at emulating his or her literary predecessors, as well as from outright forgery or plagiarism. This procedure, called *krisis poiêmatôn* 'attribution analysis', was a way of testing whether an individual wrote the works he had been credited with by tradition. It formed an integral part of the filing and cataloguing of the works of the great libraries, represented part of the investigation of Alexandrian literary biographers, and served as the highest task of the discipline of grammar.

Grammar was a discipline closely linked to Alexandria and its famous library. Echoing the rivalry between the rulers of Alexandria and Pergamum, Alexandrian scholarship found itself in conflict with a contrasting approach to literary criticism practiced at Pergamum by its librarian, Crates. In addition, the conflict between the libraries likely manifested itself in Pergamum's claim to have the very version of Homer established by Peisistratus. In contrast, the Alexandrians prided themselves on possessing Aristotle's personal library, and on their use of Aristotelian criticism to reconstruct the correct text as Homer himself had written it.

Searching for the origin of the practice of attribution analysis, Greek scholars such as Galen in the second century C.E. looked to the time of the formation of the great libraries at Pergamum and Alexandria over four centuries earlier. Galen's hypothesis was that forgery had resulted from competition for valuable texts on the part of rival Hellenistic rulers. However, ancient legends documented that Peisistratus, rather than the Alexandrians and Pergamenes, had been responsible for the introduction of literary imposture. It was almost inevitable that the story of Peisistratus and his rescue of the text of Homer would eventually be conflated with accounts of Ptolemy's creation of the library at Alexandria. Accordingly, aspects of Ptolemy's role in the translation of the Septuagint were incorporated into the account of the textualization of the Homeric epics. The resulting legend, which functions as an aetiology of literary imposture for the Byzantine discourse of grammar, also represents an attempt to take the wind out of the sails of Jewish and Christian legends about the Septuagint. It does so by implying that key elements of the Septuagint translation legend more properly applied to the textualization of the Homeric epics.

In the Jewish tradition, what mattered was the legitimacy of the textual transmission of a sacred document. Had it been preserved in the Temple archives? Was it recorded by an individual who belonged to the succession of prophets? Greek scholarship rarely assumed the accuracy of the textual attribution and typically questioned the integrity of the transmission of a given text. There were, however, some in the Greek tradition who challenged the moral legitimacy of any given writer (e.g. Plato) or the successes of the writer in encapsulating the values of Greek *paideia* 'culture'. Thus the Athenian "canonization" of the three great tragedians was likely conceived as a memorialization of Athenian values, rather than simply as a choice of the most effective playwrights.[2] Greek doubt about the authenticity of every word of a given text, and about the general applicability of the name to the text, became an important part of the methodological approach of Christian scholars evaluating the authenticity of New Testament writings. Appreciation for the moralistic tendencies in Greek criticism likely facilitated the Christian assumption of Hellenistic exegesis and scholarly methods, such as allegorical hermeneutics on the one hand, and the Aristotelian method favored by Alexandrian scholarship on the other.

Christian scholars combined Greek attribution analysis with a Jewish approach to textual legitimacy, which held that the legitimacy of a text could be validated by considering the prophetic dispensation of its textualizer and verifying the conditions of its transmission. Attribution analysis was used by these scholars to challenge the authoritativeness of works composed by anti-catholic, unorthodox, or Gnostic Christians that appeared to masquerade as scripture. But early Christian scholars also favored a legend about the textualization of the Bible associated with Ezra. The Ezra story was used to defend works viewed as scripture by the early church against charges that their textual transmission had been compromised. In effect, Christianity allowed itself a fallback clause in case attribution analysis proved too restrictive.

The combination of Greek and Jewish approaches to the relationship between names and texts achieved some startling results. On the one hand, religious confrontations between competing versions of Christianity could now take place within the discourse of grammar and its methodology of attribution analysis. Marcion claimed that the Christian New Testament had been forged by Jewish sympathizers, and produced his own copy of an anonymous gospel and Pauline letters. Christians like Tertullian responded with their own use of attribution analysis. He concluded that New Testament texts must be attributed in order to have any authority. Unnamed texts could only be persuasive to Marcionites or other heretics; according to Tertullian, each text must have its own *auctor* 'author' or 'agent'. This marks a significant development in the development of authorship, although it perhaps originates in the Jewish suspicion of unattributed texts.

St. Jerome listed himself among the famous ecclesiastical authors in his work that catalogued them. This indicates his self-awareness as a writer, and contrasts with the Alexandrian reticence towards ranking contemporaneous authors in their list of first-class writers. Jerome's action may be interpreted as a gesture of arrogance; however it is more likely that he did not conceive of the writer as having an authority only available to the giants of the past. Although in the middle Ages the Latin term *auctor* would come to refer to past authorities exclusively, Jerome, in a Callimachean vein, is probably more interested in creating a complete catalogue of church writers.[3]

St. Augustine, even more than Jerome, recognized the author's status as a biographic entity and human individual. He is perhaps the first to fully consider the implications of the fact that writers of scripture were human beings. He asserts that readers are not slaves to the writers of scripture, and should be allowed to find whatever meaning the text will allow. The words of Moses are thought by Augustine to contain multiple truths, from which each interpreter may be able to grasp less than the total. He promotes an omniscient vision of the divine author as having intended all possible interpretations, but denies human authors, including Moses, this power. Augustine's focus on will or intent of both human and divine author, combined with his acknowledgement of the existence of meanings unintended by the author, indicates a new conceptualization of authorship.

This view of the author is still far from the modern Western notion. Thus, Augustine never formulates a conception of the author as the governor of his work, as the individual who stands apart from it and to whose will or intention it is subject. He doesn't conceive of the author as a font of originality. These would be the responses of later generations of critics from the Renaissance to the Romantics, who imagined the author as a kind of creator deity. Nor does Augustine conceive of the author as the owner of his work, a legal fiction that enabled publishing houses to gain title to a work as if it were an alienable form of property. Augustine's accomplish-

ment is to acknowledge the *auctor* as a willing actor and an invol-
untary agent, at one and the same time.

    While this study has focused on what divides Greek and Jew-
ish approaches to the writers of texts, it is important here also to
take stock of their similarities. Both Greeks and Jews used the individual as a means of ascertaining the authoritativeness of the
text. For Jews, the individual amounted to the provenance of the
information conveyed in the text and the trustworthiness of this information. Greeks similarly judged the authoritativeness of information contained in a work by the name to which it was ascribed.
For both cultures, authorship was the primary way to judge authoritativeness, even if they had radically different ideas about how
much "authoritativeness" individual writers had (and the Greeks
were by no means univocal on this question).

    Nevertheless, the dominant Greek view of the writer as cre-
ative individual couldn't be more different from the Jewish conception of the prophetic scribe. It is therefore puzzling that a
combination of these two approaches could have served as the
foundation for a conceptualization of authorship promulgated by
early Christian scholars. Their version of authorship constitutes a
powerful myth about the nature of the inspired artist that has dominated Western thought ever since. It is even likely that the pre-
eminent place of the idea of authorship in Western civilization is
perversely sustained by the sense of contradiction inherent to its
cultural components.

    Christian exegetes created a new notion of authorship by com-
bining a belief in prophetic agency and divine inspiration with a focus on accuracy in the attribution of texts to individuals. The
mechanism by which decisions about the authenticity of a given
scriptural work were made involved a process of debate and discussion among respected figures of the Church, although the practices of Christian communities were also influential. This process is
perhaps a survival of the Greek *agôn* 'contest', a ritualized social
gathering traditionally employed to determine which individuals
were to be given status.[4] Of the models I have surveyed in the preceding chapters, the Christian manner of determining which works
or authors were inspired stands closest to the approach of Plato in
the *Laws* (as discussed in chapter 5). Seemingly alone among the

Greeks, Plato had depicted a society in which a panel of elders determined which individuals were to be allowed to create new literary works. This vision was not a glitch in an otherwise unbroken Greek allegiance to the poetic contest as the true testing ground for aspiring poets; it merely reconfigured the *agôn* as a juried competition to earn the right to compose. This Platonic, idealized approach tested authors for their moral fitness as poets.

The extent to which early Christianity employed an agonistic model in arriving at the contents of Christian scripture is not yet certain. If the *agôn* played a role, it was probably less in the form of the church councils; such councils have been over-emphasized by some scholars, and likely did not make truly pivotal decisions on the scriptural canon. Perhaps the debate between church congregations and church officials may be seen as a remnant of the Greek *agôn*, with "voting" accomplished through the informal polling of influential congregations and respected scholars. In any event, early Christians like Eusebius and St. Augustine did not shroud official judgements about texts in mystery. Rather than merely endorsing the opinions of the religious authorities that preceded them, they openly debated which works should be considered scripture. However, even they lacked the authority to contradict established ecclesiastical practice or the weight of previous tradition on this matter.

By incorporating Greek and Jewish approaches to the ratification of textual authority, the door was opened for these traditions to be combined in ways that were unforeseeable. Elements of Greek civilization would at times re-emerge; it may thus be said that in present day secular literary culture, the Greek *agôn* is responsible for choosing society's prophets.

The idea of an agonistic element in the formation of the Jewish canon appears to have been a fiction, resulting from a misunderstanding of one of the few verses of the Bible that gives a clue to biblical transmission — Proverbs 25:1. Spinoza, the first modern thinker to have speculated on the significance of a Council of Yavne, imagined the council to have served as a body voting on the authoritativeness of individual works of scripture, as if it were on the order of a Christian ecclesiastical council. The reality was quite different: early Judaism had no equivalent to the *agôn*. The Jews were horrified at Greek athletics and educational culture (with nakedness in the gymnasium, pagan rituals and sacrifices, and homosexuality standing out as especially odious). When Josephus describes the public ratification of the Septuagint, it is a travesty in terms of typical Greek contests, inasmuch as there are no competitors. Jews like Josephus were fundamentally opposed to Greek individualism in literature. There is also no valuation of democracy by the Jews, who praised monarchy and theocratic oligarchy instead. Individuals as well as institutions were fundamentally powerless in influencing the formation of the canon of the Hebrew Bible and disputing priestly tradition. The closing of the canon could only be described in hindsight as the ending of the succession of prophets, and was not accomplished by the decision of any council.

The consideration of valuations of the individual is essential to the investigation of the concept of canon as it existed in antiquity. From Alexandria, no list has survived, but scholars postulate the existence of a conception of an Alexandrian "canon" (although, contrary to current opinion, there is little evidence that it was referred to by this term). The Alexandrian selective lists were lists of first class authors, not lists of works. The authoritative biblical works listed by Josephus are interpreted by him as deriving from a succession of prophets, with the exception of four books of hymns and edifying literature, consisting of works credited to the greatest kings of ancient Israel, David and Solomon. Following a Jewish precedent, especially as described in the writings of Josephus, Christian works were only recognized as scripture if they had been attributed to one of eight writers from among the apostles, disciples, and their followers.

In each tradition there is a provision for ensuring that falsely attributed works not be considered part of the canon. For the Alexandrians, attribution analysis protected the authoritative list of first-class authors from being contaminated by works of inferior writers. It also protected texts from being augmented by inauthentic additions. For Josephus, the pureblooded priests of the Temple who alone had the right to approach the official biblical manuscripts stood as guarantors to the integrity of the works included in the scriptures, as well as to their transmission. Christian scriptures had to be recognized by the majority of churches and church scholars. But in Greek fashion, they had to pass the test of authenticity as well.

Jews avoided writing in their own name or attempting to gain renown from their writings. It is true that in rabbinic literature, legal rulings are often attributed to individual named rabbis (in continuation of the manner that attributions had functioned in the early Second Temple period). However, new authoritative works could only be compiled in an anonymous fashion from the statements of respected teachers. When a name is attached to an entire corpus of Jewish texts (such as the Mishnah, reputedly compiled by Rabbi Judah "the Prince"), it is meant to attest to the validity of the traditions assembled together there and to the reliability of their textual transmission. The early Christian literary tradition followed suit. The gospels were originally anonymous, and were only later attributed to Matthew, Mark, Luke, and John. The writings of Paul hang on his name and persona because they are epistles, and were not conceived as scripture at their composition. In addition to the titles that were affixed to each text, the attributions of New Testament documents to eight writers were accomplished by a complex network of interlocking references created by the editors of the collection.

One portion of the Christian amalgamation of authorship can be summed up in the following way. Authorship is the product of a classical and especially Hellenistic Greek literary discourse that sought to account for and explain the nature of a given text by linking its features to the circumstances of its origin, namely, to the life of its creator. This aetiological discourse came to employ ever more sophisticated techniques to establish the reliability of its attributions and to draw increased insight from them. Authorship is thus the creation of a social practice by which individuals were endowed with responsibility and credit for the creation of a text. As such, it is continually transformed by whatever rights, privileges, remuneration, and posthumous honors this creation is awarded by a given society.

Conversely and perversely, Christian authorship involves the societal or religious authority that derives from an author's apparent lack of agency in the promulgation of eternal truths or a divine message. This amounts to an irreducibly religious aspect of authorship. It too has a history, and can be traced back to a tendency in Judaism that allowed for the preservation of texts that were accompanied by or associated with names of unarguable stature.

Owing to its revelatory qualities, not to mention its social, legal, literary, and bibliographic dimensions, authorship cannot reveal its mysteries through any limited combination of aesthetic, psychological, sociological, theological, historical, or biographical inquiries about its nature. Moreover, the nature of authorship is typically re-mystified by studies that investigate individual authors. These investigations generally underestimate the significance of authorship itself as a historically contingent social practice. Whenever the prescient qualities of an individual's creations are pointed to, one may assume that the religious underpinnings of western authorship are at stake. Further, such investigations perpetuate the author's prophetic societal role by misidentifying these qualities as resulting from the author's innate abilities or peculiar worldview, or from a mysterious and perplexingly creative dialectic involving his or her immediate precursors, surrounding society, or readers. One such tendency, frequent in ostensibly secular literary studies, labels thinkers, writers, and artists who anticipate a cultural or historical trend as prophetic or visionary. What is characterized as such does not merely correspond to inherent features of a given work. Most would not admit that it derives from any genuine fortune-telling ability on the part of the work's creator. That which is perceived as visionary in the arts represents the underlying religious foundation of the notion of authorship showing its muscle and calling secular literary discourse on its word.

The history of interpretation is inextricably bound to the peculiar and influential Christian understanding of authorship advanced by St. Augustine. His approach to authorship is articulated in the context of a discussion on how to interpret scripture in general (*On Christian Doctrine*) and the words of Moses in particular (the *Confessions*). In the procedure outlined in these works, biblical texts are not analyzed in themselves and without reference to external factors (as in the Protestant doctrine *sola scriptura* taken to an extreme); Augustine does not separate texts from their origin as the words of an inspired but human author. Nevertheless, the relationship between author and text can never be used to explain a text in a definitive manner, nor can it foreclose possible interpretations.

The resulting Christian understanding of authorship is confusing: authorial intention is a gnawing concern for interpretation, but it is ultimately un-knowable, and in any case is not a make-or-break factor in determining textual meaning. This complex approach to authorial intention continues to haunt most forms of textual interpretation, because it was present at the birth of hermeneutics and the ascension of authorship, and because its historical origins have never been properly understood. Conversely, authorship is henceforward shaped by its intimate connection to scriptural hermeneutics (as it had previously been shaped by other approaches to interpretation). More to the point, the very nature of modern authorship is, consequently, theologically determined, and is religious through and through. Authorship is stuck with Augustine's Hellenized perspective on the strange and undeterminable relationship between Moses and scripture.

# NOTES

INTRODUCTION

1. I am employing the word 'legend' to designate a narrative composed of historical and/or fictional elements that is viewed or portrayed as a historical account by the society or individuals that created it.

2. Michel Foucault, "What is an Author?" in *The Foucault Reader*, ed. Paul Rabinow, pp. 101–120. Foucault's study is comparable in many respects to Marcel Mauss' last essay, "A Category of the Human Mind: the Notion of Person; the Notion of Self," published in 1938. Mauss sketches a social history of the evolution of the concept of the self in both Western and traditional societies. Foucault was highly influenced by the approach of the French school of sociology and ethnography represented by Mauss and his successors. See Michael Carruthers, Steven Collins, and Steven Lukes, eds., *The Category of the Person*. This monograph includes an English translation of Mauss' essay (pp. 1–25), together with a variety of articles on it.

3. See Seán Burke, *The Death & Return of the Author: Criticism and Subjectivity in Barthes, Foucault and Derrida* (Edinburgh: Edinburgh University Press, 1992).

4. Cf. Karl Kelchner Hulley, "Principles of Textual Criticism Known to St. Jerome," *Harvard Studies in Classical Philology*, 55 (1944), esp. pp. 104–109.

5. Michel Foucault, "What is An Author?" p. 108.

6. Jacques Derrida, "Signature, Event, Context," in *Margins of Philosophy*, p. 328.

7. Ibid.

8. Maurice Bloch, *From Blessing to Violence*, p. 193.

9. Ibid., p. 194.

10. Hegel, *Science of Logic*, in Stephen Houlgate, ed., *The Hegel Reader*, pp. 194–5.

11. James Kugel, "The 'Bible As Literature' in Late Antiquity and the Middle Ages," *Hebrew University Studies in Literature and the Arts* 11(1983), p. 64.

12. Rudolf Blum, *Kallimachos: The Alexandrian Library and the Origins of Bibliography*, p. 157.

13. Andrew Ford, *The Origins of Criticism*, pp. 131–57.

14. This followed from a wider trend that distinguished specialists in the arts. For instance, in the sixth century, signatures began to distinguish painters from makers of pots. Ibid., p. 134.

15. Ibid., pp. 138–9.

16. Rudolf Blum, *Kallimachos: The Alexandrian Library and the Origins of Bibliography*, p. 25 and p. 72 n. 64. Blum cites Reisch (1905) and Pickard-Cambridge (1968), pp. 71 and 84–86.

17. Ibid., p. 25 and p. 72 n. 70.

CHAPTER 1: THE SCRIBES OF THE HEBREW BIBLE

1. See the critical edition of Baba Bathra by Shraga Abramson, ed., *Massekhet Bava Batra*, with translation and commentary.

2. The *baraita* actually begins a few paragraphs earlier with the question, "What is the order of the Prophets?"

3. The reading of the Escorial manuscript here is *sefer* 'book, scroll' rather than *parashah* 'portion', although later on (II.E) the reading is reversed. See below, n. 6.

4. Several manuscripts (Munich, Florence, Paris, Escorial) insert the word *sefer* 'scroll, book' before "Judges" (i.e. "the Book of Judges").

5. In contrast, the Paris manuscript states here that Moses wrote "five books."

6. Several manuscripts (e.g., Munich, Florence) here state that Moses copied out the scroll (*sefer*) of Balaam and Job rather than their portion (*parashah*). However, *parashah* is the reading in these manuscripts in the initial statement of the *baraita*. Cf. the Escorial manuscript, which has the order reversed. On the manuscript alteration, see Sid Leiman, *The Canonization of Hebrew Scripture,* pp. 163–165 n. 260, citing R. Rabbinovicz, *Diqduqey Sofrim, Baba Bathra,* ad loc.

7. H. M. I. Gevaryahu, "Biblical Colophons: A Source for the 'Biography' of Authors, Texts and Books," *Supplements to Vetus Testamentum* 28 (1975), pp. 50–1.

8. For a detailed consideration of whether the prophets were considered the authors of their prophecies, see Y. Amir's discussion of Philo's *De Vita Mosis,* where the philosopher delineates the three varieties of revelation of God's word to his "authors." Y. Amir, "Philo," in Martin Jan Mulder, ed., *Mikra: Text, Translation, Reading, and Interpretation of the Hebrew Bible in Ancient Judaism and Early Christianity,* pp. 421–454.

9. Both Baba Bathra and Midrash Tehillim agree that Ethan the Ezrahite is the same as Abraham, but Baba Bathra includes Solomon, while Midrash Tehillim includes even David in its list, but excludes Heman and Yeduthun. On the other hand, Qoheleth Rabbah 7.19.4 seems to assume that there is no controversy over the names Adam, Abraham, Moses, David, and Solomon, yet records controversy over the rest. The list is finished off with (according to Rab) Asaph, Heman, Yeduthun, the three sons of Korah (who are counted as one), and Ezra. According to R. Joḥanan, Asaph is one of the sons of Korah yet is also counted separately because he is said to have prophesied (in 1 Chron. 25:2), while Jeduthun refers to Asaph's prophecy concerning the laws — in other words, Jeduthun is not a name of one of the ten elders. In a parallel passage (Shir Ha-Shirim Rabbah 4.4.1), it is specified that R. Joḥanan considers Asaph, Heman, and Jeduthun to be the same person. All of these texts, however, manage to arrive at the figure of ten wise authors.

10. For a discussion of medieval views on the expression, see Uriel Simon, *Four Approaches to the Book of Psalms:* "Saadiah totally ignores the Talmudic assertions that the psalms were composed by David along with 'ten elders'" (viii); "ironically, [the Karaites'] conception of the Psalms

as prophetic prayers brought these rejecters of the Oral Law close to the view of the Talmudic sages" (ix).

11. Thanks to Bernard Septimus, who writes (*per litteras* February 9, 1998): "The translation *including in it* the work of ten elders apparently derives from Rashi, who is however explaining — not translating." Rashi's words on the expression are as follows: "עַל יְדֵי עֲשָׂרָה זְקֵנִים" (including in it the work of ten elders): He wrote in it [i.e., the Book of Psalms] the words which the ten elders composed (*'amru*) [and] which were before him; some of these elders lived in his own time, namely Asaph, Heman, and Yeduthun, who were among the Levites who sang at the Temple." Rashi goes on to enumerate the Psalms that had originally been composed by Adam, Melchizedek, Heman etc. His understanding of the expression seems to be that David wrote psalms on his own and included psalms in his collection that were authored by others, including men of the past and Levite singers of his own day.

12. See for example, Richard Elliott Friedman, *Who Wrote the Bible?*, pp. 210–14.

13. Aboth deRabbi Nathan survives in two versions (A and B), both of which seem to derive from an original document (or perhaps an oral tradition) from the third century C.E. The final form of Version A likely dates from the later part of the seventh or the early part of the eighth century C.E. Much of the material in Aboth deRabbi Nathan is Tannaitic; see M. B. Lerner, "The External Tractates," in Shmuel Safrai, ed., *The Literature of the Sages*, first part, pp. 376–9. See also Strack and Stemberger, *Introduction to the Talmud and Midrash*, pp. 225–7.

14. Most editors replace "Men of the Great Assembly" with "Men of Hezekiah."

15. Thus Roger Beckwith: "It will be seen that to suppose the canonicity of Ezekiel, Proverbs or Ecclesiastes doubtful simply because the rabbis pointed out contradictions in them would be a complete mistake." Beckwith, *The Old Testament Canon and the New Testament Church*, p. 286.

16. Shabbath 30b confirms that rabbinic commentators at least had some sort of legend that some wished to store away or supress the book of Proverbs. "The book of Proverbs too they wished to withdraw, because its statements are self-contradictory. Yet why did they not withdraw it? They said: did we not examine the book of Ecclesiastes and find a reconciliation? So here too let us make search" (Shabbath 30b; Leiman, *Canonization*, p. 73).

17. Thus Leiman, *Canonization*, p. 86: "only a firmly established biblical book, or a book revered on other grounds, could qualify for גניזה [*geniza*, a storage room in which texts written in Hebrew that could not be destroyed were deposited]."

18. Modern biblical interpreters generally agree that the word originally meant 'move from scroll to scroll', and hence 'copy out'; the latter is the meaning of the word in Modern Hebrew.

19. On both questions, see the remarkable discussion by H. M. I. Gevaryahu, "Qolofonim be-sefer mishle, 'iyov, ve-qohelet," in Yizhak Avishur and Yehoshua Blau, eds., *Mehqarim be-miqre' u-va-mizrah ha-qadmon: mugashim li-Shemu'el A. Livenshtam bi-mel'ot lo shiv'im shanah*, pp. 126–7.

20. M. Fishbane, *Biblical Interpretation in Ancient Israel*, p. 33.

21. Ibid., p. 33 n. 39, citing M. Weinfeld, *Deuteronomy and the Deuteronomic School*, p. 161 n. 3. Fishbane also cites L. Zunz, "'Verfassen und Übersetzen' hebräisch ausgedrückt," *ZDMG* 25 (1871), p. 447.

22. H. M. I. Gevaryahu, "Biblical Colophons: A Source for the 'Biography' of Authors, Texts and Books," *Supplements to Vetus Testamentum* 28 (1975), pp. 50–1.

23. Among the first of the scholars of the Bible to do so was Spinoza, in the *Tractatus Theologico-Politicus*, x. He writes: "The Proverbs of Solomon were, I believe, collected at the same time, or at least in the time of King Josiah; for in the last verse of chapter 24 (= Prov. 25:1) it is written, 'These are also proverbs of Solomon which the men of Hezekiah, king of Judah, removed.' I cannot here pass over in silence the audacity of the rabbis who wished to exclude from the sacred canon both the Proverbs and Ecclesiastes, and to guard them with the remainders. In fact, they would actually have done so, if they had not lighted on certain passages in which the law of Moses is extolled. It is, indeed, grievous to think that the settling of the sacred canon lay in the hands of such men; however, I congratulate them, in this instance, on their suffering us to see these books in question, though I cannot refrain from doubting whether they have transmitted them in absolute good faith; but I will not now linger on this point."

24. "The sages sought to store away the Book of Ecclesiastes . . . And why did they not store it away? Because its beginning is words of the Law and its end [i.e., Eccles. 12:13 f.] is words of the Law."

25. "The sages sought to store away the Book of Ecclesiastes, because they found words in it which tended to heresy."

26. "Ecclesiastes does not make the hands unclean because it is [merely] Solomon's wisdom."

27. "The Jews say that . . . this book seemed fit to be consigned to oblivion, because it asserted the creatures of God to be vain [cf. Eccles. 1.2 etc.], and thought all to be for nothing [cf. Eccles. 1.3 etc.], and preferred eating, drinking, and transitory pleasures to all things [cf. Eccles. 2.24; 8.15; 11.9]; on account of this one section [i.e., Eccles. 12.13 f.] [it seemed] to have deserved its authority, that it was included among the divine books."

28. A medieval parallel to this may be seen in the writings of the Karaite Jacob al-Kirkisani, a contemporary of Saadiah Gaon, who was writing to criticize the rabbinite rejection of the Psalms as human prayer: "Their denial seems to be caused by their hatred and disdain for those who pray in this way, carried to the point, it has been said, that once upon a time they considered removing the Book of Psalms from the canon." Here a controversy over the meaning and nature of a biblical text results in a polemical attack in which the claim is raised that a book's canonicity had been questioned in the distant past. Quoted in Uriel Simon, *Four Approaches to the Book of Psalms*, p. 9.

29. According to Saul Lieberman, the word *he'etiqu* here implies the action of copying a limited selection from a complete list onto a scroll or tablet, rather than copying in the normal sense of the word. "In other words, [the passage specifies that] they didn't copy out (*he'etiqu*) from a complete list (*reshimut*) onto a scroll (cf. Shir Ha-Shirim Rabbah 71.1.3 n. 3 (63): [Solomon] wrote [*katav*] 3 books — Proverbs, etc.), or upon a tablet (see the language in Yerushalmi Pesahim 79.5.1, 26, and in the parallel in Nedarim 76), not that they [didn't] copy out (*he'etiqu*) in the regular sense of the word, like translating the LXX and the Vulgate (and Rashi comments *s.v.*: they attached merit to it [*heheziqu*], as in 2 Chronicles 31:4, for '*tq* means *hzq* 'be strong'. See Rashi *ad loc.* 8.18). Thus they said in a *baraita* in Baba Bathra 15a: Hezekiah and his companions wrote (*katvu*) Isaiah, Proverbs, Song of Songs, and Ecclesiastes. And the sense is that they copied from the writings of Solomon. And the Tanna of Aboth deR. Natan draws from this tradition." Saul Lieberman, "He'arot le–Pereq 'Alef shel Qohelet Rabbah," *Mehqarim be-Torat Erez-Yisrael*, p. 57 n. 22.

30. That the "plain-sense" of *he'etiqu* was "removed" is confirmed in rabbinic texts that repeat the arguments of Aboth deR. Natan. In Midrash

Mishle 25, it is first stated that Proverbs 25:1 indicates that the men of Hezekiah suppressed the works of Solomon.

Which the men of Hezekiah *he'etiqu*" (Proverbs 25:1): Why was this said? I say that Proverbs, Song of Songs, and Ecclesiastes had been suppressed (*genuzim*) until they were made part of the Hagiographa (*'ad she-hayu ba-ketuvin*)!

According to this argument, *he'etiqu* means 'removed, withheld, suppressed'. The statement is followed shortly thereafter by a differing view:

Another interpretation: "Which the men of King Hezekiah *he'etiqu*" (Proverbs 25:1) — they didn't *he'etiqu* 'remove/store away' but rather they *pirshu* 'interpreted', as it is said, "From there he *moved on* (*va-ya'ateq*) to the hill country" (Genesis 12:8), not to speak [of the verse], "Him who *moves* (*ha-ma'atiq*) mountains without their knowing it, who overturns them in his anger" (Job 9:5).

The second argument re-glosses *he'etiqu* as 'interpreted'. This secondary meaning employs the sense of *he'etiq* as 'move [from one meaning to another]', i.e., to explicate. The passage is clearly a restatement of the text in Aboth deR. Natan. Cf. also Yalkut Mishle 961.

31. According to the manuscript reading of Aboth deR. Natan, it was "the Men of the Great Assembly" (a body said to have originated at the time of the return from the Babylonian Exile) that interpreted these Proverbs (and removed them from out of storage). The reading seems to conclude that the Men of Hezekiah had suppressed these books, and that they must have been brought back into circulation by a later deliberative body, such as the Great Assembly. However, this story is ostensibly being used to explain Abba Saul's interpretation of *he'etiqu* in Prov. 25:1 as 'interpreted', and it cannot serve this function if the interpretation was accomplished by the Men of the Great Assembly rather than the Men of Hezekiah. The manuscript reading appears to conflate two glosses of *he'etiqu* — 'interpreted' and 'removed'. Most scholars have generally assumed that "Men of Hezekiah" was the original reading. However, correcting the text eliminates it as a witness for the plain sense of *he'etiqu* as 'removed' or 'suppressed', as well as eliminating its invention of a second institution to explain the eventual acceptance of these books into scripture. Cf. Solomon Schechter, *Aboth de Rabbi Natan*, p. 2 n. 22 and R. Beckwith, *The O.T. Canon and the N.T. Church*, p. 281.

32. See Leiman, *The Canonization of Hebrew Scripture*, pp. 72–86.

33. Ibid., pp. 120–4; see also chapter 4.

34. The text of Theodotian, Aquila, and Symmachus is taken from Frederick Field, ed., *Origenis Hexaplorum quae supersunt*, p. 361.

35. For an explication of the esoteric resonance of the word *ma'aseh* 'work' in *ma'aseh breshit* 'the work of Creation' or 'Creation work' or 'the work of Genesis', see Joseph Dan, *The Ancient Jewish Mysticism*.

36. Liddell-Scott-Jones *s.v.* cites Epistle to the Hebrews 8:13.

37. Lieberman states, "In truth, there is no difference between movement (*ha'atiqah*) from place to place and lifting (*hasa'ah*) from language to language and from subject to subject," and cites Tosefta Sota 88.45.5–6 (and parallels): "They lifted (*hesi'u*) the writing," and Mishnah Avodah Zarah 82.45 (and parallels): "they lifted (*hesi'u*) to another matter (*devar 'aher*), that is, they transferred (*hesi'u*) to another subject." Lieberman, "He'arot le–Pereq ʿAlef shel Qohelet Rabbah," in *Mehqarim be–Torat Erez-Yisrael*, pp. 57–8.

38. However, cf. the interpretation of H. Freedman in the Soncino Talmud (*ad loc.*): "this implies that they copied it out for general instruction."

39. Isaiah is included here probably because he is a contemporary of Hezekiah; this reveals much about the ideology of biblical transcription — according to Baba Bathra, proper transcription had to be performed by a witness or historical contemporary. Another factor in Isaiah's textualization being attributed to Hezekiah may be the fact that Hezekiah is referred to as the author of an epistle contained within the book of Isaiah (38:9). In this instance, the so-called *lamed auctoris* was perhaps read simultaneously as indicating authorship (of the epistle in question), and as the marker of the scribe who copied out the larger work. However, cf. Rashi *ad loc.*, who writes that because Isaiah was killed by Manasseh, he had no time to write his prophecy (for it was the custom to write this type of book before one died); this task was accomplished by the men of Hezekiah *after Hezekiah's death*, during the reign of Manasseh.

40. This passage is quoted by Simon de Magistris in Latin and Syriac from a fragment found in a Vatican codex, in his *Acta Martyrum ad Ostia Tiberina* (Rome, 1795), p. 274.

41. Cf. the Targum's adjective *'amiqe* 'deep', or the various rabbinic reports about the heretical nature of portions of the works of Solomon below.

42. See James Kugel, *In Potiphar's House,* especially the concepts of "transfer of affects" (p. 255) and "overkill" (p. 257).

43. Bernard Septimus *per litteras* (February 9, 1998) writes: "perhaps a calque developed, where Biblical Hebrew *he'etiq* was rendered as 'separate' and then glossed with Mishnaic Hebrew *peresh* 'separate' and subsequently re-evaluated as *peresh* in its other sense — 'interpret'. Cf. Sifre Numbers, no. 78 (Horovitz ed., p. 74, l. 18) where *'atiqim* is glossed as *meforashim.*"

44. These were first published in 1753–4 and later republished by his son, Jehiel Hillel Altschuler, in 1780–82; reprinted in *Mikra'ot Gedolot* (Lemberg: 1808). See *Encyclopedia Judaica, s.v.* Altschuler.

45. Cf. the word for 'to prophesize' in rabbinic literature. In general, prophets seem to 'prophesize' (*hitnav'i*) rather than *'omer* 'utter'. See Seder Olam Rabbah 30 (Leiman, *The Canonization of Scripture,* p. 66).

46. אמר רב יהודה אמר שמואל: אסתר אינה מטמאה את הידים . למימרא דסבר שמואל אסתר לאו

ברוח הקודש נאמרה? והאמר שמואל: אסתר ברוח הקודש נאמרה - נאמרה לקרות ולא נאמרה ליכתוב.

Rab Judah said in the name of Samuel: [The scroll] of Esther does not make the hands unclean. Are we to infer from this that Samuel was of opinion that Esther was not composed under the inspiration of the holy spirit? How can this be, seeing that Samuel has said that Esther was composed under the inspiration of the holy spirit? — It was composed to be recited [by heart], but not to be written.

B. Megillah 7a

47. "If you take exception to the passage [Ben Sira 30:29–30 quotation], Solomon has said the same [Prov. 12:25 quotation] (הא . . . )." שלמה אמרה)

B. Sanhedrin 100b

48. שאין לך סַדִּדר תפלות ותחנונים יותר ממשה רבינו ולסוף נאמר לו (שם ל״א) הן קרבו ימיך למות.

You have nobody who composed (*sidder*) more prayers and supplications than Moses our teacher; yet in the end it was said to him, "Behold, thy days approach that thou must die" (Deut. 31:14).

Qohelet Rabbah 9.13

49. ואימתי נאמרה מגילות קינות רבי יהודה אומר בימי יהויקים נאמרה אמר לו ר׳ נחמיה

וכי בוכין על המת עד שלא ימות אלא אימתי נאמרה אחר חורבן הבית הרי פתרונו איכה ישבה בדד:

When was the Book of Lamentations composed (*ne'emrah*)? R. Judah says: In the days of Jehoiakim. R. Nehemiah said to him, "Do we, then, weep over a dead person before he dies! When was the Book composed? After the destruction of the Temple; and behold proof is to be found in the words, 'How doth the city sit solitary!'"

Eikha Rabbah 1.1

50. James Kugel has discussed a more limited use of *'amar* in a similar compositional context. The expression אמר שיר *'amar shir* 'utter a song' indicates a technical context in which the common word *'amar* is used to apply to the uttering of a song. See James Kugel, "Is there But One Song?" *Biblica* 63 (1982) 329–50.

51. It is possible to say in rabbinic diction that Solomon "wrote down" the books of Proverbs, Ecclesiastes, and Song of Songs, but this arguably indicates his role as scribe — see Sifré on Deuteronomy 1:1 and Tosefta Yadayim 2:14. Another passage that appears to equate writing and composition is the following:

רבי הונא בשם רבי אמר דור המבול לא נימוחו מן העולם עד שכתבו גומוסיות לזכר ולבהמחץ

R. Huna said in R. Joseph's name: The generation of the Flood were not blotted out from the world until they wrote (*katvu*) nuptial songs in honor of pederasty and bestiality.

Breshit Rabbah 26.1

Such examples are infrequent, and do not at all indicate that metaphorical equation of writing and composition was primary in rabbinic diction.

52. Sid Leiman, *The Canonization of Scripture*, p. 163 n. 259.

53. Ibid., p. 163 n. 259, citing M. Simon, *Soncino Talmud:* Baba Bathra, p. 71 n. 6, end; Leiman also cites Midrash Mishle on Proverbs 25:1 and the Aboth deRabbi Nathan 1:4 to bolster this view. However, we have seen that the Aboth deR. Natan (A) cannot be used to support the idea that the *katav* was understood to mean 'write'.

54. Ibid., citing David Hoffman, "Über die Männer der grossen Versammlung," *MWJ* 10 (1883), pp. 46–47, and Willhelm Bacher, "Synagogue, the Great," in *Jewish Encyclopedia*, vol. 11, p. 642.

55. M. L. Margolis, *The Hebrew Scriptures in the Making*, pp. 20–21; quoted in Leiman, *The Canonization of Scripture*, p. 163 n. 259.

56. The Chronicler also appears to have maintained that much or all of scripture had been written down by prophets. See the discussion on Chronicles below, n. 58, and in chapter 3.

57. Elisha Qimron and John Strugnell, Discoveries in the Judaean Desert X, pp. 58–59, and M. Baillet, J. T. Milik, and R. de Vaux, Discoveries in the Judaean Desert III, p. 90.

58. See especially 1 Chronicles 29:29: "Now the acts of King David, from first to last, are written in the records of the seer Samuel, and in the records of the prophet Nathan, and in the records of the seer Gad." According to Curtis and Madsen, *The Books of Chronicles*, p. 307, "There can be little doubt that these are nothing more than references to the narratives in which Samuel, Nathan, and Gad are mentioned in our books of Samuel." Sara Japhet concurs, stating: "As the 'chronicles' mentioned here by name can hardly be regarded as actual sources, their titles should be viewed as part of the Chronicler's historiographical and theological outlook. By describing his sources as composed by prophets, and as written contemporaneously to the events in question, the Chronicler declares their ultimate validity." Japhet, *I & II Chronicles*, p. 517.

59. Joseph Heineman, *Darkhe Ha-Aggada*, chap. 1.

60. The reasons for the ordering of biblical books are not at issue here, because the goal of this study is to interpret the Baba Bathra text and the view of authorship it contains rather than to evaluate its historical veracity.

61. Cf. the ideology behind the rabbinic chronography Seder Olam.

62. The Septuagint includes the following postscript to the translation of the book of Job equating Job with Jobab:

This was translated from the Syrian Bible. Inhabiting a land in Ausiditis at the foot of the mountains of Idoumaia and Arabia, he started off with the name Jobab; He took an Arabissan wife, she bore him a son, whose name was Ennon; she herself was the daughter of Zare, son of the race of Esau, but her mother was Bossora, so he was in the fifth generation from Abraham. And these are the kings who ruled in Edom, which he also ruled over. First Balak the son of Beor, and the name of his city was Denaba; after Balak, Jobab, the one called Job; After him, Asom the ruling general from the lands of Thaimanis; After him, Adad the sun of Barad the one who repulsed Midian in the plain of Moab, and the name of his city was Gethaim. The friends who came to him: Eliphas of the race of Esau the king of Thaimanon, Baldad the tyrant of Sauchia, Sophar the king of Minaion.

The passage from the Septuagint is awkward, and does not look like it was composed in Greek. Indeed, it is uncertain whether the statement "this was translated from the Syrian Bible" refers to the entirety of Job, or rather just to the Epilogue itself. If the epilogue was originally composed

in Aramaic (the exact significance of 'Syrian' here has yet to be determined), it would seem to resemble a targumic expansion that had been
translated into Greek and appended to the translation of Job. As such, it
probably reflects an early midrashic biography of Job that predates the
Alexandrian translation of this book.

63. The Aristeas passage is found in Eusebius' quotation of Alexander Polyhistor:

> Aristeas says in his book *Concerning the Jews* that after Esau took
> Bassara as his wife in Edom, he fathered a son Job. This Job dwelt
> in the land of Ausitis by the borders of Idumaea and Arabia. He
> was both righteous and rich in cattle, for he owned 7,000 sheep,
> 3,000 camels, 500 yoke of oxen, and 500 grazing she-asses. He also
> owned substantial farmland. <u>This Job was formerly Jobab.</u> As a
> way of testing his fidelity, God overwhelmed him with great mis-
> fortunes. First, his asses and cattle were driven off by rustlers,
> then his sheep, along with their shepherds, were consumed by a
> fire which fell from heaven. Not long after this, his camels were
> also stolen by rustlers. Then his children died when his house col-
> lapsed. On the same day his body broke out in sores. While he was
> thus afflicted, Eliphaz, the king of the Temanites, and Bildad, the
> ruler of the Shuhites, and Zophar, king of the Minnaites, visited
> him. Elihu, the son of Barachiel the Zobite, also came. Although
> he was exhorted by them, he said that even without their exhorta-
> tion he himself would remain steadfast in his piety even with his
> affliction. In admiration of his fortitude God relieved him of his
> disease and made him master over many possessions.

The passage of Alexander Polyhistor is quoted in Eusebius, *Praeperatio
Evangelica* 9.25.1–4; translation in Carl Holladay, *Fragments from Hellenis-
tic Jewish Authors,* vol. I, pp. 261–75. The similarity of Aristeas and the
Septuagint postscript to Job has led Holladay to state, "it appears that
Aristeas is working with a Greek version of the Bible rather than with the
MT." See C. Holladay, *Fragments,* vol. I, p. 273 n. 4.

64. The identification is also found in the *Testament of Job,* but not in
rabbinic texts. In fact, rabbis contemporaneous with St. Jerome appear to
have denied the story, claiming that Job was not descended from Esau
(*Epistle* 73, *PL* 22 col. 677; cited in Judith Baskin, *Pharaoh's Counsellors,* p.
24), likely because of the importance of the story of Job the gentile to early
Christians. Jerome agreed with the rabbinic dismissal of the Septuagint

identification of Job with Jobab, claiming that Job was descended from Abraham's brother Nahor, whose firstborn was Uz, in Genesis 22:20 (Jerome, *Questions in Genesis, PL* 23, col. 971, cited in Baskin, p. 38 and p. 142 n. 134). However, the identification of Job with Jobab does appear in a late Targum of 1 Chronicles 1:43; see Baskin, p. 139 n. 92, citing Ginzberg, *Legends of the Jews,* 5.384 n. 14.

65. Christian exegetes such as St. Augustine (see *City of God* 18.47) typically considered Job to have been an Edomite, since they based their interpretations on the Septuagint translation of the book. At least some of these interpreters (see John Chrysostom in the passage quoted below) assumed that Moses had either textualized or perhaps composed the book. Among the most interesting treatments of the origin of the book of Job is that of Theodore of Mopsuestia (ca. 350–428 C.E.), who dated the book to post-exilic times, and also claimed that it represented the reworking of pagan oral poetry by a learned Israelite. Theodore was unfairly and inaccurately castigated by other Christians because of his unorthodox views. According to Leontius of Byzantium, Theodore had suppressed 2,000 lines from the book of Job (in fact the Masoretic Text has little more than half this many lines and the LXX less than that). Similarly, the Acts of the Fifth General Council accused Theodore of denying that the book of Job was divinely inspired; Theodore was reputed to have argued that Job, being an Edomite, had filled the book with pagan myths and fictions. However, Dimitri Z. Zaharopoulos refutes this picture of Theodore, citing the work of the ninth century Nestorian commentator, Isho'dad of Merv. Notable among Isho'dad's statements is the following: "On the evidence of many, among whom I include John Chrysostom, it was the divine Moses who wrote the book of Job during the forty years that the Israelites spent in the desert. But the opinion of the blessed interpreter (i.e., Theodore) was different. The name of the blessed Job, said he, was famous among all the people, and his virtuous acts as well as his ordeals were related orally among all the people and all the nations from century to century and in all the languages. Now, after the return of the Israelites from Babylon, a learned Hebrew who was especially well versed in the science of the Greeks committed in writing the history of the just, and in order to make it larger he mingled the story with exquisite utterances borrowed from the poets, because he composed his book with the purpose of making it more pleasant to the readers." Zaharopoulos summarizes Theodore's approach to the book of Job: "In post-exilic times a Jew, well-versed in the letters of

the Greeks, took up an Edomitic folklore which was in circulation for generations in the whole near east and committed the history of the just to
writing, fashioning it after the models of Greek poetry." Theodore's critical
investigation of Job may have appeared impious, but it amounted to a serious investigation of the work on the basis of internal evidence, a skepti-
cal approach to tradition, and an impressive awareness of oral poetics.
From this perspective, he appears to have been a forerunner of a scholar
like Giambattista Vico. See Dimitri Zaharopoulos, *Theodore of Mopsuestia
on the Bible,* pp. 45–48 and 88. Also see St. Gregory's discussion on the figure
Job: *Moralia in Job,* praefatio (*PL* lxxv.515–28, esp. 517A–B; 517C–519A);
cited in Minnis, *Medieval Theory of Authorship,* p. 37.

66. Judith Baskin, *Pharaoh's Counsellors,* p. 14.

67. E.g., J. Sota 20c.

68. Judith Baskin, *Pharaoh's Counsellors,* p. 11 and p. 131 n. 18.

69. The stories about Job's marriage to Dinah are part of a larger
rabbinic ambivalence towards Job, since Job blasphemes, questions God
(with his heart if not with his lips, cf. Job 2:10), challenges the idea of divine justice, and appears to deny the idea of the resurrection of the dead.
Thus Job is often claimed by the rabbis to be one of Pharaoh's counselors,
explaining why God allowed Satan to afflict him later. In a similar vein,
these interpreters saw Dinah's marriage to Job in a negative light. Interpreting Genesis 34:1, "And Dinah the daughter of Leah went out," Breshit
Rabbah 80.4 concludes that Dinah was forced to marry an uncircumcised
heathen. In punishment for Jacob's concealment of his daughter from his
brother Esau, God told Jacob to give Dinah in illegitimate wedlock to Job.
See Judith Baskin, *Pharaoh's Counsellors,* pp. 15–18.

70. The Jacob dating is also assumed in the texts that claim that Dinah was Job's wife (see the Job Targum translation of Job 2:9, Breshit Rabbah 57:4, pseudo-Philo's *Book of Biblical Antiquities* 8:8, and also the
pseudepigraphic Testament of Job). This dating is also found in the writing of Origen, *Homilies on Ezekiel* 4 (*PG* 13, col. 699); cited in Judith
Baskin, *Pharaoh's Counsellors,* pp. 137–8 n. 70.

71. Parallels are found in Exodus Rabbah 21:8 and Breshit Rabbah 57.

72. For the text, see Pancratius C. Beentjes, *The Book of Ben Sira in
Hebrew,* p. 81, and A. E. Cowley and Ad. Neubauer, eds., *The Original Hebrew of a portion of Ecclesiasticus,* p. 40. If Beentjes' reading of א[.]נ is correct (this reading is not given by Cowley and Neubauer), I would propose
that the text should be reconstructed נביא *navi'* 'a prophet'. This recon-

struction would indicate that Ben Sira was doubly validating Job, as mentioned by Ezekiel and as a prophet in his own right.

73. The statements in the Shulkhan Arukh and comments of R. Y. Migash, Maimonides (Rambam), Isserles (Rema) and Ha-Meiri are summarized by Adin Steinsaltz, *Bava Batra*, vol. 1, p. 62.

74. Rashi's point makes more sense when the practices regulating recitation of Torah in the Mishnah are considered. A number of rabbinic regulations ensured that Torah recitation did not typically involve the reading of long passages by a single reader without interruption. For one thing, it was forbidden for the reciter to read more than three verses of Torah in a row for the *miturgeman* to translate. Moreover, M. Megillah 4.4 requires a minimum of seven readers on the sabbath, required to recite at least three verses apiece. In B. Megillah 21b, other strictures are added: each of the three readers (the minimum required by the Mishnah on Mondays, Thursdays, and sabbath at *Minkha*) are to be commended if they read as few as four verses apiece, of the ten verses required on these occasions. The rabbis also required a benediction before and after each reader, rather than merely at the beginning and end of recitation as was originally the case (M. Megillah 4.1–2, B. Megillah 21b). Thus Rashi's directive that the last eight verses of Deuteronomy be read without interruption stands in stark contrast to the procedures that applied to the rest of the Torah. It is interesting to add here that, according to J. Megillah 4.3, those who speak foreign languages (i.e., languages other than Aramaic) are not accustomed to dividing up the reading; moreover, one person may read the entire passage. Philo also speaks of a single reader (Eusebius, *Prep. Ev.* 8.7.12–13); cited in Harry Gamble, *Books and Readers in the Early Church*, p. 325 n. 26. See also Charles Perrot, "The Reading of the Bible in the Ancient Synagogue," in Martin Jan Mulder, ed., *Mikra*, pp. 137–159.

75. See also the parallel passage in the Tosafot to B. Menaḥot 30a.

76. This interpretation derives from the sense of *yaḥid* as 'an illustrious member of the community'.

77. See M. Megillah 4.4.

78. See J. Megillah 4.1.

79. Targum Neofiti to Exod 7:1 calls Aaron the *meturgeman* of Moses when he acted as Moses' "spokesman" to Pharaoh and the Israelites. Cf. Exod. Rabbah 8:3: "And Aaron thy brother shall be thy prophet (Ex. 7:1). Just as the preacher sits and preaches whilst the interpreter sits before him, so shalt thou speak all that I shall command thee, [to Aaron] and Aaron thy

brother will speak unto Pharaoh." Thanks to Maurice A. O'Sullivan for this reference.

80. The Tosafists derive this notion from the Mishnah:

בראשונה. כל מי שיודע לקרות. קורא. וכל מי שאינו יודע לקרות. מקרין אותו. נמנעו מלהביא. התקינו שיהו
מקרין את מי שיודע ואת מי אינו שיודע.

> Originally, anyone who knew how to recite would recite, and any-one who didn't know how to recite would repeat it [after the priest]; but when they refrained from bringing [first fruit offerings to the Temple], it was decided that both those who knew how to read as well as those who didn't know would repeat the words.

> M. Bikkurim 3.7

It is unlikely that "recitation" here means reading from a written text. Nev-ertheless, the Tosafists apparently used this Mishnah to explain the origin of the *shaliah zibor*. Accordingly, the purpose of the *shaliah zibor* was to en-sure that everyone who rose to recite Torah would receive equal treatment in front of the congregation, so that those who couldn't read would not forego their duty out of shame.

81. However, in the Tosafists' commentary to B. Megillah 21b, it was pointed out that there was no *shaliah zibor* in earlier times; hence, Baba Bathra's directive that "a *yahid* reads the last eight verses [of Deuteron-omy]" could not refer to this practice. Therefore they agreed with Rashi that this must mean that the *yahid* reads the last eight verses by himself, without being interrupted by a second reader.

82. A similar connection is made by R. Samuel bar R. Isaac (J. Megillah 4:1, cited above), when he claims that the practice of simultane-ous Aramaic translation was meant to mirror the revelation of the Torah through an intermediary (Moses).

CHAPTER 2: ATTACHING NAMES TO BIBLICAL BOOKS

1. See James Kugel, *The Bible As It Was*, pp. 1–49.

2. E.g., Breshit Rabbah 8.8. See also B. Sanhedrin 99a, where an in-dividual is considered as one who despises the Lord and rejects the doc-trine that "the Torah is from heaven," simply by asserting that a single verse of the Torah, or even a single point (*diqduq*), *ad majus* deduction (*qal vehomer*), or argument from analogy (*gezerah shawah*) found in or derived from the Torah was not uttered by God but originated from the mouth of Moses himself.

3. E.g., Shir Ha-Shirim Rabbah 1:12. See Saul Lieberman, "Mishnat Shir Ha-Shirim," *Meḥqarim be-Torat Ereẓ-Yisrael*, pp. 118–126.

4. The existence of an entire Mishnaic tractate (called Megillah 'scroll') devoted to the rules concerning the textualization and public promulgation of Esther likely played a role in the re-conceptualization of all three works as already revealed to Moses. The evidence suggests that the process began with Esther, since this book had been singled out by the Mishnah. The subsequent rabbinic delineation of Ruth and the Song of Songs as *megillot*, according them a textual format not granted the other works of the Writings (*ketuvim*), as well as a marked place in the Jewish festival liturgy, may have facilitated the transformed view of their initial composition.

5. Yehoshua Amir, "Authority and Interpretation of Scripture in the Writings of Philo," in *Mikra: Text, Translation, Reading, and Interpretation of the Hebrew Bible in Ancient Judaism and Early Christianity*, p. 436.

6. See chapter 4 for an investigation of the use of this same passage from the *Timaeus* by Josephus in *Against Apion*.

7. James Kugel also suggests that the dislike of the idea of human authorship of the Bible goes back further, to the early Second Temple period: "The common practice of interpreters writing in Greek to refer to 'Moses,' 'David,' 'Solomon,' and others as the authors of this or that biblical composition — without further reference to them as mere conduits of the divine word — might suggest that, for such interpreters, the biblical compositions in question were fundamentally the product of human authors, however extraordinary the humans in question might be. But this is hardly so for a great many Greek-writing interpreters (as Philo of Alexandria, for example, makes clear), and evidence of the contrary view is occasionally explicit. In particular, a certain explanation of Gen. 34:7 found in the book of Judith gives clear testimony that its author believed the divine authorship of Scripture to extend to the ordinary narrative fabric of biblical books: God was, according to this author, the omniscient narrator of Genesis. The author of Jubilees similarly believed all of the Genesis narratives to be of divine provenance — as much as the laws of Exodus through Deuteronomy that are specifically attributed to God. Indeed, Jubilees likewise maintains that later scriptural books (apparently including, among others, Isaiah and Psalms) were inscribed in the 'heavenly tablets' long before the human transmitters of these texts had even been born. A text from among the Dead Sea Scrolls, 11QPs[a] similarly asserts that David's songs and psalms were 'given to him from the Most High,' and this belief is re-

flected as well in Philo of Alexandria and Acts 2:30–31." James Kugel, *The Bible As It Was*, p. 22.

8. The scope of the discussion of biblical attribution in this chapter largely excludes the Pentateuch and those prophetic works that became known by the name of their prophet. In the case of the prophetic works, it was clear that each prophet was responsible for the utterances contained in the book that bore his name. Attaching a prophetic name to historical books was not so straightforward. As for the Pentateuch, the early canonization of the five books of the law gave them a special significance that was not really dependent on their author or prophetic scribe (except possibly in the case of the book of Deuteronomy, which seems to have derived its status in part from its implicit claim to be the "last will and testament" of Moses). Since it is probably impossible to discover when all five books of the Pentateuch became associated with Moses and when they became authoritative, it is equally impossible to establish whether their authoritativeness followed their attribution or vice-versa. However, see the fascinating treatment of a colophon in Deuteronomy 31–34 by Jack R. Lundbom, "Scribal Colophons and Scribal Rhetoric in Deuteronomy 31–34," in Ben-Ẕiyon Lurya, ed., *Sefer Ḥayim Gevaryahu (Ḥayim M. I. Gevaryahu: Memorial Volume)*, vol. 2, pp. 53–63. Lundbom concludes, "Originally Moses was the scribe who wrote the song" (p. 63). Later, in the framing of Moses' song by a split colophon, "the impression was created that Moses wrote the entire Deuteronomic law, and from this it was but a small step to the assertion, made later in Judaism, that Moses authored the entire Pentateuch" (pp. 53–4). In any event, the belief in the divine revelation of the Law on Mount Sinai and the early authoritative status of the Pentateuch set Moses apart from the other individuals whose names were linked to biblical books. Moreover, God was believed to have spoken to Moses face to face, plainly rather than in riddles or dreams (Numbers 12:8). Because of these factors, the Mosaic attribution of the Pentateuch had a limited impact on the development of beliefs about the role of individuals in the composition and transmission of other biblical books. However, there can be no doubt that the early Mosaic attribution set the stage for biblical attribution in general.

9. Yiẕhak Heineman, *Darkhe Ha-Aggadah*, p. 28.

10. U. von Wilamowitz-Moellendorff, "Louys, Pierre: *Les chansons de Bilitis traduites du Grec pour la première fois*" (Review), *Göttingische gelehrte Anzeigen* 158 (1896) 634 n. 1; see also W. Speyer, *Literarische Fälschung*, p. 40.

11. W. Speyer, *Literarische Fälschung,* p. 40.

12. Cf. Foucault's notion of authorship as the principle of thrift. M. Foucault, "What Is an Author?"

13. It has often been postulated that the biblical heading of Ecclesiastes 1:1 about Qoheleth was a subterfuge from the start. However, the motivations of those who composed works explicitly or covertly in the name of a legendary culture-hero are outside the scope of this study.

14. Cf. Midrash Tehillim on Psalm 1 (trans. Braude):

A further comment on "Blessed is the man." R. Nehemiah began his exposition by quoting the words, "Wisdom strengthens the wise" (Eccles. 7:19) — that is, strengthened David: strengthened him "more than ten mighty men that are in the city" (ibid.) — that is, more than the ten men who were the authors of the Book of Psalms, namely, Adam, Melchizedek, Abraham, Moses, David, Solomon, Asaph, and the three sons of Korah. About these ten names, the Sages do not differ that they are names of persons. About what do they differ? [About Jeduthun as a name]. Rab maintained that "For Jeduthun" (Ps. 39:1) means "concerning the *jeduthun,*" that is, "concerning the judgments and punishments" which were imposed upon David and upon Israel.

R. Huna said in the name of R. Aha: Though certain Psalms bear the name of one of the ten authors, the book, as a whole, bears the name of David, king of Israel. As a parable tells us, there was a company of musicians that sought to sing a hymn to the king. The king said to them: To be sure, all of you are sweet singers, all of you are musicians, all of you have superior skill, all of you are men worthy of taking part in the singing of a hymn to the king, yet let the hymn, in whose singing all of you will take part, bear the name of only one man among you because his voice is the sweetest of all your voices. Thus it is written, "The saying of David the son of Jesse . . . the sweet singer of the Psalms of Israel" (2 Sam. 23:1). The singer who makes the Psalms of Israel sweet is David, the son of Jesse, a nobleman, and the son of a nobleman. Therefore what is it that is said at the end of the Book of Psalms? "The prayers of David the son of Jesse are ended" (Ps. 72:20).

As the Psalms bear the names of ten authors, so do they bear also the names of ten kinds of song, namely, glory, melody, Psalm, song, praise, prayer, blessing, thanksgiving, *Hallelujah,* and

exultation. The most excellent song of all is *Hallelujah* which, in
one word, contains both a name of God and a term for "praise."
See also Shir Ha-Shirim Rabbah 4.4.

15. Cf. the statement in B. Megillah 15a that Malachi is another
name for Mordechai, because he was near to the king (the root *m-l-k*
from which Malachi is derived means 'king'). By this gesture, Mordechai,
sometimes described as having recorded the book of Esther, was given
prophetic status.

16. James L. Kugel, "David the Prophet," in *Poetry and Prophecy,* pp.
45–55.

17. Another explanation for Davidic attribution in Second Temple
times, provided by Alan M. Cooper, is sociological rather than exegetical in
nature: "The tradition that psalmody was a Davidic institution probably
stems from the desire of the survivors or heirs of the old local guilds to legitimate their role in the Second Temple. The compelling quality of this
levitical apologetic is due in large measure to the concomitant Messianic
aggrandizement of David." Cooper's explanation successfully describes the
need to attribute as many of the psalms as possible to David. See Alan M.
Cooper, "The Life and Times of King David According to the Book of
Psalms," in *The Poet and the Historian,* ed. Richard Elliott Friedman,
p. 129.

18. In other words, all 4,050 compositions attributed to David in the
"List of David's Compositions" (see below) may be authoritative because
they are linked to David; but each and every one of these works are not
necessarily "scripture" for the community at Qumran or for any other Jewish group.

19. J. A. Sanders, *The Psalms Scroll of Qumrân Cave 11* (Discoveries
in the Judaean Desert of Jordan IV), p. 92.

20. See Eileen M. Schuller, *Non-Canonical Psalms from Qumran: A
Pseudepigraphic Collection,* pp. 9–10; p. 18 n. 28.

21. Another non-canonical psalm from Qumran (Psalm 151A) shows
that David is viewed in a more historically accurate manner as the coun-
terpart to God's prophet: "He sent his prophet to anoint me [David],
Samuel to magnify me." Similarly, the non-canonical Psalm 151B begins
with a heading which clearly states that David and God's prophet are two
separate individuals: "The first display of David's power after God's
prophet had anointed him."

22. J. A. Sanders, *The Psalms Scroll of Qumrân Cave 11,* p. 93 n.,

where he cites 1 Chron. 27:32 and B. Berakhot 45b in support of this more metaphorical sense of the word.

23. But it is significant that of the psalms found on 11QPs^a (consisting of fragments of many of Psalms 101–151), one is ascribed to an individual other than David. The first line of Psalm 127 found on the scroll includes the psalm heading *le-Shelomo* 'to Solomon'. This is an early precursor of the phenomenon in which psalms ascribed to other authors can be subsumed into a Davidic ascription — cf. Kugel's examples from the New Testament and rabbinic literature in James L. Kugel, "David the Prophet," pp. 45–55. It also may be a precursor of the idea of David as a scribe for psalms he *did not* himself compose.

24. In contrast, the Syriac translation merely says, "A Todah [or Hodayah] of David," and 11QPs^a reads "A Hallelujah of David the son of Jesse."

25. J. A. Sanders, *The Psalms Scroll of Qumrân Cave 11*, p. 58.

26. Liddell-Scott-Jones interprets the word 'specially or separately written', which would seem to speak to its transmission rather than textualization.

27. The comment by Sigmund Mowinckel on the Psalm headings is worth quoting here: "Of the 73 passages in which 'David' occurs in the heading (see above, n. 42) the word is lacking in several manuscripts or translations: Ps. 122 (2 MSS), 124 (3 MSS; Gh), 127 (G), 131 (G, H), 133 (2 MSS, G, T), 138 (Aq, Sexta); in 108 some MSS have *le-'asaf*. The note is lacking in MT, but has been added in G or other translations: Psalms 33; 67; 91; 96; 98; 104; 137. This proves at any rate that in many cases it does not represent old tradition, but secondary theory. From this, as well as from the distribution of the headings of Psalms 90–150 have on the whole been added later and gradually, and that the last two books of the Psalter were originally anonymous in the tradition. Nor does 'of Moses' in Ps. 90 represent an old tradition." Sigmund Mowinckel, *The Psalms in Israel's Worship*, vol. 2, p. 99.

28. Brevard S. Childs, "Psalm Titles and Midrashic Exegesis," *Journal of Semitic Studies*, 16 (1971), p. 148.

29. It is notable that Childs points out that this extremely late postexilic dating for the headings should be a check against a scholarly tendency to project the midrashic method back into the pre-exilic period. While the usual procedure of midrash was to construct huge edifices of narrative upon grammatical and other textual anomalies, in the case of the

Psalm headings, the broadest similarities in theme or setting gave rise to the midrashic identification.

30. James L. Kugel, "David the Prophet," in *Poetry and Prophecy*, ed. J. Kugel, p. 49.

31. Brevard S. Childs, "Psalm Titles and Midrashic Exegesis," *Journal of Semitic Studies* 16 (1971), p. 138.

32. Ibid., p. 140.

33. See esp. H. M. I. Gevaryahu, "Qolofonim be-sefer mishle, 'iyov, ve-qohelet," in Yitsḥak Avishur and Yehoshua Blau, eds., *Meḥqarim be-miqre' u-va-mizraḥ ha-qadmon: mugashim li-Shemu'el A. Livenshtam bi-mel'ot lo shiv'im shanah*, pp.107–140. Gevaryahu's works are listed in Ben-Ẓiyon Lurya, ed., *Sefer Ḥayim Gevaryahu (Ḥayim M. I. Gevaryahu: Memorial Volume)*, vol. 1, pp. 151–2.

34. Cited in H. M. I. Gevaryahu, "Biblical Colophons: A Source for the 'Biography' of Authors, Texts and Books," *Supplements to Vetus Testamentum* 28 (1975), p. 44 n. 7.

35. Herman Hunger, *Babylonische und assyrische Kolophone*, p. 9.

36. H. M. I. Gevaryahu, "Biblical Colophons," pp. 50–1.

37. Ibid.

38. Ibid., p. 46.

39. Ibid., p. 55.

40. Alan M. Cooper, "The Life and Times of King David According to the Book of Psalms," in Richard Elliott Friedman, ed., *The Poet and the Historian*, p. 118.

41. According to Shir Ha-Shirim Rabbah 1.1,10, Psalm 30 was also written by Solomon:

The Song of Songs. R. Aibu and R. Judah [joined issue on this]. R. Aibu said: '*Song*' indicates one, '*songs*' two, making three in all. R. Judah b. Simon said: The whole of the Song of Songs makes one, and two referred to in the word '*songs*' are different. How do you specify them? One is, "A song of ascents of Solomon" (Ps. 127), and the other, "A Psalm, a song at the dedication of the House of David" (Ps. 30). You would naturally think that David composed this, but in reality it is only ascribed to David in the same way as it says, "Like the tower of David is thy neck" (S. S. 4:4). So here, Solomon composed it and ascribed it to David.

The heading of Psalm 30 is here interpreted as referring to the dedication of the Temple, built by Solomon.

42. See Fred L. Horton, *The Melchizedek Tradition*, and James Kugel, *The Bible As It Was*, pp. 151–62.

43. A parallel to the question asked by R. Ḥanina is found in the commentary on the Psalms by St. Jerome:

> Si igitur psalmi isti et cantica ista Moysi sunt, quare in propriis voluminibus non habentur? Diximus ergo quomodo centesimus primus psalmus inscribitur, Oratio pauperis: et alius est qui scripsit de ipso, et ille pauper qui pro nobis deprecatur, Dominus est 'qui cum dives esset, pauper factus est propter nos' et cetera. Sic est hic Moyses, quoniam a principio caelum et terra facta sint, quomodo et homo factus sit, de conditione hominis; et iste psalmus de conditione hominis loquitur, quid sit homo, et quare natus sit. Qui ergo in Genesi scripsit de hominum conditione, ipse et nunc inducitur ab Spiritu sancto disputare quid sit homo.

> If therefore these psalms and songs are by Moses, why don't they appear in his books proper? We said that Psalm 101 [= MT Psalm 102] is entitled "Prayer of a poor man." On the one hand, he is yet another who wrote about himself, and on the other, this poor man who prays for us is the Lord, "who although he is rich, became a poor man on our behalf" etc. [2 Corinthians 8:9]. It is the same here; Moses, after [he described that] in the beginning the heaven and the earth were made, also [described] how man was made, [and] about the human condition; and this psalm speaks about the human condition, what man is, and why he is born. Thus the man who wrote in Genesis about the condition of men, he himself even now is led by the Holy Spirit to debate what man is.

> Jerome, Tractatus de Psalmo LXXXVIIII (= Psalm 90),
> *Anecdota Maredsolana* II, ed. Morin, pp. 106–7

44. But cf. Bamidbar Rabbah 12:3, where R. Huna in the name of R. Idi states that Psalm 101 was composed by Moses rather than Solomon. The Soncino edition explains that Solomon rather than David would be expected here, "Because this Psalm was altered in reference to the Temple, as is stated in the Midrash Tehillim."

45. The bishop Hippolytus comments on the procedure of counting the last heading towards all successive psalms without headings: "But the opinion of a certain Hebrew on these last matters has reached me, who

held that, when there were many without any inscription, but preceded by one with the inscription 'Of David,' all these should be reckoned also to be by David" (Hippolytus, *On the Psalms* I, in Alexander Roberts and James Donaldson, eds., *Ante-Nicene Fathers*, vol. 5).

46. Charlesworth, *OTP* II, pp. 143–176; for date, see pp. 149–50.

47. M. A. Knibb (in Charlesworth, *OTP* II, pp. 143–176) theorizes that the Martyrdom of Isaiah (the large part of chapters 1–5) was translated from Hebrew into Greek. However, the "Testament of Hezekiah" (3:13–4:22) is "manifestly Christian" and was likely composed in Greek and inserted into this text. The rest of the text (chapters 6–11) has been called "The Vision of Isaiah"; it is also Christian in origin and composed in Greek.

48. Cf. 4 Ezra 14:42–48, where Ezra copies out the books of the Bible that had been destroyed, including 24 books (i.e. the canon) which are meant for both *digni* and *indigni* 'worthy and unworthy', in addition to 70 (esoteric) books which are to have a specialized readership — *sapientiae de populo tuo* 'the wise among your people'.

49. Knibb (in Charlesworth, *OTP* II, p. 176) speculates that "then" means "in the last generation," pointing to the parallels in Daniel 12:4, 9.

50. See James Kugel, *The Bible As It Was*, p. 102: "Having — according to many interpreters — entered heaven alive, Enoch was naturally assumed to have continued living there, and in the process, to have acquired a unique knowledge of "heavenly things" — not only the ways of God and the angels, but also of natural phenomena on earth as observed from above. It is in part upon this (very old) assumption that there arose an early body of writings attributed to Enoch: several ancient authors, speaking through the figure of Enoch, set forth their own ideas as well as ancient traditions about the world and future history."

51. See also Jubilees 4: 21–24, trans. Wintermute:

[21] And he was therefore with the angels of God six jubilees of years. And they showed him everything which is on earth and in the heavens, the dominion of the sun. [22] And he wrote everything, and bore witness to the Watchers, the ones who sinned with the daughters of men because they began to mingle themselves with the daughters of men so that they might be polluted. And Enoch bore witness against all of them. [23] . . . And behold, he is there writing condemnation and judgment of the world, and all of the evils of the children of men. [24] And because of him none of the water of the Flood came upon the whole land of Eden, for he was put

there for a sign and so that he might bear witness against all of the children of men so that he might relate all of the deeds of the generations until the day of judgment.

52. M. D. Johnson, "The Life of Adam and Eve: A New Translation and Introduction," in Charlesworth, ed., *OTP* II, p. 294.

53. "Die als kanonisch anerkannten Schriften sind somit nach Meinung des Josephus und seiner Zeitgenossen nur in jener von Mose bis Esra reichenden Zeitperiode entstanden, in der der prophetische Geist in Israel lebendig war. Eine solche Anschauung gab dem rabbinischen Judentum die Möglichkeit, häretische Bewegungen abzuwehren, die sich auf die Offenbarungen der Ur- und Erzväter, wie Henoch, Enosch, oder auch Abraham beriefen." J. C. H. Lebram, "Aspekte der Alttestamentlichen Kanonbildung," *Vetus Testamentum* 18 (1968), p. 173.

54. According to the Loeb version of the *Apologeticus*, pp. 92–3, this passage is accepted as genuine by Harnack and Schanz and rejected by Rauschen.

55. Jude 14–15: "Now Enoch, the seventh from Adam, prophesied about these men also, saying, 'Behold the Lord comes with ten thousand of His saints, to execute judgment on all, to convict all who are ungodly among them of all their ungodly deeds which they have committed in an ungodly way, and of all the harsh things which ungodly sinners have spoken against Him.'"

56. James Kugel, *The Bible As It Was*, p. 39.

57. It also seems likely that works could still be attributed to legendary figures during their composition process, such as had been the case with the book of Deuteronomy; Wolfgang Speyer terms these works *echte religiöse Pseudepigraphie*. A variety of other designations, including plagiarism and forgery, should be reserved for fictitious attributions with a financial or personal motive (see chapter 6). See Wolfgang Speyer, *Literarische Fälschung*, pp. 35–6.

CHAPTER 3: THE JEWISH CRITIQUE OF GREEK LETTERS

1. Among the Greeks, a critique of the role of the *agôn* 'contest' in the determination of which poetic works should be granted the authority of the state was accomplished by Plato in the *Laws*. Plato envisions a cultural alternative to *theatrokratia* 'the rule of the theater', in which the *agôn* is modified to reward not the product of the artistic endeavor for its inherent

value, but rather the creations of societally sanctioned poets. But Plato does not offer a critique of individualism or of the Greek character. See chapter 5.

2. The difference between this claim and that of rabbinic exegetes is sharp: Baba Bathra 14b speaks to the rabbinic doctrine that a biblical book need not have been written down by the individual that first gave utterance to it — hence, the Solomonic books and the book of Isaiah were textualized by Hezekiah, rather than by Solomon and Isaiah; see chapter 1.

3. Further work on the presence or absence of these conditions remains to be done with regard to Greek and Roman literature. Greek literary forms endowed with some kind of divine authority were allegedly tampered with or forged, as we see in Herodotus' charge that the Peisistratids inserted verses into the Delphic Oracles, or Suetonius' claim that Augustus destroyed more than two thousand verses of oracular verses by either anonymous or little respected authors, and even "edited" the Sybilline oracles (Suetonius, *Augustus* 31.1). However, the very premise of both Delphic and Sybilline oracles was that they were the words of a divinity given a mystical voice by a seer, put into verse by a prophet, and written down by either the prophet or yet another individual; these verses were in no way attributed to an individual with an individual name (Sybill seems to have been a title passed on from priestess to priestess). The case is stronger in some respects for Homer as an author embodying both conditions. His works quite clearly appeal to the authority of the Muse, and were also alleged to have been forged or tampered with since the fifth century. However, it is questionable whether those asserting forgery on the part of Homer fully adhered to the notion of the Muse as a divine entity from which Homer's words drew all of their own authority. In the fifth century, Homer is cited as the pre-eminent historical document from ancient times, not as the equivalent of an oracle or other divine document. See Carolyn Higbe, "The Bones of a Hero, the Ashes of a Politician: Athens, Salamis, and the Usable Past," *Classical Antiquity* 16 (1997) 279–308.

4. See chapters 6 and 7 for a discussion of the ways Josephus' methodology affected the Christian construction of authorship and provided the basis of the Christian world's knowledge of the reasons why the Jews included and excluded biblical books from the Old Testament.

5. All translations of Josephus' *Against Apion* are taken from H. St. J. Thackeray's translation in the Loeb Classical Library, unless otherwise noted.

6. See Walter Burkert, "Zur geistesgeschichtlichen Einordnung eini-

ger Pseudopythagorica," and Holger Thesleff, "On the Problem of the Doric Pseudo-Pythagorica: An Alternative Theory of Date and Purpose," both in Kurt von Fritz, ed., *Pseudepigrapha I*, pp. 25–55 and 59–102.

7. One such instance occurs in his critique of the Egyptian anti-Jew, Manetho. Josephus criticizes this historian's use of mythic stories that are *adespotôs* (of unknown authorship): "His additional statements, which he derived not from the Egyptian records, but, as he admits himself, from fables of unknown authorship (ἐκ τῶν ἀδεσπότως μυθολογουμένων προστέθεικεν), I shall refute in detail later on and show the unbelievability of its false account (τὴν ἀπίθανον αὐτοῦ ψευδολογίαν)" (1.105). This is the only time in *Against Apion* that *adespotôs* appears. It is interesting that Menetho fails to live up to the usually high standards of Egyptian culture with regard to keeping and consulting archives, according to Josephus.

8. Sara Japhet, *I & II Chronicles: A Commentary*, pp. 20–22.

9. Edward Lewis Curtis and Albert Alonzo Madsen, *The Books of Chronicles*, pp. 23–4.

10. Cf. Kleingunther, Adolf, *"Prôtos heuretês"; Untersuchungen zur Geschichte einer Fragestellung*, on inventors in Greek culture; compare with the Alexandrian Jew Artapanus who makes Moses the *prôtos heuretês* of Egyptian religious customs.

11. H. St. J. Thackeray was responsible for the "Assistant Theory," which held that one of Josephus' Greek assistants, "the Thucydidean hack," emulated the vocabulary and style of Thucydides. For the definitive refutation of this theory, see Tessa Rajak, *Josephus: the Historian and his Society*, appendix 2. Rajak argues that Josephus himself had read Thucydides and Sophocles and was responsible for the linguistic and rhetorical affinities with these authors. In addition to emulating Thucydides' style and historical approach, he cites him as the most reliable of the Greeks, who, nevertheless, sometimes gets things wrong: "On many points even Thucydides is accused of error by some critics, notwithstanding his reputation for writing the most accurate history of his time" (1.18).

12. See Tessa Rajak, *Josephus: The Historian and his Society*, especially chapter 1, "Family, Education, and Formation"; chapter 2, "The Greek Language in Josephus' Jerusalem"; and appendix 2, "The Assistant Theory."

13. Tessa Rajak, "The Sense of History in Jewish Intertestamental Writing," p. 126.

14. Shaye J. D. Cohen, "History and Historiography in the *Against*

*Apion* of Josephus," in *Essays in Jewish Historiography*, ed. Ada Rapoport-Albert, p. 1.

15. See Rebecca Gray, *Prophetic Figures in Late Second Temple Jewish Palestine*, esp. chapter 2, "Josephus as Prophet."

16. Shaye J. D. Cohen, "History and Historiography in the *Against Apion* of Josephus," in *Essays in Jewish Historiography*, ed. Ada Rapoport-Albert, p. 6.

17. Cohen relies on a 1961 article by Klaus Oehler, "Der Consensus omnium als Kriterium der Wahrheit in der antiken Philsophie und der Patristik," *Antike und Abendland* 10 (1961) 103–129, and two encyclopedic entries on consensus.

18. Shaye Cohen, "History and Historiography in the *Against Apion* of Josephus," in *Essays in Jewish Historiography*, ed. Ada Rapoport-Albert, p. 8.

19. It is strange that Cohen should postulate that Josephus equated Epicurians with Jews, however casually. There is a long history of speculation in the pagan world that the Jews were similar to the followers of Pythagoras, but in later Jewish thought, which Josephus anticipates in many ways, "Epicurian" became in Hebrew the word for "heretic." Cf. Mishnah Sanhedrin 10.1: "These are the people who will not have a share in the world to come: those who say there is no resurrection of the dead, that the Torah is not from Heaven, and the Epicurian" (see Bickerman, "La Chaîne de la Tradition Pharisienne," p. 260 n. 22).

20. Another attempt to argue that Josephus' approach derives from classical models has been made by Robert G. Hall in "Josephus, *Contra Apionem* and Historical Inquiry in the Roman Rhetorical Schools," in Feldman and Levison, eds., *Josephus' Contra Apionem: Studies in its Character and Context with a Latin Concordance to the Portion Missing in Greek*, pp. 229–249. I disagree with Hall's claim that "Josephus does not defend his own method for *Contra Apionem* when he argues in favor of Jewish prophetic historiography, nor does he reject the Greek historical method" (p. 230). I find that comparisons with the historical methods of the Roman orators are fruitful, but not to the extent that they allow Hall to observe, "I think he has followed the method so closely that his work has that very school-boyish character he denies (1.53)" (p. 248).

21. The earliest strata of Christian writers, in contrast to the more Hellenized later periods, reveal the same dislike of personal attribution as is found in Jewish letters. F. F. Bruce states, for example, "It is remarkable,

when one comes to think of it, that the four canonical Gospels are anonymous, whereas the 'Gospels' which proliferated in the late second century and afterwards claim to have been written by apostles and other eyewitnesses." F. F. Bruce, *The Canon of Scripture*, p. 257.

CHAPTER 4: BIBLICAL AND HOMERIC TEXTUALIZATION ACCORDING TO JOSEPHUS

1. See Saul Lieberman, *Greek in Jewish Palestine*, and Martin Hengel, *Judaism and Hellenism*. Recent scholars who defend this perspective include P. van der Horst, "Greek in Jewish Palestine in the Light of Jewish Epigraphy," *Japheth in the Tents of Shem*, pp. 9–26, and Lee I. Levine, *Judaism and Hellenism in Antiquity: Conflict or Confluence?* The topic is of concern to New Testament scholars; see also Stanley E. Porter, "Jesus and the Use of Greek in Galilee," in Bruce Chilton and Craig Evans, eds., *Studying the Historical Jesus*, pp. 123–154. Porter concludes that Jesus spoke Greek at various times in his itinerant ministry, and that his actual words may be recorded in Mark 15:2 and parallels. Those minimalizing the extent of Greek influence include Louis H. Feldman, *Jew and Gentile in the Ancient World*, pp. 3–44. Treatments questioning the extent of knowledge of the Greek language in Palestine but emphasizing the pervasiveness of other manifestations of Hellenism include L. L. Grabbe, *Judaism from Cyrus to Hadrian*, vol. 1 pp. 147–170, and the new Schurer, *A History of the Jewish People in the Time of Jesus Christ*, vol. 2 pp. 29–80.

2. See Andrea Berlin, "Between Large Forces: Palestine in the Hellenistic Period," *Biblical Archaeologist* 60 (1997) 2–51, for a presentation of this idea using archeological evidence.

3. Jacob Freudenthal, *Alexander Polyhistor*, pp. 99–101, cited in Erich S. Gruen, *Heritage and Hellenism*, p. 123 n. 52; see also the citations of arguments for and against the Samaritan identity of Theodotus in Gruen on pp. 120–127, esp. p. 123 n. 53.

4. Louis H. Feldman, *Jew and Gentile in the Ancient Greek World*, pp. 28–29 and p. 471 n. 139. But see Stanley E. Porter, "Jesus and the Use of Greek in Galilee," in Bruce Chilton and Craig Evans, eds., *Studying the Historical Jesus*, esp. pp. 137–147, for a different view.

5. With regard to the epigraphical evidence, Peter W. van der Horst calls these "minimalist interpretations," citing works by Louis Feldman, Tessa Rajak, Lester Grabbe, and the new Schurer. P. van der Horst, *Japheth in the Tents of Shem*, p. 26.

6. Shaye Cohen, *From the Maccabees to the Mishnah*, pp. 36–7.

7. For the term in Alexandrian Homeric criticism, see Gregory Nagy, *Poetry as Performance: Homer and Beyond*, pp. 118–126.

8. Some of the following material is taken from the excellent chapter by Pieter W. van der Horst, "Who Was Apion?", in *Japeth in the Tents of Shem*, pp. 207–221.

9. Suzanne Netzel, ". . . wurde von den griechischen Städten mit dem Ehrennamen Ὁμηρικός *ausgezeichnet*," ed., *Apions* Γλῶσσαι Ὁμηρικαί, in vol. 3 of Sammlung griechischer und lateinischer Grammatike, p. 189.

10. Pliny, Natural History, Praef. 25. See P. van der Horst, "Who Was Apion?," *Japheth in the Tents of Shem*, p. 209.

11. In the *Deipnosophistae* of Athenaeus (1.16f–17b), it is also stated that Apion claimed to know secret details about Penelope's suitors in the *Odyssey*.

12. See P. van der Horst, "Who Was Apion?," *Japheth in the Tents of Shem*, pp. 217–220.

13. *Flavius Josèphe, Contre Apion*, ed. Th. Reinach, Paris: Les Belles Lettres, 1930, n. ad I.12; quoted in Tessa Rajak, "The Sense of History in Jewish Intertestamental Writing," p. 125, and p. 142 n. 7.

14. F. A. Wolf, *Prolegomena to Homer: 1795*, translated by A. Grafton, G. Most, and J. Zetzel, pp. 94–95; and F. A. Wolf, *Prolegomena ad Homerum*, 3rd edition, ed. Rudolf Peppmüller, pp. 58–9.

15. See Nagy, *Homeric Questions*, esp. chapter 3, "The Evolution of a Homeric Text."

16. Nagy, "Homeric Scholia," in *A New Companion to Homer*, ed. Ian Morris and Barry Powell, p. 108.

17. Minna Skafte Jensen, *The Homeric Question and the Oral Formulaic Theory*, p. 150.

18. The following table is reproduced from Jensen's study (pp. 150–151), and is used by her to argue for a common element in all the Peisistratean accounts:

| Josephus | διαμνημονευομένης διαφωνίας | συντεθῆναι |
| Plutarch | διατηρούμενος διαφερομένης | συνήγαγεν |
| Pausanias | διεσπασμένα | |
| Aelianus | διηρημένα | συναγαγών |

| | | |
|---|---|---|
| Julius Africanus | | συνράπτοντες |
| Pindar-sch. d | διῃρημένης | συνηγμένης |
| | διαδεδομένης | |
| Vita IV | | συνήγαγεν |
| Vita V | | συνέταξεν |
| D. Thr.-sch. | διασκεδασθέντων | συναγαγεῖν |
| | διασπασθῆναι | συνθεῖναι |
| | | συνερράφησαν |
| *Suda* | | συνετέθη |
| | | συνετάχθη |
| Eustathius | διῃρημένης | συνθέμενοι |
| | | συνέρραπτον |
| Tetzes | | συνήθροισεν |
| | | συναγείρας |
| | | συνθεῖναι |
| | διαφόρων | συμφορηθέντες |

19. Most scholars have assumed that the Peisistratids' role in Homeric recension was history rather than mythic history; they have also read Peisistratus into Josephus' account, though the historian makes no mention of him in this regard. Jensen implies that Josephus utilizes a vocabulary of the Peisistratean legends, and thus was referring to Peisistratus. However, not all of the legends she quotes in the table above involve Peisistratus, and if there is any common vocabulary, it merely reflects a typical way of describing Homeric transmission, and is not an argument for an archetypal version of transmission that involved Peisistratus.

20. Stories about Peisistratus "forging" lines and inserting them into his Homer text were part of an ancient Megaran polemic against Peisistratean Athens. Such resonances to the Peisistratean legend were surely not at issue by the time the Pergamene mythmakers took over the legend and refashioned it into a foundational myth for the Pergamene library.

21. Nagy, "Homeric Scholia," pp. 109–110.

22. Nagy, "Homeric Scholia," p. 110 n. 29, citing M. S. Jensen, *The Homeric Question and the Oral Formulaic Theory*, pp. 155 and 150; see also Nagy, "The Library of Pergamon as a Classical Model," in Helmut Koester, ed., *Pergamon: Citadel of the Gods*, p. 228, for a restatement of the idea that Josephus did not believe that the songs of Homer had originally been written down, and that "Josephus was using the older construct of the

Peisistratean Recension in order to undercut the ideology of his Aristarchean opponent, Apion."

23. On the problem of dating the evidence, see Jensen, *The Homeric
Question*, p. 134.

24. Nagy, "The Library of Pergamon as a Classical Model," p. 45.

25. Ibid., p. 46. He adds: "In the Homeric scholia, mentions of the
Peisistratean Recension surface very rarely: scholia T at *Iliad* X.1 and scholia H at *Odyssey* xi.604," citing Minna Skafte Jensen, *The Homeric Question*, pp. 216–18.

26. James Kugel, *The Idea of Biblical Poetry*, pp. 141–2.

27. Alcidamas, a contemporary of Isocrates, was in favor of the improvisation of speeches, and thought that the Homeric rhapsodes were
improvisators, and that he was continuing the rhapsodic tradition by advocating improvisation in oratory; apparently he retold the story of the
contest of Homer and Hesiod in *autoskhediazein* 'improvising'. Pfeiffer
p. 50 n. 5, citing the Michigan Papyrus (first published in 1925) and the
Flinders Petrie Papyrus (first published in 1891). See Albert Lord, *The
Singer of Tales*, for a discussion of how traditional poets deny that they are
adding new material to their poems.

28. Tironum gratia cum Meriano notandum est, illud φασὶν de rebus
vel certissimis usurpari in fama minime obscura, non de iis, quae a non-
nullis sive paucis traduntur. De his Graece est φασὶν ἔνιοι. φασί τινες. Eadem ratio est Lat. verborum dicunt, ferunt, tradunt, perhibent. Neque vero
per se hoc multum proficit. Quam multa perhibet fama, quorum falsi-
tatem ratio et tres testes doceant! 'For the sake of beginners, I must point
out, as Merian does, that the expression "they say" is used even for things
that are quite certain, in a *report that is by no means obscure*, not for things
that are reported by some or a few. The Greek expression for these latter is
"some say." The nature of the Latin verbs *dicunt, ferunt, perhibent,* is just
the same. Not that this is very helpful in itself. For rumor asserts (*perhibet*)
a great many things that reason and three witnesses show to be false!'
F. A. Wolf, *Prolegomena to Homer: 1795*, trans. Grafton, Most, and Zetzel,
p. 94 n. 38.

29. See Nagy, *Poetry as Performance*, pp. 136 and 187 on city editions.

30. This stands in contrast to Scholia T to *Iliad* 6.168, and the Scholia to Dionysius Thrax, p. 185, 13–17, ed. Hilgard. Cf. Zs. Ritoók, "Josephus
and Homer," *Acta Antiqua Academiae Scientiarum Hungaricae* 32 (1989) p.

143 n. 32. Ritoók also cites Chairemon (first century C.E.) who maintained that Homer knew hieroglyphs (Karl Müller, *Fragmenta Historicorum Graecorum*, 618 F 2).

31. It is uncertain whether Josephus means Artaxerxes I Longimanus or Artaxerxes II Mnemon.

32. Wilhelm Bacher, *Tradition und Tradenten*, p. 3 n. 4 writes that these words suggest a Hebrew expression הבלת האבות. However, he finds no attestation of the expression.

33. Bickerman cites Jeremiah 7:25 to support the idea that the prophets were sent by God to Israel as need arose, rather than receiving their authority from their predecessors. In other words, prophets did not hand over their authority as a king hands over his kingship. Bickerman, "La chaine de la tradition Pharisiènne," in *Studies in Jewish and Christian History*.

34. "Dans celle-ci la lignée professorale de maître à élève, est substituée à la filiation naturelle des aïeux aux descendants." Bickerman, "La chaine de la tradition Pharisiènne," p. 261.

35. Bickerman (p. 261 n. 29) quotes Horace, *Odes* I.29.14: *Socraticum . . . domum*, as well as Louis Robert, *Archaiologike Ephemeris*, 1969, p. 8 under *oikos*. Bickerman also notes that Hellenized "Barbarians" imitated the Greek example. For similar treatments of Greek institutions among Jews in the early rabbinic period, see Saul Lieberman, *Hellenism in Jewish Palestine*.

36. Saul Lieberman, "The Publication of the Mishnah," in *Hellenism in Jewish Palestine*.

37. According to Frank Moore Cross, Hillel was probably also responsible for promulgating the consonantal Masoretic (proto-rabbinic) text of the biblical works, as opposed to the Septuagint and Samaritan Pentateuch-type manuscript families that were then circulating in Palestine. See Cross, *The Ancient Library at Qumran*.

38. On the Homer of Aristotle, see Gregory Nagy, *Poetry as Performance*.

39. On the manuscript traditions of the Hebrew Bible, see Emanuel Tov, "The History and Significance of a Standard Text of the Hebrew Bible," in Magne Saebo, ed. *Hebrew Bible / Old Testament: The History of Its Interpretation*, vol. I, pp. 49–66.

40. Rebecca Gray, *Prophetic Figures in Late Second Temple Jewish Palestine*, p. 12.

41. Gray's findings on the use of the word "prophet" in the writings of Josephus stand at odds with the following position of Sid Leiman: "Once there was a break in the exact succession of the prophets, after the period of Artaxerxes, isolated instances of prophecy were possible but not literary prophecy . . . The stress may well have been on the 'historical' aspects of literary prophecy. Only a continuous history could be deemed inspired. Interrupted or sporadic histories are by definition incomplete and therefore inferior. Once the chain was broken, nothing new could be added to the biblical canon. This qualitative difference between pre- and post-Artaxerxes prophecy is also reflected in Josephan terminology. The term προφήτης is almost exclusively reserved for pre-Artaxerxes prophets. A post-Artaxerxes prophet is almost always called μάντις, or a related Greek term, but not προφήτης." Sid Leiman, "Josephus and the Canon of the Bible," in *Josephus, the Bible, and History*, eds. Louis H. Feldman and Gohei Hatta, p. 56.

42. For a discussion of this passage, see Thomas W. Allen, *Homer: Origins and Transmission*.

43. See 'Homeridai' by Rzach *RE* VIII 2147 f. Cf. also families of poets in India; see Steinthal, *Geschichte der Sprachwissenschaft bei den Griechen und Römern* I (1890), p. 30. Also, cf. the scholia vetera et recentiora partim Thomae Magistri et Triclinii to Pindar *Nemean* 2, which has the following expression: οἱ ὁμηρίδαι καὶ οἱ υἱοὶ τοῦ ὁμήρου. ἤγουν οἱ ποιηταί 'the Homeridai and the sons of Homer, or rather the poets'.

44. M. L. West, "The Invention of Homer," *Classical Quarterly* 49.2 (1999), p. 373.

45. Ibid., p. 371.

46. See M. L. West, *The East Face of Helicon*, p. 622 for the proposed etymology. He cites G. Croese, ΟΜΗΡΟΣ ΕΒΡΑΙΟΣ, *Sive Historia Hebraeorum ab Homero Hebraicis nominibus ac sententiis conscripta in Odyssea & Iliade*, Dordraci 1704, p. 59: "itaque Ὅμηρος mihi videtur nomen esse Hebraicum אמר OMER, *orator, rhetor* . . . Vel relatè magis ad opus, ut sit אמר OMER, *sermo, dictum, commentarius.*"

47. West compares this to the Cyprian Kinyradai, from whom the mythical Cinyras was abstracted; he argues that the Phoenician prototype for this guild would be *beney kinnur* 'sons of the lyre'. See M. L. West, *The East Face of Helicon*, pp. 57 and 622.

48. Steve Mason, *Flavius Josephus on the Pharisees*, esp. pp. 325–356.

49. Wilhelm Bacher, *Tradition und Tradenten*, p. 3 n. 4 compares the

Greek expression *ek paradoseôs tôn paterôn* with the Aramaic expression מסורתא דאבהתהוין found in Targum to Job 15:18, a paraphrase of the word מאבותם in that verse.

50. On the significance of the Temple archives, see R. Beckwith, "Formation of the Hebrew Bible," in Martin Jan Mulder, ed., *Mikra*, pp. 40–45. Beckwith rightly concludes that whether a book was laid up in the Temple archives had great import for the canonical reception of the book. See also A. van der Kooij, "The Canonization of Ancient Books Kept in the Temple of Jerusalem," in A. van der Kooij and K. van der Toorn, eds., *Canonization and Decanonization*, p. 31.

51. For the text, see Pancratius C. Beentjes, *The Book of Ben Sira in Hebrew*, p. 81.

52. For the text, see ibid., p. 86.

53. This reading, which accords with the Greek translation of Ben Sira, is found in M. H. Segal, *Sefer Ben-Sira Ha-Shalem*.

54. Similarly, in Josephus' version of these events, God tells Elijah that he should make Elisha a prophet "in his place" (*ant' autou*), implying that there is a prophetic office (*Antiquities* 8.352). In a departure from scripture, Josephus also writes that Elisha began to prophesy as soon as Elijah placed his mantle on top of him (*Antiquities* 8.354). Elisha is explicitly called the *diadokhos* 'successor' of Elijah in the *Jewish War* 4.460.

55. See Yehoshua Amir, *Die hellenistische Gestalt des Judentums bei Philon von Alexandrien*.

56. David T. Runia, *Philo of Alexandria and the* Timaeus *of Plato*, p. 57.

57. Maurice Bloch, *From Blessing to Violence: History and ideology in the circumcision ritual of the Merina of Madagascar*, pp. 9–10 [italics mine].

58. John Barton addresses this logical problem by pointing out that the different sides in the debate are using different definitions of "canon": "But even this degree of disagreement may in reality be less serious than it looks, since in some ways it masks a fundamental failure to agree on the meaning of the term 'canonical.' When scholars say that even as late as the second century A.D. there could still be dispute about the canonicity of a few of the books in the Writings, they usually mean by the 'canon' a closed list to which no books may be added — indeed, the idea of closure is integral to the idea of canonicity in most scholarly discussions. But when Leiman argues that the Prophets were already finished by 400 and the Writings very soon after the composition of Daniel, it is important to see

that his definition of canonicity does not include this vital ingredient. According to his understanding of the term 'canonical,' 'A canonical book is a book accepted by Jews as authoritative for religious practice and/or doctrine, and whose authority is binding upon the Jewish people for all generations'. This apparently says nothing about the *closed* character of the canon at all . . . My impression is that in practice Leiman often elides this point in his discussion, and treats the 'authoritative' books as having *exclusive* authority for Judaism just as do scholars whose definition of 'canon' does include the note of closure; but at least in principle, some of the disagreements between him and proponents of a later date for the fixing of the canon are disputes about words rather than facts." John Barton, *Oracles of God*, p. 28.

59. On the creation of the Yavne theory of canonization, see David Aune, "The Origins of the 'Council of Javne' Myth," *Journal of Biblical Literature* 110 (1991), pp. 491–3. Aune traces the theory back to Spinoza. See also Jack P. Lewis, "What Do We Mean By Jabneh?" *JBR* 32 (1964) 125–132; P. Schäfer, "Die sogenannte Synode von Jabne, II. Der Abschluss des Kanons," *Judaica* 31 (1975) 116–124; Günter Stemberger, "Die sogenannte 'Synode von Jabne' und das frühe Christentum," *Kairos: Zeitschrift für Religionswissenschaft und Theologie* 19 (1977) 14–21, and "Jabne und der Kanon," *Jahrbuch für biblische Theologie* 3 (1988) 163–174; Sid Leiman, *The Canonization of Hebrew Scripture*, pp. 120–124.

60. See, for example, Leiman, *The Canonization of Hebrew Scripture*, p. 29.

61. Ibid., p. 14.

62. Ibid., pp. 127–128.

63. A. van der Kooij, "The Canonization of Ancient Books Kept in the Temple of Jerusalem," in A. van der Kooij and K. van der Toorn, eds., *Canonization and Decanonization*, pp. 22 and 38.

64. Ibid., pp. 37–38.

65. Ibid., p. 24, citing J. L. Koole, "Die Bibel des Ben-Sira," *OTS* 23 (1965) 374–96.

66. Sid Leiman tentatively identifies the "letters of the kings about offerings" with Ezra 7:11–26, the letter that Artaxerxes I gave to Ezra; but this is not convincing, since it is only a single letter appearing within a larger work.

67. A. van der Kooij, "The Canonization of Ancient Books Kept in the

Temple of Jerusalem," p. 25, citing U. Kellermann, *Nehemia. Quellen, Überlieferung und Geschichte*, p. 122 f.

68. Cf. the comparison between Ptolemy Philadelphus and Peisistratus, where Ptolemy is imagined as a latter-day Peisistratus; see chapter 5.

69. Elisha Qimron and John Strugnell, Discoveries in the Judean Desert X, pp. 58–59.

70. Philo, *De Vita Contemplativa* 3.25: ἐν ἑκάστῃ δέ ἐστιν οἴκημα ἱερόν, ὃ καλεῖται σεμνεῖον καὶ μοναστήριον, ἐν ᾧ μονούμενοι τὰ τοῦ σεμνοῦ βίου μυστήρια τελοῦνται, μηδὲν εἰσκομίζοντες, μὴ ποτόν, μὴ σιτίον, μηδέ τι τῶν ἄλλων ὅσα πρὸς τὰς τοῦ σώματος χρείας ἀναγκαῖα, ἀλλὰ νόμους καὶ λόγια θεσπισθέντα διὰ προφητῶν καὶ ὕμνους καὶ τὰ ἄλλα οἷς ἐπιστήμη καὶ εὐσέβεια συναύξονται καὶ τελειοῦνται 'In each house there is a consecrated room which is called a sanctuary or closet and closeted in this they are initiated into the mysteries of the sanctified life. They take nothing into it, either drink or food or any other of the things necessary for the needs of the body, but laws and oracles delivered through the mouths of prophets, and psalms and anything else which fosters and perfects knowledge and piety'.

71. Luke 24:27: καὶ ἀρξάμενος ἀπὸ Μωϋσέως καὶ ἀπὸ πάντων τῶν προφητῶν διερμήνευσεν αὐτοῖς ἐν πάσαις ταῖς γραφαῖς τὰ περὶ ἑαυτοῦ 'And beginning from Moses and from all the prophets, he interpreted to them in all the scriptures events that concerned himself'.

72. 4 Maccabees 18:10: ὃς ἐδίδασκεν ὑμᾶς ἔτι ὢν σὺν ὑμῖν τὸν νόμον καὶ τοὺς προφήτας 'who taught you, while he was still with you, the law and the prophets'.

73. Cf. T. Kelim Bava Metzia 5:8, which speaks of three identical categories of scripture: the Book of Ezra (likely Ezra's recension of the Pentateuch, i.e. the book of the Temple court), Prophets, and *ḥomashin* 'fifths' (a way of referring to the five scrolls of Psalms). See also other instances of "the book of Ezra" in M. Moed Qatan 3:4; J. Sheqalim 4:2 (ed. Zhitomir, p. 27); and J. Sanhedrin 20c. Cited in Leiman, *The Canonization of Hebrew Scripture*, p. 189 n. 496.

74. Luke 24:44: Εἶπεν δὲ πρὸς αὐτούς, Οὗτοι οἱ λόγοι μου οὓς ἐλάλησα πρὸς ὑμᾶς ἔτι ὢν σὺν ὑμῖν, ὅτι δεῖ πληρωθῆναι πάντα τὰ γεγραμμένα ἐν τῷ νόμῳ Μωϋσέως καὶ τοῖς προφήταις καὶ ψαλμοῖς περὶ ἐμοῦ 'Then he said to them, These are my words that I spoke to you while I was still with you — that everything written about me in the law of Moses, the prophets, and the psalms must be fulfilled'.

75. Blenkinsopp, for example, argues that "the designation 'Former Prophets' was due not to content but to the tradition of prophetic authorship." But this explanation properly applies not only to the Former and Latter prophets, but also to many books in the Writings, with the caveat that "witnessing by a prophet" more correctly describes the textualization involved than does Blenkinsopp's formulation "prophetic authorship." Blenkinsopp, *The History of Prophecy in Israel*, p. 22.

76. I am not convinced by Joseph Fitzmyer's claim that Josephus' description of David as "prophesying" (*Antiquities* 6.166) is parallel to the comment in Acts 2:30, seeing as Josephus did not consider David part of the prophetic succession, and may not have been comfortable labeling him a prophet, even if he prophesied. J. A. Fitzmyer, "David, 'Being Therefore a Prophet . . .' (Acts 2:30)," *The Catholic Bible Quarterly* 34 (1972), p. 338.

77. A less likely explanation is that Josephus does not count David as the textualizer of all the Psalms (e.g. Psalm 137, which depicts the post-Davidic Babylonian exile). This would itself be at odds with the "list of David's compositions" (11QPs$^a$), where he is described as the textualizer of the Psalms. See chapter 2.

78. A similar point is made by Blenkinsopp: "On this showing, the primary function of the prophet was to bridge the gap between the primordial revelation at Sinai and the rabbinic leadership. Like the sages who succeeded them (cf. B. Baba Bathra 12a), *the prophets were therefore in the first place custodians and traditioners of Torah*, which implied that prophecy was clearly subordinate to law." Blenkinsopp, *The History of Prophecy in Israel*, p. 24 (italics mine). I would substitute "scripture" for "Torah" to describe how the prophets were viewed in the Second Temple period. Blenkinsopp goes on to state, "The postscript to the Pentateuch (Deut. 34:10–12) establishes a clear demarcation at the death of Moses and denies parity between the revelation accorded to him and prophetic revelation." Blenkinsopp, *The History of Prophecy in Israel*, p. 26.

79. But perhaps it is significant that in the *baraita* there is no role for Baruch, although the book of Jeremiah expressly states that he was the scribe who wrote Jeremiah's prophecies. Baruch was not a prophet, and thus could not have been responsible for the *ultimate* textualization of the books of Jeremiah, Kings, and Lamentations, according to the standards of Josephus. We are to imagine that Jeremiah later recopied what Baruch, his secretary, had initially recorded.

80. On the prophetic status of David, also see chapter 2. Ezra, who copied out his own book (probably including the book of Nehemiah, which the *baraita* does not mention explicitly) and the book of Chronicles, was legitimated by his midrashic identification with the prophet Malachi. The prophetic status of the Men of the Great Assembly was based on the fact that they included Haggai, Zechariah, and Malachi in their number. The status of Nehemiah, who finished Chronicles according to Baba Bathra 14b–15a, is less clear — yet the discussion about Nehemiah does not belong to the *baraita* itself, but rather to later commentators.

81. Cf. 2 Chronicles 33:19: "And his prayer, and how God received his entreaty, and all his sins, and his trespass, and the places where he built high places, and set up Asherim and carved idols, before he was humbled; behold, they are written among the sayings of the seers (הִנָּם כְּתוּבִים עַל דִּבְרֵי חוֹזָי)."

82. See Leiman, *The Canonization of Hebrew Scripture*, p. 165 n. 262. Leiman cites A. Neubauer, *Mediaeval Jewish Chronicles*, vol. 1, p. 174, and R. Rabbinovicz, *Diqduqey Sofrim*, ad loc.

83. See also Targum Jonathan to 1 Kings 5:13, which refers to Solomon as "prophesying" in producing wisdom; cited in A. van der Kooij, "The Canonization of Ancient Books," in van der Kooij and van der Toorn, eds., *Canonization and Decanonization*, p. 29 n. 19; van der Kooij also cites Ben Sira 24:33, where wisdom is compared to prophecy. See also Sotah 48a–b, where David, Samuel and Solomon are classified as "former prophets" by R. Huna; cited in Leiman, *The Canonization of Hebrew Scripture*, p. 69.

84. Cf. the parallel statement in Ruth Rabbah 4.5, where *megillah hazot* 'this scroll' is understood to represent the book of Ruth:

רב ור' חנינא ור' יונתן ובר קפרא ורב"ל אמרו המגילה הזאת אין נאמרה מפי בית דין מסיני נאמרה

אלא שאין מוקדם ומאוחר בתורה

Rab, R. Ḥanina, R. Jonathan, and Bar Qappara all said: This scroll [Ruth] was not composed by the Court of that time, but was said upon Mt. Sinai, [and the reason that it is written here is that] there is no chronological order in the Torah.

Ruth Rabbah 4.5

85. See Jacob Neusner, "The Religious Uses of History," *History and Theory* 5 (1966) 153–71. Chaim Milikowsky has added to the understanding of historiography in the period with his work on Seder Olam, a chronographic work that he dates to the early Mishnaic period. See C. Milikowsky, *Seder Olam: A Rabbinic Chronography*.

86. On the idea of the signature in antiquity, see W. Speyer, *Die Liter-arische Fälschung*, pp. 50–65. For an exploration of the hermeneutics of the signature in Western philosophy, see Jacques Derrida, "Signature, Event, Context," in *Margins of Philosophy*, pp. 307–330.

CHAPTER 5: PEISISTRATUS AND PTOLEMY

1. The Scholia to Dionysius Thrax were first published by Villoison and were later edited again by Bekker. Both of these editions attempted to fuse all the manuscript traditions into a single work, as if attempting to arrive at the Urtext of a single scholiastic tradition. In the case of the legend of Peisistratus, this practice resulted in the presentation of totally different and even mutually exclusive versions of the legend, which disrupted the meaning of these versions. Hilgard's 1901 edition prints the several manuscript traditions separately.

2. Pfeiffer further speculates that Asclepiades' collection of biographies *Peri Grammatikôn* was perhaps the source of the story about Peisistratus in Cicero, *De Oratore*. Pfeiffer, *The History of Classical Scholarship*, p. 273.

3. Pfeiffer, *The History of Classical Scholarship*, p. 158, especially n. 7; Pfeiffer cites G. Kaibel, *Die Prolegomena Peri Kômôidias*, Abhandlungen der Göttinger Gesellschaft der Wissenschaften, N. F. II 4 (1898) pp. 27 ff.

4. Cod. 489 is more expansive here: "Rhapsody is a part of the *poiêma;* it is comprised of and contains something small in itself and a short *peripeteia*, as Book 1 has the anger of Achilles, and Book 2, the deceitful dream, and Book 3, the duel between Paris and Menelaos. What is a *peripeteia*? A chance event (*sumptôma*) of the plot (*hupothesis*)."

5. Aelian, *Varia Historia* 13.14: "That the ancients used to sing the poetic utterances of Homer in separate parts: for example, they spoke of 'The Battle over the Ships,' 'A Story of Dolon,' 'The Greatest Heroic Moments (*aristeia*) of Agamemnon,' 'The Catalogue of Ships,' 'The Story of Patroklos,' 'The Ransom,' 'The Funeral Games over Patrokolos,' and 'The Breaking of the Oaths.' These were in place of the *Iliad*. In place of the other poem there were 'The Happenings in Pylos,' 'The Happenings in Sparta,' 'The Cave of Calypso,' 'The Story of the Raft,' 'The Stories Told to Alkinoos,' 'The Story of the Cyclops,' 'The Spirits of the Dead,' 'The Story of Circe,' 'The Bath,' 'The Killing of the Suitors,' 'The Happenings in the

Countryside,' and 'The Happenings at Laertes' Place.' At a late date, Lycurgus of Sparta was the first to bring the collected poetry of Homer to Greece. He brought this cargo from Ionia, when he traveled there. Later, Peisistratus collected it together and featured it as the *Iliad* and the *Odyssey.*" Translation after Sealey 1957, p. 344, quoted in G. Nagy, *Homeric Questions*, p. 78.

6. See J. A. Davison, "Peisistratus and Homer," *Transactions of the American Philological Association* 86 (1955) 1–21.

7. Gregory Nagy, "The Library of Pergamon as a Classical Model," in Helmut Koester, ed., *Pergamon: Citadel of the Gods*, pp. 185–232.

8. Recently, it has been argued that the approach of Crates was in reality more thematic than it was allegorical. See James I. Porter, "Hermeneutic Lines and Circles: Aristarchus and Crates on the Exegesis of Homer," in Robert Lamberton and John J. Keaney, eds., *Homer's Ancient Readers*, pp. 67–114.

9. Gregory Nagy, "The Library of Pergamon as a Classical Model," in Helmut Koester, ed., *Pergamon: Citadel of the Gods*, pp. 185–232.

10. According to Elizabeth Rawson, Posidonius defines *poiêma* as "diction that is metrical, and more elaborate than prose," while *poiêsis* is "poetic diction that is significant, and portrays, 'imitates,' things human and divine." On the other hand, for Philodemus, *poiêsis* means a whole work, and *poiêma* is a passage from it. E. Rawson, *Intellectual Life in the Late Roman Republic*, p. 280. As Minna Skafte Jensen has pointed out, "in Josephus, Plutarch, Aelianus, and two of the Pindaric scholia the words are used consistently so that ποίησις (*poiêsis*) is Homer's own work, the thing that was scattered, while *poiêmata* (or sometimes ἔπη) means the poems collected, edited, etc., generally the *Iliad* and the *Odyssey*. Thus, we find ourselves in a field that obviously has its own terminology; this is, however, used for expressing rather different subjects, a sign of the tradition being much more widespread than appears from its actual occurrences." Minna Skafte Jensen, *The Homeric Question and the Oral-Formulaic Theory*, p. 152.

11. Cf. the even stronger parallel in *Scholia Londinensia* (AE): "'Rhapsody is part of the *poiêma*.' He erred when he claimed rhapsody is part of the *poiêma*. He should have said that it is part of the *poiêsis*. For it is said that the *Iliad* and *Odyssey* are *poiêsis*, and rhapsody is *poiêma*; rhapsody is part of the *poiêsis*; it is not part of the *poiêma*" (Hilgard, p. 480).

12. Dionysius Thrax, a student of Aristarchus, would not have made the error of thinking that Peisistratus was alive in the time of his teacher.

13. For instance, according to Diogenes Laertius, "[Solon the Lawgiver] has written a law that the works of Homer are to be performed rhapsodically (verb *rhapsoideô*), by relay, so that wherever the first person left off, from that point the next person should start" (1.57).

14. These are: "Skill in reading aloud with due attention to prosodic features; interpretation, taking note of the tropes of literary composition found in the text; the ready explanation of obscure words and historical references; discovery of the origins of words; a detailed account of regular patterns; and a critical assessment (= 'poetic analysis') of poems — of all that the art includes this is the noblest part." Translation by Alan Kemp, "The *Tekhnê Grammatikê* of Dionysius Thrax Translated into English," p. 172.

15. The attribution of the grammatical treatise to Dionysius Thrax has been questioned by some who wish to date the text much later; see Alan Kemp, "The *Tekhnê Grammatikê* of Dionysius Thrax Translated into English," in Robert A. Kaster, ed., *The History of Linguistics in the Classical Period*, pp. 169–172. K. W. Göttlink tried to persuade his readers that the so-called *Ars Grammatica* of Dionysius Thrax was a Byzantine compilation. See Theodosius Alexandrinus, *Grammatica*, ed. C. G. Goettling (1882), praef. V ff. Moritz Schmidt and G. Uhlig, editor of the *Tekhnê (Grammatici Graeci* II [1883]), found the opposite. In 1958, V. di Benedetto again challenged its authorship, but Rudolf Pfeiffer raises the decisive objection that we have no evidence for a systematization of grammar a century later than Dionysius Thrax. See Moritz Schmidt, "Dionys der Thraker," *Philol.* 7 (1852) 360 ff., esp. 369 ff.; and Moritz Schmidt, "Dionys der Thraker," *Philol.* 8 (1853) 231 ff., 510 ff.; p. 231 ff. for a bibliography of the controversy. See also Cohn, *RE* v 982 on the importance of the Scholia for the history of grammatical studies; M. Fuhrmann, *Das systematische Lehrbuch* (1960) 29 ff., 145 ff., 152 ff., and 192 (Addenda); and V. di Benedetto "Dionisio Trace e la techne a lui attributa," *Annali della Scuola Normale Superiore di Pisa*, Ser. II, vol. 27 (1958) 169–210, vol. 28 (1959) 87–118.

16. For the idea of discourse and discursive formations, see Michel Foucault, *The Archaeology of Knowledge and the Discourse on Language*, esp. chapters 1 and 2.

17. Gregory Nagy states that Dionysius Thrax himself was strongly

influenced by the Cratean approach to the variety of forms in the spoken language, the *sunêtheia*. See Nagy, "The Library of Pergamon as a Classical Model," pp. 42–3, citing Pfeiffer, *Classical Scholarship*, p. 245.

18. Liddell, Scott, Jones s.v. *prolêpsis*.

19. However, the Alexandrians never claimed to have Alexander the Great's personal copy of Homer's *Iliad*. This copy was Aristotle's corrected edition that Aristotle eventually gave to Alexander. Alexander kept it under his bed together with his dagger, and later put into the box (*narthêx*) that contained the ointment vessels of Darius; thus it became the famous *Iliad* "out of the *narthêx*" (Strabo XIII.1.27 and Plutarch, *Alexander* 26). Evidently, this version was not in the possession of the Alexandrian philologists, or was of little value to them. See Blum, *Kallimachos*, pp. 69–70 n. 45.

20. Galen, *In Hippocratis Epidemiarum* III, pp. 79–80, 607.

21. Cf. Letter of Aristeas 121: οἵτινες οὐ μόνον τὴν τῶν Ἰουδαικῶν γραμμάτων ἕξιν περιεποίησαν αὐτοῖς, ἀλλὰ καὶ τῆς τῶν Ἑλληνικῶν ἐφρόντισαν οὐ παρέργως κατασκευῆς 'They had not only acquired <u>proficiency</u> in the literature of the Jews, but had bestowed no slight study on that of the Greeks also' (trans. Hadas).

22. See L.O. Bröker, "Die Methoden Galens in der literarischen Kritik," *Rheinisches Museum* 40 (1885) 415–38; and J. Mewaldt, "Galen über echte und unechte Hippocratica," *Hermes* 44 (1909) 111–34.

23. Cf. the statement found in the commentary on Aristotle's *Categories* by Philoponus:

Πτολεμαῖον τὸν Φιλάδελφον πάνυ ἐσπουδακέναι φασὶ περὶ τὰ Ἀριστοτέλους συγγράμματα, ὡς καὶ περὶ τὰ λοιπά, καὶ χρήματα διδόναι τοῖς προσφέρουσιν αὐτῷ βίβλους τοῦ φιλοσόφου. ὅθεν τινὲς χρηματίσασθαι βουλόμενοι ἐπιγράφοντες συγγράμματα τῷ τοῦ φιλοσόφου ὀνόματι προσῆγον·

They say (*phasi*) that Ptolemy Philadelphus was altogether zealous concerning the works of Aristotle, just as he was for others, and that he gave money to those offering him books of the philosopher. On which account some, wishing to be reimbursed, brought him works that they inscribed (*epigraphô*) with the name of the philosopher.

Philoponus (olim Ammonius), In Aristotelis Categorias<br>Commentarium, ed. Busse, pp. 7–8

24. Valentinus Rose, *Aristotelis Qui Ferebantur Librorum Fragmenta*, (Teubner: Lipsiae, 1886) no. 7: (Io. Philoponus ad Aristotelis *de anima* 1, 5. 1410ᵇ 28 ἐν τοῖς ᾽Ορφικοῖς καλουμένοις ἔπεσι) f. F 3ᵃ sup.: λεγομένοις εἶπεν ἐπειδὴ μὴ δοκεῖ ᾽Ορφέως εἶναι τὰ ἔπη, ὡς καὶ αὐτὸς ἐν τοῖς περὶ φιλοσοφίας λέγει· αὐτοῦ μὲν γάρ εἰσι τὰ δόγματα, ταῦτα δέ φησιν ᾽Ονομάκριτον ἐν ἔπεσι κατατεῖναι '(in the so–called Orphic verses): he said "so-called" since the verses do not seem to belong to Orpheus, as he himself also says in *Peri Philosophias*. For the teachings are his [= those of Orpheus], but he says that Onomacritus stretched them out in hexameters'. Cited by Rose here is also a statement by Cicero (*De Natura Deorum* 1.38): Orpheum poetam docet Aristoteles numquam fuisse et hoc Orphicum carmen Pythagorei ferunt cuiusdam fuisse Cercopis 'Aristotle teaches that the poet Orpheus never existed and that the Pythagoreans consider this Orphic poem to belong to a certain Cercops'.

25. Cf. Carolyn Higbe, "The Bones of the Hero, the Ashes of a Politician: Athens, Salamis, and the Usable Past," *Classical Antiquity* 16 (1997) 270–308, and Allen, *Homer: The Origins and Transmission*. In Strabo's description of the conflict, the Megarans accuse either the Peisistratids or Solon (Strabo 9.1.10).

26. Cf. Isidorus, *Etymologiae* VI.3.3–5.

27. M. Hadas states: "Tertullian (b. ca. 160) is the first writer after Josephus to mention (*Apology* 18) 'Aristaeus' by name, nor does he include the miraculous accretions of the intervening writers. The only tradition patently derived from a different source is his statement that 'to this day the libraries of Ptolemy are shown in the Serapeum with the actual Hebrew documents.'" M. Hadas, *Aristeas to Philocrates*, p. 76.

28. See Nagy, *Pindar's Homer*, pp. 160 ff.

29. It is important to note here that in the reports about Ptolemy's role in the translation of the Septuagint, his "zeal" is also foregrounded. An example of this is found in Aristobulus's account of the translation: "But the complete translation of everything in the law occurred at the time of the king surnamed Philadelphus, your ancestor, who brought great zeal (φιλοτιμία) to this undertaking, while Demetrius Phalereus attended to matters relating to these things" (Aristobulus frag. 3). Aristobulus frag. 3b expands on this: ". . . or according to some, in the time of Ptolemy surnamed Philadelphus, when Demetrius of Phalerum brought to this task the greatest zeal (φιλοτιμία), [and] attended to the matters of translation

with painstaking accuracy." Cf. Carl R. Holladay, *Fragments from Hellenistic Jewish Authors* III, pp. 156–7.

30. Later meanings of the word *spoudê* in Byzantine Greek may have influenced the trajectory of these legends: *spoudê* means 'haste' or 'zeal' in classical Greek, but also 'scholarship' and even 'the making of artistic transcripts' in later Greek.

31. Thanks to Timothy Power for this reference.

32. Scholia to Dionysius Thrax, ed. Hilgard, *Grammatici Graeci* III 160.32; cited in Pfeiffer, p. 224 n. 1.

33. On the censorius epithet *perisson* 'superfluous' see Pfeiffer, *History of Classical Scholarship*, p. 232.

34. Marc Shell, *Money, Language, and Thought*, p. 105.

35. Ibid., pp. 110–11.

36. Thamyras continued to expiate his sins in the underworld in the Nekuia of the *Minuas*, fr. 3, 4, along with Amphion. See Allen, *Homer: The Origins and Transmission*, p. 89 n.

37. Andrew Ford, *Homer: The Poetry of the Past*, p. 97.

38. Ibid., p. 99.

39. From Euripides' perspective, Orpheus does not come off so powerless. Admetus, the husband of Alcestis, yearns for the poetic powers of Orpheus in order to restore his wife to life (*Alcestis* 357–63).

40. A similar attempt at providing an etymology connecting "obolus" (the Latin form of the Greek coin) and "obelus" (the dagger-shaped mark that Aristarchus employed to mark inauthentic lines) is found in *Anecdotum Parisinum*, Parisian codex 7530 (780 C.E.). Cited in G. Veltri, "Tolomeo Filadelfo, emulo di Pisistrato," *Laurentianum* 32 (1991), pp. 162–3.

41. "70 et 72 renvoie aux Anciens qui assistent Moïse et qui prophétisent. Il n'y a aucune prétention historique derrière ces chiffres." Gilles Dorival, "La Bible des Septante: 70 ou 72 traducteurs?" in Gerard J. Norton and Stephen Pisano, eds., *Tradition of the Text: Studies offered to Dominique Barthélemy in Celebration of his 70th Birthday*, pp. 45–62.

42. One may compare the *kat' idian* theme with the use of *idiôtês* 'unaffiliated' in Strabo, *Geography* 13.1.54 C 609:

> Theophrastus bequeathed (*paradidômi*) it to Neleus, who brought it home (*komizô*) to Scepsis and bequeathed (*paradidômi*) it to his followers, <u>non-affiliated (*idiôtês* pl.) men</u>, who kept the books locked up but not carefully stored.

Affiliation in some way is perceived as casting doubt on the authenticity of the works contained in Aristotle's library; hence there is a need to add that the followers of Neleus were unaffiliated men, who did not add to these works out of some sense of allegiance to an individual or philosophical school. Or perhaps the lack of affiliation of these men rather explains why they were not interested enough in the books to prevent them from being damaged by moths and mold.

43. Moses Hadas, *Aristaeus to Philocrates*, pp. 71–2.

44. See Giuseppe Veltri, *Eine Tora für den König Talmai*, for an extensive treatment of the rabbinic polemic against the Septuagint.

45. The elements of the LXX version that substantively differ from the Masoretic Text are underlined.

46. Found in B. Megillah 9a and its parallels. See Veltri, *Eine Tora für den König Talmai*, pp. 78–88 for details on the rabbinic texts and variations on the spelling of יומימ in the manuscripts.

47. Cf. A. Pickard-Cambridge, *The Dramatic Festivals of Athens*.

48. Naomi Janowitz, "The Rhetoric of Translation: Three Early Perspectives on Translating Torah," *Harvard Theological Review* 84 (1991) 129.

49. According to G. Nagy, *Homeric Questions*, pp. 80–1, this expression probably referred to rhapsodic performance of the portions of Homer in relay.

50. Parallels can be found in Massekhet Soferim 1:8, Mekilta Exodus 12:40, Shemot Rabbah 5.5, Tanhuma Exodus 22. In Massekhet Soferim, however, there are no longer 72 translators, but only 5 (one for each book of the Pentateuch); Braverman suggests, "the source for Soferim 1:7 seems to be Aboth deRabbi Natan ch. 37, second version (ed. S. Schechter; New York: P. Feldheim, 1945), 94. Schechter's n. 1. ad loc cites a variant referring to ten translators." J. Braverman, *Jerome's Commentary on Daniel*, p. 16 n. 5.

51. See J. Braverman, *Jerome's Commentary on Daniel*, p. 33 n. 67.

52. Cf. ibid., p. 16 n. 5: "This technique was used by Alexandrian scholars to arrive at the text of Homer . . . The author of the Letter of Aristeas seems to be pointing out this analogy regarding the production of the texts of the LXX and Homer. Thus it is clear here that the translation was not divinely inspired, but the result of careful scholarly teamwork."

53. In a process we have not explored here, the rabbinic world highlighted the discrepancies of the Septuagint translation with the Hebrew original. Examining these two sets of responses to the Septuagint reveals a

significant correspondence: forgery as a challenge to Greek authoritative-ness is somehow equivalent to mistranslation as a challenge to the author-itativeness of the Bible in the Jewish world.

54. Something similar likely occurred in the comparison of Judas Maccabee to Nehemiah as collectors of a library of Hebrew scriptures (2 Maccabees 2:13–14). It is unlikely that the author of 2 Maccabees knew much about Nehemiah's collection of a "library," and it shouldn't be ruled out that the comparison was part of Judas' self-promotion. I suggested in chapter 4 that the library of Nehemiah was imagined in 2 Maccabees as a finite collection of scriptures merely re-assembled by Judas. However, the notion of "Nehemiah's library," if it in fact existed, might better be con-ceived as the archive he set up. Thus Nehemiah likely took on attributes of Judas only in retrospect; likewise, it was Judas who turned the archive into a finite collection which he thought to derive from centuries before.

55. Cf. the illusory absence of use-value in paper money, where the il-lusory absence is created by an undervaluation of money's metaphorical relationship to the commodity.

CHAPTER 6: ARISTOTLE AND EZRA

1 According to Rudolf Blum (*Kallimachos*, p. 61), the library of the Museion was merely augmented by the library of Aristotle and Theophras-tus that had been inherited by Neleus.

2. Aristotle, frag. 7, Rose.

3. Cf. the discussion on homonymy in chapter 5.

4. See Blum, *Kallimachos*, p. 202.

5. For example, [Plutarch] *Vitae Decem Oratorum* 836A describes 233 or 425 speeches ascribed to Lysias as *gnêsioi* 'legitimate'.

6. Pfeiffer, *History of Classical Scholarship*, p. 269.

7. Blum, *Kallimachos*, p. 18 and p. 67 n. 25, where he cites Jacoby (1957) no. 4, fragment 74–84 with commentary, and also Regebogen, "Pinax," column 1413 f.

8. Blum, *Kallimachos*, p. 19.

9. Jacoby, *Die Fragmente der griechischen Historiker*, 1957 no. 6, frag-ment 2 with commentary.

10. Eratosthenes is the founder of critical chronology in antiquity. Eratosthenes wrote *Olympionikai* and *Khronographiai*, first expounded the principles of scientific chronology, and worked out a complete chrono-

logical table on the foundation of the Olympic lists. 776/5 was fixed as the first year of the first Olympiad; see Van der Waerden, *Science Awakening* (1954) 228 ff. For the period prior to this, he had to use local lists, especially the list of the Spartan kings (preserved in Eusebius' *Khronika*) which goes back to the year 1104/3, the time of the *kathodos* of the Herakleides. See E. Schwartz, "Die Königslisten des Eratosthenes und Kastor," *AGGW* 40 (1894/5) 60 ff. Eratosthenes fixed the *akmê* of Homer to 100 years after the Trojan War but before the Ionian migration, and claimed that Hesiod had lived later than Homer.

11. Blum, *Kallimachos*, p. 34.

12. Blum, *Kallimachos*, p. 237. Jerome also cites Greek predecessors Hermippus the Peripatetic, Antigonus Carystius, the learned Satyrus, and Aristoxenus the musician, as well as Latin authors Varro, Santra, Nepos, and Hyginus.

13. He admits that *De Scriptoribus Ecclesiasticis* might be the more logical title, if he had not been following the example of Suetonius.

14. Blum, *Kallimachos*, p. 213 n. 34 cites Wehrli, *Hermippos der kallimacheer,* Die Schule des Aristoteles: Suplementband I, fragment 1.

15. On this kind of authorial biography, see Mary R. Lefkowitz, *The Lives of the Greek Poets.*

16. Blum, *Kallimachos*, p. 190, citing Friedrich Leo, *Die griechisch-römische Biographie nach ihrer literarischen Form.*

17. See Blum, *Kallimachos*, pp. 188–194.

18. David Trobisch, *The First Edition of the New Testament*, p. 46.

19. Ibid., p. 59.

20. Ibid., p. 47.

21. Ibid., p. 55.

22. Ibid., p. 45.

23. To get a more complete sense of the scope of Christian attribution analysis, see W. Speyer, *Literarische Fâlschungen*, pp. 179–217, and Armin Daniel Baum, *Pseudepigraphie und literarische Fälschung im frühen Christentum*, pp. 198–261, where the principle texts in Greek and Latin are assembled, together with a German translation.

24. Although Marcion did not admit that Luke had composed the gospel, it seems possible that Marcion chose the gospel of Luke as the basis for his reconstructed version on the grounds that Luke was a disciple of the favored Paul, and that he was as far away from the time of Jesus and the "Jewish" apostles who tampered with his words and deeds as possible.

25. The charge that the Jews had suppressed the Apocrypha in an effort to correct history is also implied by Augustine, who in *De Doctrina Christiana* II.15.22 states, "Therefore, even though something is found in Hebrew versions different from what they [the Septuagint translators] have set down, I think we should cede to the divine dispensation by which they worked to the end that the books which the Jewish nation refused to transmit (*nolebat prodere*) to other peoples, either out of envy or for religious reason (*vel religione vel invidia*), might be revealed so early, by the authority and power of King Ptolemy, to the nations which in the future were to believe in Our Lord."

26. Quoted in *Ecclesiastical History* 6.25.14.

27. Tertullian, *Adversus Marcionem* IV.5.4. See D. Guthrie, "Tertullian and Pseudonymity," *ET* 67 (1956) 341–342. Cf. the similar position of Iamblichus in *De Vita Pythagorica* 29.157–158 and 31.198 with respect to the writings of the disciples of Pythagoras being credited to Pythagoras himself.

28. In *De Pudicitia* 20, Tertullian attributes the Epistle to the Hebrews to Barnabas, a companion of Paul. Cited in Bruce Metzger, *The Canon of the New Testament*, p. 159.

29. Examples of Eusebius' citations of the attribution analysis of his predecessors are abundant. He cites Clement's defense of the authenticity of the Epistle to the Hebrews, in which it was claimed that Paul had not attached his own name to Hebrews because he was apostle to the Gentiles only, whereas the Lord himself was apostle to the Hebrews (cf. Heb. 3:1; Rom. 15:8). Clement thought that Paul had written the letter in Hebrew and that Luke published its Greek translation for Greek-speaking readers. (See Clement's *Hypotyposeis*, quoted by Eusebius, *Ecclesiastical History* 6.14.4, and cited in Bruce p. 190.) Eusebius also discusses the attribution analysis of Dionysius, bishop of Alexandria from 247/8 C.E. to 265 C.E. Dionysius had concluded that Revelation was not written by James the son of Zebedee (the author of the Fourth Gospel and 1 John) on stylistic grounds. Instead, he speculated that it was written by a man called John as it claims to be, who was not the apostle, but a "holy and inspired person." Accordingly, it should not be given the same status as a work written by an apostle (Eusebius, *Ecclesiastical History* 7.25–27).

30. F. F. Bruce, *The Canon of Scripture*, p. 199.

31. Eusebius, *Ecclesiastical History* 1.2.9; see chapter 4 on Ben Sira.

32. Ibid., III.10.

33. Karl Kelchner Hulley, "Principles of Textual Criticism Known to St. Jerome," *Harvard Studies in Classical Philology* 55 (1944), esp. pp. 104–109.

34. Courcelle, *Late Latin Writers,* pp. 81–86, credits Jerome with reading Josephus' complete works. Cited in Thomas P. Halton, *Saint Jerome On Illustrious Men,* p. 29 n. 1.

35. See *Ep.* 70 (*Corpus Scriptorum Ecclesiasticorum Latinorum* 54, 705): Iosephus antiquitatem approbans Iudaici populi duos libros scripsit contra Appionem, Alexandrinum grammaticum et tanta saecularium profert testimonia ut mihi miraculum subeat quomodo vir Hebraeus et ab infantia sacris litteris eruditus cunctam Graecorum bibliothecam evoluerit 'Josephus, commending the antiquity of the Jewish people, wrote two books against Apion, an Alexandrian grammarian. He brings forth such testimonies of our age, that it seems to me miraculous the way which a Hebrew man, also trained from childhood in the sacred books, studied the whole library of the Greeks'.

36. See chapter 3, together with Shaye J. D. Cohen, "History and Historiography in the *Against Apion* of Josephus," in *Essays in Jewish Historiography,* ed. Ada Rapoport-Albert, p. 1.

37. See Quintilian I.4.3.

38. Jerome cites Tertullian's discussion of the authenticity of works traditionally ascribed to Paul (*DVI* 5.10): "The epistle which is called the *Epistle to the Hebrews* is not considered to belong to him, on account of its difference from the others in style and language, but it is reckoned either, according to Tertullian, to be the work of Barnabas, or, according to others, to be by Luke the evangelist or by Clement afterwards bishop of the church at Rome, who, they say, arranged and adorned the ideas of Paul in his own language, though, to be sure, since Paul was writing to Hebrews and was in disrepute among them, he may have omitted his name from the salutation on this account." Jerome also cites Eusebius with regard to Clement the Bishop, who had been credited with writing a disputation between Peter and Apion (presumably to have taken place when Apion came to Rome)! "A second Epistle is also ascribed to [Clement's] name, which has not been accepted by the ancients, and a *Disputation of Peter and Apion,* written in a prolix style, which Eusebius rejects in the third book of his *Ecclesiastical History*" (*DVI* 15.2–3).

39. Other examples of Jerome questioning a work's attribution on stylistic grounds include the case of Theophilus the Bishop (*DVI* 25.3): "I

also have read *Commentaries on the Gospel* and on *The Proverbs of Solomon* ascribed to his authorship, which do not seem to me to match the elegance and style of the previous volumes."

40. Guiseppe Veltri has suggested that the story of Ezra, often connected with the story of the Septuagint, helped originate the textual destruction motif found in the Peisistratus legend in the Scholia to Dionysius Thrax. However, it now seems certain that this idea went back to the Alexandrian Homeric critics, and did not derive from the Septuagint legend. See G. Veltri, "Tolomeo Filadelfo, emulo di Pisistrato," *Laurentianum* 32 (1991) 146–166.

41. Influence in the other direction — from the Classical world to Jewish sources — also seems unlikely. G. Veltri doubts but does not exclude the possibility that the story of the Peisistratus recension had an influence on rabbinic reports: "Dass die rabbinischen Nachrichten von der Beschreibung einer solchen Revision beeinflusst worden sind, is theoretisch nicht auszuschliessen, jedoch schwer beweisbar" (G. Veltri, *Eine Tora für den König Talmai*, pp. 166–7). It would be similarly difficult to argue that the story of the destruction of the Bible in 4 Ezra was influenced by the Homeric legends.

42. See G. Veltri, *Eine Tora für den König Talmai*.

43. The figure of 700,000 scrolls is clearly wrong, and merely represents a combination of the two numbers of books given in the Letter of Aristeas (200,000 scrolls were in the possession of Ptolemy, and they were to be augmented by another 500,000). See L. Canfora, *The Vanished Library*, p. 187.

44. The second of these disasters — the burning of the library at Alexandria — has also been challenged by scholars such as Fraser and Canfora. Besides Gellius and Isadore of Seville, the event is only described by Ammianus (XXII.16.13 f.), who places the conflagration during the dictatorship of Caesar. Canfora has questioned the assumptions of scholars like Carl Wendel, who tried to show that the passage in Gellius (paralleled in Isadore of Seville) derived from Varro, author of the *De Bibliothecis* and appointed by Caesar to oversee the care of the library. According to Canfora, Gellius and Ammianus consulted the Letter of Aristeas (187) rather than Varro, and retrojected library conflagrations which occurred during the Christian era into the past. Ammianus writes: ". . . templa, inter quae eminet Serapeum . . . in quo bibliothecae fuerunt inaestimabiles: et loquitur monumentorum veterum concinens fides septingenta voluminum

milia, Ptolemaeis regibus vigiliis intentis compositis bello Alexandrino, dum diripitur civitas sub dictatore Caesare conflagrasse . . . Sed Alexandria ipsa non sensim ut aliae urbes, sed inter prima aucta per spatiosos ambitus internisque seditionibus diu aspere fatigata, ad ultimum multis post annis Aureliano imperio agente civilibus iurgiis ad certamina internecia prolapsis dirutisque moenibus amisit regionis maximam partem, quae Bruchion appellabatur, diuturnum praestantium hominum domicilium" (XXII.16.13 f.). See Canfora, *The Vanished Library,* esp. pp. 183–9.

45. Cited in Canfora, *The Vanished Library,* p. 183.

46. It is attested for example in Indian traditions. The text of the Pañcapadika of Padmapada (ca. eighth cent. C.E.), a commentary upon Shankara's commentary on the Vedanta Sutras, was destroyed and reconstructed from memory. As the story goes, Padmapada, a disciple of Shankara, showed the text he had composed to his uncle and entrusted to him his work until his return. The uncle of Padmapada, a disciple of an opposing school of philosophy, destroyed the text in the realization that he could not refute the arguments of his nephew. Padmapada returned without his commentary, but Shankara his teacher recited it for him, and thus the text was saved. The theme is common in Indian literature, and suggests that stories of textual destruction and reconstruction need not be traced back to a single source; see Vidyaranya, *Sankara-Dig-Vijaya: The Traditional Life of Sri Sankaracharya.* I thank Carlos Lopez for this illuminating parallel.

47. See the still pertinent discussion in H. E. Ryle, *The Canon of the Old Testament,* pp. 239–72.

48. Jacob Myers, *I & II Esdras,* pp. 115–119; 129–131.

49. Because none except Daniel could read it, which implied that the Assyrian characters were not popularized until the days of Ezra.

50. Cf. the change in scripts in fifth century Athens. Under the archonship of Euclides (403/402) B.C.E.) the Ionic alphabet was officially adopted for public documents in Athens instead of the local Attic script (Theopompus 115, *Fragmenta Historicorum Graecorum* 155, ed. Karl Müller).

51. Cf. the Samaritan allegation that Ezra had rewritten the Bible in the Aramaic language, not just the Aramaic script.

52. See B. Moed Qatan 18b. Cf. T. Kelim Bava Metzia 5:8; M. Moed Qatan 3:4; J. Sheqalim 4:2 (ed. Zhitomir, p. 27); and J. Sanhedrin 20c for

possible references to this "edition" of the Pentateuch. Cited in Leiman, *The Canonization of Hebrew Scripture*, p. 189 n. 496.

53. Although the canon was also associated with the twenty-two letters in the Hebrew alphabet, it has been shown that both 22 and 24 refer to a stable number of biblical books (achieved through counting certain works together). See for example Roger Beckwith, *The Old Testament Canon of the New Testament Church*, pp. 235–273, who argues that the number 22 actually derives from 24.

54. See Sid Leiman, *The Canonization of Hebrew Scripture*, pp. 86–120 on "Outside Books," "Status of the Book of Ben Sira," and "Books Defile the Hands." On early esoteric Jewish texts, see Joseph Dan, *Ancient Jewish Mysticism*.

55. The text in Arabic and Latin was edited by Fabricius, "S. Hippolyti episcopi et martyris opera," vol. II, p. 33; The Latin translation of the Arabic text, found in *Patrologia Latina* 10.704–5, is as follows:

> Dixit Armius, auctor libri Temporum: Anno decimo nono regni Ptolemei regis, jussit ut congregarentur seniores filiorum Israelis, ut sibi in manus praesentarent librum legis, et ut singuli eorum praesto essent ad explanandos sensus ejus. Astiterunt itaque seniores, secum habentes legem praestantissimam. Tunc jussit ut unusquisque eorum interpretaretur sibi librum legis. At ille repubgabat (dissentiebat ab expositione) expositioni, quam transtulerant seniores. Et jussit seniores detrudi in carceres et vincula. Et arreptum librum legis conjecit in altam fossam, et immisit super illam ignem et cineres fervidos, per septem dies. Tum postea praecepit, ut conjicerent lutum civitatis in illam fossam, in qua erat liber legis. Et impieta fuit fossa usque ad summum. Mansit lex sub stercore in illa fossa per septuaginta annos, et non periit, neque corruptum fuit ex ea vel unum folium. Anno vigesimo primo regni Apianuti regis eduxerunt librum legis e fossa, et ne unum quidem folium ex ea erat corruptum.

56. A fragment of a Greek version of 4 Ezra also establishes a link between the inspired retextualization of the Bible by Ezra and the equally inspired Septuagint:

> οὐ δὴ ξένον ἐπιπνοίᾳ θεοῦ τοῦ τὴν προφητείαν δεδωκότος καὶ τὴν ἑρμηνείαν οἱονεὶ Ἑλληνικὴν προφητείαν ἐνεργεῖσθαι. ἐπεὶ κἀν τῇ ⟨ἐπὶ⟩ Ναβουχοδονόσορ αἰχμαλωσίᾳ διαφθαρεισῶν τῶν γραφῶν κατὰ τοὺς

Ἀρταξέρξου τοῦ Περσῶν βασιλέως χρόνους ἐπίπνους Ἔσδρας ὁ
Λευίτης ὁ ἱερεὺς γενόμενος πάσας τὰς παλαιὰς αὖθις ἀνανεούμενος
προεφήτευσε γραφάς.

It is certainly not strange that this could be accomplished by the
spirit of the Lord, giving prophecy and its translation [= the Sep-
tuagint] as if it were Greek prophecy; just as (since the scriptures
had been destroyed during the captivity of Nebuchadnezzar) the
inspired Ezra, being both a Levite and a priest, prophesied during
the time of Artaxerxes the king of Persia, and revived all the ancient scriptures again.

Apocalypsis Esdrae Quarta
This text gives yet another example of the way Ezra's deed is cited as an
undisputed example of the kind of textual miracle that a prophet inspired
by God can accomplish. Especially noteworthy here is the description of
the translation of the Bible in a manner *hoionei hellenikên prophêteian* 'as
if [it were] Greek prophecy'. The passage appears in A.–M. Denis, *Fragmenta pseudepigraphorum quae supersunt Graeca* [*Pseudepigrapha veteris
testamenti Graece* 3], pp. 130–132.

57. It is not surprising that Jerome rejects 4 Ezra, although he claims
never to have read it. For one thing, Jerome followed the Jewish tradition
above all else. In addressing the problem of translating the Old Testament
and the various discrepancies between existing translations and the
Hebrew text, he consistently values the Hebrew text as the true original.
Jerome similarly followed the Hebrew canon, and rejected apocryphal
books solely on the ground that they were omitted in the Hebrew scriptures. In reference to 4 Ezra, Jerome rebukes Vigiliantius for using the
book to argue against prayers after death: "As for you, when wide awake
you are asleep, and asleep when you write, and you bring before me an
apocryphal book which, under the name of Esdras, is read by you and
those of your ilk, and in this book it is written that after death no one dares
to pray for others. I have never read the book." *Patrologia Latina* vol. 23,
cols. 359–60, quoted in J. Myers, p. 133.

58. Nahum Sarna, *Ancient Libraries and the Ordering of Biblical
Books*.

59. It should be noted that the stated purpose of the Hexapla according to Origen in his letter to Africanus is not to correct the inspired
Septuagint with reference to the Hebrew, but rather to foster awareness of
the differences between these texts. Origen developed for this purpose a

system of asterisks and daggers to mark passages missing in either the Hebrew or in the Greek but present in the other, 'so that in our debates with the Jews we do not quote passages which are lacking in their texts, and so that we can make use of those which are in their texts but not in ours' (*Epistola Ad Africanum* 5). See N. R. M de Lange, *Origen and the Jews*, p. 51.

60. It is also possible that Origen here means the Mishnah (or the Jewish oral law in general), or that the book of the Law which Ezra read from was in fact the book of Deuteronomy. However, it seems more likely to refer to the copy of the Torah referred to in Deut. 17:18.

61. Origen's expression τὰ ἐπ' αὐτοῦ γεγονότα 'the events of his own time' recalls the wording given by Josephus in *Against Apion*: (1.37) τὰ δὲ καθ' αὑτοὺς ὡς ἐγένετο 'the events of their own time', in the discussion of the role of prophets as record-keepers of events rather than historiographers. Elsewhere, Origen quotes from *Against Apion* extensively, for example in the *Contra Celsum*.

62. See R. Joseph Hoffmann, ed. and trans., *Porphyry's Against the Christians*, p. 18 and pp. 21–23; and Adolf von Harnack, *Porphyrius: "Gegen die Christen," 15 Bücher: Zeugnisse, Fragmente und Referate.*

63. Origen, *Contra Celsum*, IV.22.41. See also Carl Andresen, *Logos und Nomos: Die Polemik des Kelsos wider das Christentum,* pp. 149 ff.

64. Lazarus-Yafeh, *Intertwined Worlds*, pp. 63–4.

65. Al-Tha'labī, *Qisis*, p. 310, quoted in Lazarus-Yafeh, *Intertwined Worlds*, p. 58.

66. Lazarus-Yafeh, *Intertwined Worlds*, p. 69. On other Islamic charges of falsification (Taḥrīf) and alteration (Tabdīl) of both Old and New Testaments, as well as charges of the lack of reliable transmission (Tawātur), see Lazarus-Yafeh, ibid., pp. 19–49. On the attribution analysis of Islamic scriptures, see the list of bibliography on p. 42 n. 61.

67. Moses Gaster, *The Samaritans*, p. 28.

68. Ibid., pp. 29–30.

69. John Bowman, *Samaritan Documents*, p. 103.

70. However, see Lazarus-Yafeh, *Intertwined Worlds*, p. 62: "Samaritan literature apparently contains no explicit references to falsification of the Torah by Ezra the Scribe. Only the 'Dustan,' a small group that split away from the other Samaritans, mentions Ezra and especially his new Torah — but in a positive way."

71. John Bowman, *Samaritan Documents*, pp. 126–135.

CHAPTER 7: FROM CANON TO AUTHORSHIP

1. Pfeiffer, *The History of Classical Scholarship*, p. 204.

2. *Comicorum Graecorum Fragmenta* I, pp. 3.3, 58 165, 81 ad test. 10, ed. Kaibel; cited in Pfeiffer, *The History of Classical Scholarship*, p. 204 n. 8.

3. *Suda* v. Deinarchos, cited in Pfeiffer p. 206 n. 2.

4. See Cicero, *Academica* II.73: "qui mihi cum illo collati quintae classis videntur."

5. Pfeiffer, *The History of Classical Scholarship*, p. 207.

6. Ibid., p. 208.

7. David Ruhnken, *Historia Critica Oratorum Graecorum* in his edition of Rutilius Lupus 1768 and often reprinted: *Opuscula* I (1823) 386; cited in Pfeiffer, p. 207 n. 1.

8. H. W. Beyer, "Kanôn," *Theological Dictionary of the New Testament* 3 (1985) 596–602.

9. H. W. Beyer, "Kanôn," p. 600.

10. τὸν ἐκκλησιαστικὸν φυλάττων κανόνα, μόνα τέσσαρα εἰδέναι εὐαγγέλια μαρτύρεται, cited in Pfeiffer, p. 207 n. 4.

11. The term appears in Rufinus' translation of Origin's *Homily* on Joshua 2:1. According to F. F. Bruce, "the words are those of Rufinus" (*The Canon of Scripture*, p. 77 n. 37). This judgment bolsters Bruce's claim that Athanasius is the first writer to have used the word to denote a selective list (Bruce, p. 77), a view that ultimately derives from H. Oppel, *KANÔN*, p. 70 ff. and others, according to Pfeiffer. Apparently, these scholars did not know that the Eusebius passage came first, and ignored the role of Origen in the formulation of Eusebius' use of the term. See Pfeiffer, p. 207 n. 4.

12. *De Decretis Nicaenae Synodi* 18.3 (ed. H. G. Opitz, *Athanasius Werke* II, 1 [1935], 15), cited in H. W. Beyer, "Kanôn," *Theological Dictionary of the New Testament* 3(1985), p. 601 n. 25.

13. F. F. Bruce, *The Canon of Scripture*, p. 209; Harry Gamble, *The New Testament Canon*, pp. 54–5.

14. H. W. Beyer, "Kanôn," *Theological Dictionary of the New Testament* 3 (1985), p. 601

15. See Photius, *Bibliotheca* 20b.25: Αἰσχίνην . . . καὶ Φρύνιχος . . . εἰς τοὺς ἀρίστους ἐγκρίνει, κανόνα μετά γε τοὺς πρώτους Ἀττικοῦ λόγου τοὺς ἐκείνου ἀποφαινόμενος λόγους, cited in Pfeiffer, *The History of Classical Scholarship*, p. 206 n. 2.

16. Cf. Jacques Derrida on the iterability of the signature, in "Signature, Event, Context," in *Margins of Philosophy*, pp. 307–330.

17. For instance, Eusebius' canon, his personal feelings about individual scriptural books notwithstanding, appears to have been that of his ecclesiastical milieu. Although he probably had concluded that Revelation was inauthentic, he nevertheless included it in his fifty copies of the Christian scriptures requested by Constantine after 330 C.E. F. F. Bruce, *The Canon of Scripture*, pp. 204–5 and p. 205 n. 35.

18. Ibid., p. 231.

19. See Schaff and Wace, eds., *Nicene and Post-Nicene Fathers* (Eerdmans), series 2, XIV, pp. 453 ff., cited in F. F. Bruce, *The Canon of Scripture*, p. 97 n. 71.

20. F. F. Bruce, *The Canon of Scripture*, p. 97. See also Bruce Metzger, *The Canon of the New Testament*, p. 160 n. 28, where Metzger dismantles the idea of early synods that rejected the Shepherd of Hermas and approved the Gospel of Matthew. Metzger concludes that there is not a trace of a canon issued by a synod or a collective agreement among churches or bishops during the lifetime of Eusebius (ca. 260–340 C.E.); Metzger, p. 202.

21. Metzger, *The Canon of the New Testament*, p. 237.

22. Significantly, the limits of the canon were debated within the church until the Council of Trent in 1564; thus the process did not completely end in 397 C.E.

23. Harry Gamble, *The New Testament Canon*, p. 56.

24. It should be pointed out here that a Catholic-Protestant argument has helped to obscure the real dialectic at work. Catholic scholars have traditionally stressed the role of the Church (especially church councils) in the formation of the canon, while Protestant scholars have emphasized the intrinsic and self-authenticating authority of the canon (as if neither individual scholars nor churches played a role in the process). The real question is how tradition is shaped in history by multiple influences. This argument is in some ways comparable to the debate over an early or late date in the formation of the canon of the Hebrew Bible (see chapter 4). On the Catholic-Protestant debate, see Harry Gamble, *The New Testament Canon*, pp. 82–92.

25. "There is no doubting the wide dissemination of the major works; André Wilmart's survey of "La tradition des grands ouvrages de saint Augustin" (in *Miscellanea Agostiniana* II [1931] 257–315 at 295–315) lists 258 manuscripts for the *Confessions* and 376 for the *City of God* (cited

in David. F. Wright, "Augustine: His Exegesis and Hermeneutics," p. 727). "Augustine was by far the most heavily used exegetical quarry of the Carolingian commentary compilers, but more significant still was the use of material from him in the standard Bible commentary of the central and later Middle Ages, the *Glossa Ordinaria*" (David F. Wright, p. 728).

26. Jude 14–15: "Now Enoch, the seventh from Adam, prophesied about these men also, saying, 'Behold the Lord comes with ten thousand of His saints, to execute judgment on all, to convict all who are ungodly among them of all their ungodly deeds which they have committed in an ungodly way, and of all the harsh things which ungodly sinners have spoken against Him.'"

27. Augustine's knowledge of Josephus' work has been neglected by scholars working on both authors. Whether this influence derived from Augustine reading a Latin translation of *Against Apion* or by his reading of other Christian authors influenced by Josephus cannot be ascertained without further study.

28. See David Quint, *Origins and Originality in Renaissance Literature: Versions of the Source*, for a treatment of the impact of classical views on originality on poetics during this period.

29. It is also notable that, according to A. Momigliano, Josephus (unlike St. Augustine and Gregory of Nizianzus) did not create his autobiography for the purpose of describing himself, his character, or his inner life. Like Isocrates (in *About the Exchange*) and Demosthenes (in *On the Crown*) who had written four centuries before, Josephus was still writing his autobiography or life (*bios*) in self-defense, in the tradition of juridical speeches. A. Momigliano, "Marcel Mauss and the quest for the person in Greek biography and autobiography," in Michael Carrithers, Steven Collins, and Steven Lukes, eds., *The Category of the Person*, p. 90.

30. Bertrand de Margerie, *An Introduction to the History of Exegesis, III: St. Augustine*, p. 77.

31. Albrecht Dihle, *The Theory of Will in Classical Antiquity*, p. 123. This view is echoed by Richard Sorabji, who states that Augustine brings together a number of different criteria that had only occurred separately in previous philosophers. These criteria included the idea of the will belonging to the rational soul, the connection of the will with freedom and responsibility, the idea of will-power and its failure, a conceptualization of willing as ubiquitous in all action, and the notion of a perverted or bad will. Richard Sorabji, *Emotion and Peace of Mind*, pp. 335–7.

32. A. Momigliano, *The Development of Greek Biography*, p. 18.

33. G. Misch, *A History of Autobiography in Antiquity* (originally *Geschichte der Autobiographie*); cited in A. Momigliano, "Marcel Mauss and the quest for the person in Greek biography and autobiography," p. 84.

34. A. Momigliano, "Marcel Mauss and the quest for the person in Greek biography and autobiography," pp. 84–5.

35. Krister Stendahl, "The Apostle Paul and the Introspective Conscience of the West," *Harvard Theological Review* 56 (1963) pp. 199–215, and Jean-Pierre Vernant, "The Individual Within the City State," in Froma Zeitlin, ed., *Mortals and Immortals*, pp. 318–333.

36. Phillip Cary, *Augustine's Invention of the Inner Self: The Legacy of a Christian Platonist*.

37. Albrecht Dihle, *The Theory of Will in Classical Antiquity*, p. 138.

38. Charles Kannengiesser, "Interrupted *De doctrina christiana*," in Arnold and Bright, eds., *De doctrina christiana, A Classic of Western Culture*, p. 5.

39. See Bertrand de Margerie, *An Introduction to the History of Exegesis, III: St. Augustine*, especially his chapter, "Does Augustine's Moses Stand for Multiplicity in Unity?," pp. 47–88.

40. De Margerie writes, "many of Augustine's interpreters from Thomas Aquinas to Zarb thought they could summarize his doctrine by distinguishing the primary literal sense, which the inspired author mainly had in mind, from other literal, secondary, derived and adapted senses of the same passage, which are meanings willed by God, who intended them to be expressed by specific biblical verses." Bertrand de Margerie, *An Introduction to the History of Exegesis, III: St. Augustine*, p. 58 and p. 82 n. 20, citing Thomas Aquinas' discussion of literal meaning in the *Summa Theologica* I.1.10, in *Quodlibet* VII, art. 14–16, and in *De Potentia* IV.1.

41. Augustine, *De Doctrina Christiana* III.3.6.

42. Sed cum verba propria faciunt ambiguam scripturam, primo videndum est ne male distinxerimus aut pronuntiaverimus. Cum ergo adhibita intentio incertum esse perviderit quo modo distinguendum aut quo modo pronuntiandum sit, <u>consulat regulam fidei, quam de scripturarum planioribus locis et ecclesiae auctoritate percepit,</u> de qua satis egimus cum de rebus in libro primo loqueremur. <u>Quod si ambae vel etiam omnes, si plures fuerint partes ambiguitatis, secundum fidem sonuerint, textus ipse sermonis a praecedentibus et consequentibus partibus,</u> quae ambiguitatem

illam in medio posuerunt, restat consulendus, ut videamus cuinam
sententiae de pluribus quae se ostendunt, ferat suffragium eamque
sibi contexi patiatur.

But when proper words make Scripture ambiguous, we must
see in the first place that there is nothing wrong in our punctuation or pronunciation. Accordingly, if, when attention is given to
the passage, it shall appear to be uncertain in what way it ought to
be punctuated or pronounced, let the reader consult the rule of
faith which he has gathered from the plainer passages of Scripture, and from the authority of the Church, and of which I treated
at sufficient length when I was speaking in the first book about
things. But if both readings, or all of them (if there are more than
two), give a meaning in harmony with the faith, it remains to consult the context, both what goes before and what comes after, to
see which interpretation, out of many that offer themselves, it pronounces for and permits to be dovetailed into itself.

Augustine, *De Doctrina Christiana* III.1.2, trans. Shaw

43. Rarissime igitur et difficillime inveniri potest ambiguitas in
propriis verbis, quantum ad libros divinarum scripturarum spec-
tat, quam non aut circumstantia ipsa sermonis, qua cognoscitur
scriptorum intentio, aut interpretum conlatio aut praecedentis
linguae solvat inspectio.

It is therefore very rare and very difficult to find any ambiguity in the case of proper words, as far at least as Holy Scripture is
concerned, which neither the context, showing the design of the
writers, nor a comparison of translations, nor a reference to the
original tongue, will suffice to explain."

Augustine, *De Doctrina Christiana* III.4.8, trans. Shaw

44. "When we read the inspired books in the light of this wide variety of true doctrines which are drawn from a few words and founded on
the firm basis of Catholic belief, let us choose that one which appears as certainly the meaning intended by the author (*id potissimum deligamus quot
certum adparverit eum sensisse quem legimus*)" (*De Genesi Ad Litteram*
I.21.41).

45. A passage in *De Doctrina Christiana* expresses a similar condemnation of readers who grow overly attached to their own inaccurate interpretations:

Sed quisquis in scripturis aliud sentit quam ille qui scripsit, illis non mentientibus fallitur ... Asserendo enim temere quod ille non sensit quem legit, plerumque incurrit in alia quae illi sententiae contexere nequeat. Quae si vera et certa esse consentit, illud non possit verum esse quod senserat, fitque in eo nescio quo modo ut amando sententiam suam scripturae incipiat offensior esse quam sibi.

But anyone who understands in the Scriptures something other than that intended by them is deceived, although they do not lie ... in asserting rashly that which the author before him did not intend, he may find many other passages which he cannot reconcile with his interpretation. If he acknowledges these to be true and certain, his first interpretation cannot be true, and under these conditions it happens, I know not why, that, loving his own interpretation, he begins to become angrier with the Scriptures than he is with himself.

Augustine, *De Doctrina Christiana* I.36.41–I.37.41, trans. Shaw

46. This conception of authorial intention (where what the author means is everything the text means) finds a modern analog in the New Pragmatism of Steven Knapp and Walter Benn Michaels. See Seán Burke, *The Death and Return of the Author*, pp. 138–142.

47. The confusion resembles the debate between Neo Pragmatists (Steven Knapp and Walter Benn Michaels' "Against Theory") and New Critics (represented by Wimsatt and Beardsley's "The Intentional Fallacy"). As Seán Burke states, "Intentionless meaning is thus for Knapp and Michaels as fallacious as meaningful intention was for Wimsatt and Beardsley. Strange as it might seem then, 'Against Theory' finds itself in full agreement with 'The Intentional Fallacy' on at least one issue. Both articles maintain that it is fruitless to inquire into an author's intention, that there is never any need to step outside the text in search of an author: on the pragmatist case, because what the author meant is everything the text means; for the New Critics, because what the author means cannot find its way back into his or her text." Seán Burke, *The Death and Return of the Author*, p. 139.

48. Thus Augustine warned his admirers not to look upon his writings as they would upon the scriptures, but to accept only those things which, upon examination, they found to be true. See A. J. Minnis, *Medieval Theory of Authorship*, p. 59.

49. However, this is not the view of Bertrand de Margerie: "Augustine may even have been the very first author explicitly to face this question: what should be my present attitude toward all the future interpretations of my writings?" Bertrand de Margerie, *An Introduction to the History of Exegesis, III: St. Augustine*, pp. 49–50.

50. See, for example, David Quint, *Origins and Originality in Renaissance Literature: Versions of the Source*, and M. H. Abrams, *The Mirror and the Lamp: Romantic Theory and the Critical Tradition*. On the absence of a notion of *creatio ex nihilo* in ancient Greek poetics, see Andrew Ford, *The Origins of Criticism*, p. 134.

CONCLUSION

1. Cf. the phenomena of "Aristotle's Books" as discussed in chapter 5.

2. On the nature of Greek *paideia*, see Werner Jaeger, *Paideia: The Ideals of Greek Culture* I–III.

3. On authorship in the middle ages, see A. J. Minnis, *Medieval Theory of Authorship*.

4. On the precise role of judges and voting in the awarding of prizes at the dramatic contests in Athens, see A. Pickard-Cambridge, *The Dramatic Festivals of Athens*, pp. 96–99.

# BIBLIOGRAPHY

Abbenes, J. G. J., S. R. Slings, and I. Sluiter, eds., *Greek Literary Theory After Aristotle: A Collection of Papers in Honour of D. M. Schenkeveld* (Amsterdam: VU University Press, 1995).

Abrams, M. H., *The Mirror and the Lamp: Romantic Theory and the Critical Tradition* (New York: Oxford University Press, 1953).

Abramson, Shraga, ed., *Massekhet Baba Bathra*, in Y. N. Epstein, ed., *Talmud Bavli* (Jerusalem: "RAZAL" Company Ltd., 1958).

Allen, Thomas W., *Homer: The Origins and the Transmission* (Oxford: Clarendon Press, 1924).

Altschuler, David and Jehiel Hillel Altschuler, *Mikra'ot Gedolot* (Lemberg: 1808).

Amir, Yehoshua, "Authority and Interpretation of Scripture in the Writings of Philo," in Martin Jan Mulder, ed., *Mikra: Text, Translation, Reading, and Interpretation of the Hebrew Bible in Ancient Judaism and Early Christianity* (Philadelphia: Fortress Press, 1988), 421–454.

———, *Die hellenistische Gestalt des Judentums bei Philon von Alexandrien*, Forschungen zum jüdisch-christlichen Dialog (Düsseldorf: Breklumer Druckerei Manfred Siegel, 1983).

Andresen, Carl, *Logos und Nomos: Die Polemik des Kelsos wider das Christentum* (Berlin: W. de Gruyter, 1955).

Arnold, Duane W. H. and Pamela Bright, eds., *De doctrina Christiana: A Classic of Western Culture* (Notre Dame: University of Notre Dame Press, 1995).

Athenaeus, *The Deipnosophists* I–III, trans. Charles Burton Gulick, Loeb Classical Library (Cambridge: Harvard University Press, 1927).

Augustine, Saint, *Concerning the City of God Against the Pagans*, trans. Henry Bettenson (New York: Penguin Books, 1984).

———, *De Doctrina Christiana*, Corpus Scriptorum Ecclesiasticorum Latinorum, vol. 80, ed. W. M. Green (Vienna: Hoelder-Pichler-Tempsky, 1963).

———, *On Christian Doctrine*, trans. J. F. Shaw, *Select Library of Nicene and Post-Nicene Fathers*, vol. 2 (Grand Rapids, Michigan: Eerdmans Pub. Co., 1956).

Aune, David, "The Origins of the 'Council of Javne' Myth," *Journal of Biblical Literature* 110 (1991) 491–3.

Avishur, Yitzḥak, and Yehoshua Blau, eds., *Meḥqarim be-miqre' u-va-mizraḥ ha-qadmon: mugashim li-Shemu'el A. Livenshtam bi-mel'ot lo shiv'im shanah* (Jerusalem: A. Rubinshteyn, 1978).

Baar, Johannes, *Index zu den Ilias-Scholien*, Deutsche Beiträge zur Altertumswissenschaft, vol. 15 (Baden-Baden: Bruno Grimm Verlag für Kunst und Wissenschaft, 1961).

Bacher, Willhelm, "Synagogue, the Great," in Cyrus Adler and Isidore Singer, eds., *Jewish Encyclopedia*, vol. 11 (New York: Funk and Wagnalls, 1925), 640–3.

———, *Tradition und Tradenten in den Schulen Palästinas und Babyloniens* (Leipzig: Buchhandlung Gustav Fock, 1914).

Baer, Y., "Jerusalem in the Times of the Great Revolt," *Zion* 36 (1971) 127–190.

Baillet, M., J. T. Milik, and R. de Vaux, *Les 'Petites Grottes' de Qumran*, Discoveries in the Judaean Desert of Jordan III (Oxford: Clarendon Press, 1962).

Barthes, Roland, "The Death of the Author," in Roland Barthes, *Image / Music / Text*, ed. and trans. Stephen Heath (NY: Hill & Wong, 1977), 142–8.

Barton, John, "'The Law and the Prophets': Who are the Prophets?" *Oudtestamentlische Studiën* 23 (1984) 1–18.

———, *Oracles of God: Perceptions of Ancient Prophecy in Israel after the Exile* (New York: Oxford University Press, 1986).

Baskin, Judith R., *Pharoah's Councellors: Job, Jethro, and Balaam in Rabbinic and Patristic Tradition* (Chico, California: Scholars Press, 1983).

Baum, Armin Daniel, *Pseudepigraphie und literarische Fälschung im frühen Christentum* (Tübingen: Mohr Siebeck, 2001).

Beckwith, Roger, "The Formation of the Hebrew Bible," in Martin Jan Mulder, ed., *Mikra: Text, Translation, Reading and Interpretation of the Hebrew Bible in Ancient Judaism and Early Christianity,* Compendia Rerum Iudaicarum ad Novum Testamentum (Philadelphia: Fortress Press, 1988), 39–86.

———, *The Old Testament Canon of the New Testament Church and its Background in Early Judaism* (London: SPCK, 1985).

Beentjes, Pancratius C., *The Book of Ben Sira in Hebrew: A Text Edition of All Extant Hebrew Manuscripts and A Synopsis of All Parallel Hebrew Ben Sira Texts* (Leiden, New York, Köln: E. J. Brill, 1997).

Berger, Michael S., *Rabbinic Authority* (Oxford: Oxford University Press, 1998).

Berlin, Andrea, "Between Large Forces: Palestine in the Hellenistic Period," *Biblical Archaeologist* 60 (1997) 2–51.

Beyer, H. W., "*Kanôn,*" *Theological Dictionary of the New Testament* 3 (1985) 596–602.

Bialik, Hayim Nahman and Yehoshua Hana Ravnitzky, *The Book of Legends (Sefer Ha-Aggadah): Legends from the Talmud and Midrash,* trans. William G. Braude (New York: Schocken Books, 1992).

Bickerman, Elias, "La Chaîne de la Tradition Pharisienne," in *Studies in Jewish and Christian History,* vol. 2 (Leiden: E. J. Brill, 1980), 256–269.

———, "Faux Littéraires dans l'Antiquité Classique," in *Studies in Jewish and Christian History,* vol. 3 (Leiden: E. J. Brill, 1986), 196–211.

———, *Four Strange Books of the Bible* (New York: Schocken Books, 1967).

Blackman, Edwin Cyril, *Marcion and His Influence* (New York: AMS Press, 1978 [1948]).

Blenkinsopp, Joseph, *The History of Prophecy in Israel* (Philadelphia: Westminster Press, 1983).

Bloch, Maurice, *From Blessing to Violence: History and Ideology in the Circumcision Ritual of the Merina of Madagascar,* Cambridge Studies in Social Anthropology (Cambridge: Cambridge University Press, 1986).

————, *Ritual, History and Power: Selected Papers in Anthropology*, London School of Economics Monographs on Social Anthropology (London: The Athlone Press, 1989).

Bludau, August, *Die Schriftfälschungen der Häretiker* (Münster: Verlag der Aschendorffschen Verlagsbuchhandlung, 1925).

Blum, Rudolf, *Kallimachos: The Alexandrian Library and the Origins of Bibliography*, trans. Hans Wellisch (Madison: University of Wisconsin Press, 1991 [1975]).

Bourdieu, Pierre, *Distinction: A Social Critique of the Judgement of Taste*, trans. Richard Nice (Cambridge: Harvard University Press, 1984).

Bowman, John, ed. and trans., *Samaritan Documents: Relating to Their History, Religion, and Life* (Pittsburgh: Pickwick Press, 1977).

Braude, William G., trans., *The Midrash on Psalms (Midrash Tehillim)*, Yale Judaica Series, vol. 13 (New Haven: Yale University Press, 1959).

Braverman, Jay, *Jerome's Commentary on Daniel: A Study of Comparative Jewish and Christian Interpretations of the Hebrew Bible*, The Catholic Biblical Quarterly Monograph Series, vol. 7 (Washington, D.C.: The Catholic Biblical Association of America, 1978).

Bröker, L. O., "Die Methoden Galens in der literarischen Kritik," *Rheinisches Museum* 40 (1885) 415–38.

Brown, Francis, S. R. Driver, and Charles A. Briggs, eds., *Hebrew and English Lexicon* (Peabody, Massachusetts: Hendrickson Publishers, 1906, 1979).

Brox, Norbert, ed., *Pseudepigraphie in der Heidnischen und Jüdisch-Christlichen Antike*, Wege der Forschung, vol. 484 (Darmstadt: Wissenschaftliche Buchgesellschaft, 1977).

Bruce, F. F., *The Canon of Scripture* (Downers Grove, Illinois: InterVarsity Press, 1988).

Buber, Solomon, ed., *Midrash Tehillim Ha-Mekhuneh Shoḥer Tov* (Jerusalem: 1966 [1891]).

Burke, Seán, *The Death & Return of the Author: Criticism and Subjectivity in Barthes, Foucault, and Derrida* (Edinburgh: Edinburgh University Press, 1992).

Burkert, Walter, "Zur geistesgeschichtlichen Einordnung einiger Pseudopythagorica," in Kurt von Fritz, ed., *Pseudepigrapha I* (Geneva: Vandoeuvres, 1972), 25–55.

Busse, Adolf, ed., *Eliae in Porphyrii Isagogen et Aristotelis Categorias Com-*

*mentaria,* Commentaria in Aristotelem Graeca, vol. 18 (Berlin: Georgii Reimeri, 1900).

———, *Philoponi (Olim Ammonii) in Aristotelis Categorias Commentarium,* Commentaria in Aristotelem Graeca, vol. 13, pt. 1 (Berlin: Georgii Reimeri, 1898).

Canfora, Luciano, *The Vanished Library: A Wonder of the Ancient World* (Berkeley and Los Angeles: University of California Press, 1990 [1987]).

Carrithers, Michael, Steven Collins, and Steven Lukes, eds., *The Category of the Person: Anthropology, Philosophy, History* (Cambridge: Cambridge University Press, 1985).

Cary, Phillip, *Augustine's Invention of the Inner Self: The Legacy of a Christian Platonist* (Oxford: Oxford University Press, 2000).

Charles, R. H., *The Apocrypha and Pseudepigrapha of the Old Testament in English* (Oxford: Oxford University Press, 1913; 1963).

Charlesworth, James H., ed., *The Old Testament Pseudepigrapha,* 2 vols. (London: Darton, Longman and Todd, 1983–1985).

Childs, Brevard S., "Psalm Titles and Midrashic Exegesis," *Journal of Semitic Studies* 16 (1971) 137–150.

Clement, of Alexandria, *Stromateis* Books 1–3, trans. John Ferguson (Washington, D.C.: Catholic University of America Press, 1991).

Clift, Evelyn Holst, *Latin Pseudepigrapha: A Study in Literary Attributions* (Baltimore: J. H. Furst Co, 1945).

Coats, George W. and Burke O. Long, eds., *Canon and Authority: Essays in Old Testament Religion and Theology* (Philadelphia: Fortress Press, 1977).

Cohen, Shaye J. D., *Josephus in Galilee and Rome,* Columbia Studies in the Classical Tradition, vol. 8 (Leiden: E. J. Brill, 1979).

———, *From the Maccabees to the Mishnah,* Library of Early Christianity (Philadelphia: The Westminster Press, 1987).

———, "History and Historiography in the Against Apion of Josephus," *History and Theory* 27 (1988) 1–11.

Cohn, Leopold, "Dionysius Thrax," in Wissowa-Kroll-Mittelhaus, eds. Paulys *Real-Enzyklopädie der klassischen Altertumswissenschaft* 5 (1905) 978–983.

Collins, John J., *Between Athens and Jerusalem: Jewish Identity in the Hellenistic Diaspora* (New York: Crossroad Publishing Co., 1983).

Collomp, Paul von, "Der Platz des Josephus in der Technik der hellenistischen Geschichtsschreibung," in Abraham Schalit, ed., *Zur Josephus-Forschung* (Darmstadt: Wissenschaftliche Buchgesellschaft, 1973), 278–293.

Conway, Moncure Daniel, *Solomon and Solomonic Literature* (New York: Haskell House Publishers Ltd., 1973).

Cooper, Alan M., "The Life and Times of King David According to the Book of Psalms," in Richard Elliott Friedman, ed., *The Poet and the Historian: Essays in Literary and Historical Biblical Criticism* (Chico, California: Scholars Press, 1983), 117–131.

Cornford, Francis Macdonald, trans., *Plato's Cosmology: The Timaeus of Plato* (New York: Harcourt, Brace, and Company, 1937).

*Corpus Scriptorum Ecclesiasticorum Latinorum* (Vienna, Leipzig, and Prague: Vindobonae, F. Tempsky, 1866–).

Costello, Charles Joesph, *St. Augustine's Doctrine on the Inspiration and Canonicity of Scripture* (Washington D. C.: The Catholic University of America, 1930).

Courcelle, P., *Late Latin Writers and Their Greek Sources* (Cambridge: Harvard University Press, 1969).

Cowley, A. E., and Ad. Neubauer, eds., *The Original Hebrew of a Portion of Ecclesiasticus (39:15 to 49:11)* (Oxford: Clarendon Press, 1897).

Cramer, J. A., *Anecdota Graeca Oxoniensia* 4 (Oxford, 1837; reprint Amsterdam, 1963).

Crenshaw, James L., ed., *Studies in Ancient Israelite Wisdom* (New York: Ktav Publishing House, Inc., 1976).

Croese, G., ΟΜΗΡΟΣ ΕΒΡΑΙΟΣ, *Sive Historia Hebraeorum ab Homero Hebraicis nominibus ac sententiis conscripta in Odyssea & Iliade* (Dordraci, 1704).

Cross, Frank Moore, *The Ancient Library of Qumran*, 3rd ed. (Minneapolis: Fortress Press, 1958; 1995).

Curtis, Edward Lewis, and Albert Alonzo Madsen, *The Books of Chronicles* (Edinburgh: T. & T. Clark, 1910).

Dalbert, P., *Die Theologie der hellenistischen-judischen Missionsliteratur unter Ausschluss von Philo und Josephus* (Hamburg: Volksdorf, 1954).

Dan, Joseph, *The Ancient Jewish Mysticism* (Tel-Aviv: MOD Books, 1993).

Daniélou, Jean, *Origène* (Paris: La Table Ronde, 1948).

Davison, J. A., "Peisistratus and Homer," *Transactions of the American Philological Association* 86 (1955) 1–21.

de Lange, N. R. M., *Origen and the Jews* (Cambridge: Cambridge University Press, 1976).

———, ed., Origen, *Philocalie 1–20 sur les Écritures, et la Lettre à Africanus sur l'histoire de Suzanne* (Paris: Les Éditions du Cerf, 1983).

Denis, A.–M., *Fragmenta Pseudepigraphorum Quae Supersunt Graeca Una Cum Historicorum et Auctorum Judaeorum Hellenistarum Fragmentis* (Leiden: E. J. Brill, 1970).

Derrida, Jacques, "Signature, Event, Context," in *Margins of Philosophy*, ed. Alan Bass (Chicago: University of Chicago Press, 1982), 307–330.

di Benedetto, V., "Dionisio Trace e la techne a lui attributa," *Annali della Scuola Normale Superiore di Pisa*, Ser. II, vol. 27 (1958) 169–210.

———, "Dionisio Trace e la techne a lui attributa," *Annali della Scuola Normale Superiore di Pisa*, Ser. II, vol. 28 (1959) 87–118.

Dihle, Albrecht, *The Theory of Will in Classical Antiquity* (Berkeley and Los Angeles: University of California Press, 1982).

Dionysius Thrax, *Ars Grammatica*, ed. G. Uhlig, Grammatici Graeci pars 1, v. 1 (Hildesheim: G. Olms, 1965 [1883]).

Dorival, Gilles, "La Bible des Septante: 70 ou 72 traducteurs?" in Gerard J. Norton and Stephen Pisano, eds., *Tradition of the Text: Studies offered to Dominique Barthélemy in Celebration of his 70th Birthday* (Göttingen: Vandenhoeck & Ruprecht, 1991), 45–62.

Drachmann, A. B., ed., *Scholia Vetera in Pindari Carmina* (Stuttgart: B. G. Teubner, 1927).

Droge, Arthur J., *Homer or Moses? Early Christian Interpretations of the History of Culture* (Tübingen: J. C. B. Mohr, 1989).

*Encylopedia Judaica*, ed.-in-chief Cicil Roth (New York: Macmillan, 1971–2).

Erbse, H., ed., *Scholia Graeca in Homeri Iliadem*, 7 vols. (Berlin: De Gruyter, 1969–88).

Eusebius, *The History of the Church from Christ to Constantine*, trans. G. A. Williamson (New York: Penguin Books, 1965).

Eusebius, *Preparation for the Gospel*, trans. Edwin Hamilton Gifford (Grand Rapids, Michigan: Baker Book House, 1981).

Evans, Ernest, ed. and trans., *Tertullian: Adversus Marcionem* (Oxford: Clarendon Press, 1972).

Fabricius, Alberto, ed., *S. Hippolyti Episcopi et Martyris Opera* (Hamburg: Chr. Liebezeit, 1716–18).

Fallon, F., "Theodotus: A New Translation and Introduction," in James H. Charlesworth, ed., *Old Testament Pseudepigrapha*, vol. 2 (London: Darton, Longman and Todd, 1983–1985), 785–93.

Feldman, Louis H., *Jew and Gentile in the Ancient World* (Princeton: Princeton University Press, 1993).

———, *Josephus and Modern Scholarship (1937–1980)* (Berlin: Walter de Gruyter, 1984).

Feldman, Louis H. and Gohei Hatta, eds., *Josephus, the Bible, and History* (Leiden: E. J. Brill, 1989).

Feldman, Louis and John Levison, eds., *Josephus' Contra Apionem: Studies in its Character and Context with a Latin Concordance to the Portion Missing in Greek* (Leiden: E. J. Brill, 1996).

Field, Frederick, ed., *Origenis Hexaplorum Quae Supersunt* (Oxford: Clarendon Press, 1875).

Fishbane, Michael, *Biblical Interpretation in Ancient Israel* (Oxford: Clarendon Press, 1985).

Fitzmyer, Joseph A., "David, 'Being Therefore a Prophet . . .' (Acts 2:30)," *Catholic Biblical Quarterly* 34 (1972) 332–339.

Ford, Andrew, *Homer: The Poetry of the Past* (Ithaca: Cornell University Press, 1992).

———, *The Origins of Criticism: Literary Culture and Poetic Theory in Classical Greece* (Princeton: Princeton University Press, 2002).

Foucault, Michel, *The Archaeology of Knowledge* (New York: Pantheon Books, 1972).

———, *The Care of the Self* (New York: Random House, 1986).

———, *Language, Countermemory, Practice: Selected Essays and Interviews by Michel Foucault* (Ithaca: Cornell University Press, 1977).

———, "What is an Author?," in *The Foucault Reader*, ed. Paul Rabinow (New York: Pantheon Books, 1984), 101–120.

Fraade, Steven D., *Enosh and his Generation*, Society of Biblical Literature Monograph Series, no. 30 (Chico, California: Scholars Press, 1984).

Fraser, Peter Marshall, *Ptolemaic Alexandria* (Oxford: Clarendon Press, 1972).

Freedman, H., and Maurice Simon, eds., *Midrash Rabbah: Ruth*, trans. L. Rabinowitz; *Song of Songs*, trans. Maurice Simon (London: Soncino Press Ltd., 1983).

———, *Midrash Rabbah: Genesis*, 2 vols., trans. H. Freedman and M. Simon (London: Soncino Press Ltd., 1983).

————, *Midrash Rabbah: Deuteronomy*, trans. J. Rabbinowiz; *Lamentations*, trans. A. Cohen (London: Soncino Press Ltd., 1983).

————, *Midrash Rabbah: Numbers*, trans. J. J. Slotki (London: Soncino Press Ltd., 1983).

Freudenthal, J., *Alexander Polyhistor und die von ihm erhaltenen Reste jüdaischer und samaritanischer Geschichtswerke*, in *Hellenistische Studien*, vols. 1 and 2 (Breslau: H. Skutsch, 1875–9).

Friedländer, M., *Geschichte de jüdischen Apologetik als Vorgeschichte der Christentums* (Zürich: Caesar Schmidt, 1903).

Friedman, Richard Elliott, ed., *The Poet and the Historian: Essays in Literary and Historical Biblical Criticism* (Chico, California: Scholars Press, 1983).

————, *Who Wrote the Bible?* (New York: Harper & Row, 1987).

Fritz, Kurt von, ed., *Pseudepigrapha I: Pseudopythagorica, lettres de Platon, littérature pseudépigraphique juive: huit exposés suivis de discussions* (Vandoeuvres: Fondation Hardt pour l'Étude de l'Antiquité Classique, 1972).

Fritzsche, Otto Fridolinus, *Libri Apocryphi Veteris Testamenti Graece* (Lipsiae: F. A. Brockhaus, 1871).

Fuhrmann, Manfred, *Das systematische Lehrbuch; ein Beitrag zur Geschichte der Wissenschaften in der Antike* (Gottingen: Vandenhoeck & Ruprecht, 1960).

Gager, John G., *Moses in Greco-Roman Paganism*, Society of Biblical Literature Monograph Series 16 (Nashville: Abingdon Press, 1972).

Galen, *Scripta Minora* I, ed. Marquardt, Müller, Helmreich (Amsterdam: A. M. Hakkert, 1967).

Gamble, Harry Y., *Books and Readers in the Early Church: A History of Early Christian Texts* (New Haven: Yale University Press, 1995).

————, *The New Testament Canon: Its Making and Meaning* (Philadelphia: Fortress Press, 1985).

Gaster, Moses, *The Samaritans: Their History, Doctrines, and Literature* (London: Oxford University Press, 1925).

Gellius, Aulus, *The Attic Nights*, trans. John C. Rolfe, Loeb Classical Library (Cambridge: Harvard University Press, 1927).

Gerber, Christine, *Ein Bild des Judentums für Nichtjuden von Flavius Josephus: Untersuchungen zu seiner Schrift Contra Apionem*, Arbeiten zur Geschichte des Antiken Judentums und des Urchristentums, vol. 15 (Leiden: E. J. Brill, 1997).

Gerhardsson, Birger, *Memory and Manuscript: Oral Tradition and Written Transmission in Rabbinic Judaism and Early Christianity*, Acta Seminarii Neotestamentici Upsaliensis, vol. 22 (Uppsala: Almquist & Wiksells, 1961).

Gevaryahu, H. M. I., "Biblical Colophons: A Source for the 'Biography' of Authors, Texts and Books," *Supplements to Vetus Testamentum* 28 (1975) 42–59.

———, "Qolofonim be-sefer mishle, 'iyov, ve-qohelet," in Yizḥak Avishur and Yehoshua Blau, eds., trans. M. D. Rutter *Meḥqarim be-miqre' u-va-mizraḥ ha-qadmon: mugashim li-Shemu'el A. Livenshtam bi-mel'ot lo shiv'im shanah* (Sheffield, Almond, 1987), 107–140.

Gill, Christopher and T. P. Wiseman, eds., *Lies and Fiction in the Ancient World* (Exeter: University of Exeter Press, 1993).

Ginzberg, Louis, *The Legends of the Jews* (Philadelphia: Jewish Publication Society, 1968).

Goldin, Judah, "Be Deliberate in Judgement," *Tarbiz* 62 (1992–3) 617–619.

———, *The Fathers According to Rabbi Nathan: A Translation and Commentary* (New Haven: Yale University Press, 1955).

Goodenough, Erwin R., *By Light, Light: The Mystic Gospel of Hellenistic Judaism* (New Haven: Philo Press, 1935, 1969).

———, *The Politics of Philo Judaeus: Practice and Theory* (New Haven: Yale University Press, 1938).

Grabbe, L. L., *Judaism from Cyrus to Hadrian*, 2 vols. (Minneapolis: Fortress Press, 1992).

Grant, R. M., *The Letter and the Spirit* (London: S.P.C.K., 1957).

Gray, G. Buchanan, "The Additions in the Ancient Greek Version of Job," *The Expositor* 19 (1920) 422–38.

Gray, Rebecca, *Prophetic Figures in Late Second Temple Jewish Palestine* (New York: Oxford University Press, 1993).

Greenspahn, Frederick E., "Why Prophecy Ceased," *Journal of Biblical Literature* 108 (1989) 37–49.

Gruen, Erich S., *Heritage and Hellenism: The Reinvention of Jewish Tradition* (Berkeley and Los Angeles: University of California Press, 1998).

Gudeman, Alfred, "Literary Frauds among the Greeks," in Henry Drisler, *Classical Studies in Honour of Henry Drisler* (New York: Macmillan and Co., 1894).

Gunkel, Hermann, *The Folktale in the Old Testament* (Sheffield, England: Sheffield Academic Press, 1987).

Guthrie, David, "Tertullian and Pseudonymity," *Expository Times* 67 (1956) 341–342.

Gutman, Yehoshua, *Ha-Sifrut Ha-Yehudit Ha-Hellenistit* (Jerusalem: Mosad Byalik, 1963–69).

Hadas, Moses, ed., *Aristeas to Philocrates (Letter of Aristeas)*, Jewish Apocryphal Literature (New York: Harper & Brothers, 1951).

Halbertal, Moshe, *People of the Book: Canon, Meaning, and Authority* (Cambridge: Harvard University Press, 1997).

Hall, Robert G., "Josephus, *Contra Apionem* and Historical Inquiry in the Roman Rhetorical Schools," in Louis Feldman and John Levison, eds., *Josephus' Contra Apionem: Studies in its Character and Context with a Latin Concordance to the Portion Missing in Greek* (Leiden: E. J. Brill, 1996), 229–249.

Halton, Thomas P., *Saint Jerome: On Illustrious Men* (Washington D.C.: The Catholic University of America Press, 1999).

Harlow, Daniel C., *The Greek Apocalypse of Baruch (3 Baruch) in Hellenistic Judaism and Early Christianity*, Studia in Veteris Testamenti Pseudepigrapha 12 (Leiden: E. J. Brill, 1996).

Harnack, Adolf von, *Der Kirchengeschichtliche Ertrag der Exegetischen Arbeiten des Origenes* (Leipzig: J. C. Hinrichs'sche Buchhandlung, 1918).

———, *Porphyrius: "Gegen die Christen," 15 Bücher: Zeugnisse, Fragmente und Referate* (Berlin: Verlag der Konigl. Akademie der Wissenschaften, in Kommission bei Georg Reimer, 1916).

Hatch, E. and H. A. Redpath, *A Concordance to the Septuagint and the Other Greek Versions of the Old Testament Including the Apocryphal Books* (Oxford: Clarendon Press, 1897).

Hayward, C. T. R., *Saint Jerome's Hebrew Questions on Genesis* (Oxford: Clarendon Press, 1995).

Heineman, Yiẓḥak, *Darkhe Ha-Aggadah* (Jerusalem: Magnes Press, Hebrew University, 1970).

Heinemann, Joseph, *Studies in Jewish Liturgy*, ed. Avigdor Shinan (Jerusalem: The Magnes Press, Hebrew University, 1981).

Hengel, Martin, "Anonymität, Pseudepigraphie und 'Literarische Fälschung' in der jüdisch-hellenistischen Literatur," in Kurt von Fritz, ed., *Pseudepigrapha I* (Vandoevres: Fondation Hardt, 1972).

———, *Judaism and Hellenism* (Philadelphia: Fortress Press, 1974).

Hennings, R., *Die Briefwechsel zwischen Augustinus und Hieronymus und ihr Streit um den Kanon des Alten Testaments und die Auslegung von Gal. 2, 11–14* (Leiden: E. J. Brill, 1994).

Herford, R. Travers, *Pirke Aboth* (New York: Jewish Institute of Religion, 1945).

Hieronymi, *De Viris Illustribus*, ed. Giulelmi Herdingii (Lipsiae: B. G. Teubner, 1879).

Higbe, Carolyn, "The Bones of a Hero, the Ashes of a Politician: Athens, Salamis, and the Usable Past," *Classical Antiquity* 16 (1997) 279–308.

Hilgard, Alfred, *Scholia in Dionysii Thracis Artem Grammaticam* (Hildesheim: Olms, 1901; 1965).

Hoffman, David, "Über die Männer der grossen Versammlung," *Monatsschrift für Geschichte und Wissenschaft des Judentums* 10 (1883) 45–63.

Hoffmann, R. Joseph, ed. and trans., *Porphyry's Against the Christians* (Amherst, N.Y.: Prometheus Books, 1994).

Holladay, Carl R., *Fragments from Hellenistic Jewish Authors*, Society of Biblical Literature: Texts and Translations Pseudepigrapha Series, nos. 10, 12, 13, 14 (Chico, California: Scholars Press, 1983).

Horsley, Richard A., "'Like One of the Prophets of Old': Two Types of Popular Prophets at the Time of Jesus," *The Catholic Bible Quarterly* 47 (1985) 435–463.

Horton, Fred L., *The Melchizedek Tradition*, Society for New Testament Studies Monograph Series 30 (Cambridge: Cambridge University Press, 1976).

Houlgate, Stephen, ed., *The Hegel Reader* (Oxford: Blackwell Publishers, 1998).

Hulley, Karl Kelchner, "Principles of Textual Criticism Known to St. Jerome," *Harvard Studies in Classical Philology* 55 (1944) 87–109.

Hunger, Hermann, *Babylonische und assyrische Kolophone* (Kevalaer: Butzon u. Bercker; Neukirchen-Vloyn: Neukirchener Verlag des Erziehungsvereins, 1968).

Irenaeus, *The Writings of Irenaeus*, trans. Alexander Roberts and W. H. Rambaut, Ante-Nicene Christian Library, vols. 5, 9 (Edinburgh: T. & T. Clark, 1868–69).

Isaac, E., *I (Ethiopic Apocalypse of) Enoch: A New Translation and Introduction*, in Charlesworth, ed., *Old Testament Pseudepigrapha*, vol. 1 (London: Darton, Longman and Todd, 1983–1985), 5–89.

Jacobs, Irving, "Literary Motifs in the Testament of Job," *The Journal of Jewish Studies* 21 (1970) 1–10.

Jacoby, Felix, *Die Fragmente der griechischen Historiker* (Berlin: Weidmann, 1923–58).

Jaeger, Werner, *Paideia: The Ideals of Greek Culture,* 3 vols. (New York: Oxford University Press, 1939–1944).

Janko, Richard, *The Iliad: A Commentary,* vol. 4, ed. G. S. Kirk (Cambridge: Cambridge University Press, 1992).

Janowitz, Naomi, "The Rhetoric of Translation: Three Early Perspectives on Translating Torah," *Harvard Theological Review* 84 (1991) 129–140.

Japhet, Sara, *I & II Chronicles: A Commentary* (Louisville: Westminster/ John Knox Press, 1993).

Jastrow, Marcus, *Dictionary of the Targumim, Talmud Babli, Yerushalmi, and Midrashic Literature* (New York: Judaica Press, Inc., 1992 [1971]).

Jellicoe, Sidney, ed., *Studies in the Septuagint: Origins, Recensions, and Interpretations,* Library of Biblical Studies (New York: Ktav Publishing House, Inc., 1974).

Jensen, Minna Skafte, *The Homeric Question and the Oral-Formulaic Theory* (Copenhagen: Museum Tusculanum Press, 1980).

Johnson, M. D., "The Life of Adam and Eve: A New Translation and Introduction," in Charlesworth, ed., *The Old Testament Pseudepigrapha* (London: Darton, Longman, and Todd, 1983–1985), 249–296.

Josephus, Flavius, *Antiquities of the Jews,* trans. H. St. J. Thackeray, Ralph Marcus, Allen Wikgren, and L. H. Feldman, Loeb Classical Library (Cambridge: Harvard University Press, 1930–1965).

———, *The Life; Against Apion,* trans. H. St. J. Thackeray, Loeb Classical Library (Cambridge: Harvard University Press, 1926).

———, *Jewish War,* trans. H. St. J. Thackeray, Loeb Classical Library (Cambridge: Harvard University Press, 1997).

Kaibel, G., ed., *Comicorum Graecorum Fragmenta* I (Berlin: Weidmann, 1899).

———, *Die Prolegomena Peri Kômôdias,* Abhandlungen der Göttinger Gesellschaft der Wissenschaften, N. F. II 4 (Berlin: Weidmannsche buchhandlung, 1898).

Kamesar, Adam, *Jerome, Greek Scholarship, and the Hebrew Bible* (Oxford: Clarendon Press, 1993).

Kannengiesser, Charles, "Interrupted *De doctrina christiana,*" in Arnold and Bright, eds., *De doctrina christiana, A Classic of Western Culture* (Notre Dame: University of Notre Dame Press, 1995), 3–13.

Katz, Peter, "The Old Testament Canon in Palestine and Alexandria," *Zeitschrift für die neutestamentliche Wissenschaft* (1956) 191–217.

Keaney, John J., and Robert Lamberton, eds., *Homer's Ancient Readers* (Princeton: Princeton University Press, 1992).

———, *[Plutarch] Essay on the Life and Poetry of Homer* (Atlanta: Scholars Press, 1996).

Keble, John, *Five Books of S. Irenaeus, Bishop of Lyons; Against Heresies* (Oxford and London: James Parker and Co., 1872).

Kellermann, Ulrich, *Nehemia. Quellen, Überlieferung und Geschichte*, Beihefte zur Zeitschrift für die alttestamentliche Wissenschaft 102 (Berlin: Töpelmann, 1967).

Kemp, Alan, "The *Technê Grammatikê* of Dionysius Thrax, Translated into English," in Daniel J. Taylor, ed., *The History of Linguistics in the Classical Period* (Amsterdam, Philadelphia: John Benjamins Publishing Company, 1987), 169–189.

Kieffer, René, "Jerome: His Exegesis and Hermeneutics," in Magne Saebo, ed., *Hebrew Bible / Old Testament: The History of Its Interpretation, vol. I: From the Beginnings to the Middle Ages (Until 1300)* (Göttingen: Vandenhoeck & Ruprecht, 1996), 663–681.

Kleingunther, Adolf, *"Prôtos heuretês"; Untersuchungen zur Geschichte einer Fragestellung* (Leipzig: Dieterich, 1933).

Knapp, Steven, and Walter Benn Michaels, "Against Theory," in W. J. T. Mitchell, ed., *Against Theory: Literary Studies and the New Pragmatism* (Chicago: University of Chicago Press, 1985), 11–30.

Koester, Helmut, ed., *Pergamon: Citadel of the Gods* (Harrisburg, Pennsylvania: Trinity Press International, 1998).

Kohen, Yekutiel, ed., *Ginze Ha-Geonim 'al Massekhet Bava Batra* (Jerusalem: Otsar Ha-Poskim, 1994).

Koole, J. L., "Die Bibel des Ben-Sira," *Oudtestamentische Studiën* 23 (1965) 374–96.

Knibb, M. A., "The Martyrdom and Acsension of Isaiah," in Charlesworth, ed., *The Old Testament Pseudepigrapha* (London: Darton, Longman, and Todd, 1983–1985), 143–176.

Knight, Jonathan, *Disciples of the Beloved One: The Christology, Social Setting and Theological Context of the Ascension of Isaiah*, Journal for the Study of the Pseudepigrapha Supplement Series, vol. 18 (Sheffield: Sheffield Academic Press, 1996).

Kraft, Robert A., "'Ezra' Materials in Judaism and Christianity," in *Aufstieg und Niedergang der Römischen Welt* II.19.1 (Berlin: De Gruyter, 1979), 119–136.

——, "Scripture and Canon in Jewish Apocrypha and Pseudepigrapha," in Magne Saebo, ed., *Hebrew Bible / Old Testament: The History of Its Interpretation*, vol. I (Göttingen: Vandenhoeck & Ruprecht, 1996), 199–216.

Kugel, James L., *The Bible as it Was* (Cambridge: The Belknap Press of Harvard University Press, 1997).

——, "The 'Bible as Literature' in Late Antiquity and the Middle Ages," *Hebrew University Studies in Literature and the Arts* 11 (1983) 20–70.

——, "David the Prophet," in James Kugel, ed., *Poetry and Prophecy* (Ithaca: Cornell University Press, 1990), 44–55.

——, *The Idea of Biblical Poetry: Parallelism and its History* (New Haven: Yale University Press, 1981).

——, "Is there But One Song?" *Biblica* 63 (1982) 329–350.

Kugel, James L., and Rowan Greer, *Early Biblical Interpretation* (Philadelphia: Westminster Press, 1986).

La Bonnardière, Anne-Marie, "Le Canon des divines Écritures," in Pamela Bright, ed., *Augustine and the Bible* (Notre Dame, Indiana: University of Notre Dame Press, 1986), 26–41.

Lambert, W. G., "A Catalogue of Texts and Authors," *Journal of Cuneiform Studies* 16 (1962) 59–77.

——, Hermann Hunger: *Babylonische und Assyrische Kolophone* (Review), *Die Welt des Orients* 5 (1970) 290–1.

Lambropoulos, Vassilis, *The Rise of Eurocentrism: Anatomy of Interpretation* (Princeton: Princeton University Press, 1993).

Lazarus-Yafeh, Hava, *Intertwined Worlds: Medieval Islam and Bible Criticism* (Princeton: Princeton University Press, 1992).

Lebram, J. C. H., "Aspekte der Alttestamentlichen Kanonbildung," *Vetus Testamentum* 18 (1968) 173–189.

Lefkowitz, Mary R., *The Lives of the Poets* (Baltimore: The Johns Hopkins University Press, 1981).

Leiman, Sid Z., ed., *The Canon and Masorah of the Hebrew Bible: An Introductory Reader*, The Library of Biblical Studies (New York: Ktav Publishing House, Inc., 1974).

——, *The Canonization of Hebrew Scripture: The Talmudic and Midrashic Evidence* (Hamden, Connecticut: Archon Books, 1976).

———, "Josephus and the Canon of the Bible" in Feldman and Hatta, eds., *Josephus, the Bible, and History* (Leiden: E. J. Brill, 1989).

Leo, Friedrich, *Die griechisch-römische Biographie nach ihrer literarischen Form* (Leipzig: B. G. Teubener, 1901).

Lerner, M. B., "The External Tractates," in Shmuel Safrai, ed., *The Literature of the Sages,* first part, Compendia Rerum Iudaicarum ad Novum Testamentum, section 2 (Philadelphia: Fortress Press, 1987), 367–409.

Levison, John R. and Louis H. Feldman, ed., *Josephus' Contra Apionem: Studies in its Character and Context with a Latin Concordance to the Portion Missing in Greek,* Arbeiten zur Geschichte des Antiken Judentums und des Urchristentums, vol. 34 (Leiden: E. J. Brill, 1996).

Lévy, Isadore, *Recherches Esséniennes et Pythagoriciennes,* Hautes Études du Monde Gréco-Romain, vol. 1 (Geneva: Librairie Droz, 1965).

Lewis, Jack P., "What Do We Mean By Jabneh?" *Journal of Bible and Religion* 32 (1964) 125–132.

Liddell, H. G., R. Scott, and H. Stuart Jones, eds., *Greek-English Lexicon,* 9th ed. (Oxford: Clarendon Press, 1940).

Lieberman, Saul., "He'arot le–Pereq 'Alef shel Qohelet Rabbah," in *Meḥqarim be–Torat Erez-Yisrael* (Jerusalem: Magnes Press, 1991), 53–69.

———, *Hellenism in Jewish Palestine: Studies in the literary transmission, beliefs and manners of Palestine in the I Century B.C.E.–IV century C.E.* (New York: Jewish Theological Seminary, 1950).

———, *Greek in Jewish Palestine* (New York: Philipp Feldheim, Inc., 1965).

———, "Mishnat Shir Ha-Shirim," in *Meḥqarim be–Torat Erez-Yisrael* (Jerusalem: Magnes Press, 1991), 118–126.

Lindsay, Hugh, "Strabo on Apellicon's Library," *Transactions of the American Philological Association* 114 (1984) 290–298.

Linke, Konstanze, *Die Fragmente des Grammatikers Dionysios Thrax,* Sammlung griechischer und lateinischer Grammatiker, vol. 3 (Berlin: Walter de Gruyter, 1977), 1–77.

Lord, Albert B., *The Singer of Tales* (New York: Atheneum, 1965).

Lundbom, Jack R., "Scribal Colophons and Scribal Rhetoric in Deuteronomy 31–34," in Ben-Ẓiyon Lurya, ed., *Sefer Ḥayim Gevaryahu (Ḥaim M. I. Gevaryahu: Memorial Volume),* vol. 2 (Jerusalem: World Jewish Bible Center, 1990), 53–63.

Lurya, Ben-Ẓiyon, ed., *Sefer Ḥayim Gevaryahu (Ḥaim M. I. Gevaryahu:*

*Memorial Volume)*, 2 vols. (Jerusalem: World Jewish Bible Center, 1990).

Lütcke, Karl Heinrich, *"Auctoritas" bei Augustin* (Stuttgart: W. Kohlhammer Verlag, 1968).

Mack, Burton, "Under the Shadow of Moses: Authorship and Authority in Hellenistic Judaism," *Society of Biblical Literature, Seminar Papers* 21 (1982) 299–318.

Marcus, Ralph, "The Pharisees in the Light of Modern Scholarship," *The Journal of Religion* 32 (1952) 153–164.

Margerie, Bertrand de, *Introduction to the History of Exegesis, vol. 3: St. Augustine*, trans. Pierre de Fontnouvelle (Petersham, Massachusetts: Saint Bede's Publications, 1991).

Margolis, M. L., *The Hebrew Scriptures in the Making* (Philadelphia: Jewish Publication Society of America, 1922).

Marmorstein, A., "Les Epicuriens dans la Litterature Talmidique," *Revue des Études Juives* 54 (1907) 181–193.

Martínez, Florentino García, and Eibert J. C. Tigchelaar, *The Dead Sea Scrolls Study Edition*, 2 vols. (Leiden: E. J. Brill, 1998).

Mason, Steve, *Flavius Josephus on the Pharisees: A Composition-Critical Study* (Leiden: E. J. Brill, 1991).

———, "The Problem of the Pharisees in Modern Scholarship," in Jacob Neusner, ed., *Approaches to Ancient Judaism: New Series*, vol. 12 (Atlanta: Scholars Press, 1993), 103–140.

Mason, Steve, with Robert A. Kraft, "Josephus on Canon and Scriptures," in Magne Saebo, ed., *Hebrew Bible / Old Testament: The History of Its Interpretation*, vol. I (Göttingen: Vandenhoeck & Ruprecht, 1996), 217–235.

Mauss, Marcel, "A Category of the Human Mind: the Notion of Person; the Notion of Self," trans. W. D. Halls, in Michael Carrithers, Steven Collins, and Steven Lukes, eds., *The Category of the Person: Anthropology, Philosophy, History* (Cambridge: Cambridge University Press, 1985), 1–25.

Meade, David G., *Pseudonymity and Canon: An Investigation into the Relationship of Authorship and Authority in Jewish and Earliest Christian Tradition* (Tübingen: J. C. B. Mohr, 1986).

Meecham, Henry G., *The Letter of Aristeas: A Linguistic Study with Special Reference to the Greek Bible* (Manchester: Manchester University Press, 1935).

Metzger, Bruce M., *The Canon of the New Testament: Its Origin, Development, and Significance* (Oxford: Clarendon Press, 1987).

———, "Literary Forgeries and Canonical Pseudepigrapha," *Journal of Biblical Literature* 91 (1972) 3–24.

———, "Seventy or Seventy-two Disciples?" *New Testament Studies* 5 (1959) 299–306.

Mewaldt, J., "Galen über echte und unechte Hippocratica," *Hermes* 44 (1909) 111–34.

Migne, J.-P., *Patrologiae cursus completus; Series Graeca* (Paris: J.-P. Migne, 1857–1866).

———, *Patrologiae cursus completus; Series Latina* (Paris: J.-P. Migne, 1844–1891).

Milikowsky, Chaim, "The End of Prophecy and the End of the Bible in the View of Seder Olam," *Sidra* 10 (1994) 83–94.

———, *Seder Olam: A Rabbinic Chronography* (Ph.D. diss., Yale University, 1981).

Minnis, A. J., *Medieval Theory of Authorship: Scholastic Literary Attitudes in the Later Middle Ages* (London: Scholar Press, 1984).

Miron, Dan, *A Traveler Disguised* (Syracuse: Syracuse University Press, 1996).

Misch, G., *A History of Autobiography in Antiquity* (London: Routledge & Kegan Paul, 1950 [1907]).

Momigliano, Arnaldo, *Alien Wisdom: The Limits of Hellenization* (Cambridge: Cambridge University Press, 1971).

———, *The Development of Greek Biography* (Cambridge: Harvard University Press, 1993).

———, "Marcel Mauss and the Quest for the Person in Greek Biography and Autobiograpy," in Michael Carrithers, Steven Collins, and Steven Lukes, eds., *The Category of the Person: Anthropology, Philosophy, History* (Cambridge: Cambridge University Press, 1985), 83–92.

Morin, D. Germanus, ed., *Commentarioli in Psalmos*, Anecdota Maredsolana, vol. 3 part I (Oxford: J. Parker & Co. Booksellers, 1895).

Mowinckel, Sigumund, "'Ich' und 'Er' in der Ezrageschichte," in Arnulf Kuschke, ed., *Verbannung und Heimkehr: Beiträge zur Geschichte und Theologie Israels im 6. und 5. Jahrhundert v. Chr.* (Tübingen: J. C. B. Mohr [Paul Siebeck], 1961), 211–233.

———, *The Psalms in Israel's Worship* (Nashville: Abingdon, 1962).

Mulder, Martin Jan, ed., *Mikra: Text, Translation, Reading and Interpretation of the Hebrew Bible in Ancient Judaism and Early Christianity*, Compendia Rerum Iudaicarum ad Novum Testamentum (Philadelphia: Fortress Press, 1988).

Müller, Karl, ed., *Fragmenta Historicorum Graecorum* (Frankfurt/Main: Minerva, 1975).

———, *Oratores Attici Graece Cum Translatione* II (Parisiis: A. Firmin-Didot, 1858–1877).

Murray, Oswyn, "Aristeas and Ptolemaic Kingship," *The Journal of Theological Studies* 18 (1967) 337–371.

Myers, Jacob, *I & II Esdras*, Anchor Bible (Garden City: Doubleday, 1974).

Nagy, Gregory, "Homer and Plato at the Panathenaia: Synchronic and Diachronic Perspectives," in T. M. Falkner, D. Konstan, and N. Felson Rubin, eds., *Contextualizing Classics* (Lanham, Maryland: Rowman and Littlefield, 1999), 127–155.

———, *Homeric Questions* (Austin: University of Texas Press, 1996).

———, "Homeric Scholia," in Ian Morris and Barry Powell, eds., *A New Companion to Homer* (Leiden: E. J. Brill, 1997), 101–122.

———, "The Library of Pergamon as a Classical Model," in Helmut Koester, ed., *Pergamon: Citadel of the Gods* (Harrisburg, Pennsylvania: Trinity Press International, 1998), 185–232.

———, *Pindar's Homer: The Lyric Possession of an Epic Past* (Baltimore: The Johns Hopkins University Press, 1990).

———, *Poetry as Performance: Homer and Beyond* (Cambridge: Cambridge University Press, 1996).

Neitzel, Suzanne, *Apions Γλῶσσαι Ὁμηρικαὶ*, Sammlung griechischer und lateinischer Grammatiker, vol. 3 (Berlin: Walter de Gruyter, 1977), 185–328.

Neubauer, Adolf, *Mediaeval Jewish Chronicles and Chronological Notes, Ed. From Printed Books and Manuscripts* (Oxford: Clarendon Press, 1887–95).

Neusner, Jacob, *The Fathers According to Rabbi Nathan: An Analytical Translation and Explanation*, Brown Judaic Studies no. 114 (Atlanta: Scholars Press, 1986).

———, "The Religious Uses of History," *History and Theory* 5 (1966) 153–71.

Norton, Gerard J. and Stephen Pisano, eds., *Tradition of the Text: Studies* offered to Dominique Barthélemy in Celebration of his 70th Birthday (Göttingen: Vandenhoeck & Ruprecht, 1991).

Oehler, Klaus, "Der Consensus omnium als Kriterium der Wahrheit in der antiken Philsophie und der Patristik," Antike und Abendland 10 (1961) 103–129.

Opitz, H. G., Athanasius: Werke (Berlin, Leipzig: W. de Gruyter, 1934– ).

Oppel, Herbert, KANON: Zur Bedeutungsgeschichte des Wortes und seiner lateinischen Entsprechungen (Regula-Norma), Philologus, Supp.-Band 30.4 (Leipzig: Dieterich, 1937).

Pelletier, André, Lettre d'Aristée à Philocrate, Sources Chrétiennes, vol. 89 (Paris: Les Éditions du Cerf, 1962).

Perrot, Charles, "The Reading of the Bible in the Ancient Synagogue," in Martin Jan Mulder, ed., Mikra: Text, Translation, Reading and Interpretation of the Hebrew Bible in Ancient Judaism and Early Christianity, Compendia Rerum Iudaicarum ad Novum Testamentum (Philadelphia: Fortress Press, 1988), 137–159.

Pfeiffer, Rudolf, The History of Classical Scholarship from the Beginnings to the End of the Hellenistic Age (Oxford: Clarendon Press, 1968).

Philo, Collected Works, trans. F. H. Coleson and G. H. Whitaker, Loeb Classical Library (Cambridge: Harvard University Press, 1924–1962).

Pickard-Cambridge, A., The Dramatic Festivals of Athens (London: Oxford University Press, 1969).

Plato, Laws, trans. Bury, Loeb Classical Library (Cambridge: Harvard University Press, 1999).

Plato, Lysis, Symposium, Gorgias, trans. W. R. M. Lamb, Loeb Classical Library (Cambridge: Harvard University Press, 2001).

Pliny, Natural History, trans. W. H. S. Jones, Loeb Classical Library (Cambridge: Harvard University Press, 1967–1975).

Polzin, Robert, "Deuteronomy," in Robert Alter and Frank Kermode, eds., The Literary Guide to the Bible (Cambridge: Harvard University Press), 92–102.

Porter, James I., "Hermeneutic Lines and Circles: Aristarchus and Crates on the Exegesis of Homer," in Robert Lamberton and John J. Keaney, eds., Homer's Ancient Readers (Princeton: Princeton University Press, 1992), 67–114.

Porter, Stanley E., "Jesus and the Use of Greek in Galilee," in Bruce Chilton and Craig A. Evans, eds., Studying the Historical Jesus (Leiden: E. J. Brill, 1998), 123–154.

Purvis, James D., *The Samaritan Pentateuch and the Origin of the Samaritan Sect* (Cambridge: Harvard University Press, 1968).

Qimron, Elisha, and John Strugnell, *Qumran Cave 4: V: Miqṣat Maʿase Ha-Torah*, Discoveries in the Judaean Desert X (Oxford: Clarendon Press, 1994).

Quint, David, *Origins and Originality in Renaissance Literature: Versions of the Source* (New Haven: Yale University Press, 1983).

Quintilian, *Institutiones Oratoriae*, ed. and trans. Donald A. Russell, Loeb Classical Library (Cambridge: Harvard University Press, 2001).

Rabbinovicz, Raphael, *Diqduqey Sofrim*, 12 volumes (Jerusalem: ʾOr Ha-Ḥokhmah, 2001 [1868–1897]).

Rad, Gerhard von, *Studies in Deuteronomy*, Studies in Biblical Theology (London: SCM Press Ltd., 1953 [1948]).

————, *Wisdom in Israel* (Valley Forge, Pennsylvania: Trinity Press International, 1970).

Rahlfs, Alfred, ed., *Septuaginta*, 5th ed. (Stuttgart: Privileg. Württ. Bibelanstalt, 1952).

Rajak, Tessa, *Josephus: The Historian and His Society* (London: Duckworth & Co. Ltd., 1983).

————, "The Sense of History in Jewish Intertestamental Writing," in Johannes Cornelis de Moor, ed., *Crises and Perspectives: Studies in Ancient Near Eastern Polytheism, Biblical Theology, Palestinian Archaeology and Intertestamental Literature*, Oudtestamentische Studiën vol. 24 (Leiden: E. J. Brill, 1986), 124–145.

Rawson, Elizabeth, *Intellectual Life in the Late Roman Republic* (London: Duckworth & Co. Ltd., 1985).

Reese, James M., *Hellenistic Influences on the Book of Wisdom and its Consequences*, Analecta Biblica, vol. 41 (Rome: Biblical Institute Press, 1970).

Regebogen, Otto, "Pinax," in Wissowa-Kroll-Mittelhaus, eds. *Paulys Real-Enzyklopädie der klassischen Altertumswissenschaft* 40 (1950) 1409–1482.

Reider, Joseph, *The Book of Wisdom: An English Translation with Introduction and Commentary* (New York: Harper & Brothers, 1957).

Reisch, Emil, "Didaskaliai; Didaskalos," in Wissowa-Kroll-Mittelhaus, eds., *Paulys Real-Enzyklopädie der klassischen Altertumswissenschaft* 5 (1905) 394–401; 401–406.

Riedweg, Christoph, *Mysterienterminologie bei Platon, Philon und Klemens von Alexandrien*, Untersuchungen zur antiken Literatur und Geschichte, vol. 26 (Berlin: Walter de Gruyter, 1987).

Reinach, Theodore, ed., *Flavius Josèphe, Contre Apion* (Paris: Les Belles Lettres, 1930).

Ritoók, Zs., "Josephus and Homer," *Acta Antiqua Academiae Scientiarum Hungaricae* 32 (1989) 137–152.

Robert, Louis, *"Oikos," Archaiologike Ephemeris* 108 (1969) 8.

Roberts, Alexander and James Donaldson, eds., *The Writings of Tertullian* vol. 1, *Ante-Nicene Christian Library: Translations of the Writings of the Fathers*, vol. 11 (Edinburgh: T. & T. Clark, 1869).

———, *Hippolytus, Cyprian, Caius, Novatian, Appendix*, trans. S. D. F. Salmond, *Ante-Nicene Fathers*, vol. 5 (Peabody, Massachusetts: Hendrickson Publishers, 1994).

Rose, Valentinus, *Aristotelis Qui Ferebantur Librorum Fragmenta* (Lipsiae: Teubner, 1886).

Ruhnken, David, *Opuscula Varii Argumenti, Oratoria, Historica, Critica* I (Lugduni Batarorum: S. et J. Luchtmans, Academie typographos, 1823).

Runia, David T., *Philo of Alexandria and the* Timaeus *of Plato*, Philosophia Antiqua, vol. 44 (Leiden: E. J. Brill, 1986).

Ryle, H. E., *The Canon of the Old Testament* (London: Macmillan, 1892).

Rzach, Aloisius, 'Homeridai,' in Wissowa-Kroll-Mittelhaus, eds., *Paulys Real-Enzyklopädie der klassischen Altertumswissenschaft* 8 (1913) 2145–2181.

Saebo, Magne, ed., *Hebrew Bible / Old Testament: The History of Its Interpretation, vol. I: From the Beginnings to the Middle Ages (Until 1300)* (Göttingen: Vandenhoeck & Ruprecht, 1996).

Sagnard, F., ed., *Irénée de Lyon: Contre les hérésies* III, Sources chrétiennes (Paris: Éditions du Cerf, 1952).

Safrai, Shmuel, ed., *The Literature of the Sages* (Philadelphia: Fortress Press, 1987).

Saldarini, Anthony J., *The Fathers According to Rabbi Nathan, a Translation and Commentary* (Leiden: E. J. Brill, 1975).

Salvesen, Alison, ed., *Origen's Hexapla and Fragments: Papers Presented at the Rich Seminar on the Hexapla, Oxford Centre for Hebrew and Jewish Studies, 25th–3rd August 1994* (Tübingen: Mohr Siebeck, 1998).

———, *Symmachus in the Pentateuch*, Journal of Semitic Studies Monograph, vol. 15 (Manchester: University of Manchester, 1991).

Sanders, J. A., *The Psalms Scroll of Qumrân Cave 11*, *Discoveries in the Judaean Desert of Jordan* IV (Oxford: Clarendon Press, 1965).

———, *Torah and Canon* (Philadelphia: Fortress Press, 1972).

Sarna, Nahum, *Ancient Libraries and the Ordering of Biblical Books* (Washington D.C.: Library of Congress, 1989).

Satran, David, *Biblical Prophets in Byzantine Palestine*, Studia in Veteris Testamenti Pseudepigrapha, vol. 11 (Leiden: E. J. Brill, 1995).

Schäfer, P., "Die sogenannte Synode von Jabne, II. Der Abschluss des Kanons," *Judaica* 31 (1975) 116–124.

Schaff, Philip and Henry Wace, eds., *Jerome: Letters and Select Works*, second series, trans. W. H. Freemantle, *Nicene and Post-Nicene Fathers*, vol. 6 (Peabody, Massachusetts: Hendrickson Publishers, 1994).

Schäublin, Cristoph, "Josephus und die Griechen," *Hermes* 110 (1982) 316–341.

Schechter, Solomon, *Aboth de Rabbi Natan* (New York: P. Feldheim, 1945).

Schmandt-Besserat, Denise, *How Writing Came About* (Austin: University of Texas Press, 1996).

Schmidt, Friedrich, *Pinakes des Kallimachos* (Berlin: Verlag von Emil Ebering, 1922).

Schmidt, Moritz, "Dionys der Thraker," *Philologus* 7 (1852) 360–382.

———, "Dionys der Thraker," *Philologus* 8 (1853) 231–253; 510–520.

Schuller, Eileen M., *Non-Canonical Psalms from Qumran: A Pseudepigraphic Collection*, Harvard Semitic Studies 28 (Atlanta: Scholars Press, 1986).

Schürer, Emil, *A History of the Jewish People in the Time of Jesus Christ (175 B.C.–A.D. 135)*, revised edition, eds. Geza Vermes, Fergus Millar, and Matthew Black (Edinburgh: T. & T. Clark, 1979 [1886]).

Schwartz, Eduard, "Die Königslisten des Eratosthenes und Kastor," *Abhandlungen der Königlichen Gesellschaft der Wissenschaften zu Göttingen, Mathematisch-Physikalische Klasse* 40 (1895) 1–96.

Schwartz, Seth, *Josephus and Judaean Politics*, Columbia Studies in the Classical Tradition, vol. 38 (Leiden: E. J. Brill, 1990).

Scott, R. B. Y., "Solomon and the Beginnings of Wisdom in Israel," in James L. Crenshaw, ed., *Studies in Ancient Israelite Wisdom* (New York: Ktav Publishing House, Inc., 1976 [1955]), 84–101.

Segal, M. H., *Sefer Ben Sira Ha-Shalem* (Jerusalem, 1933).

Seneca, *Epistles*, trans. Richard M. Gummere, Loeb Classical Library (Cambridge: Harvard University Press, 1996 [1920]).

Shell, Marc, *Money, Language, and Thought* (Berkeley and Los Angeles: University of California Press, 1982).

Shinan, Avigdor, *The Embroidered Targum: The Aggadah in Targum Pseudo-Jonathan of the Pentateuch* (Jerusalem: Magnes Press, 1992).

Silverstone, A. E., *Aquila and Onkelos* (Manchester: Manchester University Press, 1931).

Simon, Uriel, *Four Approaches to the Book of Psalms: From Saadiah Gaon to Abraham Ibn Ezra*, SUNY Series in Judaica (Albany: State University of New York Press, 1991 [1982]).

Skehan, Patrick W., "St. Jerome and the Canon of Holy Scriptures," in Francis X. Murphy, ed., *A Monument to St. Jerome* (New York: Sheed & Ward, 1952), 259–287.

Skehan, Patrick W. and Alexander Di Lella, *The Wisdom of Ben Sira: A New Translation with Notes*, Anchor Bible (New York: Doubleday & Company, Inc., 1987).

Smith, Jonathan Z., *Imagining Religion: From Babylon to Jonestown* (Chicago: University of Chicago Press, 1982).

Smith, Morton, "Pseudepigraphy in the Israelite Tradition," in Kurt von Fritz, ed., *Pseudepigrapha I* (Geneva: Vandoevres, 1972).

Smith, Wilfred Cantwell, *What is Scripture? A Comparative Approach* (Minneapolis: Fortress Press, 1993).

Sorabji, Richard, *Emotion and Peace of Mind: From Stoic Agitation to Christian Temptation* (Oxford: Oxford University Press, 2000).

Speyer, Wolfgang, *Die Literarische Fälschung im Heidnischen und Christlichen Altertum*, Handbuch der Altertumswissenschaft, 1,2 (München: C. H. Beck'sche Verlagsbuchhandlung, 1971).

Spinoza, Benedictus de, *Tractatus Theologico-Politicus* (New York: Dover, 1951).

Steinthal, Heymann, *Geschichte der Sprachwissenschaft bei den Griechen und Römern* I (Hildesheim: G. Olms, 1971 [1890]).

Steinsaltz, Adin, *Bava Batra* vol. 1, in *Talmud Bavli: meturgam u-mevo'ar: 'im kol ha-mefarshim 'al ha-daf ka'asher nidpas mi-qedem*, vol. 18 (Yerushalayim: ha-Makhon ha-Yisre'eli le-firsumim Talmudiyim, 1998).

———, *The Talmud, the Steinsaltz Edition: A Reference Guide* (New York: Random House, 1989).

Stemberger, Günter, "Jabne und der Kanon," *Jahrbuch für biblische Theologie* 3 (1988) 163–174.

———, "Die sogenannte 'Synode von Jabne' und das frühe Christentum," *Kairos: Zeitschrift für Religionswissenschaft und Theologie* 19 (1977) 14–21.

Stendahl, Krister, "The Apostle Paul and the Introspective Conscience of the West," *Harvard Theological Review* 56 (1963)199–215.

Stern, David, *Parables in Midrash: Narrative and Exegesis in Rabbinic Literature* (Cambridge: Harvard University Press, 1991).

Stern, Sacha, "Attribution and Authorship in the Babylonian Talmud," *Journal of Jewish Studies* 15 (1994) 28–51.

Stone, Michael E., "The Metamorphosis of Ezra: Jewish Apocalypse and Medieval Vision," *Journal of Theological Studies* 33 (1982) 1–18.

Strack, H. L. and Günter Stemberger, *Introduction to the Talmud and Midrash*, trans. Markus Bockmuehl (Edinburgh: T & T Clark, 1991).

Stummer, Friedrich, *Einführung in die lateinische Bibel* (Paderborn: Verlag Ferdinand Schöningh, 1928).

*Talmud: Hebrew-English ed. of the Babylonian Talmud*, ed. I. Epstein (London: Soncino, 1960–).

*The Talmud of Babylonia*, trans. J. Neusner, Brown Judaic Studies, (Atlanta: Scholars Press, 1992).

*The Talmud of the Land of Israel: a preliminary translation and explanation*, trans. Jacob Neusner (Chicago: University of Chicago Press, 1982–1994).

*Tanakh: The Holy Scriptures: The New JPS Translation According to the Traditional Hebrew Text* (Philadelphia: Jewish Publication Society, 1985).

Tarn, W. W., *The Greeks in Bactria & India* (London: Cambridge University Press, 1938).

Tcherikover, Victor, *Hellenistic Civilization and the Jews* (Philadelphia: Jewish Publication Society, 1966).

———, "The Ideology of the Letter of Aristeas," *Harvard Theological Review* 51 (1958) 59–85.

———, "Jewish Apologetic Literature Reconsidered," *Eos* 48 (1956) 169–93.

Tertullian, *Apology; De Spectaculis*, trans. T. R. Glover, Loeb Classical Library (Cambridge: Harvard University Press, 1977 [1931]).

———, *The Writings of Quintus Sept. Flor. Tertullianus*, in *Ante-Nicene Christian Library*, vols. 11, 15, 18, trans. S. Thelwall (Edinburgh: T. & T. Clark, 1869–70).

Theodosius Alexandrinus, *Spuria*, ed. C. G. Göttling (Leipzig: 1822).

Thesleff, Holger, "On the Problem of the Doric Pseudo-Pythagorica: An Alternative Theory of Date and Purpose," in Kurt von Fritz, ed., *Pseudepigrapha I* (Geneva: Vandoevres, 1972), 59–102.

Tomson, P. J., "The New Testament Canon as the Embodiment of Evolving Christian Attitudes Towards the Jews," in A. van der Kooij and K. van der Toorn, eds., *Canonization and Decanonization* (Leiden: E. J. Brill, 1998), 107–131.

Torrey, Charles Cutler, *The Lives of the Prophets: Greek Text and Translation,* Journal of Biblical Literature Monograph Series, vol. 1 (Philadelphia: Society of Biblical Literature and Exegesis, 1946).

Tov, Emanuel, *The Greek and Hebrew Bible: Collected Essays on the Septuagint* (Leiden: E. J. Brill, 1999).

———, "The History and Significance of a Standard Text of the Hebrew Bible," in Magne Saebo, ed., *Hebrew Bible / Old Testament: The History of Its Interpretation, vol. I: From the Beginnings to the Middle Ages (Until 1300)* (Göttingen: Vandenhoeck & Ruprecht, 1996), 49–66.

———, "The Rabbinic Tradition Concerning the 'Alterations' Inserted into the Greek Pentateuch and their Relation to the Original Text of the LXX," *Journal for the Study of Judaism* 15 (1984) 65–89.

Trobisch, David, *The First Edition of the New Testament* (Oxford: Oxford University Press, 2000).

Untersteiner, Mario, *Problemi di Filologia Filosofica* (Milan: Cisalpino-Goliardica, 1980).

Urbach, E. E. "Halakhah and Prophecy," *Tarbiz* 18 (1947) 1–27.

———, "When Did Prophecy Cease?" *Tarbiz* 17 (1946) 1–27.

van der Horst, Pieter W., *Japheth in the Tents of Shem: Studies on Jewish Hellenism in Antiquity* (Leuven: Peeters, 2002).

van der Kooij, A., and K. van der Toorn, eds., *Canonization and Decanonization: Papers Presented to the International Conference of the Leiden Institute for the Study of Religions (Lisor), Held at Leiden 9–10 January 1997* (Leiden: E. J. Brill, 1998).

van der Kooij, A., "The Canonization of Ancient Books Kept in the Temple of Jerusalem," in A. van der Kooij and K. van der Toorn, eds., *Canonization and Decanonization* (Leiden: E. J. Brill, 1998), 17–40.

van der Waerden, B. L., *Science Awakening,* trans. Arnold Dresden (Groningen: P. Noordhoff, 1954).

Veltri, Giuseppe, *Eine Tora für den König Talmai* (Tubingen: J. C. B. Mohr, 1994).

———, "Tolomeo Filadelfo, emulo di Pisistrato," *Laurentianum* 32 (1991) 146–166.

Vermès, Geza, "La figure de Moïse au tournant des deux testaments," *Moïse, l'homme de l'alliance* = *Cahiers Sioniens* 8 (1954) 63–92.

———, *Jesus the Jew: A Historian's Reading of the Gospels* (London: Collins, 1973).

———, "A Summary of the Law by Flavius Josephus," *Novum Testamentum* 24 (1982) 289–303.

Vernant, Jean-Pierre, "The Individual Within the City State," in Froma I. Zeitlin, ed., *Mortals and Immortals: Collected Essays* (Princeton: Princeton University Press, 1991), 318–333.

Vidyaranya, *Sankara-Dig-Vijaya: The Traditional Life of Sri Sankaracharya,* trans. Swami Tapasyananda (Madras: Sri Ramakrishna Math, 1978).

Villalba I Varneda, Pere, *The Historical Method of Flavius Josephus,* Arbeiten zur Literatur und Geschichte des Hellenistischen Judentums, vol. 19 (Leiden: E. J. Brill, 1986).

Visotzky, Burton L., *Midrash Mishle* (New York: The Jewish Theological Seminary of America, 1990).

Vitruvius, *De Architectura,* trans. Frank Granger, Loeb Classical Library (Cambridge: Harvard University Press, 1962).

Wehrli, Fritz, ed., *Hermippos der Kallemacheer,* Die Schule des Aristoteles: Suplementband I (Basel: Schwabe, 1974).

Weinfeld, M., *Deuteronomy and the Deuteronomic School* (Oxford: Clarendon Press, 1971).

West, M. L., *The East Face of Helicon: West Asiatic Elements in Greek Poetry and Myth* (Oxford: Clarendon Press, 1997).

———, "The Invention of Homer," *Classical Quarterly* 49 (1999) 364–382.

Wilamowitz-Moellendorff, Ulrich von, "Louys, Pierre: *Les chansons de Bilitis traduites du Grec pour la première fois*" (Review), *Göttingische gelehrte Anzeigen* 158 (1896) 623–638.

Williams, James G., *Those Who Ponder Proverbs: Aphoristic Thinking and Biblical Literature* (Sheffield: The Almond Press, 1981).

Wilmart, André, "La tradition des grands ouvrages de saint Augustin," in *Miscellanea Agostiniana*: testi e studi, pubblicati a cura dell'Ordine eremitano di s. Agostino nel XV centenario dalla morte del santo dottore II (Rome: Tipografia poliglotta vaticana, 1930–1931), 257–315.

Wimsatt, W. K. and Monroe C. Beardsley, "The Intentional Fallacy," in

W. K. Wimsatt Jr., *The Verbal Icon: Studies in the Meaning of Poetry* (Lexington: University of Kentucky Press, 1954), 3–18.

Winston, David, *Logos and Mystical Theology in Philo of Alexandria* (Cincinnati: Hebrew Union College Press, 1985).

———, "Two Types of Mosaic Prophecy According to Philo," *Journal for the Study of Pseudepigrapha* 4 (1989) 49–67.

———, *The Wisdom of Solomon*, Anchor Bible (Garden City: Doubleday & Company, Inc., 1979).

Wintermute, O. S., *Jubilees: A New Translation and Introduction*, in Charlesworth, ed., *Old Testament Pseudepigrapha*, vol. 2 (London: Darton, Longman and Todd, 1983–1985), 35–142.

Wolf, F. A., *Prolegomena ad Homerum*, ed. Rudoph Peppmüller (Halis Saxonum: E Libraria Orphanotrophei, 1795; 1884).

———, *Prolegomena to Homer*, trans. Anthony Grafton, Glenn W. Most and James E. G. Zetzel (Princeton: Princeton University Press, 1985).

Wolfson, Harry Austryn, *Philo: Foundations of Religious Philosophy in Judaism, Christianity, and Islam* (Cambridge: Harvard University Press, 1947).

Wright, David F., "Augustine: His Exegesis and Hermeneutics," in Magne Saebo, ed., *Hebrew Bible / Old Testament: The History of Its Interpretation, vol. I: From the Beginnings to the Middle Ages (Until 1300)* (Göttingen: Vandenhoeck & Ruprecht, 1996), 701–730.

Zaharopoulos, Dimitri Z., *Theodore of Mopsuestia on the Bible: A Study of his Old Testament Exegesis* (New York: Paulist Press, 1989).

Zarb, Séraphin M., "Unité ou multiciplité des sens littéraux dans la Bible?" *Revue Thomiste* 37 (1932) 251–300.

Zevit, Z., "The Second-Third Century Canonization of the Hebrew Bible and its Influence on Christian Canonizing," in A. van der Kooij and K. van der Toorn, eds., *Canonization and Decanonization* (Leiden: E. J. Brill, 1998), 133–160.

Zsengellér, J., "Canon and the Samaritans," in A. van der Kooij and K. van der Toorn, eds., *Canonization and Decanonization* (Leiden: E. J. Brill, 1998), 161–171.

Zunz, Leopold, "'Verfassen und Übersetzen' hebräisch ausgedrükt," *Zeitschrift Deutsche Morgenländische Gesellchaft* 25 (1871) 435–448.

# INDEX